THE PHARISEES

The Sociological Background of Their Faith

II

Professor Morris Loeb, of New York, the distinguished chemist, scholar and public worker, who died on October 8, 1912, by his last Will and Testament, created a Fund under the following terms: "I give and bequeath to The Jewish Publication Society of America the sum of Ten Thousand Dollars as a permanent fund, the income of which alone shall, from time to time, be utilized for and applied to the preparation and publication of a scholarly work devoted to the interests of Judaism."

The present work, published in 1938, is the second issued under this Fund. The first, *Saadia Gaon—His Life and Works,* by Henry Malter, was published in 1921. The third, *The Jews in Spain—Their Social, Political and Cultural Life During the Middle Ages,* by Abraham A. Neuman, was published in 1942. The fourth, *The Jewish Community—Its History and Structure to the American Revolution,* by Salo Wittmayer Baron, was published in 1942. The fifth, *The Jews of Ancient Rome,* by Harry J. Leon, was published in 1960.

This new edition of *The Pharisees—The Sociological Background of Their Faith* was made possible by the generous participation of the Stroock Publication Fund.

THE MORRIS LOEB SERIES

THE PHARISEES

The Sociological Background of Their Faith

LOUIS FINKELSTEIN

Chancellor and Solomon Schechter Professor of Theology
at the Jewish Theological Seminary of America

VOLUME

WITH SUPPLEMENT  THIRD EDITION

The Jewish Publication Society of America

Philadelphia 1966–5726

Second Edition, Revised, 1940

Third Impression, 1946

Third Edition, Revised, 1962

Second Impression, 1966

Library of Congress Catalog Card Number: 61-11709

Manufactured in the United States of America

TABLE OF CONTENTS

VOLUME II

PAGE

XVIII. THE IDEALS OF PEACE AND HUMAN EQUALITY DURING THE EXILE 443

XIX. SOCIAL AND POLITICAL CONFLICT UNDER THE PERSIAN RULE 500

XX. THE STRUGGLE AGAINST ASSIMILATION: JUDAISM BECOMES THE SYNAGOGUE 546

XXI. HELLENISTS, HASIDEANS AND PHARISEES ... 570

SUPPLEMENT

I. THE UNIQUENESS OF PHARISAISM 627

II. THE BACKGROUND OF THE SADDUCEAN VIEWS .. 637

III. THE *'Am ha-Arez* 754

IV. THE ORIGIN OF THE SADDUCEES AND BOETHUSIANS AS SECTS 762

V. THE SOCIOLOGICAL BASIS OF THE CONTROVERSIES WITHIN PHARISAISM 780

ABBREVIATIONS 800

APPENDIX A. THE UNITY OF ISAIAH 40–66, AND THE PLACE AND DATE OF THE AUTHOR 801

APPENDIX B. THE MEANING OF EZEKIEL 1.1–2 ... 806

APPENDIX C. ADDITIONAL CONTROVERSIES BETWEEN THE SECTS 811

NOTES 821

NOTES TO THE SUPPLEMENT 882

BIBLIOGRAPHY 903

INDEX TO PASSAGES 949

INDEX TO SUBJECTS 973

XVIII. THE IDEALS OF PEACE AND HUMAN EQUALITY DURING THE EXILE

The Babylonian exile, properly considered, was epochal not only for the history of the Jews, but for civilization generally. It was the first time in history that a considerable community dissociated the worship of its God from its ancestral soil. This may seem, at first glance, an advance in thought which can interest only theologians; actually, it was the basis for the development of the whole conception of human brotherhood and the breakdown of that prejudice which transforms love of one's own people and country into the hatred of all others. At last the principle was established that God has no special home on earth, but that all countries and people are alike before Him. This truth, which thoughtful men today accept as axiomatic, was quite unknown, except in the limited prophetic circles, twenty-six centuries ago. Men actually believed that their gods had a preference for their own native countries and their own peoples. Athene was the goddess of Athens; Chemosh the god of Moab; Melkart the god of the Tyrians; Marduk the god of the Babylonians. This comforting superstition, satisfying as it was to the vanity of our ancestors, was a great peril to the world, for it bestowed on opposing national prejudices supernatural sanctions which rendered them impossible of reconciliation. The Moabite went forth to battle not only for his people and for his land, but for his god; and so did the Edomite; and every one of the other nations round about. Patriotism ceased to be, like love of one's family, relative to the accidents of birth and life, and quite compatible with similar feelings by other people for their homelands. It became absolute, bigoted, and intolerant. It was not only non-rational, but irrational, like a demand of a son that all people see in his mother the grace and lovableness with which his own memories endow her.

For generations the prophets had inveighed against this narrow and false conception of the God of Israel. They had claimed that He was the God not only of Canaan, but of the whole world. He had brought Israel out of Egypt, the Philistines out of Kaphtor, and the Arameans from Kir.[1] He was the Lord of Hosts, the Creator of heaven and earth. But the doctrine of a transcendent Deity had been accepted only by a limited circle of intellectually advanced pietists. Even David, driven to seek shelter from Saul among his people's enemies, the Philistines, declared himself condemned to idol-worship (I Sam. 26.19). Naaman, the Syrian general, becoming converted to the God of Israel, took some Palestinian earth with him to Damascus, so that he might worship YHWH on His own soil (II Kings 5.17), somewhat as the Shah of Persia is said to have put Persian sand between the soles of his shoes when he visited Europe before the World War, to free him from the necessity of stepping on foreign soil.

The population of the Ten Tribes, which were deported by the Assyrians to the cities of Media, apparently shared this view. Unable to take any Palestinian soil with them into their exile, the Ten Tribes soon became assimilated to the surrounding population. It is significant for the influence of prophecy in Judah that the garrison of Judaite soldiers stationed on the island of Yeb in Egypt did not forsake the worship of YHWH, but served Him as well as other gods.[2] Whether Assyrian and Babylonian soil was brought to Jerusalem when the imperial worship was introduced there under Ahaz, Manasseh, and Jehoiakim, is not recorded. Perhaps that was held to be unnecessary because the reduction of a country to provincial or semi-provincial status involved its subordination to its conqueror's gods. It became the territory not only of the Emperor, but ipso facto of his deities.

Be that as it may, it was certainly a revolutionary thought for Jeremiah to demand that the exiles of Judah, who had been taken as captives to Babylonia, continue to worship the God of their fathers on the foreign soil (Jer. 29.7). The acceptance of his doctrine, which had been so unpopular in Palestine, by the exiles of the years 597 B.C.E. and 586 B.C.E., can only be explained in terms of the social forces which the deportation itself created. This involves an analysis of the constituency both of the Palestinian and the Babylonian Judaite societies during the exilic period.

The opinion has generally prevailed, until recent times, that Nebuchadnezzar's deportation in 586 B.C.E. practically emptied Judah of its people. The saying of an ancient sage that "for fifty-two years not a single person passed through the country,"[3] was accepted by the modern historian as well as by the traditional teacher.

No one seems to have realized the inherent difficulty of imputing to Nebuchadnezzar such folly as this interpretation of events implies. How could any ruler wantonly leave an important border province uninhabited and exposed to the first invader? Archaeological evidence does indeed prove that the "walled cities" of Judah were razed and burned,[4] and biblical record leaves no doubt that the two deportations of 597 B.C.E. and 586 B.C.E. brought to Babylonia a considerable section of Jerusalem's population, including both members of the dominant nobility and the plebeian craftsmen and traders. Together with them came also a large group of the wealthier country squires, who formed the backbone of the army. But these classes together constituted a small minority of the country's population. Even if we add to them the large number who died in battle, starved in the post-war famine, were sold as slaves, or fled to foreign lands, there still remains a goodly fraction of the Judaite community unaccounted for. These were the "poor of the people of the soil," the masses of the peasantry, whom Nebuchadnezzar left on their farms and in their vineyards, and who were quite unaffected by the fortunes of the war.

The contemporary writers are careful to describe the catastrophic events of 597 B.C.E. and 586 B.C.E. as relating only to Jerusalem and its inhabitants. Chroniclers and poets regularly speak of a "deportation of Jerusalem" rather than of Judah.[5] They mention the reduction of the country's minor fortresses, but reserve their main laments for the capture of its capital. This habit cannot be attributed to the distorted perspective and narrow arrogance peculiar to inhabitants of a metropolis, who so frequently write as though the countryside did not exist. For the Prophet of the Restoration, too, thinks of the exile as affecting primarily the Holy City. It is Jerusalem which needs consolation, not the land of Judah (Isa. 40.1). The evidence definitely establishes the fact that the countryside of Judah did not suffer any permanent injury in the invasions of 597 and 586.[6]

The situation in Judah after the year 586 B.C.E. becomes clearer when we compare it with that which followed the Roman War in the year 70 C.E. On both occasions Jerusalem, with its Temple, its wealth, its commerce, and its instruments of authority, disappeared; yet the life of the hinterland remained undisturbed. There was only one difference between the periods which must be kept in mind. When Jerusalem was destroyed by the Romans, two sister-cities of her own country divided her inheritance: Ludd succeeded to her commerce, and Yabneh to her spirit. Nothing like that happened in 586. In that first destruction, the commerce of Jerusalem was deflected to Tyre, and her culture was deported to even more distant Babylonia.

The difference was due not to governmental planning, but to accidents of history. There could be no important commercial center in Ludd in 586, because that city depended for its growth on the development of a Jewish diaspora which looked to Jerusalem as its holy city. It was only toward the end of the Second Commonwealth that the trade routes from Egypt to Damascus, which pass through Ludd,[7] became busy with the enormous traffic of the pilgrims traveling to and fro, and the caravans taking the goods of Judah to its children abroad, and bringing their produce and their wealth back to the mother country. When the head of the body politic was destroyed, this sub-cerebral center could still carry on its functions.

The Babylonian conquest produced no Yabneh as spiritual successor to Jerusalem for the simple reason that the only men capable of establishing such a center were prevented from doing so. Gedaliah, the governor, was murdered two months after his appointment; Jeremiah, the prophet, was forcibly taken to Egypt (Jer. 41.2; 43.2).

We can understand the situation in Judah after Gedaliah's death and Jeremiah's removal if we try to imagine what would have happened in the year 70 C.E. if Johanan ben Zakkai and one or two of his leading disciples had perished with Jerusalem. There would have been no conclave or academy at Yabneh; no talmudic traditions would have developed; no conflict of parties would have arisen. The chapters of Jewish history after the year 70 C.E., which are filled with records of rabbinic achievements and sagas of their learned battles, would have been empty. Our information about the period would have ended with Josephus's record of the Roman destruction. The lack of all contemporary documents, written or orally transmitted, would have left us with the impression that the country was practically devastated.

How correct this is can be seen from the fact that the period for which there were no rabbinic traditions, i. e., after the sixth century C.E., was actually described by historians as one of utter devastation. The talmudic schools were suppressed; and it was long supposed that with the men of learning the whole population disappeared. It is only within the last few decades that documents have been unearthed proving definitely the continued existence and development of an important Jewish community until the time of the Crusades.

Darkness like that which enveloped the Second Jewish Commonwealth five centuries after its conquest, fell on the First Commonwealth immediately after the murder of Gedaliah. Yet a careful examination of the available evidence enables us to reconstruct something of the character of Palestinian life even during that period.

It is clear that the Judaite peasant who remained in the land did not fully realize just what was involved in the destruction of his country's spiritual center. He was keenly aware, of course, of the inconvenience and loss he sustained in the absorption of metropolitan commerce by Tyre. And he was touched even more nearly by the changes in the government of the country. His taxes were possibly higher than they had been under Judaite kings; he doubtless found the alien factors less tractable than his own countrymen had been; and his patriotic feelings were outraged by the transfer of a large section of Judaite territory — the Negeb — to Edom, Babylonia's tiny ally in the late war.[8] He must have been chagrined when he thought of the foreign governors in Mizpah, and the Babylonian gods, Bel, Nebo, and Marduk, who were worshiped there. The establishment of that city as a place of prayer for those who remained faithful to YHWH could hardly serve as a balm to his wounded national pride.

But, deprived of the leadership of the city groups, the peasant was unable to offer any effective resistance to the Babylonian conquerors. The astute Nebuchadnezzar had foreseen this; and that had of course been his reason for the destruction of the cities, especially Jerusalem. It was an incident of his military tactics that the country was thrust back into pre-Davidic economy and lost the civilization which had been built up through four centuries of patient effort. No trace remained of the commercial revolution of the tenth and ninth centuries B.C.E. Together with the remainder of Jerusalem's cultural life, prophetic tradition disappeared. Isaiah's doctrines of Universal Peace and of Jerusalem's Holiness; Habakkuk's conception of Divine Justice among nations as among individuals; Zephaniah's reliance on the "humble of the earth"; Jeremiah's differentiation between act and intent — all vanished. The worship of YHWH remained, but not in the form in which Isaiah or Jeremiah had envisaged it. In some localities it was syncretized with the worship of Baal; in others it remained pure, yet primitive and anthropomorphic. In none did it attain the nobility with which metropolitan teachers had surrounded it.

The only seers who could arise in the backward environment of exilic Palestine were those of a rural stamp — the successors of Nahum the Elkoshite. Narrow nationalists, they were characterized by an utter blindness to social conflict, a refusal to deal with individual unrighteousness, and a burning desire for vengeance against their people's enemies and conquerors. They had nothing to say in denunciation of the syncretistic village worship in their midst. They attained their highest eloquence not in appeals to return to YHWH, but in horrifying pictures of their enemies' destruction.

The fragments of their addresses which have been preserved are to be found in Isaiah, chapters 13, 14, 21, 34, and 35; and in Jeremiah, chapters 50 and 51.[9] Both the peculiar style and content of these writers make it easy to separate their work from the context, fixing their country as Judah and their date as the period of the exile. They describe the parched wilderness of southern Judah, the bituminous wastes of the Dead Sea district, and the blistering sand-laden whirlwinds of the desert, with the vividness of eye-witnesses. They compare the rejuvenated country of their vision with the typical Palestinian scenery of Carmel, Lebanon, and Sharon. They all predict the fall of

Babylonia. Yet it is easy to see that most, if not all, of them, lived at the beginning of the exilic period, long before their prophecy was fulfilled, for they know nothing of Cyrus and the Persians. The instruments of divine vengeance on which they rely are the Medes, Babylonia's most powerful rival in the first half of the sixth century B.C.E.

The spirit which animates their prophecies is not that of the gentle, pacific Jeremiah, but of his opponents, the "false," ultra-nationalist, provincial-patrician seers. Gloating over the future destruction of their enemies, these writers are silent about any wrong-doing among their own people. Yet they were neither wicked nor godless; they were simply deluded fanatics, patriotic visionaries, who confused wish with reality, and naïve hope with reasonable expectation.

Had prophetic religion found no other spokesmen during the exile it would inevitably have degenerated into another Near Eastern mythology, and deservedly been lost. Fortunately its true spirit, banished from Palestine, found a safe haven in Babylonia, where Nebuchadnezzar had quite unwittingly contributed to its development and preservation.

While the Palestinian population during the exile was almost exclusively peasant in character, that of the Babylonian deportation included members of the lay patricianship, the Temple hierarchy, the city artisans, as well as the country gentry. Each class among the exiles responded to the catastrophe in characteristic manner. The outcry of the lay nobility has been preserved by one of its members in the fourth chapter of Lamentations.[10] The author reveals his class prejudice in almost every verse he writes. He says nothing of the destruction of the Temple;

he wastes no words on the devastation of Judah's smaller cities. He is concerned solely with the sufferings of "the precious sons of Zion.... that did feed on dainties" and "were brought up in scarlet." His vision is haunted by the princes, who "were purer than snow," "whiter than milk," "more ruddy in body than rubies" (4.2–7). He cannot suppress his disappointment that Egypt failed his people. But above all he mourns Zedekiah, "the breath of our nostrils, the anointed of the Lord.... of whom we said: 'Under his shadow we shall live among the nations' " (4.20). It never occurs to him to impute the sin for which the city was punished, to the King, the princes, or the people. It all happened, he thinks, because of the rigors of the reformation of Josiah, and its aftermath. "Because of the sins of her prophets, and the iniquities of her priests, *that have shed the blood of the just in the midst of her.*" The reference to King Josiah and his counselors is unmistakable. Only under that unfortunate king had prophets joined priests in destroying their common enemies, those who worshiped at the rural altars. The poet betrays his sympathy for his fellow-landowners of the countryside by calling their priests "the just," and at the same time indicates his own high governmental position by blaming the conflict not on the civil authorities who doubtless waged it, but on the Temple priests and the prophets who instigated it.

The poet has no plans for the future. The restoration of Judah as a state is impossible; and the prospect for the survival of its faith offers the writer no comfort. He definitely belongs to the group who held that "the Lord seeth us not; the Lord hath forsaken the land" (Ezek. 8.12). He can weep over the past; he cannot harbor any aspiration for the future. His only consolation is the hope that Edom, too, though it escaped Jerusalem's fate for the moment, will ultimately share it!

Equally narrow and fatuous is the message of Psalm 137, which was obviously composed by exiled priests of the Temple who had returned to their land.[11] "How shall we sing the Lord's song, in a foreign land?" they had asked when the Babylonian captors asked them for "one of the songs of Zion." They did not refuse to utter the hymns because that might gratify their victors. They simply could not worship God except on His own soil. Their ritual was associated with the Temple; when they were removed from that, their religion lost all meaning.

This poem,[12] too, ends with an invective against Edom. Perhaps it was written before 586 by some priests who managed to return to Palestine from their exile and were therefore free to utter imprecations against the Imperial power as well as against its little ally. The poem may even have been intended to stir the people to revolt. In any event the author belonged to the party of ultra-nationalists, who actually dared carry on their propaganda against Babylonia, even in the exile. Two of them, in fact, were burned alive by Nebuchadnezzar for their seditious activities.[13]

Far different from the attitude of these lay and ecclesiastic Nationalists was that taken by the prophetically minded priest who wrote the Second Chapter of Lamentations.[14] The author's association with the Temple is clear. He cannot understand how God rejected "in the indignation of His anger *the king and the priest;*" how He could forget "His footstool," "cast off His altar," and "abhor His sanctuary;" how He could be silent when the enemy murdered "priest and prophet in the sanctuary of the Lord." The poet is particularly moved when he thinks of the desolation of Zion on the Sabbath and "the appointed season," once such festive occasions. The crowds and tumult of the "days of assembly" continue to haunt his imagination. When he recalls the scene of the approaching armies, as they gathered to besiege Jerusalem, he can find no more appropriate simile for them than that of the gathering pilgrims on Passover, Shabuot, and Sukkot. Even when the enemy had burst into the sanctuary, uttering their pagan shouts of victory, it seemed to the priest that they made a tumult "in the House of the Lord as in the day of a solemn assembly."

The contrast between the pietism of the second chapter and the secularism of the fourth chapter of Lamentations is strikingly shown by the fact that the name of God occurs thirteen times in the former and only thrice in the latter poem. The difference involves more than statistics. The Divine Name occurs again and again in Lamentations 2 because the author of that poem regards Him as the true source of Israel's sufferings. Its defeat is a punishment for its sins. The human enemy is but the instrument of God's anger, and may well be left out of account. In Lamentations 4, it is the mortal conqueror who is primarily considered. God might have defeated him, had He chosen, it is true. But He had obviously decided not to interfere.

Characteristically, the pietist utters no imprecations against the enemies of his people. He is convinced that Judah has suffered just punishment for its sins, in following the false prophets who saw visions "of vanity and delusion" (2.14) and failed to expose the nation's transgression. There is but one hope for it: "Arise, cry out in the night, at the beginning of the watches; pour out thy heart like water before the face of the Lord" (2.19).

In this rejection of any thought of vengeance, and in his call to the people to return to God, the poet most nearly approaches the doctrine of contemporary prophecy. But prayer alone did not satisfy the prophets. They worked out a program for the preservation of Judaism in the midst of the exile. They accepted the exile with resignation, but were determined to resist assimilation in Babylonia, as their ancestors had resisted it in Palestine. They could not establish a temple on foreign soil; Deuteronomic law forbade that. But they could, and would, gather for prayer-meetings; they would observe their Sabbaths and their festivals; continue the practice of circumcision; abstain from forbidden meats; and patiently await the restoration of their Commonwealth and its sanctuary.

The cornerstone of their communal life was to be social righteousness, and the practice of justice by each of their people in his relation with his neighbors.

These doctrines which within a generation were adopted by the vast majority of Babylonian Judaites were at first espoused only by the urban plebeians among the exiles. This is obvious from an analysis of the composition of the exilic community, which the scriptural historians, as though conscious of its importance, describe with precision. The first deportation, they record, consisted of ten thousand able bodied men (many of whom were accompanied by their families). One thousand of them were smiths and carpenters; seven thousand, members of the country gentry, the backbone of the army; the remaining two thousand, apparently, were drawn from the hierarchy and the nobility.[15]

It was this community to which Jeremiah addressed his famous epistles, calling on its members to "build houses and dwell in them," and to seek "the peace of the city whither

I have led you captive, for in its peace shall ye have peace."[16] Apparently the prophet, whose party in Jerusalem was too insignificant to prevent his imprisonment, had a sufficient following in the exile to make this exhortation effective. For such was the response to it that the ultra-nationalists in Babylonia demanded that the authorities of Jerusalem prevent his further writing.[17]

But who were Jeremiah's followers in Babylonia? The members of the nobility were those who persecuted him; the gentry were the backbone of the nationalist movement, which he opposed. Obviously, Jeremiah's following was derived, as a rabbinic tradition indicates,[18] from the third group, the smiths and the carpenters: the plebeians of Jerusalem's market place.

Various social factors combined to give these urban plebeians greater influence in Babylonia than they had ever possessed in Palestine. Of these we may enumerate the following: (1) their comparatively large number; (2) the ease with which they could adjust themselves to the new environment; (3) their possession of a definite program of action; (4) the disappearance of the motive to assimilation from most of the former nobility; (5) the erosion of those groups who were subject to assimilation; and (6) the reduction of practically the whole community to the status of plebeians.

(1) It may seem curious that one thousand people should exercise a determining influence on the Babylonian deportation, especially when they were outnumbered nine to one by other groups. But it must be recalled that the prophetic following formed a more compact, determined, and positive group than the rest. And for such a group a proportion of ten percent is considerable. The Pharisees, whose enrolled

membership constituted only a small fraction of their contemporary Commonwealth, controlled its culture completely.[19] It is obvious that the urban plebeians of Babylonia, being relatively more than twice as strong, were quite irresistible.

That they were without equal influence in Judah was due in the main to the fact that their proportion to the rest of the population was much smaller. It is a plausible conjecture that they formed only one fifth of the population of Jerusalem, or less than one fiftieth of that of the country. That was a sufficiently large minority to preserve its traditions, but was far too small to influence national policy.

(2) But aside from numerical strength, the urban plebeians were the only ones among the deportees who could easily adjust themselves to the new life. The resources of all the other captives, namely their land and their possessions, had been left behind; but the skill of the artisan and the cunning of the tradesman were inalienable from their persons. The farmer might have to seek a post as manager or tenant; the craftsman, given permission to work, had no difficulties before him. The brilliant suggestion has been made that the great clan of the Senaa, which constituted the largest single group of returning exiles in 538 B.C.E., were really descendants of these exiled artisans.[20] In Jerusalem they had been called *senua*, "the hated," or "the despised." Their class consciousness made them retain the name, but transformed it, as so frequently happens in history, to one of honorific connotation. Their large number testifies to the prosperity which met them because of their ready acceptance of their new life.

(3) The plebeians prepared themselves for exile not only by their economic status, but by their intellectual outlook.

For generations, their leaders had taught them that the Palestinian community was doomed and that they must be ready for deportation and purification. The program of their life in the Dispersion had been worked out for them. In any crisis those who have a plan of adjustment have an advantage over those who lack it; the confused nobility and gentry, who had spurned the prophets in Palestine, had no alternative but to accept their guidance in Babylonia.

(4) The sociological forces making for assimilation in Palestine were practically without influence in Babylonia. There was little possibility for free mingling between Judaite captive and Babylonian victor. And even had the Babylonians been willing to accept the Judaites as equals, the resentment which the Judaite bore toward his conqueror and enslaver would have made association difficult.

(5) On the other hand, the limited group which was admitted to Babylonian society doubtless rapidly lost their Judaite consciousness. It was possible for a noble in Palestine to imitate the ways of the Canaanites and the Egyptians and yet remain within the fold of the Judaites, who were his people. In Babylonia, where the only ties holding the Judaites together were the common memories of the past, assimilation to the Babylonian habits of life meant abandonment of the Judaite community.

(6) Finally and most important of all, the Babylonian community became converted to plebeian theology, because it had been reduced to plebeian economy. Nebuchadnezzar had brought into being the classless society of which the prophets had for centuries been dreaming. Instead, however, of sharing equally in the national prosperity, all were partners in the national adversity. It was not the

unlanded, but the landed, class which had disappeared. The former patrician or provincial might glory in the estates which nominally he still owned in Palestine; but they provided him with no food, clothing, or shelter. Shorn of his power, the victim of far greater tyranny than he had ever exercised over his subordinates, he quickly absorbed the doctrine of the submerged.

The exile thus served as a social electrolysis. The landed and the landless groups which had been carrying on their cultural battle for centuries were at last separated. The landowners and their retainers were in Judah; the landless plebeians were in Babylonia. The division enabled the prophetic following, for the first time in history, to develop its traditions without the interference of an opposing majority.

Only in one respect did the Babylonian Judaites depart from the natural development of prophetic teachings — in their reverence for everything which reminded them of their home country and its capital city. The Temple which Jeremiah had rebuked, the priests whom he had contemned, the King and the princes whom he had denounced, became sacred memories. The local patriotisms of the provincials and the family connections of the patricians were both handed down from generation to generation. With something of the feeling which prompted the pilgrim fathers to name the place on which they landed Plymouth Rock after the port whence they had sailed, and to transplant throughout New England names of English cities which they had left, the Judaite squires in Babylonia recalled that they had come from Bethlehem, from Ludd, from Ono, from Jericho. The more aristocratic emigrés recalled their noble ancestors; but with pride, rather than arrogance. In the humiliation of common poverty, and under the urgent necessity to gain a livelihood, social prestige could be a consolation, but might also be a danger. In pioneering life, only the humble and the democratic, who forgot their splendid past and accepted equality with the meanest, could survive. Curiously, however, as soon as he ceased to demand respect, the aristocrat received it. The splendor of the setting sun gilded even the darkest clouds of the vanishing past, and made many plebeians recall with sentimental pangs "the good old days" which had been anything but good for them. Their reverence and admiration helped the patrician to retain his self-respect, and to recall throughout the exile the family connections of which he had so arrogantly boasted in Jerusalem.

The reverence of the plebeians for the patrician ancestral connections was in part associated with their resistance to assimilation. Many writers have confused the affection of the exiles for their traditions with nationalist chauvinism,[21] from which it was poles apart. It was precisely because the urban plebeian was not a nationalist in the ordinary sense of the word, that he could not yield in his loyalty to his traditions. If he could have expressed his love for his people by bold assertions of national superiority and by activities looking to his country's restoration as an independent kingdom, perhaps he would have found it unnecessary to stress the validity of his people's customs and institutions. But, convinced that his restoration could come only from God, and firmly believing that all men — other peoples as well as his own — were made in the image of God and were therefore equal, he could escape the self-abasement of artificially stimulated assimilation only by his cultural and religious particularism. He did not claim that his ways were obligatory for other peoples. Indeed, he specifically denied this. Other nations were bound by certain ethical regulations which God had fixed for all mankind. The ceremonial obligations of Judaism were binding on the Judaite alone.

The plebeian Judaites, on the other hand, were disposed to admit into their ranks those of the Babylonians who desired to join them. Regarding their distinction from other peoples not as racial or national, but as simply religious, intellectual and cultural, they could see no reason to reject those who became convinced of the truths they taught and were prepared to adopt the customs they observed. The word *Ger*, which had meant "landless" in pre-exilic Palestine, came to connote among them the "one who cleaved unto the Lord" from other peoples. They insisted that his rights in Israel were the same as those of the native born Judaite.

That this policy was not theoretical but had practical application is obvious from the record which tells us that no less than 652 out of the forty-two thousand persons who returned in 538 B.C.E. (about one and one-half percent) could not tell whether they were descended from Judaite ancestry (Ezra 2.59).

It is important to master this doctrine, for it is basic to appreciation of post-exilic plebeian philosophy, Pharisaism, and its interpretation of the Torah, notably the so-called Priestly Code, which gave Proto-Pharisees and Pharisees so much inspiration. The usual indictment of this major section of the Torah as narrow and bigoted amazes one who has lived according to its main regulations. As analyzed in current biblical studies, the code avers equality of the sexes[22] and of nations,[23] establishes Palestine as an economic as well as political democracy,[24] in which every person is allotted an inalienable right to an equal amount of land, and no distinction is permitted between the native and the alien,[25] and yet its formulation is described as a backward step in the development of religion!

True, it demands, together with social justice, adherence to traditional custom. It insists that the Judaite observe his Sabbath[26] and the law of circumcision,[27] that he desist from eating forbidden food,[28] and that he observe the rules of Levitical purity.[29] It definitely sets up barriers between Israel and the world. But that the barriers are neither racial nor national, but only religious and ceremonial, does not seem to have occurred to students. Any pagan might become an Israelite through the process of conversion and acceptance of the principles of the Law. Once the pagan joined the community of Israel, he obtained all the rights of any other member, and the Israelite was specifically commanded to love him as himself (Lev. 19.34). Yet it is only when we realize their further significance that we can understand the true spirit of this legislation, which is fundamental to the whole Law. Far from being a backward step in the development of either Judaism or religion, it is the climax of the whole prophetic teaching.

The universal acceptance of the prophetic doctrine in Babylonia necessarily involved the decay of the prophetic movement as a formal institution. Prophecy had been the voice of the protesting, submerged, disinherited minority. In the deportation, where this minority became a dominating majority, there was need not for protest and criticism, but for guidance and legislation. The prophet became the scribe; the critic became the teacher. Instead of telling people what they must not do lest they die, it became his task to tell them what they ought to do that they might live. It was thus in Babylonia that the first steps were taken to transform prophetic religion into the system of norms and rules which is usually denominated legalism.

This transformation is usually described as a descent, as though the constructive effort of the legislator were in some manner inferior to the critical work of the prophet. Actually, of course, there was neither rise nor fall in the change. The scribe was the disciple of the prophet. "Moses," the ancient tradition properly records, "received the Law from Mount Sinai, and handed it over to the elders; the elders handed it over to the prophets; and the prophets handed it over to the men of the Great Assembly."[30] The alteration was due entirely to the circumstances of the times. There was only one loss in the substitution of legalism for prophecy; poetry was replaced by prose. So long as the representative of prophetic religion had merely to create a general yardstick with which to measure specific evils in the Commonwealth, he could — indeed, he had to — resort to poetical composition. He could spend chapter after chapter in denunciation of social wrong-doing, in painting the outlines of a future ideal commonwealth, in describing the wrath of God against those who violated His will. But when he found himself faced with the task of nation-building, he realized that the time for the grand style had passed. Precision, accuracy, and brevity were far more important than beauty and magnificence. The imagination which this task required was mathematical and technical rather than dramatic and artistic. The times needed blueprints to guide the craftsmen, the carpenters and the masons, rather than landscapes to inspire the esthetes. Some of the rarest individuals in history, like Moses and Isaiah, have combined both gifts in themselves. The Book of Deuteronomy possesses a poetic loftiness of expression and at the same time devotes itself to detailed questions of life, in a manner which demonstrates it to be the work of the most inspired of all prophets. Unfortunately for the human race, such geniuses appear only once in many generations, perhaps centuries. In their absence, their work must be carried on by lesser men, who still reflect something of the majesty of their Master's power. As the sages, with their usual insight, put it: "The face of Moses was like that of the sun; that of Joshua was like that of the moon."[31] In Jewish history, there have been a few dazzling, brilliant suns; but of course these have been outnumbered by the many lesser, though almost equally important and distinguished, luminaries. Those who were endowed with these gifts became the foremost teachers in the history of Jewish legalism — Simeon the Righteous, Akiba ben Joseph, Saadia Gaon, and Moses Maimonides. Most of their comrades became craftsmen of the Law.

Perhaps, however, a special imaginative gift was needed by the Babylonian pioneers in the field of legalism. They legislated not only for their own generation; they instituted the habit which, we have already observed,[32] had such profound effect on later Palestinian life, of creating norms for the future. Realizing that Babylonian life did not allow for the realization of their conception of justice, and convinced that God would restore them ultimately to the land of their fathers, they carefully prepared a program for the Ideal Commonwealth which they hoped to establish in Judah. The dream of this Ideal Commonwealth added zest to their hope for a return and was doubtless one of the forces which kept alive the "Zionist" movement of that day.

The visionary aspirations of the plebeian idealists coincided with the more concrete hopes and ambitions of the former patricians and provincials, who hoped to return to their ancestral estates, and of the priests, who eagerly awaited the restoration of the Temple. The whole of the Babylonian Judaite community was thus permeated with the urge for a return to the Holy Land.

For many years the aspiration seemed impossible of realization. The most optimistic dreamer could find no encouragement for his hopes. Suddenly, however, a new light dawned upon them. In the year 562 B.C.E. Amil-Marduk liberated Jehoiachin, who had been held in prison for thirty-seven years, ever since his surrender to Nebuchadnezzar (in 597), and set his "throne above the thrones of all the [subject] kings," who were with him in Babylonia.[33]

There can be little doubt that the liberation of Jehoiachin was part of a determined policy which Amil-Marduk felt essential for the preservation of the Empire. Nebuchadnezzar had conquered the distant lands, but had done nothing to ensure their loyalty. His successor apparently believed that the conquests could be consolidated if the various provinces and peoples were treated with liberality. He knew well that Babylonia was surrounded by powerful empires, the Medes to the north and east, and the Lydians to the west. There was every reason to fear that when they attacked her, they would find powerful allies within her domains. There was only one thing to be done — to win the loyalty of the subject peoples.

We may easily imagine the delight of the exiled Judaites when they saw their King released from imprisonment and made the household guest of the Great King. The historian of the period attached such importance to the event that he considered it a suitable climax to his history of Israel. King Jehoiachin himself, doubtless moved with unutterable joy in his innermost heart, named the son who was born to him after his release, *Pedaiah*, "YHWH hath redeemed."[34] And, indeed, it must have seemed to many observers that it was not only the King, but his people, who had been restored to divine favor. The hope of a restoration suddenly took on new life and strength; the impossible was fast becoming the probable.

But the dream was destined to be brief. The leaders of the Babylonian army had no faith in Amil-Marduk's policy of conciliation. They had helped Nebuchadnezzar seize the provinces by force; and by force alone would they be kept. Kindness would be misinterpreted as weakness and would only lead to difficulties. The leader of this faction seems to have been one Nergal-Sar-Usur (perhaps the biblical Nergal-sar-ezer), a leading general, and brother-in-law of the King. In the year 559 a rebellion broke out against Amil-Marduk, who was slain, and Nergal-Sar-Usur became King in his place.

The death of Amil-Marduk must naturally have been a severe blow to the most hopeful of the Judaites. Yet it did not crush them. Perhaps Ezekiel's prophecy about Gog and Magog, with its symbolism of Babylonia's destruction on the hills of Palestine, was uttered when the good King

Amil-Marduk fell before the army leaders, and the prophet realized that only the destruction of Babylonia's power could lead to Israel's restoration.

The prophet did well to retain his faith. The policies which Amil-Marduk had favored, rejected for the moment, were to be revived by a far greater ruler, who was destined to make them the foundation stone of his Empire: Cyrus the Great. The year of Amil-Marduk's death witnessed the rise of Cyrus to the principate of Anshan, an obscure subject province of Median dominion. Before many years had passed, however, this prince was to become a world figure. Ezekiel probably died, however, before the new ruler showed his prowess. The mantle of prophetic leadership taken from Ezekiel was given to another, greater teacher, whom he did not know, and who apparently knew nothing of him, the Second Isaiah. A native of Palestine during the exile, this man, whose real name has been forgotten but whose words will ever be remembered, became the most majestic figure in Hebrew prophecy. The equal of Isaiah in eloquence and political sagacity, of Jeremiah in tenderness and sense of the pathetic, and of Ezekiel in dramatic power and poetic imagination, he surpasses both predecessors and successors in clarity of thought, universality of outlook, theological insight, and philosophical understanding. Combining in himself the poet and the thinker, the patriot and the internationalist, he loves humanity the more deeply because of his intense affection for his own people. With singular receptivity to new ideas, his mind continues to grow even after he has entered on his prophetic career, and we perceive with increasing admiration and respect the continual widening of his intellectual horizons. No prophet spoke with more complete awareness of the permanent significance of his message or with greater confidence in his ability to interpret it; yet none was more truly self-effacing and fit to become the Great Unknown.

In his country origin and his early travels, as well as in one other phase of his career — his transformation into a teacher of the urban doctrine of social justice — Deutero-Isaiah resembles Ezekiel, from whom he is otherwise far apart.[35] In the twenty-seven chapters of his work, we can follow his development step by step, from the early days when, overwhelmed with the possibilities of a restored Commonwealth, he poured forth his joy in a torrent of unsurpassed eloquence, through the period of pain and disillusionment when, his hopes frustrated, his ideals crushed, he sat down to reconstruct his philosophy and to adjust it to the changed phenomena he saw about him and finally into the years of his wise and melancholy old age, when he realized that he had been called neither to build nor to announce a great commonwealth, but to help reform and improve a small people. The careers of few men are more illuminating or more instructive; none is as replete with both pathos and grandeur, tragedy and spiritual majesty.

The youth of the prophet coincided with that of Cyrus. His first prophecy was apparently delivered about the year 550, shortly after the great Persian conqueror mad his epochal advance into Asia Minor. The Babylonian power in Palestine had already begun to wane; everyon could see the dangers which were facing the Empire. The son of prosperous parents, Deutero-Isaiah was given th opportunity to travel; doubtless he visited Tyre, perhap even Egypt and the cities of Syria.[36] It must have been during one of these journeys that he became convinced tha

Judah's fundamental need was a metropolis. Every other country had an urban center; Judah alone remained bucolic, countrified. As he pondered over the problem, he realized that there was no obstacle to the rebuilding of Jerusalem save the inertia of the people. The Babylonians, who had destroyed the city almost half a century earlier, would hardly object to its reconstruction; in fact, they might welcome it as a bulwark on the outposts of their Empire. A Voice cried to him, "Call," but his heart told him that there was no audience for him to move. "How shall I call?" he answers. "All flesh is grass, and its goodliness as the flower of the field" (40.7). Yet the Voice would not be silenced; "The word of our God will be established forever," it said. The time had come for Zion's children to comfort her. God who had willed her destruction now called for her restoration.

The prophet said nothing in this first call of rebuilding the Temple; he held out no hope for Jewish autonomy; he made no reference to the return of the exiles from Babylonia or the gathering of the dispersed from other lands; and certainly he had nothing to say about social injustice or the significance of his message to the peoples of the world. His concern was with Jerusalem, and with her alone.

Suddenly the world scene shifted. The much traveled and well-informed prophet followed with amazement the issue of the struggle between the hitherto little known Cyrus and the supposedly indomitable Croesus, King of Lydia, in Asia Minor. Less than a decade had passed since Cyrus had become prince of his native province; and already he had proven himself the "man of destiny." Within six years after he attained the principate of Anshan, he had proclaimed himself King of Persia, broken the power of the

Medes, and made himself master of their huge dominions. Not satisfied with these memorable victories, he had had the temerity to attack the kingdom of Lydia in Asia Minor, whose ruler, Croesus, was said to be the richest man on earth. Croesus, underestimating the ability and power of the young upstart, had taken insufficient precautions for defense, and soon found himself besieged and helpless in his capital, Sardis. Before long he had to yield, and the former subject princeling of the Medes became the world's foremost potentate, with a dominion extending from the Indus River to the Aegean Sea.

The prophet of Israel, surveying the scene from the hills of Palestine, realized with all other intelligent observers that a new era in history had opened. Curious, unutterable hopes stirred in his breast. Might not the rôle of Cyrus have some significance for Israel? Might it not be a divine portent, indicating the path which Israel's future development was to follow? To ask the question was to supply the answer. The dreamlike fancy of one day became the dominating ideal of the next. What Anshan had accomplished in the sphere of mundane government, Israel would undertake in the far more important sphere of spiritual influence. The Persian had imposed his rule on the nations; Israel would impart its knowledge to them. For the moment the problem of Jerusalem's restoration was overshadowed in the prophet's mind; other, broader issues were at stake. The future of mankind hung in the balance, its fate was to be decided by the tiny people of Israel. Was it to continue in idolatry and ignorance, or would it rise to monotheism and truth? The ferment in religious faith evident everywhere in the world, the advance of Zoroastrianism in Babylonia and Persia, the confusion of doctrine observable in western cities, together with the international situation — the imminence of a destructive war between Persia and Babylonia — offered an unexampled opportunity for a widespread religious movement which Israel might initiate.

When, after deep cogitation, the prophet finally uttered his call, it was with the passion of innermost conviction. His reference to Cyrus was, naturally, cautious, recondite, even ambiguous. The Babylonian governor, who still ruled in Mizpah, might resent undue enthusiasm by a Judaite orator for the foreign conqueror, who was probably preparing to subdue the Empire. The prophet couched the description of Cyrus in terms which might conceivably refer to Abraham, the ancestor of Israel, though, to be sure, the prophet would then appear in a guise quite unknown to the Book of Genesis.

> "Who hath raised the victorious[37] one out of the east,
> Calling him to His feet;
> Giving nations before him,
> And making him rule over kings;
> He maketh them as dust with his sword,
> And as driven stubble with his bow.
> He pursueth them, and passeth on safely,
> He treadeth no way with his feet" (41.2 ff.).

Even more emphatically did he express himself at the end of the prophecy:

> "I aroused one from the north and he has come;
> Yea from the east, calling on My name;
> He trampleth princes like mire,
> As the potter treads upon clay" (41.25).

The Judaite hearers of the address doubtless recognized at once the portrait of Cyrus, who came both from the "North" and from the "East." But for the Babylonian spies and traducers, the camouflage was complete. How could they suspect that a Hebrew prophet would hail the pagan prince, as one "who called on the name of Israel's God." Yet the prophet could do so with a clear conscience; for Cyrus called on God with his acts, if not in words. Heathen conqueror as he was, he fulfilled to the letter — so it must have seemed to Deutero-Isaiah — the words of the earlier prophets. Whom else could Jeremiah, for instance, have described with such vigor and enthusiasm as the northern invader?

But if Cyrus had indeed come to fulfill the words of the prophets, that fact was itself of importance to all the world. It had but to be made manifest to the nations and all would realize that in Israel's God alone is there truth.

Any doubt they might entertain would be dissipated by the coincidence of Cyrus's conquests with the rebuilding of Jerusalem. Either event alone might be an accident of history; together they offered an accumulation of evidence which would be irrefutable.

> "The beginnings of Zion, behold them!
> I give Jerusalem a herald of joy."

The optimistic prophet did not for a moment doubt that the Israelites would at once undertake the reconstruction of their metropolis. In the midst of his fiery passion, he could not repress a smile at the discomfiture of the idol-makers, when they saw themselves defeated by the onrush of events. They would flee, each one to his place, confessing their works "vapor and vanity."

Yet how was the demonstration of God's truth, be it ever so dramatic and cogent, to be brought to the peoples of the world? The answer was simple — through the scattered communities of Israel's diaspora. It was not in vain that Israelites were to be found in every important center the prophet had visited. There were some in Egypt; there was a large deportation in Babylonia; there was a colony in Tyre; and there were the remnants, doubtless, of the ten tribes in Media. A frontal attack on idolatry might fail; but "the worm of Israel" making its way through the mountains of unbelief would grind them to dust even more effectively than threshing-sledges of iron. Who has not seen the hills of sand which the tiny worms dig up from the ground? And who will say that given determination and a purpose, these worms could not reduce great masses of earth?

Perhaps ordinarily the task might seem formidable. But the world was thirsting for the message of Israel. Like wanderers in a wilderness, the nations' throats were parched with scepticism, unbelief, and superstition; it was God's will that their need be answered — through Israel.

The shift in the prophet's interest from the physical restoration of Jerusalem to the spiritual reformation of humanity was probably altogether unconscious. Soon, however, he realized that the two ideals were not opposed to each other but supplementary. It was not as a boring worm — through the diaspora — that Israel was to influence mankind, but as a human teacher, a Servant of God, having his home in the world's spiritual center, Palestine.

There was no need for violence;[38] the prophet had no mind to contest the government of the world with the prince of Anshan. Israel had but to develop the true faith and become conscious of its mission; and all nations would ultimately hearken to it.

> "Behold My Servant, whom I sustain; My chosen in whom My soul delighteth;
> I have put My spirit upon him; he will make the right to go forth to the nations.
> He will not cry nor shout aloud; nor make his voice heard in the street.
> A bruised reed he will not break; and a dimly burning wick he will not quench;
> He will make the right to go forth according to the truth.
> He will not chide nor deal harshly,
> Till he have set the right in the earth, and the isles await his teaching."

Turning to the people themselves, he cries out:

> "I, the Lord, have called thee in righteousness,
> I took thee by the hand and kept thee,
> And have made thee My pledge to the peoples, the light of the nations;
> To open sightless eyes, to bring captives out of prison, from the dungeon those who sit in darkness" (42.1ff.).

Did anyone challenge these claims? Did they deny the prophet's prediction that soon the whole world would be united in the service of God? Let them beware. The physical victories of Cyrus had been foretold and had come to pass; so would the spiritual victories of Israel. Only the blindness and deafness of Israel, the "Servant of God," prevented it from seeing its opportunity and its task. Israel looked upon itself as a small people, entrapped and imprisoned, not realizing that only its sins brought evil upon it; and that freedom, service and spiritual leadership were beckoning to it, as soon as it returned to God.

There were moments, of course, when the prophet realized how fanciful his vision was. His heart wanted to believe; but his mind remained unconvinced. The whole dream was manifestly absurd. The sober rationalist who had seen Tyre and Zidon, Egypt and Asia Minor, who knew their culture and their civilization, their commerce and their wisdom, their art and their poetry, their wealth and their taste, could not, try as he might, persuade himself that their moral leadership must come from tiny, subject, rural Judah, with its ignorant, narrow-minded, crude-mannered peasantry. Still, backward as his countrymen were in every other phase of life and intellect, they alone, by some miracle — it could not possibly be anything else — had been informed of God's true being. With prophetic insight, which the history of later centuries was so amply to confirm, he returned to the solution which had suggested itself to him at the beginning — the use of the diaspora. The enlightened Israelites of the Dispersion, the traders of the great world centers, who knew Israel's ideals and understood the life of foreign countries, would serve as the interpreters of God to mankind.

True, so long as they remained scattered in their distant ports, they were spiritually impotent. The prophet had seen them at close range. He knew their weakness as well as their strength. Their religion was syncretistic;

their habits of mind assimilationist. They had lost contact with the sources of their own faith; they were engrossed in their daily tasks; they admitted themselves descendants of Jacob; some of them proclaimed themselves followers of YHWH; only a few definitely wrote on "their hands the name of YHWH, and announced themselves part of Israel." How were such men to be inspired to take over the task of recasting the mind of the world?

At last the prophet realized the significance of the call which had come to him at the beginning of his career. The men of the Dispersion who were carrying on the commerce of pagan cities would be brought back to Jerusalem; they would raise it to its former glory; and then, with their help, the divine message might go forth to the nations of the world. The restoration of Jerusalem and the reformation of humanity were thus not at all rival ideals; they were different phases of the same effort. Jerusalem had to be rebuilt that Israel might be exalted; Israel had to be exalted that Man might be saved.

The gathering of the dispersed of Israel was not, as the prophet now saw it, so hopeless as it might appear at first glance. Cyrus was about to attack Babylonia; his advent would be not merely a portent for Israel, but also a means for its reëstablishment. His conquest of Babylonia would enable the exiles in that country — the largest contingent of the Israelite diaspora — to return and would inaugurate the culmination of the prophetic program. In an address, full of humor and irony, the prophet envisages the assembling of the nations and their idols to see the glory of Israel and its God. In a single dramatic act, such as the situation demanded, God would demonstrate His truth before all the nations.

> "Sing, ye heavens, for the Lord has wrought it,
> shout, ye depths of the earth;
> Break forth, ye mountains, into song; forest, and every tree therein;
> For the Lord hath ransomed Jacob, He glorifies himself in Israel.
> Thus saith the Lord, thy Redeemer, He who formed thee from the womb,
> I am the Lord, maker of all . . . .
> Who confirms the word of His servant, and perfects the counsel of His messenger,
> Who says to Jerusalem, Be peopled, and to the cities of Judah, Be builded; yea, all its ruins will I restore;
> Who says to the deep, Be dry, and all thy rivers shall I make dry ground;
> *Who says of Cyrus, He is My shepherd, and he shall fulfil all my pleasure*" (44.23 ff.).

That the prophet should have dared to mention the Persian King while the Babylonians still ruled Judah may seem singular. Obviously, however, Cyrus had not yet attacked the Empire. It was only in the prophet's mind that he appeared as the world conqueror; and it was by implication, rather than with explicit statement, that the prophet indicated his belief in the Persian as the future victor.

Suddenly, Cyrus fulfilled the prophet's expectations and attacked Babylonia. There could no longer be any question of the trend of world events. The prophet can hardly contain himself:

> "Thus saith the Lord to his annointed, to Cyrus
> Whose right hand I hold,
> To trample nations before him, and loosen the loins of kings,
> To open before him the doors, and that the gates may not be shut;
> I will go before thee, and make the crooked places straight,
> I will break in pieces doors of brass, and cut in sunder bars of iron,
> And I will give thee treasures of darkness, the hoards long hidden in secret.
> That thou mayest know that I am the Lord,
> Who calleth thee by thy name, even the God of Israel . . .
> Maker of light, and creator of darkness, author of peace and creator of evil, I, the Lord, perform all this" (45.1ff.).

Almost as though he expected his words to be literally transmitted to the Conqueror, the Prophet carefully indicates that Israel's God of light and darkness, and not the Zoroastrian Ahura-Mazda, had given Cyrus his victory.[39] But the teacher's main concern is after all with Israel. He was more than ever impatient with Israel's slowness to understand her place in the world. "Alas," he cries, "for him that strives with his Maker; a potsherd with the maker of the earth. Shall the clay say to him that fashions it, What doest thou? Or thy work has no value at all? Can one say to a father, What begettest thou? Or to a mother, With what dost thou travail?" (45.10). It was impossible for Israel to escape the divine destiny put upon it. Cyrus would rebuild Jerusalem, he would restore the exiles, the metropolis would develop, distant nations would come to it to worship God; almost against the will of its children it would become the spiritual capital of the world. "Yea, Thou art a God, who veils Himself," the prophet cannot help calling out, "the God of Israel, the saviour" (45.15).

The prophet would have been less than human had the fall of Babylonia not moved him to cogitate on her career, her arrogance, her tyranny, and her end. He expects his people to come flocking back to the land of their ancestors, convinced at last that their destiny is fixed by God. Not only those in Babylonia, but those in Egypt and those in distant Media will return to rejoice in the miracle which was performed for them. "The self-despised, world-abhorred servant of nations" (49.7) will receive the homage of kings and prostrations of princes.

The exultation of the prophet was short-lived. At the supreme moment of his life, two terrifying disappointments were in store for him. Neither Cyrus nor Israel was ready to accept the prophetic mission. The expected edict of Cyrus, obtained doubtless through the unrecorded but heroic efforts of Babylonian Judaites, was at last issued. It reduced the aspirations of the Judaites to an almost negligible minimum.[40] There was no call to the exiles to return to the land; there was no announcement of the special place of Jerusalem in the religious history of the world. Judah was offered no rights of autonomy; its limits remained those fixed by Nebuchadnezzar in 597 B.C.E.; the *Negeb* was not restored to Judah; and there was no possibility of extending the Judaite domain to include the land of the Samaritans. The "redemption" had reduced itself to the return of a few exiles; the appointment of a Judaite *Pehah* (governor), Sheshbazzar, the scion of the late King Jeconiah;[41] the permission to rebuild the Temple, within definitely fixed limits; and the return of the sacred vessels which the Babylonians had taken from the sanctuary.

Even more disappointing was the exiles' response to this edict. The first return consisted of some forty thousand souls (Ezra 3.64). Whether they all came at once, or in the course of years, is not stated; but we may assume that they were not transplanted suddenly, or without regard to the necessity of orderly, slow settlement. In any event, the migration of forty thousand people seems impressive enough from the distance of twenty-seven centuries. Yet the prophet had expected more. He had hoped that the Babylonian exiles would rise as one man and seek their ancient home. Was this meager group of pioneers the Commonwealth he had foreseen? Was this the beginning of mankind's conversion to God? Was this insignificant ripple in the history of an obscure province and a despised people a sign which would demonstrate to the world the greatness of the God of Israel? For a moment the prophet was dumbfounded. The failure of the pagan King could be explained. Other potentates had proven themselves unworthy of prophetic confidence. Obviously Cyrus was not God's anointed. But what had happened to the people of Israel? The uncompromising, enthusiastic prophet could not realize that the immediate return of forty thousand people to a devastated country from a land in which they and their fathers had been settled for almost half a century, was an astonishing demonstration of loyalty. Surely, it seemed to him, the exiles could not understand the significance of the events which were occurring about them.

> "Wherefore did I come and find no one; call, but with none to answer?
> Lack I aught of power to ransom? Is there not in Me strength to rescue?" (50.2).

Did Israel consider herself divorced from God? Did she think He was without power to help her that she refrained from returning to His open arms?

There was little to be gained by these expostulations with an absent, distant, unhearing audience. Those who remained in Babylonia and the other seats of the diaspora had failed the prophet; he must see what could be achieved with those who had returned. They, too, were disheartened; and the prophet's manifest duty was to reawaken their courage and their hope, to show them that they were the nucleus of the Commonwealth of which he and they had both dreamed. Neighbors might laugh at their pretensions; might scoff at their weakness; might deride their aspirations. But they must not falter. He, himself, had "set his face like flint," knowing that ultimately he would be vindicated. He called on them to do likewise. On no other occasion did the prophet so manifestly transfer his own feelings to the people. Ostensibly it is Israel, the idealized Servant of God, who speaks; but the passions are clearly those which the prophet felt in his own spirit.

> "The Lord hath given me a tongue for teaching,
> To know how to help the fainting with a word,
> He wakeneth me early,
> Yea, early he quickeneth my ear,
> To hear as a pupil . . . .

I gave my back to the smiters, my cheeks to those
who plucked the beard;
My face I shielded not from insult and spitting.
The Lord, God, is my helper; therefore I am not
confounded" (50.4 ff.).

They were not the mighty torches which he had hoped God would hold up to the nations; they were the first sparks of gradually increasing flame.

"Who among you feareth the Lord, listening to the
voice of His servant,
Walketh in darkness, without light,
Let him trust in the name of the Lord, let him rely
on his God;
Behold, ye are all kindlers of fire; lighters of brands;
Go then in the light of your flame, in the brands ye
have kindled.
Ye have this from My hand,
For My sake, cleave ye to it" (50.10 ff.).[42]

Even as he spoke, however, the prophet's heart sank within him. He was trying to hold up the courage of his followers; but how could he hold up his own courage? He tried to find consolation in Israel's past. The wonders of the creation no longer interested him; what he needed was evidence not of God's power but of His interest in Israel. He looked back to Abraham. Abraham had been only one, but God had "blessed him and given him increase" (51.2). He thought of the exodus from Egypt. Certainly the arm which "had cleft Rahab, which had pierced the dragon" (51.8), was able to redeem Israel once more. What concern had he then with the decisions of "a mortal man, or the son of man who is made as the grass?" (51.12). How could he have forgotten that his true reliance must be on "the Lord, his Maker?" Yet he could not help weeping when he thought of the fate of Jerusalem, deserted by her own offspring, with "none to lead her of all the sons she bore, none to take her by the hand of all those she had reared" (51.18). Impatient with the dereliction and betrayal of the unresponsive diaspora, he distinguishes, for the first time, the righteous in Israel from the wicked. He had always, before, thought of Israel as a unit; but it was obviously multifold, compound, and complex. Those who had returned are "the pursuers of righteousness, who seek the Lord"; "those who know righteousness, people in whose heart is My Law." Never again would he utter the call to "Israel and Jacob," which is found in almost every one of his earlier prophecies. Except with reference to the God, or the Holy One of Israel, or events in Israel's past, the name disappears from his vocabulary.[43] There were those who responded and those who failed to respond; no tie united the two parts of the people.

The prophet was too powerful a spirit to withdraw from his task in the face of this collapse of his expectations. He continued to strive for his ideal — the conversion of mankind to God. But his prophecies had lost their youthful exuberance and sense of exultation. A note of sadness, almost a confession of failure, runs through almost all his subsequent addresses. With one or two exceptions they are all set in the minor key; indeed some of them even lack the poetic beauty of his earlier verse. The Prophet had suddenly become old, dispirited, prosaic. He was still wise, far-sighted, and more than ever liberal and great-hearted. Yet crushed and defeated, he permitted a certain impatience and bitterness to enter his soul. He had no doubt that

Zion would ultimately be rebuilt, God vindicated, and the world converted; but clearly it was not to be in his day or generation.

"The heavens shall vanish like smoke,
And the earth wear out like a garment,
Its people must likewise perish;
But My salvation abideth forever,
My triumph shall never be ended" (51.6).

And then, instead of anticipating a quick flight of all the exiles to Palestine, he remarks:

"Depart, depart, go out thence,
Touch no unclean thing!
Forth from the midst of her, purify yourselves,
Ye bearers of the Lord's utensils.
For not in haste shall ye go forth,
And not in flight shall ye remove;
For the Lord goeth before you,
And the God of Israel is your rearguard" (52.11f.).

The painful cogitations which filled the prophet's mind during these months of heart-rending disappointment, ultimately led to a moral discovery which must rank among the foremost events in the annals of human religion. Could it be, he asked himself, that the shame, suffering, and disappointment of his people were themselves part of the intricate divine plan to bring salvation to the nations? Was it necessary for the spiritual glory of the New Commonwealth that it begin humbly, with apparent failure? The questions had only to be raised for the answer to appear. It was manifest that had Israel returned from the exile through the decree of Cyrus, the sceptical would have explained the event in purely human terms. Israel had to return into the land, a humble and low group of immigrants, so that nations might watch it attain greatness as a divine symbol which could be neither mistaken nor disregarded. It had to be reduced to the lowest depths of suffering and humiliation, that its rise might be the more dramatic, magnificent, and impressive.

He called on his people to accept this fate with submission, and even with joy. If their suffering was necessary to bring about man's spiritual restoration, they should accept it, not only resignedly, but gladly. They were to be the martyr-nation, the self-effacing Servant of God. They could ask for nothing; they lived only to give.

The superb Idea, finally formulated, gushed forth in a torrent of eloquence, such as had rarely come even from the prophet's inspired lips.

"Behold, My servant shall prosper,
He shall be honoured and greatly exalted.
For as much as many were appalled at him,
For his face was marred more than any other,
And his visage than the children of men,
So shall the mighty ones be startled at him,
Kings shall be silent before him,
For what had not been told them they shall see,
What they had not heard, they shall understand.
'Who had believed what we report?' [they shall say]
'And to whom was the Lord's arm revealed?
For he grew up as a slender shoot before us,
As a root out of the arid ground;
He had no form nor charm, that we should notice him;
No beauty that we should admire him.

He was despised and forsaken of men, a man of sorrows
and acquainted with pain;
As one from whom men hide their faces he was despised,
and we esteemed him not.
*Yet it was our woes that he bore, and our sorrows that
he carried;*
*While we accounted him punished, smitten of God,
and afflicted.*
*But he was wounded for our transgressions, bruised
for our iniquities;*
*On him fell the chastisement that made us whole, and with
his stripes were we healed.*
*All we like sheep had gone astray, we had turned each
to his own way;*
*And the Lord laid on him the penalty, charged upon him
the guilt of us all*' " (52.13—53.6).

But the suffering of his Servant is not to be in vain. The Lord assures him:

"When his life shall make atonement for sin,[44]
He will see his seed, will prolong his days,
And the Lord's purpose will prosper in his hands.
He will see the fruit of his mortal travail,
In knowing himself true will be satisfied;
My servant will bring many to the right,
For he will carry their sins" (53.10–11).

The powerful call has rung across the centuries, moving generations of men as have few other passages in literature. It has been the inspiration of poetry, music, and legend, no less than of religious devotion and martyrdom. Yet so high is the ideal that few even in the most enlightened day can be said to attain it. There are thousands, even tens of thousands, who are willing to give their own lives for great causes, and sometimes even for small matters. But how many are there who can think of their people, their extended ego, as a means to aid other people more distant from them? Yet this is exactly what the ancient prophet demanded from his fellow-Palestinians. They were not to seek independence or national greatness, they were not to hope for power or mastery, they were to find contentment in the mission which God had assigned to them, to be hated because they loved, to be persecuted because they were right, to be spurned because they were magnanimous.

Like the other visions of the prophets, this one was destined to be fulfilled with an accuracy which would have amazed his most devoted followers. The religion of Palestine was ultimately carried to the ends of the earth; the day was to come when kings and princes were to prostrate themselves before the Holy City; the God of Deutero-Isaiah was to be worshiped by half the human race. The prophet was destined to be vindicated also in his belief that his result could be achieved only after the religion of Israel had been purified in the enlightenment of a restored Jerusalem; and that the bearers of the message were to be primarily the Jews of the diaspora. In the curious paradox of history, however, the people who gave this religious guidance to the western world became the Suffering Servant, being exposed to the most continuous and persistent religious persecution ever inflicted on any group. When the ancient world collapsed, and all Europe was thrown back into primeval darkness, the continued existence of Israel helped restore something of the classical light in the first renaissance of the twelfth century;[45] Israel's curious devotion to ancestral customs, language and literature enabled later generations to comprehend fully the teachings of the prophets and the apostles; its survival as a submerged minority which, in the midst of economic and political suffering, yet retained high cultural, intellectual, ethical, and religious interests, raised from among it a whole series of tribunes of the people, who have kept alive the prophetic traditions of human equality even until our own day. But how could the prophet know that the conversion of the world, which he foresaw, would take place only after eight centuries, and that the Suffering Servant would in truth enter on his tragic rôle almost at the same moment?

If the future was partly concealed from the prophet, it was altogether unintelligible to his audience. The description of the Suffering Servant must have fallen on their ears like a terrifying malediction. For them its sweet cadences were not imaginative poetry, but grim reality. The program was too heavy for mortals to accept without protest. So discouraging must have been the effect of his words that the prophet soon felt impelled to brighten the gloom with a vivid picture of Jerusalem's ultimate glory. Jerusalem might be barren, he cried, but she would ultimately produce more children than many a fruitful mother; there was no reason for either shame or fear; her future spiritual leadership of the world was assured by God Himself. Yet even as he spoke with conviction and encouragement, the prophet let drop a word which showed how deeply his own spirit was suffering. He had begun his career with a call to his people to "comfort" Jerusalem; he had to confess that after years, perhaps after decades of preaching, she still remained "uncomforted."

"Thou afflicted, and disquieted, and uncomforted,
See, I lay thy foundations with beryl,
And ground thee with sapphires;
I will make thy battlements with rubies;
And thy gates of carbuncle-stones,
Wholly of gems thine enclosing walls" (54.11f.).

It is altogether probable that the prophet, having delivered this message, was silent for some years. If the future of Israel was to be an eschatological redemption, there was nothing more to be said. At any rate an obvious lacuna separates the address to the "barren one" in chapter 54 from the renewed call in chapter 55. The difference is far from sufficient to justify the theory of another author, especially in view of the fundamental similarities in style and thought which persist throughout the work.[46] But it does indicate a profound crisis in the prophet's career. It is clear that the teacher had been mingling with the exiles of Babylonia and had come, partially, under the influence of their teachings of the significance of the Sabbath, the moral responsibility of the individual, and the fundamental importance of social justice. His disappointment in Israel had already freed him from belief in it as a moral unit. But he had still failed to recognize the ethical implications of his new frame of mind. The social conflict, the struggle of man to dominate man, and the injustice of exploitation, were quite invisible to his country-trained eyes. His contact with the Babylonian Judaites removed the scales from his eyes. Suddenly he saw the world as it was, and at once he emerged as the teacher of social righteousness, human equality, international peace, and loyalty to Judaite ceremonials.

His first reference to the problem of individual justice occurs in his comforting address to the "barren one." It was a somewhat hesitant, almost embarrassed suggestion, yet sufficiently definite to be unmistakable. Addressing Jerusalem, he said merely:

> "With righteousness shalt thou be established;
> Be far from oppression,
> That thou mayest not fear,
> And that terror may not approach thee" (54.14).[47]

The remark may seem to us quite innocuous; yet so foreign is it to the content of preceding addresses that as careful a commentator as Duhm removes it as a gloss![48] The truth, however, is that the prophet must be taking his first step in the direction of social teaching; the next chapter reveals him in his full stride. With the passing of time, he accepted not only the principle of individual responsibility and the concern with social righteousness, but he even alluded to angelic intermediaries between God and man, and became the foremost exponent of prophetic internationalism.

His new doctrine of universalism is of especial interest because of its relation to his youthful teachings. He had always been concerned with the conversion of mankind to a knowledge of God. But it had never occurred to him that in the spiritual empire to be established, Israelite and converted pagan would be equal. He did not discuss the problem in detail; but it is clear that Israel was to remain the "guide" of all the other nations. Like the apostle Paul many centuries later, he conceived of two measures of observance — one for the Jew, another for the Gentile.[49]

Such a doctrine was entirely opposed to the mentality of the returning exiles. The equality of all men was a fundamental principle of their faith; and they looked forward to a time when everyone would be equal before God. The acceptance of proselytes into Judaism had been practiced by them throughout their sojourn in Babylonia; they could not conceive of any different policy being adopted now.[50]

It was apparently a curious incident which brought the prophet out of his retirement and thrust him once more into the arena of public debate.[51] A eunuch, attached to the governor's court, wanted to become Judaized; were the Jews ready to accept him? The prophet considered the problem so important that he devoted a whole chapter to it.

"Ho, everyone who thirsts, come ye to the waters [he cries],
Yea, come he who has no money;
Buy and eat, without money,
And without price both wine and milk . . .
Incline your ear, and come unto Me,
Hear, that your soul may live,
And I will make an eternal compact with you,
The favor assured to David . . .
Let not the stranger say,
Who has joined himself unto the Lord,
Separate indeed am I,
By the Lord from His people.
Nor be it said by the eunuch,
Behold I am a withered tree . . .
And the strangers who join themselves

Unto the Lord, to do His bidding,
To love the Name of the Lord
And to prove themselves His servants,
All who keep the Sabbath, not profaning it,
And who lay fast hold of My covenant,
And I will bring them to My holy mountain,
And give them joy in My house of prayer;
Their whole-burnt offerings and sacrifices
Shall be offered for acceptance on My altar;
For My house a house of prayer
For all peoples shall be called.
'Tis the word of the Lord, God,
Who gathereth the scattered of Israel:
Yea, others to him will I assemble, My own to be ingathered" (55.1ff.).

No more fervid plea for the equality of all peoples in worship had yet been heard in Israel. What followed this announcement is not recorded; but it may be inferred from the following address, in which the prophet leaves the high rostrum from which he had delivered all his earlier utterances and undertakes a fierce, bitter, personal arraignment of his opponents. All the suppressed passion of his soul breaks forth in an invective which is almost without parallel in Scripture. The prophets (obviously those of rural, Judaite origin) who opposed him, are "blind, unable to discern"; they are "dumb dogs, unable to bark, dreaming, napping, loving slumber," forsaking the flock which is entrusted to their care. "Yea, and the dogs are greedy, they cannot be satisfied!" As if to make clear that he is speaking of village prophets, of the same type Amos had denounced more than two hundred years earlier,[52] he accuses them of crying, "Come, I will fetch wine! Let us revel with drink. And thus shall be yet the morrow, a great day, surpassing!" (56.12).

From the provincial prophets he turns to an equally relentless denunciation of their followers. The accusations he makes against them could hardly be valid for all the villagers. But in his bitter anger, he makes no distinction between those of the villagers who are purist in their worship of YHWH, and those who are syncretist; both are alike in their opposition to his universalist teaching; and both are condemned. And, indeed, if the purists were willing to admit the syncretist Judaites as their brethren, how could they reject the pagans, who were hardly more idolatrous? It is almost impossible to reproduce in translation the fire and vehemence of the original.

> "But as for you, come ye hither, sons of the sorceress,
> Seed of the adulteress and the harlot! Whom are ye mocking?
> At whom do ye make wide mouths and thrust out the tongue?
> Are ye not the offspring of sin, the seed of falsehood?
> Ye who burn with lust at the terebinths, under each green tree;
> Who slay your children in the valleys, in the clefts of the rocks" (57.2 ff.).

Adopting Hosea's and Ezekiel's metaphor of idolatrous Israel as the faithless wife,[53] he cries out with increasing wrath:

> "On a lofty, o'ertopping mount, hast thou placed thy couch,
> Thither hast gone up to offer sacrifice,

Behind the door and the post, hast thou set thy symbol.
Yea, deserting Me, hast thou gone up, hast made wide thy bed;
Thou hast taken thee a compact from them, preferring their couch" (56.6 ff.).

Never before had the prophet used such words of either Israelite or pagan; never before had he said a word in criticism of the village prophets; never before had he attacked the sin of rural syncretism. The whole chapter is clearly a reply to the criticisms which had been raised against his decision. He was not defending himself, but his views; his anger was aroused not by personal chagrin, but by fear of disaster to his cause. His cry is still, "Build up, build up, prepare the way, take the stumbling blocks from the way of My people." The God who dwelleth "on high and in sanctity," but also with the "contrite and the lowly of spirit," having smitten Israel, has healed him. He has given "in full measure consolation to him and his mourners," crying "peace, peace, *to the far* as well as to the near!" Whoever trusts in Him, whether Judaite or Gentile, "will inherit the land," but "for the wicked, there is no peace!"

The fierce denunciation of the syncretists had somewhat calmed the prophet's temper. But the controversy had opened his eyes to a far subtler difference between the villagers and the "pursuers of righteousness." Even when the provincials were followers of YHWH, and worshiped only at the sanctuary in Jerusalem, they were not without grave blemish. They might be guiltless of the enormities he had described, but they were mere ritualists, blind to the true significance of divine religion. Rising up before them on one of the fast days, he ruthlessly denounced them in a poem which is still appropriately read in all synagogues on the Day of Atonement:

"Is not this the fast I desire:
That ye loose unrighteous bonds, and burst the bands of the yoke?
That ye set the crushed at liberty, and unbind every grievous burden?
Is it not to share the bread with the hungry, bringing the poor and oppressed to thy house?
When thou seest one naked, that thou shalt clothe him, and hide not from thine own flesh?" (58.6 ff.).

It was social unrighteousness which prevents the development of Israel as the moral teacher of the world, as the true Servant of God.

"Behold, the hand of the Lord lacks not power to rescue,
His ear is not dull of hearing;
Nay, your own sins are barring you,
Withholding you from your God . . .
For your hands are defiled with blood,
And your fingers with evil-doing;
Your lips have spoken falsehood,
Your tongue repeateth iniquity.
No one cries out with righteousness,
No one gives truthful judgment,
Trusting in vanity, speaking lies,
Conceiving trouble, and bringing forth deceit . . .
Dealing wickedly, falsely
Turning back from following our God;

Speaking oppression with rebellion;
Conceiving and uttering in the heart lying words.
Justice is made to turn back,
Righteousness stands afar off;
For truth has fallen in the street,
And rectitude cannot approach" (59.1 ff.).

Yet even this cannot ultimately prevent the realization of the prophet's dream. The Covenant of the Lord will be fulfilled; His light will burst on Israel as a new sun; Jerusalem will still attain its place as the spiritual metropolis of mankind. Finding Himself without human help, God will appear in eschatological might; He will crush His opponents and usher in a new world.

And so, having lost hope in human endeavor, and waiting for God alone, the prophet approached his end. In a psalm of heart-rending appeal, he recalls God's aid to His people in former times, and asks why He has forsaken them now. The prophet had answered the question before; they were the Suffering Servant. Yet the failure of any light to break through the dark clouds, the passing of decade after decade without any sign of God's appearance, called for some more realistic explanation. The prophet who, like Ezekiel,[54] continued until the end to ignore the problem of human intent, asks God why He makes Israel so sinful.

"Why dost Thou cause us to err from Thy ways,
And harden our hearts that we fear Thee not?" (63.17).

In the next chapter, the prophet gives us the divine reply. God had offered His help, doubtless through the prophet's first call, to a people which had not yet turned to Him; He had spread His hands to them all day, begging them to build their ideal nation. But — once again the prophet inveighs against the village worship which he had tolerated so amiably in the first half of his ministry —

> "The people that give provocation to Me, to My face, without ceasing,
> Offering sacrifice in the gardens, burning incense on brick altars;
> Who make their abode in the tombs, and lodge in the secret caverns;
> Who eat the flesh of the swine, and defiling broth in their vessels;
> They who cry out, Stand back! Touch me not, I am holy for thee! . . .
> These who burn incense on the mountains, and on the hilltops have defiled Me; I will measure out their payment in their lap" (65.3 ff.).

At last the prophet had arrived at the principle of individual reward and punishment. The wicked in Israel will perish; the righteous alone among them and among the other nations will be saved.

> "Behold My servants shall sing from gladness of heart, but ye shall cry out from anguish of heart;
> From anguish of spirit ye shall wail, and your name ye shall leave for a curse" (65.14).

Those who mourned for Jerusalem would join in rejoicing with her in her restoration; but those who neglected her, who worshiped at the village altars, would suffer the judgment of the Lord. Not that the prophet believed that God was in any way limited to His Temple:

> "Thus saith the Lord, The heaven is My throne [he begins],
> And the earth the footstool of My feet;
> What manner of house will ye build for Me,
> And where is the place of My abiding?
> Rather upon this will I look, upon the lowly,
> Him of contrite spirit, that trembleth at My word" (66.1 ff.).

Yet man needed a center of worship; and this was to be the sanctuary in Jerusalem. There would be no superiority of Jew over Gentile in the ritual; even priests and Levites would be accepted from the heathen who would come to it.

> "And it shall be from new moon to new moon,
> And from one sabbath day to another,
> That all flesh shall come to offer
> Their worship before Me, saith the Lord" (66.23).

Thus with a last glance at the Promised Land, toward which he had been striving all his life but which he was not destined to enter, the prophet disappears. He had lifted prophecy to unprecedented heights; he had brought a large section of native Judaites under the influence of the advanced doctrines of the returned exiles; above all, he had created an idea which was ultimately destined to affect, in a measure, the contour of western thought. The hope of the conversion of the world to prophetic religion did not die with its originator. Centuries later the Pharisees traveled over land and sea to win converts to their views, and proselytes to Judaism were to be found in Rome, in Egypt, and in the midst of Arabia. And finally, when Judah, weary with its struggle against Rome, was beginning to withdraw into itself, the task was in part taken over by the apostles of Christianity. Victory came; but to a prophet who could no longer enjoy it, and to a Jerusalem which was not even aware of it.

XIX. SOCIAL AND POLITICAL CONFLICT UNDER THE PERSIAN RULE

Either toward the end of the Second Isaiah's life or soon after his death, there occurred a series of events which left a permanent impression on the contemporary prophetic writings. Cambyses, the son and successor of Cyrus, undertook the conquest of Egypt; in his absence, a pretender, Gaumata, posing as the King's murdered brother Smerdis and supported apparently by a large group of the Median nobility, whose tool he was, seized the throne of the Empire. So powerful did this pseudo-Smerdis become that Cambyses, hurrying back from Egypt, apparently despaired of regaining his authority and committed suicide. Since Cambyses had no direct heirs, Darius, son of Hystaspes, the next in the order of succession, undertook to avenge his death, and in the year 522 B.C.E. became King.

Darius's kingship was at first only nominal; large sections of the Empire were in open revolt against him. His struggle with the rebels occupied almost two full years; and it was not until April of the year 520 B.C.E., that he could truly call himself King of Persia.

Meanwhile, Sheshbazzar, the first governor of Judah, had been succeeded by his nephew, Zerubbabel.[1] While neither Zerubbabel nor his people took any part in the widespread disturbances, both he and they were, of course, deeply concerned with the course of events. It must have occurred to many of them that the troubled times were propitious for the completion of the sanctuary in Jerusalem. The Government of the Empire, engrossed with larger concerns, and grateful for the loyalty of the people as well as eager to please them, would probably not interfere. The responsible heads of the community, Zerubbabel, the governor, and Joshua, the High Priest, realized however that the very circumstances which to inexperienced minds favored the undertaking, in reality surrounded it with perils. In a time of unrest, any effort to further an important piece of construction in the devastated city of Jerusalem might be interpreted as the first step toward revolution. "The time is not come," they pleaded with their enthusiastic followers; "the time that the Lord's house should be built" (Hag. 1.2). Only when peace had been restored throughout the Empire, did Zerubbabel and Joshua consider these objections removed. When Haggai, who had doubtless been a leader in the movement to rebuild the Temple even before this time, arose toward the end of August, 520, and demanded immediate action, he met with a willing response even from those who had been hesitant.

Only two chapters by the prophet, who thus made his appearance on the stage of history, have been preserved. Yet such was the chiseled sharpness and distinctiveness of his personality that these few verses are almost sufficient for a reconstruction of his character and philosophy.

His diction and his imagery betray rural associations and indicate that he was descended of the peasantry who had survived in Palestine during the whole period of the exile. Indeed, his whole appeal is based on the belief that greater piety will result in better harvests. A reconstructed Temple is a prerequisite, he insists, to increased productivity of the soil:

"Ye have sown much, and brought in little,
Ye eat, but ye have not enough,
Ye drink, but ye are not filled with drink" (1.6).

"Therefore over you the heaven hath kept back, so that there is no dew, and the earth hath kept back her produce" (1.10). "Through all that time, when one came to a heap of twenty measures, there were but ten; when one came to the winevat to draw out fifty press-measures, there were but twenty; I smote you with blasting and with mildew and with hail in all the work of your hands; yet ye turned not to Me, saith the Lord" (2.16 ff.). "Is the seed yet in the barn? yea, the vine, and the fig tree, and the pomegranate, and the olive tree hath not brought forth — from this day I will bless you" (2.19).

The naïveté of this prediction is entirely consonant with the whole outlook of this prophet, which is identical with that of the earlier rural seers. Like them he denies, as we have already observed, the existence of angels.[2] But no less important is the emphasis which he, in common with the Wisdom writers, lays on the increased wealth.[3] The goal of material success which he places before the people is altogether out of accord with the philosophy of the plebeian prophets. Naturally, he does not utter a word about individual righteousness, and has nothing to say about the problems of social injustice and human equality.

There can be little doubt therefore that the prophet represented the views of the purist faction of the provincials, the worshipers of YHWH whom Deutero-Isaiah had denounced for their ritualism, but who were guiltless of any apostasy.[4]

Like his fellow-provincials, Haggai was an extreme nationalist; and when the world cataclysms of the year 521–520 occurred, they suggested to him new possibilities for Israel. The prophet realized that for the moment Darius was victorious over his enemies; but Haggai could not believe that the revolutions which had broken out spontaneously in various parts of the Empire could in reality be put down as completely as they seemed to be.

At any rate, it pleased the prophet to think that the peace which had been restored was merely a lull in the storm. God had offered the Judaites a sign. As soon as His house was completed, the world would be thrown into new confusion.[5] The Empire would be disrupted and then—. The prophet did not dare explore the Messianic vistas which opened before him. Had not the Second Isaiah promised Israel a glorious kingdom? His words were speedily to be fulfilled. "Yet a little while more," said Haggai, "and I will shake the heavens and the earth and the sea and the dry land; and I will shake all nations, and the choicest things of all nations shall come, and I will fill this house with glory, saith the Lord of hosts" (2.6 ff.). A few months later, he says even more pointedly: "Speak to Zerubbabel, governor of Judah, saying, I will shake the heavens and the earth; and I will overthrow the throne of the kingdoms . . . . and I will overthrow the chariots, and those that ride in them; and the horses and their riders shall come down, every one by the hand of his brother. In that day, saith the Lord of hosts, will I take thee, O Zerubbabel, My servant, the son of Shealtiel, saith the Lord, and will make thee as a signet; for I have chosen thee, saith the Lord of hosts" (2.23).

These dangerous words show how easily the "quiet" nationalism of Deutero-Isaiah's early prophecies could transform itself into the fiery militarism against which Jeremiah and Isaiah had struggled. The farmer's acceptance of Persian rule was superficial; a little scratch showed the ancient war spirit still alive and strong. But while the resurgent nationalism won some support from Haggai, it met opposition from his contemporary, Zechariah,[6] who followed in the pacifist tradition of the pre-exilic urban teachers, and the Babylonian immigrants.[7]

Just as Haggai is patently rural in his manner and his address, so Zechariah is artisan and in the urban tradition. In one vision he sees a man with a measuring line in his hand, trying to find the length and breadth of Jerusalem (2.6); in another, he is shown "a candle-stick all of gold, with a bowl upon the top of it, and its seven lamps thereon; there are seven pipes, yea, seven to the lamps, which are upon the top thereof" (4.2); in a third, he notices a "flying roll," and makes special mention of its dimensions, "the length thereof is twenty cubits, and the breadth thereof ten cubits" (5.2); the fourth vision is that of a measure and a piece of lead (5.7); he then sees four chariots coming between two mountains, "and the mountains were mountains of brass" (6.1). There is hardly a single reference in all the visions to vegetables or animals, such as we might expect from a man surrounded with rural scenes and spending his life in agricultural activity. But most convincing of all is his statement that taking gold and silver from some Babylonian pilgrims, he made crowns for Joshua, the High Priest, and perhaps also for Zerubbabel (6.11).

Zechariah was then a craftsman. Apparently he had learned his trade not in rural Palestine but in the Judaite settlement of Babylonia, and had come with the other pioneers between 538 and 520 B.C.E. As we might expect, he shows close kinship not to the Palestinian prophets, but to Ezekiel, the teacher of the exile. God speaks to him not directly but through an angelic intermediary; less frequently in words than in pictures; and with an emphasis on the world and the individual rather than on the nation of Israel.

In the midst of his concern with the momentous events of the day, he finds time to denounce iniquity and wrong-doing within the nation.[8] "Thus hath the Lord of hosts spoken, saying: Execute true judgment and show mercy and compassion every man to his brother, and oppress not the widow, nor the fatherless, the stranger, nor the poor; and let none of you devise evil against his brother in your heart" (Zech. 7.9, 10). "These are the things that ye shall do: Speak ye every man the truth with his neighbour; execute the judgment of truth and peace in your gates, and let none of you devise evil in your hearts against your neighbour; and love no false oath; for all these are things that I hate, saith the Lord" (8.16, 17).

Like Isaiah and Jeremiah he is deeply opposed to the empty ritualism of fasting. When he is asked by the people whether they should continue their traditional days of mourning and fasting, now that the Commonwealth had been restored, he says: "Then came the word of the Lord of hosts unto me, saying: 'Speak unto all the people of the land, and to the priests, saying: When ye fasted and mourned in the fifth and in the seventh month, even these seventy years, did ye at all fast unto Me, even to Me? And when ye eat, and when ye drink, are ye not they that eat, and they that drink?' " (7.4 f.).

Inevitably he was at odds with Haggai, the spokesman of the native, agricultural party. Neither prophet mentions the other, though they were active not merely in the same generation but in the same months. A later writer credits both with inaugurating the movement to establish the Temple; but in Haggai's book not a word is said of any support from Zechariah. It simply records that, "Then Zerubbabel, the son of Shealtiel, and Joshua, the son of Jehozadak, the high priest, with all the remnant of the people, hearkened unto the voice of the Lord their God, and unto the words of Haggai the prophet, as the Lord their God had sent him" (1.12). But a close study of the two prophets reveals not only indifference to each other, but clear and definite hostility and opposition between them. Haggai was the militant nationalist urging rebellion, Zechariah the traditional pacifist urging quiet and submission. When Zerubbabel was about to yield to the importunities of the war party Zechariah cried out: "This is the word of the Lord unto Zerubbabel, saying: Not by might, nor by power, but by My spirit, saith the Lord of hosts" (4.6). He does indeed promise Zerubbabel future greatness — "Who art thou, O great mountain before Zerubbabel? Thou shalt become a plain; and he shall bring forth the top stone with shoutings of grace, grace unto it" (4.7) — but this must come from divine, not human, activity. He has no wish for a physical wall about Jerusalem, "For I, saith the Lord, will be unto her a wall of fire round about, and I will be the glory in the midst of her" (2.9). He accepted the doctrine of the Second Isaiah welcoming the pagans into the worship of God. "And many nations," he says, "shall join themselves to the Lord in that day, and they shall be My people" (2.15). They shall not become Israelites; they will remain members of their own peoples; but they will be recognized as servants of God.

Haggai had uttered his prophecy of imminent world cataclysm on the twenty-fourth day of the ninth month of the year 520–519 B.C.E., the second year of Darius's reign. Zechariah allowed precisely two months for some sign of this approaching catastrophe to make its appearance. On the twenty-fourth day of the eleventh month Zechariah arose to give his views. In a vision, he had heard the divine messengers, who had been sent to investigate conditions on earth, report to their Master, that "We have walked to and fro through the earth, and, behold, all the earth sitteth still, and is at rest" (1.11). When the angel asks God when He will have mercy on Jerusalem, God replies "with good words, even comforting words" (1.13), "I return to Jerusalem with compassions: My house shall be built in it, saith the Lord of hosts" (1.16). Nothing is said of empire, or riches, or material power, or even autonomy. Such implicit denials of the nationalist aspirations might be "comforting" to Zechariah; they could hardly seem so to Haggai and his followers.

It was not long before Haggai's reckless enthusiasm brought on the danger Zerubbabel and Joshua had foreseen. The prophet's harmless Messianic dreams were represented to Zerubbabel's superiors as incitements to rebellion. Perhaps Zerubbabel had himself been imprudent in his replies to Haggai's words, or in his failure to repress him. He may have taken it for granted that his quietism during the upheavals had put his loyalty beyond question, and overlooked the obvious fact that his descent from the Davidic dynasty made him especially subject to suspicion. He may not have realized that the memory of the widespread revolts which had greeted the accession of Darius inclined the

Imperial officials to deal harshly with the slightest sign of disaffection. They could least of all afford to tolerate it in Palestine, the bridge between their empire and the newly conquered, still restive province of Egypt. In any event, before Haggai could utter a third nationalist prophecy, he disappeared from the scene, and shortly thereafter Zerubbabel followed him into obscurity. Whether they were banished from the land or met an even worse fate, our records do not say. That the country escaped punishment and that the building of the Temple was completed, indicates the trust of Darius in the peace party. Perhaps we may even surmise that the permission which the Persian government granted the Jews to build their Temple, was intended as a conciliatory, compromise measure, to strengthen the peace party and to discourage the nationalists. But thereafter, and until the days of Nehemiah, the governors of Judah were Persians. The house of David continued to receive recognition and honor from the people, but was definitely repressed by the government.

The foremost Jewish authority henceforth, and practically until the end of the Commonwealth, was the High Priest. Whatever autonomy the Persians granted the Jewish community was vested in him and in the Council of Elders. A lay associate was, indeed, recognized;[9] but his position was completely overshadowed by that of the Temple Chief.

The elevation of the High Priest involved a similar promotion for his whole tribe. Under the new order, the priests were possessed of a threefold advantage, which they did not hesitate to use for their own advancement, and which gave them an unprecedented control of the whole Commonwealth. They were the foremost patricians and landowners; they were the heads of the Temple; and they were the recognized agents of the Persian government. Of these their most important advantage was doubtless their possession of the land.

They had taken their farms in violation of the express commandment of Deut. 18.1, which forbids priests to own land. But, as we have seen, their teachers had discovered a way to escape this prohibition, by limiting it to times when all the twelve tribes were settled in Palestine. As a result, their holdings became so large that the Egyptian historian, Hecataeus of Abdera, in the third century B.C.E., was actually under the impression that Jewish law assigned to the priests larger portions of the country than to other classes![10]

It is true, of course, that the permission to hold land was originally given the priests out of dire necessity. When the first immigrants from Babylonia had returned under Cyrus, they were not in a position to maintain a leisure priest class. The priests had to work as farmers on the soil in order to obtain their livelihood. But having acquired their holdings when they had no ecclesiastical perquisites, the priests refused to yield them when prosperity made it unnecessary for them to enjoy secular income.

It was to the interest of the Persians, on the other hand, as well as to those of the priests to deal with these representatives of the people rather than with the masses. All alien rulers consider it a great convenience to have a section of the subject population loyal to them and acting as their agents. Finding the priests their willing tools, the Persians could not begrudge them the substantial crumbs which fell from their own lordly tables. It thus happened that by the middle of the fifth century B.C.E., the priests were an important part of the aristocracy, and by the beginning of the fourth century B.C.E. they were without any rival whatsoever.

No such good fortune attended the patrician clans of laymen who, having retained their family affiliations through half a century of exile, returned with the priests to the New Jerusalem. Like the priests and the other immigrants, they had to be content with whatever lands had remained unoccupied during their absence. Perforce most of them settled with their less aristocratic fellows in the hill country near Jerusalem, since the more fertile lands of the *shefelah* and the plains were occupied by settlers. The patricians, whose ancestors had lived in Jerusalem, were probably in worse case than the village gentry in this respect; for while the farmer might still be remembered in the district where he had been brought up and his lands returned to him, the scion of a noble family which had never visited their estates had much less chance to recover his ancestral property. Struggling to gain a foothold in the new land, the descendants of the ancient nobility had at length to yield the close clan relationships which they had so carefully guarded in Babylonia. The sentiments which attached to Palestinian memories while they were in distant exile disappeared in face of reality; the glamour of aristocratic memory faded; the hope of restoration to ancient position was gone. There was left nothing but the wretched present, with its daily drudgery and difficulty. The inertia of pride spent itself at length — as soon as threadbare gentility became more ignominious than confessed poverty. The great-grandchildren of princes lost their inhibiting consciousness of social superiority and thought, and acted like their neighbors, who were descended from commoners. In the middle of the fifth century B.C.E., Ezra still found and identified a record of the returning clans;[11] but by the time of the Chronicler (about 300 B.C.E.) most of the families had already been forgotten, and he does not even mention them.

Only one family, the *Senaa*, preserved its identity and actually forced its way into the new aristocracy. It had come in far larger numbers than any other. As we have already seen, this fact, together with its name (meaning the "hated") has led historians to surmise that it was originally not a patrician family at all, but a proletarian group.[12] As usual in antiquity, the class name ultimately became recognized both by its own members and by others as a clan designation; and a fictitious eponym was invented as ancestor of the tribe. Being proletarians by tradition, the Senaa were more able than others to detach themselves from the Babylonian soil and also to make their way as pioneers in Palestine. With their large numbers they had an advantage over other families both in point of power and persistence. In the age of the Chronicler (I Chron. 9.7), they traced their descent from the tribe of Benjamin, which means that they had at length obtained for themselves land in the fertile valleys which had once belonged to that tribe. But they were destined to rise still higher, for it appears from a talmudic record that the family ultimately forced its way into the priesthood.[13]

This forcible entry of a lay family into the priesthood need not surprise us. Wealth and power are tempting baits to the near aristocrat. As it became evident that authority and aristocracy in the new community must be the prerogative of priesthood, many who would not associate themselves with the Temple service out of love for God chose it out of desire for Mammon. The foreign governors who ruled Judea were always ready to interfere in the Temple government for a price; Herod and the Romans sold the high-priesthood to the highest bidder, as did some of the Seleucids before them. And while we have no documentary evidence of similar activities by the Persians, there is good reason to believe that their governors were not blind to this important source of income. The Book of Maccabees tells us explicitly that Menelaus, a member of the tribe of Benjamin, was appointed High Priest in the days of Antiochus;[14] and we can be certain that similar influences led to the admission of the whole Senaa family. Of the family Hakoz,[15] we are definitely told that, rejected from the priesthood by the first settlers because they could not establish their priestly descent, they ultimately were admitted.[16]

What happened to whole families must have occurred more frequently to individuals. The Talmud frequently discusses the status of men claiming to be priests without being able to produce sufficient evidence for it. Many described themselves as priests whose fathers had in fact been mere slaves in priestly families.[17] Others had even less connection with the priesthood. Even in modern times,[18] when the priesthood involves only religious burdens and provides no privileges, there are cases on record of men who desired the distinction without any right to it. How much stronger must have been the urge to be accepted into priestly families in the early days before the questions of genealogy had become as fixed and settled as they were in the talmudic age or as they have become today. The Chronicler (I, 24.7 ff.) enumerates twenty-four priestly families in his day, of whom several are not mentioned in any of the earlier records preserved in Ezra and Nehemiah.

In fact, the clan of Jehoiarib, which is listed in our texts of Chronicles as the first of the priestly clans, hardly was known in the fifth century B.C.E.[19] Other radical transformations of the priestly organization become apparent as soon as we compare the different records with one another. They leave us with the definite impression that the priesthood during the Persian period, like any other symbol of nobility, was obtainable by those who could afford to pay for it. Thus two forces were at work to make the priesthood all powerful: the continual enrichment of the ecclesiastics through their varied sources of income, and the accretion to their number of the patricians originally outside of it.

The priesthood of the Second Commonwealth inevitably became as fully secularized as the aristocracy of the First Commonwealth whose place they had seized. Though few or none of them were lineal descendants of the ancient Judaite nobility, they fell heir, not only to their place in the community but also to their motives and ideals. Holding the same relative place in the body politic as the defenders of Queen Athaliah and the counselors of Ahaz and Manasseh, these priests necessarily held the same opinions. They did not indeed seek to introduce the foreign idol worship, for their whole existence and authority depended on the Temple and its prestige. But in every other way they were as assimilationist as any generation of nobles before them had been. We shall see what momentous consequences this betrayal by those who should have been the nation's spiritual leaders had for Judaism.

It was characteristic of the Second Commonwealth, with the violent social changes it effected, that the Levites, descended from the priests who worshiped at the country shrines, and for the most part inhabitants of Palestine during the exile, should have become the plebeian teachers.[20] Driven from their country shrines by propaganda emanating from Jerusalem, they had no choice but to accept the secondary place which the Law granted them in Jerusalem. A continual struggle ensued between them and the priests who, during the whole period of the Second Commonwealth, strove to identify their status with that of the former Temple servants, the *Nethinim* and the gate-keepers. Such, however, was the caste consciousness of the sanctuary officialdom that even in the last decade of the Second Commonwealth, the singers, who were apparently descended from the true Levites, refused to admit the gate-keepers to equality with them; and a hundred years after the destruction of the Temple, the defenders of the Levites still quarreled furiously with the protagonists of the priesthood when the latter tried to identify certain Temple ministers with "the servants of the priests."[21]

The oppression which the Levites of all groups suffered at the hands of the priests inevitably drove them to make common cause with the other oppressed groups, the plebeians of the city and the small farmers of the highlands. Yet, descended from the countryside, and sheltered from the outside world by the walls of the Temple, these Levites could not fully share the impatience of the other plebeian teachers with the arrogance and oppression of wealth. Some Levites, moreover, were sufficiently strong economically to avoid the Temple and the degraded service which it offered them. Their village shrines, like the Temple itself, had become possessed of landed estates; and when the surrounding peasantry ceased to come to them for worship, the Levites simply appropriated the ecclesiastical property to themselves. On no other basis can we explain, for instance, the possession of vast estates by the family from which the great Levitical rabbi, R. Eliezer ben Hyrcanus, of the first century, was descended.[22] Certainly the revenues which the priests grudgingly permitted these inferior ecclesiastics to collect could not have enabled them to acquire large landed properties and to attain the status of squires and near-nobility.

The social divisions of the Second Commonwealth were thus closely related to those of the earlier Kingdom. The country still had its ecclesiastical aristocracy, its lay patricians, its country gentry, and its urban plebeians. Yet the philosophies of some of these groups had undergone basic changes during the exile. The most important of these was the willingness of the plebeians to admit proselytes into their ranks. They befriended and welcomed the Calebites, the Jerahmeelites, and the Kenites who presented themselves for conversion to Judaism. The number of these people who became Judaites was indeed considerable.[23] They were deeply impressed with the miracle of the Restoration and the tales which the Judaites told of its prediction by their prophets. Disappointing as the new Commonwealth was to those who had dreamed of it, who had carried about visions of gates of emerald and houses of sapphire, it was an overwhelming revelation of divine power to the semi-nomadic wanderers who lived a far more precarious life than the poorest of the settled population. The provincials, on the other hand, and the pietist priests, who shared their views, opposed proselytization of the heathen. To the provincials Judaism was a status into which one was born, not a faith which one might join. The struggle between these views continued for centuries. Long after the plebeians had obtained formal sanction for their interpretation of the Law, the patricians, the provincials, and the priests still resisted its application to individual cases. As late as the first century B.C.E., Shammai, the leader of the provincial faction of the Pharisees, was as famous for his rejection of proselytes as his plebeian opponent, Hillel, was for accepting them.[24] Indeed, a hundred years after their time, Eliezer ben Hyrcanus and Eleazar of Modin, both Shammaites, opposed the plebeian, Joshua ben Hananya, on the same issue.[25] The aversion of the pietist Aaronids to proselytization led to their refusal to marry women converts. They found a basis for this rule in a peculiar interpretation of Scripture; and it has remained their practice until our own time.[26]

The principles of social justice and human equality within the Jewish Commonwealth were the cornerstones of plebeian doctrine. The demands of the group had become clearly formulated in Babylonia, and from them they would not recede. The ideal kingdom would certainly, they were convinced, bring about the readjustment of rights which the Second Commonwealth had failed to effect. The country gentry and their prophets, knowing as little about social conflict and oppression as their forbears in the First Commonwealth, continued to ignore the inequalities and injustices of the present. So far as the social relations within the Jewish community were concerned, the present seemed ideal.

Aside from the controversies about the ritual, the division between the rural and urban teachers of the early Second Commonwealth bears an uncanny correspondence to that between the leaders who are arising today to guide the destinies of the new Homeland in modern Palestine. No one conversant with affairs in Palestine today can be blind to the diverse social forces which find expression in the continual conflict between the labor groups which draw their following from the artisans and traders of Tel Aviv and the plebeian peasantry of the Emek Jezreel, and the parties whose strength lies in the farmers of older "private property" colonies and among the new arrivals in the large cities of Tel Aviv and Jerusalem. Both in their concern for political rights and wider boundaries for Palestine, and in their social views, the bourgeois following shows itself heir to the ancient gentry of the Second Commonwealth; while the plebeian spirit once more appears in the modern labor groups. The situation is slightly confused by the influences which the conditions in their home countries have on the immigrants, but in general the observer may notice how with the resurrection of the ancient Commonwealth there has been brought into renewed life the traditional struggle of the urban plebeian with his humanist ideals against the complacent farmer with his dreams of political power and imperialism.

The one essential difference between partisan conflict today and 2400 years ago is the relatively unimportant rôle which modern parties assign to religious forms. Whether this is to be a permanent characteristic or merely a passing phase of the Third Commonwealth, it would indeed be rash to predict. Historical parallels usually do not fit in all details. But the believer in religion, and particularly in Judaism, may be pardoned if he discerns in the darkness of a foggy twilight the signs of a new dawn, heralding another sun, rather than the passing of an old order into blackest night. This hope is based, in part, on the conviction that the ancients were not all as God-fearing, and that the moderns are not as godless, as many would lead us to believe. The situations which developed in the ancient Jewish community might easily be duplicated today, and the ideals which today find expression in purely humanistic terms may once more be given their natural, fundamental and permanent expression in their relation to God.

By applying the touchstone of the threefold issue between the country and the plebeian teacher we can readily assign the prophetic messages which have been preserved out of the fifth and fourth centuries B.C.E. to their respective parties. Almost all the material is anonymous, but so distinctive is the style of the period as well as of each party that identification both of person and of party is almost certain.

A. The Rural Prophets of the Persian Period

Three prophets represent the views of provincial pietists of the period: Joel, Obadiah, and Deutero-Zechariah (the author of Zechariah 9–11).

The most rural of all, both in his imagery and in his sympathies, is Joel. His very first verses indicate a sympathy for drinkers of wine, which would seem ironical in the mouth of a prophet, but is proven by later reference to be meant in earnest. The prophet, like provincial Judaites of all generations, sees nothing shameful or wicked in drinking wine; and he considers the destruction of the grapes a national calamity. It is not an accident that the occasion of his prophecy is a plague of locusts which, as frequently happens, followed a severe drought. The prophet sees the fig tree languishing, the pomegranate tree, palm tree and the apple tree withering, "for joy is withered from the sons of men" (1.12). The vividness of the portrayal and the passion of utterance demonstrate the personal relation of Joel to the catastrophe; he feels it deeply because it touches him nearly.

Like the other provincial pietists, Joel is a confirmed adherent of ritual. His cure for the trouble is fasting and sackcloth. The contempt of Deutero-Isaiah for fasting without righteousness, Zechariah's derisive question, "When ye fasted and mourned in the fifth and in the seventh month, even these seventy years, did ye at all fast unto Me, even unto Me?" (7.4), ring in our ears when we hear Joel's call to repentance:

"Gird yourselves, and lament, ye priests,
Wail, ye ministers of the altar;
Come, lie all night in sackcloth, ...
For the meal-offering and the drink-offering is withholden
From the house of your God.
Sanctify ye a fast,
Call a solemn assembly,
Gather the elders
And all the inhabitants of the land
Unto the house of the Lord your God,
And cry unto the Lord" (1.13 ff.).

"Blow the horn in Zion,
Sanctify a fast, call a solemn assembly;
Gather the people,
Sanctify the congregation,
Assemble the elders,
Gather the children,
And those that suck the breasts;

Let the bridegroom go forth from his chamber,
And the bride out of her pavilion.
Let the priests, the ministers of the Lord,
Weep between the porch of the altar,
And let them say: 'Spare Thy people, O Lord' " (2.15 ff.).

We can see that of all his people's distresses the one which troubles the prophet primarily is the necessary interruption of the meal-offering and the drink-offering. Like the priests of later days who continued, in the midst of a starving city, to offer the daily sacrifice on the altar, this earlier prophet bemoans among the tragic woes of his day the interference with the usual temple customs. He reaches a climax in his portrayal of suffering when he finally says:

"Lament like a virgin girdled with sackcloth
For the husband of her youth.
The meal-offering and the drink-offering is cut off
From the house of the Lord;
The priests mourn,
Even the Lord's ministers" (1.8 f.).

"Yet even now, saith the Lord,
Turn ye unto Me with all your heart,
And with fasting, and with weeping, and with lamentation;
And rend your heart, and not your garments,
And turn unto the Lord your God;
For He is gracious and compassionate,
Long-suffering, and abundant in mercy,
And repenteth Him of the evil.
Who knoweth whether He will not turn and repent,

And leave a blessing behind Him,
Even a meal-offering and a drink-offering
Unto the Lord your God?" (2.12 ff.).

The touching phrase, "rend your heart, and not your garments," is a call for sincere repentance but not for the improvement of social conditions. Rural prophet as Joel is, he has met the urban traders and those coming under their influence; he can recognize hypocrisy which, under a cloak of mourning, carries a heart untouched. But he does not recognize, as did Deutero-Isaiah and the author of Jonah, that even heartfelt remorse is inadequate unless the penitent searches his conscience for wrongs to man, as well as for sin against God.

Finally the locust disappeared and the land was saved. The prophet thereupon used the opportunity to foretell the future glory and restoration of the people. The God who saved them from destruction through the natural force of the locusts will come to their aid again against the nations who oppress them. But the picture of the ideal future which this prophet paints is full of wars and battles and bloody conflicts and final vengeance on all Israel's enemies.

Almost shamelessly, one is tempted to say, Joel parodies his urban predecessor's call to peace:

"Proclaim ye this among the nations,
Prepare war;
Stir up the mighty men;
Let all the men of war draw near,
Let them come up.
Beat your plowshares into swords,
And your pruning-hooks into spears;
Let the weak say: 'I am strong' " (4.9).

"Put ye in the sickle,
For the harvest is ripe;
Come, tread ye,
For the winepress is full, the vats overflow;
For their wickedness is great" (4.13).

The vengeance which the prophet foresees for the other nations is reminiscent of that prophesied by the Palestinian seers during the exile:

"Egypt shall be a desolation,
And Edom shall be a desolate wilderness,
For the violence against the children of Judah,
Because they have shed innocent blood in their land" (4.19).

"And also what are ye to Me, O Tyre, and Zidon, and the regions of Philistia? Will ye render retribution on My behalf? And if ye render retribution on My behalf, swiftly, speedily will I return your retribution upon your own head. Forasmuch as ye have taken My silver and My gold, and have carried into your temples My goodly treasures; the children also of Judah and the children of Jerusalem have ye sold unto the sons of the Jevanim [the Greeks], that ye might remove them far from their border; behold I will stir them up out of the place whither ye have sold them, and will return your retribution upon your own head; and I will sell your sons and your daughters into the hand of the children of Judah, and they shall sell them to the men of Sheba, to a nation far off; for the Lord hath spoken" (4.4 ff.).

Note how in this passage, as throughout his book, this rural prophet continually mentions Judah before Jerusalem.

When finally he has completed his picture of the terrible judgment in the valley of Jehoshaphat, he returns to his original theme, the pleasure of the wine drinkers for whom he has such natural sympathy:

"And it shall come to pass on that day,
That the mountains shall drop down sweet wine,
And the hills shall flow with milk,
And all the brooks of Judah shall flow with waters;
And a fountain shall come forth from the house of the Lord,
And shall water the valley of Shittim" (4.18).

Like the other contemporary prophecies, that of Joel has suffered much at the hands of the interpolator, this time a citizen of Jerusalem, who felt his city neglected and the principles of its prophets violated. The additions are so foreign to the text that they have been marked off on purely literary grounds by the critical commentators.[27] Thus when the prophet is describing the impending return of prosperity and enumerates the agricultural products of the country one by one, the interpolator, suddenly remembering the permanent water difficulties in Jerusalem, has to mention the blessing which will come to her in plentiful rains:[28]

"Be not afraid, ye beasts of the field;
For the pastures of the wilderness do spring,
For the tree beareth its fruit,
The fig tree and the vine do yield their strength.
Be glad then, ye children of Zion, and rejoice
In the Lord your God;
For He giveth you the former rain in just measure,
And He causeth to come down for you the rain,
The former rain and the latter rain, at the first.

And the floors shall be full of corn,
And the vats shall overflow with wine and oil,
And I will restore to you the years that the locust hath eaten,
The canker-worm, and the caterpillar, and the palmer-worm,
My great army which I sent among you" (2.22 ff.).

More serious was the insertion of what is now chapter 3, foretelling the universalization of prophecy among all classes. The message is so completely opposed to the whole trend of Joel's thought, which in the following chapter regards the future world as belonging to native Israel alone, that we should be entitled on that ground alone to reject it as an addition. The loose connective which the interpolator supplied to attach it to what precedes is confirmatory proof of the spuriousness of the passage. Having described the immediate bliss of returning crops, the prophet concludes:

"And ye shall know that I am in the midst of Israel,
And that I am the Lord your God, and there is none else;
And My people shall never be ashamed" (2.27).

Thereafter followed originally the prophecy of doom for the nations, beginning with the words:

"For, behold in those days and in that time,
When I shall bring back the captivity of Judah and Jerusalem,
I will gather all nations,
And will bring them down into the valley of Jehoshaphat" (4.1 f.).

But the urban writer cannot accept the decision of the Valley of Jehoshaphat as a complete and adequate picture of the New World, and so he prefaces it with a chapter of his own:

"And it shall come to pass afterward,
That I will pour out My spirit upon all flesh;[29]
And your sons and your daughters shall prophesy,
Your old men shall dream dreams,
Your young men shall see visions;
And also upon the servants and upon the handmaids
In those days will I pour out My spirit . . . .
And it shall come to pass, that whosoever shall call on the name of the Lord shall be delivered;
For in mount Zion and in Jerusalem there shall be those that escape,
As the Lord hath said,
And among the remnant those whom the Lord shall call" (3.1 ff.).

Even without the allusion to Jerusalem and Mount Zion we could be sure that the prophet who promised the gift of prophecy to slaves and handmaids was not among those who owned them. Slaveholders are hardly likely to foresee their servants as inspired guides for themselves and the world. But the prophet is not satisfied with turning slaves into seers; he must provide in the world's spiritual center an escape for "whosoever shall call on the name of the Lord." The doom predicted over the nations in the next chapter by Joel could apply, this interpolator felt, only to those who refused to join the Lord after they had received due warning. Without such warning how could the nations be expected to return? But, the prophet assures us, there will be sufficient signs and portents to convert those who will wish to be converted:

"And I will show wonders in the heavens and in the earth,
Blood, and fire, and pillars of smoke.
The sun shall be turned into darkness,
And the moon into blood,
Before the great and terrible day of the Lord shall come" (3.3 f.).

Closely allied with the prophecy of the original Joel is that preserved in the tiny Book of Obadiah, the smallest in the Hebrew Scriptures. Various critics have maintained that its twenty-one verses are derived from different writers,[30] and have pointed out, indeed, that its first nine verses are practically identical with a passage in the present book of Jeremiah.[31] Without entering into the very complicated question of the priority of authorship of these verses, it is sufficient to point out here that in its present form the Book dates from the end of the fourth century — the period under discussion, and that its author was a rural prophet, of the stamp of Joel. The message of the prophet is the doom of Edom. He reproaches that tiny nation with self-sufficiency, but above all with injustice to Judah, when she sided with Babylonia in 597 and 586 B.C.E. But having settled the fate of Edom, the prophet proceeds to other nations:

"For the day of the Lord is near upon all the nations;
As thou hast done, it shall be done unto thee;
Thy dealing shall return upon thine own head.
For as ye have drunk upon My holy mountain,
So shall all nations drink continually,

Yea, they shall drink, and swallow down,
And shall be as though they had not been ....
And the house of Jacob shall possess their possessions"
(v. 15 f.).

He expects the territory of Judah to be greatly extended. It will include the Negeb, which Nebuchadnezzar had transferred to Edom in reward for its assistance against Judah,[32] and which remained in foreign hands until the Hasmonean days; the land of the Philistines on the coast, Samaria on the north, and Gilead in Transjordan. "And the captivity of this host of the children of Israel, that are among the Canaanites, even unto Zarephath, And the captivity of Jerusalem, that is in Sepharad, Shall possess the cities of the South" (v. 20). In other words, the ambitions of the patricians of Saul's day will at last be fulfilled;[33] the whole coastal valley will be in the hands of the Israelites. The conquered country will be divided in a manner peculiarly satisfying to patrician landowners. The inhabitants of the *shefelah*, already possessed of Judah's richest soil, will inherit in addition the even more fertile country of the Philistines and Mount Ephraim. The Judaites of the Negeb will obtain the land of Edom, but in turn they will have to surrender their country to the restored exiles who were at the moment in Phoenicia!

The resurrection of the patrician ideal from the obscurity in which it had been hidden for seven centuries indicates better than anything else can the constancy of the group conflict in Palestine, and the class associations of the prophet.

The comparatively modest boundaries which the prophet predicts for Palestine — neglecting the whole of Damascus[34]—

indicates perhaps a hope for the speedy realization of his program. We may plausibly conjecture that he was addressing the people on the eve of Alexander's invasion of the land; and that his hopes were pinned on a reallotment of the Palestinian soil through the favor of this new western conqueror. He expected his country to side with Alexander and to be given in reward the same rights over Edom that Edom had been given over it when the tables were turned.

The Second Zechariah was far more hopeful. It is generally assumed that he, too, spoke at the advent of Alexander,[35] but he expected the Greek conqueror to give Judea the whole of David's empire. It may seem incredible to us that anyone capable of the style and thought of the Second Zechariah should seriously harbor such fancies. But then, for us, Alexander's conquest is merely an episode in history, important in the development of human civilization, but like all other human achievements transient both in itself and its effects. To the contemporary, particularly the Jewish contemporary, it must have seemed much more. For centuries the prophets had promised a "day of the Lord" when the whole plan of the world would be rearranged, when the Persian Empire would fall, its satrapies be set free, its subject peoples made independent. The Jews had been led to expect that Israel as a nation or Judaism as a faith would attain a new world-status in that day. The visions had been dreamed and spoken, they had been repeated and written down, without anyone taking them sufficiently to heart to alter his daily business on their account. People believed in the prophets, indeed, as Marxians believe in the inevitable revolution, without permitting the conviction to interfere with their occupation or business, their marriage or the foundation of their families.

In the midst of this day-dreaming and prophesying there appeared suddenly from the West a young conqueror before whom the mighty Empire lay as helpless as a paralyzed giant. The suddenness of this victory must itself have overwhelmed the Judean peasant, who lacked our knowledge of the preceding events in the light of which a Greek invasion of Asia was inevitable. Was not this the Day of the Lord, for which the prophets had been waiting since the time of Isaiah? Those of us who were adults in the fateful years of 1914–1918, remember well how vulnerable even twentieth-century sophistication is to Messianism. Man's pathetic yearning for an ideal world is such that whenever powerful forces sweep the earth his expectations run high. Indeed sometimes men become sufficiently aroused to realize their ideals, at least in part. No wonder, then, that the Judaite prophets, listening to the approach of the Macedonian phalanxes, thought the country's opportunity had come. Humble Obadiah was content with an enlarged Judea; the more ambitious Second Zechariah was prepared to demand not only the whole of Palestine, but Syria and Phoenicia as well. He expected Judah to become the ally of Alexander: "And I will stir up thy sons, O Zion, with thy sons, O Javan (Greece), and will make thee as the sword of a mighty man" (9.13).[36]

Like Joel, this prophet enjoys the prospect of battle.

> "For the Lord of hosts hath remembered His flock the
> house of Judah,
> And maketh them as His majestic horse in battle.
> Out of them shall come forth the corner-stone,
> Out of them the stake,
> Out of them the battle bow,

Out of them every master together.
And they shall be as mighty men,
Treading down in the mire of the streets in the battle,
And they shall fight, because the Lord is with them;
And the riders on horses shall be confounded" (10.3 ff.).

It would seem almost as though the prophet were endeavoring to arouse the war spirit of his comrades to enlist in Alexander's armies. He reminds them that they, too, can fight and that assistance will come especially to them from God:

"And the Lord shall be seen over them,
And His arrow shall go forth as the lightning,
And the Lord God will blow the horn,
And will go with the whirlwinds of the south" (9.14).

Both Obadiah and the Second Zechariah realize that in order to be effective in battle Judah cannot stand alone, but must seek union with the Samaritans. It is this practical suggestion, especially significant since it comes from the otherwise chauvinistic gentry, that lends the color of near-certainty to the theory that both prophecies were uttered about the time of Alexander. Obadiah tells us that in the conflict with Edom, "the house of Jacob shall be a fire, And the house of Joseph a flame, And the house of Esau for stubble, And they shall kindle in them, and devour them; And there shall not be any remaining of the house of Esau" (v. 18). In the same spirit, the Second Zechariah says:

"For I bend Judah for Me,
I will fill the bow with Ephraim" (9.13).
"And I will strengthen the house of Judah,
And I will save the house of Joseph,

And I will bring them back, for I have compassion
upon them,
And they shall be as though I had not cast them off;
For I am the Lord their God, and I will hear them.
And they of Ephraim shall be like a mighty man,
And their heart shall rejoice as through wine" (10.6 f.).

But, as we know from Josephus,[37] the plan for union between the two communities was frustrated. The rivalries and the enmities which had been fostered for centuries could not be wiped out even in the sight of a golden opportunity to enhance the glory of a united kingdom. The Samaritans complained to Alexander of the Judaites; the Judaites of the Samaritans. The prophet describes bitterly and with anguish his disappointment at this turn of events. He had undertaken to offer the nation political advice only because its official leaders were selfish and greedy. This thought he expresses in the following symbols: "Thus said the Lord my God: 'Feed the flock of slaughter; whose buyers slay them, and hold themselves not guilty; and they that sell them say: Blessed be the Lord, for I am rich; and their own shepherds pity them not' " (11.4–5). The prophet then continues, "So I fed the flock of slaughter, verily the poor of the flock. And I took unto me two staves; the one I called Graciousness, and the other I called Binders; and I fed the flock" (11.7). The prophet later explains that the staff called Graciousness had relation to the foreign nations, and the staff called Binders was to unite Judah and Ephraim. He means then that he urged two policies: Graciousness toward the Greek, and Union between Judah and Israel. "And I cut off the three shepherds in one month; 'for My soul became impatient of them, and their soul also loathed Me.' Then said I: 'I will not feed you; that which dieth, let it die; and that which is to be cut off, let it be cut off; and let them that are left eat every one the flesh of another.' And I took my staff Graciousness, and cut it asunder, 'that I might break My covenant which I had made with all the peoples'" (11.8 f.). In other words, he found it impossible to bring sufficient strength from Judah to weigh heavily in the counsels and plans of Alexander. "And it was broken in that day; and the poor of the flock that gave heed unto me knew of a truth that it was the word of the Lord" (11.11).

But the disappointing denouement was still in the future, when the prophet delivered his first calls to the people. Then he foresaw Judah rising like a newly revived people and living an ideal, bucolic life on its ancestral soil: Judah once more united to Ephraim. Being from the country, like Joel in an earlier day he does not hesitate to give wine a prominent place in his picture of the Good. The slight suggestion of drinking in the passage already cited does not stand alone. A little further the prophet remarks:

> "The Lord of hosts will defend them;
> And they shall devour, and shall tread down sling-stones;
> And they shall drink, and make a noise, as through wine;
> And they shall be filled like the basins, like the corners of the altar . . . ." (9.15).

As in Joel, also in Second Zechariah, a whole passage has been added which thoroughly contradicts both the ideals and the thoughts set forth in the main prophecy. When the prophet warmly asserts that the Philistine cities shall be seized by Judah and be made to observe Jewish ritual law:[38]

"And I will take away his blood out of his mouth,
And his detestable things from between his teeth" (9.7),

the interpolator continues:

"And he shall be as a chief in Judah,
And Ekron as a Jebusite."

The Jebusite was the tribe which, originally dwelling in Jerusalem, had become integrated into Judah. The interpolator thus declares that the conquered peoples shall have all the privileges of native Judaites. Not satisfied with this frustration of the original prophet's intention, the interpolator proceeds:

"And I will encamp about My house against the army,
That none may pass through or return;
And no oppressor shall pass through them any more;
For now have I seen with Mine eyes.
Rejoice greatly, O daughter of Zion,
Shout, O daughter of Jerusalem;
Behold, thy king cometh unto thee,
He is triumphant, and victorious,
Lowly, and riding upon an ass,
Even upon a colt the foal of an ass.
And I will cut off the chariot from Ephraim,
And the horse from Jerusalem,
And the battle bow shall be cut off,
And he shall speak peace unto the nations;
And his dominion shall be from sea unto sea,
And from the River to the ends of the earth" (9.8 ff.).

The king of the ideal Judah will not be a warrior at all; he will have nothing to do with "his majestic horse in the battle" (10.3); in fact, God will destroy horses out of Jerusalem and chariots out of Ephraim. The new king is to be a poor plebeian, riding upon an ass as he makes his way into the Jerusalem, which God will prepare for him. He will govern the nations, not by force but by peaceful persuasion; and his gentle rule, as representative of God on earth, will include the whole world. Nothing could be further from the mind of the original writer than this transfer of the culmination of Judah's bliss to the end of days, or its realization through the peaceful miracle of divine intervention. It is incredible that this pacifist passage should have been written by the warlike author of the remainder of the booklet. It belongs to a totally different school of thought, the urban plebeians as opposed to the rural gentry.

Perhaps it was this interpolator who composed the magnificent chapters in which the Book of Deutero-Zechariah ends (Zech. 12–14). In any event they reflect his spirit. Belonging, however, to the final stratum of prophecy, they must be considered separately in connection with the conditions of the age to which they belong.

B. The Urban Prophets

The Second Zechariah's prediction of the conversion of the Philistines to the Jewish dietary laws indicates a deep change in the religious mentality of the provincials. No more than two hundred years earlier Deutero-Isaiah had condemned the provincials for their adherence to the ancient syncretistic worship, for eating the flesh of the swine, the detestable thing, and the mouse. Now the villagers had become so converted to the ritual law that they adhered to it more firmly than the urbanites themselves. The forces which brought this conversion will be discussed more suitably in the next chapter. Here we have merely to record the interesting fact that the rural preacher, about 330 B.C.E., considers renunciation of blood and other forbidden food a fundamental principle of Judaism, so important that it is the first commandment imposed on the new proselyte.

Four centuries later, the earliest Christian apostles, gathered for their famous council in Jerusalem, announced the same conviction. Drawn from the provinces, they, too, held the belief that the dietary ritual is an essential of religion.[39]

The acceptance of the ritual law among the provincials freed the later urban prophets from the task which had burdened their predecessors so heavily, that of denouncing village worship and custom. The newer group of urban prophets, in the fourth century, were free to devote all their eloquence to the social problems of human equality and the relations of the Jews to their neighbors. But the prophets preferred to present their ideas on these subjects through constructive suggestions rather than through destructive criticism. They had learned from Ezekiel the art of projecting their pictures of an ideal state on a distant eschatological screen. This device combined in itself the threefold merits of sound pedagogy, effective rhetoric, and personal prudence. The proletarian follower of the prophet was entranced by his picture of an ideal future and became a zealous missionary for its realization. And even the opponent of prophecy came to see in it no longer choleric scolding, but wise and philosophical statesmanship. At the same time the powerful rulers of the land could not consider the prophet the dangerous enemy he might have seemed had he confined his words merely to depicting their detailed transgressions. Thus wisdom and art combined to transform the prophet into the apocalyptist.

The most important of the apocalypses which have been preserved in prophecy is that contained in Isaiah 24–27. This booklet, it will be recalled, is the earliest work in Scripture definitely to assert the belief in resurrection (26.19). It likewise adopts the plebeian doctrine of semi-human angels (24.21). Indeed, it appears to hold, with the later Book of Daniel and the Book of Jubilees, that each nation has its particular angel in heaven. Hence the prophet believes that when God will visit the nations on earth, He will also visit "the angels of heaven in heaven." The prophet's belief in human equality appears in his first verses:

"Behold the Lord maketh the earth empty and maketh it waste,
And turneth it upside down, and scattereth abroad the inhabitants thereof.
And it shall be, as with the people, so with the priest;
As with the servant, so with his master;
As with the maid, so with her mistress;
As with the buyer, so with the seller:
As with the lender, so with the borrower;
As with the creditor, so with the debtor" (24.1f.).

Like the other plebeian prophets, he is not concerned with the power which will come to the people of Israel after the world cataclysm, but with the recognition which will be accorded their faith.

"Then the moon shall be confounded, and the sun ashamed;
For the Lord of hosts will reign in mount Zion, and in Jerusalem,
And before His elders shall be Glory" (24.23).

"And He will destroy in this mountain
The face of the covering that is cast over all peoples,
And the veil that is spread over all nations.
He will swallow up death forever;
And the Lord God will wipe away tears from off all faces;
And the reproach of His people will He take away from off all the earth" (25.7).

"For thus shall it be in the midst of the earth, among the peoples,
As at the beating of an olive tree,
As at the gleanings when the vintage is done.
Those [who remain] yonder lift up their voice, they sing for joy;
For the majesty of the Lord they shout from the sea:
'Therefore glorify ye the Lord in the regions of light,
Even the name of the Lord, the God of Israel, in the isles of the sea' " (24.13 ff.).

"Thou hast gotten Thee honour with the nations, O Lord,
Yea, exceeding great honour with the nations;
Thou art honoured unto the farthest ends of the earth" (26.15).

A far more graphic and touching appeal for tenderness toward other nations was made by the writer of the Book of Jonah, a work unsurpassed in the whole of Scripture for its breadth of sympathy and its love of mankind. The incidental episode of the whale and the absurd efforts of theologians to rationalize it, have, as usual, covered the ethical gem contained in this book with hills of casuistic dust. The well-known story describes the effort of Jonah, the son of Amitai, to escape the duties of prophecy. The word of the Lord comes to him urging him to predict the destruction of Nineveh. Unwilling to take the message to the doomed city, he flees from God. But a storm arises, Jonah is thrown into the sea, swallowed by a whale, thrown back on land, and compelled to proceed to Nineveh. Coming there, he perforce delivers the terrible message: "Yet forty days, and Nineveh shall be overthrown." "And the people of Nineveh," continues the story, "believed God; and they proclaimed a fast, and put on sackcloth, from the greatest of them even to the least of them. And the tidings reached the king of Nineveh, and he arose from his throne, and laid his robe from him, and covered him with sackcloth, and sat in ashes. And he caused it to be proclaimed and published through Nineveh by the decree of the king and his nobles, saying: 'Let neither man nor beast, herd nor flock, taste any thing; let them not feed, nor drink water; but let them be covered with sackcloth, both man and beast, and let them cry mightily unto God; yea, let them turn everyone from his evil way, and from the violence which is in his hands. Who knoweth whether God will not turn and repent, and turn away from His fierce anger, that we perish not?' And God saw their works, that they turned from their evil way; and God repented of the evil, which He said He would do unto them; and He did it not" (3.5–10).

The talmudic sages remind us that what moved God, according to the story, was not the ashes and sackcloth, but their repentance and their "turning from their evil way."[40] *En passant*, the writer thus takes the opportunity to align himself with Deutero-Isaiah, and against Joel, in holding the ritual of fasting worthless unless it is accompanied by ethical improvement.

But whereas God was stirred to pity the people of Nineveh, Jonah, represented as a typical rural prophet, was exceedingly displeased and he was angry. He was so disturbed by the turn of events that he begged for death. Thereupon God prepared a gourd — a quickly growing plant with widespreading leaves and branches — under which Jonah sat while he waited for the fulfillment of his prophecy. A day later the gourd was struck by a worm and it withered. "And it came to pass, when the sun arose, that God prepared a vehement east wind; and the sun beat on the head of Jonah, that he fainted, and requested for himself that he might die, and said: 'It is better for me to die than to live.' . . . . And the Lord said: 'Thou hast had pity on the gourd, for which thou hast not laboured, neither madest it grow, which came up in a night, and perished in a night; and should not I have pity on Nineveh, that great city, wherein are more than sixscore thousand persons that cannot discern between their right hand and their left hand, and also much cattle?' " (4.8–11).

On that note the book ends. Even at this distance in time and space, the significance of the treatise cannot be lost. The writer caricatures the contemporary prophets, particularly of the provincial variety, who were more anxious to see their predictions fulfilled than their admonitions obeyed. Their haunting fear was that the sinful would repent and escape punishment. He seizes on the figure of Jonah the son of Amitai for the subject of his tale, because the Book of Kings tells us that this prophet was a villager, hailing from Gath-hepher, and was a nationalist who foretold victories for Israel. Had the author invented a name, the point of the story would have been lost. He does not maintain that the prophets are false or insincere; he simply holds them unworthy bearers of the divine message, who themselves need a lesson in human kindness and generosity.

Even more simply and effectively does the writer of Ruth bring to his readers the message of international sympathy. This author has in mind, particularly, the opposition among the chauvinistic gentry to the admission of proselytes into Judaism and marriage with them. With astounding boldness he traces the royal dynasty of David back to a Moabite woman who had chosen to come into the Jewish fold. A genteel family of Beth-lehem had fled from Judah to Moab during a famine; there the two sons had married native women. When the father and the sons die, the three widows, the mother-in-law and the two daughters-in-law, undertake the journey back to Judah. On the road, Naomi, true to the prejudices of her class, tries to dissuade her daughters-in-law from coming with her. The elder turns back, but the younger, Ruth, declares: "Entreat me not to leave thee, and to return from following after thee; for whither thou goest, I will go; and where thou lodgest, I will lodge; thy people shall be my people, and thy God my God; where thou diest, will I die, and there will I be buried; the Lord do so to me, and more also, if aught but death part thee and me" (1.16). This is sufficient avowal of Jewish faith for the author. Arriving in Beth-lehem, Ruth is fortunately brought to the field of Boaz, a near relative of her husband, who ultimately marries her, becoming through this union the ancestor of Jesse, the father of David.

The moral of the tale was the more important because in the Law Moabites are expressly excluded from the Jewish community.[41] Apparently the writer, with the later rabbis, holds that this limitation applies only to Moabite men and does not include the women.[42]

The universalist message is further emphasized by a group of Wisdom writers who, in their zeal for the recognition of the heathen, made them the heroes of their books and attributed their own ideas to them. The chief product of this movement was the book of Job, who is described as an Arab chieftain, while his friends, Eliphaz, Bildad and Zophar, are made to come from different parts of the wilderness. With extraordinary sensitivity for words and language the author substitutes unusual Arabic-sounding expressions for the more common ones in use in Jerusalem's vernacular. He is equally adept in his selection of desert pictures for his imagery. Yet despite all his care, the Jerusalem scene protrudes itself through the Arab façade, and behind the tents of Kedar we see the curtains of Solomon. A similar attempt to attribute a book of Jewish wisdom to a Gentile was made by the author of the treatise ascribed to Agur son of Yakeh.[43] We have already seen how in both these works the plebeian teachings of human equality are emphasized, but obviously neither of these works could emphasize the plebeian teachings of the Jewish faith. That was left to the Hasidean proverbs and psalms which, equally humanitarian, are more definitely pietistic, combining in themselves a denial of any claim to special rights for the Jewish people with an avowal of the unrivaled superiority of the faith they had given the world.

C. Trito-Zechariah: The Inevitable Conflict

One prophet, looking over the Jewish Commonwealth, saw the significance of all the partisan divisions and predicted that they would end in armed conflict. Living about the year 200 B.C.E., the prophet to whom we owe the last three chapters of Zechariah portrays to us the bitterness between city and country, and hints at the wide separation between the lower and upper classes in the city itself. The prophet is himself a plebeian from Jerusalem; like his fellow-plebeian prophets, he asserts the existence of angels (12.8; 14.5), and looks forward to the time when Jerusalem will be the religious center of the world (14.16 ff.). Without giving the Jewish people any special status, God will reign in Mount Zion and all nations will come there once a year, during the Feast of Tabernacles, to offer their fealty to Him. Those who desist will lose their rain; and if Egypt, which needs no rain, should fail to come, it will suffer by the plague which is in store for the disobedient.

The prophet realizes what great convulsions must take place before Egypt and the other peoples are ready to accept the spiritual suzerainty of Jerusalem. All the nations, including Judah, will ultimately mass, the prophet imagines, in a world war against Jerusalem (12.2–3; 14.2). The victory will at first be with the investing Judaites, "that the glory of the house of David and the glory of the inhabitants of Jerusalem be not magnified above Judah" (12.7; 14.3). Half of the city shall go forth into exile, but "the residue of the people shall not be cut off from the city" (14.2). It seems reasonable to suppose that this "residue," who are to remain in the city, are the plebeians, overlooked by the conqueror as they were despised by their rulers.

In any event, the victory of Jerusalem's enemies will be followed by their swift discomfiture:

> "Then shall the Lord go forth,
> And fight against those nations,
> As when He fighteth in the day of battle....
> And the Lord, my God, shall come,
> And all the holy ones with Thee....
> And the Lord shall be King over all the earth;
> In that day shall the Lord be One, and His name one" (14.3 ff.).

The prophet expects the new order to be accompanied by a vast increase in the world's light. This had already been predicted by the First Isaiah (30.26), and this later prophet is merely repeating his prophecy when he foresees a time when "there shall be one day which shall be known as the Lord's; not day and not night; But it shall come to pass, that at the evening time there shall be light" (14.7).[44] The ideal further confirms our surmise of the urban origin of the prophet, for additional light would hardly be a blessing to the farmers, whose crops need the shelter of darkness as much as the rays of the sun. Uninterrupted sunshine would not only burn the crops but, in the sub-tropical climate of Judea's lowland, would be unbearable. The idea, introduced perhaps from Babylonia and Persia, suited much better the needs of the metropolitan city which, in antiquity as today, seeks to prolong the waking hours so far as possible. We can readily understand how the urban prophet would dream of the new world as perpetually sunlit.

Finally, having in mind Jerusalem's primary need for water, the prophet, like Ezekiel before him, promises as part of the new dispensation, a permanent river flowing through the capital. "And it shall come to pass in that day, that living waters shall go out from Jerusalem: Half of them toward the eastern (Dead) sea, and half of them toward the western (Mediterannean) sea; In summer and in the winter it shall be" (14.8). Such was the general plebeian faith in the coming of such a stream that the Chronicler projects its existence also back into the golden age of the past, maintaining that it was stopped from flowing only in the days of Hezekiah to prevent Sennacherib's army from finding much water (II Chron. 32.4). Geological observation and archaeological excavation have alike shown that there could not have been such a stream; nor can any arise short of a miracle or a violent change in the configuration of the land. But the need for water was keen and it necessarily gave wings to both hope and imagination.

But more important than either the lengthened day or the living waters is the new peace which will descend upon the country. Since the abolition of the local shrines and their syncretistic services, the most important difference between city and country had concerned the laws of Levitical purity which we have already discussed. The trader and artisan of Jerusalem, like the priest, observed these laws, which were, however, neglected and ignored at a distance from the holy precincts. The prophet expects this wound in the body politic to be healed, when all the people of the land will observe the Levitical regulations. So diligent will all the people, both urban and provincial, be in the observance of the laws of purity, that the vessel used in anyone's home will be fit for the offerings in the Temple. The various gradations still recalled in the Mishna between the property of the provincial and the observant citizen, between the observant citizen and the priest, and between the ordinary priest and those engaged in offering sacrifice,[45] will disappear. The ordinary peasant in his farm will be as scrupulous in the ideal future as the functioning priest at the altar is today. Hence it will come about that "every pot in Jerusalem and in Judah shall be holy unto the Lord of hosts; and all they that sacrifice shall come and take of them, and seethe therein." The very bells on the horses shall be holy unto the Lord (14.20 ff.);[46] and the pots used for the priestly food in the House of the Lord shall be like the basins before the altar. With this improvement in the people's morale, the prophet foresees the removal of an institution which must have been irksome to every sensitive-minded Jew, the merchant who sat in the Temple to provide clean vessels and fit animals for sacrifice. Since only few possessed Levitically pure utensils, these business men in the Temple were still a necessity, but in the future there "shall be no more a trafficker in the house of the Lord of hosts" (14.21).

XX. THE STRUGGLE AGAINST ASSIMILATION: JUDAISM BECOMES THE SYNAGOGUE.

The articulate philosophies which were born out of the social struggle during the Persian period have been analyzed in the preceding chapter. They were brilliant tongues of fire which, issuing out of the hearth of the Jewish Commonwealth, have offered light and heat to all succeeding generations. The sociologist and the historian, however, must, like chemists, pass beyond the beautiful vision into the very heart of the contending elements and seek to understand the mass actions and reactions which underlay the spectacle; for the members of the various groups were neither prophets nor philosophers, but simple men and women who followed their natural instincts and impulses. Their ideas rarely attained logical formulation; they were vague and inchoate. Like all reality it was a hopeless medley of movements and counter-movements, incapable of exact definition. Not all the plebeians were idealist eschatologists, any more than every member of Washington's continental army was a Thomas Jefferson, or every Independent of 1640 an Oliver Cromwell. The farmers of the day were indeed sincere patriots, like their prophetic spokesmen, but they had other interests and weaknesses which the single-minded prophet no longer shared. The nobility were in general the opportunists we have described, but they were more than that: they were husbands, wives, masters, courtiers and, most of them, priests. Inevitably the pious teachings of their craft affected the hearts and minds of some of them deeply, and a critical hour found many of them greater men than their usual actions would indicate.

The most important single problem with which the men of the new Commonwealth had to deal concerned the neighboring peoples, primarily the Samaritans. This people consisted largely of descendants of the ancient ten tribes, who had torn away from the Davidic dynasty after the death of Solomon. In 722 B.C.E., Assyria had destroyed their capital, Samaria, and carried off a considerable portion of the population into exile. The land left vacant was colonized by equally unfortunate captives from Syria and Babylonia. It is an error, however, to suppose with some historians that the Samaritans of the sixth century were wholly, or even primarily, of non-Israelitish stock. Biblical writers in the fifth and fourth century B.C.E. still speak of the people as Ephraim,[1] and recognize their kinship to the Jews. But aside from this evidence, it is a priori impossible to assume that any king would uproot a whole people, leaving none of its original inhabitants behind. In transferring peoples from place to place the Assyrian conquerors were not simply exerting themselves to be cruel; they were, like Nebuchadnezzar in later times, pursuing a prudent imperialistic policy. They knew that their interests lay in division among their subjects, and they found it to their advantage to destroy the racial uniformity and supposed purity of the conquered peoples. R. Joshua ben Hananya, living in the first century of the Common Era, realized this much better than many modern writers. Discussing the status of the Ammonites in his day, he denied that there was any longer a pure Ammonite, in the sense which the Pentateuch used the term. "Sennacherib long ago came up on these lands and confused the whole world," the wise rabbi remarked.[2] He does not say that the Assyrian transplanted the various nations, but that he "confused" or "mixed" them. He had created in every land a hybrid people, partly indigenous and partly alien.

But if the new immigrants were fewer than the original inhabitants, they were culturally more advanced; for, the same policy which led the Assyrians to deprive Israel of her nobility, the wealthier gentry, the priesthood, and the metropolitan traders, was followed also in other countries. It was the upper classes which were transplanted from land to land, in order to separate the potential leaders of revolutions from the necessary following.

The superior mentality of the newcomers gave them a disproportionate influence over the culture of the land, which thus became more truly composite than the racial strain. Just as the modern civilization of England inherits its legends from the Britons, its religion from the Romans, its basic language from the Saxons, and its more elegant forms of speech, its forms of government, and its architectural monuments from the Normans, so the Samaritans derived their religion from the Israelites, their language from the Arameans, and their favorite name (the Cutheans) from their principal contingent. The use of this name for the whole people indicates the glory which descent from the noble, patrician deportees shed on those who could claim it. No one who could identify himself with the aristocratic captives from Cutha, would admit descent from the humble fellahs, whom the Assyrian had contemptuously permitted to remain on their ancestral soil. In one of their quarrels with the Judaites (about the end of the sixth century B.C.E.) a group of Samaritans boasted that they were brought into the land by Assur-bani-pal, King of

Assyria.[3] The pride with which the fact is mentioned indicates the common state of mind. The social élite of the community were not the native Israelites, but the immigrant Babylonians and Arameans, and ultimately the whole nation came to claim kinship with them.

Yet the belief that each land had its own god or gods prevented the newcomers from foisting their ancestral faith on the rest of the people. The Book of Kings tells us that the immigrants were brought into the Israelitish faith by the fear of lions, which infested the country in the aftermath of the destructive wars. The people, believing that the lions were sent by the local deities who were not being worshiped in the accustomed way, asked the Assyrian Emperor for a native priest who might teach them the "manners of the gods of the land."[4] In accordance with this request, the shrine at Beth-el was reëstablished, and a priest from among the Israelitish exiles sent back to superintend its ritual. The truth of this story cannot be doubted, and the events which it describes were certainly a factor in the conversion of the newcomers to the ancient religion of the land. But a solitary priest in Beth-el, and a single untoward incident, can hardly account for the victory of one faith over another. To understand fully the conversion of the heathen immigrants to the service of God, we must look for deeper, sociological forces. These become clear when we realize that Shechem, the most ancient capital of the northern tribes, rather than Beth-el, the shrine which the Assyrian emperor had sanctioned, became the central sanctuary of the Samaritans. Obviously, the conversion of the people had less to do with the episode of the lions than with the persistent spread of current folklore. In the particular district of Beth-el, a certain group may have been won to the Israelitish God through the fear of wild beasts; the Samaritans as a whole became worshipers of God as "true proselytes."[5]

The common worship of God was the only tie between Judah and the new, hybrid people to the north. The bonds of language and supposed kinship had snapped; for the Samaritans no longer spoke Hebrew, or regarded themselves as descended from the patriarchs. Even in respect to worship there was a fundamental difference between Judean and Samaritan, for the Judean regarded Jerusalem as the main sanctuary of God, while the Samaritan preferred the shrines of his northern country.

Yet the feeling that both nations belonged to YHWH, had a powerful influence on their relations to each other. It kept alive the sense of close relationship and the memory of the transient unity of the days of Saul, David and Solomon. It was the basis of a lasting conviction that Palestine was a single unit — the land of God. From the day when Israel lost its independence, in 722 B.C.E., it was a cardinal point in Judah's national policy to regain the Samaritans for God. This was one of the major purposes of Hezekiah's confederacy with Babylonia and Egypt and his ill-fated rebellion against Assyria. To symbolize his sense of unity with the North, Hezekiah named his heir Manasseh, after one of the northern tribes — the only time in recorded biblical history when an individual was called after a patriarchal eponym.

But so long as Assyria was in the heyday of its strength, nothing could be done to reunite the kingdoms. No sooner, however, had she shown signs of fatal weakness than Josiah made open approaches to the northern tribes. Jeremiah speaks of Ephraim with touching tenderness and hopes that the reunion of the kingdoms is now at hand.[6] There may have been some hope that the compromise offered in Deuteronomy, making Jerusalem the only place of sacrifice but declaring Shechem, and particularly the neighboring Mount Gerizim, a place of "blessing," would be accepted.[7] But nothing permanent developed out of these efforts, for the Samaritans were in no mood to seek subjection to a Judaite King as an escape from bondage to Assyria.

When, in 586 B.C.E., Judah, too, lost its independence, its exiles in Babylonia continued nevertheless to dream of a reunited kingdom. They had been promised a restoration of their own commonwealth, and that implied for them as an essential factor the recovery of the ten tribes. Ezekiel again and again iterates his promise that in the new Commonwealth Judah and Ephraim will join hands (cf. Ezek. 16.59 ff.; 35.10; 37.15 ff.; 48.1 ff.). But he apparently realizes that there may be difficulty in securing the loyalty of the northern tribes to a capital and a sanctuary situated so far south as Jerusalem. He therefore carefully avoids the assertion that Jerusalem will again be the seat of the government and of worship. To the suggestion that a temple be constructed in Babylonia, he answers that only "in My holy mountain, in the mountain of the height of Israel, saith the Lord God, there shall all the house of Israel, all of them, serve Me in the land" (20.40). The carefully worded reply does not make Jerusalem the sole place of worship. With intentional vagueness and ambiguity it leaves the exact spot of the future sanctuary doubtful; it insists only that the Temple be located in Palestine. This is further clarified when Ezekiel undertakes to apportion the land of the future Commonwealth among the tribes. Palestine is to be divided into twelve equal horizontal strips, each possessed by one of the tribes. In the middle of all will lie Reuben and Judah. South of Judah, between it and the still more southerly territory of Benjamin, will be an extra-tribal area, for the Temple, the priests, the Levites, and the "prince." Having seven tribes north of it and only five to the south, the sanctuary will not be in the exact center of the country, but much nearer the middle than Jerusalem. Ezekiel takes no pains to tell us which city he would choose for the Temple; that is a matter for the future. "The name of the city," he says, "from that day shall be, The Lord is there" (48.35).

Seen in the light of Ezekiel's plan, the arrangement which the Pentateuch records for the tribes in the wilderness is especially significant. The Ark, the Tent of Meeting, the priests and the Levites were in the middle of the Israelite encampment. The tribes were massed in groups of three on the four sides of this sacred area. The plan, and the care with which it is outlined, are mystifying until we realize that it is intended to be a model for the Ideal Commonwealth of Palestine. The Law regards the Holy Land as a square rather than a rectangle, and scatters the tribes in all parts instead of giving each a horizontal strip of territory stretching from the east to the west. The sanctuary is to be in the exact center of the land, and each of the tribes is to be in the same relative position to it. The whole scheme is fully in accord with the ideal of the Torah, to make of Israel a holy community, deriving its meaning and its inspiration from the sanctuary, to which each member will resort at frequent intervals. Jerusalem is, of course, unmentioned. Not a single law deals with the rights of the capital, not a single institution is associated with it. The Law recognizes only two gradations of holiness; that of the

Temple, and that of the camp of Israel, the whole Jewish settlement.

These benign plans were all doomed to frustration. The policy of "divide and rule" prevented the two provinces of Israel and Judah from becoming a single domain after 586 B.C.E. So distinct were they from one another that although by the end of the sixth century Aramaic had become the vernacular in the North, Hebrew was still the main language in Judah. The Persian Emperor who permitted the Judaites to return to their land was careful to give them no rights in Samaritan territory. The country assigned to the returning exiles was carefully delimited; it consisted of a tiny strip of land round about Jerusalem.

Yet even such a small measure of deliverance aroused the astonishment of the Palestinian world. The Samaritans, seeing the exiles come back from Babylonia, were deeply impressed by the divine miracle which had been worked for them. Jeremiah's great prediction had been fulfilled at last; God had reversed the actions of Nebuchadnezzar. To the inhabitant of Palestine who knew nothing of imperialistic intrigues and rivalries it was clear that God had raised Cyrus to power for the sole purpose of restoring His Temple and His people. The insistence of Deutero-Isaiah on this vindication of prophecy shows how powerful an argument it was. It was altogether natural, therefore, that the Samaritans should approach the returning exiles with the offer to join them in building the Temple to God. The chronicler, to whom we owe our information about the period, tells the story in these words: "Now when the adversaries of Judah and Benjamin heard that the children of the captivity were building a temple unto the Lord, the God of Israel; then they drew near to Zerubbabel, and to the heads of the fathers' houses, and said unto them: 'Let us build with you; for we seek your God, as ye do; and we do sacrifice unto Him since the days of Esarhaddon, king of Assyria, who brought us hither.' But Zerubbabel and Jeshua, and the rest of the heads of the fathers' houses of Israel, said unto them: 'Ye have nothing to do with us to build a house unto our God; for we ourselves together will build unto the Lord, the God of Israel, as king Cyrus, the king of Persia hath commanded us' " (Ezra 4.1ff.). The tale is usually rejected as spurious because it seems incredible either that the Samaritans would offer help to the returning band of poor Judaites or that the Judaites, offered help from any quarter, would dare to reject it. Some historians have even suggested that we have in the chronicler's record an inversion of the original fact; that in actuality the Judaites had begged for the Samaritans' help and were denied it. But the supposed difficulties arise, like so many others in the interpretation of the Bible, from reading into Scripture more than the text says. The chronicler does not say that the Samaritans offered to join the Judaites in the construction of a temple *at Jerusalem.* Such an offer certainly could not have been rejected. After all, why should not the Samaritans have been taken into the Congregation of God? Their worship was indeed rural and partly Canaanite, but so was that of the Judaites who had remained in the land, and with whom the returning exiles gladly joined hands. The admixture of foreign races among the Samaritans could not have worried the returning exiles. They knew well that the Judaite stock itself was not without Canaanite and other alien blood, and they had brought with themselves from Babylonia no less than 800 souls whose Judean descent was open to question. But the difficulty lay in the implied demand that the new temple be built *in Shechem*. If the Samaritans were to join the returning exiles, they would naturally expect the temple to be built in their territory. To this the exiles properly replied that they intended to carry out the command of Cyrus authorizing them to build a temple in Jerusalem, and no other place would enter into consideration. By this decision all hope of reuniting the northern Israelites with the Judaites disappeared; hereafter they were doomed to be separate, rival, and at times even hostile peoples.[8]

But the rejection of the Samaritans did not destroy them as a living reality. They were the nearest relatives of the Judaites, and never during the next two centuries did they cease to be in close relations with the southern kingdom.[9] To many Judaites this friendship seemed more dangerous than hostility. The Judaite community, containing so many pioneers, and therefore suffering like all pioneer communities from a scarcity of women, was threatened with spiritual disaster through intermarriage with the surrounding nations. As usual, the tendency toward assimilation was strongest among the poor and the most affluent, and was weakest among the middle classes. This was especially true in the first days of the Second Commonwealth, when the poor were driven to exogamy by necessity, and the wealthy drawn to it by ambition. The lowest classes simply could not afford to compete for the Judaite women against their wealthier brethren, and had to find mates among the more numerous neighboring peoples. At the same time, the richest nobility sought to enhance their position by marriage alliance with native patrician families.[10] Opposed to both these tendencies, among the bulk of the peasantry who formed the middle class, was their intense chauvinistic nationalism. Sufficiently wealthy to bid successfully for Judaite women, they had no need nor desire for aliens. But while both patricians and plebeians sought wives among the foreign nations, there was this difference to be observed between the two classes. The plebeian had to seek his wife among people still poorer than himself, the nomadic tribes living in the grazing lands of southern Judah, the Calebites, the Jerahmeelites, and the Kenites. These tribes provided Judah with many male converts and now supplied the poorest, also, with proselyte wives. Adhering to the traditions which the immigrants brought from Babylonia, the plebeian considered the man or woman who accepted Judaism as fully a member of the faith as a native Israelite. That a pagan woman who became married to a Judaite would continue to follow her childhood worship never occurred to the plebeian, whose family was far too poor to maintain two separate religious forms. Hence while intermarriage among the plebeians was frequent, it did not weaken the Judaite community, but strengthened it. The writer of the Book of Ruth defends the marriage of Judaites to Moabite women, and according to the Chronicler several Judaite families originated in mixed marriages. He even admits that the builder of the Solomonic Temple was a half-Jew (II Chron. 2.13; cf. I Chron. 4.18). To be sure, this statement is simply repeated from Kings; but as the Chronicler was not above suppressing facts which did not agree with his notion of right, his special mention of this indicates his approval of it.

Far more serious, however, was the intermarriage which the patricians, particularly the high-priestly families, practiced. Too proud to marry below their caste, they had to turn for wives to the neighboring aristocracies, and in the first place chose, naturally, Samaritans. Within eighty years after 538 B.C.E., when the Babylonian exiles had begun to return, this evil became so widespread that Ezra, coming to Palestine from Babylonia, in 458 B.C.E., was amazed and horrified.[11] In Babylonia, marriage with the unproselytized heathen was held to be nothing less than treason to the Jewish community; to see it practiced by the children of the High Priests was intolerable. In a passionate scene, which he vividly describes, Ezra appealed to the transgressors who had married heathen wives to divorce them. Some of these women were mothers of children, but Ezra knew no compromise. The mixed families had to be purified.

Ezra's ruthlessness did not escape prophetic censure. Living at the time was Malachi, a plebeian prophet, the burden of whose message was a demand for priestly purification. It is from him that we know how corrupt the priesthood had already become. "If then I be a father," he says in God's name, "Where is My honour? And if I be a master, Where is My fear? Saith the Lord of hosts unto you, O priests, that despise My name" (1.6). The priests, accustomed to their own rich fare, had been heard to mutter, "The table of the Lord is contemptible" (1.7). They were capable of offering as sacrifice blind and lame and sick beasts, such as were no longer fit for work or human food (1.8). "Present it now unto thy governor," says the prophet, "Will he be pleased with thee? Or will he accept thy person?" "Oh, that there were even one among you that would shut the doors," he finally cries, "that ye might not kindle fire on Mine altar in vain! I have no pleasure in you, saith the Lord of hosts" (1.8 ff.). "The priest's lips should keep knowledge, and they should seek the law at his mouth; for he is the messenger of the Lord of hosts" (2.7).

The prophet could not then be accused of undue friendship for the secularized priesthood. But he felt that Ezra had gone too far. "Have we not all one father? Hath not one God created us?" the plebeian in him asks. "Why do we deal treacherously every man against his brother, profaning the covenant of our fathers?" (2.10). He admits that Judah "hath dealt treacherously, and an abomination is committed in Israel and in Jerusalem; for Judah hath profaned the holiness of the Lord which He loveth, and hath married the daughter of a strange god" (ibid. 2.11). To Malachi it seemed that a curse against committing the sin in the future would have been sufficient. "May the Lord cut off to the man that doeth this, him that calleth and him that answereth out of the tents of Jacob, and him that offereth an offering unto the Lord of hosts." He denies, however, any justification for breaking up families (2.12):

> "And this further ye do:
> Ye cover the altar of the Lord with tears,
> With weeping, and with sighing,
> Insomuch that He regardeth not the offering any more,
> Neither receiveth it with good will at your hand.
> Yet ye say, 'Wherefore?'
> Because the Lord hath been witness
> Between thee and the wife of thy youth,
> Against whom thou hast dealt treacherously,
> Though she is thy companion,
> And the wife of thy covenant.
> For I hate putting away,
> Saith the Lord, the God of Israel" (2.13 ff.).

Opposed by both the prophet and the leading priests, Ezra, who had been so successful in his initial efforts to bring the Judaite community within the Law, yielded, and apparently returned to Babylonia.[12] But the bitterness he had aroused between the Judaites and the Samaritans remained. Some of the Judaites had actually divorced their Samaritan wives; and unquestionably difficulties had arisen in every home based on mixed marriages. The proud northern people could not forget that its southern neighbors had even considered offering it the gross insult suggested by Ezra. When, a decade after Ezra's departure, plans were brought forward to rebuild the walls of Jerusalem, the Samaritans opposed them with unprecedented vigor. They wrote to the Persian capital, accusing the Judaites of being a rebellious people, and asserted that "if this city is builded, and the walls finished, they will not pay tribute, impost, or toll, and so thou wilt endamage the revenue of the kings." Indeed, they concluded, "by this means thou shalt have no portion beyond the River [Euphrates]" (Ezra 4.13, 16).

The strong protest bore fruit; and Artaxerxes, who was then King, forbade the building of the walls. The Samaritans, to whom the King's reply was addressed, lost no time in approaching the city with sufficient force to prevent the workers from continuing their labor.

The Judaites, refusing to resign themselves to defeat, appealed for assistance to the Imperial representatives in their country, who in turn sent a long memorandum on the subject to the central government.[13] It is doubtful whether they would have achieved success, however, had not Nehemiah, a Jew, happened to be cup-bearer to the King at the time. The representatives of the Judaite community reached Nehemiah, who obtained permission from Artaxerxes to visit Jerusalem and to rebuild its walls.

The struggle between Nehemiah and the Samaritans, his ousting of Tobiah the Ammonite from the Temple, his insistence on the suppression of trade on the Sabbath day, his attempt to prevent the spread of mixed marriages, all reflect the attitude natural to a pious exilic Jew. As such, Nehemiah must have expected the whole-hearted coöperation of the prophets. It was with amazement, therefore, that he found them resisting some of his favorite projects. While they applauded his opposition to the creditors, who had enslaved their Hebrew brethren, they rejected those of his policies which tended to arouse rancor among the neighboring populations; for the prophets were pacifists and afraid, above all, of quarrels and battles.[14] This attitude Nehemiah could not appreciate. He respected the religious principles of the urban prophets, and even their social doctrines. But, having been a high officer of the Empire, he could not understand what seemed to him their pusillanimity. When he was building a wall about Jerusalem, carrying out the main purpose of his coming, they actually discouraged him. Loyal to the teachings of Zechariah, who had prophesied that God would be "a wall of fire"[15] about the city, they felt it sacrilege to put up a wall of stone. Perhaps, as Nehemiah suggests, some of his pacifist opponents were insincere hirelings of the Samaritans and merely assumed the mantle of prophecy to conceal their nefarious dealings. But there can be no doubt that the prophetic party, as such, without suggestion from elsewhere, opposed Nehemiah's warlike and provocative maneuvers. They were consistent pacifists and could see nothing to be gained from bloody battles, from the protection of walls, and from irritation of their neighbors. Nehemiah, with all good will toward the plebeians, could not enter into this frame of mind. It seemed to him that Jerusalem ought to be at least a walled city, protected from marauders and raiders; it was shameful that the city of God should be humbled to the earth. When the prophets opposed him, he held them little better than traitors (Neh. 6.12 ff.).

The failure of Ezra and Nehemiah to impose their will on the Judaites reflects the fact that the Palestinian community had reached its maturity. The problems of Judaites in their native land were different from those of the Jews in the Dispersion, and it was no longer possible for the great leaders of the Dispersion, no matter how high their imperial position might be, to dominate Palestinian thought. The infant community which, in the last decades of the sixth century B.C.E., had had to rely on the spiritual strength which came to it from Babylonia, was soon to become the maker and dispenser, rather than the recipient, of Jewish thought.

Under the leadership of these native teachers, the relations between Judaite and Samaritan which the activities of Ezra and Nehemiah had done so much to strain, became friendly once more. The prophets of the fourth century B.C.E. could even conceive of both peoples presenting a united front to their conquerors and enemies. Certain it is that the Samaritans accepted the authority of the Pentateuch and became firm observers of its tenets.

Mixed marriages between the Samaritans and the Judaites continued; and there were even marriages between Judaites and pagans. In spite of the opposition of the priesthood generally to marriage even with proselytes, the highest members of the tribe continued to marry heathen women, almost until the end of the Second Commonwealth. As late as the first century B.C.E., the writer of the Testaments of the Twelve Patriarchs has still to take them to task, because "the daughters of the Gentiles do ye take to wife, purifying them with an illegal purification."[16] But with the passage of time and the end of the disproportion between men and women in the New Commonwealth, the demand for patrician ladies of foreign nations lessened. The Jewish aristocracy grew in power, in numbers, and in influence; and the self-consciousness of the people increased. With the arrival of the Greeks, the Jewish nobility turned to them rather than to the neighboring Samaritans and Ammonites and Tyrians for cultural guidance. Indeed, the Judaites began to feel contempt for their foreign cultural standards.

While Ezra failed in his effort to prevent mixed marriages, he achieved immortal fame through the movement he initiated for the abolition of the village shrines. These local temples and altars had been the scenes of mixed, sometimes degraded and vile forms of worship, and had been the objects of protest from prophets since the days of Isaiah. They had been forbidden in Deuteronomy, suppressed by Hezekiah and Josiah, and yet they continued. The fulminations of Deutero-Isaiah against them were probably as ineffective as those of Jeremiah a century before him. In an age when religion combined in itself all the arts and the sciences, when its priests and prophets were not only theologians but also physicians, economists, political leaders, rhetoricians, dramatists, musicians and teachers, it was impossible to confine its functions into a single city. The provincial could not undertake a trip to the capital whenever he sought God; he expected God to come to him.[17]

Ezra seems to have realized that the village worship would never be overcome either by force or by denunciation; it was necessary to find a moral substitute for the provincial sacrifice. Fortunately, there was one readily available in the synagogue. The origin of this great institution, the mother of the church and the mosque, as well as of the modern synagogue, is lost in the mists which fill the dawn of Jewish life. The oldest synagogue structures which archaeologists have recovered date from the third century of the Common Era. Presumably that is because the older synagogues were destroyed to the foundations during the persecutions of Hadrian (132–135 C.E.); for synagogue buildings are mentioned in a Maccabean psalm (Ps. 74.8), which tells how they were burnt by the soldiers of Antiochus Epiphanes (ca. 168 B.C.E.). But the synagogue as an institution is much older than the edifices in which it ultimately found its home. We can trace its origin back to the Babylonian commonwealth, and to the prayer gatherings which the prophets instituted at a much earlier time.[18] What may be the earliest reference to such prayer meetings occurs in the story of the Shunamite woman who had befriended Elisha and who went to him when her child suddenly died. Her husband, who did not yet know of the child's death, said to her: "Wherefore wilt thou go to him to-day? it is neither new moon nor sabbath" (II Kings 4.23). The implication is clear that on Sabbaths and new moons, visits to the prophet were customary. We may be certain that these were not in the nature of social calls but rather of religious pilgrimages. The people came to the prophet to hear words of religious exhortation and to have him intercede for them with God.

We cannot doubt that many of the prophecies which have been preserved for us in the biblical books were delivered at just such meetings. The usual picture of the prophet as the street orator haranguing a motley mob which listened to him because they had nothing else to do, hardly suits the recorded facts. The prophets took their messages seriously and spoke them where they would be most effective. Amos sought out the great festive gathering in Beth-el for his denunciation of Israel; Jeremiah frequently resorted to large assemblies in the Temple. Isaiah walked about Jerusalem for three years without clothes or shoes to impress the people with the message he wished to bring them, that the Egyptians on whom they relied for help would thus be carried off in captivity by the King of Assyria. We know how effectively the early Christians used the synagogues as places to deliver their messages, for after all it is in an orderly gathering of men attuned to religion that educational efforts for religion are most effective.

If Isaiah, Jeremiah, and their colleagues wanted to influence public opinion they had, like all other orators, to seek out audiences which were sympathetic or were ready to listen seriously. The prophets would have wasted their energies and accomplished nothing had they, except on the most extraordinary occasions, addressed their words to the hostile. The direct purpose of their prophecies was, after all, not to convince the recalcitrant or the intransigent, whose interests they opposed and whose methods they denounced. They might indeed from time to time effect an extraordinary conversion, but that would be the miraculous exception, not the daily occurrence. What they tried to do in their prophecies was to strengthen the faith of those who already believed in them and to supply them with arguments and ideas which they might use in their daily intercourse with others who might be subjects for conversion. That, after all, is the task and the aim of the moral and political philosopher in any generation and at any time. But to reach these sympathetically minded followers, formal gatherings were essential, and for these apparently the Sabbath and new moon meetings at the prophet's place of abode were used.

The suggestion has already been put forward that regular prayer meetings under the guidance of the prophets were instituted during the persecutions of Manasseh. This surmise is considerably strengthened by the emphasis on prayer which we find among the prophetic writers immediately after that King's reign. The repeated warnings to Jeremiah not to pray on behalf of the people, and the petitions for them which he incorporates into his book, indicate apparently that he took part in prophetic prayer meetings even during the reign of Josiah (cf. Jer. 14.11; 15.19; etc.). More important, perhaps, than this evidence is the fact that in the prayer attributed to King Solomon at the dedication of the Temple there is not a word said of the use of the building for the sacrificial system. The beautiful prayer, fully worthy of the great occasion in retrospective celebration of which it was written, contains 31 verses (I Kings 8.23–53), in the course of which there might certainly have occurred some reference to the main purpose of the structure, the offering of sacrifices to God. Instead, the author who, according to the consensus of opinion among biblical scholars, lived about the year 600 B.C.E., speaks of the various people who might come and pray in the sanctuary or, living in a distant land, turn toward it. The conception of the Temple as a house of prayer, could hardly occur to one who had never seen any such institution, who lived in a community *all* of whose shrines were for sheep and bullocks.

When the Judaites were carried off to Babylonia, the institution of the synagogue was thus prepared for their use. It has long been noticed that some of Ezekiel's prophecies were uttered at synagogue gatherings. In fact, independently of his evidence we should have to suppose that the Judaites in Babylonia either built themselves a temple (which we know they did not do) or established some kind of synagogue assembly for prayer worship. For it is altogether inconceivable that a deeply religious people should for half a century live without any form of worship.

Linguistic evidence likewise points to the pre-exilic development of the synagogue. The lecture house which in later days was separated from the synagogue, but was originally identical with it, is called regularly *Bet Ha-Midrash.* The term is used for the first time in extant literature by Ben Sira[19] (ca. 200 B.C.E.) and is usually translated "House of Exposition." But the root, *darash,* means not to "explain" but rather to "inquire," or to "seek out," and the expression must therefore have meant originally "house of inquiry." The verb is the technical term used of consultation with the prophet (Cf. Gen. 25.22). The *Bet Ha-Midrash* thus appears to have been in origin the Oracle, where people came to seek God, to find out His will, or to invoke His aid.

While the followers of the prophets who were among the leaders of the Babylonian exile maintained the synagogue in their new land, it apparently was forgotten in Palestine during the exile. The few surviving members of the prophetic persuasion huddled about the governorate at Mizpah and maintained a "house of prayer" there; but elsewhere throughout the land the people worshiped, as we have seen, at village shrines.

Ezra understood that in any struggle between the Temple of Jerusalem and the local high places, the provincials would inevitably side with their village institution. It was obviously necessary to offer them some place of worship which would wean them away from the shrines at which they and their ancestors had sacrificed for centuries. The synagogue offered itself once more, as it had in the Babylonian exile, as a savior of Judaism. On Sabbaths and festivals, in addition to the sacrifices offered in Jerusalem, the people were urged to assemble in their villages to hear the reading of the Torah, the exhortation of a prophet, the prayer of a pietist, and the blessing of a priest. Where no prophet of original powers was available, some one read from the recorded prophecies of ancient times. Frequently the priest, as the most learned in the congregation, performed the whole of the service, but it was not essential that he do so.

The Temple officials might have looked askance at the synagogue as a rival institution were they not threatened with graver dangers from the village shrine. Realizing the need for some provincial houses of worship, they decided to accept the synagogue and make it a means for propaganda on behalf of the central sanctuary.[20] The portions of the Torah and the Prophets which were read in the synagogue asserted the superior holiness of Jerusalem and its Temple. Whenever priests were available they were made the primary functionaries of the prayer meetings; above all, they alone could offer the priestly benediction which concluded the service.

Given the choice of synagogue with its prayer service and the traditional shrine with its bloody sacrifices, the villagers could not long hesitate. On the side of the synagogue were ranged the authority of the Torah, the prophets, and the priests of Jerusalem; in the balance against all these were mere inertia and the local keeper of the country altar. In addition to its great spiritual advantages over the local altar, the synagogue was the simpler institution. It required no sacrifice, it asked for no lambs, it demanded no meal offerings.

There can be little wonder that the synagogue won an easy victory over its adversary, the village altar, a victory all the more memorable because for centuries the Temple had failed to achieve it whether by force or persuasion. When the Persian period ended and the contest between Judaism and Hellenism began, the synagogue had become a fundamental institution in the land. Its services were no longer limited to Sabbath and festivals; such was its hold on the peasant that whenever he came into town to buy his supplies he would make his way also into the synagogue for instruction and prayer. The services which were originally held only on Sabbaths and festivals were extended to the market days, Monday and Thursday. Ultimately, a shortened service, in which the reading of the Torah was omitted, but which included only prayer and the priestly blessing, was established in most communities every day.

The synagogue, established as a foil to the village high places, never became a serious rival of the Temple. It never claimed for itself any prestige beyond that of a "small sanctuary,"[21] far inferior and secondary to that of the holy place in Jerusalem. Yet its existence enabled large groups, such as the Essenes and the Sect of Damascus,[22] to shun the Temple altogether because they disliked the priests who ministered there. But more than that, it offered a forum to the Pharisees to spread their doctrine among the farming community. Not in essence a Pharisaic or a plebeian institution, for it had outgrown by far its prophetic beginnings, it yet served as a channel through which the artisan or merchant or Levitical scholar in Jerusalem could reach the common people. If Jewish life survived the destruction of the Temple, that was because the synagogue had been prepared to take over the whole burden and carry it onward for generations to come.

XXI. HELLENISTS, HASIDEANS, AND PHARISEES.

While the Synagogue was attaining its full strength and development, Alexander's easy victory over Persia brought Judaism face to face with the most formidable adversary it had yet encountered. The simple religion and theology of the nomadic tribes who had settled in Palestine between the fourteenth and the twelfth centuries B.C.E. had shown themselves stronger than the opposing Canaanite worship and superstition. The prophets had been able to persuade the people that Egypt's technical skill was no warrant for the truth of her polytheistic faith or the value of incestuous institutions. The quick destruction which overtook Phoenicia, Aram, Assyria and Babylonia had dissipated whatever belief in their respective gods their momentary success might have evoked. But none of these peoples could compare with the new challenger to the traditions of Israel. Hellas, long first in arts, in science, in philosophy, in literature, and in commerce, at last took her place also at the head of world government, and added to all her other laurels those of physical conquest. No nation had yet appeared with half the virtues of this western people, which had produced a Homer, an Aeschylus, a Phidias, a Pericles, a Plato, Athenian wisdom and Spartan courage, and now was to reach the climax of its military power in the demi-god, Alexander.

The passion which the aristocracy of Jerusalem had felt for foreign cultures in preceding ages was lost in their new love. They threw themselves into Hellenism with the zeal and energy of neophytes. Their own laws, customs and traditions were forgotten in this last infatuation. They built a gymnasium, like those of the Greeks, in Jerusalem and shocked the Semitic sense of propriety by taking their exercise and playing Hellenic games quite naked. Ashamed, in their own country and amidst their own people, of the circumcision which all Palestinians (except the Philistines) had practiced from time immemorial, some of them underwent the excruciating pain of an operation — twenty centuries before the discovery of anesthesia — to obliterate this sign of the Covenant. They endeavored to speak the language of their new rulers and called themselves by the sweet-sounding Greek names. Hundreds of children were called Alexander, of course; what more could a mother wish for her child than that he might prove a pale reflection of the world conqueror? But there were others named after mythological heroes; Jason, Menelaus and the like. It is symptomatic of the form which Asiatic Hellenism took on that the assimilation centered altogether on the development of the sound body, without any regard to the sound mind.

But this impulse toward assimilation in externals was not universal. The plebeians, more convinced than ever that their Torah was from God, could listen with complaisance to the tales of Greek glory. Pacifists to the core, they had no mind to emulate the physically powerful. On the other hand, their well trained intellects were able to assay at their true value the drops of Greek learning which trickled into Asia from Athens. They continued to believe, as had their fathers for generations, that true knowledge could be found only in the Law and the Prophets, and that the beginning of Wisdom was the fear of the Lord (Prov. 9.10). The only desire which contact with current Hellenism evoked in them was to prove the superiority of their own traditions.

Yet there were two lessons which they learned from the Greeks: the strength inherent in organization and the value of formulated doctrines. They derived the first from the Macedonians, the second from the Athenians.

Like the rest of the Orient the Jewish plebeians had been deeply impressed by the manner in which the well-massed Macedonian phalanxes had torn through the armies of the Great King. But while others could see in this only an exhibition of superior Greek prowess, the keen eyed leaders of Jerusalem's market place realized that it demonstrated another, more important truth: properly disciplined and ordered, a small group might rout outnumbering hosts.

They understood at last why their predecessors had made such little headway in spreading their teachings among the people. The prophetic following had never been a party in the true sense of the word. It had had the advantages of truth, reason, piety, and determination. It had produced wise leaders, capable thinkers, eloquent orators, and gifted writers. But that was not enough. It had lacked fundamental requisites for human victory—numbers, wealth, and organization. The first two were beyond its power to secure; but why could not the third be provided? Never before had the plebeians made any attempt to attain group solidarity, to formulate a definite program of action, to demand that everyone declare himself either for them or against them. They had permitted their wealthier adherents to be court officials of Kings who persecuted, imprisoned, and even executed their leaders. The plebeians had even permitted the more backward elements to hold views which were denounced as subversive and false by the more progressive. The reformation of Josiah, in which some of their leaders had participated, had been rejected by others; the building of Jerusalem's walls which Haggai had advocated, had been denounced as evidence of little faith by Zechariah.

No wonder that such confused movement had had only a limited influence. From the perspective of centuries, it seemed miraculous that it had even survived. But now a change was to take place. The plebeians became the Hasideans, "the Pietists." The assumption of a name indicated a fundamental change in the whole attitude of the groups. The followers of Isaiah, Jeremiah, and Deutero-Isaiah could not be identified; their disciples of the third century B.C.E. stood out as a definite unit in the body politic. It is altogether probable, however, that the naming of the group was merely one of the minor changes in its development. The character of the Pharisaic and Essenic Orders, which were Hasidism's spiritual children, indicates that the earlier group, too, had its recognized membership, its rules for admission and expulsion, its period of trial, its recognized beliefs, its duly chosen leaders, and its method for reaching party decisions.

No less important than these externalities of organization was the systematization of plebeian belief. For the first time in Jewish history, an attempt was made to formulate some of the fundamental doctrines of the faith. The concept was so definitely foreign to the Judaite mind, which always liked the concrete and shunned the abstract, that we cannot be wrong in imputing the tendency to the influence of the example set by the Athenian philosophical schools. But while the method was Hellenic, the content was definitely prophetic. The principles asserted by the

Hasideans were those taken over by Pharisaism in later times, the belief in the resurrection, in the existence of angels, in Divine Providence as relating to the individual in all aspects of his life, and in the validity of the Oral Law.

The fear of Trito-Zechariah, that a war between Jerusalem and the rest of Judah was in the offing, may have been produced, in part, by the growing strength of the Hasidean Order in the capital. Certain it is that by the year 168 B.C.E., the new organization had become sufficiently established to exercise a determining influence on the course of Palestinian history.

It is doubtful, however, whether the Order could have attained this prestige without the assistance which came to it through a curious series of events in the third century B.C.E. Palestine was then under the rule of the Egyptian Ptolemys. The High Priest was the first local functionary and combined in himself the ecclesiastical duties of the Aaronid with the official prerogatives of the governor. Chief of the aristocracy, he was naturally also first of the assimilationists. Neither he nor his subordinates were apparently conscious of the contradiction involved in their queer position. They could not realize that by deserting Judaism and cleaving to Hellenic-Egyptian culture, they were breaking down the ladder on which they had ascended.

The weakness of the high-priestly family became clear as soon as it encountered formidable opposition. Joseph ben Tobiah, who was fated to be its first challenger, was an opulent Judaite, with large landholdings east of the Jordan and with powerful friends in Samaria. He was not of the high-priestly family, but his mother was the sister of the High Priest. The family connection was, however, of slight importance in a day when kinship was reckoned only through the father. In fact, it was Joseph's mother, the sister of the High Priest, who gave him the first opportunity to utilize his economic wealth in order to gain political power.

The High Priest, Onias II, had withheld the taxes from Ptolemy III Euergetes, hoping doubtless to gain some special privileges from him because of the difficulties then ensuing between Egypt and Syria. As a result of the quarrel that arose, Onias sent his nephew, Joseph, to Egypt to pacify the government there. Either on this trip or subsequently, Joseph took advantage of the Egyptian friendships he formed to obtain the right of chief tax collector of all Syria on behalf of the Egyptian government. This official recognition placed him in a position superior to that of the High Priest — in fact, above that of any Judaite or Syrian alive.[1]

We may imagine how the High Priests in Jerusalem, who had held the first place in the Commonwealth for almost three centuries, accepted the promotion which had come to a simple member of the laity. They suddenly discovered that, having cast aside their spiritual claims, they might easily be bereft of all temporal power as well. They were the more terror-stricken when they noticed that Joseph ben Tobiah, who even before his rise had had intimate associations with the Samaritans and the pagans, pursued more energetically than ever his Hellenistic policies, which threatened to undermine the last vestige of priestly authority.

Onias II, who had himself played the assimilationist all his life, could not easily change his ideals or his habits. But his successor, Simeon II, realized with statesmanly understanding in what direction the true interests of the priesthood lay. He broke completely with the assimilationists, who had until that time claimed the whole aristocracy and priesthood, and became the leading exponent of Hasidean doctrine, in which alone he saw promise of permanent influence for the Temple and its ecclesiastic officials. He knew that the hybrid culture which had been developing in Jerusalem under the joint influence of a weakening tradition and a corrupt Hellenism was even more dangerously materialistic and selfish than the negativism which had been characteristic of the aristocrats before his day. The spiritual life of the people could be saved only by accepting the plebeian doctrine that Judaism was Torah, a philosophy, greater than any other, because it emanated from God.[2]

In order to carry out his program, Simeon convoked a "Great Assembly," similar to that which had met on Mount Carmel in the days of Ahab and Elijah.[3] Such importance, however, attached to the decisions of this Assembly that it became known in later Jewish history as "*The* Great Assembly" (*Keneset Ha-Gedolah*), par excellence.

And, indeed, the measures which the Assembly took were of a most revolutionary nature. The most important of them was the admission of the plebeian scholars into the *Gerousia* or Governing Council of the community. For a suitable parallel to this revolutionary change, which was the first step in the transformation of Judaism from an aristocracy into a sophocracy, or government by the learned, we must turn to the admission of the Commons into Parliament by Simon de Montfort in 1265. The traditions which derived from the earliest days of Israelite settlement in Palestine were broken down; the rights which had been vested solely in the "heads of the families" and the "elders" or sheiks of the clans, were to be shared by them with men of learning, who might be smiths, carpenters, or traders.

It is a pity that no records have been preserved of the deliberations which led to this epochal decision. Surely nothing but the determination of the High Priest could have carried the day for the plebeians. A generation earlier, the Chronicler had vainly pleaded for the admission of some Levites into the Council, basing his demand on the grounds of historical precedent. Now, the privilege was extended to men who had no ecclesiastical standing whatever.[4]

The innovation necessitated an alteration in the name of the Council. It could no longer be called the *Gerousia*, or Gathering of Elders; it had become simply the *Bet Din Ha-Gadol*, the Great Court, or in Greek, for governmental purposes, the Synhedrion, or Council.

The new plebeian members were to be selected by the Court itself. Whether any fixed number was assigned to them, whether they were admitted to all meetings or only to some, and whether they also met separately from the elders, is not recorded. It seems probable, however, that from the first they were permitted to select one or two advisers to the High Priest from among their midst; and that their superior knowledge of the ceremonial Law made them especially responsible for its development.

Second only to the reorganization of the *Gerousia*, and in a sense ancillary to it, was the announcement that the period of prophecy was at an end. This decision had been adumbrated by the declaration of Trito-Zechariah, who may himself have been a member of the Great Assembly, denying that any true prophets would arise in the future.[5] And indeed, the admission of the plebeians into the Sanhedrin made a prophetic opposition superfluous. The struggle between the classes was at last removed from the market place into the Council Chamber, where it belonged.

The end of the period of literary prophecy, which had extended over six centuries, could not be better marked than by the collection and edition of the prophetic works. It is probable that a standard text was produced, which ultimately became the basis for all future codices, and thus explains the remarkable uniformity of all the extant manuscripts of the prophets.[6]

A record of later date ascribes to the Great Assembly more than the collection of the ancient prophetic works; it maintains that the sages of that day actually "wrote" the Books of Ezekiel, the Twelve Prophets, Daniel and Esther.[7] Apparently, the chronicler to whom we owe this report meant that the men of the Great Synagogue reduced the scattered fragments of these works or perhaps their memorized texts into written, book form.[8] Whether he was correct in this it is of course impossible to say. The fact that he included the Book of Daniel in his list — although it was not composed for more than two generations after the time of the Great Assembly — naturally casts doubt on the authenticity of his tradition. And yet there are a number of considerations in the textual analysis of Ezekiel and the Twelve Prophets which support him.

Not satisfied with the major achievement of finally fixing the prophetic canon, the Great Assembly turned its attention to the ritual of the Temple and the synagogue. The innovation which they introduced into the temple service, in the daily reading of the *Shema'*, has already been described.[9] The synagogue service, which had grown up without official direction, was put on a recognized basis, and a fixed formula was established for its daily and Sabbath prayers.[10] The service probably began with the reading of prescribed portions of the Torah; this was followed by the informal petitions of the individual members of the congregation; after which the leader recited aloud his prayer for the whole group. As formulated by the Great Assembly, it seems to have read as follows: "Blessed art Thou, O Lord, our God and the God of our fathers, the God of Abraham, the God of Isaac, and the God of Jacob, the most-high God, Possessor of heaven and Earth. Hear our cry, O Lord, our God, have pity and mercy upon us. Blessed art Thou, O Lord, who dost hear prayer." On Sabbaths and festivals, when petitions for daily needs could not be offered, the second and third verses read, "Grant us joy, O Lord our God in this Sabbath [*or*: festival] day. Blessed art Thou, O Lord, who dost sanctify Israel and the Sabbath [*or*: the Festivals]." Where a priest was present, the service ended with his benediction.

It is noteworthy that the first verse of these prayers reflects the same theological trend of thought that is indicated in the selection of the *Shema'* for the Temple service: the combination of the universalist and the particularist elements in the Jewish conception of God. God is appealed to first as the Deity of the Patriarchs, and then as the Creator of heaven and earth.

The same conception reappears in the Blessing after Meat, which, in its original form, was apparently also fixed by the Great Assembly. The first paragraph praised God as the one "Who feeds the whole world in His grace"; the second thanked Him for having granted Israel the land of Canaan and its produce.[11]

Finally, the Great Assembly summarized its principles in a norm calling on the judges of the villages and towns to combine with their judicial duties also those of teachers of the young. "Be deliberate in judgment, set up a hedge about the Law and make many disciples."[12] In later times the second phrase was construed as a justification for the addition of various prohibitions to those enumerated in Scripture;[13] but originally it was apparently intended merely to urge the strengthening of the tradition as opposed to assimilation. Like their leader the High Priest, the members of the Great Assembly realized that Hellenism as a cultural movement could be offset only by a strong educational effort among the masses.

Simeon's services to the Torah won him the title *Ha-Zaddik*, the Righteous, among the loyalists. His conversion was not individual, however. Large numbers of the aristocratic laity realized the peril to which their unbridled assimilationism was leading and turned back into cultural nationalism. This movement was further stimulated by a conflict which broke out among the Hellenizing descendants of Joseph ben Tobiah himself.

The seven older sons of this mighty tax farmer quarreled bitterly with his favorite youngest son, Hyrkan, who was a half-brother of theirs. Various stories were told of his ignoble birth; according to some he was the child of an Egyptian dancer with whom Joseph had fallen in love. But Hyrkan himself always maintained that he was of legitimate birth. According to his story, Joseph had indeed fallen in love with an Egyptian dancer, but through a ruse had been prevented from living with her. One of Joseph's brothers was ordered to bring the dancer to Joseph's house, but brought his own daughter in her place, and this girl, Joseph's niece, became his legitimate wife, and the mother of Hyrkan.

Whatever be the truth about this ancient scandal, there can be no doubt of Hyrkan's hostility to his older brothers.

Joseph decided to send Hyrkan to Egypt to protect him from the anger of his brethren; but once there, Hyrkan spent a fortune in winning the favor of the rulers to himself. His father, fearing that the young man might supplant him in his high office, recalled him, but durst not hurt him, since he came armed with letters of commendation from Ptolemy.

When Joseph ben Tobiah died, the quarrel about the succession broke out in earnest. Two of the older brothers were killed in the fray between the various factions. But the High Priest, Simeon the Righteous, sided with the older brothers, and ultimately Hyrkan left Jerusalem to retire into his ancestral estates across the Jordan, where he seems to have set up a petty, feudal principality.

The struggle was, however, destined to reach wider dimensions. The sons of Tobiah, angered at the favor shown Hyrkan at the Egyptian court, and fearful lest he ultimately supplant them, also favored the Seleucids. We may take it, although the records are silent on the matter, that the majority of the plebeians in Jerusalem agreed with this pro-Syrian policy.

This assumption is further confirmed by the events which occurred in 198 B.C.E., when Antiochus III, the Great, vanquished the Egyptians and seized control of Palestine. In a document preserved by Josephus,[14] the authenticity of which is generally recognized, Antiochus acknowledges the assistance given his army by the Jews in the struggle against the Egyptians, and in gratitude he grants them autonomy, "to let them live according to the laws of their own country;" he makes gifts to the Temple, including not only sacrifices but also the right to import wood from Lebanon tax-free; and finally he discharges from the crown tax and poll tax "the *Gerousia*, the priests, the scribes of the Temple and the sacred singers." The men whom the Greek king describes as "scribes of the Temple" were, we may be sure, the *soferim*, whom we know from Jewish literature, the sages and scholars who preserved the Oral Law, and whom Simeon the Righteous had admitted into the Great Assembly and the Council it established. The composer of the document calls them "scribes of the Temple," although they had no direct association with sacrifice, because the Council met within the Temple portals, and because it was necessary to distinguish them from the professional secretaries, who were also called scribes. As late as the Talmud, the central court is called the "*Bet Din* of the Chamber of Hewn Stones." It was natural, therefore, that in earlier times, and especially in a government document, the scholars should be mentioned as those associated with the Temple. It is equally significant that the Levites, "the sacred singers" of the sanctuary, are given the same relief from taxes as the priests. This further indicates a recognition by Antiochus that the party which sided with him was composed largely of the plebeian scholarly group, with whom the oppressed Levites were so closely associated. Bearing in mind the antagonism between the priests and the Levites which became traditional during the Second Commonwealth, we cannot believe that those who obtained this recognition for the lower temple ecclesiastics were the high-priestly aristocrats of Jerusalem. On the contrary, it is apparent that the negotiations with Antiochus III were carried on by the recognized *Gerousia*, in which the Levites and scholars sat on equal terms with the priests. It was this body which contained within itself representatives of the humbler castes, which insisted that they be granted the privileges and immunities which in earlier times belonged to the priests alone.

But together with the priests, scholars and Levites, Antiochus felt bound to recognize his other powerful allies in Jerusalem: the Tobiads, the older sons of Joseph ben Tobiah,[15] who, taking sides against Hyrkan, had joined Simeon II in espousing the cause of the Syrians. An aristocrat by the name of Simeon, who was either one of them or closely affiliated with them, was appointed to the high position of "Prince of the Temple" (Heb. *Sar Ha-Birah*). Presumably this office had formerly been filled by a member of the high-priestly family; its assignment to an "outsider" must have been a painful humiliation, for according to the records before us, this Simeon the Tobiad was not even a priest, but a member of the tribe of Benjamin (II Mac. 3.4).

The high-priestly families blamed the philo-Syrian policy of Simeon the Righteous for this further rise of the upstart Tobiads. Far from regaining control of the Commonwealth for them, the High Priest had actually entrenched their rivals in power. He might indeed claim — and with justice — that he had saved for the hierarchy all of its prestige and influence that could be saved. Yet they could not bear with equanimity the arrangement which compelled them to share their religious authority with the plebeian scholars and the despised Levites, and their temporal government with the lay Tobiads.

So long as Simeon the Righteous lived, he managed to keep the arrogance of the Tobiads under restraint, and to impose his own loyalist policy on the Temple priests. But when he died and his own son, Onias III, succeeded as High Priest, a quarrel between the House of Tobiah and the disappointed Aaronids, who had so recently been its allies, broke out.

Simeon the Tobiad, not satisfied with being Prince of the Temple, wanted to become also the *Agoranomos*, which would have given him full power over the market and thus over the economic life of the city. When Onias III declined to give him this office, he appealed to the Syrian government and pointed out to them that the Temple contained immense treasures of gold and silver which ought to be turned over to them. Seleucus IV, who reigned at the time, was, like all the Syrian kings, greatly in need of funds, and immediately despatched Heliodorus, a general, to obtain the Temple treasures. Onias III resisted the Greek demands, and finally succeeded in persuading Heliodorus not to confiscate the Temple funds. So unusual was such yielding by the Syrian governors that a legend arose of some miracle which occurred just in time to prevent the desecration of the sanctuary.

The Tobiad, temporarily defeated, did not drop his plan. After some time he again appeared before Seleucus to traduce Onias III as a traitor. Onias was summoned to defend himself; but apparently while the matter was still undecided Seleucus died and Antiochus IV Epiphanes came to the throne.

The charge against Onias was probably not without foundation. Seeing that the covenant with Syria had failed the ruling class, Onias reverted to the Egyptophilism which was natural and traditional with the Judaite aristocracy. He sought out Hyrkan, the illegitimate son of Joseph ben Tobiah who was living in Transjordan, and joined hands with him in upholding the cause of the Ptolemys, just as the nobility of Jeohiakim's day had sided with the Pharaohs. The Tobiads, on the other hand, and a large number of their friends, continued to uphold the cause of the Syrians. The struggle between the pro-Egyptians and the pro-Syrians had now ceased to be religious or social. The plebeian pietists could accept neither the one nor the other, for both were assimilationist. The High Priest and his following, who looked to Ptolemy for guidance, were no less Hellenistic than the Tobiads, though perhaps their interest in the Temple made them less extreme. The Tobiads, on the other hand, did not hesitate to inform Antiochus "that they were prepared to leave the laws of their country and the Jewish way of living according to them, and to follow the king's law and the Grecian way of living: wherefore they desired his permission to build a gymnasium in Jerusalem. When he had given them leave, they hid the sign of the circumcision, so that even when they were naked they might appear to be Greeks. Accordingly, they left off all the customs which belonged to their country and imitated the practices of other nations" (II Macc. 4.9).

These reforms hardly needed the consent of Antiochus, and it has been justifiably assumed that their real purpose was to bring about the transformation of Jerusalem into a Greek *polis*, with the organization, manners, language and custom of any other Hellenic community. This is indicated particularly in the record preserved in the Second Book of Maccabees (4.10), which tells us that the Helenists prayed to the King to "register the inhabitants of Jerusalem as Antiochians."

Together with these changes in the city's organization and culture, the Tobiads obtained the removal of Onias from the high-priesthood, and the substitution of his brother, Jason, who was more amenable to their purposes. Led by the new priest and the powerful Hellenists, the young men were trained in the ephebic system of the Greeks. "The noblest of them," we are told, "wore the Greek cap, and there was an extreme of Greek fashions and an advance of an alien religion by reason of the extreme profaneness of Jason, that ungodly man and no High Priest. The priests had no more zeal for service at the altar, but despising the sanctuary and neglecting the sacrifices, they hastened to enjoy that which was unlawfully provided at the palaestra, after the summons of the discus, making no account of the honour of their fathers, and thinking the glories of the Greeks best of all" (II Macc. 4.12 ff.).

But the time came when the Tobiads, wearied of governing through Jason, who was their puppet, decided to seize the high-priesthood for themselves. Menelaus, a brother of Simeon the Tobiad, going on a mission to Antiochus, persuaded the King to appoint him to the holy office, "outbidding Jason by three hundred talents of silver" (ibid. 4.24). Jason was now driven into exile across the Jordan, while Menelaus established himself in his place, "bringing [to it] nothing worthy of the high-priesthood, but having the passion of a cruel tyrant and the rage of a savage beast."

Menelaus, who thus supplanted the ancient Zadokite dynasty of High Priests, was not even an Aaronid. As we have seen, his brother Simeon is expressly described as a Benjaminite, which implies, of course, that he, too, belonged to that tribe. Recent apologetes, unable to believe that an outsider could have been elevated to the highest ecclesiastical office without provoking armed rebellion, explain that the term *phyle Binyamin* (used in the Book of Maccabees to describe Simeon) refers not to the tribe, but to a priestly clan of *Miyamin*. They insist, therefore, that Menelaus was actually a priest, though not of the high-priestly families. Others who suppose that Simeon was also a son of Joseph, go so far as to transform the whole Tobiad family into priests.

But these statements rest on unverified and unverifiable surmises. Whether Simeon and Menelaus were actually sons of Joseph ben Tobiah or not, cannot be stated definitely. But that they were not priests seems evident from the record. It is altogether unlikely that a contemporary writer would confuse a priestly family with a whole tribe, and it is further improbable that a Greek author, sufficiently ignorant to make the confusion, would have known the clan-genealogy of the priesthood. It is true that none of the books describing the events, the First or Second Maccabees or Josephus, mentions the astonishing event of the rise of a non-priest — for the first time in recorded history — into the high-priesthood. But there was good reason for their silence. The Jews were by no means willing to publish the facts about the desecration of their highest ecclesiastical office. Josephus, in his *Antiquities*, is so anxious to cover up the ignominy which the Jews felt in that *coup d'état* that, in one passage, he makes Menelaus a son of Onias III.[16] This is in startling opposition to what he says elsewhere; but he considers it preferable to misstate the facts and to be guilty of an obvious contradiction than to admit the painful truth. It was the same attitude, doubtless, that led older writers to be silent about Menelaus's Benjaminite ancestry.

While the Hellenists were thus playing havoc with the Temple and the whole of Jewish life, the plebeians were organizing their school and pursuing their studies. In spite of all the oppression they underwent, they were not without capable teachers and leaders. The new converts whom they gained during the favorable era of Simeon the Righteous remained with them, and many more were doubtless added to their ranks from sheer disgust with the methods pursued by the Hellenists, both pro-Egyptian and pro-Syrian. Of those who stood in the first rank of the loyalists at this time, tradition recalls the names of two — Jeshua ben Sira, and Antigonus of Socho. These men, deserting the social ambitions and materialistic interests of their class, became — doubtless to the horror and dismay of their friends — proctors and scribes like the humble plebeians.

Whether they worked together or separately we do not know, but both of them were, of necessity, intermediaries between the two contending classes, the plebeian Hasids and the aristocratic patricians. They realized that if Hasidism was to win converts among the patricians, it would have to be transformed and reinterpreted. The nobility and the upper class gentry might accept the Hasidic teaching of pacifist nationalism, but they would never accept such doctrines as the resurrection, personal angels, and human equality, or the negation of free will and the value of mundane achievement. Ben Sira created his own form of loyalist teaching, which is preserved in the book bearing his name. He outlines what he considers to be the essential of plebeian ideology, its piety, its reverence for the Jewish past, its loyalty to Jewish literature and thought. At the same time, he specifically denies any faith in its theology. He approves the plebeian doctrine of kindness to the slave under certain circumstances, but holds that at other times patrician severity is the wiser policy. He regards learning as the highest of human values, but considers it more appropriate for the patrician than for the artisan. Ben Sira's book thus becomes a medley of beautifully expressed compromises and casuistries. We flit from sage maxim to pious psalm, from cold prudence to saintly faith, from patrician pride to plebeian comradeship. But a close inspection shows us that the book is not a confused notebook of literary jottings, but a carefully planned pedagogic treatise, aimed to win the patrician child, and incidentally his father, to the new faith of what we may call neo-Hasidism.

In Ben Sira's mind, Hasidic cultural nationalism became violently political. He could not share the sense of complete independence from paganism which was characteristic of the plebeian. In his efforts to win over some of his assimilationist comrades, he had to exaggerate the virtues of his people and the vices of its rivals. Hence we find him uttering sentiments regarding the Edomites and the Samaritans which no plebeian Hasid could have brought himself to repeat:

> "With two nations is my soul vexed,
> And the third is no nation:
> They that sit on the Mountain of Seir and the Philistines,
> And that foolish people that dwelleth in Sichem" (50.26).

With such feeling toward the surrounding peoples, Ben Sira must necessarily have been deeply averse to intermarriage with them. Yet, not a single denunciation of mixed marriages occurs in his book, although according to the First Book of Maccabees it was still a rampant social evil, especially among the patricians to whom Ben Sira is addressing himself. Did Ben Sira perhaps fear that any mention of exogamy as an evil might alienate some of those whom he wished to attract to his doctrine, the children and grandchildren of mixed marriages? And can this apprehension have been the true reason for his amazing omission of Ezra, the iron-willed opponent of such unions, from his list of Jewish heroes?[17]

From Antigonus of Socho there has been preserved only a single maxim which, as we have observed, was an effort to compose the theological quarrels of the day by declaring them irrelevant.[18]

It was probably at this time that the Sanhedrin boldly appealed to Antiochus Epiphanes against the injustices and oppression of Menelaus. This act shows that the organization of the Sanhedrin had not been changed through the various coups which had taken place at the Temple. The pietist scholars still sat in the High Court side by side with the Levites and the priests. But Antiochus was not at all moved by the petitions and protests of these Judaite teachers. On the contrary, a timely gift of Menelaus to the King's favorite brought about the execution of the agents "who," says the historian, "had they pleaded before the Scythians, would have been discharged uncondemned" (II Macc. 4.47).

A year later, 169 B.C.E., Antiochus, returning from an Egyptian campaign, appeared in Jerusalem and, in violation of Jewish Law, was led by Menelaus into the innermost chamber of the Temple, which was never entered except by the High Priest on the Day of Atonement. The King seized the Temple treasuries, taking from them a thousand and eight hundred talents of gold, including all the gold and silver vessels which had been treasured there for generations before him. The pietists who opposed these ravages were ruthlessly slaughtered or sold into slavery. Not satisfied with these brutalities, Antiochus appointed a Phrygian,

Philippos, "in character more barbarous than him that set him there," to assist Menelaus in carrying out his assimilationist programme. And in further pursuit of his determination to Hellenize the country, the King appointed a similar governor over the Samaritans at Shechem.

In 168 B.C.E. Antiochus undertook another expedition against Egypt. This time he had before him every prospect of a complete victory when, as is well known, C. Popilius Laenas, the representative of the Roman Senate, commanded him to withdraw at once from the campaign. Infuriated at this peremptory order, which he had no choice but to obey, the King decided to wreak his vengeance on the helpless Judeans. His determination became adamant when he heard that Jason had returned to Jerusalem and was inciting a revolt against him. The truth was that Jason had met with nothing but hostility from all sections of the people. But the King either did not, or would not, hear these mitigating reports. He dispatched Apollonios, a regimental commander, to Jerusalem with twenty-two thousand men to reduce the city. Coming to Jerusalem, the wily Syrian commander played the man of peace until the Sabbath when the Jews, being at rest from their work, were attacked by his soldiers, mercilessly cut down in the streets, and searched out for destruction in the retreats of their houses. The walls of the city were broken down and in place of the old Hebrew city a new Hellenic *polis* was founded south of the Temple, near the old citadel of David. The observance of the Law, by either Jew or Samaritan, was made punishable by death; the Temple at Jerusalem was rededicated to the Olympian Zeus, and that of the Samaritans on Mount Gerizim to Zeus Xenios. Throughout the land, synagogues and sacred scrolls were burned and local idolatrous altars were set up. The people's feelings were outraged by the sacrifices of swine, both in these new sanctuaries and in the old Temple of Jerusalem.

The priests, no less than the plebeians, were dismayed by these events. With one fell swoop they lost the ecclesiastical authority by which, after all, they had ruled. Their assimilationist tendencies might move them to disport themselves naked in heathen gymnasia, to call themselves by Greek names, to speak the Hellenic language, and to stutter over Homeric masterpieces, but the suppression of the Jewish ritual was a grave spiritual and economic disaster for them. Yet they had no choice but obey the inexorable tyrant, whose word was law and whose will was enforced by his armed bands.

Many of the plebeian Hasids, however, would not yield to the infamous decrees. Life had given them little but the delight in the Law and the commandments, the knowledge that they were serving God, and the hope in a future world; were all of these to be sacrificed at the whim of a deluded pagan? Leaving their shops and their markets, many fled to caves where, as outlaws from the human ruler, they could the better serve their divine King. But even in these hiding places Antiochus's soldiers ferreted them out and slaughtered them in cold blood. Pacifist by their plebeian tradition, they made no effort to organize opposition, and had no faith in the possibilities of insurrection. They looked to God for a miraculous delivery, which they were certain must be near. The Book of Daniel preserves a series of stories which one of the Hasids composed to keep up the courage of his comrades. Like Daniel and his three colleagues, they were to choose death rather than sacrilege; martyrdom was to be preferred not only to idolatry, but to the surrender of an iota of the Law.

The hopes of the plebeians were indeed to be fulfilled, but in a different manner than they had expected. Mattathias, a priest living at Modin, a village near Jerusalem, was one of the converts to the New Hasidism. He believed uncompromisingly in God and the Law, but he added to this faith the courage and warlike spirit of the farmer. When the royal agent came to set up the heathen altar in his village, he did not flee, nor did he stretch out his neck for slaughter. A member of the gentry as well as a priest, he slew the King's representative and raised the banner of revolt. He had to escape into the wilderness, of course, like so many plebeian Hasids, but he fled not from, but to battle. Gathering about him a number of other loyalists and those Hasids whom he could inspire, he formed a small band ready to become the divine instruments for the people's freedom. He died in the early stages of the war and handed over the command to his son, Judah, the best soldier in the family.

In a series of brilliant exploits Judah defeated the armies sent against him and finally forced his way into Jerusalem, where he rededicated the Temple, cast out the statue of Zeus and restored the traditional ritual.

During the war Antiochus died and was succeeded by Demetrius, a pretender to the throne, who slew Antiochus V, the son of Epiphanes. The new king, seeking a solution of the Jewish problem, was persuaded by Alcimus, a member of the old high-priestly nobility, that peace could be restored if he would withdraw the oppressive decrees of Epiphanes and permit the Temple to function and Jewish law to be observed. It was now (162 B.C.E.) that the difference between the pacifism of the Hasids and the warlike spirit of the Maccabees and gentry was to show itself. Judah and his military commanders would not hear of any peace with Alcimus; they demanded the recognition of themselves as the Jewish leaders. But, the Book of Maccabees tells us, "there was gathered together unto Alcimus and Bacchides [the general whom Demetrius had sent with Alcimus into Judah] a company of scribes, to seek justice. And the Hasidim were the first among the children of Israel that sought peace of them, for they said, 'One that is a priest of the seed of Aaron is come with the forces, and he will not do us wrong' " (I Macc. 7.12).

Once in power, Alcimus and Bacchides treacherously slaughtered sixty of the leaders of the late rebellion, among them the famous scholar, Jose ben Joezer of Zeredah,[19] Alcimus's uncle. Judah and his followers were driven from Jerusalem, and the Hellenistic priests again governed the Temple.

Judah now strengthened his forces and reached the climax of his career in a brilliant victory over Nicanor, a Syrian general who had been sent against him. This led to nothing, however, for Bacchides returned with a huge army before whom Judah's followers melted away. The pacific gestures of the Syrians and Alcimus, the hopelessness of the struggle against overwhelming odds, and Hasidean love of peace, left Judah with no more than 800 men. Daring battle with these few, he was overcome and killed.

Yet his intransigent band would not yield. Under Jonathan, the brother of Judah, they continued to carry on guerilla warfare against Alcimus and the Syrian soldiers. The rebels gained some strength when, in 159 B.C.E., Alcimus died of a sudden stroke which the people interpreted as punishment for his sin. Somewhat later Jonathan, who added to his military ability diplomatic cunning of a high order, arranged a truce which permitted him to live at Michmash in peace with the government. So far as we can see, the peace was entirely satisfactory to the Hasids who could now pursue their studies and religious practice without interference. But Jonathan's ambition had been kindled, and in 153 B.C.E. he managed, by playing off rival pretenders to the Syrian throne against each other, to obtain for himself the high-priestly office.

By this time it became evident that the passion for the Law, which had been the motivating ideal of the Hasmoneans in their youth, had cooled and had been replaced by a selfish desire for aggrandizement, mixed with a patriotic hope of gaining power and independence for Judea. Jonathan doubtless outraged Hasidic feeling when, as High Priest, he continued to lead armies in battle.[20] The readers of the Chronicles remembered that David had been denied the privilege of building the Temple because he had shed much blood (I Chron. 28.3), yet now the High Priest himself was an active general. Moreover, he was leading armies not against the enemies of the Lord and the Torah, but was involving himself in dynastic war about the Syrian succession in which Judea had little interest. But success atones for many sins, and the continual good fortune which came to Jonathan seemed a token of divine blessing. When he died by the hand of treachery, in 145 B.C.E., Simeon, his brother, the only surviving member of the family, succeeded without difficulty to the high-priestly dignity. He pursued the diplomacy which had brought such success to Jonathan, and was finally rewarded when in the year 143 B.C.E. he was recognized as civil ruler of the Jewish people who were not only autonomous but at last independent.

The ancient Hellenizing aristocracy which had been in control of land and Temple till 168 B.C.E. now gave way to the upstart Hasmonean house, who were destined during the next seventy-five years, to hold the first place in the Commonwealth. The priestly clan of Jedaiah or Seraiah (both names are used of it in the ancient records) was removed to second place, yielding the first to the previously hardly known family of Jojarib, to which the new rulers belonged. But the social forces which had made the grandchildren of pious priests, returning from Babylonia to Palestine, impious renegades and assimilationists, operated no less effectively against the continued idealism of the new priesthood. Simeon, himself, met death seven years after his accession to complete rule, at the hands of a son-in-law, bearing the ominous name of Ptolemy (135 B.C.E.). Presumably this Ptolemy was a Jew, but certainly he was an assimilationist, calling himself by the traditional name of the Egyptian kings. In his ambition to rule he was capable of murdering his father-in-law, seeking the death of his brother-in-law, and brutally torturing his mother-in-law, whom he had captured, to save himself from his deserved fate. That Simeon should have married his daughter to such a creature is evidence of his own fatal desire to be "accepted" by the patrician families of the disappearing past.

Still neither the people nor their rulers could forget, in the early days, what a miracle God had performed through the Hasmoneans, giving them the marvelous, unpredictable victory over the Syrians. The Law had been vindicated and it became, inevitably, the constitution of the land. The Sanhedrin was reestablished; the High Priest sat once more at its head; and each of the wings of the new pietist group was represented in the leadership of the Council—the wealthier gentry by Joshua ben Perahya, who was head of the "judicial committee," and the humbler plebeian group by Nittai the Arbelite.[21]

Among the first decisions taken by this Council was one fixing the status of the heathen in the new Commonwealth. In accordance with Deuteronomic Law the government was authorized to stamp out the worship of idols; but no effort was to be made toward forcible proselytizing. The Gentiles were prohibited from uttering blasphemy, worshiping idols, committing murder, theft or sex crimes, tearing the limbs of living animals (a common pagan practice of the day), and were made subject to the established civil law. Otherwise they were left free to follow their own religious or irreligious inclinations.[22]

It is clear from this and other decisions taken during this period that so far as the interpretation of the Torah was concerned, the plebeian scholars were in full control of the Sanhedrin. The compromise which gave to them control of the inner life of the people, and to the ruling Hasmoneans, who retained their warlike spirit, the political power, was continued under John Hyrkan, the son and successor of Simeon. While the plebeian scholars were developing the Law within the land, John Hyrkan carried on furious warfare against the neighboring peoples. Since Deuteronomic Law, now the land's basic constitution, forbade conscription, the King resorted to mercenary troops, with whose assistance he conquered the Samaritans and the Idumeans (Edom). The Samaritan Temple on Mount Gerizim was destroyed and, in violent opposition to the Hasidean teachings, the Idumeans were forcibly proselytized. Finally, Hyrkan added to his high-priestly title also the coveted name of King,[23] combining in himself the traditional dignities of the Davidic and Aaronid dynasties.

The brilliant victories of the Hasmoneans, the deep indebtedness which the pious owed them, the miracles which had been worked through them, and the natural infectiousness of war fever, had gradually won away the Hasidean peace party. The pacifism of its leaders during the trying days of Alcimus, and their continual efforts at a compromise with the Syrians, seemed to their contemporaries treacherous defeatism, and inevitably brought about the dissolution of the whole group. In the joy and pride of victory, principles were forgotten and no one wished to associate himself with those who had openly preached "ignoble" submission. But the disappearance of the party could not prevent the resurrection of its ideology as soon as the people returned from the madness of war to the sanity of normal life. War fever rises very quickly but it cannot last. The excited revelry of the night ends soon enough in the pains and sickness of the morning; what seemed the *summum bonum* a few hours before appears hateful and disgusting in the light of a new day. As soon as good fortune deserted the Hasmoneans and they began to lose battles instead of winning them, the old pacifism of the plebeian would once more make its appearance.

But this did not affect the new aristocracy which the Hasmonean victories had brought into being. To them and their children pacific teachings seemed freakish and absurd. Their wealth was fast increasing through the seizure of new lands and the capture of slaves; they were rising rapidly from peasantry into nobility; they were definitely supplanting the older aristocracy in wealth, position, prestige and power. The House of David, for instance, which as late as Trito-Zechariah (ca. 200 B.C.E.) still was an important clan in Jerusalem (12.12), had now disappeared from "society." Some of the ancient priestly groups were submerged with it. In their place new priestly clans had arisen, whose widened estates and increasing slave-holdings enabled them, like the earlier nobility, to take up residence in the metropolis.

The military captains and lieutenants, who felt that they supported the state, resented the control exerted over them by the peace-loving scholars who ruled the Sanhedrin. On the other hand, the plebeians were becoming restive at the growing influence of rural custom in Jerusalem. They had thought that when victory came to the people it would bring the realization of the dreams which they had carried about for centuries. Now victory had indeed come to the Jews and to the Torah; yet not to the plebeian interpretation of it. True, the plebeian scholars had great influence in the Sanhedrin, but they were without power over the Temple and its forms. There the priests with their traditional ritual, with their observance of Shabuot on Sunday, their disregard of urban Sabbath prohibitions, their refusal to kindle Sabbath lights, were supreme.

In addition to these differences and difficulties there were, sharper than ever, the fundamental disputes in theology. Though plebeian pacifism had been quite submerged in the excitement of war, its associated religious doctrines had survived. Indeed, the plebeians had been confirmed in their faith in the resurrection by the martyrdom of their comrades, which had left the less individualistic gentry quite untouched. The kindred problems of Providence and personal angels were being disputed with almost equal fervor. In addition to these, there were the great perplexing questions whether the Maccabean victories would culminate in a Messianic Age, and whether the Anointed of God would be a priest and one of the Hasmoneans, as the ruling class hoped, or a simple Judaite and a descendant of David, as the prophets had foretold?

Above all, there was the inclusive conflict about the validity of the Oral Law and the authority of the scribes. The new aristocratic priests could, no more than their predecessors among the Hellenists, brook the rivalry of the lay scholars. The priests could not forget that biblical Law had vested in them alone the sole religious authority, which was now being usurped, they felt, by the Sanhedrin, which was composed and largely controlled by contemptibly poor, plebeian academicians. Having arrived at power, the priests felt themselves unwarrantably hampered by the rules which prevented them from following aristocratic fashions in religion as in other matters. It was a source of shame to have to observe Pentecost on the day fixed for it by artisans and craftsmen, when the fashionable nobility favored another time. The Hasmoneans preferred by far the associations, companionship and ideology of the remnants of the old priesthood to the doctrines of the plebeians with whom they had been comrades in arms.

The keener observers of the day realized that these controversies were dividing the people as effectively as had the problem of Hellenism and Nationalism in the preceding century. Two authors undertook to bring about peace between the rival groups before any final schism occurred. One of them, a priest, wrote a deeply nationalist work, the

Book of Jubilees, through which he tried to unify the nation in hate for all other peoples. Passing over the moot doctrine of resurrection in silence, he asserts instead the immortality of the soul, which was less objectionable to the patricians and the gentry because it had never become an issue, and because it had come from the philosophy of the Greeks. He gives the ultimate throne and victory to the priests, but yields to their opponents the belief in angels, and in Divine Providence. He accepts some of the urban Hasidean customs, but in general prefers those of the patricians and the country.

Among the intricate problems which he proposed to settle, perhaps the foremost related to the calendar. Already in those early days it was a moot question whether the priestly or the scholarly section of the Sanhedrin ought to fix the time of the new moon. The question may seem trivial, perhaps ridiculous, to us because we no longer realize its full implications; but the ancient Jewish calendar depended not on mathematical calculations and arrangements, but was set from month to month according to the physical reappearance of the new moon. Witnesses who had seen the first sign of the crescent on the horizon after sunset were expected to report the fact to the authorities, who thereupon published throughout the country the fact that a new month had begun. The year consisted of twelve months whose limits were determined by these observations. But, since the lunar year consists of only 354 days, eleven less than the solar year, it was necessary from time to time to "intercalate" a thirteenth month before the Passover, to prevent its being moved back into the winter. This intercalary month was a "second Adar" and was added whenever a consideration of the sun's position in the heavens, the state of the crops, or of the new-born lambs, made it appear necessary.

The intercalation of the additional month had, however, not only ritual but also important economic implications, for according to the Law, no new Palestinian grain could be harvested or eaten before the Passover. We can readily see what financial stakes were involved, in consequence of this, in the postponement of Passover both for the native grower of barley, who watched his harvest ripen but durst not touch it, and for the importer who was preparing to sell the products of neighboring countries, Ammon and Egypt. Such was the interest in this question that in talmudic times the most careful safeguards were thrown about the deliberations regarding it. The committee met in gravest secrecy; none but those specially invited were permitted to be present.[24] The decision had to be reached at the seat of the Council; only under the most serious conditions of persecution was it permitted to have the committee meet in Galilee, for instance. The same importance naturally attached to the matter also in the earlier times which we are discussing. And because of that the question of who was the authority in the matter was long mooted. The priests of the Temple considered the calendar and its fixing one of their functions. So far as they were concerned, the calendar has but one purpose — to tell them when the special festival sacrifices were to be offered. That the Jewish communities throughout the land were equally concerned with the festivals and the calendar, they could not appreciate. True, work was prohibited on the holidays, but that appeared to the ritualist, then as now, secondary to the Temple celebration. The Sanhedrin, on the other hand, dominated by the plebeians, endeavored to seize this power which had formerly been held by the priests. They considered the calendar a matter of national interest to the individual Jews, to the synagogues throughout the land, to the commercial classes who had business dealings dependent on it. It seemed to them that the Temple's connection with the calendar was secondary and not primary; and held, therefore, that the fixing of the new moon and the intercalary month should be referred to themselves as the general judicial and legislative body. The conflict regarding these opposing rights was long and bitter. As late as the first century of the Common Era the witnesses regarding the new moon had to satisfy both parties by appearing first before the priests and then before the Sanhedrin.[25] The decisions of the two bodies did not necessarily agree, and we may well imagine the confusion and difficulty which arose from two rival calendar-fixing authorities. Long before the problem had become as embittered as it did in those later years, the author of the Book of Jubilees proposed to settle the question forever by establishing a simple solar year of 364 days, divided into four equal quarters of 91 days or three months each. In this calendar the festivals, new moons, and other holidays would fix themselves and the troublesome problem removed from the field of politics and institutionalized religion, as it were.

The Book of Jubilees had wide influence and was in some circles accepted as authoritative. It has been preserved for us by the Ethiopian Church, which considered it canonical. Some of its provisions are still actually observed by the Ethiopian Jews, the so-called Falashas.

A similar, but far more definitely partisan effort at unification was made by the author of the Testaments of the Twelve Patriarchs. This book, which purports to record the last wills of the sons of Jacob, the eponymous ancestors of the Twelve Tribes, accepts without qualification the plebeian contentions regarding resurrection, angelology, Divine Providence and pacifism. But the author, like the extreme Pharisees, adheres to the doctrine of non-resistance and the negation of the world. He approaches the Essenes in his contempt for the comforts and satisfactions which life offers. Unlike the priestly writer of the Book of Jubilees, he is very little concerned with the ritual; and rarely discusses its observance. Only once does he digress in this regard to urge the priests in the Temple to accept the Pharisaic prescriptions regarding the service. Otherwise his concern is only with questions of moral right and wrong. He skillfully uses incidents in the lives of the various patriarchs to point moral lessons to their children. Judah attributes his troubles to his sin of mixed marriage with a Canaanite woman; Reuben considers his sufferings a just punishment for his violation of his father's concubine. There are some indications that the writer was an artisan and lived in Jamnia, the small village on the Mediterranean which was later to succeed Jerusalem as the center of Jewish learning.[26] But the author has muffled himself too completely in his disguise to enable us to make any definite statements about his life.

Pharisee as he is, the author of the Testaments of the Twelve Patriarchs, no less than the priestly writer of the Book of Jubilees, accepts the rights of the Hasmoneans to the throne, as well as to the high-priesthood. He regards them as chosen by God and urges that they stand higher than the tribe of Judah, from which the Davidic dynasty was descended. It is clear from the insistence on the point in both books that there was, even in the heyday of

Maccabean power and prestige, a minority which could not reconcile itself to the displacement of the House of David. It is also significant that a pacifist and believer in non-resistance, like the writer of the Testaments, should yet take pride in the Hasmonean victories over their enemies. With the writer of the Book of Jubilees he records with evident glee the struggles between Judah and the Canaanites, and with excusable fiction chooses for the places of those battles the localities where the Hasmonean army beat the Syrians. This ancient pacifist, who had been able to tear all rancor out of his heart, yet looked like many of his modern successors with satisfaction on the military achievements of his people in the past, and used their pride in these accomplishments as a means to mould them into a united group.

But the differences between the opposing groups, the patricians and the plebeians, were too deep-seated and all-embracing for such palliatives as these books offered. The nationalist warriors were not to be satisfied in their aspirations by tales of the brilliant exploits of their fathers, nor could their desire for new lands and slaves be stilled with a promise of infinitely greater glory in the future world, if they would only be quiet now. The quietistic plebeians who desired peace could not, on the other hand, become sufficiently non-resistant to tolerate militarism. Their tolerance of the heathen did not extend to the wicked among their own people. Like the author of Isaiah 66, they acknowledged the equality of Gentile and Jew in the worship of God, but like him, too, they could not repress a feeling of deep hatred and disdain for the wayward in Israel. They joined the prophet wholeheartedly in picturing an ideal future when the nations coming to greet God would "go forth, and look upon the carcasses of the men that have rebelled against Me; for their worm shall not die, neither shall their fire be quenched; and they shall be an abhorring unto all flesh" (Isa. 66.24). The gentlest and most non-resistant of pacifists still bore the birthmark which proved the descent of their doctrine from primitive, savage ferocity.

The Society of Pharisees, organized to maintain the Levitical laws of purity, now fell heir to the mantle which had fallen from the weakened shoulders of the Hasideans. They continued the missionary activities which the early Hasidean movement had inaugurated, but added to it the new zeal which derived from pride in the divine victory of Judah over its enemies.

The founders and chief exponents of the new puristic movement were the scholars and scribes. These teachers, who had made the study of the Law the main purpose of their lives, could not brook the rejection of a large part of it by a majority of the population. They tried to extend the habits of study and observance, as well as the belief in their favorite doctrines, such as resurrection and Divine Providence. As the Hasmonean parvenus lost the friendship of the plebeian masses, the Pharisaic party gained numbers and power. Yet the official purpose of the Society was still the propagation of the laws of purity; the ethical and theological views which divided it from the priestly aristocracy remained in the background. It was only toward the end of John Hyrkan's reign that a series of events occurred which transformed the society into a political party of the opposition prepared to take up arms in defense of its rights.

Rancor between the patricians and the plebeians was fomented primarily by those most dangerous of all Iagos, the hypocrites, demagogues, slanderers, and defamers, who tried to curry favor with particular groups by spreading libel about others, caring nothing about the fate of either, so long as they satisfied their own ambitions. They denounced the plebeians to the patricians, principally to the King, John Hyrkan; and the King to his people. They spread a rumor that his mother had been taken captive during the Maccabean wars, and that he was therefore unfit to serve as High Priest. They told him that the scribes believed the rumors. The latent electricity was discharged in a terrific thunderbolt when, at a feast in honor of one of John Hyrkan's victories, a flattering adviser suggested that he adorn himself with the high-priestly vestments. This ostentatious flaunting of the high-priestly dignity at a "victory dinner" was certain to pain and embarrass the peace-loving scholars who were present.

It happened as the evil counselors had foreseen. One reckless scholar arose and said: "Hyrkan, is not the royal crown sufficient for thee? Leave the crown of priesthood for the sons of Aaron!" After this public reference, the malicious rumor of Hyrkan's birth could no longer be ignored. The Sanhedrin thereupon made formal investigation of the charge, discovered it to be without foundation, and condemned the rash accuser to the comparatively light punishment of public scourging. But Hyrkan and his counselors, flushed with the pride of victory and far less reluctant than their opponents to shed blood, demanded the death penalty. When the Sanhedrin refused to impose it, Hyrkan seized the opportunity to expel the plebeian scribes, and to restore the old *Gerousia* of priests and clan chieftains.

Like other momentous events, the quarrel between King Hyrkan and the Pharisees is important not only for its lasting effects on the future, but because of the changes which culminated and became manifest in it. By disbanding the Sanhedrin of scholars and reverting to the displaced *Gerousia* of family-heads, the Hasmoneans and their followers symbolized their rise from rural patriotism into aristocratic opportunism. For the first time in their history they took action in the interests of their class and against the obvious unity of the nation. When Jonathan, against the advice of the Hasideans, had still carried on the war against the Syrians, he was moved by a deep feeling of patriotism; he identified his family ambitions with his love for his people. But Hyrkan's attack on the plebeian scholars was a clear effort to subject the national good to that of the ruling class. In his expulsion of the scribes John Hyrkan did not limit himself to those of urban plebeian derivation, the main source of the earlier Hasidean, and later Pharisaic, pacifism. He and his associates were determined to make descent rather than erudition the qualification for membership in the ruling assembly; and hence drove from it the rural scholar, as well as his urban colleague. The Hasmonean dynasty had now definitely allied itself with the patricians, and the Sadducean party of which it was the nucleus became the spiritual heir of the pre-Maccabean Hellenism. The two groups of Pharisaic scholars, the wealthier rural class together with the humbler urban plebeians, became a united opposition. Their efforts were now directed less to win the peasantry to observe the Law, particularly in its Levitical aspects, than to wrest the power over the Temple and other religious institutions from the hands of the patrician Sadducees. The Pharisees did not break away from the worship of the sanctuary though the Sadducean priests officiated there, nor did they make any effort at rebellion. They simply intensified their propaganda and sought by educational and peaceful methods to win back their position in the community.

Josephus records that at one time the organized membership of these Pharisaic units numbered about six thousand.[27] They could not all have been residents of Jerusalem, but perhaps we may assume that at least two thirds of them were. Since the organization admitted only men, and presumably only those who were self-supporting and had families, we may take it that the 6000 affiliated members represented an actual following of 30,000 souls, of which 20,000 were residents in Jerusalem. The probable population of Jerusalem at the time was about 75,000; so that these figures imply that about one in every four city families was formally associated with Pharisaism. When we add to that number the much larger group of unorganized sympathizers which so formidable a movement always has, we can readily see that the larger part of Jerusalem's population was on the Pharisaic side of the controversy. But the directing powers of the city, its aristocracy, and the people of influence were Sadducees.

The assumption that one third, or 2000, of the members of the Pharisaic orders lived outside of Jerusalem is a liberal estimate, for while the Pharisees doubtless converted the peasants to their ideas, the tiny Jewish villages were so compact and united that formal organization inside of them was a superfluity. The strength of Pharisaism on the land could not, therefore, be judged from the numbers of organized adherents it had; every synagogue was its forum, and every prayer service its meeting. The peasant might hesitate to accept the rigorous discipline of the Pharisaic laws of purity which gave the sect its name, yet he agreed with their doctrine of resurrection, and willingly followed those customs which were not too burdensome.

How far the virus of Hellenism and aristocratic ambition had infected the Hasmonean family became evident when John Hyrkan died (104 B.C.E.) leaving the throne to his wife and the high-priesthood to his eldest son, Aristobulus. The Greek name which the new High Priest bore is unimpeachable testimony to his preference for the culture against which his family had so valiantly and successfully struggled. Hyrkan had been known among the Jews by his Hebrew name, Johanan. Even when he decided to take a foreign name in addition, he had chosen one of Persian, rather than Hellenic origin. But the new High Priest officially called himself Aristobulus, "the good adviser," and as if to emphasize his cultural leaning—Philhelene, lover of Greece.

Aristobulus's character, dominated by selfish ambition, was revealed in his first acts. Breaking with the great traditions of the Hasmoneans who had always acted as a closely knit family, he threw his mother into prison and seized the temporal power for himself. Together with the reigning Queen he imprisoned also three of his four brothers, permitting only Antigonus, for whom he had special affection, to share the administrative duties with him. When, however, slanderers denounced Antigonus to the King, the young prince was executed as a rebel.

Yet such was the paradox of Sadducism, in which loyalty to the Jewish ritual was mingled with slavish imitation of Greek culture,[28] that Aristobulus continued his father's efforts to extend the Judean boundaries, and compelled the conquered peoples to be circumcised and accept Judaism.

Fortunately, Aristobulus reigned but one year, dying at the end of it of a loathsome disease, in which his mind became disordered. His widow, Salome Alexandra, immediately released his three brothers from their bonds. In accordance with the levirate law, she married her oldest brother-in-law, Alexander Jannai, who now succeeded both to the throne and to the high-priesthood.

The new ruler pursued the policies inaugurated by his father and carried on by his brother, waging warfare almost continuously against his neighbors, and declining to give the pacific Pharisees any voice in either the religious or temporal government. The conflict between the King and the Pharisees came to a head, however, when in his brutal arrogance Alexander undertook to deride the libation of water during the Sukkot festival.[29] Angered beyond control, the assembled populace, who stood with their palm branches and citrons in their hands awaiting the ceremony, threw the fruits at the King. Alexander called out his mercenary troops, who killed six thousand people in the ensuing affray.

The riot brought the more restive element among the Pharisees into the leadership of their party, and when the King departed to carry on a campaign across the Jordan, they raised the banner of revolt in Jerusalem. Alexander, defeated in an ambush by the Arabs whom he had attacked, rushed back to the city to protect his throne. Harassed by internal opposition as well as by foreign enemies, Alexander's trained mercenaries and Jewish troops were for six years unable to quell the rebellion. Fifty thousand Jews are said to have perished in the Civil War; but the opposition, aroused to fury, would not yield. When Alexander finally begged for terms of peace they declared that they would be satisfied with nothing less than his death.

In the midst of these troubles the King died (76 B.C.E.)

and Salome Alexandra, a widow for the second time, again ruled in her own right. The new Queen immediately made overtures to the Pharisees, and promised to restore them to power in the Sanhedrin. Their leader, Simeon ben Shattah, was recalled from Egypt whither he had fled from Alexander's wrath, and was placed, in association with Judah ben Tabbai, at the head of the judicial and religious activity of the Sanhedrin, as Joshua ben Perahya and Nittai of Arbel had been during the beginning of Hyrkan's reign, more than a generation before. The high-priestly office was to be held by Alexander Jannai's eldest son, Hyrkan, while the younger son, Aristobulus, was to head the army for his mother.

The internal peace which returned to the country under the new Queen was matched by a cessation of hostilities against the neighboring princes. Such was the prosperity which this lull in the continual storms of war brought, that the later sages looked back at the reign of Salome Alexandra as a golden age. "During the time of Queen Shelemzia and Simeon ben Shattah, wheat grains grew as large as the kidneys of an ox,"[30] one of them said, with usual oriental hyperbole.

The Pharisees, now come to power, demanded much more influence and authority than they had had in earlier days. During the thirty years of suppression their partisan ideology had become crystallized and formulated. They insisted that the Temple ritual, over which they had had no authority in Hyrkan's day, be conducted in accordance with their prescriptions, that the regulation of the calendar be made a function of the Sanhedrin, and that the head of their group, rather than the High Priest, be recognized as the highest judicial officer. They enacted decrees giving formal legislative sanctions to numerous Pharisaic opinions, and even asked for summary judgment against those army chieftains and members of the Sadducean nobility who had most actively opposed them. Queen Salome was willing to grant all their requests, save those of revenge against their enemies, who had incurred their anger in the service of her house.

Such was the power of the Pharisees over the government that they prevented it from carrying on those foreign wars which had been the pride of the Hasmonean house since its foundation. Aristobulus did indeed undertake an invasion of Damascus, but unsupported from home he achieved nothing. When Tigranes, King of the Armenians, threatened attack on the country, the pacifist government, casting aside the military traditions of the dynasty, openly bribed him to desist. We may imagine with what chagrin conquerors like Hyrkan and Alexander Jannai would have regarded such political defeatism.

But the good days of Queen Alexandra were destined to be short; she died at the age of seventy-three, hoping that the nine years of partisan truce which she had given the land might prove the basis for a lasting peace. But no sooner had her older son, Hyrkan, who had previously been High Priest, also taken the throne, than his warlike brother, Aristobulus, marched against him. The fraternal struggle was the more grave because it represented a real social cleavage. Aristobulus had, even in his mother's day, associated himself with the Sadducees, who admired his military spirit and enterprise, and despised the High Priest, Hyrkan, for his willing acceptance of the Pharisaic prescriptions regarding the Temple service. But the qualities which made the older brother hated by the Sadducees endeared him to the Pharisees who, by the same token, could not brook the younger militarist, Aristobulus, in whom they saw the reincarnation of their old enemy, Alexander Jannai.

When Hyrkan attempted to defend himself against Aristobulus, a large part of the army, sympathizing with the warlike militarist who had been their commander during the former Queen's life, went over to Aristobulus. The pacifist Pharisees, who preferred Hyrkan as king, were not prepared to fight for him against his brother, who had as yet done them no injury. Provided their own position in the Sanhedrin, which had been gained during the preceding reign, was untouched, it did not matter very much to them whether the older or younger son of Alexandra officiated at the Temple. Deserted by his army and unsupported by his friends, the sluggish and pacific Hyrkan offered to withdraw from the throne and the high-priesthood, provided he would be permitted to live in peace as a private citizen. The two brothers met in the Temple, where peace was concluded on these terms. "They departed," says Josephus, "the one, Aristobulus, to the palace; the other, Hyrkan, a private man, to the former house of Aristobulus."

But now the Hasmonean house was to reap the whirlwind which it sowed when John Hyrkan had conquered and forcibly proselytized the Idumeans. The time was approaching when a scion of the defeated people was to take bloody vengeance from the family which had given him occasion and opportunity. Among the friends and advisers of Hyrkan the most wily and ambitious was Antipater, an Idumean noble. He persuaded the gentle, but unwise, Hyrkan that his life was in danger in Jerusalem, and urged him to flee to Aretas, King of the Arabs, whose capital was at Petra, on the borders of Judea. Aretas, happy at the chance which came to him to put Hyrkan on the Judean throne and thereafter claim from him gratitude and, perhaps, vassalage, marched with an army to Jerusalem.

The economic interpretation of the struggle between the brothers receives support from the fact that Hyrkan and the invading army met no opposition on its entry into Jerusalem. Apparently the Pharisees and their large plebeian following welcomed him. We know from Josephus that the city's defenses were strong; indeed, a few years later when Pompey besieged it he found its position impregnable except in the north. Surely the Arabian soldiers could not have taken the city more easily than the Roman legions, had they not been assisted from within. We must assume, therefore, that the chiefs of the Sanhedrin, who were the Pharisaic leaders, advised the people to offer no resistance to Hyrkan and his allies, but to admit them. Aristobulus, helpless against the union of the men of Jerusalem with his enemies, retired to the Temple, which was strongly fortified, and where the Sadducean priests, rather than the Pharisaic scholars, were in control.

The non-resistant attitude of the pacific Pharisees was well expressed on this occasion by Honi (or, as Josephus calls him, Onias) when, being asked to pray for the invaders, he said, "O God, King of the whole world, since those who stand with me are Thy people, and those who are besieged are Thy priests, I beseech Thee not to hearken to the prayers of either party against the other."[31]

The siege was raised by the Roman general, Scaurus, a lieutenant of Pompey, to whom both Aristobulus and Hyrkan had appealed for assistance. Aretas was sent home by the Romans under threat of war if he should continue to interfere in Jewish affairs, and Aristobulus was reëstablished as King. But Hyrkan and Antipater would not be quiet, and when Pompey approached Judea they appealed to him once more for a decision in their favor. This recognition of the Roman suzerainty in Judea marked the complete reversion of the Hasmonean dynasty to the policies of the aristocratic Hellenists whom they had displaced. John Hyrkan's rejection of the Pharisees had shown that the Hasmoneans were as impatient with the plebeian scholars and Jewish culture as had been the earlier high-priesthood. But at that time they had still retained, by sheer inertia, the warm nationalism which their forefathers had inherited from the country environment. The internal quarrels and personal rivalries had destroyed this last vestige of idealism in them. The conversion from patriotism to opportunism becomes painfully evident as we read in Josephus of the policy pursued by Aristobulus in this critical time. His wavering decisions remind one of Isaiah's description of Ahaz's actions under similar conditions: "And his heart, and the heart of his people, shook, as the trees of the forest shake in the wind." He was continually alternating between the warlike advice offered him by the war-hungry squireage and the caution urged by his own self-interest and the foremost of his fellow-patricians. His wife, we learn from Josephus, was an ardent lover of Rome, and believed that Judea should voluntarily submit to its yoke; many others must have agreed with her. In his indecision Aristobulus committed blunder after blunder, and was finally driven to seek refuge in Jerusalem. But when the Roman army encamped at Jericho and was about to undertake a march against the city, Aristobulus's heart failed him and he appealed to Pompey, offering bribes, homage and admission to the city. Thereupon Pompey sent one of his generals, with Aristobulus, to Jerusalem to receive the promised gifts and capitulation; but as the Romans, with Aristobulus, approached Jerusalem, the soldiers within closed the gates against them, renouncing the peace terms which their King had accepted.

Pompey, enraged at this treatment, imprisoned Aristobulus and proceeded toward the capital. According to Josephus, "Some thought it best to deliver the city to Pompey, but Aristobulus's party exhorted them to shut the gates because he was held in prison." Clearly the followers of Aristobulus, who had failed before to persuade the citizens of Jerusalem to protect their city against Hyrkan, sought to move them by the argument that the present invader was a Roman, a heathen. But the pacifist populace of Jerusalem admitted Pompey without a blow. It was only the Temple area that he, like Aretas, had to besiege, and its walls and towers that he took by storm. We are not to suppose that the civil population of the city was less brave or patriotic than the priests. It was rather that they saw no occasion or justification for the war. The Sadducean priests were ready to defend themselves like the Spartans at Thermopylae; the Pharisaic citizenry would gladly have died for the Law, but refused to give up their lives for national independence.

Pompey, having robbed the Temple, massacred his enemies, and taken many captives, reinstated Hyrkan as High Priest and ruler of the people, but without the title of king. Aristobulus and his two sons were carried off to Rome. One of them, Alexander, escaped on the way, and came back to Palestine to rebel against Hyrkan II and the Roman rule. The Roman proconsul of Syria defeated him easily, but took the opportunity to reorganize the government of the country, dividing it into five districts, each with a presiding council of its own. Through this division the political power of the central Sanhedrin was destroyed and, it was hoped, the possibility of united action in the country was ended.

Hyrkan and the high-priestly aristocrats were convinced that the independence of Judea was lost and that their interest and future lay in open sympathy with Rome. During the conflict between Pompey and Caesar which broke out in the year 49 B.C.E., Hyrkan prudently urged support of Caesar. He actually sent three thousand men into the field with him and exhorted the Jewish population in Alexandria to side with the Roman against Ptolemy. Caesar gratefully rewarded Hyrkan with the title of Ethnarch and reëstablished the unity of the country. But the patriotic lower priesthood and the country gentry remained dissatisfied, particularly because Caesar also granted a special position of political power to Antipater the Idumean and his two sons Herod and Phezael. After the battle of Philippi (42 B.C.E.) when Antony became master of the Near East, the Jews sent a delegation to him opposing the Idumean rulers. But Hyrkan defended them before Antony and they were confirmed in their power.[32]

When, however, Antony fell a victim to the charms of Cleopatra, the Parthians, who seized this opportunity to invade Syria and Palestine, placed Antigonus, the son of Aristobulus, on the Judean throne as King and High Priest. Herod, appealing to Rome for assistance, was named King of the Jews by the Senate (39 B.C.E.). Proceeding to Palestine with this authority, he obtained the assistance of two Roman legions. Rural Galilee, the last stronghold of the nationalist gentry, was already then beginning to show its mettle and offered him resistance. But he speedily overcame his enemies and besieged Jerusalem. Again, as when Aretas and Pompey had besieged the city, the Pharisaic teachers advised yielding. But Antigonus had prepared himself for emergency and prevented the surrender. After a siege of five months, Herod and his Roman followers took the city by storm and put an end to the Hasmonean dynasty and their claims. Thereafter Judea, nominally independent under an Idumean ruler, was actually in bondage to Rome.

The fraternal wars of the Hasmoneans, their abject surrender to the Romans, and finally their treacherous betrayal of the Jewish cause, when they defended Antipater, proved conclusively that they had ceased to be patriots, and had become pure assimilationists, like the Hellenists whom they had supplanted. It was inevitable that this exhibition of moral and spiritual decadence by the once exalted family, who were the center of the Sadducean nobility, should strengthen the morale and increase the numbers of the Pharisaic opposition to them. What had happened in the days of Elijah thus repeated itself: the group which had come into power on the platform of nationalism had betrayed its cause and compelled the patriotic peasants to join hands with the cosmopolitan townspeople in increasing numbers.

This fact, together with the arrangement for bi-factional control which had been traditional in Pharisaism from the beginning, ultimately brought about a fissure in the Order. The provincial group and their representative scholars became the School of Shammai; the townspeople, and their sympathizers, the School of Hillel.[33] But while the opposition between the factions became permanent, and sometimes even attained bitterness, it never led to sectarianism. Hillel and Shammai, like their disciples Gamaliel I and Akabiah ben Mahalalel, R. Simeon ben Gamaliel I and R. Johnanan ben Zakkai, R. Eliezer ben Hyrcanus and R. Joshua ben Hananya, R. Ishmael and R. Akiba, recognized each other as true Pharisees, devoted to the fundamental principles of their society and unshakable in their loyalty to it.[34]

And thus the conflict which had begun in the earliest days of Israelitish history entered on a new and final phase. The struggle between the followers of God and the worshipers of Baal, the class-conscious militarist and the egalitarian peace-lover, the aristocratic Hellenist and the democratic Hasid, the nationalist Sadducee and the universalist Pharisee, was now to assume the form of an academic, deliberative and juridical discussion among the leading scholars of the Pharisaic Order.

The common interest of the contending groups in the advancement of Jewish learning, in the search for truth, and the universal recognition of God and His Law, engendered in each of them a respect for the other which was without precedent in the annals of Palestinian, or indeed any other, social conflict. For centuries sages assembled to discuss every aspect of human life — religious ceremonies, civil and criminal law, philosophical and theological concepts, political ideals, daily manners, and even questions of science, art, and daily amusement. For no less than three hundred and fifty years, from the origin of the Pharisaic Order about the middle of the second century B.C.E., until the Roman rule had destroyed the class conflict by reducing the whole population to a common misery (about the end of the second century C.E.), the discussions continued. The sages found themselves in almost continual disagreement with regard both to their general outlook and the detailed applications of their principles.

Curiously enough, this division of opinion did not interfere with popular respect for the Pharisaic teachers. Throughout Palestine, and indeed even in the diaspora, in Babylonia, as well as in Egypt and in Rome, the words of the Pharisaic scholars were accepted as authoritative interpretations of the Laws of Moses. "If you were not Theodotus the Physician," wrote the president of the Conclave to a Jew in Rome who was noted for his piety as well as for his learning, but who had acted contrary to the ruling of the Conclave in one matter, "I should declare you excommunicate!"[35] And similarly, when some Palestinian emigré scholars attempted to regulate the calendar from Babylonia, their colleagues in Palestine suppressed the effort without difficulty.[36]

But the Pharisaic scholars were leaders not only for their own generation; to this day their decisions affect the lives of millions of Jews all over the world. Talmudic scholars have, of course, always known that the decisions of the Conclave were by no means unanimous; and are able to follow the arguments used by the opposition as well as by the majority. Yet in civil litigation and in ceremonial regulation, involving losses of considerable sums, and at times severe hardships, the view which prevailed in the Conclave or emerged as authoritative under the general rules of talmudic codification has been accepted as binding.

No litigant who has been enjoined to pay damages in accordance with the view of R. Meir has announced that he adheres to the views of R. Judah, for instance; and no observant scholar would prepare his meat in accordance with the lenient views of R. Jose the Galilean, when the prevailing opinion was otherwise. Interpretations have been changed, but only by universally recognized scholars, whose opinions are themselves binding on all the people of their generation.

The authority which thus attached to the ancient Conclave made it a Jewish Senate, of the same type but of far greater significance in the course of history than that which met at Rome. No wonder that the founders of the Christian Church realized the need for establishing some such institution in their midst, and almost from the beginning met in council in Jerusalem, when difficult problems arose to perplex them.[37]

The ancient Conclave which thus became an integral part of Christianity disappeared, however, from Judaism. With the spread of rabbinical scholarship to the ends of the earth, assemblies of all or even a majority of the learned men of any generation were no longer feasible.

And yet the essential unity of the Pharisaic interpretation of the Law has been preserved. Bitter controversies have arisen between different communities, and also between individuals, with regard to the correct interpretation of the Law. But rabbinic Judaism, the first-born child of Pharisaism, remains a unit until this day.

The feat of maintaining such unity amidst the wide diversity of personal opinion and local environment has been achieved through the establishment of an institution which has replaced the ancient Conclave: the consensus of scholarship. This has practically the same significance in Judaism as it has in science and in the humanities.

Without establishing any formally recognized authority or hierarchy, the rabbinic teachers of each generation tend to agree on a common interpretation of Scripture and Talmud and generally look to one or two among themselves as the foremost guides in legal decisions.

It was by this mode of common consent — expressed in no formal vote or plebiscite, but simply spreading among the teachers and the people — that the Babylonian Talmud has been accepted as more authoritative than that of Palestine; that such teachers as Rabbenu Gershom (ca. 960–1040), Rashi (about 1040–1105), Alfasi (1013–1103), Maimonides (1135–1204) and Caro (1488–1575) became definitive interpreters of rabbinic Judaism. Perhaps the latest in this long chain of teachers who have given form to rabbinic Judaism in each generation was that famous scholar-statesman, Isaac Elhanan Spektor (1817–1896), the rabbi of Kowno, in Lithuania, during the latter part of the nineteenth century.

This consensus of scholarship does not mean that rabbinic Judaism as at present observed is altogether uniform. There are wide differences of practice among Jews of various regions of the world and almost a score of different forms of the synagogue prayer ritual. The best known are those of Ashkenaz or Germany, used also by the Jews of Austria, Poland, Lithuania, Russia, and Eastern Europe generally; and Sepharad or Spain, still used by the descendants of the Jews who were expelled from that country in 1492.

But the differences between communities involve far more than the forms of prayer. The Jews of Palestine observe the festivals only on the dates set for them in Scripture; those of the diaspora observe an additional day for each festival, save the Sabbath and the Day of Atonement. There are different attitudes with regard to what is to be regarded as leavened food and therefore forbidden on the Passover; there are different observances with regard to the separation of milk and meat foods; there are different marriage and funeral customs; and there are even slight differences in the manner of the observance of the Sabbath and the festivals. But these variations are themselves recognized and regulated by the consensus of opinion.

The manner in which this unity of the faith has been preserved, without any attempt to impose uniformity on various groups, reminds us of the tolerance which was one of the fundamental characteristics of Pharisaism from its origin. The phenomenon indicates, as do the histories of modern science and liberal scholarship in their special fields, how easy it is for free men to follow their trend of thought and at the same time to coöperate in the achievement of a common spiritual goal, without any of the limitations implied in formal organizations. Perhaps it also suggests that the contribution of Pharisaism to the world, unique as it has been, is still incomplete; and that its most important influence on world thought is yet to be exerted. Far more of its ethical teachings than have thus far been made available to western thought lie hidden in the great tomes of the Talmud and its kindred works. As they are studied by minds trained in western literary technique and faced with new world problems, these volumes will be found to contain a more profound understanding of human values and human potentialities than any of us dares imagine.

We can all see today how the shadows that fell on the world with the decay of ancient Rome were dispelled, in part at least, through the light that came from Palestine; is it not possible that the teachings of the prophets have been preserved in unaltered form, and at such great sacrifice, because they have still a greater purpose to serve during the years of mingled darkness and light, which are before us in the reconstruction of Western Civilization?

SUPPLEMENT

I. THE UNIQUENESS OF PHARISAISM

Pharisaism was a unique phenomenon in the ancient world. A phase in a social battle continued in Judea for a millennium and a half, it bore only a limited resemblance to the similar struggles convulsing other Mediterranean areas during the same period. Writing this book more than twenty years ago, I was impressed with the similarities between the controversies in Jerusalem and those in Athens and Rome. Everywhere urbanization led to conflict between the inhabitants of the town and the landed aristocracy. Emphasis on the individual personality was widespread; and resistance to it by the provincials and large landowners was universal. But the central issues of the struggle in Jerusalem, and the individuals who emerged in its market place, were virtually without analogue. Prophecy, Pharisaism, Hillelism, and (through the momentum of the cultural tradition, even after the fall of Jerusalem) the School of Rabbi Akiba and the academies of some of his disciples, each in turn articulated in its own way the same basic attitudes toward life. In their contests with their opponents all dealt with the relation of the individual person, as child and servant, to God. All alike resisted the doctrine that the individual was simply part of a community which could serve God through a chosen priesthood.

On rereading the book it is evident that the analogies suggested in it could be misleading unless supplemented with a discussion of the unique qualities of Pharisaism. No wonder the late Henry Sloane Coffin, having read and generously reviewed this book, once remarked to me that he could go along with everything except the explanation of the Psalmists. "That is really too much!" he cried. Immersed in my theory, I had failed to remark on the miracles of Prophecy, Psalmody, Pharisaism, and Talmudism. I had taken these so much for granted that I neglected to emphasize their singularity.

For, unlike all other urban struggles known to me, Pharisaism (and the longer process of which it was part) was a demand not for rights, but for the opportunity to serve. The Pharisee and his predecessors were not rebelling against the prerogatives of the priestly clan, nor against inequality with the aristocracy in ownership of land. They objected to doctrines which interfered with their concept of all life as a tenure of service, of the world as a school and a Temple, and of all men as quasi-priests. The question raised by the Pharisee and the prophet resembled that raised the world over; their answer was, it seems to me, unique. Like other plebeian town-dwellers, the Proto-Pharisee learned that he was not merely a member of his group. Toiling with his own hands for his own wages, making friends in the market place, meeting freely with other tradesmen and workers, some of them foreigners, his horizons reached beyond membership in his family or clan.

This discovery resembled that being made by townsmen elsewhere. But in Jerusalem the Proto-Pharisee and the Pharisee, instead of becoming revolutionaries concerned with rights in the present world, became theologians, affirming human immortality and equality before God.

Hence, unlike most other urban plebeians,[1] the Pharisee

was far more meticulous in his piety than the contemporary local peasant. Indeed, the Pharisee's main contention with the peasantry arose from his demand that they give themselves completely to God and to Torah. They observed the main rituals and were willing to follow all but the most rigorous dictates of the Law.[2] He desired to build a Kingdom of God and considered no demand of the Torah unreasonable in the light of that goal.

It can scarcely be an accident that of the recorded controversies between the Pharisees and their opponents, not one was based on a Pharisaic desire for material goods. It was a singular revolt of the underprivileged which demanded neither better pay, shorter hours, preferment in office, nor redistribution of land, but was preoccupied with the proper date of Shabuot, the ritual of the Day of Atonement, the water-libations of Sukkot, the nature of man's soul, and the laws of Levitical purity. The Pharisees, to be sure, asserted that their traditions derived from the prophets, and that Pharisaic exegesis of Scripture was more authoritative than that of the High Priests. Beginning with the time of Simeon the Righteous, Proto-Pharisees apparently demanded and (at various times) obtained the right to sit in the national Sanhedrin as unsalaried judges.[3] But this participation in the national court was (as we shall see)[4] incidental to the need to protect Scriptural law from invasion by vested interests of the High Priests and their subordinates. Nowhere in the Talmud is there a demand, like that voiced in the Book of Jubilees,[5] for an immediate Jubilaic reapportionment of the land among all the peasants. This issue, like others of the same type, the Pharisees left for the final Messianic redemption of mankind. The immediate problems belonged to quite a different realm.

No effort has been made in this book to explain the origin of the uniqueness of Prophecy or Pharisaism. A naturalist may call it the maturing of the human mind; to the theologian it seems nothing less than Divine revelation. In either event, Pharisaic piety, stemming from that of the Prophets, included ideas—such as the conviction of God's Oneness, the value of spiritual life, and the insignificance of temporal goals—which cannot be related to specific human motivations and situations.

While Pharisaism was in essence unique, opposition to it was not. However spiritual and selfless the claim of the Pharisee might be, the governing groups, lay and ecclesiastic, were bound to resist it. Even the assertion that all men were immortal servants of God appeared to the upper classes of the early Second Commonwealth, and perhaps their predecessors, to be an infringement on their special theological status. The struggle of Sadducism against Pharisaism has, therefore, a counterpart in the effort of all agrarian aristocracies to preserve special privileges.

The type of piety characteristic of the ancient Pharisee inevitably clothed him with another singular quality. He was passionately devoted to his principles, but he was non-aggressive. His opponents' desire to suppress him transformed academic differences of opinion into live controversy.

Everywhere else the aggressors in the urban-rural conflict were the urban plebeians, demanding rights traditionally denied them. In Jerusalem, the Proto-Pharisee did not have to struggle for equality. He gave it to himself—in another world. The aggressors were the High Priests who wanted to deny him this liberating doctrine. Such eminent scholars as Wellhausen and Geiger have misinterpreted Pharisaism in large part because they failed to perceive how one-sided originally was the conflict between Pharisaism and Sadducism. The Pharisee suffered in patience; his opponents continued to goad and persecute him.

No less significant than the Pharisees' preoccupation with theological issues, was the irenic manner in which their position was originally and generally stated. It is, after all, remarkable that the earliest clear and emphatic references to personal immortality in Judaism should be negation of the rising doctrine, rather than its affirmation.[6] It cannot be without significance that the name Pharisees, meaning "sectarians,"[7] attached itself permanently to the group and came to be used by them, as well as by their enemies. Not until Pharisaism had entered a phase which its foremost teachers deplored, becoming a pawn in struggles of rival Hasmonean priests, did some of its leaders lay claim to power. And only in later generations, after the high-priesthood had brought Israel to the brink of destruction, was Sadducism actually declared apostasy by the Pharisee. Sadducean aberration from the normal aims of Pharisaism seriously concerned many of its teachers, and they regarded the ages in which this occurred as "those tainted with a blemish."[8]

The unique quality of the Pharisaic effort is underscored, in fact, by its insistent protection of institutions used to undermine and discourage it. From the beginning, Pharisaism, seeking to establish the synagogue as a house of prayer and study, also demanded full and generous support of the Temple. The basic document of the movement, preserved in the Book of Nehemiah,[9] prescribes the duty of the Proto-Pharisee to the Temple and its hierarchy, and pledges the movement to support these institutions.[10] One test of loyalty to Pharisaism was willingness to pay the tithe to the Levite. The *'am ha-arez*, who theoretically accepted the authority of the Temple hierarchs, gave his heave-offering to the priests, because, ritually holy, it was forbidden to the laity.[11] The tithe was not ritually holy in itself. It was secular grain. But it had to be given to the Levite. The *'am ha-arez* did not recognize failure to perform this obligation as "theft from the [Levitical] tribe."[12] The Pharisee did, and paid his tithe.

So unwilling was early Pharisaism to engage in struggle against the high-priesthood that rabbinic tradition has preserved in the Passover service a whole series of anti-Pharisaic. documents, prepared by Temple authorities to counteract Proto-Pharisaic theological influence in the community.[13] The anti-Pharisaic tone of these works did not prevent the Pharisee from repeating them at his Passover service. He recognized the right of the Temple authorities to determine the liturgy for the paschal night, and probably came to interpret the passages in a manner congenial to his theology.

Perhaps the remarkable docility of the Pharisees was born out of supreme confidence in themselves and in the right. We have already observed that these ancient saints were far too wise to bother about the trivialities which engage the lives and energies of lesser men. Their aspirations soared to heaven, and nothing earthly could seduce them from this main concern.

The Pharisaic views, rooted in the Torah and free from material motivation, had special appeal to the market place of Jerusalem. Indeed, some, dealing with issues on which the Written Law is either silent or ambiguous, reflect traditions which presumably developed in Jerusalem's trading center, perhaps in pre-exilic times.[14] That is why they aroused such opposition among the aristocracy and rural landowners.

That is also why they were able to survive generation after generation, in the teeth of a hostile hierarchy which also governed the land.

The thesis of the book, therefore, stands. Pharisaism, as a movement, was the product of the market place of Jerusalem; Sadducism, of the priesthood which was of provincial origin. However, generally the views of the Sadducees require explanation—not those of the Pharisees. The Pharisees adhered to the text of the Commandments and the words of their fathers. The motives of the priesthood, deviating in so many instances from the Torah, need analysis.

Within Pharisaism itself, two traditions emerged, represented ultimately in the Schools of Hillel and Shammai, but far more ancient than those sages.[15] Unlike the controversies in which Pharisaism as a whole engaged, those between its factions and later among its sages always concerned issues where the word of Scripture is unclear, either out of ambiguity or out of silence. In these marginal issues, left to their own devices, the sages were inevitably guided by their predisposition, which might be personal and usually also reflected group and regional attitudes. It could scarcely be otherwise. The judges were not guided by arbitrary whim. Since equally able and dedicated men disagreed in the interpretation of the Law, it must have been ambiguous. Each faction and its leaders were thus left to make decisions which seemed to them most clearly "right in the eyes of the Lord,"[16] a discovery inevitably dependent on personal background.

Thus, the divergences of opinion and practice within Pharisaism differed radically from those which separated the whole movement from Sadducism. The argument with Sadducism rarely dealt with issues about which Scripture is unclear. Controversies which the Torah left to the sages for decision did not, by their nature, become sectarian. There would almost always be Pharisaic scholars to side with the priesthood and the landed aristocracy in such matters. These controversies have come down to us as dividing the Pharisaic schools and scholars, not the Pharisees from the Sadducees.

Because in Pharisaic theology the world is a Temple, every gesture assumes for the Pharisee the importance of the proper note for a musical composer, of rhythm and word for the poet, of color and shade for the painter. Nothing is too insignificant for comment and analysis. As nothing in human life is too trivial for Divine concern, so no action by His servant is too unimportant to be weighed carefully for its merits.

Pharisaism encouraged debate on such issues. Disagreement among its sages did not provide embarrassment. On the contrary, the controversies reflected the group's determination to serve God with as much dedication and with as much discernment as possible. Difference of opinion, when justified, was, at least in the early ages of Pharisaism, the glory of the whole movement.[17] In their disagreements, as in their agreements, the Pharisees applied the principle that all life must be holy.

Quite aside, therefore, from the detailed issues separating Pharisee from Sadducee, there were two overriding ones. The first was the definition of holiness. The other was the relation of controversy, when the Torah is ambiguous, to the holy life. Pharisaism considered all life to be capable of holiness; and also insisted that in the search for holiness, finite human beings will sometimes find two opposite forms of action both right. Sadducism sought to limit holiness to the Temple and its appurtenances, and clearly regarded as nonsense the concept that two inconsistent opinions could both be correct.

The analysis of the controversies, in the present discussion, will necessarily sometimes take us far afield. For the historian the ancient argument, like the archaeologist's potsherd, subjected to painstaking examination, provides great illumination.

One of the most remarkable aspects of Pharisaism was its ability, despite preoccupation with minutiae of conduct, to retain its sense of humor. It never lost its tolerant, joyous, affectionate and earthy attitude to the world and to life. A passage my revered teacher, the late Professor Louis Ginzberg, was fond of citing clearly reflects the whole Pharisaic attitude toward the pious life. Rabban Johanan ben Zakkai, persuaded that the Messiah would ultimately come to redeem Israel and the world, nevertheless did not lose his perspective or sense of reality. "If, while engaged in planting a tree, you hear that the Messiah has come, finish your work, and then follow him," he advised his disciples.[18]

Other-worldliness did not lead to rejection of this world. Dedication to God did not lead to depreciation of man. The desire to serve was consistent with a desire to savor the permissible joys of life. The courtier in the Divine Palace, which is the whole earth, devoted endless hours to the discovery of just what gestures might please his Creator. But error neither dismayed nor disconcerted him. He approached God as a King, but he knew that God would treat him as a beloved son. He tried his utmost to avoid transgression, but he knew beforehand that, no matter how grave, sin would be forgiven; and it might even miraculously be transformed into constructive good.

In the pages of the Talmud the sagacity and the naïveté of the ancient scholars are equally astonishing. Their faith was essentially simple. Yet their judgments were surprisingly wise. With intuitive feeling for the right which later generations vainly sought to emulate, they were able to educate large masses in love and fear of God and to create institutions which preserved tradition in perilous times which could hardly have been foreseen. The stamp put on all future Western thought by Pharisaism offers clear demonstration of its profundity as well as its universality.

To demonstrate, once again, the main thesis of this book as I now understand it, I shall first undertake a reappraisal of the recorded controversies between Sadducees and Pharisees, indicating the underlying issues, supplementing those in the text of the book, and sometimes suggesting a new approach, based on more recent, perhaps more mature, investigation. It seems better to leave the original argument, even when modified by this supplement. The student and reader are entitled to reach their own decisions regarding varying interpretations to be put on the controversies.

From this discussion of recorded differences between the Sadducees and the Pharisees, I shall turn to a re-appraisal of the talmudic view of the contemporary peasant; and to an analysis of the talmudic record of the origins of Sadducism and Boethusianism, showing how distinctly the Rabbinic Sages recalled these great events. I shall conclude with a discussion of the record within talmudic literature of the role of social predisposition in decision-making.

II. THE BACKGROUND OF THE SADDUCEAN VIEWS

While the Pharisees opposed Sadducism, they frequently expressed admiration and respect for the piety of individual Sadducees.[1] The Sadducee of the Talmud often appears to be a well-intentioned if misguided priest. Such, indeed, was the piety of many that, recognizing the superior learning of the Pharisaic scholars, while formally opposing them,[2] Sadducees would obey their injunctions in daily behavior. This seems to have been especially common with Sadducean women, who were guided almost entirely by Pharisaic traditions in such laws as those appertaining to menstrual impurity.[3]

Yet, as the following analysis will show, the Sadducean controversies with the Pharisees almost all sprang from self-serving intersets of the high-priesthood. Finding parts of the Pentateuchal law difficult to observe, the high-priesthood rejected it, substituting more convenient forms, and even pagan rites and notions which the Law of Moses had tried to eradicate.

This materialistic self-serving background of the Sadducean views has an important bearing on the origin of the sect as well as that of the controversies.

As the argument will show, A. Geiger's failure to perceive this basic difference between the sectarian controversies of Pharisee against Sadducee, and the factional arguments within Pharisaism itself, sometimes led him into confused, often surprising misinterpretation and misreading of ancient texts.[4]

The deviations from Scripture urged in Sadducean exegesis could not, as this book shows,[5] have arisen in Maccabean times. The first Hasmonean High Priests, the brothers Jonathan and Simon, were dedicated and devoted Jews who courted martyrdom for Torah. John Hyrkan retained their traditions. None of these men would have stooped to distortion of the Law to serve temporal interests. By the time of the later Hasmonean High Priests, who could be cynical toward the Torah, Sadducism and Pharisaism had already developed their final forms. The Sadducean views originated long before. Various passages in Scripture and early Apocalyptic literature plainly demonstrate the pre-Maccabean origin of the controversies.

Recognition of these facts led me to the view that the ritual and juristic controversies arose during the Persian and Hellenistic periods, when to serve its purposes the cynical, assimilationist priesthood was willing to violate the Law. However, during the past twenty years I have become increasingly impressed with evidence, which I originally tried to ignore, that at least some of the controversies between the Pharisees and the Sadducees arose before the Exile. During a large part of the pre-exilic period the priests of the Temple were no less cynical and self-serving than during the Persian and Hellenistic periods. Under some reigns they were frankly idolatrous.

For example, one of the issues which demonstrably arose at an early date concerned the water-libations on the Feast of Tabernacles.[6] Only an institution long established could have compelled conformity from Alexander Jannaeus who, as a Sadducean, did not believe in it. But these water-libations, unmentioned in the Pentateuch, could scarcely have assumed such importance except in the crowded market place of Jerusalem where the end of the dry season found a large population parched and concerned, not for the following harvest, but for the indispensable rainfall of the morrow. These conditions hardly correspond to life in Persian and Hellenistic Jerusalem, which was no more than a large village. Moreover, the association of Sukkot with rainfall is mentioned in the last chapters of Zechariah.[7] When I wrote this book I followed the prevailing opinion of scholars who then dated these chapters in the late Hellenistic period.[8] It now seems probable that they were really composed five or six centuries earlier.[9] Accordingly the association of Sukkot with a period of judgment for rain and with appropriate rituals developed during the First Commonwealth. There is equally good reason (shown below)[10] to believe that the controversies about the ritual of the Day of Atonement, the date of Shabuot, the *'erub* and the *lex talionis*, as well as some theological issues, arose during the First Commonwealth in the time of the prophets.

Both the Pharisaic and Sadducean systems were inherited by the Temple High Priests and the Pharisees of the Second Commonwealth from earlier ages. The issues became bitter, partisan, and sectarian under the Hasmoneans.

To ascertain the facts about these controversies, we must now re-assess them individually. They may be considered in six categories:

A. Ritual and Juristic Issues, in which Sadducism Contravened the Word of Scripture

1. The Controversy Regarding the *Omer* and the Date of Shabuot
2. The Incense on the Day of Atonement
3. The Use of Fire on the Sabbath

4. The Controversy Concerning the Red Heifer
5. The Meal-Offerings and Libations Accompanying Animal Sacrifice
6. The Impurity of Metals
7. The Law of Inheritance
8. The Law of False Witnesses
9. The Responsibility of a Master for Damages Committed by His Slaves
10. Ransom in Lieu of Capital Punishment

B. Issues where Sadducism Opposed the Spirit of Biblical Law, Not Any Specific Statement

11. The Water-Libations on Sukkot
12. Judicial Leniency in Punishment

C. Issues where Scripture is Inexplicit

13. Equal Participation of All Jews in Daily Sacrifices
14. The *Nizzok*

D. Institutions Described by the Pharisees as Post-Biblical

15. Hand-Washing
16. The *'Erub*

E. Priestly Traditions Opposed by Some Pharisaic Scholars, and Denounced by Them as Sadducean

17. The Priestly Interpretation of the *Lex Talionis*
18. The Priestly Tradition Regarding Death by Burning
19. The Impurity of a Mother after Childbirth
20. Proof of Virginity by a Bride under Suspicion
21. The Ceremony of *Halizah*

F. Theological Controversies

22. The Doctrines of the Resurrection and of the Immortality of the Soul
23. The Doctrine of Personal Angels

A. Ritual and Juristic Issues, in which Sadducism Contravened the Word of Scripture

1. The Controversy Regarding the *Omer* and the Date of Shabuot

The ceremony of the *Omer* sacrifice consisted of cutting a sheaf of barley at the beginning of the harvest, and its sacrifice as the first fruit (Lev. 23.10 f.). Forty-nine days after this sacrifice was Pentecost, the Feast of Shabuot. On that festival two loaves of leavened bread were presented as the first offering of the wheat harvest "unto the Lord."[11]

The ritual of cutting the *Omer* and its sacrifice are to be performed on "the morrow of the Shabbat" (ibid., 23.11). Shabuot is also described as occurring "on the morrow of the seventh Shabbat" after the offering of the *Omer* (ibid., v. 16).

According to Pharisaic tradition, Shabbat in v. 11 means the first day of Passover.[12] The festival of Shabuot occurs on the fiftieth day thereafter.

The Sadducean tradition holds that in both verses Shabbat means "weekly Sabbath."[13] Accordingly the *Omer* is always to be cut on the Saturday night of the Passover week, and sacrificed on Sunday; and the festival of Shabuot always occurs on a Sunday.

A third view, preserved in the Book of Jubilees[14] and among the modern Falashas,[15] insisted that Shabbat in v. 11 meant the *last* day of Passover; but agrees that in v. 16, it meant week.

Those identifying Shabbat in these verses with the weekly Sabbath are uniformly described in rabbinic literature as Boethusians. But we now know that the controversy antedated by centuries the origin of that sect.[16] The Book of Joshua, in fact, refers to it (see above p. 116). The Book of

Jubilees, certainly pre-Herodian and probably pre-Maccabean, had as one of its main purposes the resolution of this controversy, which must therefore have arisen long before the time of Boethus the High Priest.[17] Why then did the Talmud ascribe the deviationist view only to the Boethusians?

The solution of this riddle requires a new approach, which sheds light on the controversy itself.

As already indicated, the date of the Feast of Weeks (Shabuot) depends on the time of the *Omer* sacrifice.

The months of the Jewish calendar could be "long" or "short," because they were determined by observation of the New Moon, which sometimes appears on the thirtieth night after the preceding New Moon, but at other times on the thirty-first night.

Despite this variability in the monthly date of Shabuot, the Pharisees considered the festival the anniversary of the Revelation on Mt. Sinai. The festival, they held, always occurred "in the season" of the Revelation, and was intended to celebrate that most important event in human history. There was some disagreement, even among the later Rabbis, regarding the precise date of the Revelation.[18] But this disagreement did not involve any question regarding the nature of Shabuot. According to all Pharisees, the Revelation occurred on the fifty-first day after the Exodus; and that anniversary was marked by Shabuot.

The controversy about the date of the *Omer* sacrifice is essentially secondary to that about the date of Shabuot. In this book,[19] I assumed that the basis of that controversy was essentially theological and historical. I held that the Pharisees considered Shabuot a feast celebrating primarily the Revelation, and therefore believed it had to have a fixed date, at least in reference to Passover. The Sadducees adhered to the view that it was the festival of the wheat harvest, and therefore need not occur on a fixed date.

Further study has shown that the issue was far more complex. Doubtless the Pharisaic and Proto-Pharisaic attitude toward Revelation played a part in the insistence of the Pharisees on the correctness of their view; while the provincial unconcern with Torah as study made it natural for Sadducees to regard Shabuot as simply an agricultural festival, that of the wheat harvest. But the controversy was deeply rooted in material interests. The priests from whom Sadducism inherited its views in this regard were concerned to avoid personal discomfort and expense; and were also inclined to accept the provincial, semi-pagan concept of the Sabbath, opposed by both Scripture and the Pharisees.

The material interest of the priesthood in fixing the date of Shabuot on Sunday derived from the system of priestly service in vogue at the Temple.

The Aaronid priesthood consisted of twenty-four clans,[20] each gathered to perform the Temple service for one week in the winter, and for another in the summer.[21] On the three pilgrimages all the priests assembled to look after the vastly increased numbers of sacrifices, when the priestly portions of the offerings sufficed to attract virtually all of them to the capital.

For the priests gathered in the Temple during the long festivals, Passover and Tabernacles, the opportunities for service and the ecclesiastical emoluments associated with these major pilgrimages justified the journey to Jerusalem even from distant parts. When the festivals occurred during the week, the clan then officiating at the Temple found its term of service and income curtailed. Yet the loss was more than offset through the sacrifices brought by the hosts of pilgrims.

Not so on Shabuot. This was a one-day festival, bringing a comparatively small number of pilgrims to the Temple. In Ezekiel Shabuot is not even mentioned as a pilgrimage.[22] When Shabuot occurred in the middle of the week, the priestly clan then in charge of the Temple service lost very little. True, it had to share the Temple emoluments of the festival with other priests who came for the pilgrimage. But the loss was presumably less than the gain provided by the festival emoluments.

However, the clans in charge of the service during the preceding and the following weeks were aggrieved. Those whose terms had expired on the previous Sabbath had to choose between losing the festival emoluments by going home, or finding food and lodging in Jerusalem outside the Temple for the few days preceding the festival. Similarly, the clan about to begin its term of service on the Sabbath following Shabuot would either lose its portion of the festival, or its members would have to fend for themselves during the few days separating the festival from the following Sabbath.

These difficulties were obviated when Shabuot occurred on Sunday. The priests ministering the preceding week had but to remain in Jerusalem one day to share in the festival income. The clan entering on its service on the Sabbath preceding Shabuot joined the other priests in the celebration of the pilgrimage, receiving part of the additional emoluments of the festivals, besides the regular ones from sacrifices which would be offered also on weekdays.

So convenient was this arrangement, that the priests must naturally have wondered why it could not become regular. The temptation to read into Leviticus an interpretation permanently fixing Shabuot on Sundays must have been very great, actually irresistible. The Proto-Pharisaic and Pharisaic interpretation of the word Shabbat in the relevant verses was rejected out of hand.

After several millennia, and in the perspective of another civilization, the difficulty confronting the priests in observance of the literal command of Scripture may hardly seem to justify a schism. But anyone acquainted with the way slight personal advantage sways judgment, even in those trained to objective thought, will be prepared to find the ancient priesthood interpreting the Bible in congenial ways, particularly priests who were less than dedicated servants of God.

That such an issue seemed far from trifling also to devout priests is clear from the record (Mishna Sukkah 5.7–8). This passage tells us: "When a festival occurs immediately before or after the Sabbath [so that all priests have assembled in the Temple before the Sabbath, or remained through it] all the clans share equally in the division of the shewbread. If one day intervenes between the Sabbath and the festival, the clan in whose term the Sabbath occurs receives ten loaves, and all other priests [who arrived early for the festival, or remained over the Sabbath after the festival] receive two loaves." This norm was necessary to obviate unseemly quarrels among the priests under the circumstances mentioned. The more complex problem of providing work and income for priests during an intervening period, when the festival was the brief Shabuot, led to a schism.

Perhaps, however, we do some of the ancient priests injustice in this ascription of their exegesis only to personal convenience. A more profound issue was also involved: the nature of the biblical Sabbath. The Pharisaic interpretation of the word Shabbat in the chapter dealing with the *Omer* and Shabuot emphasized the conception of the Sabbath as a day of delight. According to this view, the etymological kinship of the Hebrew word Shabbat and the Mesopotamian *shabbatu* did not imply that both words had the same meaning. The Mesopotamian *shabbatu*, widely marked as a day of ill-omen even in Persian and Hellenistic times, was for the Proto-Pharisees institutionally unrelated to the biblical Sabbath, a day of blessing, of dedication to God, and of supreme happiness. The issue was fundamental to Prophetic and Pharisaic theology. The word Shabbat in the biblical text of Leviticus, chapter 23, was probably used to stress the distinction between the Sabbath of Israel and the *shabbatu* of the Mesopotamians. The context shows that the Pharisaic exegesis corresponded to the literal meaning of the biblical verse.[23]

The passage reads: "When you come into the land which I give unto you, and shall reap the harvest thereof, then ye shall bring the sheaf of the first fruits of your harvest unto the priest. And he shall wave the sheaf before the Lord, to be accepted for you; on the morrow after the Shabbat the priest shall wave it" (Lev. 23.11). The mere fact that the preceding paragraph describes the Passover festival cannot fix the Shabbat mentioned in this verse as that of the Passover week. Moreover, within the same section the word Shabbat is used for "week" (v. 15), and in the form *Shabbaton* definitely means "festival" (vv. 24, 39). The Day of Atonement is described as *Shabbat Shabbaton*, "A supreme Shabbat" (v. 32). These repeated uses of the words *Shabbat* and *Shabbaton* for "festival" and "holiday" suggest a deliberate effort to stress a particular notion. Scripture is emphasizing the idea of the Sabbath as a day of festivity.

The description of Yom Kippur concludes with the verse, "on the ninth day [of the seventh month] in the evening, from evening to evening, shall ye observe your Shabbat" (v. 32). Again the word Shabbat occurs in the sense of holiday.

Dominated by provincial, semi-pagan notions, the priesthood of the Temple rejected the implication of the biblical text, and interpreted it to suit their own needs.

The literal and Proto-Pharisaic interpretation of the biblical text would scarcely be opposed by priests dwelling in Jerusalem or its environment, who then belonged to the lower ranks of the priesthood, without large estates in the provinces. Trained to resist the teachings of the Proto-Pharisees, but without objection to the celebration of the *Omer* and Shabuot in the middle of the week, the spokesmen of this group apparently proposed a compromise. They agreed that Shabbat meant festival; but the last day of Passover, rather than the first. This is the tradition preserved among the Falashas, and probably was current in wide circles in Jerusalem of the early centuries. In the Book of Jubilees,[24] this principle was adopted; but according to the peculiar solar calendar of the book, Shabuot always occurred on the seventh Sunday after the last day of Passover, which always fell on a Saturday. According to talmudic records, the barley harvest of the highlands did not always ripen in time to be garnered for the *Omer* sacrifice on the sixteenth of Nisan. To make sure of grain for the sacrifice, a field was set aside in the Valley of Kidron,[25] facing the southern sun,[26] and therefore ripening before that of the highlands. The barley of Jericho and the surrounding valley often ripened earlier.[27] The peasant population of the highlands therefore was not discommoded by postponement of the *Omer* to the day after the last day of Passover. No new grain was usually available in their farms before that time. Nor were the rich landowners in Jericho and other lowland areas put to any inconvenience; they had stored sufficient grain from their earlier crop season to take care of their needs. The community which suffered through delay of the *Omer*, permitting use of the new barley, was the landless urban population of Jerusalem. Its members looked forward so eagerly to the new grain, that the traders in its markets obtained a supply even before the *Omer* was sacrificed; preparing it for distribution as soon as the offering would be made.[28]

Delay in the date of the *Omer* and of Shabuot was also welcomed by the priests for another reason.

The later the festival, the more plentiful and the more varied would be the first fruits brought to the Temple on Shabuot. Even the postponement of the *Omer* for a few days, from the sixteenth of Nisan until the Sunday following, would to that extent be useful, because it would delay the festival of the first fruits by that much.

True, anyone could bring the first fruit of his orchard or farm to the Temple even after Shabuot. But he was far less likely to do so than on the occasion of the pilgrimage. As this first fruit was given the priests, the loss of their emolument through early celebration of Shabuot was considerable.

Of all the sectarian controversies raging in the Second Commonwealth, that concerning the dates of the *Omer* and Shabuot inevitably became the most bitter and the most prominent. Each group denied that its opponents really observed the festival of Shabuot, for observance of a festival on the wrong date could not offset the sin of its violation on the correct date, while wrongful observance was itself a violation of the Law.

Whatever the origin of the anti-Pharisaic interpretation of the relevant verses in Leviticus, some of the later priests, having received that tradition from their ancestors, were convinced of its truth. They were deeply concerned at what they regarded as their opponents' widespread and flagrant violation of the Law. On the other hand, the Proto-Pharisees, without authority in the Temple during long periods, could not fulfill the law of the Shabuot pilgrimage in accordance with their tradition. They could come to Jerusalem on the day set for the festival in their own calendar, but at the Temple that day was marked with no festive sacrifice. They might abstain from labor on the day they considered the holiday, but their neighbors would be violating it. Proto-Pharisees would have difficulty in explaining to their children that the Temple priests violated the Law through a misinterpretation.

No less serious, of course, was the problem of eating new grain, after the first day of Passover. If the Boethusians or those identifying the Sabbath of Leviticus 23 with the seventh day of Passover were right, the Pharisees were violating the Law by eating new grain before that day. Granted that the issue involved only a few days, at most a week, it was still important for the poor, waiting impatiently for the *Omer* and the new barley.

None of the other controversies involved such profound public and private considerations. The ceremonies of the red heifer and the Day of Atonement concerned directly only the officiating priests. The Pharisees might be aghast at its violation of the Law; but they were not themselves thwarted in regard to their own observance. The kindling of the

Sabbath lights, the *'erub*, the issue of the impurity of metals involved only private behavior, regarding which each man followed his convictions. The problem of the inheritance law arose only on rare occasions, and was a matter for the judiciary. The water-libations on Sukkot and the ritual of the willows concerned only those present in the Temple, and were not resisted by the Sadducean priests.

But the problem of the date of the *Omer* and of Shabuot served as continuous reminders of the sectarian cleavage in Jewry, and of the opposition of the Temple priesthood, in general, to the whole Prophetic-Pharisaic tradition.

Hence the energetic efforts made by the Pharisees to obtain recognition for their views on the issue of the *Omer* and Shabuot. On the Sabbaths between Passover and Shabuot each Pharisee was expected to recite the passages of the ancient Mishna, detailing how the Pharisaic tradition came to be and associating it directly with Moses, at the Revelation on Mt. Sinai. This part of the Mishna became the core of the treatise, *Abot*, and its discussion constituted the first section of the *Abot of Rabbi Nathan*.

Every Pharisee was required literally to count the days from the sacrifice of the *Omer* (or the time when it should have been sacrificed) until Shabuot. On each of these nights he reminded his family and his disciples that the Temple priests were without authority in the interpretation of the ritual Law, and that their views in regard to the *Omer* and Shabuot were erroneous.

Perhaps the association of the Revelation with the festival of Shabuot, nowhere mentioned in Scripture, was part of the Proto-Pharisaic endeavor to obtain support regarding the date of the festival. Association of the festival with an historical event would render absurd the Sadducean exegesis, superficially so attractive to the priests.

The connection of the festival of Shabuot with the Revelation antedates the writing of the Book of Jubilees; and if that book be, as I believe,[29] pre-Maccabean, the argument must also have been of pre-Maccabean origin. It is mentioned in the liturgy of Shabuot (according to the Babylonian rite), apparently deriving from the fourth century B.C.E. Association of Shabuot with the anniversary of the Revelation on Mt. Sinai was congenial to the urban scholars. The concept of a wheat harvest festival, with no fixed calendar date, seemed more congenial to the aristocrats with peasant background.

As already observed, the sacrifice of the *Omer* following the Sadducean doctrine posed very difficult ceremonial questions for the Pharisees. Leviticus 23.14 forbids new grain to be eaten before the offering of the *Omer* sacrifice. The verse specifically states: "And ye shall eat neither bread, nor parched corn, nor fresh ears, until this selfsame day, until ye have brought the offering of your God." *Omer*, sacrificed on the wrong day, was not *Omer*. How then could the Pharisees eat grain at all under a Temple regime violating their interpretation of Scripture?

Fortunately, Scripture provides for this contingency. The prolix statement, "until this selfsame day, until ye have brought the offering of your God," suggests that use of the new grain is permitted on the sixteenth of Nisan, whether or not the sacrifice has been offered. This in fact was probably the interpretation of the Pharisees, who held that when the *Omer* was not sacrificed, grain might be used after the sixteenth day of Nisan. The decision became overwhelmingly important after the destruction of the Temple, when the Jews could not offer the *Omer* sacrifice at all. At that time Rabban Johanan ben Zakkai formulated the norm that new grain might be eaten after the sixteenth day.[30] R. Judah ben

R. Ilai, transmitting, as he frequently did, traditions going back to the market place of Jerusalem generations before, maintained that this was no innovation by Rabban Johanan ben Zakkai, but had always been recognized law.[31]

In the final generations of the Second Commonwealth, when the Pharisees controlled the Temple ritual, their opponents, the Boethusians, resorted to various stratagems to bring about the sacrifice of the *Omer* and the determination of the date of Shabuot in accordance with their views. We are told that Boethusians hired false witnesses to delude the Pharisees. This happened when the New Moon of Nisan was expected to appear on either Friday night or Saturday night. If on Saturday night, the *Omer* would, according to Pharisaic Law, be cut on a Sunday night and offered on the sixteenth of Nisan, a Monday. In that event, Shabuot would also be on a Monday, seven weeks later. On some occasions when actually no New Moon was visible that Friday night, the Boethusians, partly from desire to annoy their opponents, but also to escape the necessity of spending even a single day without priestly income, bribed witnesses to testify falsely before the Pharisaic authorities to the appearance of the New Moon on that night. Once a witness so bribed betrayed the conspiracy.[32] Thereafter, the Pharisaic courts would not accept witnesses to the New Moon without proof of their reliability.

The conduct of the Boethusians suggests that they were as corrupt and self-seeking as were many priests of the Persian-Hellenistic period and of the First Commonwealth. To mislead the authorities regarding the New Moon could only bring about widespread and grievous violation of Scriptural Law according to all views. Sacrifices would be omitted on days when they should rightly be offered; and offered when forbidden. The sacrifices of the New Moon and of Passover would be wrongfully offered on the Sabbath. Observing the Passover beginning with the wrong day, the whole community would be eating leavened bread on what was actually the seventh day of Passover. No pious Jew, whatever the temptation, would resort to such measures, even in the heat of controversy. It is instructive that we know of no such efforts by the Sadducees. Whatever their errors might be, the Sadducees were in the main God-fearing and respectful of Temple worship.

The fact that the Boethusians, whose cynicism will presently be further demonstrated,[33] resorted to these measures reveals the underlying materialistic interest. In earlier times such interest had led to misinterpretation of Scripture and the origin of the Sadducean concept itself; in Pharisaic times, to an effort to corrupt the calendar.

The Mishna (Menahot 10.3) states specifically that the complicated ceremonial attending the cutting of the *Omer* was necessary because of "the Boethusians, who say that the time for cutting of the *Omer* is not the night after the festival day." In another passage (Hagigah 2.4), we are told that when Shabuot occurred on a Sabbath (and according to the Shammaites, even when it occurred on a Friday), the "day of slaughtering" the whole-burnt offerings of the festival was the following Sunday. But in that event, the High Priest did not don his special garments, and the day was not observed (as otherwise customary) as a half-holiday "so as to give no substance to the words of those who say Shabuot is always on Sunday."

The authors of the Mishna and the other talmudic works had good reason for their silence regarding the Sadducean and pre-Sadducean origin of the deviationist view: unwillingness to ascribe this view to an ancient tradition, even one held to be erroneous. To attribute the deviationist view to the legitimate high-priestly dynasty and its followers would certainly have embarrassed the Pharisees. While their interpretation of the Law might be accepted as superior to that of the High Priests who were known to be ignorant, the determination of the calendar was widely considered the prerogative of Temple authorities. The Pharisaic scholars themselves agreed that the New Moon was "hallowed" even if the Court determining it was in error.[34] It was not easy to understand why Temple authorities were obeyed in the determination of the date of Passover, Rosh ha-Shanah, Yom Kippur, and Sukkot, all of which depended on the time of the New Moon, but were disobeyed when they fixed the time of Shabuot, following their Sadducean tradition. The Pharisees persuaded themselves that the exegesis of their opponents had not really originated with earlier High Priests, was totally without traditional basis, and was merely a self-serving device of Boethusian cynics. The analysis offered above shows, however, that while the deviationist interpretation was self-serving, it was not an invention of the Boethusians. This sect arose no earlier than the latter half of the first century B.C.E., whereas the heretical exegesis was already extant when the Book of Joshua was composed.

2. The Incense on the Day of Atonement

As indicated in this book on p. 118, the Sadducees and Boethusians required the incense offered on the Day of Atonement in the Innermost Temple Shrine to be put on a censer of fire, before entry into the Holy of Holies. The Pharisees, following the literal word of Scripture, held that the incense must be put on the fire in the Holy of Holies itself.

When the book was written I adopted the view of J. Z. Lauterbach that in this instance the underlying issue between Sadducism and Pharisaism was theological. According to the Sadducees the Divine Presence was visible in the Holy Shrine. They therefore dared not enter it unprotected by the smoke-screen arising from the burning incense.

I still believe that the issue of the visibility and the anthropomorphic nature of God played a decisive role in this controversy.[34a] But other issues were also involved.

The Sadducean way of offering the incense corresponded not only to the usual pagan practice, but also to that prevalent in wealthy households. After a festive meal a servant put incense on fire in an outside room, and brought it smoking to his master who passed his hands over the incense, so the fragrance removed from them the smell of the food he had touched.

The idolatrous use of incense derived from this and similar customs of wealthy households. Idols were approached by worshipers like masters by slaves.

This was undoubtedly one reason for the rejection of this form of worship in Scripture. The Bible sought to eradicate the concept of sacrifice as a meal presented to the Deity. That is also why no beer or honey could be offered on the altar;[35] or indeed any meats, except those specifically commanded in Scripture.[36]

Beyond this objection, Scripture sought to eradicate other theological implications of the pagan rite. The use of the smoke-screen of incense to protect the High Priest from the Vision of the Deity, suggesting that this Vision might be fatal, was associated with the pagan concept of holiness as a source of peril. Scripture consistently sought to eliminate this view. It described the scene in which the sons of Aaron and seventy of the elders of Israel "saw the God of Israel; and there was under His feet the like of a paved work of sapphire stone, and the like of the very heavens for clearness. And upon the nobles of the sons of Israel, He laid not His hand; and they beheld God, and did eat and drink" (Ex. 24.10–11). True, when Moses asks God to "show him His glory" (ibid. 33.18), God replies "Thou canst not see My face, for man cannot see Me and live" (v. 20). But clearly this is not because God is a source of death; on the contrary, the whole context shows that He is the source of life, of forgiveness, of mercy. It is merely that living man cannot endure the overwhelming Glory of the Divine Presence. This Glory would not, of course, be manifest in the Holy of Holies to the High Priest, any more than it was to Moses, to whom God spoke "mouth to mouth, even manifestly, and not in dark speeches, and the similitude of the Lord doth he behold" (Num. 11.8.).

Disobedience to the Divine commandment might be fatal, as is evident in various texts. But a rite performed as commanded could not be harmful, whatever Vision might appear to the High Priest in the Sacred Shrine.

Finally through its commandment Scripture implicitly rejects the doctrine that God actually appeared in the Holy of Holies.

In reply to the literal and simple interpretation of Scripture urged by the Pharisees, the Sadducees frankly said in defense of their position: "If the incense is prepared in the outer hall for a human master, how much more should be done for the King of kings of kings."[37]

To this logic the Pharisees could only reply that Scripture commanded otherwise.

Perhaps the Sadducean High Priests might have been less adamant had the Pharisaic norm been less difficult to execute. To put the incense on the fire outside the Temple shrine was easy. The coals would be taken from the altar in a censer, and the incense poured over them.

The Pharisaic norm, in contrast, required much effort and great dexterity.

According to it, the High Priest had to take a censer of coals from the altar in one hand, and a spoon of incense in the other. Holding them before him, he had to walk through the Temple hall into the dark Innermost Shrine. There, guided only by the glow of the coals in the censer, his hands burdened, he had to grope to the rock on which the offering was to be made. He placed the censer upon the rock, and poured the incense over the coals in the censer. The Law required this part of the ritual to be performed with his hands rather than with the spoon. To put the incense into the palms of his hands, he might place the spoon handle in his mouth, between his teeth, so that the incense poured into his palms. Or he might put the handle between his fingers in such a way that the contents could be dropped into his palms. Having achieved this feat he transferred the incense directly from his hands onto the flaming censer.[38]

Dressed in highly inflammable linen garments, the High Priest performing this service was in great peril. A spark from the burning incense might readily set his linen clothes afire.

No wonder that this ritual is described in the Talmud as one of the most difficult in the whole Temple service.[39]

The Pharisees insisted upon it because of their faithfulness to the command of Scripture, and because that command seemed logical and was congenial to their theology.

The difference between the ordinary way of presenting incense, whether to mortal kings or to pagan idols, and that of the Day of Atonement, gave them no concern. On the contrary, they assumed that the Torah deliberately rejected the usual custom, substituting its own norm to widen the gulf separating God from human masters and idols.

The deviationist view is generally ascribed in the Talmud to the Sadducees.[40] But in the light of what we have already observed about the controversy regarding the *Omer*[41] (and shall presently discover in regard to other controversies), we may assume that the issue arose in very early times. The priests of the First Commonwealth were surely as unwilling as the Sadducean High Priests of the Second to undertake the rigorous tasks imposed on them by the Scriptural words and inclined to perform the offering in the manner usual among idol-worshipers.

To prevent the High Priest from following the Sadducean ritual, the Pharisees when in power compelled him to swear that he would obey their norm.[42] This oath was necessary for he would be alone within the Temple building during the ritual and could, without detection, put the incense on the coals outside the Innermost Shrine.

The oath was directed to conscientious High Priests, suspected of Sadducism but not of cynicism, but would not prevent a Boethusian political High Priest, really contemptuous of religion, from following his own bent. Such a High Priest could, during the period of Pharisaic domination in the Temple, be prevented from observing the Sadducean ritual in its most natural way which was heaping the incense on the fire in the Temple courts next to the altar itself. Unable to perform the service in this easy manner, he would gain little from violation of Pharisaic ritual afterward by putting the incense on the fire outside the Innermost Shrine.

But a conscientious Sadducean High Priest might be tempted to do this. Holding that the Law required the incense to be put on fire outside the Veil and prevented from doing so in the Courts of the Sanctuary, he might secretly follow his own tradition alone in the outer halls of the Temple.

Strict Sadducean doctrine charged one who acted otherwise with a mortal sin. Therefore the Pharisees extracted an oath from the High Priest to follow their view. Regardless of his belief in the authenticity of Sadducean doctrine, the High Priest would hesitate to violate a solemn oath on the Day of Atonement. To give him further courage the Pharisaic elders, imposing the oath on him, assured him that he was acting as agent for them and for the Pharisaic courts. Presumably according to Sadducean jurisprudence, as later according to that of the Shammaites, a principal is responsible for the acts of his agents.[43] Thus the Pharisaic elders absolved the High Priest from any sense of guilt he might feel in obeying them, and took on themselves the full responsibility for his actions, if he followed their instructions.

Yet, the Talmud relates, on at least one occasion a Boethusian High Priest boasted that he had flouted the will of the Pharisees.[44] He brought the burning incense into the Shrine only after he had put it on the fire in the outer hall of the Temple building. His father, told of the incident, reprimanded him, saying, "Although we teach our own tradition, we act according to the teaching of the sages. I wonder whether you will live long." When the son died shortly afterward, the event was ascribed to his transgression. The father must have shared the conviction of many contemporary Sadducees that the Pharisaic tradition was authoritative and binding.

The provincial, primitive theology reflected in the Sadducean norm, its cynical disregard of the plain command of Scripture, and its intimate relationship to practices of pagan temples suggest pre-Maccabean, perhaps pre-exilic origin.

3. The Use of Fire on the Sabbath

The Pharisaic norm, maintaining that fire kindled on Friday need not be extinguished before the Sabbath, seems amply supported by the language of Exodus 35.3, which reads: "Ye shall kindle no fire throughout your habitations upon the Sabbath day." The verse implies permission to *utilize fire already kindled.*

The belief that fire was tabu on the Sabbath apparently prevailed among provincials, dominated by the idea of the Mesopotamian *shabbatu* and identifying the Jewish Sabbath with it. We have already seen how Scripture sought to eradicate this view of the Sabbath and how the issue was reflected in the controversy regarding the proper date of Shabuot.[45]

The Proto-Sadducean bias in favor of the Mesopotamian concept in this regard was fortified by the conditions of life in provincial, lowland Judea. The warmer weather made fire on the Sabbath unnecessary even in winter months; the habit of going to bed early made lights on the Sabbath unnecessary. Otherwise the Hellenized priests and aristocrats would scarcely have gone beyond the letter of the law in their observance of the Sabbath.

The nature of this controversy, like that of the two others already discussed, suggests very early origin. Even the word of Scripture was insufficient to free the Palestinian peasant from his fear of the use of fire on the Sabbath day.[46]

4. The Controversy Concerning the Red Heifer

The book indicates[47] that the controversy about the red heifer really involved the whole institution of ritual impurity. Early Pharisaic law asserted that a person ritually defiled was in general purified by bathing, and could after that properly be described as "clean."[48] He still could not eat the holy meats.[49] But this disqualification was related only to the laws of ritual holiness attaching to those meats, and not to ritual purity.

For the Pharisee, as for Scripture, this distinction between the laws of ritual holiness and of ritual purity was fundamental. In biblical and Pharisaic religion, ritual holiness and ritual impurity were not by any means opposite, although that which was impure had generally to be kept apart from that which was holy. The ritually holy and the ritually impure were in fact related, each having a special ritualistic status, given by Divine Law.[50] No merit attached to ritual holiness, and no demerit to ritual impurity. Hence Scripture, defining the duties of the priests, authorized them to "put differences between the holy and the common, and between the unclean and clean" (Lev. 10.10). In both divisions, the exceptional state is mentioned first. The holy was to be distinguished from the profane; and that which was impure from that which, being pure, could be used in daily life.

This theory of ritual holiness and purity, basic to Prophetic and Pharisaic theology, opposed the general trend of Near Eastern religious thought, and was particularly objectionable to the priesthood.[51] The Pharisee, like the Prophet, affirmed the sanctity of the Temple, of the priests, of the holy meats, and of everything related to the sacrificial system. But this "sanctity" involved nothing more than special regulations. Similarly, the Prophet, like the Pharisee, recognized the existence of ritual impurity; and held that it, too, involved nothing more than distinctive regulations.

The Pharisee, like his predecessors, sought to live his secular life "in purity," which he regarded as normal. He took the position that the whole community was "holy," and that therefore, although not a priest, he was required so far as possible to live in "purity," that he might not defile the community of the Lord. The Temple was "holy" in a special degree, and therefore to contaminate it was to court death; but the community, too, should be kept as "pure" as possible. With few exceptions, such as a woman after childbirth, anyone permitted to enter the "camp" of Israel was permitted (as we shall see) to enter at least the outer precincts of the Temple, but not of course the holy shrine itself. Hence the Proto-Pharisee or the Pharisee tried to keep his food and drink, the vessels containing them, and his own body ritually "undefiled." If he became defiled through contact with a dead body, he cleansed himself as soon as possible, according to the norms set down in Numbers, chapter 19. If he was afflicted with a "flow," he sought purity as required by Leviticus, chapter 15. If he became impure in a minor degree, for one day, either through marital congress, or through contact with a source of minor defilement, he bathed as soon as he could, to wash away the "impurity."

His status after this ritual bath underlay the controversy dealing with the red heifer. The Pharisee thought he was now "pure."[52] His profane food was not defiled.[53] The vessels he touched remained "pure."[54] The prohibition which kept him from consuming holy meats (otherwise permitted), he saw not as symbolic of his "impurity," but of their superior "holiness."

A similar principle applied to a woman after childbirth. For the first seven days after the birth of a son and for fourteen days after the birth of a daughter the mother was "impure."[55] Anything she touched was "defiled." She might not be approached by her husband. But, having bathed at the end of this period, she ceased to be "impure," although she was still debarred from the Temple and the holy meats.

She held this new status for thirty-three days if her child was a son and for sixty-six days if a daughter. During this period, marital congress with her husband was permitted according to the Pharisees, for she was "pure" in every relationship, save that she could not eat the holy meat nor enter the Temple precincts.[56]

The principle that the *tebul yom* was in fact "pure" had other, more practical, consequences for the residents of Jerusalem. The Second Tithe might not be eaten in impurity (Deut. 26.14). This tithe, separated in the first, second, fourth, and fifth years of the Sabbatical cycle, had to be consumed in Jerusalem. Because of the abundance of the produce separated as Second Tithe, it often had to be given to residents of Jerusalem by the pilgrims whose stay did not offer time for them to consume all they had brought to the Holy City. If the *tebul yom* were to be declared "impure," he could not taste grain or fruit which belonged to the Second Tithe. Only because the *tebul yom* was considered pure, could most pilgrims and inhabitants of the Holy City enjoy the Second Tithe.[57]

True, Deuteronomy 23.10 provides that after a seminal issue a soldier, because of his impurity, should remain outside the camp until the sun has set after he has bathed. But the provision explicitly speaks of an army on the march in wartime. Scripture requires of such an army holiness beyond that demanded in civilian life and comparable to that of the Temple itself. The temptation to transgression, and particularly sexual laxity, was far greater in war than in normal life. Resistance had correspondingly to be encouraged. The concept of God's presence in the army as in the Temple itself doubtless contributed to the preservation of moral and religious standards.

But, aside from the army, a *tebul yom* was "clean."[58] The Pharisee and Proto-Pharisee who was a *tebul yom* could participate in the normal activity of his household and community. He could eat with his family without fear that he might defile the bread or drink he touched, rendering them unsuitable for those "who ate profane food in a state of purity."

The Sadducees did not prohibit the *tebul yom* from eating profane food, although they apparently forbade a woman after childbirth to engage in marital congress during the period of her "purification."[59] But the Sadducean notion of the *tebul yom* differed radically from that of the Pharisees. The Sadducee did not take the trouble to observe most laws of ritual purity outside the Temple. Like the *'am ha-arez* and his own predecessors, he related the laws requiring one to be "pure" only to the Temple and its appurtenances. Therefore, regarding the *tebul yom* as *tamé*, ritually defiled, the Sadducee was able to pursue his normal life. As *tebul yom*, he remained outside the Temple, and refrained from eating the heave-offering or sacrificial meat. But his household was unaffected by this stringency. Even the special rule of the Sadducees, prohibiting a woman to engage in marital intercourse during this period, did not seriously discommode

Sadducees and their predecessors who practiced plural marriage.

The issue dividing the Sadducee and the Pharisee ceased to be one of private behavior and became subject to public controversy because the ceremony of the red heifer, obviously sacred, was performed outside Temple precincts. Scripture distinctly states that "a man that is clean should gather up the ashes of the heifer after it is burnt" (Num. 19.9). It also provides that the water, containing the ashes, should be sprinkled on the impure person, to cleanse him, only by a "clean" one (ibid., v. 19).[60]

The Pharisees, holding the *tebul yom* technically "clean," considered him fit to gather the ashes of the red heifer, to sprinkle the water and, if a priest, even to prepare the red heifer itself. Even a vessel which had been defiled could be used for the waters of purification after immersion in a pool of water, when it became *tebul yom*.

The Sadducees, holding that the *tebul yom* was in defilement, denied all this — a denial threatening the whole Pharisaic concept of secular life in purity.

The importance attached by the ancients — both Pharisees and pious Sadducees — to the ritual purity of the ashes of the red heifer can scarcely be exaggerated. If these ashes were defiled, the whole system of Levitical purity would come to an end. A person rendered impure through contact with a corpse could only be "purified" through sprinkling these ashes upon him, provided they had not themselves been defiled (Num. 19.18). If impure ashes were sprinkled upon a defiled person he remained impure.

Therefore the greatest possible care was taken to prevent the ashes, or the waters containing them, from defilement in any way. The priest who was to burn the red heifer was separated from his wife for seven days, and made to live in the Temple precincts, lest it turn out that she had menstruated during that time, and he had lived with her or touched her, and thus become contaminated for seven days (Mishna Parah 3.1; cf. Sifra *Zav* end, 37, 43a). On each of these days in the Temple, ashes of all the earlier red heifers were sprinkled on him, lest it turn out that through contact with a corpse or a grave (Mishna Parah 3.1), he had at any previous time been defiled. If defiled in this way, seven, six, five, three, or two days before his removal into the Temple, he would require sprinkling of the ashes on the first day of his restraint, and then on the fourth. If defiled a day before his incarceration, he required purification on the second and the fifth: if just before his removal to the Temple precincts, on the third day and on the seventh (see Num. 19.12). Through all the centuries ashes of each sacrificed red heifer were kept, so the priest who engaged in this act of worship could be purified with a sprinkling which included samples from each of the red heifers previously sacrificed, to make sure of his purity, for surely not all of them could have been defiled. (Mishna Parah, loc. cit., and commentary of R. Elijah Gaon, ad loc.).

During the week of his detention at the Temple, the assigned priest touched only stone utensils, incapable of defilement (Mishna Parah, loc. cit.). The waters to be used in the ceremony were drawn by boys of eight, too young to be contaminated through a seminal issue. These children were born and reared in specially chosen courts in Jerusalem, which they never left. These courts were on rocks overhanging large caves or other openings in the ground, so that there was no possibility of the children becoming contaminated through passing over a forgotten grave (ibid. 3.2). (The rule underlying this norm is that a grave defiles only those standing on solid ground above it, but not those separated from it by empty space.) On their way to the ritual of drawing water from the Siloah for the ritual of cleansing, the boys were seated on broad boards, effectively protecting them from contamination from any forgotten grave over which they might pass (loc. cit.). The cups in which they drew the water from the Siloah were of stone, impervious to Levitical defilement (loc. cit.). Complicated arrangements were made for them (if necessary) to draw the water without leaving the boards on which they were riding (loc. cit.). Similarly, very complicated arrangements were made when they were required to put the ashes of earlier burnt heifers in the water, to purify the priest about to officiate at the ceremony of the red heifer (Mishna Parah 3.3).

The Temple, its courts, the surrounding area, and the place where the heifer was burned on the Mount of Olives were all built over open caves, lest a forgotten grave be situated in the solid earth (ibid. 3.3).

Assigned to officiate at the ritual of the red heifer, the priest (usually the High Priest) kept within the Temple precincts was not touched by any fellow-priest during the week of preparation, presumably lest any of them had suffered a flow without being purified.

The priest, about to burn the red heifer, walked to the Mount of Olives on a wooden bridge, supported by a series of complicated arches, so that at no time was there solid ground between him and the earth below (ibid. 3.6), lest he be contaminated through passing over solid earth containing a forgotten grave.

(It is interesting that no provision was made to purify the priest from possible contamination through a flow which had been cured. Nor was such purification required of the

High Priest even in preparation for the Day of Atonement. Apparently it was the view of the early Hasideans that the *zab* [like the *zabah*] became pure at nightfall after his immersion in water; and that his purity did not depend on the sacrifices offered on his behalf. This view seems to have been preserved by the School of Hillel in later times, as will be observed below, pp. 677 ff.

The members of the secular community could not avoid contact with persons themselves "impure" in a severe degree, or with vessels which had been in the house of the dead. Marital congress itself ritually defiled both the men of the secular community and their wives. If, adopting the Sadducean view, they could not consider themselves "clean" until the following evening, virtually all their lives would be spent in impurity; and the biblical ideal of a community observing the laws of purity would remain unfulfilled.

The letter and spirit of the Law seem, in this instance as in others, entirely on the side of the Pharisees. It is true that the expression "and he shall be impure until evening" is used by Scripture in a number of connections. The rule applied to one touching the carcass of creeping things (Lev. 11.24); or that of a beast (ibid. v. 27) or one carrying them (ibid. v. 28; cf. further ibid. vv. 39,40). Similarly anyone touching a *zab* (a person afflicted with a flow) or sitting in his chair or touching his bed (Lev. 15.5,6,7) or touching the bed of a woman afflicted with a flow, or her chair (ibid. v. 27), or touching the bed or chair of a menstruating woman (ibid. v. 20), as well as a man and woman engaged in marital intercourse (ibid. v. 18), or a man suffering a seminal issue (ibid. v. 18), and likewise vessels in contact with the carcass of an animal (ibid. v. 32) were all "impure" until evening, even after the ritual of immersion. But Scripture does not explain wherein this impurity consists. Was such a person defiled so that even after bathing he contaminated others and might not enter Temple courts, or did his impurity simply bar him from holy meats?

Various passages indicate that the "impurity" until evening, discussed in these contexts, refers only to eating sacrificial meat.

Thus we are told that a person with a flow is to be impure even after his cure for seven days, but immediately after immersion (presumably on the seventh day) he is declared "pure" (Lev. 15.13). Likewise a leper, healed of his disease, while required to remain outside his tent for seven days (Lev. 14.8) refraining from cohabitation, is specifically declared "pure" (ibid.).

Presumably, the ritual "purity" of the *zab* after bathing, and of the healed leper after the initial ceremonies of purification, freed them from the possibility of communicating impurity to others or to things, and therefore permitted them to come into the camp, whence the diseased leper and *zab* were barred (according to Numbers 5.2 ff.). As no distinction was made between priest and other Israelite in this connection, it must be assumed that the priest did not, according to early Hasidean law, contaminate the heave-offering during this period; and as nothing is said about any prohibition to enter the Temple courts, the cured leper (having undergone his preliminary rites of purification) and the healed *zab* (having bathed) might enter them.

In the passages discussing the purification of the woman afflicted with a flow (the *zabah*) or the menstruating woman, nothing is said in Scripture about ritual immersion. But doubtless the rules applying to the *zab* applied also to them. The *zabah* was declared impure for seven days after her cure, the menstruating woman for seven days after the beginning of her period. But doubtless in both instances this "impurity" simply prohibited the women from cohabitation during that period. If they bathed on the seventh day, their status was equivalent to that of the *zab* after his ritual immersion, and to the healed leper after his preliminary rites of purification.

Nothing was said barring the healed leper, the *zab* or the *zabah*, or the menstruating woman, after the rites of their purification, from the Temple courts, or from use of the heave-offering, although they were specifically prohibited from eating the sacrificial meat (Lev. 22.7 ff.). Indeed, this specific prohibition suggested that they were not otherwise impure, and were particularly not prohibited from eating the heave-offering or entering the Temple courts. Only the woman after childbirth might not enter the Temple, even during her "purification," and even if she had undergone immersion (Lev. 12.4).

(We may assume that the special regulation for the woman after childbirth was intended to protect the overzealous from prematurely undertaking the journey to the Sanctuary, a consideration not applying to any of the other instances mentioned.)

Two significant passages confirm this interpretation of the Scriptural verses. In the discussion of the status of persons engaged in the ceremony of the red heifer, we are told that they were defiled until evening (Num. 19.7, 8, 10). On the other hand, the person taking the scape-goat to the Wilderness on the Day of Atonement and the priest who burned the special sacrifice of atonement on that day, were ordered only to wash their clothes and their bodies, and immediately afterward were declared "pure." No mention was made of defilement until evening regarding them (Lev. 16.28).

The difference in the text suggested that the norms declaring a person impure until nightfall dealt only with the consuming of the sacrificial meat. Because the Day of Atonement is a fast day there was no need to prohibit the defiled person from eating holy meats after his ritual bath.

The Proto-Pharisees and the Pharisees could therefore rightly hold that whenever the word "impure" was used for persons who had bathed after defilement, whether on the day of their contact with impurity for minor cases, or on the seventh day for major impurities, the prohibition applied only to eating sacrificial meats. The *tebul yom* might enter the Temple courts or eat the heave-offering.

The right of the *tebul yom* to consume the tithe did not reflect on its holiness. The Second Tithe had in this regard the same status as the heave-offering. It could be eaten by anyone including the *tebul yom.*

The Proto-Sadducean and Sadducean rejection of this exegesis, while apparently an example of stringency, actually came from a denial of the application of norms of purity to secular life.

The Pharisees insisted that the High Priest about to participate in the sacrifice of the red heifer become defiled, and then bathe. He would thus be a *tebul yom.* In officiating at the sacrifice afterward, he proclaimed the validity of the Pharisaic thesis. Presumably this refinement of the argument developed only in Maccabean times. Earlier, the Proto-Pharisees could hardly have compelled the High Priest to follow their dictates. But the underlying issue was far more ancient. Like the other controversies it was pre-Maccabean; and perhaps even pre-exilic in origin.

The Pharisaic concept of the *tebul yom* is sufficiently discussed in this book. But the Sadducean opposition to it remains unexplained. Why did they and their predecessors oppose the Pharisaic concept, well rooted in Scripture? Why were they inflexible on this issue?

The Proto-Sadducean and Sadducean view derived from several considerations. Of these perhaps the most important was the great inconvenience caused the priests through the suspicion that they violated the biblical laws of purity.

In general, Levitical purity of an individual could be established only on faith, because Levitical impurity could be caused through private circumstances, such as conjugal intercourse. However, in the case of a priest, such defilement involved public interests. A priest having had marital relations with his wife during the night was forbidden to enter the Temple until he became pure.[61] The sacrificial food he touched became unfit either for him or his fellow-priests.

If he violated the laws separating him from his wife during her menstrual period, he was defiled for seven days.[62] If he touched a corpse he was defiled for seven days. To avoid violation of these norms by High Priests, the Proto-Pharisees compelled them to dwell in the Temple precincts for the week preceding the Day of Atonement.[63] Similar arrangements were made for the priest about to officiate at the ceremony of the red heifer, Mishna Parah, 3.1.) It was impractical to impose such arrangements on all officiating priests.

Various theories had to be developed to reassure the people regarding the possible defilement of the sacrifices by "impure" priests. One was that Levitical defilement did not invalidate community sacrifices.[64] (This rule did not, of course, prevent the Pharisees from doing their utmost to see that the priests offering public sacrifices were "pure." Sacrifices should be offered by qualified priests;[65] but public offerings were not invalidated through the impurity of the priesthood.)

Another norm declared that the blood sprinkled on the altar, though defiled, did not disqualify the sacrifice even of a private person. The "plate" worn by the High Priest on his forehead "atoned" for this type of impurity.[66] Thus, if the vessel in which the blood was received to be carried to the altar had been defiled by an "impure" priest touching it, the sacrifice was still valid. R. Eliezer held that even if the meats to be eaten by the priests or the persons offering the sacrifices became contaminated, that did not invalidate the sacrifice.[67] The blood might be sprinkled as though the meat were pure. R. Joshua held that under the circumstances the blood should not be sprinkled on the altar, but if it had been sprinkled the sacrifice was valid. R. Eliezer in this instance, as so frequently, transmitted Temple traditions. The conscientious priest, about to sprinkle the blood on the altar, did not have to worry lest one of his less meticulous fellows, touching the meat of the sacrifice, had contaminated it.

Even if the portions of the animal to be offered on the altar (and in the case of a whole-burnt offering, this included of course the meat of the whole beast) were contaminated, once they had been taken to the altar for sacrifice, the ceremony could be completed and was valid.[68] Moreover, a priest defiled through contact with the dead did not disqualify the sacrifice he offered, unless his defilement was known.[69] Indeed, his own knowledge of his defilement did not disqualify the offering. His impure state had to be known also to others before a sacrifice could be declared invalid.[70] (The major concern of the pious was lest the priest, like the *'am ha-arez*, might fail to observe the rule of purity requiring him to avoid contact with a corpse or visit to a cemetery; and if he did, to undergo the complex ritual of purification, described in Numbers, chapter 19. There was less concern lest the priest violate the other laws of purity; for they were heeded even by the *'am ha-arez.*)

Despite all these leniencies, the Proto-Pharisees sought to lessen the possibility of defilement of the priests officiating at the Sanctuary. The Proto-Pharisees were concerned not only about the priest whose piety resembled that of the *'am ha-arez*; they had to consider also the apostate, heretical, and cynical priests, who observed none of the laws of purity. How real these problems were, is illustrated by the doubtless authentic record of a priest, who, although uncircumcised, participated in the ceremonies of the purification of the "impure" through sprinkling on them the waters containing the ashes of the red heifer (Yer. Nazir 8.1, 57a). The Rabbis decided that such "purification" was valid. Nevertheless, anyone conversant with the general attitude of the Talmud toward Jews violating the Covenant of Abraham will readily appreciate how painful and difficult this decision must have been. According to the norms just mentioned, sacrifices offered by priests, wittingly violating the laws of purity (in some regard other than the impurity deriving from contact with a corpse), were invalid. To meet these difficulties, at least in part, the Proto-Pharisees required anyone about to perform any act of worship in the Temple to bathe, even if known to be pure.[71] It was hoped that at the barest minimum this requirement would remind of his impurity a defiled priest who had contracted minor impurity lasting only one day.[72]

Apparently even if he were to enter the Temple courts as a *tebul yom*, the priest — recalling his impurity and therefore intending to be purified — according to early Pharisaic theory would not invalidate the sacrifices.[73] This seems to be the correct explanation of the peculiar formulation of Mishna Zebahim 2.1, whose present form has so vexed the commentators. It reads:

> "Any sacrifice, the blood of which has been collected by a non-priest, a bereaved priest before the burial of his dead, a *tebul yom*, a priest not wearing the priestly garments, a priest under obligation to offer a sacrifice of purification [like a healed leper or one healed from a flow], or who has not washed his hands and feet, or who is uncircumcised, *or defiled*, or who is sitting down, or who is standing on material other than the Temple ground itself, including an animal, or the feet of his colleague, is invalidated."

It seems strange that the *tebul yom* should be mentioned apart from one more severely defiled (that is, one who had not bathed) and long before him. Probably the most ancient text of the Mishna made no reference either to the *tebul yom* or the priest required to offer a sacrifice of purification. As already observed, nowhere in Scripture is there any hint that sacrifice offered by such a priest was invalid. And, in fact, in the final generation of the *tannaim* R. Simai encountered difficulty in finding an argument justifying this norm (Sanhedrin 83b).

Nor does it seem to have been the view of the early Hasideans that a *tebul yom* defiled sacrificial meats through contact with them. That is why in the discussion of what is to be done about meats defiled through contact with an impure person, the Mishna, like the Sifra, discusses only meats defiled through a primary source of impurity or a secondary one, but omits all reference, either in the words of the School of Shammai or in those of the School of Hillel, to sacred meat contaminated through contact with a *tebul yom*, or with one still under obligation to offer a sacrifice of purification (like a cured *zab* or leper: cf. Mishna Shekalim 8.6; Sifra, *Zav*, *perek* 8.6, 33b). So also R. Hanina, the associate of the High Priest, discussed (Mishna Pesahim 1.6) only the question whether one might burn the sacrificial meat defiled in a primary degree with that defiled in a secondary degree. But he made no mention of meat contaminated through a *tebul yom*, as did R. Akiba in a later generation. This early Pharisaic concept was not only opposed by contemporary Sadducism, but repudiated in later times by many Pharisees themselves. In their endeavor to prevent the priest in the status of *tebul yom* from eating or touching the heave-offering, some later Pharisaic scholars ultimately declared him no less impure than had the Sadducees of an earlier age. The change in Pharisaic outlook led to great confusion both in talmudic texts and in their interpretation.

As a result of this change in the Pharisaic attitude toward the *tebul yom*, such great authorities as Maimonides and his critic, Rabbi Abraham B. David, disagreed regarding the talmudic law on the subject. There was a similar disagreement between Rashi and some of his critics, the authors of the *Tosafot*. The contradictory interpretations of the Talmud apparently had their source in its ambiguity, which, in this instance, arose from difference of opinion between early and later Rabbinic scholars.

This difference is obvious from a study of various talmudic texts. Thus, Mishna Parah 11.4 reads: "Anyone required by Scriptural law to bathe [after impurity], defiles the sacred meat and the heave-offering as well as profane food and the tithe and is forbidden to enter the Temple precincts [until he has bathed]. After immersion, he continues to *defile* the holy meat and the heave-offering, according to R. Meir; whereas the other sages say that he *invalidates* the holy meat but may eat profane food and the tithes. *If he enters the Temple whether before or after immersion, he is guilty.*"

The final norm which has troubled all the commentators is irreconcilable with the opening statement, forbidding entry into the Temple courts only before ritual immersion, and not afterward. Nor does the opening passage of the Mishna impute "guilt" to all such persons. According to many scholars, some "defiled" persons, while forbidden to enter the Temple courts, incur no guilt in doing so.[73a]

Presumably, the opening passage of the Mishna reflected the earliest Hasidean and Pharisaic position. According to it, one required to undergo a ritual bath defiled the sacred meat and the heave-offering, and might not enter the Temple. The clear implication seems to be that after immersion he would not defile the sacred meat (although forbidden to eat it), nor the heave-offering, and might enter the Temple.

The second part of the Mishna preserves the view of R. Meir who, adopting the views of his teacher, R. Akiba, held that a *tebul yom* did defile the sacred meats and the heave-offering. R. Meir's colleagues agreed that a *tebul yom* defiled the sacred meats, but denied that he defiled the heave-offering. (This follows the reading of most manuscripts and early editions. In later editions, the words "and the heave-offering" were inserted even in the statement of R. Meir's colleagues.)

The final passage of the Mishna declaring one deserving death or requiring a sacrifice of atonement, if he entered the Temple even after immersion, clearly derives from the

School of R. Akiba, who did not distinguish the *tebul yom* from the *tamé*.

Sifra, too, transmits views like those of the early Mishna. Enumerating those required to offer a sacrifice for entry into the Temple during impurity, Sifra mentions those who having passed the period of "severe" defilement (as when suffering a flow) are in their "lenient" period (still defiled, but no longer ill).[74] It says nothing about the *tebul yom*, implying that according to the most severe interpretation of the Law the *tebul yom* who entered the Temple needed to offer no sacrifice of atonement.[75]

In Sifre Numbers 125, p. 161, the issue is the subject of a controversy between disciples of R. Ishmael.

The Mishna itself records the change in the views of the Pharisees in regard to the *tebul yom*. It reads: "Originally, a woman, in the days of purity [after childbirth, when she has the status of *tebul yom*] was permitted to pour water over the paschal lamb [without defiling it]. Later the School of Shammai put her in the same class with one who has had contact with a corpse."[76]

The norm of the early Hasideans, requiring every priest about to enter the Temple for worship to bathe, prevented according to their views infraction of the Law. Later Pharisees, particularly of the School of R. Akiba, rejecting the earlier concepts, found difficulty in reconciling this norm with their own positions, just as it was irreconcilable with those of the Sadducees.[77] Nevertheless, once formulated by R. Akiba and his School, the norm was insisted upon by all scholars.

Such importance was attached by the Pharisees to immersion before worship that they compelled the High Priest to bathe five times on the Day of Atonement, once before each of the main acts of worship he performed.[78] The Testaments of the Twelve Patriarchs (T. Levi 9.11) mention immersion immediately before entering the Temple, and it seems to be required also by Jubilees 21.16.

The requirement to bathe before entering the Temple to worship worked hardship, for the priests, some elderly or ill, found immersion in a cold pool in winter months trying. But beyond that, the suspicion implicit in the norm made it objectionable. Even those guilty of the negligence imputed to them by the Proto-Pharisees must have resented the implications.

Hence the Sadducean insistence that nothing was gained through this ritual. The *tebul yom* was not a whit less defiled after the ritual bathing than before; there was no point to the requirement imposed by the Proto-Pharisees.

However, another consideration may have entered into the Sadducean attitude toward the *tebul yom*. This concerned the authority of the priests over the heave-offering and other portions, given them outside the Temple. The priests naturally claimed that the heave-offering had virtually the same status as the sacrificial meat. And therefore, just as they would brook no interference of lay authorities in regard to the ritual of the Temple, they claimed the right to decide all questions arising in regard to the other priestly emoluments. The Hasideans held that the priestly authority was limited to the Temple, and indeed was questionable even there. They certainly would not grant the right of the priests to determine questions bearing on priestly portions, like the heave-offering, given them outside the Temple.

If the claim of the priests to authority over the heave-offering was accepted, it would — like other holy meat — be forbidden for use as food by the *tebul yom*. If it were not really holy meat, but in a class by itself, the Hasideans might be justified in their claim that it could be eaten by the *tebul yom*.

It seems probable that the issue of the holiness of the heave-offering and of the priestly authority regarding it was one on which virtually the whole Aaronid clan was in agreement. Hence, when after the Hasmonean rebellion (or even before their time, during the High Priesthood of Simeon the Righteous) the Hasidean group came to include many Aaronid priests, division arose regarding the issue of the *tebul yom*, so far as the heave-offering was concerned.

No controversy arose within Pharisaism regarding the ritual of the red heifer, for the Hasidean view had in that respect crystallized in earlier centuries. The preparation of the red heifer was a public act; and the Pharisaic and Proto-Pharisaic authorities had forcefully presented their views to early generations of priests, opposing the doctrine that the *tebul yom* was impure. Likewise, no controversy arose within Pharisaism with regard to the requirement that any priest, about to enter the Temple for the purpose of worship, had to bathe. The right to decide which priests might enter the Temple for worship was one with which the Hasidean courts had dealt for generations, as will be seen below, pp. 726 ff. The insistence of the Hasideans that particular priests could not enter the Temple, effectively barred them from its precincts, but permission given by them to priests to offer sacrifices could be overruled by the priestly authorities.

Thus the priest who was a *tebul yom*, while permitted to participate in worship according to early Hasidean law, was barred from the Temple by his fellow-Aaronids. On the other hand, the priest who regarded himself as "pure," was barred from the Temple by the Pharisees and their predecessors, unless he underwent immersion and became (if he had been impure) at least a *tebul yom*.

Whether a particular priest ate the heave-offering as a *tebul yom* was a question he decided for himself. If, following his tribal tradition, he held that as a *tebul yom* he might not eat the heave-offering, no Hasidean authority could compel him to do so.

Within the Temple itself, the rules regarding the *tebul yom* were, of course, determined by the Aaronids themselves. Thus, if a priest, during his term of service at the Temple and residing in its outer precincts, suffered a nocturnal emission, he was required by his fellow-Aaronids to desist from worship that day, even after he had bathed (Mishna Tamid 1.1; Middot 1.9).

On two recorded occasions, High Priests who found themselves defiled on the Day of Atonement were replaced by others; although apparently according to Hasidean tradition the defilement of the High Priests might have been removed by ritual baths (see Tosefta Yom ha-Kippurim 1.4, ed. Lieberman II, p. 221; and Abot of R. Nathan, I, chap. 35, 53a).

Obviously no Hasidean court could compel a priest to perform an act of worship for which he felt himself unfitted. The Hasideans and the Pharisees would therefore not interfere with the Temple rule requiring a *tebul yom* to desist from participation in the service.

Perhaps special significance attached to the question of the authority of priests over the heave-offering, because that question also involved their right to regulate and administer the giving of the tithes. This was because the Levites were required by the Law (Num. 18.28) to separate a tithe from their tithe, for the benefit of the priests. This tithe of the tithe had the same ritual status as the heave-offering. If the jurisdiction over the heave-offering were in the hands of the priests, so was that over the tithe given by the Levitical tithe, and therefore over the tithe itself. If not, the latter was under the jurisdiction of lay authorities.

That the question of the authority of the priesthood over the heave-offering was in fact a subject of discussion within Pharisaism itself seems evident from Sifre Zutta, Num. 18.7, p. 292. The passage discusses the verse, "And thou and thy sons with thee shall keep your priesthood in everything that pertaineth to the altar, and to that within the veil" (Num. 18.7). Sifre Zutta remarks: "This verse teaches that the responsibility for transgression in regard to sacrifices is given over *only* to the priests. One might suppose that this rule applies only to the most holy sacrifices [such as the whole-burnt offering, the sin offering, etc.]. How do we know that it applies also to the lighter sacrifices [such as the peace offering]? One might suppose that the rule applies only to the parts of these lighter sacrifices that are eaten. Whence do we know that it applies also to those parts that are not eaten [but are consumed on the altar]? Therefore Scripture says, 'in everything that pertaineth to the altar.' We might then presume that the rule applies also to the heave-offering, the priestly share of the tithe, and the portions separated from the loaves (according to Num. 15.20). Therefore Scripture adds, 'And to that within the veil.' Just as the community cannot know what happens within the veil, so the rest of the verse deals only with what the community cannot know about (and therefore cannot control)."

The exclusion of the heave-offering and similar priestly contributions from the rule announced in this verse is the more remarkable as, according to both Sifre (Num. 116, p. 133) and Sifre Zutta (loc. cit.), the rest of the passage deals precisely with those gifts.

It seems clear that the argument in Sifre Zutta was intended to counter an opposing view — that of the Shammaitic priests — who demanded the authority and claimed the responsibility for collection of the heave-offering and its supervision.

It is indeed a plausible conjecture that in the early Shammaitic Midrash to the Book of Numbers from which Sifre Zutta ultimately derives, the whole passage was held to refer to the heave-offering no less than to the sacrificial meats. Sifre (loc. cit.) holds that the first part of the verse dealing with the altar and the veil simply establishes the right of the priests themselves to determine who was a priest. (While Sifre Numbers in its present form derives from the School of R. Ishmael, and generally follows the views of the School of Hillel, it can be shown that in a very early form, it, like the other tannaitic Midrashim, was composed by Proto-Shammaitic scholars, and came to R. Ishmael from R. Nehunyah b. Hakkanah, a great Shammaitic sage of the final generation of the Second Temple. See my discussion of his views in *Mabo*, pp. 54 ff.)

Indeed, such was the claim of the priesthood to responsibility for the heave-offering, as well as to rights over it, that early priestly authorities (presumably the Hasmonean High Priests) refused to permit pilgrims from other lands to bring *hallah* (which had the same ritual status as the heave-offering) to the Holy Land (Mishna Hallah 4.10. For the early date of this section of the Mishna, see J. N. Epstein, *Mabo le-Sifrut ha-Tannaim*, p. 273.) The reason for this refusal, to accept priestly offerings brought to the Holy Land from the Diaspora, is of great interest. R. Hoshaya explains that had offerings been accepted, priests feeling responsible for the execution of the law requiring separation of the priestly portions would be lured to leave the Holy Land to collect these contributions (Yer. Shebi'it, chap. 6, end; cf. Professor Saul Lieberman in *Tosefta Ki-Fshutah*, Shebi'it, p. 547).

The Court of Priests could exercise its authority in the Land of Israel. Outside the Land the responsibility, it might be felt, devolved on individual priests. No such sense of responsibility would be felt at all, unless it was considered the *duty* of the priesthood to collect the gifts of the heave-offering.

The many controversies between the Schools of Shammai and Hillel in the Mishnaic treatise, *Tebul Yom*, become intelligible once we appreciate that the Shammaites considered the *tebul yom tamé*, and the School of Hillel did not. It would take us too far afield to discuss the individual norms of that treatise in detail here. The Talmud tries to interpret the differences otherwise, in order to reconcile the views of the School of Hillel with those later promulgated by R. Akiba, who held that the *tebul yom* was *tamé*.

Thus the Shammaites preserved the tradition of the Pharisaic priests that the *tebul yom*, while *tahor* ("pure") in regard to the red heifer (following the norm set down by the ancient Hasidean authorities), was *tamé* ("impure") in regard to the heave-offering. Yet even the Shammaites did not declare the *tebul yom* forbidden to enter the Temple courts, or even to participate in sacrificial ceremonies. That is why the discussion in Sifra, *Hobah*, *perek* 12.1, 22d, emanating from "the ancient elders" who were in fact the Shammaites (see Yer. Gittin and *Mabo*, p. 23) made no reference to the *tebul yom* as obliged to offer a sacrifice for entry into the Temple.

Thus the Shammaites like the Hillelites and the predecessors of both Schools, could rightly demand that any priest, about to enter the Temple for worship, bathe.

However, in their apprehension lest a priest eat the heave-offering while in the status of *tebul yom* (a procedure they considered forbidden), the Shammaites declared the heave-offering touched by him unfit to be eaten. They succeeded in obtaining general consent to this extension of the Law during the Conclave, held under their guidance in preparation for the Great Rebellion against Rome (Mishna Zabim, end, and see above p. 678).

This drastic action was necessary precisely because the Hillelites held that the *tebul yom* could eat the heave-offering. This view of the Hillelites seems to have prevailed even in the time of R. Joshua b. Hananya, according to whom priests "were purified to eat the heave-offering as soon as they had bathed" (B. Berakot 2b). The expression "from the time when the priests are permitted to eat the heave-offering," in Tosefta Berakot 1.1, ed. Lieberman, p. 1, suggests (according to Professor Saul Lieberman, *Tosefta Ki-Fshutah*, beginning) that many priests, following the Hillelite view, actually consumed the heave-offering while still in the condition of *tebul yom*, i.e., before nightfall.

Following the views of the School of Hillel and particularly R. Joshua, R. Ishmael and his School insisted that the *tebul yom* was in fact "pure." According to this view, the ancient Pharisaic requirement, that everyone about to enter the Temple for worship must bathe, was quite intelligible. Even if such a person was defiled, the ritual bath would make him a *tebul yom*, and therefore would permit him to enter the Temple courts and participate in worship. The position of this School is clarified in several comments preserved in Sifre

Numbers. Thus in Sifre Numbers 125, p. 161, the issue of the *tebul yom* apparently became the basis of argument between disciples of R. Ishmael. According to R. Josiah, the purpose of the emphatic assertion of Numbers 19.13, "He shall be unclean; his uncleanness is yet upon him," was to suggest that all defiled persons (and not merely those defiled by contact with a corpse) were barred from the Temple. R. Josiah did not mention the *tebul yom* who thus appears, according to him, to be subject to no punishment for entering the Temple and might even be permitted to do so. R. Jonathan, his colleague, who frequently reflected the influence of the School of R. Akiba, maintained that the emphasis was intended to cover the case of the *tebul yom*.

According to the School of R. Akiba itself, not only the *tebul yom*, but also one required to offer a sacrifice of purification (such as a leper or a person afflicted with a flow and cured of the disease, or a woman after childbirth) was barred from the Temple until the sacrifice had been offered (B. Makkot 8b).

R. Josiah's view coincided with that of R. Ishmael himself. Holding that a *tebul yom* was included under the term "pure" (as the early Hasideans had maintained), R. Ishmael sought no further evidence in Scripture to prove that a *tebul yom* might participate in the ceremony of the red heifer. The use of the word *tahor* describing the participants indicated this norm, he held. R. Akiba, maintaining apparently that a *tebul yom* could not really be called *tahor*, found support for the early Pharisaic view regarding the red heifer in the following argument. Scripture used the word *tahor* both in describing the man gathering up the ashes of the heifer (Num. 19.9) and in describing the one sprinkling the water of purification (ibid. v. 18). This repeated emphasis was taken by R. Akiba, in accordance with a general talmudic rule of exegesis, to suggest that even one not absolutely pure, but who could possibly be included in the category of "pure," qualified for the ritual (Sifre, Num. 129, p. 166; cf. ibid., 124, p. 157, where various commentators suggest the text should be emended).

Thus, while R. Akiba held that a *tebul yom* was not really *tahor*, but in a certain degree *tamé*, R. Ishmael and his disciple, R. Josiah, retained the attitude of early Hasideanism.

We may be sure that the Proto-Sadducean and Sadducean priests were no less concerned about the priestly prerogative outside the Temple, than were the priestly Shammaites. Hence, we must assume that the Sadducees and their predecessors considered a *tebul yom* forbidden to eat the heave-offering, precisely as a defiled person might be; for in their view, as in that of the Shammaites, the heave-offering had the ritual status of sacrificial meat.

R. Tarfon, sharing the general Hillelite view, would say when he ate the heave-offering, "I have performed an act of worship." It is noteworthy that he did not say, "I have eaten sacred food." This was because he would eat the heave-offering both in the morning and in the evening (Sifre Zutta 18.7, p. 293), holding that while a *tebul yom* might eat the heave-offering, he might not eat the sacred meat.

We have observed that the practice of the Temple priests, barring the *tebul yom* from the Temple courts and from any act of worship, was in fact associated with the priestly tradition, holding him *tamé*, and was inconsistent with the original Hasidean view which declared him *tahor*. Mishna Tamid simply records what happened at the Temple, without entering into the question of whose views were implemented in particular decisions. Mishna Middot likewise is a faithful record of Temple procedure. Moreover, both treatises emanated from priestly Shammaitic authors quite in sympathy with the traditions followed in the Temple.

We have also observed that these traditions, opposed by the early Hasideans, and later — after the organization of Pharisaism — by the Proto-Hillelites and Hillelites within it, were logically associated with the doctrine rejected by the Pharisees forbidding a *tebul yom* to participate in the ceremony of the red heifer.

R. Akiba, in his effort to reduce the whole tradition to logical consistency, could not accept this approach. He could not agree that the Temple authorities conducted its affairs in violation of the Hasidean tradition; nor that the priestly tradition, recorded in Mishna Tamid and Middot, opposed that of the Pharisees.

Moreover, living a generation after the destruction of the Temple, when the issues arising from the possibility that defiled priests might officiate had long ceased to be relevant, R. Akiba no longer interpreted as an effort to deal with possible defilement the requirement that a priest, entering the Temple for the purposes of worship, should bathe. On the other hand, R. Akiba doubtless thought it necessary to stress the holiness of the heave-offering as sacred meat, so as to be sure that every Jew would give the appropriate portions to the priests. To overcome any reluctance on the part of the people to do so, because the priests no longer could perform their function as ministers at the altar, R. Akiba insisted that the heave-offering was virtually as sacred as the sacrificial meats had been. Therefore, except for the now purely theoretical issue of the red heifer, he reverted to the position taken by the Sadducees in a much earlier period, namely, that the *tebul yom* was "impure." According to R. Akiba, a *tebul yom* touching the heave-offering defiled it according to *biblical Law*, and was likewise forbidden to eat it according to that Law.

Sifra, following the views of R. Akiba, interpreted the passage in Leviticus 22.4 ff. dealing with sacrificial meats as applying also to the heave-offering (Sifra, *Emor*, *perek* 4, 97c). Most of R. Akiba's disciples adopted his views. The preservation of their assertions, together with the earlier norms of the Schools of Shammai and Hillel, introduced many complexities into Rabbinic *halakah* which later *amoraim* struggled vainly to resolve.

The Babylonian Talmud, adopting R. Akiba's view that the *tebul yom* defiled the heave-offering according to biblical Law, was forced to emend the text of Mishna Zabim, quoted above, through the elimination of the reference to the *tebul yom* (see B. Shabbat 14b). The Talmud of Jerusalem held that the norm is of Rabbinical origin (See J. N. Epstein, *Mabo le-Nusah ha-Mishna*, p. 592; Professor Saul Lieberman, *Ha-Yerushalmi Ki-Fshutah*, p. 39).

However, in view of the categorical assertion of Mishna Parah 11.4, in its present form, no question was raised in either Talmud as to the right of the *tebul yom* to enter the Temple courts. Likewise Mishna Zebahim, 2.1, in its present form, left no room for doubt that the *tebul yom* invalidated any sacrifice in which he participated. Both of these passages, however, in their present formulation follow the view of R. Akiba. As we have seen, the earlier text, which can still be discerned, held an opposing view, emanating from the early Hasideans.

The Sadducee could not effectively resist the demand of the Pharisees (or their predecessors) for ritual bathing before entering the Temple. But he was glad to discover a ceremonial in which his views of purity proved more rigorous than those of the Pharisees. On the other hand, the Pharisees strove to validate their views through the emphasis given in connection with the ceremonies of the red heifer.

The norm formulated by the Proto-Pharisees, declaring that the red heifer might be sacrificed by a *tebul yom*, and that a *tebul yom* might cleanse an impure person by sprinkling the purifying waters on him, was preserved, even after the Pharisaic attitude toward the *tebul yom* had become much more rigorous.

Holding, on the one hand, that the *tebul yom* was *tamé* and relying on priests who knew of their defilement not to enter the Temple courts for worship; while, on the other hand, accepting the ancient Hasidean rule that all priests entering the Temple for worship were required to bathe, the Shammaitic priests seem to have developed a curious theory to explain the apparent paradox. They held that the clothes of an *'am ha-arez*, even if immersed, defiled one accustomed to living in purity outside the Temple, namely, the Pharisee. The clothes of the Pharisee, even if purified, they said, likewise defiled a priest who ate the heave-offering. The clothes of priests who underwent immersion so as to partake of the heave-offering, also even if immersed, were not sufficiently pure to enable them to eat the holy meats. Those permitted to eat the holy meats required a special immersion to participate in the ritual of the red heifer.

The Mishna records simply that anyone knowingly sitting on garments of a person Levitically "pure" as indicated, but to a lesser degree than needed for the state one desired to enter, had to bathe and wait until evening until he could consider himself "pure." Presumably, this record which places the priests above the Pharisees emanates from priestly sources.

Moreover, a priest, bathing with the thought that he would eat the heave-offering, was still impure so far as the holy meats were concerned. One who had bathed to partake of the holy meats was still disqualified from participating in the ceremonies of the red heifer. Each higher degree of care required immersion, intended to remove impurity in regard to it (Mishna Hagiga 2.6-7).

However, it was agreed that these special immersions were not required biblically. While therefore a person knowing that he should undergo them, and having failed to do so, was barred from participating in the rituals for which he was unprepared, his failure did not disqualify the service. Thus, a priest about to enter the Temple to worship could be required to bathe, lest he might have sat on the clothes of a Pharisee, or his own secular clothes, even if he had bathed thereafter without intent to enter the Temple. His defilement, not stemming from Scriptural Law, would be removed sufficiently to prevent him from defiling the sacrifices.

The age of these rules, and the theory underlying them, seems fixed by the record which states that "José ben Joezer was a *hasid* among the priests. Yet his clothes [after immersion to eat the heave-offering] were considered defiling for those about to eat the holy meats" (Mishna, ibid.). The date of José ben Joezer is known; he was a contemporary of Judah the Maccabee. It thus appears that the Hasmoneans adopted the Hasidean norm as required for all priests, but provided reasons for them, which could hardly have stemmed from the Proto-Pharisees.

Furthermore, accepting the Hasidean norm that the priest

about to officiate at the ritual of the red heifer had to be defiled, and then purified through immersion, the Hasmoneans nevertheless sought to protect him from any other type of impurity, no matter how theoretical. Hence, their rule that even priests permitted to participate in the sacrifices and to eat holy meats might be "defiled" so far as the ritual of the red heifer was concerned.

Perhaps nothing can show more clearly the untenability of Geiger's general thesis concerning the "Old Halakah" and the "New Halakah" than this development. According to him, Sadducean norms belonged to the "Old Halakah," and the Pharisaic norms belonged to the "New Halakah."[79] In the same way, he insisted that within Pharisaism there was a continuous trend toward a New Halakah which carried further the ideas developed in the original Pharisaic norms. Yet in regard to the *tebul yom*, it is demonstrable that the later trend within Pharisaism was not toward greater leniency for the *tebul yom*, but toward greater severity.

5. The Meal-Offerings and Libations Accompanying Animal Sacrifice

According to Leviticus 6.9 ff., meal-offerings could be eaten by priests after a handful had been offered on the altar.[80] (This rule did not apply to meal-offerings of the priests themselves.)[81] The question arose whether the meal-offering required along with animal sacrifices might likewise be eaten after an appropriate portion had been sacrificed on the altar. Presumably the argument dealt only with the meal-offerings brought with "peace-offerings," when the meat was eaten by the priests, after appropriate portions were sacrificed. It is improbable that the priests demanded for themselves meal-offerings accompanying whole-burnt offerings.

The early priests demanded the right to eat these meal-offerings like any other. The Proto-Pharisees, perhaps even in Prophetic times, resisted this claim; for Scripture (Num. 15.4 ff.) seems specifically to imply that whether the animal sacrifice is a whole-burnt offering or a peace-offering, the accompanying sacrifice of meal and wine must be offered on the altar itself.

The priests could of course present an argument in favor of their view. The libations, offered with the sacrifices, are specifically described as "a sweet savor unto the Lord" (ibid., 15.7, 10). The question is whether the phrase, following immediately after the mention of the libations, refers to them alone, or also to the meal-offering, described before the libations. Perhaps the issue may have arisen as to whether the words describing the meal-offering, "then shall he that bringeth his offering *present unto the Lord* a meal-offering," can possibly refer to one that is given the priests, as representatives and agents of the Lord. Doubtless the priests could maintain the position that while the libations of wine were forbidden to them, because they could not drink wine at all during their period of service at the Temple (Lev. 10.8 ff.), no such injunction applied to meal-offerings accompanying meat sacrifices, the rules regarding which ought not (in their opinion) to differ from those applying to all other meal-offerings, not brought by priests.

The argument seemed specious to the Proto-Pharisees, for it seemed far more natural to them to interpret the expression, "sweet savor unto the Lord," as referring to all the sacrifices accompanying the meat-offerings.

6. The Impurity of Metals

Although metalware is not specifically mentioned in discussion of the norms of impurity in Leviticus,[82] there can be little doubt that the Pharisees were correct in holding that under Scriptural law metalware is subject to impurity. This is obvious from the passage from Numbers 31.22, cited in this book on p. 129. The Sadducees, relying on the passages in Leviticus dealing with the impurity of vessels and making no mention of metalware, considered them free from the possibility of contamination.

The issue became controversial under Simeon ben Shattah, who insisted that the priests at the Temple follow Pharisaic law in this respect. This seems to be the meaning of the tradition that "Simeon ben Shattah declared metalware subject to impurity."[83]

7. The Law of Inheritance

In the discussion of the controversy between the Pharisees and the Sadducees on the law of inheritance (pp. 138 ff.), I indicated that the Sadducean law conformed to Roman jurisprudence and may have been influenced by it, and that the issue was one which would naturally divide the groups because of their opposed sociological background.

The controversy concerned a daughter's right of inheritance when the other survivor was a granddaughter by a deceased son. The Sadducees declared both heirs equal. The Pharisees held that the son's issue, though a daughter, had priority over the daughter of the deceased himself.

The book demonstrates that plebeian groups, even among the Pharisees of later times, generally opposed division of estates among heirs. The plebeian properties were small. One family could eke out its living from a farm, but two would be reduced to starvation. Wiser policy gave the whole property to one heir, compelling the other to solve his or her economic problem in trade or labor. Perhaps this norm was less harsh because the issues before the plebeian judges arose among owners of land in the immediate neighborhood of Jerusalem, where the dispossessed heir could be expected to earn a livelihood in the community in which he had been reared.

The early Pharisees took this general view of justice and public policy.

However, the text of this book does not explain the unity of Pharisaic judges regarding the inheritance of the granddaughter when there was a surviving daughter, despite their division in analogous situations.

The Pharisees were unanimous on the right of a son's daughter to inherit in preference to her aunt, because that was the natural interpretation of Scriptural law. Scripture definitely stated: "If a man die, and *have no son*, then ye shall cause his inheritance to pass unto his daughter" (Num. 27.8). The words "and have no son" occur once more in another connection, namely, the law of the Levirate marriage.[84] But there the word *ben* (rendered in that verse, "child," in the current translations) included grandchildren, and really means "issue." If the widow had any descendant by the deceased brother, she was not subject to the Levirate marriage. By argument from analogy the Proto-Pharisaic scholars inferred that "son," as used in the law of inheritance, also meant "issue"—in this instance, from the context, issue by a male child.

The early Hasidean scholars felt that, influenced by Roman law, their opponents disregarded the express word of Scripture. Even if Scriptural word had seemed illogical to them, the Hasideans would have felt bound by it, considering it a reflection of Divine wisdom. But their own attitude toward the division of estates persuaded them that the biblical provision was quite logical, and what they, as human judges, would readily maintain.

Perhaps the early Hasideans, like the later Hillelites, took the same position regarding all division of properties when the situation was unclear. However, after a large part of the priesthood became Hasideans, the priestly tradition was accepted as a valid view within Pharisaism for all cases not specifically covered in the Pentateuch. Hence there arose a factional dispute within Pharisaism regarding division of inheritance generally. But there could be no dispute within the group regarding the right of a granddaughter to inherit in place of her aunt.

8. The Law of False Witnesses

As in the law of inheritance, so in the controversy about the law of false witnesses, the Sadducees appear to have followed the example of Roman law.[85]

The controversy revolved about the punishment of witnesses whose testimony had led a court to a wrong decision. According to the Sadducees, "witnesses cannot be executed [for false evidence in a capital case] unless their victim has been executed." The Pharisees declared witnesses guilty although the court had corrected itself in time to save the defendant.

The basic issue between the Pharisees and the Sadducees concerned the principle of the *lex talionis*. According to the Sadducees, false witnesses, found guilty, suffered the injury they had inflicted on their victim. The Sadducees based their position on Deuteronomy 19.21, "And thine eye shall not pity: life for life, eye for eye, tooth for tooth, hand for hand, foot for foot." (We shall presently see[86] that their interpretation of this verse was probably erroneous.) But this harsh punishment could hardly be justified for unsuccessful attempts to inflict injury. Therefore, when the decision was not carried out on the accused, the witnesses should not suffer the prescribed punishment.

The Pharisees (as will become clear)[87] rejected the literal interpretation of the *lex talionis*. The penalty exacted by them for bodily injury was monetary compensation, reasonably imposed even though the conspiracy of the witnesses had been discovered in time to save the accused. However, punishment could not be imposed unless the court had rendered its decision on the basis of the false testimony. [But see Additional Note, p. 899.]

The Pharisaic position has ample support in Scripture, which says, "Then ye shall do unto him, *as he purposed* to do unto his brother" (ibid., v. 19). Scripture clearly declared false witnesses guilty even when their purpose is frustrated.

Accepting the principle of punishment for false testimony in the absence of actual injury, the Pharisees insisted that even in capital cases false witnesses be executed despite the escape of their intended victim.

When Simeon ben Shattah became chief judge in the reign of Queen Salome a case involving this controversy occurred.[88] Two witnesses had testified in a capital case. The defendant had been convicted, but before he could be executed one of the witnesses was proved false. Simeon ben Shattah, following the classic Pharisaic position, held that the false witness was subject to the extreme penalty. Simeon may have been determined to carry out this judgment because it offered an opportunity to reject dramatically the opposing Sadducean view.

Simeon's colleague, Judah ben Tabbai, only heard of this action later, perhaps because it had occurred before Judah's return from Egypt, whither he had fled during the troublesome reign of Alexander Jannaeus.[89] Told of Simeon's decision, Judah commented: "By the Temple service, you have shed innocent blood" for neither witness could be punished for false testimony unless both were convicted. Simeon ben Shattah, hearing this view, accepted it.[90]

Page 144 shows that in writing this book I interpreted the incident otherwise. But my earlier interpretation runs counter to all the four passages in which it is recorded, and must therefore be corrected.

9. The Responsibility of a Master for Damages Committed by His Slaves

Discussion of the controversy about the responsibility of masters for slaves on pp. 283 ff. of this book does not take sufficient account of the fact that Scripture in this instance, too, sides entirely with the Pharisees. The issue was whether a master could be made to pay damages for wrongs committed by his slave without the master's knowledge or, further, against his will. The Pharisees held that he could not; the Sadducees that he could.

In my analysis of the issue I cited the view of Shammai, holding a principal responsible for the actions of his agent even when these are criminal. The Hillelites held that only the agent is responsible. While the Hillelites' view is an extension of that taken by the Pharisees generally, the issue dividing the Pharisaic factions is quite different from that between the Pharisees and Sadducees. Responsibility for damage by an agent—slave or free—is very different from that for damages done without one's consent or against one's will. The controversy between the Pharisaic schools involved an issue on which the Bible is admittedly ambiguous. Nowhere in Scripture are we definitely informed whether a principal should be punished for actions done at his behest. On this marginal problem the Pharisaic scholars divided according to their natural propensities without the guidance of a specific rule.

But, whereas the Torah discussed the responsibility of an owner for damages done by his cattle (even against his will),[91] nothing was said about similar depredations by slaves. So obvious an omission could not be an oversight. The failure to discuss a master's responsibility for damages by his slave can have only one meaning: there was no such responsibility.

This omission may not have worked serious hardship in early times. Rural, slave-owning landowners who were neighbors were usually also kinsmen or at least fellow-clansmen. A slave would no more dare inflict injury on a neighbor than on his own master. But in the large metropolitan centers, a slave might readily come into contact with a neighbor whom his master did not know or even hated. Injury to such a neighbor would scarcely invite punishment from the slave's master, unless the master were held responsible. Hence, in early times, patrician judges in Jerusalem held a master responsible for damages done by his slave *against the master's will.* The Proto-Pharisees, concerned at once for the letter of the Law and the preservation of the dignity of the human slave, contrasted with a beast, refused to hold the master responsible.

10. Ransom in Lieu of Capital Punishment

A most interesting, although hitherto baffling passage in Sifra states: "Whence do we know that a person, about to be executed, on whose behalf another offers his value [to the Temple], must nevertheless be killed? Because Scripture states, 'None devoted, that may be devoted of men, shall be ransomed; he shall surely be put to death' " (Lev. 27.29).[92]

Sifra assumed the existence of judges who would accept ransom to exculpate those condemned to death. We may presume that these judges were Proto-Sadducean or Sadducean. The Pharisees held that no one justly condemned could be redeemed through monetary payment.

Scripture explicitly formulated this rule in cases of murder. It said: "Moreover, ye shall take no ransom for the life of a murderer, that is guilty of death; but he shall surely be put to death. And ye shall take no ransom for him that is fled to his city of refuge, that he should come back to dwell in the land, until the death of the priest" (Num. 35.32 f.). The dictum of Sifra simply expanded the rule to all those condemned to death, and to those ransomed by others, rather than themselves. But surely the rule set down in Sifra was implied in that of Scripture; and only prohibited evasion of the Law. Sadducean judges, encouraged by general Near Eastern practice,[93] against which the Scriptural passage inveighed, apparently often permitted the wealthy, guilty of death, to buy their own lives through compensatory payment. This practice created differences between rich and poor before the Law, differences equally abhorrent to Scripture and the Pharisees.

B. Issues where Sadducism Opposed the Spirit of Biblical Law, Not Any Specific Statement

11. The Water-Libations on Sukkot

The controversy regarding the water-libations on Sukkot is recorded in both the Talmud and in Josephus. The ceremony consisted of pouring water on the altar each day of the Sukkot week. On the seventh day especially joyful and complicated ceremonies accompanied this offering and there was also a procession seven times about the altar carrying willows of the brook. After the ceremonies the willows were beaten against the ground.

Some authorities in the Talmud maintain that the customs of beating the willows and the water-libations were "established by the Prophets."[94] But other teachers ascribe them to Moses as part of the Oral Law revealed on Mt. Sinai.[95] R. Akiba found support for the custom of water-libations in Scripture itself, as other scholars did for the custom of beating the willows.[96] According to others it was introduced after the Exile.[97]

The Sadducees rejected all these ceremonies because they had no warrant in the Pentateuch. However, this book (pp. 102 ff.) gives evidence that water-libations were offered in biblical times on specific occasions. As already noted, we learn from the Book of Zechariah (14.16-17) that the festival of Sukkot was early identified as a season of judgment in regard to rain. The water-libation and its associated ceremonies were intended as a sacrifice to bring the rain.[98]

According to Josephus, Alexander Jannaeus, in his desire to indicate his contempt for the Pharisees and their teaching, poured the water handed him for these libations not on the altar, but on his feet.[99]

Referring to this incident, the Mishna Sukkah 4.8 warned the priest pouring the libation to hold his hand high, so that all might see that he was performing the ceremony properly, "because it happened that a priest poured the water on his feet, and the people pelted him with their citrons." A *baraita* cited in B. Sukkah 48b identified the priest as a Sadducee.

But Tosefta Sukkah 3.16, p. 197, maintains that he was a Boethusian. The difference may be due to nothing more than a copyist's error, for Alexander Jannaeus lived before the rise of the Boethusians.

On the other hand, the description of the priest as a Boethusian *may* be deliberate. Perhaps the transmitter of the Tosefta did not believe that a Sadducean priest, whatever his personal predilection, would treat a Temple ceremony with contempt.

Significantly, the Mishna does not describe the priest thus accused of violation of the Law and pelted with citrons, as a High Priest. Neither does the Tosefta nor the *baraita* cited in Babli. The ancient teachers considered it unwise to record rejection of the Pharisaic tradition by a High Priest, or to report that the congregation in the Temple pelted a High Priest with citrons. But the record in Josephus is corroborated by the Talmud of Jerusalem which implies that the priest involved was a High Priest.

The Talmud of Jerusalem asserts that the priest who poured the libation on his feet was the very one recorded as having performed the ritual of the Day of Atonement and of the red heifer according to Sadducean, rather than Pharisaic, practice.

Contemptuous of the ceremony, it was curious that Alexander Jannaeus participated in it. And if compelled to do so, it is strange that he should risk offense to the people by pouring the water on his feet.

The hint in the Mishna that the riot occurred because he *seemed* to pour the water on his feet, rather than because he did so, probably points to the truth. Sadducee though he was, Alexander Jannaeus performed the ceremonies to please the people. Through an error, word spread through the assembled crowds in the outer Temple courts—some distance from the altar—that he was pouring the water on his feet and he was pelted with citrons.

While Alexander Jannaeus submitted to the direction of the Pharisees regarding this ceremony, headstrong Boethusians of a later period sought to frustrate them. Unable to resist the multitudes on ordinary occasions, they resorted at least once to a ruse to prevent the performance of the rituals.[100]

The seventh day of Sukkot that year occurred on a Sabbath. (The modern Jewish calendar is arranged to make this impossible;[101] but in ancient times, when the New Moon was determined by actual reappearance of the moon, it happened from time to time.)[102] The Boethusians, denying the Pharisaic Oral Law and therefore holding that the ceremony of the willows had no foundation, objected with particular vehemence to beating the willows on the ground on the Sabbath day. Such action might be a violation of the Sabbath, except in performance of a ritual.

Unwilling to violate the Sabbath by carrying the willows to the Temple for the ceremony, the Pharisees brought them on Friday. The Boethusians, always ready for horseplay, covered the willows with rocks. The Law forbade the removal of the rocks on the Sabbath,[103] so the Pharisees would be prevented from using the willows for the customary ceremonials.

However, the *'am ha-arez*, ignorant peasants who had come to witness the spectacular procession, did not observe some of the minutiae of the Sabbath Law. Eager like the Pharisees to have the ceremonies performed, the peasants removed the rocks which the Pharisees would not touch, and the ritual proceeded as usual.

The incident should not deceive us. The *'am ha-arez*, mentioned in the record, accepted Pharisaic guidance only in rituals which commended themselves to the populace.[104] The rigors of Pharisaic Law did not appeal to them. Nor had their rural ancestors invented the ceremonies associated with the water-libations. But having come as pilgrims to the Temple, even on the Sabbath they would not permit sectarian hair-splitting controversies to cheat them from participation in customs sanctioned by an authoritative group.

The rabbinic sources identifying the people who covered the willow-branches with stones as Boethusians rather than Sadducees, are apparently meticulously correct. The higher social strata of the priesthood would not have demeaned themselves to pile rocks on the willows. Such stratagems were employed only by Boethusians.

The talmudic record, according to which the ceremony of beating the willow-branches against the ground originated with "the Prophets," seems correct. So primitive a rite would scarcely have been invented by the sophisticated Proto-Pharisees of the fourth and third centuries B.C.E. Moreover, the High Priests of the Persian and Hellenistic ages would not have permitted the custom to become prevalent had it been of recent origin.

The rite of water-libations therefore must have originated with the leaders of the market place in Jerusalem in the First Commonwealth, or they may have been preserved as customs originating in an earlier wilderness tradition.

Perhaps we may ascribe the enthusiasm for the ceremony to the urgent need felt by the Proto-Pharisees for a ritual replacing, in the popular imagination, the fertility rites culminating in the vineyard dances and pagan festivities customary among the provincials on the tenth of Tishri, the biblical Day of Atonement.[105] This theory would account for the strange mixture of solemnity and levity characteristic of the ritual of the water-libations. The Proto-Pharisees were glad to develop a rite through which they could offer the pilgrim the equivalent of the sensual joy which Judaism denied him on the Day of Atonement. Guided by Prophetic and Hasidean teachers, the populace would be protected from temptation to behave in unseemly fashion and would find even greater happiness in the worship of God than did their neighbors in the rituals of Baal.

Unopposed by early High Priests who happened to be friendly to the Prophetic following, the water-libation became part of the Temple ceremonial, although it had no clear authorization in the Pentateuchal system of sacrifices.

The ceremony was continued by the Hasmoneans. We have already observed that such an antagonist of Pharisaism as Alexander Jannaeus performed it, although no rule required the High Priest to do so.

The issue became bitter because it touched the very life of the common people in Jerusalem. Sukkot occurred at the end of the dry season when the need for water was urgent. Belief that the ceremonies could bring the needed rains was widespread; disrespect for this view led to violence.

But why were the usually cynical, worldly-minded Boethusians so deeply concerned lest the willows be beaten on the Sabbath? And why, indeed, did the Sadducees and Proto-Sadducees oppose the custom of water-libations and its attendant ceremonies? Granted that the ceremonies were especially congenial to the people of Jerusalem's market place, why were they resisted anywhere?

I suggested in this book[106] that these ceremonies were opposed by the priests because, according to them the Day of

Atonement was the time when the High Priest performed all the rituals of propitiation. Having obtained forgiveness for their sins, the people could rely on a year of prosperity and sufficient rainfall. The festival of Sukkot was not in their opinion a "day of judgment" at all.

But now I believe that the priests had more profound motives for objecting to these ceremonies. The ceremonies associated with Sukkot were the only ones at the Temple in which the community, rather than the priesthood, was the main participant. All the rituals of the Temple prescribed in the Pentateuch had to be performed by Aaronid priests or Levites. But the procession around the altar, with willow-branches during each day of Sukkot, and beating the willow-branches on the seventh; the chanting of the verse

"We beseech Thee, O Lord, save us now;
We beseech Thee, O Lord, make us now to prosper"
(Ps. 118.25);

the dancing with the torches on the second and succeeding nights of Sukkot; the singing of songs throughout the night—were ceremonies performed by the people at large.[107] The community singing and dancing were led by "Hasideans and men of piety,"[108] the instruments were played by the Levites.[109] The role of Aaronid priests in the ceremonial was minor.

Such happiness attended these celebrations that the Mishna remarks, "He who has not seen the celebration of the libations has not seen joy in his life."[110] R. Joshua ben Hananya, who as a young man had participated in these ceremonies, reported that there was scarcely time for sleep during the Sukkot week. In the ecstasy of the joyous worship no one minded. "We would begin," he says, "with the morning sacrifice. After that we would rush to the synagogue for prayers. Thence to the house of study. Then to the *musaf* [the additional sacrifice of the festival]. Then for a meal. After that for afternoon prayers. Then to the afternoon sacrifice. Finally, to the celebration of the libations [which apparently lasted until early in the morning]."[111]

One of the leading scholars of the day, Rabban Simeon ben Gamaliel I, esteemed both for his own merit and for his ancestry, used to perform memorable feats of dexterity in this celebration. Forgetting his dignity, he would dance about, throwing eight flaming torches into the air, and catching each as it came down, before it fell to the ground.[112]

The priests could not encourage such a celebration. Their natural impulse was to regard it with disdain, and to seek means to suppress it.

The priests had further reason to object to these ceremonies. We know that the priests discouraged crowds at the pilgrimages.[113] The assemblage of large groups in the Temple courts, and the need to look after hundreds, perhaps thousands, of sacrificial offerings, were trying to the priests, no matter how much they might welcome the emoluments associated with the offerings. R. Joshua ben Hananya recounted with delight his lack of sleep caused by the ceremonies during the Sukkot week, but the labor of officiating at the sacrifices, slaughtering, skinning, and preparing the bullocks, the rams, the lambs, the pigeons, and the meal-offerings did not fall on him or other Levites. The priests, who had to supplement their regular duties with attendance at the popular ritual of the water-libation, must have endured almost superhuman strain. Hence they opposed the ritual as an unnecessary burden and a provocation to chaos and trouble.

It speaks volumes for the popularity of the ceremonies

and for the urgent need of water in Jerusalem that they could not be suppressed. If, as seems probable, the custom arose in primitive times, its survival through the ages of idolatry, of assimilationism under the Persians and the Greeks, and finally in opposition to the Sadducean High Priests, is indeed remarkable testimony to its hold on the population.

On the other hand, this very popularity made the ceremonies the more obnoxious to institution-minded and clan-minded ecclesiastics. The priests persisted in their opposition. The Boethusians, usually so heedless of Jewish custom and ritual, went so far that they appealed to the Sabbath laws to prevent the ceremonies from proceeding.

12. Judicial Leniency in Punishment

Josephus informs us that the Pharisees inclined to leniency in punishment, whereas the Sadducees tended toward severity.[114] His view is amply corroborated in the Mishna which, imposing the death penalty on many transgressors, discovered procedures by which transgressors escaped punishment. The necessity for eyewitnesses, as well as for evidence that a crime has been committed knowingly, deliberately, and without mitigating circumstances, made certain that almost all brought before Pharisaic judges would be acquitted. Self-incrimination[115] and double jeopardy[116] were outlawed. Indeed, the Law made it possible for R. Tarfon and R. Akiba to maintain that, had they sat in the Sanhedrin while it possessed the authority to impose capital punishment, no one would have been executed.[117] All agreed that a Sanhedrin which ordered an execution once in seven years was to be called "murderous."[118]

In this attitude toward punishment the Pharisees simply

applied the principles of the Torah, whose genius combines normative severity with procedural leniency. The rule is sometimes harsh; its application is always merciful.

This approach to the Law was demonstrated in the very beginning of Genesis. Adam was told that if he ate of the Tree of Knowledge he would die.[119] He transgressed the Law, but lived for 930 years.[120] No effort was made to explain the failure of God to fulfill His threat. It was assumed that in punishment the righteous Judge would temper judgment with mercy.

Condemned for the death of Abel, Cain is given a sign to protect him from anyone seeking to slay him, because he was then bound to be a stranger on the face of the earth (Gen. 4.15). Even a willful murderer is not subject to execution on the basis of his own confession.

Leniency in judicial procedure is further implied in the passage dealing with the ox which killed a man (Ex. 21.28). "If the ox was wont to gore in time past, and warning hath been given to its owner, and he hath not kept it in, but it hath killed a man or woman; the ox shall be stoned, and its owner also shall be put to death." Scripture continued, however, "If there be laid on him a ransom, then he shall give for the redemption of his life, whatsoever is laid upon him."

The two cases mentioned in the Torah in which transgressors were executed were decided not by Moses but by God Himself (Num. 15.32 ff.; Lev. 24.6 ff.). Despite the express norm of Scripture condemning to death him who violates the Sabbath, it was felt that in a specific instance, "it had not been declared what should be done to him" (Num. 15.34). Even more explicitly the blasphemer was "placed in ward, that it might be declared unto them at the mouth of the Lord" (Lev. 24.12). Capital punishment, theoretically within the jurisdiction of human courts, really belonged to God and not to man.

C. Issues where Scripture is Inexplicit

13. Equal Participation of All Jews in Daily Sacrifices

The Sadducees held that the daily sacrifice might be paid for by individuals, instead of from the Temple coffers. The Pharisees denied this, insisting that the sacrifice could be offered only out of the *shekalim* paid by everyone equally.

In this book (pp. 282 ff.) I assumed that the issue revolved about the principle of human equality. The Pharisees and their predecessors held that the daily offering, and all public offerings, should come from funds in which every Jew had a share equal to that of his brother.

Now there is evidence that another, far less theoretical, issue was also involved in the argument. We know that in the final days of the First Commonwealth the priests considered themselves free from the obligation to pay the annual *shekel* for support of the Temple. According to the Mishna,[121] R. Judah says, "Ben Bokri testified in Yabneh that a priest contributing the *shekel commits no transgression.*" Rabban Johanan ben Zakkai replied [to Ben Bokri], "Not so. On the contrary, a priest failing to contribute his *shekel* violates the Law."

The discussion showed that many priests did not contribute the *shekel.* Ben Bokri defended their practice, although he admitted that they might contribute it, if they chose. Rabban Johanan ben Zakkai held that the payment was mandatory for priests as for all other Jews.

The priests refusing to contribute the *shekel* did not agree that the cost of the daily sacrifice had to fall equally on each Jew. According to them the sacrifice was offered on behalf of all Israel, but who paid for it did not matter.

While the priests whose views Ben Bokri reflected may have been Pharisees, the principle underlying their behavior could justify the Sadducees. If priests were not required to contribute to the daily sacrifice which was offered on their behalf as well as on behalf of all other Jews, it might follow that a wealthy man could contribute the sacrifice for the whole community.

The opinion of the Sadducean priests opposed the explicit assertion of the Covenant of the Great Assembly (Neh. 10.33). By this Covenant, an annual gift of a third of a *shekel* was to be made by each Jew for public offerings. The document pledging the gifts had been signed by Israelites, Levites, and priests.

This repudiation of the document by the Sadducees offers additional evidence that the covenant preserved in Nehemiah stems from the founders of Hasideanism.[122]

In the Talmud, the norm established in Nehemiah is associated with that in Exodus 30.11 ff.[123] On the first of Adar if it fell on a Sabbath, or on the preceding Sabbath, if Adar began on a weekday, that portion of the Law was actually read in all synagogues, to remind the people of the annual contribution to the Temple.[124] But this chapter dealt only with a census, and the Sadducees could well argue that neither priests nor Levites were included in any census of Israel mentioned in the Pentateuch.

The unwillingness of the priests to contribute the *shekel* to the Temple had far deeper roots than mere niggardliness. The issue involved the status of the priesthood and the function of the sacrificial system. The priests considered themselves Divine courtiers, chosen by the Deity, for reasons of His own, for superior holiness, and therefore for near approach to Him as ministers.[125] The Hasideans considered them simply agents of the people of Israel, assigned to particular service to God and commanded to follow a holy life because of this service.[126] According to the first view, the priestly prerogative of worship derived from superior sanctity; according to the second, their holiness derived from their particular service.[127]

The nature of the sacrificial system itself was also involved. By the priestly view, the purpose of sacrifices was to give delight to the Deity—not sensuous delight in the consumption of food[128] (as the pagans and the simple-minded believed) but delight in the odor of the sacrifices (which seemed less anthropomorphic) and in the number offered.[129] They took the verses, describing sacrifices as a "sweet savor," literally.

Their opponents held that the enjoyment God derived from the sacrifice was the same as He found in their fulfillment of other commandments: "It is a joy for Me that My commands are obeyed."[130]

In the priestly theories, God desired the sacrificial meat, and did not care who paid for it. In the Hasidean theory, He was not concerned with the sacrifice, but only with those who provided it. Following the priestly argument, failure of priests to share in the cost of the sacrifice did no harm. Following that of the Hasideans, the priests, failing to contribute to the daily sacrifice, violated the Divine will, and to that extent displeased Him.

The Hasidean view was as usual well grounded in Scripture. Leviticus 21.8 specifically asserts that the priests "shall be holy unto their God, and not profane the name of their God; for the offerings of the Lord, made by fire, the bread of their God, they do offer; therefore they shall be holy." The holiness of the priests was thus a specific commandment imposed on them. Their status resulted from their function, not their function from their status.

In Leviticus 16.21, Aaron is told to put his hands on the scapegoat destined to carry the sins of all Israel into the wilderness, confessing while he did so "all the iniquities of the children of Israel."

In this ritual, Aaron, and all later High Priests, acted as agents of the whole community. This concept of the priesthood reappears in Exodus 28.29, 38; 29.1; and in Numbers 18.1 ff., and prevails in the Torah. In each of these passages, Aaron and his sons are told that they are to bear the responsibility for the iniquities of the people of Israel. This responsibility is perhaps most dramatically expressed in the rule permitting an unwitting murderer to return from exile after the death of the High Priest (Num. 35.38). The premise of this law seems to be that the guilt of the assassin is absolved with the death of the High Priest.

At any rate, this interpretation was put on these passages by the Hasidean and talmudic authorities. Hence, as already stated, on the evening of the Day of Atonement the Hasidean elders described the High Priest as their agent and themselves as the agents of the Hasidean court representing all Israel.

The priests and Sadducees could counter these arguments with the observation that at least two sacrifices were offered by an individual, namely, the High Priest, on behalf of the community, showing that individuals could pay for public offerings. The sacrifices were the bullock on the Day of

Atonement, which, the priests held, atoned for the transgressions of not only the High Priest and his immediate family, but the whole priesthood;[131] and the daily meal-offerings, sacrificed by the High Priest morning and evening.[132] That these were public offerings was implied in the rule permitting them even on the Sabbath, when private offerings were forbidden.[133]

To these objections the later Rabbis offered three different replies, all of them presumably originating in early times. According to R. Judah, the bullock, sacrificed by the High Priest on the Day of Atonement, was intended for the purification of the Temple and the Temple courts and for the atonement of the High Priest and his family, not for the tribe.[134] R. Simeon, agreeing that the ritual of the bullock atoned for the tribe, insisted that the atonement was made in the confession recited by the High Priest before the sacrifice.[135] R. Meir[136] and R. Jacob[137] insisted that the bullock was not a public sacrifice at all, but a private one, offered on the Sabbath because its time was fixed. The bullock atoned for all the priests because they were part of Aaron's household, and it was to his household that Scripture referred, not to that of the contemporary High Priest.

It seems probable that these different opinions derived from older sources. On the Day of Atonement the High Priest confessed twice over the bullock.[138] In his first confession he mentioned only himself and his family.[139] Because some interpreted the biblical phrase in a narrow sense, limiting his family to his personal household, the High Priest mentioned only its members in his first confession. To satisfy those who argued that the whole clan was his household, he confessed once more, asking forgiveness for the whole priesthood.

The meal-offering, sacrificed daily by the High Priest, was, according to R. Judah, a private sacrifice.[140] Yet it could be offered on the Sabbath, because it enabled the hierarchy to function. R. Simeon maintained[141] that, although presented by the High Priest, the meal-offering was actually a public sacrifice, for the priest, unlike other donors, was the agent of the community. During the interim between the death of one High Priest and the appointment of another, R. Judah required the heirs of the first one to bring the meal-offering. R. Simeon held that it was given by the community.

On Hasidean theory neither example bore on the question of the daily sacrifices, in which each person should share as part of his duty to fulfill.

The Sadducees argued that if the priests contributed the *shekel*, the meal-offerings brought by the community, being in part sacrifices of priests, would have to be consumed on the altar.[142] But these offerings included the shewbread, the two loaves of new grain on Shabuot, and the remainder of the *Omer*, all traditionally given to the priests. The Hasideans denied that the shewbread and the two loaves could be considered meal-offerings in the sense used by Scripture. Neither could the *Omer*, as interpreted by scholars before R. Akiba's time. However, the demonstration of this early attitude toward the *Omer* would require analysis beyond the scope of this book.[143]

A curious textual difference among the versions of a synagogue prayer recalls the ancient conflict regarding the status of the priesthood. In the oldest forms of the prayer, beseeching God to bestow on Israel the blessings He commanded the priests to give them, the priests are called "the priests of Thy holy people."[144] In later versions this expression was altered and made to read, "the priests, Thy holy people." When Sadducism ended, opposition to their doctrine also weakened.

Similarly, some Rabbinic authorities interpreting literally the passage, "So they shall put My Name upon the children of Israel, and I shall bless them" (Num. 6.27), take the word "them" to mean the children of Israel.[145]

In this exegesis the priests are considered functionaries, beseeching God's blessing for Israel, but incapable of bestowing a blessing themselves. That is the prerogative of the Deity. Other priestly scholars assert that "them" in this passage means "priests." The people of Israel, they say, are blessed by the priests; and the priests by God.[146] In their view, as in that of earlier Proto-Sadducism, the priests belonged to a special category, chosen by God for service in His court, and granted prerogatives denied other Jews.

So completely had the early controversy and its implications been forgotten among the later rabbinic authorities, that in the Babylonian academies the nature of the priesthood was argued at some length, but no definite conclusion was reached.[147]

14. The *Nizzok*

The famous controversy between the Pharisees and the Sadducees concerning the *nizzok*, mentioned in Mishna Yadayim 4.7 and discussed in this book (pp. 811-813), can now be shown to have arisen from a natural difference of approach by priests and scholars of the market place. The traditional interpretation of this controversy, accepted by Professor Louis Ginzberg, is doubtless correct.[148] The issue was whether a stream of water in flowing from one vessel to another unites the two bodies of liquid. If so, an impure vessel receiving the liquid would defile both that being poured into it and the source in the "pure vessel."

In Pharisaic law such a stream of water is not unifying (Mishna Makshirim 5.9); the Sadducees said that it was.

The Torah offered no clear rule regarding this problem. Therefore later scholarship had to follow its own judgment in the matter.

The Temple priests considered the liquid being poured from one vessel into another a continuous body, ruling that if the liquid in the contaminated vessel was impure it defiled the liquid flowing into it and also that in the original container.

Such interpretation of the Law was feasible for priests in the Temple, who could avoid pouring liquid into defiled vessels. So could the wealthy householder on his farm or in his mansion. When wine or other liquid was poured by a slave into an impure vessel only a minor calamity occurred unless the original source contained a considerable amount of water or oil.

The situation was different for city traders. Most of their customers were presumably defiled, many with major impurity, such as that resulting from attendance at a funeral or from a "flow," and the vessels they brought to the shops were therefore also impure. The trader often had to pour wine from his jug directly into that brought by a customer, often held in the hands of the purchaser while it was being filled. To declare the stream of liquid "impure" was to defile the liquid in the original container and in fact to forbid all customary dealing in the market place. The Pharisee and his predecessors would not have objected to this sacrifice, as they did not object to other great sacrifices, had it been commanded in the Torah. But there was no evidence of such a command in the Torah. The Hasidean (and perhaps the Prophetic exegete before him) therefore followed the usual norm, that "one who declares something prohibited, should produce evidence for his view."[149] In the absence of such evidence, one could not assume a prohibition.

The Sadducean argument that the liquid in the original container, the stream, and the vessel into which it was being poured constituted a single physical unit seemed to the Pharisees illogical. Sadducean exegesis, if accepted, would lead to the conclusion that a brook is physically a unit and that contamination of a part contaminated the whole. Why then was a stream flowing through a cemetery not impure? The Sadducees themselves did not in this instance go to the extreme of considering a whole river a physical unit. Why then should a jet of water unite physically, for the purpose of ritual law, the contents of two flasks?

D. Institutions Described by the Pharisees as Post-Biblical

15. Hand-Washing
and
16. The '*Erub*

Two institutions, opposed by the Sadducees, were declared by the Pharisees to be innovations by post-biblical authorities. One was the norm according to which contact with sacred books "defiled" the hands.[150] The second was the '*erub*, or merging of households, which permitted carrying objects from one's house into a common court on the Sabbath.[151]

The Sadducees rejected the whole principle that hands could be defiled,[152] and their opposition to the rule declaring hands defiled through contact with sacred books was only a specific instance of their general view. Similarly, their opposition to the *'erub* seems to derive from their view that carrying on the Sabbath from one's house into a common court was permitted.

Both regulations (i.e., washing the hands and the *'erub*) are ascribed by the Talmud to King Solomon.[153] The association of the ritual of hand-washing with that sovereign is easily understood. His building of the Temple and the establishment of Jerusalem as the main center of worship brought to it priests and laymen in large numbers. It was difficult to be sure that each participating priest had purified himself before eating sacrificial food. And it was even more difficult to be certain that the laymen, permitted to eat some types of sacred meat, had purified themselves for this purpose.

While impurity could usually be removed only through immersion of the whole body in water, one passage in Scripture suggests that a *zab* (a person suffering from a "flow") did not communicate impurity through touch if he had previously rinsed his hands in water (Lev. 15.11). According to no less an authority than R. Eleazar ben Arak, this verse served as the foundation on which the scholars erected the institution of "purification of the hands."[154]

We do not know how the Sadducees interpreted this verse. But presumably they found intolerable the suspicion that the many Temple priests were, in fact, impure;[155] and therefore did not consider necessary the requirement to wash one's hands before eating sacred meats.

To assuage their feelings the Pharisaic scholars urged that eating of the sacred food and also the heave-offering were acts of worship; and that the hand-washing, on which they insisted in preparation for such meals, was analogous to that required in Scripture before performing an act of worship at the altar.[156] Later, this doctrine led to the custom of washing one's hands before any meal.

It is, at first glance, more difficult to see why King Solomon should be credited with the institution of the *'erub*. However, consideration of life in ancient Jerusalem clarifies the problem. The prohibition against carrying objects from a house into the common court on the Sabbath perhaps did not ordinarily fall very heavily on city-dwellers. While the houses of the poor were tiny, one could manage to have meals in them. There was no necessity to use the court on the Sabbath in a way requiring utensils or other objects.

The situation was different during the pilgrimages. Then the owners of houses would frequently sleep in the courts, leaving the enclosed shelter to the pilgrims.[157] With a vastly enlarged population, meals had to be eaten in the courts; and on the Sukkot festival there was need to provide for the Sukkah in the court for all. Under these circumstances, Jerusalem simply could not have provided housing for the pilgrims, had not the law of the *'erub* been established. The Talmud thus concludes that the *'erub*, like the ritual of hand-washing, was actually initiated by King Solomon when he erected the Temple.

E. Priestly Traditions Opposed by Some Pharisaic Scholars, and Denounced by Them as Sadducean

17. The Priestly Interpretation of the *Lex Talionis*
18. The Priestly Tradition Regarding Death by Burning

One rabbinic record recalls a controversy between Pharisees and Sadducees regarding the *lex talionis*: the Sadducees applied it literally; the Pharisees substituted monetary compensation, except for murder.[158]

Geiger accepted the authenticity of this record,[159] and supports his argument by reference to R. Eliezer ben Hyrcanus, one of the foremost Pharisaic scholars, reported to have accepted the literal interpretation of the *talio*. Hence, Geiger maintained, the "Old Halakah" accepted the literal interpretation, represented by both the Sadducees and R. Eliezer. The rejection of this interpretation was part of the "New Halakah." However, it now seems probable that Geiger erred in his explanation of R. Eliezer's position and of the rabbinic record regarding the controversy.

To understand the controversy between the Pharisees and the Sadducees the biblical law of the *talio* needs to be reconsidered. We have already observed[160] that the genius of biblical law requires normative severity, and judicial clemency. Moral indignation and horror were expressed through the threat of dire punishment. But the rigor of the law was constantly mitigated in actual practice through procedural protection of the accused. Nowhere is this genius of biblical law reflected more clearly than in the discussion of the *lex talionis*.

Scripture (Ex. 21.22 ff.) provides that "if two men strive together, and hurt a woman that is with child, so that her fruit depart, and yet no harm follow, he shall surely be fined, according as the woman's husband shall lay upon him; and he shall pay as the judges determine. But if any harm follow, then shalt thou give life for life, eye for eye, tooth for tooth, hand for hand, foot for foot, burning for burning, wound for wound, stripe for stripe."

The word translated "harm" apparently means fatal accident, presumably to the mother. U. Cassuto has suggested[161] that the words "life for life," etc., in this passage are simply a stereotype, archaic phrase from Near Eastern Common Law, recalling the primitive punishment; but that the Scripture in reality envisages only monetary compensation for the injury. This seems clear from the fact that a few verses earlier (v. 13) Scripture provides the death penalty only for *willful* murder. Accidental homicide was punishable through exile. But homicide resulting from a quarrel between two antagonists was not placed in the same category as an accident. The person causing death must make appropriate compensation to the husband and father injured.

The use of the archaic stereotype, however, still requires explanation. It was intended, as already indicated,[162] to express the horror of Scripture at the deed; and to suggest that morally, though not necessarily judicially, the *talio* ought to be invoked.

This was clearly the interpretation put on the passage by the Shammaitic Pharisees. We know that R. Eliezer, who imposed the *talio* for willful injury to a person's limb, recognized the propriety of monetary ransom for unintentional injury,[163] like that described in this passage. His views may have been shared by the Sadducean judges.

However, R. Eliezer's view that willful injury to a person's body may be punished by the *talio* was challenged by his colleagues. Presumably he reflected the attitude of the School of Shammai, they that of the School of Hillel. The Shammaites derived their position not from the passage in Exodus, but from another, Leviticus 24.19 ff. This passage reads:

> "And if a man maim his neighbor, as he hath done, so shall be done to him, breach for breach, eye for eye, tooth for tooth, as he hath maimed a man, so shall it be rendered

unto him. And he that killeth a beast shall make it good, *and he that killeth a man shall be put to death.*"

R. Eliezer followed the passage literally. But, to the Hillelite Pharisees, the prolixity and repetitiousness of the passage presented grave difficulties. It seemed that the passage in Leviticus, like that in Exodus (21.24 ff.), dealt primarily with moral justice, and assumed mitigation of the Law by judges.

The Torah asserted that the person guilty of mayhem ought to suffer precisely the injury inflicted. Yet "life for life" in the case of a beast meant payment; hence "breach for breach" might likewise be interpreted by the judges to mean payment.[164]

But the passage concluded that such leniency might not be extended to capital cases, for "he who killeth a beast shall make it good, while he who killeth a man must be put to death."

This interpretation seemed appropriate also to the passage already mentioned dealing with false witnesses (Deut. 19.18 ff.). It was scarcely conceivable that mere purpose to do another person bodily injury should be punished through the suffering of similar injury. As already observed,[165] the Sadducees who interpreted the passage in Deuteronomy literally were compelled to disregard the words, "as he had purposed to do."

Support for the Shammaitic view might be found in the command of Scripture, Numbers 35.31, "Ye shall take no ransom for the life of a murderer, that is guilty of death; but he shall surely be put to death. And ye shall take no ransom for him that is fled to a city of refuge, that he shall come back to dwell in the land, until the death of the High

Priest." The verses imply that lesser penalties than death or exile might be replaced with monetary ransom.[166] However, the Hillelite position was by no means refuted from these verses; for according to it, there was no *talio*, except for murder.

Presumably the difference between the Shammaites and the Hillelites derived from their opposing attitudes toward equality before the Law. The Shammaitic principle imposing the *talio*, but permitting substitution of monetary compensation for it, would have involved different rules for rich and poor. The poor man, unable to pay for the injury he inflicted, would undergo equivalent suffering; the rich would escape through payment of damages. This attitude the Hillelites could not tolerate.

Josephus, discussing the law of the *talio*,[167] appears (as so frequently) to follow the Shammaitic interpretation of the Law.

But how does it come about that R. Eliezer, one of the leading Pharisaic scholars of his time, should in this instance be siding with the Sadducees?

The answer to this puzzle must be sought in the judicial system of ancient Jerusalem toward the end of the Second Commonwealth. The civil courts, insofar as the Romans permitted them to have jurisdiction, were dominated at that time by the Pharisaic scholars, as was the religious life of the country. The Sadducees, although high in social rank, were comparatively few and without influence even on the Temple ritual. They could not determine judicial policy.

But there did exist a "Court of Priests," claiming jurisdiction over the Temple, and in a degree over the whole priestly tribe. The existence of the "Court of Priests" is well attested in rabbinic literature, but the authority attaching to it is by no means clear. The vagueness of the Talmud on the subject was due to the obsolescence of the institution when the talmudic records were compiled, to the opposition by Pharisaic scholars, and to the controversies surrounding the Court's authority during its existence.

The Court of Priests definitely claimed jurisdiction in marital cases arising within the tribe.

We are told that while the usual dower of a widow or a divorcee was two hundred *zuz* if she had been a virgin when married, and otherwise one hundred *zuz*, "the Court of Priests used to collect four hundred *zuz* for a virgin, and two hundred *zuz* for others. The sages did not interfere with the Court."[168]

Another record suggests that the witnesses to the New Moon, on whose evidence the beginning of the month was proclaimed, appeared first before "the Court" (i.e., the Pharisaic authorities), and then before "the priests."[169] On one occasion a witness came to testify with his son and his slave. The "Court" accepted him and the slave, and rejected the testimony of the son, holding that witnesses to the New Moon could not be members of the same family. But when they appeared before the priests they accepted him and his son, but rejected the slave as unfit to testify.

More light is shed on the authority wielded by the "Court of Priests" in the tannaitic commentaries on the Pentateuch. Thus in Sifra,[170] the verse: "So Moses spoke unto Aaron, and to his sons, and to all the children of Israel" (Lev. 21.24), is interpreted, "He admonished Aaron concerning the sons, and the sons concerning Israel, and the sons concerning one another." This means, the commentators state, that the responsibility (and therefore the authority) to enforce Levitical law in the Temple was entrusted to Aaron so far as his children were concerned; to his children so far as the people generally were concerned; and to his children for one another.

This "admonition" is addressed to a "Court of Priests," for the admon tion could be helpful only if there was a body[170a] clothed with authority to execute the rule. This is demonstrably the general implication of the term "admonished" in such contexts. Rashi, who did not recognize the existence of a "Court of Priests" clothed with authority in the Temple, and yet did recognize the force of the statement, actually seems to emend the text of Sifra, and suggests that "the Court [i.e., the Pharisaic Sanhedrin] was admonished concerning the behavior of the priests." But the text of the Sifra as cited is found in all the editions and manuscripts and can scarcely be wrong. The author intended to rest responsibility for the observance of the Law in the Temple in a Court of Priests.

This view is forcefully expressed in Sifre Numbers 116 (ed. Horowitz, p. 133). The verse under discussion is "And the Lord said unto Aaron, Thou, and thy sons, and thy father's house with thee shall bear the iniquity of the sanctuary and thou and thy sons with thee shall bear the iniquity of your priesthood." Sifre (Num. 18.1) seems to hold that the contrast between "the iniquity of the sanctuary" and "the iniquity of your priesthood," is deliberate. The first is entrusted to Aaron, his sons, *and his father's house*. The second, to Aaron and his sons. The difference according to Sifre is that transgressions affecting the Sanctuary were to be dealt with by a Court, whereas each priest was himself responsible for observance of the priestly laws. The "Court" discussed here, could only be the "Court of Priests"; for it would be difficult for the general Sanhedrin, including non-priests, without access to the Temple, to supervise its ritual.

This seems to be the clear meaning of R. Ishmael's remark in Sifre (loc. cit.), "To whom is authority given? To the one entrusted with the responsibility." R. Josiah illustrates the point through the suggestion that sins of individual priests regarding sacrifices fall on the priesthood as a whole. Sifre suggests later, in the same passage, that the words "iniquity of your priesthood" refer to transgressions responsibility for which is entrusted to the priesthood as a whole, i.e., to each individual priest for himself; whereas the verse: "And thou and thy sons with thee shall keep your priesthood in everything that pertaineth to the altar (Num. 18.7) refers to transgressions "entrusted to the Court." This interpretation is accepted by virtually all the commentators. The one exception, Rabbi David Pardo, was compelled to read into the text a farfetched interpretation which cannot be accepted.

Yet Sifre itself indicated that this view was by no means unanimous. The opposing view derived its strength from the statement, "and ye shall keep the charge of the holy things, and the charge of the altar, that there be wrath no more upon the children of Israel" (Num. 18.5). The need to protect the people of Israel from Divine wrath, according to the passage of Sifre dealing with this verse, indicated that the general Sanhedrin (consisting of non-priests as well as priests) had authority in the Temple itself. "This verse is an admonition to the *Court of Israel* to admonish the priests, so that the ritual of the Temple be performed properly; for when the ritual is performed properly they prevent catastrophe from coming upon the world." On the other hand, a later verse which reads: "And thou and thy sons with thee shall keep your priesthood in everything that pertaineth to the altar" (ibid., v. 7), was explained by R. Eleazar ha-

Kappar to mean: "Anything pertaining to the altar is in thy charge and that of thy sons." R. Eleazar ha-Kappar shared the view of R. Ishmael, and the first passage cited from Sifre above, placing the conduct of the Temple in the hands of a "Court of Priests."

The difference of opinion was accentuated by the further remark of Sifre, "There was a place behind the Innermost Shrine where the genealogies of the priests were examined" to make sure of their right to participate in the worship.[171] This statement seems to contradict that in Mishna Middot, chapter 5, end, which specifically speaks of "The Chamber of Hewn Stones [adjacent to the Temple, but not part of it] where the Great Sanhedrin *of Israel* sat and judged the priesthood" to decide who could enter the Temple service. The inconsistency between the two norms did not, of course, escape the commentators, who suggested various ways to reconcile them. Yet none of these explanations seems adequate.

The norm in Mishna Middot was taken from life. Therefore we must assume that the Sanhedrin in the Chamber of Hewn Stones actually had authority to decide whether a person, claiming to be a priest, could exercise those functions. On the other hand, it is clear from Sifre that any decision reached by the Sanhedrin was subject (at least in certain periods) to review by a Court of Priests meeting in a chamber behind the Inner Shrine of the Temple.

Mishna Eduyyot 8.3 refers to this dual system of judging the priests in its cryptic reference to a decision by Rabban Johanan ben Zakkai. As reported in the Mishna, Rabban Johanan ben Zakkai "decreed" that the ordinary courts should not deal with the rights of men to recognition as priests; "for," he said, "the priests will accept your negative decisions, but not your affirmative ones." In other words, Rabban Johanan ben Zakkai, finding that the Court of Priests insisted on authority to review the decisions of the Sanhedrin in regard to priesthood, and powerless to prevent the Court of Priests from doing so, held that there was no point in trying such cases at all. The Court of Priests would not admit one rejected by the Sanhedrin, for such action might lead to riots. But it did refuse admission to the priesthood to some approved by the Sanhedrin.

Rabban Johanan ben Zakkai felt justified in this stand because, according to him, even Elijah the Prophet will not reverse decisions taken by established Courts, even the Court of Priests, regarding ancestral privileges. He will reject only those who have been admitted to the priesthood by sheer force; and will readmit only those wrongfully ejected by force.

In another passage dealing with the Court of Priests (Tosefta Sanhedrin 4.7) we are told that the Scroll of the Torah, written for the King, should be gone over by "a *Bet Din* of Priests, or one of the Levites, or one of Israelites entitled to marry their daughters into the priesthood." According to Yerushalmi,[172] however, the Scroll was examined by the Sanhedrin of seventy-one members, the "Court of Israel."

Sifre Deuteronomy 160, p. 211, disagrees with both Tosefta and Yerushalmi, asserting that the Scroll was examined only by priests. During the Second Commonwealth the preservation of the text of the royal Scroll was originally a responsibility of the Court of Priests. The view, reflected in Tosefta, implies an extension of this rule, permitting any properly constituted Court eligible to judge capital cases to review the text. The view of the Yerushalmi followed the trend of later exegesis to confer all such authority on the Great Sanhedrin.

Sifre further preserves traditions suggesting that the "Court of Priests" originally claimed even greater authority; and that it was, at least at one time, recognized as the ultimate Court of Appeal in all religious issues. Thus, Sifre Deuteronomy 351, p. 408, comments on the verse, "They shall teach Jacob Thine ordinances, and Israel Thy Law" (Deut. 32.10): "Hence we learn that all [ritual] decisions are to be made by them [the priests]." A special rôle for the priests in the judiciary seems to be implied in another comment in Sifre. The reference in Deuteronomy 1.15 to "officers" associated with the Courts is explained in Sifre 15, p. 25, to mean "the Levites, who flog [the guilty] with a strap." The belief that this office belonged to the tribe of Levi was suggested also in Josephus.[172a] If the assistants to the judges were Levites, we would expect the judges themselves often, maybe usually, to have been priests.

In the light of this information, the reason Hillel argued with the Elders of Bathyra concerning the paschal lamb becomes intelligible.[173] Hillel, maintaining that the paschal lamb ought to be sacrificed even when the fourteenth day of Nisan fell on a Sabbath, was confronted by the Elders of Bathyra who had no tradition on the subject. They argued the matter all day. Finally he persuaded them to follow his view, by laying approval of his views to the authority of his teachers, Shemayah and Abtalyon.

The Sanhedrin, i.e., the Court of the Chamber of Hewn Stones, does not appear in this discussion. The omission of any reference to the Sanhedrin is curious, for most scholars assume that it controlled the whole Jewish ritual, including that of the Temple. But the Sanhedrin's authority did not extend to the Temple service, which was determined by a

Court of Priests. This Court of Priests had assigned to the Elders of Bathyra responsibility for the observance of the Sabbath in the Temple. So Hillel argued with the Elders of Bathyra.

There is an interesting reference in the Mishna to "the High Priests" who acted as judges in various cases.[174] The Mishna mentions "two civil judges in Jerusalem," transmitting some of their opinions. The High Priests rejected both views ascribed to Hanan ben Abishalom. R. Dosa ben Arkenas, the great Shammaitic scholar, agreed with the judgment of the High Priests. Rabban Johanan ben Zakkai, the Hillelite leader, agreed with Hanan. Presumably "the High Priests" constituted the "Court of Priests," and the judges of Jerusalem mentioned, Admon and Hanan, were Israelites, that is, non-priests, sitting in the market place or the gate of Jerusalem to adjudicate civil cases.

The manner in which the priestly judiciary performed its functions is nowhere clearly described, but can be reconstructed from various records. Thus we are told that the Levites had to stand guard at twenty-one points on the Temple mount. "The officer of the Temple mount" was charged with the responsibility for these guards. He would pass from one to the other, holding a torch before him. Reaching a post the officer would cry out "Peace on thee."[175] If the guard had fallen asleep the officer was entitled to beat him with a stick and burn his clothes. "Thus they say, 'what is the noise in the Temple courts about?' [And the answer would usually be] 'A Levite is being beaten, and his clothes are being burned, because he fell asleep at his post'." This was no mere theory. R. Eliezer ben Jacob recorded that when his maternal uncle, a Levite, fell asleep at his post his clothes were burnt.

Nowhere in the judicial procedure of the rabbinical courts do we find anything analogous to this high-handed discipline. Throughout the talmudic writings, a person accused of transgression is entitled to offer a defense and to be judged in proper fashion. To strip him of his clothes, burn them, and beat him, without trial, was unheard of. In contrast, on the Temple mount, the officer of the Temple mount had full authority to use his judgment without inquiry into the circumstances or opportunity for judicial procedure.

We can now understand, too, the curious norm of the Mishna which has perplexed commentators: "A priest who performed the Temple service during impurity is not brought before the Court by his fellow-priests; but the young priests take him out of the Temple courts and split his skull with logs."[176] Surely the transgressor was not simply seized by his fellow-priests and lynched. The accusation would have to be proved and the sin shown to be willful. This would require investigation of the facts and judgment regarding the Law. The Mishnaic norm therefore must mean that the accused was not brought before the ordinary courts for judgment but was tried by fellow-priests, and when found guilty executed in the manner indicated.

The summary punishment applied not only to one who performed the ritual in impurity, but was apparently inflicted on others who violated Temple norms. Thus, R. Eliezer maintained that even "a High Priest who steps between the altar and the 'porch' [before the Temple structure] is liable to have his skull split with logs."[177] Once more it is clear that this fearful punishment would not be inflicted without trial and proof of guilt. Yet the Mishna and Talmud know of no such judicial penalty.

Apparently the Court of Priests, authority in the Temple, tried the accused, and if he was found guilty instructed the young priests to perform the execution.

The existence of such a Court of Priests, with authority to execute transgressors, explains a puzzling talmudic tradition. R. Eleazar ben R. Zadok asserted that as a child he saw the execution of a priest's daughter who had committed adultery. She was surrounded by fagots, which were set afire.[178] To his colleagues, death by burning meant molten lead poured down the throat of the condemned, so "that his soul would depart, but the body remain intact." Therefore the Mishna asserts that "the Court did not know the Law." Rab Joseph explained that the Mishnaic aspersion on the Court meant that "it was a Sadducean court."[179] In another version R. Eleazar's testimony was rejected because childhood memories are unreliable.[180]

The controversy between R. Eleazar ben R. Zadok and his colleagues seems to be reflected also in the argument concerning the death of Nadab and Abihu. According to one tradition, their bodies were burned to ashes;[181] according to another, their bodies remained intact.[182] The two traditions reflected differences regarding the penalty of burning.

There is no reason to doubt the evidence of R. Eleazar despite its inconsistency with the whole Rabbinic tradition. Presumably he would not have offered his evidence had he suspected that the Court which sentenced the adulteress was either ignorant or Sadducean. We must assume that in his opinion, based on what he learned later in life, it was an authoritative Court. The issue between him and his colleagues became the question whether a Court, acting in the manner described, could be called a proper Court. He considered it a duly authorized Court: apparently a Court of Priests judging a member of its own tribe. His colleagues declared a Court acting as reported unfit.

These various records shed light on a curious tradition, handed down by R. Eliezer ben Jacob, the priestly sage whose Levitical uncle was punished as already described. "I have a tradition," R. Eliezer reports, "that a Court may [under certain circumstances] flog a person and otherwise punish him without reference to the norms of the Torah — not to violate the Torah, but to protect it. During the period of the Greek rule, a man who rode a horse on the Sabbath was brought to Court, and stoned; not because the sin deserves this punishment but because the time needed such rigor. In another instance, a husband who had had conjugal relations with his wife in the shelter of a fig tree, was brought to Court, and flogged. The sin was not punishable, but the time needed such rigor."[183] Presumably, the Courts, inflicting these illegal punishments during the period of the Greek rule, were those of the Hasmonean rebels, who had not yet established their State.

In that anarchic period the priestly Court of the Hasmoneans apparently took extreme measures to prevent even the slightest infraction of the Sabbath laws, lest it lead to worse, and sought to maintain levels of modest sexual behavior, with severity unknown to the Torah.

In the light of these records, we may understand the contradiction between two passages in Sifre. According to Sifre Deuteronomy 351, p. 408, all matters relating to the discovery of a slain person, whose murderer has not been identified, are under the jurisdiction of the priests, precisely as with the ceremony of the red heifer or the ordeal of the woman suspected of adultery. But this is certainly not the impression given by Mishna Sanhedrin 1.3, or Sifre Deuteronomy 205, p. 241. Because according to Scripture failure to punish a murderer defiles the land (Num. 35.34), the Court of Priests apparently claimed jurisdiction over such cases. Perhaps the disagreement between R. Judah and R. Simeon, as to whether five or three "judges" act in such matters, depends on the issue of whether the High Court of the Israelites, i.e., the Sanhedrin alone, is represented or also the Court of Priests.[184]

This discussion also explains the curious passage in Sifre Deuteronomy 208, p. 243, interpreting the verse (Deut. 21.8), "And the priests, the sons of Levi, shall come near — for them the Lord Thy God hath chosen to minister unto Him, and to bless in the name of the Lord; *and according to their word shall every controversy and every stroke be.*" The word rendered "stroke" (*nega'*) is interpreted by the Talmud to mean leprosy, following the usage of Leviticus, chapter 13. Hence Sifre explains the verse as follows: "Scripture compares controversies to leprosy. Just as lepers are examined only by day, so controversies are decided only by day. Just as controversies cannot be decided by relatives, so issues of leprosy cannot be decided by relatives." The discussion assumes that the judges in issues of controversy are priests, precisely as in cases of leprosy.

Another record seems to ascribe far broader power to the Court of Priests. The existence of a Court of Priests, with jurisdiction of its own, seems further confirmed by the curious record, Numbers 25.7, describing Phineas, about to impose punishment on Zimri, "arising out of his Sanhedrin."[185] By implication Phineas was a member of "the Court of Priests," but in this instance did not consult his colleagues. Finding the guilty engaged in the act of copulation, he was entitled to execute them. Interestingly enough, the reference to the Sanhedrin of Phineas was omitted in both Targum Onkelos and in Targum Ps. Jonathan, although it occurred in the Targum Yerushalmi. The ancient authorities were not in complete agreement about the rights of such a tribal or clan Sanhedrin.

We have already observed that a tradition concerning the summary execution of transgressors of Temple laws was transmitted by R. Eliezer ben Hyrcanus.[186] Other sources prove his intimacy with Temple traditions and the close relation of his views to those of the Temple priesthood. Perhaps, then, it is not farfetched to speculate that his view, adopting a more or less literal interpretation of the *lex talionis*, derived from the Court of Priests, which was also the source of Josephus' interpretation of the Law. Both R. Eliezer and Josephus agreed that the condemned could "ransom" his limb through appropriate compensation but, at least according to Josephus, when compensation was not made the *talio* could be enforced.

This view, followed at times by the Court of Priests, was considered Sadducean by most Pharisees and so was the view that execution by burning meant burning at the stake.

19. The Impurity of a Mother after Childbirth

We have already observed[187] that in Pharisaic law a *tebul yom* (i.e., one who has bathed to remove impurity ending at nightfall) was considered "pure" for all purposes except eating the heave-offering and other sacred meats and entering the Temple.

According to Leviticus, a woman after childbirth is unclean for seven days for a son, and fourteen days for a daughter. Thereafter she "shall continue in the blood of her purity" (Lev. 12.5). During this period of thirty-three days for a son and sixty-six for a daughter she might not enter the Temple nor eat the holy meat. In fact, she had the status of a *tebul yom*.

But what about her relations with her husband? The Talmud consistently denied any prohibition of marital intercourse in this period.[188] It even insisted she could not be defiled either menstrually or through a "flow," during this time, for the blood is the "blood of purity."[189]

However, the Samaritan text of Scripture and the Karaite interpretation of the Law held that a woman was "impure" during this period, and that marital relations with her husband were forbidden.[190]

A. Geiger expressed the belief that the Sadducees shared this view,[191] and the Talmud shows that customary practice prohibited marital congress during the period of purification.[192] One of the sins of the sons of the priest, Eli, was that "they lay with the women that did service at the door of the tent of meeting" (I Sam. 2.2). The Talmud denied this, asserting that they were accused of this gross transgression, because "they delayed the offering of the pigeons of purification, and thus prevented the women *from consorting with their husbands*."

This rabbinic interpretation assumes that women after childbirth could not enter into marital relations before bringing the prescribed sacrifice, at the end of forty days for a son and eighty days for a daughter.

The tradition, with its apology for the sons of Eli, seems of priestly origin, reflecting the attitude crystallized into a norm by the Sadducees, forbidding marital congress during the period of "purification." The Sadducean interpretation of the Law in this instance simply preserved an early priestly tradition which Proto-Pharisaism opposed as beyond the requirements of Pentateuchal Law. Perhaps the Pharisees and their predecessors were the more vehement in their opposition to the priestly exegesis because it implied a rejection of their whole concept of *tebul yom.*

The controversy probably arose in early times and seems to underlie the explanation of the law in the Book of Jubilees. According to that book (3.9 ff.) the rule dealing with impurity after childbirth commemorates the time when Adam and Eve were admitted to the Garden of Eden. Adam came into the Garden of Eden at the end of forty days after Creation; Eve after eighty days. Hence mothers were prohibited to enter the Sanctuary for forty days after the birth of a son and for eighty days after the birth of a daughter. The book stresses the fact that because of its sanctity Eve was kept out of the Garden of Eden for eighty days after her creation; while Adam was there. This passage suggests that mothers after childbirth were not only forbidden to enter the Temple, but also to engage in marital intercourse. The author thus supported the Sadducean view, forbidding marital relations during "the days of purification."

Geiger, following his concept of the "Old Halakah" and the "New Halakah," greatly confused his argument through an attempt to establish a relationship between the Sadducean view and that of the Shammaites.[193] However, we have shown that[194] his theory of the relations of the Shammaites to Sadducism is baseless. The Shammaites were as anti-Sadducean as the Hillelites. The controversies between the Schools of the Pharisees differed in their very nature from those between the Pharisees and the Sadducees.

On the other hand, evidence that the Shammaitic views cited by Geiger were unrelated to those of the Sadducees does not undermine his theory that the Sadducees forbade marital relations after childbirth, even during the period of purification. This view, upheld by many priests not necessarily associated with Sadducism as a movement, was bitterly opposed by non-priestly scholars in the Pharisaic tradition.

20. Proof of Virginity by a Bride under Suspicion

Deuteronomy 22.13 ff. provides that "if any man take a wife, and go in unto her, and hate her, and lay wanton charges against her, and bring up an evil name upon her, and say: 'I took this woman, and when I came nigh unto her, I found not in her the tokens of virginity'; then shall the father of the damsel, and her mother, bring forth the tokens of the damsel's virginity unto the elders of the city in the gate." The passage continues that if the charges are proved false, the husband shall be chastised, pay a fine of a hundred silver *shekels*, and be denied the right to divorce the woman at any future time. If the charges were shown to be true, she was executed.

A gloss in *Megillat Ta'anit*[195] reports that the Sadducees took literally the passage of Scripture describing the evidence to be produced by the parents of the accused bride. It reads: "And they shall spread the garment before the elders of the city." R. Eliezer ben Jacob in Sifre[196] maintains the same position, which reflects a priestly tradition.

Yet the glossator to *Megillat Ta'anit* would scarcely have invented the report that the doctrine was Sadducean. His tradition must therefore be correct. The Sadducees interpreted this biblical passage literally. But so did other early priests with whose opinions the glossator was apparently not acquainted.

The Sadducean view was perhaps more extreme than that of R. Eliezer ben Jacob, who held that the parents' failure to display the stained garment should result in the husband's acquittal. Therefore he would be free to divorce his wife without paying her dower, but she could not be executed. For, granted that she was not a virgin at the time of her marriage, she might have been seduced before her betrothal, and therefore would not be subject to capital punishment as having betrayed her husband.

Sadducean law does not seem to have made this distinction. Its rigorous norms may have imposed capital punishment even on an unmarried woman found unchaste. Hence the Sadducees may have taken the whole passage literally, maintaining that a bride who was found to have lost her virginity before marriage was subject to capital punishment.

Pharisaic law required witnesses for such a penalty. The husband had to prove that his bride had been unfaithful to him *during the period of their betrothal.*[197]

By Pharisaic interpretation two separate legal actions are discussed in this passage. The first is the husband's demand for summary divorce of his wife without payment of dower. This action might be sustained if the parents could not disprove the charge. Some Pharisaic priests held display of the garment was one way to disprove the charge.[198] But there might be other ways of doing so.

In another Pharisaic tradition of interpretation, while the whole passage deals with an accusation leading to capital punishment, it is interpreted metaphorically. The husband must produce witnesses to his wife's infidelity; the parents must produce witnesses impugning the testimony of the other witnesses.

This difference within the Pharisaic tradition is reflected in a controversy between R. Meir and his colleagues recorded in Mishna Sanhedrin.[199] Taking — as so often — the priestly view, R. Meir held that "the person bringing wanton charges" against a bride was, in the first instance, asking only for civil remedy. Therefore the case was to be tried before three judges. If there were witnesses to the charge of infidelity during the period of betrothal, another action might ensue, requiring like all capital cases twenty-three judges. Other scholars held that to be sustained at all the charge required witnesses; and the case was from its very beginning in the category of those possibly leading to capital punishment. They therefore required twenty-three judges for any case of "wanton charges."[200]

21. The Ceremony of *Halizah*

The same gloss, which asserts that the Sadducees insisted on a literal interpretation of Deuteronomy 22.15 ff., imputes a similar Sadducean approach to another passage.[201] In the ceremony of *halizah* releasing a childless widow from the obligation to marry her brother-in-law, the Bible includes the provision[202] that she shall "loose the shoe from off his foot" (i.e., her brother-in-law's foot), "and spit in his face [*befanav*]."

In Pharisaic exegesis, the word *befanav* means "before him." The Sadducees apparently took it to mean literally "in his face."

We have no reason to doubt the glossator's authenticity in this respect, especially because evidence has confirmed the remainder. Pharisaic judges naturally assumed that the amphibolous word *befanav* meant "before him"; for in their society no one ever spat at another's face. Equally naturally the peasantry, among whom many Proto-Sadducees were reared, took the word to mean "in his face."

F. The Theological Controversies

22. The Doctrines of the Resurrection and of the Immortality of the Soul

In this book's discussion[203] of the Pharisaic concepts of the Resurrection of the Dead and of the Immortality of the Soul, I was guilty of a number of errors both of omission and of commission. In some form the doctrine of man's immortality was even in Palestine much older than Pharisaism. Paleolithic men buried their dead in a manner suggesting that even they regarded death as merely a state in vital existence, and transcending it. The shade was believed to survive in the grave; and among some groups of the people the shade or spirit was worshiped.

This popular tendency toward worship of ancestral shades explains, as suggested in this book,[204] the unwavering resistance of the Prophets to the bare mention of spirits. Nevertheless, hints of popular belief in "spirits," scattered in the Pentateuch, Prophets, and Hagiographa, indicate that the superstition was widespread.

Since this work was published, Ezekiel Kaufmann has clearly established the Isaianic authorship of chapters 24-27 of this Prophet's book.[205] It follows that the first clear reference to the future Resurrection of the Dead was made by Isaiah in the eighth century B.C.E. All theories ascribing the emergence to the Second Commonwealth should therefore be discarded.

Yet the Hasideans of the Persian age, as well as their opponents, introduced a new element in the discussion of man's future. I have shown elsewhere,[206] that at least two concepts concerning this future were current among the Pre-Maccabean Hasideans. One stressed the Immortality of the Soul; the other, the future Resurrection of the Dead.

These ideas were not originally confused. Maimonides in some works seems to suggest that they are not only independent of one another, but in a way mutually inconsistent.[207] Assuming that man is essentially an immortal spirit and that his life on earth is simply prelude to a nobler existence in Paradise, the resurrection of the body to further sensuous being seems superfluous and even undesirable. On the other hand, if man's eschatological future inheres in return to physical life with a body, how will the soul survive without a body, and what will the soul do during the aeons separating death from resurrection?

Full analysis of the interplay of the two doctrines in Hasidean, Pharisaic, and rabbinic literature requires a volume which I hope to write. For the present discussion, it is sufficient to note that the term *'olam ha-ba* ("the coming aeon"), used so often in the rabbinic literature to describe man's future state, is deliberately ambiguous. It is no accident that such scholars as Maimonides[208] and Nahmanides[209] disagree about its meaning. The great commentators perceive different meanings in the *'olam ha-ba* because ambiguity was intended. Formulated probably as early as the fourth century B.C.E., the Mishna uses the term *'olam ha-ba* to suggest man's future bliss. But recognizing the existence of different concepts of this bliss, the author of the Mishna (as frequently in other controversies) takes no sides, and uses language acceptable to either view. That the term *'olam ha-ba* is amphibolous is by no means an original opinion of mine.[210] It was expressed centuries ago by Rabbi Joseph Albo[211] and following him by Rabbi Issachar Baer, author of the brilliant commentary called *Beer Sheba* on a number of talmudic treatises, including the final chapter of Sanhedrin.[212]

Belief that man's soul is immortal, and that the righteous do not really die, but at the moment of death become virtually angels, must have seemed to many teachers of early centuries perilous to religion. The Prophets Isaiah, Jeremiah, and Ezekiel avoided mention of "angels" because the word might mean personal angels with wills of their own, and such angelology might compromise Prophetic monotheism.[213] The Prophets would naturally be very careful to avoid the suggestion in public addresses that at death every human being might become a "spirit" residing in Heaven with God Himself. Such a concept might encourage prayer to ancestors, perhaps sacrifice to them and deification of them. The negation in virtually all biblical psalms of Thanksgiving of the possibility of the dead offering prayer to God was therefore deliberate.[214] It was not unnatural for one recovering from serious illness to include in his prayer of gratitude an expression of delight in ability to utter it. But the Thanksgiving hymns go far beyond this. They consistently declare that *only* the living can give praise to the Lord.

The attitude of the biblical psalmists to the doctrine of immortality is in sharp contrast to that of the authors of the Thanksgiving hymns emanating from the Cave Sect. Reaction to negation of immortality in the biblical hymns led the sectarians to emphasize the doctrine in their own compositions.[215]

Such an assertion as "The heavens are the heavens of the Lord; but the earth hath He given to the sons of men. The dead praise not the Lord, neither any that go down into silence" (Ps. 115.10-11), was intended to offset or discourage the increasingly popular concept of man's immortality.

Doubtless many primitive men, like some in the present age, concerned over severe illness of someone dear to them, were impelled to seek the intercession of their dead ancestors before the Heavenly Throne. To obtain this intercession they might visit the graves of the dead. To prevent the person restored to health from believing that such petitions to the dead had indeed helped, he was required to recite psalms denying any such possibility.

The doctrine of immortality must have appeared particularly dangerous to the religious teachers of the countryside, where ancestor worship and spirit worship were still rife as late as the Hellenistic and talmudic periods. That may have been the reason for the emphatic negation of belief in immortality in pilgrim hymns, such as those included in the *Hallel* recited by the peasant on his visit to Jerusalem.

None of these hymns deny the future resurrection. That doctrine could in no way be held inconsistent with the absolute monotheism which the Prophets sought to preserve in the teeth of widespread polytheism. On the contrary, as we have already seen,[216] Isaiah affirms the doctrine of the Resurrection of the Dead. Ezekiel symbolically raised the dead to life, and thus suggested that physical resurrection of the righteous might well be expected in the future time. Elijah[217] and Elisha[218] both are reported to have resurrected persons who had been dead. Thus the eschatology of the Psalms and of Prophetic passages dealing with the hereafter differs markedly from that implied in such works as those of Ben Sira, who denies the Resurrection of the Dead.[219]

We may conclude that earlier teachers of Judaism did not resist the almost universal conviction that ultimately the dead will rise to life, but they were concerned lest the doctrine of individual immortality, unlike the doctrine of the resurrection, lead to ancestor worship or deification of the dead. In contrast, the concept of resurrection by its implications offered hope for the nation as a whole.

Resistance to the doctrine of immortality in such obviously

early compositions as the various Thanksgiving hymns is evidence of the ancient origin of the concept. The notion may have developed during the First Commonwealth. If this is correct, the usual approach to the emergence of Pharisaic eschatology requires thorough re-examination.

Religious teachers of the countryside would resist, as related to ancestor worship, such a concept of immortality. The doctrine was particularly congenial to the city, where urban cosmopolitanism and emphasis on the individual combined to make the idea of personal immortality especially attractive. The sharp contrast between rich and poor in the metropolis brought special urgency to the problem of the theodicy for its religious teachers and special welcome to the concept of the Immortality of the Soul.

Jerusalem during the Persian and the early Hellenistic periods was not so different from the countryside that it would develop notions distinctive of a metropolis. The main growth of Jerusalem during the Second Commonwealth seems to have occurred during the Ptolemaic and Hasmonean periods. The author of the Book of Jubilees could still conceive of all the pilgrims to Jerusalem eating the Second Tithe within the Temple courts (Jub. 32.14).[220] Even if the "Sanctuary" was held to include the whole area of the Temple mount, the number of pilgrims accommodated then would be very small indeed. The paschal lamb was also eaten only in the courts of the Sanctuary (ibid., 49.20), although the Book of Jubilees attempted to meet resultant overcrowding by requiring only males, twenty years and over, to participate in the paschal feast (ibid., 49.17). But the book specifically demands that the paschal lamb be eaten in "the courts of the house." All this would have been impossible in the time when Jerusalem was hardly large enough to hold the pilgrims.

While Jerusalem in Persian and early Hellenistic times may have been little more than a village, it probably had expanded into quite a city during the reigns of Hezekiah and Josiah.[221] Therefore the origin in Judaism of the concept of personal immortality may perhaps be dated in these reigns. Virtually all the ritualistic controversies between Pharisee and Sadducee seem to have arisen before the Exile, and it now appears that the issue of man's immortality was possibly also of pre-exilic origin.

The Pharisaic view on the subject was not found in Scripture, because belief in man's immortality was not then (even by its proponents) regarded as essential to faith and religion. As we shall presently see,[222] it was not even stressed in the earliest synagogue liturgy. The issue was far more metaphysical than theological, religious, or moralistic. The Prophets appealed to men to seek justice out of love for God, out of desire to obtain mercy for their people, and out of fear of punishment in the present world. Their preserved utterances contain no discussion of whether immortality awaits the righteous who suffer in the present world. This was natural. They faced an idolatrous, assimilated opposition which either rejected the doctrine of immortality, or accepted it as ancestor worship, anathema to the Prophets.

On the other hand, the doctrine of the Resurrection of the Dead apparently became a cornerstone of Proto-Pharisaic theology in the fourth century B.C.E. Taught perhaps for centuries in Prophetic schools, possibly associated with the doctrine of the future Messiah, implied in at least one passage in Deutero-Isaiah, the idea of a future resurrection of the pious in which the wrongs of this world would be righted, ultimately became a cardinal doctrine of the faith in the market place of the restored Jerusalem.

In Persian, Hellenistic, and later times, the priests, aristocrats, and provincial leaders opposed the concept, not because it was unmentioned in Scripture, for Isaiah had distinctly spoken of it, but rather because in aristocratic circles the idea was held detrimental to the morality of the youth. Ben Sira emphatically rejected it.[223] A moralist, he, like the authors of large sections of Proverbs, sought to inculcate morality through appeals to prudence, to persuade children of the wealthy of the perils lurking in the ways of the wicked, to encourage in his disciples thrift, diligence, caution, and respectability.

His patrician ethics was directed toward the encouragement of practicality in human relations, energetic pursuit of one's business, and protection of one's material interests. But all these tended to become insignificant under Proto-Pharisaic theology. The child raised on a rural estate, when he arrived in Jerusalem and heard of the current Hasidean eschatology, might not necessarily join their pious ranks or adopt their high moral standards, but he might begin to reappraise the goals of life highly regarded in his own class.

Anxiety of the Judean aristocracy about the spreading doctrine of the future world was forcefully expressed in the Sadducean taunt: "It is a tradition of the Pharisees, that they should deny themselves the goods of this world; but in the future world, they will have nothing."[224] The apothegm was addressed not to the Pharisees, but to young Sadducees. The Sadducean teachers, worried lest their charges become other-worldly, insisted on negation of the future rewards of righteousness claimed by the Pharisees. This was apparently the view also held by Ben Sira and other Proto-Sadducees.

As in other theological controversies, each side exaggerated the perils inherent in the other's views. The patrician leaders overstated the problem posed in the education of their children by the Proto-Pharisaic doctrine. Yet Pharisaic theory did tend to undermine some notions among patrician virtues. The convert to Proto-Pharisaic eschatology would take the Torah seriously not only in its formal rituals, but also as a way of life which to the patrician seemed dangerously unrealistic.

The Proto-Sadducean opposition to the doctrines of immortality and to resurrection was thus of a piece with the general outlook of the priesthood of pre-Maccabean generations. The insistence on fulfillment of the Divine command, even when that involved great sacrifice and, above all, the demand that all life be conducted as a sacred enterprise, were encouraged by the theology of an after-life. The Proto-Sadducean theory of the importance of worldly practicality was inconsistent with it.

Emphasis on the individual in the doctrine of the Immortality of the Soul made it no less repugnant to those placing central emphasis on the family and the nation. Not only did the doctrine of immortality, like that of the resurrection, tend to corrupt youth from the patrician point of view, but it also seemed to render irrelevant many Prophetic promises to the nation. In a Cosmos where, after death, the righteous virtually become angels, it might appear inconsequential to inquire what mundane bliss and power were reserved for Israel alone as a nation among the nations of the world.

From the beginning the Hasideans asserted that Immortality of the Soul could be achieved by Gentiles as well as by Jews, being a prerogative of righteousness, not of nationhood or of race.[225] This concept worked against the widespread notion of the priests that (like their own) Israel's holiness was one of status, rather than of function.

Finally, as indicated in the book,[226] the very democracy of the doctrines of immortality and resurrection made them repugnant to many. From the patrician viewpoint, any notion that the meanest subject in the Commonwealth might at the moment of death become — simply by virtue of righteousness and saintly living — the foremost member of his generation in Paradise, was obnoxious.

Because they had inherited from Prophetic predecessors both the concept of the Immortality of the Soul and that of the resurrection, the Proto-Pharisees considered either view consistent with tradition. Hence their invention of a term, *'olam ha-ba*, to be used for either the one or the other.

In the early generation of the Synagogue its leaders had no desire to oust from its membership those denying immortality and the resurrection. They accepted into the canon of the Psalter hymns definitely rejecting these doctrines and recognized the Books of Job and of Ecclesiastes as sacred works. Such prayers as the *Kaddish*, formulated in early times, as well as apparently the earliest forms of the *'amidah*, contained no reference to either doctrine.[227]

Only after the doctrines were denounced as heretical by the Proto-Sadducees did the Proto-Pharisees come to insist that, on the contrary, belief in *'olam ha-ba*, in one or the other of its forms, was a basic principle of the faith.

The benediction asserting the Pharisaic eschatological doctrine (intended to prevent Sadducees from leading the synagogue in prayer) was, in the ritual of the Holy Land, as ambiguous as the term *'olam ha-ba* itself.[228] The term, *mehayyeh ha-metim* applied to God, might mean either "He Who keeps the dead alive," or "He Who resurrects the dead."

Similarly, the Mishnaic norm:[229] "The following have no share in the future life — he who denies the *tehiyyat ha-metim*, of the Revelation, and the Epicurean," might admit to the future life those who accept *either* Immortality of the Soul *or* the Resurrection of the Dead. Maimonides, at least in one stage of the development of his thought, clearly interpreted the Mishna in this way.[230]

This analysis seems to confirm the theory that Sadducism was essentially a product of upper-class Jerusalem and of provincial thought, while Hasideanism had its roots in the market place of Jerusalem. But the development of the notion of the resurrection suggests, and other research indicates, that Pharisaism at an early time spread into the countryside of Judea, and even into the lowland villages of Benjamin and distant Galilee.

23. The Doctrine of Personal Angels

The argument in this book[231] indicates that, like so many other issues dividing Pharisee and Saducee, the theological debates originated in pre-exilic times. The question whether angels had individual personality was of particular concern to the Prophets and the Psalmists who feared lest man pray to "angels" and dilute the pure monotheism of their faith.

Avoidance of the word *malak* in so many pre-exilic works, substitution of the word *seraphim* for it in Isaiah, and development of the concept of living "beasts" and "wheels" carrying the Divine Chariot, further emphasized the distinction drawn by the Prophets between the creatures above man and God Himself. In the Torah the *malak* never had independent being. Inclusion in the sixth chapter of Genesis of the tale of the *nephilim* and the *bené elohim* who consorted with the daughters of men was intended to suggest the material, physical, and un-Divine nature of these beings, in sharp contrast to God. Psalm 82 was an effort to assert the mortality of these superhuman creatures who, whatever their nature, were not Divine.

It is instructive that the term, translated in the English Bible, "Lord of Hosts," never occurs in the Torah or the Book of Ezekiel, although it is quite common elsewhere. The precise meaning of the expression has not yet been clarified, but its omission in the Torah, and by Ezekiel, is surely significant and suggests resistance to the doctrine of personal angels.

The Passover *Haggadah*, compiled in its earliest form in the fourth or third centuries B.C.E.,[232] includes most emphatic denial of the existence of angels, except perhaps as emanations of the Divine Personality itself.

This negation did not prevent use of the Passover *Haggadah* in Pharisaic and rabbinic homes. But the desire to offset its rejection of an idea favored in some Pharisaic circles led to inclusion in the *Haggadah* of some rituals of a passage supplementing and in fact contradicting the main text.

The term *malak* never occurs in the Mishna, nor in any of the main texts of the prayer book according to the ancient rites. Despite the fact that the first benediction of the *Shema'* and the *kedushah* both deal with the angelic hymn of praise to God, the ancient Pharisaic liturgists were careful to speak of *seraphim*, *'ophanim* (wheels), and holy "beasts." Some prayers suggest that the hymns, ascribed by the Prophets to the *seraphim* and the "holy beasts," are uttered by the visible heavenly bodies: the sun, the moon, and the stars. Once more the inserted reference to angels (*malakim*) in later rituals only serves to emphasize their curious omission from the earlier texts.

Even within Pharisaism some groups held the belief in personal angels inconsistent with the tradition. Presumably these groups emanated from the upper strata of Jerusalem, the priesthood and allied circles who, having accepted Pharisaism, nevertheless considered references to angels in prayer unwarranted.

Yet many Pharisees accepted the concept of personal angels, without concern lest it compromise belief in the One God. This book shows[233] that for them any compromise of the Prophetic emphasis on the dignity of the individual creature, through an assumption of the existence of personal angels, was a far graver issue than a reconciling of monotheism with the existence of these angels.

Summary of the Discussion

From the preceding analysis it is evident that many underlying ideas of Sadducism had their origin in high antiquity. The ritualistic point of view attributed to the Sadducees reflects, in the main, the aristocratic and provincial attitudes of Judea in the later centuries of the First Commonwealth. This was apparently true also of the theological issues raised by Sadducism. Sadducean civil law included rules deriving from the priestly tradition and others which, like the ritual and theology of the Sadducees, probably originated among the aristocratic landowners of the First Commonwealth.

Pharisaism inherited most of its notions from the Prophetic schools. The Pharisaic contention that "the Prophets transmitted [the tradition] to the Men of the Great Synagogue,"[234] thus seems to be validated by analysis of their traditions.

III. THE *'AM HA-AREZ*

The impression conveyed by a cursory reading of the relevant talmudic texts that the *'am ha-arez* was impious requires reappraisal. By the standards of townsmen, he was ignorant, vulgar, boorish, but — like peasants all over the world — he was genuinely God-fearing.[1] Only comparison with the Hasidean preoccupation with service to God and transformation of all life into successive acts of worship reduced the *'am ha-arez* to a person neglectful of his faith. Study of the accusations made against him, and of those not made, offers better appraisal of his mentality.

Talmudic works show that the term *'am ha-arez* was applied primarily to the small landowners and tenant farmers,[2] who barely eked out their livelihood from the land they tilled. The term did not properly apply to the wealthy landowners, whose neglect of the Law was due, not to grinding poverty, but to willful disobedience.

Unlike some sinful townsmen, the *'am ha-arez* was afraid of incurring the wrath of God; and he often translated this fear into tabus. Perhaps he accepted in theory the Pharisaic concepts of the Resurrection and the Future Life; but these ideas did not affect him as they did the Hasidean and the Pharisee. He could not conceive of the future so vividly that expectation of reward in another life would make him give up real joys in the present one. Fearing the Deity, he was concerned lest transgression bring upon him immediate ill-fortune or strike him dead.

While his fear of God enabled the peasant to avoid transgression, like everyone else he found it easier to overcome small temptations than great ones. For instance, confronted with the demand that he deny himself and his family necessary food, he found a way to assuage his conscience without making what was to him undue sacrifice. Thus the *'am ha-arez* separated the heave-offering from his grain and delivered it to the priest.[3] The peasant considered the heave-offering sacred; and he feared that he might die if he consumed it, or grain from which it had not been separated.[4] He entertained no such fear of the First Tithe, assigned to the Levite, or the Second Tithe which had to be eaten in Jerusalem, or the tithe of the poor which in the third and sixth years of the Sabbatical cycle was set aside for charity. These were not "holy," for they could be eaten by anyone. Consequently, the peasant did not regard the laws surrounding them as comparable to those dealing with the heave-offering. The Hasidean scholar might insist that untithed grain was forbidden (*tebel*) like that containing the heave-offering. The Law might denounce eating such *tebel* as mortal sin. The *'am ha-arez* was not convinced. He understood the severe tabu attaching to the heave-offering. So far as he was concerned, no such tabu attached to the tithe which was not reserved for priests, and which (even according to the Hasideans) he and his fellows could consume as guests of a Levite or in Jerusalem.

The fact that the heave-offering was only one fiftieth of the harvest was a further argument not to withhold it. Similarly some *'am ha-arez* set aside the tithe for the poor; but having done so, appropriated it for themselves. And indeed their own poverty was only slightly less crushing than that of the landless orphans and widows to whom the tithe for the poor was assigned.

Again, the peasant tended to disregard the laws relating

to the Sabbatical year.[5] The Midrash suggests that the rigor of this law accounted for its neglect. Therefore the Midrash[6] asserts that those who observe the laws of the Sabbatical year should be considered "the mighty in strength that fulfill His word" (Ps. 103.20). "It is usual," noted the ancient Rabbi, "to see a person observe a commandment necessitating sacrifice on a particular day, or a particular week, or a particular month. But what commandment imposes sacrifice for a whole year? Yet this poor peasant watching his field or vineyard barren, is compelled to pay government imposts on it and suffer in silence. Is there a mightier man than he?" Some rabbinic authorities held that the laws of the Sabbatical year applied only as part of the Jubilaic system,[7] and that the latter was dependent on equal distribution of land among the people of Israel.[8] We do not know whether the peasant shared this view. In any event, the *'am ha-arez* was, doubtless justly, suspected of violating the laws of *Shebi'it* (the Sabbatical year).

But he observed the weekly Sabbath. We have seen that he either did not know or did not concern himself with the norms forbidding various objects, such as rocks and stones,[9] to be moved on the Sabbath day. These norms were "rabbinical" in origin. A peasant would find it difficult to see how moving a rock in order to take a willow from under it for religious use could be a violation of the Sabbath.

On the other hand, in common with other peasants of the Near East regarding the Sabbath as a day of peril,[10] the *'am ha-arez* would not utter a falsehood on that day.[11] He could be trusted on the Sabbath where he might be suspect during the rest of the week.[12]

A trustworthy tradition reports that the peasantry (when compelled to do so, because of crowded conditions in Jerusalem during the Passover) would eat their paschal meal on the Mount of Olives, within an area sanctified only by post-exilic governments.[13] The more meticulous *haberim* (formally accepted members of the Pharisaic order) recognized as part of the Holy City only the area sanctified during the First Commonwealth.

The *ʻam ha-arez* did not accept the Hasidean norm requiring even profane food to be kept pure so far as possible and to be consumed only in a state of purity.[14] The Hasideans themselves admitted that these norms were not "biblical" in the usual sense of the term; but regarding the world as a Temple they insisted that all normal life should be in a state of purity. This was a general commandment. The man violating it might not be a *haber*, but neither was he a transgressor.

On the other hand, the Talmud assumes as a matter of course that the *ʻam ha-arez* could be trusted to observe the laws of Levitical purity during a pilgrimage, when about to enter the Sanctuary.[15]

He could also be trusted to do nothing which might lead to defilement of a sacrifice.[16] R. José reported some sense of Pharisaic duress in the Pharisaic acceptance of the norm asserting confidence in such trustworthiness of the *ʻam ha-arez*. Had the *ʻam ha-arez* been considered suspect in such matters, he might have been tempted to set up a local altar in his own village,[17] rather than resort to the central Sanctuary. The lesson taught the Judaites by the Samaritan schism was not lost, and the authorities realized that undue rigor and severity could only lead to difficulties. Nevertheless, the Pharisees and their predecessors would never have accepted the word of the *ʻam ha-arez* regarding the Levitical purity of his produce for use in libations and other sacrifices, without evidence that this confidence was in general justified.

Nowhere was the *'am ha-arez* accused of laboring or engaging in commerce on the Sabbath day, of eating forbidden food, of seething meat in milk, of violating the holiness of the Sanctuary, of transgressing the laws of purity in marital intercourse, of failing to observe the major laws of purity dealing with the afflictions of "a flow" or leprosy. His clothes (but not he) were declared impure for the Hasidean, "lest his wife happen to have sat on them during her impurity."[18]

The *'am ha-arez* would not permit a menstruating woman to sit on his garment. But he did not regard his wife as "impure" during the whole period of seven days when he was forbidden to have intercourse with her. He distinguished, as the Talmud strongly hints others did, between the days when she was actually "defiled"[19] and those when she was simply waiting for the period of separation from her husband to end. During those additional days she might well sit on his garment. Yet the Hasidean considered the garment defiled in a major degree.

The peasant's honesty is suggested not merely by the norm declaring that he would not even for a considerable gain tell a falsehood on the Sabbath day,[20] but in many other ways as well. A woman housekeeper belonging to this class might, it is said, be suspected of substituting food of her own preparation for that entrusted to her by a *haber*.[21] She might without permission of her husband give household food to her neighbor.[22] But in such instances, the *'am ha-arez* could justify as generous the action held wrong by the stricter Hasideans.[23]

While the *'am ha-arez* was pious and observant by standards other than those of Hasideans,[24] he retained a number of rituals condemned by Prophecy and Pharisaism as virtually pagan. He would hesitate to start work on Fridays or Saturday evenings, or New Moons, preserving the Mesopotamian doctrine that the Sabbath and New Moon were days of ill-omen, but transferring the Sabbath tabu to other times. He was given to other superstitions associating relics of the dead with good or ill luck.[25] He continued the pagan fasts and celebrations, and his defenders tried hard to find support for his views in a reconstruction of history.[26] In the text of this book,[27] we indicate how the talmudic term *bet ha-baal*, meaning "field fed by rains" derives ultimately from discourse in which the *baal* was conceived as the god of rain and fertility. In some passages of the Mishna,[28] particularly sensitive editors apparently felt the impropriety of the use of the term *bet ha-baal*, and replaced it with the expression *bet ha-geshamim* (meaning literally, rain-watered field).

The curious term *minhah* for "afternoon" seems to derive from the usage at the local altars.[29] II Kings 3.20 placed the time of the *minhah* (meal-offering) slightly before noon; I Kings 29.36, in the late afternoon.[30] But the passages are not contradictory. There were two meal-offerings at the local altars whose owners could not afford, or regarded themselves as forbidden, to sacrifice a lamb each morning and afternoon. One was about midday, corresponding to the main meal of the day in the homes of royalty and wealth, the other was toward evening.

When the central Sanctuary in Jerusalem was defiled under King Ahaz, he introduced into it the pagan ritual which sacrificed a whole-burnt offering in the morning and a meal-offering in the afternoon (II Kings 16.15). But this meal-offering was specifically described as that "of the evening," presumably because at most local altars there was also a morning meal-offering instead of an animal sacrifice. By the time of Ezra the term "the meal-offering of the evening" had become a standard phrase to describe late afternoon, and was used in that sense in his memoirs (Ezra 9.4), as innocently as the term *bet ha-baal* is used in the Mishna. The "meal-offering of the evening" appeared in the more general sense of evening sacrifice in Psalms 141.2 and as a designation for late afternoon in Daniel 9.21.

The two meal-offerings of the local altars are still recalled in the expressions *minhah gedolah* ("the large meal-offering") and *minhah ketanah* ("the small meal-offering"), used in the Talmud to describe early and late afternoon, respectively. These terms have greatly troubled the talmudic commentators, for within Temple ritual, the two meal-offerings were indistinguishable from one another and the time of the day could not be fixed by them.

But derived from the village worship at the high places, the term was natural. Its penetration into the language of the Rabbis indicates its prevalence among provincials.

Because of the semi-pagan origin of these terms, they were never used in the Mishna, Tosefta, or other Palestinian sources.[31] The terms, employed by the Babylonian authorities, occurred in the Babylonian Talmud,[32] because their origin and associations were not recognized in that country.

Survival of the local altars to a later period justified the apprehension of early authorities (reflected in the remark of R. José ben Halafta, already cited)[33] that on slight provocation country folk might revert to the practice of village worship.

However, the outstanding characteristic of the *'am ha-arez* was his simplicity. The Talmud assumes as a matter of course that the peasant would not know when the beginning of a new month had been announced by the Temple priests or the Pharisaic courts.[34] He might be confused regarding the precise date of any event, although by the middle of the month he might be presumed to know the approximate date.[35]

The epithet *ʻam ha-arez* was not, however, given the peasantry by the Hasideans, but was applied to the "country people" by the landowning aristocracy whose main homes were in Jerusalem. The description thus corresponds to the expression "natives," for which it was used in the Books of Ezra and Nehemiah. The *ʻam ha-arez* mentioned in the last chapters of Kings[36] as a significant and recognized body in the Commonwealth, apparently represented the "country" in contrast to the "city." The term *ʻam ha-arez* should not therefore be rendered "people of the soil," but "country people" or "country person."[37]

IV. THE ORIGIN OF THE SADDUCEES AND BOETHUSIANS AS SECTS

While we have already suggested that Sadducean views originated very early,[1] possibly during the First Commonwealth, no organization of the Sadducean sect existed before the Hasmonean age. In pre-Hasmonean times, Sadducean notions needed no sectarian organization to protect them. The hierarchy which governed the community was committed to what later became known as Sadducean views. The Hasidean opposition to the hierarchy maintained its own traditions, transmitting them from master to disciple, as the correct interpretation of the Law. Only in details outside the area of Temple practice or national policy could Hasideans actually follow their convictions.

All this was changed when Simeon the Righteous admitted the "Sages of Israel,"[2] i.e., the Hasidean scholars, into the national *Gerousia*. Participation of the Hasideans in the leadership of the community inevitably involved at least partial acceptance of their doctrines even regarding Temple ritual. However, the Sadducean *halakah* was not forgotten. Driven underground, it survived through transmission from parent to child in the high-priestly families.

The authority gained by the Sages of Israel was apparently increased under the early Hasmoneans. The continued Hasmonean battle for independence, after the Syrian government had annulled its decrees against Jewish worship, may have alienated some Hasideans. But the obvious esteem and affection for John Hyrkan in Pharisaic tradition (at least up to his final years)[3] and the fact that he asked the *Pharisees* to punish the calumniator of his family[4] indicate sufficiently that under Hyrkan the Sages of Israel were in control of the judiciary and national religious policy.

Toward the end of his reign, as Josephus[5] and the Talmud[6] (although there the story is referred to Alexander Jannaeus) record, the Pharisaic scholars left the Sanhedrin and apparently their schools were suppressed. Perhaps in his attempt to free himself from them, Alexander dubbed them *Perushim*, or heterodox. Various considerations support the conjecture that this was the moment when those siding with the Hasmonean government came to be known as Sadducees, i.e., descendants of Zadok, the High Priest.

The name Sadducee would not have been applied to the defenders of the Hasmonean dynasty during the first period of its rise. At that early time they would still be widely regarded as upstarts and revolutionaries against the legitimate Zadokide high-priestly dynasty. Only Hasmonean reiteration, for half a century, that they were descended from Zadok would account for their adherents being named Sadducees.

The cleavage between John Hyrkan and the Sages of Israel, described by Josephus, is recorded with great detail in a *baraita*[6a] which may have been his source. However, this *baraita* in its present form replaces John Hyrkan with King Alexander Jannaeus. The reason is clear. The Babylonian transmitters of the *baraita* could not believe that the saintly John Hyrkan, of whom so many miracles were told, drove the Sages of Israel from the Sanhedrin.

On the other hand, another record curiously overlooked by commentators (including the present writer in his earlier studies) definitely associated the rise of Sadducism with the quarrel between the Sages of Israel and John Hyrkan. An historical document of primary significance, its meaning has been distorted through a strange conflation of textual readings, rendering it for a long time useless to historians.

This record was preserved in *Abot of Rabbi Nathan*, I. Solomon Schechter's great edition of that work and of the alternative version makes possible, for the first time, a reconstruction of the text of the original *baraita*. According to *Abot of Rabbi Nathan*, I, chapter 5, 13b, it reads:

> "Antigonus of Socho received the tradition from Simeon the Righteous. He used to say, 'Be not like servants, who serve their master in order to receive wages. Be rather like servants who serve their master without expectation of wages. But let the fear of Heaven be upon you, *so that your reward may be doubled in the future.*'
>
> "Antigonus had two disciples, who studied his words. They taught them to their disciples, who in turn taught them to their own disciples.
>
> "There arose [a group] critical of them [these disciples]. These men said, 'Why did our ancestors [i.e., Antigonus and perhaps also his teacher, Simeon the Righteous] say these things? Is it possible for a laborer to work all day and receive no wages at night? If our ancestors had known that there was another world, and there was [to be] a Resurrection of the Dead, they would not have spoken thus.' Thereupon they arose and separated themselves from the Torah. Out of them there arose two factions: Sadducees and Boethusians — the Sadducees called after Zadok; the Boethusians after Boethus. Boethus used vessels of silver and gold all his life. But this was not because of arrogance. The Sadducees hold that the Pharisees have a tradition which leads them to

self-denial in this world. Yet nothing awaits them in the future world."

An analysis of this record is indispensable for understanding the origin of the Sadducean sect.

We observe that the final words of the first paragraph, "so that your reward may be double in the future," are missing in the citation of Antigonus' maxim in the Mishna.[7] They seem to be an editorial addition by transmitters who tried to harmonize the saying of Antigonus with the Pharisaic doctrine of immortality. Had Antigonus actually included those words, the discussion recorded in the rest of the passage could not have occurred.

To understand the remainder of this record, it is necessary for the student to rid himself of the preconceptions engendered by the classical commentaries to the Mishna of Abot. In the prevailing interpretation, the disciples of Antigonus to whom the *baraita* referred bore the names Zadok and Boethus. The Sadducean sect was called after Zadok, the Boethusian after Boethus.

This interpretation had its origin in the *Aruk*[8] of Rabbi Nathan ben Yehiel of Rome. It was popularized by Rabbi Samuel ben Meir[9] and by Maimonides.[10] Historically it seems far more likely that the Sadducees were named after the High Priest Zadok who founded the hierarchal dynasty ministering in the Temple, and the Boethusians after the High Priest Boethus appointed by Herod.[10a] Therefore modern writers generally have rejected the authenticity of the record before us.

But unprejudiced study of the *baraita* in the form transmitted in *Abot of Rabbi Nathan*, I, and cited above, shows that it does *not* identify by name the disciples mentioned. The *baraita* merely states that Antigonus had two disciples who in turn taught their own pupils. The author of the *baraita* did *not* believe that the Sadducees and Boethusians were named after disciples of Antigonus. Had he held this view, he could scarcely have omitted so focal a point from his record. Moreover, we know from the Mishna of Abot,[11] as well as from *Abot of Rabbi Nathan* itself,[12] that Antigonus had two very famous disciples. They were the heads of the Pharisaic schools in the generation after him, namely José ben Joezer of Zeredah and José ben Johanan of Jerusalem. If the two disciples mentioned in our *baraita* were indeed named Zadok and Boethus, why does the record ignore his far more distinguished pupils, the leaders of Pharisaism in the following generation?

No Pharisaic record referring to the disciples of Antigonus could state that he had two disciples and then proceed to mention only the schismatics, without any reference to his *real* followers, the heads of the Pharisaic academies.

It seems evident that the two disciples mentioned in *Abot of Rabbi Nathan*, I, as particularly associated with Antigonus, were in fact those known to us from the Mishna, namely, the two Josés. We are told in this record that they transmitted his teachings to their pupils; and these pupils to another generation.

We know that José ben Joezer died a martyr's death at the hands of his nephew, Alcimus, who became High Priest during the Maccabean revolt.[13] But apparently José ben Johanan survived him as head of Pharisaism for many years. The disciples and successors of these early Pharisaic leaders were well known from the record in Mishna Abot and other sources. They were Joshua ben Perahya and Nittai of Arbel.[14] Their disciples and successors, in turn, are likewise well known. They were Judah ben Tabbai and Simeon ben Shattah.[15]

The *baraita* recorded with remarkable precision the course of events after the time of Antigonus. His teachings, transmitted by his disciples to theirs, and then to a third generation, ultimately encountered questioning: "There arose a group critical of them which asked, 'Why did our ancestors say these things?' "

The origin of the sectarian controversy is thus definitely dated in the time of Judah ben Tabbai and Simeon ben Shattah. Opponents rejecting their doctrines regarding another world and the Resurrection of the Dead, appealed to the authority of Simeon the Righteous and Antigonus of Socho who were recognized by all Jews as saints and masters of the tradition. Critics of the Pharisaic leaders spoke of Antigonus and presumably his teacher, Simeon the Righteous, as "our ancestors." These critics were not simply disciples of these sages, but their descendants. In brief, they belonged to the high-priestly families and the aristocracy of the land.

Unable to accept the interpretation put on the words of Antigonus by the heads of the Pharisaic academies, these men "separated themselves from the Torah." That is to say, they rejected the Pharisaic tradition, as transmitted by the Sages of Israel.

"There arose out of them two factions: the Sadducees, named after Zadok; the Boethusians, named after Boethus."

The Zadok now mentioned for the first time in this *baraita* could be no other than the most famous person bearing the name, the founder of the high-priestly dynasty. He needed no identification. The author of the *baraita* assumed that his hearers would know he meant *the* Zadok of Solomonic times. Nor was there need to identify Boethus. Everyone knew the notorious Herodian High Priest.

The chronicler did not claim that the Sadducees named for Zadok the High Priest, and the Boethusians named for Boethus, arose at the same time. He merely indicated that ultimately two factions developed in opposition to the Torah, as expounded by the Sages of Israel. One was called Sadducees, the other Boethusians.

Associating the Boethusians with the High Priest Boethus, the author nevertheless described him as a Sadducee. An upstart, Boethus, the record informs us, was not accustomed to the use of the gold and silver dishes. He resorted to them not out of a sense of refinement nor even out of arrogance. Rather, he followed a principle of the Sadducean group which insisted on enjoyment of the pleasures of this world. The Sadducees ascribed more significance to their earthly hedonism which underlay their disbelief in any future life, a conception they considered schismatic and, as we shall see, unethical.

It may seem curious to us, of course, that the taunt described as Sadducean should be used to explain the conduct of the central figure in Boethusianism. But the author of the record was aware of no contradiction. Boethus was a Sadducee. It was only as a result of his high-priesthood that a group of his followers came to be known as Boethusians.

Herod had appointed various upstart protégés to the high-priesthood. His supporters in this policy could scarcely be called Sadducees, for it was directed against the family whom tradition identified with the High Priest Zadok. The upstarts and their following came to be called Boethusians, after the best known and least respected of the Herodian High Priests.

In the taunt directed against the Pharisees and apparently reporting the *ipsissima verba* of the Sadducees, the future life normally described in talmudic literature as *'olam ha-ba*[16] ("the coming aeon" or "the coming world") is called *'olam aher* ("another world"). We have already remarked that the term *'olam ha-ba* was invented and employed by the Hasideans and Pharisees with deliberate ambiguity.[17]

It could refer either to the future aeon of the Resurrection or to the Paradise into which man's spirit entered immediately after death. The Sadducees distinguished the two ideas. They spoke of the world of immortal souls as "another world," and they insisted that their forebears, accepting either that doctrine or that of the resurrection, could not have made the assertion included in Antigonus' maxim.

The Sadducean terminology was in one version of the Targum[18] interestingly imputed to Cain. In the argument between Cain and Abel, which led to the latter's death, Cain said (according to the Targum), "There is neither judgment nor Judge, nor *another* world; *and there is no reward for the righteous nor punishment for the wicked.*" To this Abel replied, "There is judgment, and there is a Judge. And there is another world. There is reward for the righteous and there is punishment for the wicked." In this discussion Cain thus appeared as the spokesman for later Sadducism and Abel as the representative of Pharisaism.

Entering on his studies of Genesis in the Pharisaic schools, the boy was being fortified through the quotation in the Targum against the argument with which Sadducean children and teachers would endeavor to seduce him.

No theological issue divided the Boethusians from the Sadducees. Both belonged to the same ecclesiastical tradition. Both opposed the Pharisees and their traditions. But politically Sadducees and Boethusians were poles apart. The first were supporters of the ousted Hasmonean dynasty, and belonged to the old aristocratic families. The second were supporters of Herod and his flunkies, being upstarts from the lower ranks of the priesthood.

The Boethusians are therefore those whom the early Christians termed Herodians.[19] The Christians called them after their political affiliation; the Talmud, after the high-priestly house they supported.

The clear distinction between Sadducees and the Boethusians made in *Abot of Rabbi Nathan* is also reflected in the Babylonian Talmud. A record, preserved in the Talmud,[20] reports "If one lives in the same court with a Gentile, a Sadducee or a Boethusian, one may not carry anything [into it from the house or from it into the house] on the Sabbath day. Rabban Gamaliel holds that Sadducees and Boethusians do not necessarily make the court prohibited." (They could waive their rights to it, and then it would be used. In the case of a Gentile neighbor, waiving his rights would not suffice; one must pay him for the unqualified use of the court on the Sabbath day.)

The precision of the record in *Abot of Rabbi Nathan* need not astonish us. It occurs in the first of the five documents constituting that book. I have elsewhere demonstrated that this document was edited by Shammaites,[21] shortly after the destruction of the Temple and included a number of remarkably clear and precise ancient records.

The *baraita* did not state whether the Sadducean break "from the Torah" occurred at the beginning or toward the end of the careers of Judah ben Tabbai and Simeon ben Shattah. Nor can the dates of these scholars be determined with absolute precision. Joshua ben Perahya and Nittai of Arbel headed the Pharisaic academies after the death of José ben Johanan. It is reasonable to surmise that the period in which Joshua and Nittai presided over Pharisaism coincided with the first part of the reign of John Hyrkan.

The passing of these great scholars may have been one of the causes leading to the quarrel of John Hyrkan with the Pharisees. Judah ben Tabbai and Simeon ben Shattah in their youth may have been unable to guide Pharisaism with the maturity and understanding characteristic of their teachers, and had perhaps not yet been appointed to office when the crisis came.

It is certainly instructive that neither Joshua ben Perahya nor Nittai of Arbel, Judah ben Tabbai nor Simeon ben Shattah, was mentioned in the record of the quarrel between John Hyrkan and the Pharisees. None of these scholars was at the moment at the helm of Pharisaism. The older generation had passed; and the new one had not yet come into its own.

In any event, the *baraita* in *Abot of Rabbi Nathan*, I, definitely placed the quarrel between Sadducism and Pharisaism after the passing of Joshua ben Perahya and Nittai of Arbel, and therefore at the end of the high-priesthood of John Hyrkan.

One of the most astonishing aspects of this record is its understanding of Sadducism. This chronicler saw Sadducees not as heretics or apostates. He did not read them out of Judaism. He still belonged to the time when Pharisees quite willingly worshiped in a Temple presided over by a High Priest suspected of Sadducism, and when the Pharisaic sages gladly participated in a Sanhedrin containing Sadducean members, indeed, a Sadducean majority.

The *baraita* simply stated that the Sadducees broke away from "the Torah" — that is, the Hasidean tradition — not out of malice or wickedness, it would seem, but because Pharisaic doctrine seemed to them inconsistent with the maxim of Antigonus.

The question raised by the Sadducees, according to this *baraita*, suggests that they were trying to *protect* the observance of the Law, threatened, they thought, by Pharisaic other-worldliness. "Is it possible," the *baraita* quotes them as asking, "for a laborer to work all day and to receive no wages at night?" At first glance this seems a peculiar query in the mouths of Sadducees; for, far more than the Sadducees, the Pharisees had been insisting that the laborer would be recompensed — in another world. How does it follow from this question, that Antigonus did not believe in "another world" and the Resurrection of the Dead?

The answer is that the Sadducees did not question for a moment the principle of reward and punishment, but held that reward and punishment occurred *on earth.* Antigonus had not questioned the doctrine of reward and punishment, according to them. Could he really expect a laborer to work all day without expectation of wages? Apparently, they argued, what Antigonus was denying was not reward and punishment as such, but reward and punishment *in another world.*

Like Ben Sira, the Sadducees who thus broke with the Hasidean tradition were presumably convinced that the Hasidean eschatology was undermining the structure of moral education. The piety of the Sadducees, like their ethics, was entirely prudential. They had to deal with children of aristocracy, for whom life on earth offered many satisfactions. The threat that these satisfactions might be lost in punishment for sin, and the promise that they might be prolonged as reward for the good life, was far more significant to this system of education than the promise of a happy hereafter could be. The promise attracted the Pharisee who had little in this world and no prospects of improvement in his lot.

Disagreeing with the Sadducean approach, the ancient chronicler, perhaps a contemporary of Hillel and Shammai and therefore of Herod, still tried to explain it fairly and forthrightly to his own disciples. It was the more necessary to do this, because only through absolute frankness could he hope to bring his disciples to understand how the contemporary Temple hierarchy could be so misled as to be Sadducean or Boethusian.

This respect for the Sadducees has already been noted as characteristic of much rabbinic literature. Nowhere were the Sadducees described as seeking, like the Boethusians, to subvert witnesses through bribery in order to mislead Pharisaic courts. The issue of the date of the *Omer* sacrifice and of Shabuot was consistently attributed to the Boethusians, not the Sadducees. This was not because the two groups disagreed in the matter, but because the Pharisees wished to present the opposition in the ugliest light. The Mishna and kindred works explained again and again that many Sadducees in their piety would follow Pharisaic traditions, for fear of falling into transgression.[22]

From the standpoint of these early Pharisees, while John Hyrkan erred grievously in accepting some Sadducean traditions and restoring them to the Sanhedrin, that did not destroy his reputation as a man of piety and dedication. He could still be regarded in Pharisaic literature as a saintly person and stories of his almost prophetic qualities could be transmitted in the academies.

When the "men of Jerusalem," presumably the Pharisaic population of the Holy City, decided to appoint Judah ben Tabbai their *Nasi*, he fled from this honor,[23] trying presumably to avoid the inevitable quarrel with the Hasmonean priests which would result from his acceptance of the office. Therefore he sought refuge in Alexandria, not from the wrath of John Hyrkan or Alexander Jannaeus, but from the ill-timed tribute of his own colleagues. Thus Pharisaism remained without recognized heads for its schools and for the movement as a whole, from the defection of John Hyrkan until the time of Queen Salome.

The struggle between the Sadducee and Pharisee became acute during the civil war under Alexander Jannaeus. Although his father had broken with the Pharisees, Alexander Jannaeus, interestingly enough, still performed the ritual of the water-libations in accordance with their views;[24] therefore the break between the Hasmoneans and the Pharisees had not become complete under John Hyrkan. He merely had adopted some Sadducean ways and readmitted them to the Sanhedrin. His view had wide support among the priests, but through its application the control of the Sanhedrin was handed over exclusively to the Sadducees, whereupon the Pharisaic scholars left in anger.

Yet never, while the Temple stood, did the tension between the groups become such as to prevent many Pharisees from worship there. Even the Boethusian High Priests appointed by Herod and his successors were generally recognized as fit to perform the service.

Final denunciation of the Sadducees as apostates occurred

only after the destruction of the Temple. The Schools of R. Ishmael and R. Akiba both agreed in this judgment.[25] But whereas the School of R. Ishmael still held that the Sadducees should be differentiated from the Epicureans or atheists, the School of R. Akiba could perceive no distinction between the groups. The view of R. Akiba is reflected in the second version of *Abot of Rabbi Nathan*, where the *baraita* cited above occurred in much altered form. To quote this *baraita*,

"He [Antigonus of Socho] had two disciples, named Zadok and Boethus. Having heard this maxim [of Antigonus], they taught it as they had received it from their master. But they [Zadok and Boethus] omitted the explanation harmonizing Antigonus' words, with the views of the Pharisees. Hence they [the disciples of Zadok and Boethus] said to them [i.e., to Zadok and Boethus], 'Had you known that there will be a Resurrection of the Dead and a future reward of the righteous, (they) [you] would not have said this.' Thus they became apostates; and there arose out of them two families: the Sadducees, named for Zadok; and the Boethusians, named for Boethus."

We observe in this *baraita* that the Boethusians and Sadducees are described not only as having abandoned the Torah, but as having become apostates; also that the groups are described as being named not after the High Priests, but after disciples of Antigonus of Socho. Finally, the disciples of Zadok and Boethus are held to be the founders of the sects.

This theory of the origin of Sadducism and Boethusianism may (as we shall see) be ascribed to the School of R. Akiba.

The Talmud records the opposition between this School and the older scholars regarding the status of Boethusians and Sadducees. In the record already cited from B. 'Erubin, 68b, we are told that, according to Rabban Gamaliel II,

Sadducees and Boethusians were not in a class with Gentiles respecting the Sabbath law. The colleagues of Rabban Gamaliel held they were. Rabban Gamaliel derived his tradition, he himself stated, from the practice of his father who apparently took the older view, tolerating the deviationists. The sages opposing Rabban Simeon ben Gamaliel I and his son belonged to the School of R. Akiba. For them, no distinction would be drawn between these sectarians and Gentiles in regard to the Jewish Sabbath law.

(This interpretation of the controversy between Rabban Gamaliel II and his colleagues was given by R. Meir who, despite his relationship to R. Akiba, often transmits priestly and Shammaitic traditions. According to R. Judah, even Rabban Gamaliel held that the schismatics were to be considered as Gentiles regarding their attitude toward the Sabbath.)

The ascription of this section of *Abot of Rabbi Nathan*, II, to R. Akiba and his School is amply supported, for it bears the stamp of R. Akiba's editorship. Several basic differences between *Abot of Rabbi Nathan*, I and II, in this part of the book prove the latter's relation to R. Akiba. Whereas *Abot of Rabbi Nathan*, I, holds (in this first section of the book) that a woman, in the time of her impurity, might not adorn herself (a teaching of the Shammaites),[26] *Abot of Rabbi Nathan*, II, includes no such prohibition, adopting the more lenient view of R. Akiba. *Abot of Rabbi Nathan*, I, stated that Rabban Johanan ben Zakkai was received with great friendship by Vespasian, even before the prophecy that the latter would become Emperor, while *Abot of Rabbi Nathan*, II, held that Rabban Johanan obtained leave to establish an academy at Yabneh only after that prediction. This view suggests that held by R. Akiba, who blamed Rabban

Johanan ben Zakkai for failing to demand that Vespasian abandon the war against Jerusalem.[27] Surely R. Akiba could have considered such a request possible only *after* the fulfillment of Rabban Johanan's prediction. *Abot of Rabbi Nathan*, II, further included a severe stricture against the descendants of Hillel, especially Rabban Simeon ben Gamaliel I and Rabban Gamaliel II, because "they were rigorous in their own observance, and lenient to all Israel."[28] This complaint may naturally be ascribed to R. Akiba and his School, who were irked by some of the pro-Shammaitic tendencies of these scions of the dynasty of Hillel.[29]

Evidently it was the view of R. Akiba and his School that the Shammaitic tendencies of these descendants of Hillel could not be excused on the ground that they followed the more rigorous view in their own practice.

These examples indicate that *Abot of Rabbi Nathan*, II, (at least in its first section) has come to us in the form given by the School of R. Akiba. This School maintained that the Sadducees, denying the Resurrection, the Future Life, and the Oral Law, were renegades and apostates and could not really be included within the fold of Judaism.

R. Akiba also found the differences between the Sadducees and the Boethusians to be only those of a family. The age of Herod had long passed. R. Akiba saw no reason to distinguish the Sadducee from the Boethusian on any issue. It seemed to him clear that the groups divided only socially.

As in other matters, so in regard to the theory of sectarian origins, R. Akiba's view came to dominate the Babylonian academies. Babylonian scholars generally equated Sadducism with apostasy. John Hyrkan's defection from Pharisaism was cited as an example of a man having served as pious High Priest for eighty years who became an apostate in his old age.[30] For the Babylonian scholars, the incident aptly illustrates the maxim, "Do not feel certain of thyself [i.e., thy piety] until the day of thy death."[31] Following the *baraita* as taught in the School of R. Akiba, the Babylonian scholars further concluded that the breach between John Hyrkan and the Pharisees occurred, not in the time of Judah ben Tabbai and Simeon ben Shattah (the third "Pair" after Antigonus), but in that of Joshua ben Perahya. Hence according to the Babylonian Talmud it was Joshua ben Perahya, not Judah ben Tabbai, who fled office.[32] With courageous anachronism, the Babylonian Talmud held that Joshua ben Perahya was recalled from Alexandria by Simeon ben Shattah, when the latter attained power under Queen Salome.

On the other hand, the prevalent view of the Talmud of Jerusalem favored the account given in *Abot of Rabbi Nathan*, I. In this view John Hyrkan never abandoned his saintliness, despite his error. The maxim, "Do not feel certain of thyself until the day of thy death," is illustrated by a story of a pious scholar who was seduced to transgression by a spirit.[33]

At the same time, for reasons already mentioned, the whole talmudic tradition was unanimous in its contempt for the Boethusians.

The record of *Abot of Rabbi Nathan*, I, regarding the origins of Sadducism and Boethusianism, issuing from an author almost contemporary with the events, agreed wholly with the conclusions of modern historical research. While Sadducean views originated among early cynical, self-serving High Priests whose attitudes and spirit remind one of the later Boethusians, many Sadducees of the Hasmonean period and thereafter were men of genuine piety. They followed the traditions received from their ancestors, but usually also heeded the prescriptions of the Pharisees. These priests may never have become converted to the doctrine that the "Sages of Israel" had a place in the Sanhedrin; but that prejudice was natural to the priestly class and its clients.

Almost all medieval scholars, identifying contemporary Karaism with ancient Sadducism, were unwilling to differentiate Sadducees from Boethusians; and declared that neither could be considered Jews, so far as the ritual of the Sabbath was concerned.[34]

V. THE SOCIOLOGICAL BASIS OF THE CONTROVERSIES WITHIN PHARISAISM

The unique and astonishing durability of Pharisaism — the only interpretation of Judaism to have retained its vigor across the centuries — may be attributed to many causes. One was almost certainly its hospitality to varying interpretations of Scripture regarding marginal and doubtful issues.[1] Unlike the sectarian interpreters of Judaism, the Pharisees never permitted their doctrine to become monolithic. So long as the letter and spirit of Scripture were preserved intact, Pharisaism tolerated wide flexibility in doctrine as well as in ritual. Thus, while (as already noted)[2] the controversies between the Pharisees and their opponents generally center about issues where the meaning of Scripture was not really in doubt, controversies within Pharisaism all dealt with problems where Scripture offered no clear guidance. It is the thesis of this book that many of the controversies which arose over such issues within Pharisaism had their basis in differences of sociological, cultural, and economic background. The relation of some controversies to such differences of background is suggested in the text of this book as well as in my *Akiba*.[3] A full examination of the theory would require more than one volume and cannot be undertaken here. However, the discussion aroused by the thesis in the first edition of this book in 1938 necessitates at least the presentation of further evidence in its support.

The theory that many rabbinic decisions were largely determined by local, group, or family considerations, preconceptions and even bias, was not invented by me, nor even by the late Professor Louis Ginzberg.[4] It is far older than Nahman Krochmal or Geiger, who explained a number of otherwise inexplicable controversies in this way. The theory is clearly stated in the Talmud and developed by the great medieval commentators. Neither the Talmud nor the medieval scholars applied the principle consistently to the interpretation of rabbinic controversies, because they were primarily concerned with decision-making rather than history or biography.

Identification of the sociological background of a position taken by ancient scholars is of no help to decision-makers in determining the Law. That is a problem of objective exegesis. To take account of the bias implied in the original view is to argue *ad hominem*. Hence the Talmud and the medieval commentators, fully cognizant of the relation of specific views of ancient teachers to local conditions and tribal traditions, devoted their energies to the discovery of a dialectic by which decisions could be objectively evaluated. For the modern temper, concerned no less with history and biography than with exegesis, the sociological background of the various rabbinic sayings, particularly when there is conflict among the sages, is highly significant.

Differences among rabbinic scholars arose in at least three ways. Some of them deal with marginal issues, on which earlier texts were unclear; others with new situations not defined in earlier texts. But a third group preserves different traditions, going back possibly to the very origins of Judaism. Early differences of custom became hardened, in these instances, into differences of opinion.

It would be beyond the scope of the present essay to discuss the last group of differences. The Talmud itself recognizes its existence; for this type of difference illustrates the principle that until the time of José ben Joezer, the Torah was studied as it was given to Moses; thereafter, it was not studied as it was given to Moses.[5]

Whether hardening of variations of custom into controversies between factions was itself due to changes in sociological background is an issue to be discussed in another connection. But certainly the Talmud accepts the view that many controversies regarding marginal issues and new issues had their genesis in personal or group need, bias, or preconception.

The Talmud recognizes, for example, that disagreement in interpretation of the Law between Babylonia and the Land of Israel often arose because of the different conditions prevalent in the two countries. Thus when Rab said that "Ninety-nine percent of the people die because of an evil eye, and only one percent through the decree of Heaven,"[6] whereas R. Hanina remarked that "Ninety-nine percent die because of cold, and only one percent because of the decree of Heaven," the Talmud adds that they disagreed "Because Rab lived in Babylonia where the evil eye was common, whereas R. Hanina lived in Sepphoris, where the climate is cool."[7]

In halakic issues the Talmud was equally clear in its realization of the inevitable impact of locality on opinion. In the discussion of the different views of R. Johanan and Rab Hisda about the formula to be used in the benediction after eating certain fruits, the Talmud remarks that R. Johanan's opinion was natural for a resident in the Land of Israel, Rab Hisda's for a resident in Babylonia.[8]

A similar comment is made by the Talmud in the discussion of another difference of opinion between R. Hanina and Rab. The issue revolved about the precise moment when a meal may be said to have begun. The law forbids one to begin a meal after the time for afternoon prayers, before reciting them. However, having begun one's meal, it need not be interrupted for prayer. What then is the "beginning" of a meal, which justifies its continuance even though the time has arrived for the *minhah* prayer? R. Hanina says "the loosening of one's girdle" as one sits down to eat. Rab says "the washing of one's hands" in preparation for the meal.[9] "But," adds the Talmud, "they do not disagree. One was discussing the norm applying to the Land of Israel" (where, says Rashi, girdles were worn loosely and did not have to be unfastened before a meal); the other is speaking of Babylonia (where girdles were worn tightly fastened).

There are no fewer than eight controversies which the Talmud maintains are not controversies at all, but reflect differences of background between the Land of Israel and Babylonia.

The Talmud goes further: it insists that many apparent controversies, even between authorities living in the same country, reflect differences of local situation or dialect.

R. Eleazar ben Azariah and his colleagues disagreed regarding the sacrifice to be offered by one who said simply, "I vow to bring a whole-burnt offering." R. Eleazar maintained that the man must bring a pigeon or a dove; the other scholars said, a lamb.[10] The Talmud explains that both actually held the same view, namely, that under the circumstances one is required to bring the least costly offering. But in the locality of R. Eleazar pigeons and doves were cheaper than lambs, whereas in the locality of his colleagues they were more expensive.[11]

A controversy between R. Meir and R. Judah about the precise form of the ritual of the Day of Atonement performed by the High Priest in the Temple is explained in the Talmud as deriving from differences of dialect.[12] The High Priest, offering the blood of the sacrifice in the Holy of Holies, had to aim one drop directly in front of him and seven downward. To make sure that he did not violate the rule by offering more or less, he counted each drop. And to prevent confusion, he would say, "One," as he sprinkled the first drop, directly before him. And then as he added the seven others, he would say, "One and one; one and two; one and three," etc. This is the ritual according to R. Meir. According to the tradition of R. Judah, the High Priest said, "One and one; two and one," etc. The Talmud explains that each rabbi ascribed to the High Priest the language he would himself use; and that the difference of opinion is therefore nothing more than dialectal.

According to Mishna Nedarim 6.1, "One who takes a vow not to eat cooked food, may eat roast." The Babylonian Talmud (ad loc.) cites an opposing view by R. Josiah, who held that roasting is included in the term "cooking." The Talmud adds that no controversy is involved; only a difference of dialect. In R. Josiah's country, roasting was called cooking; in that of the majority of the scholars, it was not.

Again, according to Mishna Nedarim 6.5, "One who vows not to drink milk is permitted to drink skimmed milk; but R. José forbids it." The Talmud explains that this controversy, too, really reflects a difference not of opinion but of dialect. "In the locality of the majority group, skimmed milk was not called milk; in R. José's town it was."[13]

Mishna Baba Mezi'a 3.8 maintains that if wine placed for safe-keeping cannot be identified, the person to whom it is entrusted, returning its equivalent to the owner, may deduct one-sixth of the volume because of the absorption by the earthenware containers. R. Judah holds that the trustee may deduct a fifth. "But," adds the Talmud,[14] "there is no real disagreement among the scholars. Each one rendered the decision according to the local custom." In the locality of the majority group the container would be covered with a coating of wax, which absorbed less wine. In that of R. Judah a more absorbent tar coating was used. Another view holds that there was a difference in the earthenware used for the container itself. Some pottery is more absorbent than others; and the two opinions arose out of differences in the type of earthenware in use.

In another chapter of the same treatise (10.2), the Mishna discusses the allocation of the cost of rebuilding a house in which the lower floor belonged to one person, and the upper story or attic to another. "The one owning the ground floor," says R. José ben Halafta, "provides the ceiling. The one owning the upper story provides the cement put on top of the ceiling [to serve as floor for his home]." R. José ben Hanina and R. Simeon ben Lakish seemed to disagree regarding the precise meaning of the word *tikra* (ceiling) as used by R. José ben Halafta. According to R. José ben Hanina, "ceiling" here means "mats." According to R. Simeon ben Lakish it means "boards." The Talmud continues: "But no controversy is involved. In the place of R. José ben Hanina mats were used to separate the two stories from one another; in the place of R. Simeon ben Lakish, boards."[15]

According to Mishna Baba Batra 1.6, a field belonging to two partners cannot be divided between them, except by mutual consent, unless it is large enough to provide each with nine *kab* (a *kab* is a sixth of *seah*, which contains 2,500 square cubits, approximately 10,000 square feet). R. Judah says, "Nine half *kab* would be sufficient." "But," says the Talmud again, "there is no controversy. Each sage decided according to [the needs of] his locality."[16] According to the *Tosafot*, the talmudic comment means that R. Judah's country was very fertile, and therefore it paid to cultivate even a small plot. This was not true in the country of his antagonists. However, perhaps we may also interpret the difference as arising from the standard of living and property of the two authorities. In R. Judah's poor community, a field of nine half *kab* was a respectable piece of property. In the locality of his opponents it was considered too tiny for a family.

The Talmud (according to one view) ascribes to R. Judah ben Ilai the opinion that "A person suspect of violating the law of the Sabbatical year is necessarily suspect regarding the tithes." This assertion opposes R. Akiba's view that "One suspect of transgressing the laws of the Sabbatical year is not necessarily suspect regarding the tithes."[17] Explaining R. Judah's view, the Talmud comments, "In the locality of R. Judah, the laws of the Sabbatical year were observed meticulously," and therefore heeding them did not necessarily imply equal concern for the tithes. The region from which R. Akiba's norm derived differed in this respect from that in which R. Judah's originated. (We shall observe hereafter that the Talmud is referring not to R. Judah's native country, or that in which he spent his mature life, but to the highlands of Judea, the traditions of which he usually transmits.)

The Mishna itself asserted that judicial decisions and norms announced as applying generally often really were dictated by local situations. Thus, the Mishna, Ketubot 5.8, stated as a general norm, that "A trustee appointed to provide for the maintenance of another person's wife is required to supply her with two *kab* of wheat, or four *kab* of barley, each week." R. José ben Halafta added the following comment (included in the Mishna itself), "The scholar who required this measure of barley was R. Ishmael, who lived near Edom." According to the Babylonian scholars, R. Ishmael's reason was that the barley of that region was particularly poor; and no less than twice the amount of wheat needed to sustain life would be required of that type of barley.[18]

According to Mishna Nedarim 8.4, "One who takes a vow, 'until the harvest,' is bound only until the beginning of the harvest." " 'The harvest,' " the Mishna continues, "means the wheat harvest and not the barley harvest" (which began approximately seven weeks earlier).

The Talmud of Jerusalem commenting on the passage countered, "But Scripture specifically states [of Ruth] that 'She kept fast by the maidens of Boaz to glean until the end of the barley harvest and the wheat harvest' " (Ruth 2.23). Surely Scripture implied that the word "harvest" may be used for the reaping either of barley or of wheat. The Talmud replied, "The Scriptures refer to conditions in the South (Judea) [and therefore use the terminology, natural to it]; the Mishna refers to Galilee."

In Tosefta Hallah 1.17, ed. Lieberman, p. 276, R. Judah explained the difference between the proportion of the loaf given the priest by a baker and that given by a private person. According to the Mishna, bakers were required to give the priest only one forty-eighth of the loaf but other persons one twenty-fourth. R. Judah offered as reason for this difference, "that a baker is necessarily niggardly in regard to his dough, whereas a private person is not." That is to say, a baker whose business it was to sell bread, necessarily counted on each part of his dough for his livelihood. To give away an additional one forty-eighth of each loaf might mean the difference between starvation for his family and their having sufficient food. A private person could better afford to be generous.

R. Judah's explanation was opposed by his colleagues. They maintained that the fraction required from a private person was large, because otherwise the priest would receive little more than a few crumbs. A baker, giving the priest one forty-eighth of his loaves, would be making a considerable contribution.

We may justly ascribe this very controversy between R. Judah and his colleagues to a difference of background. R. Judah frequently transmitted traditions of the market place of Jerusalem. The baker of the metropolis, faced with severe competition, had to consider even a small fraction of his dough very carefully. To give away an additional forty-eighth of it might drive him, faced with less scrupulous competitors, into bankruptcy. R. Judah's colleagues were discussing the situation of bakers in small towns and villages, without such competition, who could indeed afford to give away the full one twenty-fourth of the dough to the priest, merely passing on the additional cost to their purchasers. But the scholars, according to the authorities emanating from the countryside, made no such demand on the bakers, because even one forty-eighth of the dough they baked was a considerable portion. Perhaps in the villages it would have been difficult to find priestly consumers for larger amounts.

(There is a variant reading in Tosefta according to which the private person is less likely to be generous than a baker;

but that need not be discussed here. Even according to that reading, R. Judah explained the norm on the basis of different attitudes of the people to whom it was addressed.)

Another controversy was explained by R. Johanan as deriving from a difference of economic status. Mishna Eduyyot 3.3 states that according to R. Dosa, the peeling of herbs given as heave-offering might be eaten by non-priests. R. Dosa's colleagues forbade it. The underlying issue was whether peelings of herbs were to be considered normal human food. R. Dosa held that they were not. His colleagues maintained that they were, and therefore as part of the usual heave-offering were forbidden to anyone but priests.

R. Abbahu, transmitting a tradition received from R. Johanan, asserted that R. Dosa's colleagues ascribed holiness as heave-offering only to peelings of herbs belonging to private farmers.[19] Those from producers of herbs for the market were not considered heave-offering by anyone. As Professor Saul Lieberman[20] explains, the producer for the market who had to be concerned with his margin of profit, tended to peel his herbs carefully. What he cut off from the stalk could therefore not be considered human food. On the other hand, the private farmer who used his produce only for his family, often peeled part of the flesh of the herb with its outer covering. Such peelings might still be used for food by the poor, according to R. Dosa's colleagues.

R. Johanan's explanation of the controversy implied that it arose out of difference in social background; and that R. Dosa, reflecting the traditions of the richer provincial groups and the aristocracy of Jerusalem, permitted the peelings — even those made by private farmers — to be eaten by non-priests, because in his circles they were not considered suitable food for anyone.

According to the Mishna a special norm applied to grapes produced by a vine in its fourth year, if situated within a day's journey from Jerusalem. Fruits of a tree during its first three years were forbidden (Lev. 19.20 ff.). Those of the fourth might be eaten only in Jerusalem. However, they could be "redeemed" on the same basis as the Second Tithe. In that event, the money obtained in exchange for them had to be spent in Jerusalem.

Grapes grown within a day's journey of Jerusalem could not be exchanged for money outside the city.[21] They had to be brought to Jerusalem for consumption there.

The Talmud[22] explained this law on practical grounds. Grapes were a rare commodity in Jerusalem markets. The grapes of the surrounding country were almost wholly used for the manufacture of wine, needed in especially large quantities for the Temple service. The consumption of the grapes of the fourth year in Jerusalem necessarily lessened the demand for fruits in the market of Jerusalem, which thus tended to become plentifully supplied with produce.

When the Temple was destroyed, holy food could no longer be eaten within the precincts of Jerusalem. Yet the fruit of the fourth year could also not be consumed outside the city.[23] It became customary to exchange such fruits, as well as the Second Tithe, for money — perhaps a nominal sum. This exchange or redemption removed the prohibition against eating the produce outside Jerusalem. The money could be set aside to be brought to Jerusalem, whenever the Temple might be rebuilt.

However, vineyard owners living within a day's journey from Jerusalem could benefit from this device only if the rule against exchanging grapes for money outside the walls of the Holy City was abrogated. This Rabban Johanan ben Zakkai persuaded the court, over which he presided, to do.[24]

Many disagreements among scholars are ascribed by the Talmud to differences of conditions in various times. The disagreement between R. Johanan and R. Ammi about the measure of grain needed to sow a field was explained on the ground that R. Ammi lived at a time when the land had lost much of its fertility and needed twice the amount of seed used in the time of R. Johanan.[25] This is astonishing, for only a single generation had elapsed between the two scholars. Perhaps, however, R. Johanan was transmitting an older norm which R. Ammi felt compelled to change because the land had lost its productivity.

Yerushalmi Maaser Sheni 1.1 frankly states that the prohibition against selling the fruit of the Second Tithe was intended to encourage personal participation in the pilgrimages. Compelled to utilize the Second Tithe in Jerusalem or give it away, the provincial would find it profitable to undertake the journey to the Holy City.

When the question was raised as to why certain types of work, prohibited during the week of the festivals, were permitted during the Sabbatical year, one authority replied, according to Yerushalmi Moed Katan 1.1: "Because the Sabbatical year involves long cessation from work, they had to permit this. Because the festival week is obviously short, they prohibited it."

According to the view of R. Johanan,[26] marriages were prohibited during the week of the festivals because, had they been permitted, there would be a tendency to postpone all marriages until that vacation period.

The Talmud of Jerusalem asserts that a view of R. Meir,

seemingly intended for general application, was valid only for villagers. Perhaps the Talmud meant to suggest that R. Meir made this decision only for villagers.[27]

The Talmud of Jerusalem asserted further that when the issue arose as to whether the tithe could be given the priests as well as Levites, the colleagues of R. Joshua ben Levi (who was a Levite) assumed that he would side against the claims of the priesthood. Although he defended the claims of the priests, the candor of the Talmud in suggesting that his siding with the priests astonished his colleagues, indicates that in such marginal issues, when a logical argument could be built up for either view, one might expect a scholar to be swayed by personal or tribal predisposition.[28]

Similarly, according to Yer. Pesahim 5.5, 32c, when someone remarked that one of the customs of the Temple had for its purpose the prevention of theft by the priests, R. Zeira retorted, "Say it with half your mouth." That is to say, "Do not articulate the issue so clearly, but mumble it." As Professor Saul Lieberman has shown,[29] this is the real meaning of the passage, somewhat obscured in the current texts and misunderstood by earlier commentators. R. Zeira, himself a priest, felt called upon to defend the honor of the clan. The Talmud makes no effort to conceal this partiality.

The French Tosafists adopt this talmudic approach to rabbinic controversies as reflecting differences of circumstance. Thus, according to Rabbi Samson of Sens in his commentary on the Mishna Hallah, 2.6, Rabbenu Jacob Tam ascribes the disagreement between Shammai and Hillel there discussed to variation in social background. The issue dividing Shammai and Hillel in that passage is the size of a loaf subject to the laws enumerated in Numbers 15.17 ff. In this passage the Torah demands a gift to the priest from every loaf of bread baked. According to Mishna Eduyyot 1.2, Shammai held that a loaf containing a *kab* was subject to the norm; Hillel said, only if it contained two *kab*. Rabbenu Tam maintained that Shammai based his view on the practices appropriate to an individual.[30] Because the *kab* was the equivalent in size to twenty-four eggs, an individual obeying the law would give the priest at least the measure of an egg in dough, a minimum gift. Hillel, deriving his norm from the practice of the professional baker, required the loaf to be at least two *kab* in size. Otherwise, the portion given the priest would not even be the size of an egg. The implication of Rabbenu Tam's explanation seems clear. Hillel's decision for the community generally was based on the practices which developed among bakers; Shammai's derived from those current among farmers.

Rabbenu Tam went further. He maintained[31] that an apparent controversy between R. José the Galilean and his colleagues regarding the penalty to be imposed on one who strikes his neighbor derived from difference in economic status. According to Mishna Baba Kamma 8.6, one who struck his neighbor had to pay a *sela*. R. Judah stated in the name of R. José the Galilean that the penalty was a *mina*. From the discussion in the Talmud[32] it seems clear that the *sela* mentioned in the Mishna was half a *dinar*, or about one two-hundredth of the penalty fixed by R. José the Galilean. Rabbenu Tam, commenting on the unusually wide divergence in judgment between the authorities, explained that the smaller penalty applied when a person of low social status was the victim and the larger one when a person of high standing had been hurt. "Even," add the later authors of the *Tosafot*, "if we assume the existence of a real controversy among the scholars, it still is obvious that the penalty imposed on one who strikes a man of wealth [and position] would be higher than that imposed on one who had no such standing."

It can scarcely be accidental that the same medieval scholar is responsible for the sociological interpretation of the two controversies or that, in both instances, it seems clear to the modern student that his interpretation is right.

Presumably Rabbenu Tam had thought through similar interpretations of many controversies. He did not record them, being far less interested in such matters than in the reconciliation of difficult passages and their philological interpretation.

However, according to Rabbi Joseph ibn Habib, the learned author of the commentary *Nimmuke Joseph* on Alfasi, the view of that great scholar of the eleventh century was closely akin to that ascribed to Rabbenu Tam.[33] According to Rab Isaac Alfasi, each authority fixed the extreme limits of the penalty — R. José the Galilean the maximum, his colleagues the minimum. R. José the Galilean indeed fixed the penalty to be exacted for striking a man of wealth, but held that even for a poor person it would be more than a *sela*. On the other hand, his colleagues, fixing the penalty for striking a poor man at a *sela*, held that even for a man of wealth and position it would be less than a *mina*.

While we do not have the *ipsissima verba* of Rab Isaac Alfasi, which were probably (as Rabbi Solomon Adeni suggested) included in a responsum, we must assume that, like Rabbenu Tam later, Rab Isaac Alfasi held that R. José the Galilean and his colleagues were setting standards of punishment according to the circles in which they respectively moved. But if this view was really held by Rab Isaac Alfasi, it almost certainly derived from the Gaonic schools.

We are thus led to assume that there was a continuous tradition in the great rabbinic schools which, in addition to the formal arguments of talmudic dialectic, recognized the human background of the opposing views of the sages.

As already indicated,[34] the Talmud and its commentaries are naturally far less interested in this approach than in the dialectical discussion justifying opposing views. This is because the subjective preferences of scholars cannot be used as a basis for decision-making. The student who has to decide whether to follow the views of Shammai or Hillel, and the judge who has to impose a penalty either according to the standards of R. José the Galilean or his colleagues, are not helped by such considerations as those advanced by Rabbenu Tam. These permit too much ground for subjective decisions, whereas the student and judge seek objective law. Recognizing that many decisions in marginal issues are affected by personal, group, or other bias, the student and judge have to evaluate the opposing views in some objective manner. A rationale has to be discovered for objective decision.

Talmudic literature is thus largely an effort to discover the logic underlying decisions which are recognized as originating in approaches which are largely subjective and therefore beyond argument.

But the historian, living long after the event and especially one who strives to accept as guide to his life the decisions determined by talmudic dialectic, may well be forgiven for his desire to discover the sociological genesis of opposing views. As he does so, he finds to his astonishment that much which appeared confused and inconsistent in the talmudic dialectic becomes clear and coherent. The dialectical method pursued in the classical discussions of the Talmud and the commentaries reduced talmudic jurisprudence to a coherent system based on accepted principles, whether of law or of exegesis. But they cannot alone guide one in the continuous process of reaching new decisions in unprecedented cases. That is because no accepted principles apply themselves to the infinite complexities of much of human life, and the issues raised in the Talmud always involve cases which, by their very nature, elude classification.

It is only when the dialectical argument is supplemented with insight into the inevitable personal bias of the judge, academician, or school, that we can discover the rationale for many differences of opinion among the rabbinic sages.

The discovery is most valuable in the process of making decisions. To discover the rule of law applying in a special situation it was necessary for the Talmudists and the earlier Pharisees to seek logical objectivity, even when they knew that their decisions had been reached in the first instance through subjective and emotional bias. Yet the relation of their judgments to the group interests they sought to defend is extraordinarily illuminating for those who seek to extend the method of talmudic thought to new areas and new circumstances. The validity of the decisions offered by such scholars as Hillel and R. Akiba derives in the final analysis, not from their arguments (which were generally countered by equally cogent logic from the opposition), but from the correctness of the mental attitude which led to their decision in the first place. The recovery of this attitude may be one way to achieve the type of wisdom characteristic of these great sages.

But this wisdom was by no means confined to one group of scholars; it belonged to Shammaites, no less than Hillelites; to R. Eliezer, no less than R. Joshua; to R. Ishmael in precisely the same measure as to R. Akiba. If these great luminaries were led to disagree, not by opposition of moral approach or legal reasoning, but by difference of situation, background, and predisposition, we may justly conclude that the opposing systems were not really in conflict, but represented either equally valid approaches to human dilemmas or applications of the same approach to differing circumstances.

To one today seeking guidance in the murk and confusion of daily life, trying to discern the Voice in the babble of confusing words from all sides, understanding the manner in which the ancient sages and saints reached their conclusions becomes as important as understanding the manner in which they defended these conclusions.

Moreover, for a reconstruction of the genius of Pharisaism the rejected decisions are of no less consequence than those accepted: granted that only the accepted, definitive, and codified rule is important for the rituals of worship. The Shammaitic system of morals and religion, surviving only in fragments, is of permanent value equal to that of their opponents. The argument of the Palestinian schools, whose decisions are in general not considered binding when opposed by the Babylonian academies, might be extremely valuable from the general standpoint of education in morals and ethics.

Thus, a later age returning to study the talmudic literature may find vast opportunity for more than historical research in these great, enduring classics. Both those following the rituals and laws of Pharisaism and those outside its fold may discover in the genius which animated its great teachers inspiration and encouragement — no less than example — in the effort to formulate an approach to the Good Life.

Significantly, since the close of the talmudic period the foremost effort to recover the implicit genius of Pharisaism was that of Maimonides, whose genius so frequently cut through the perplexities of the transmitted discussion to the heart of the moral issues raised long before him. It is conceivable that his method later adopted by other scholars may inspire students of the future to return to the Talmud for fresh guidance. The task of formulating the codes has not been completed. The task of bringing the talmudic method to bear on decisions, not subject to codification but penetrating every aspect of life, is the challenge Pharisaism presents our generation.

APPENDICES
NOTES

ABBREVIATIONS

AJSL	*American Journal of Semitic Languages and Literature*
HTR	*The Harvard Theological Review*
HUCA	*Hebrew Union College Annual*
JBL	*The Journal of Biblical Literature*
JQR	*The Jewish Quarterly Review*
MGWJ	*Monatsschrift fuer Geschichte und Wissenschaft des Judentums*
Palaestina-jahrbuch	*Palaestinajahrbuch des deutschen evangelischen Instituts fuer Altertumswissenschaft des heilingen Landes zu Jerusalem*
REJ	*Revue des études juives*
ZAW	*Zeitschrift fuer die alttestamentliche Wissenschaft*
ZDMG	*Zeitschrift der deutschen morgenlaendischen Gesellschaft*

APPENDIX A

The Unity of Isaiah 40–66, and the Place and Date of the Author

The study of Deutero-Isaiah, like that of Ezekiel, has today reached a critical stage. The analytical studies of Gressmann (*ZAW*, XXXIV, 1914, p. 254 ff.), L. Koehler (*Deuterojesaja, stilkritisch untersucht*), and S. Mowinckel (*ZAW*, XLIX, 1931, p. 87 ff.) have now been followed by the masterly and careful investigation of W. Caspari (*Lieder und Gottessprueche der Rueckwanderer*), for whom they prepared the way. They have all proceeded on the assumption laid down by Duhm in *Das Buch Jesaia* that the only part of the book which can be called Deutero-Isaiah consists of chapters 40–55. The remainder of the work is assigned either to a third prophet, Trito-Isaiah, or to a group of writers.

This view is also adopted by P. Volz (*Jesaia II, uebersetzt u. erklaert*, in Sellin's *Kommentar*).

The unity of the book attacked by these scholars has, however, found two vigorous and able defenders in Ludvig Glahn, whose work *Hjemkomstpropheten* published in Danish in 1929, appeared in German translation in 1934 under the title, *Der Prophet der Heimkehr*, Kopenhagen-Giessen, and more especially in C. C. Torrey, who includes in the work of the Second Isaiah also chapters 34 and 35 (*The Second Isaiah*, New York, 1928).

Torrey's work is of especial interest because it is not only in his conclusion that he disagrees with his opponents; he differs from them in his whole approach to the subject. He sees in the Second Isaiah a prophet who developed his thought in a series of consecutive addresses, the logic of which can be followed from chapter to chapter. Indeed, he points to several instances where successive chapters apparently discuss different phases of the same general subject.

Even Mowinckel and others, however, who maintain that the work is to be divided either among two or more prophets, or is the product of a "school," admit that there is much to be said regarding the similarity of style and thought between chapters 56–66 and 40–55 (see Mowinckel, op. cit., p. 252, n. 1). What leads these scholars to divide up the work are the obvious differences of mood between the first and second part of the work. But in stressing the significance of these differences, both the creators of the compilation theory and those who hold to the doctrine of a Third Isaiah fail to take cognizance of the versatility which is one of the main characteristics of the genius of Deutero-Isaiah. He was one of the few men in whom passion is combined with intellectual freedom; he could see each question in all its facets, and when he felt that he had overstated his side of the question made haste to restore the balance with another address clarifying the issue (see ch. XVIII, note 32). From such a genius one would naturally expect differences of approach and expression which might suggest difference of authorship. So a comparison of *Hamlet* or *Macbeth* with *Two Gentlemen of Verona*, might suggest that they could not both be the product of Shakespeare's pen. Yet they were. Not indeed, as we now know, from the same period; but certainly from the same personality. And it cannot be denied that the similarity of style and approach between the most dissimilar parts of Isaiah 40–66 is greater than that between the later tragedies of Shakespeare and his first comedies.

In addition to this vital difference in interpretation, there arises the question of the date of the author of whatever chapters are assigned to Deutero-Isaiah. Most writers adhere to the older belief that he spoke about the years 546–538 B.C.E. and is the prophet of the exile; Torrey insists that he belongs to the fourth century.

Finally, there is wide disagreement concerning the home of the prophet. Duhm (op. cit., p. 15) and A. Causse (*Les Dispersés d'Israël*, Paris, 1929, pp. 34 ff.) place him in Phoenicia; others, in Egypt (H. Ewald, *History of Israel*, English translation, London, 1874, V, p. 42; Hoelscher, *Geschichte der israelitischen Religion*, p. 123; and even more definitely in *Die Propheten*, p. 321); still others, in Palestine itself (Mowinckel, op. cit., p. 244, note 1; Torrey, op. cit., p. 53 ff.; W. H. Cobb, in *JBL*, XXVII (1908), 48 ff.; J. A. Maynard, ibid., XXXVI (1917), pp. 213 ff.; Buttenwieser, ibid., XXXVIII (1919), p. 94 ff.; G. Dahl, ibid., XLVIII (1929), p. 374), a view which, as stated in the text, I share. Indeed, it seems to me that the following considerations for his Palestinian environment are irrefutable. How could anyone living in the exile say to his fellows: "Depart ye, depart ye, go ye out from thence; touch no unclean thing; go ye out of the midst of her; be ye clean, ye that carry the vessels of the Lord"? (52.11). To whom was the prophet speaking when he said: "For your sake have I sent to Babylon and will bring all of them down as fugitives"? Why does the Second Isaiah conceive of his omnipresent God as "sending" to Babylonia? Was he a henotheist believing God's presence limited to Palestine? Is it not obvious that the expression is used because Isaiah himself was in

Palestine, and Babylonia was far away from him? The people of whom he speaks as "them" are not his hearers, for *they* resided in the Holy Land, but the exiles, on the Tigris and the Euphrates, which he had never seen. It is to them he calls, in notes clearly modulated to carry across the desert, and not addressed to his immediate audience: "Go ye forth from Babylon, flee from the Chaldeans" (48.20).

His scenic background is Palestinian rather than Babylonian. The low Mesopotamian valley could hardly suggest that the announcer of good tidings "go up into the mountain" (40.9). Only a native Judaite, knowing the lack of water which is the main peril of the hill country, would promise as part of the new order, "I will open rivers on the high hills" (41.18). The prophet must have seen herds of sheep and goats, such as the modern traveler still meets on the rocky slopes of Judea, to say: "They shall feed in their ways, and in the high hills shall be their pasture. They shall not hunger nor thirst, neither shall the heat nor the sun smite them" (49.9).

The prophet is altogether unaware of the true conditions of his exiled countrymen in Babylonia. He believes that Babylonia laid its yoke very heavily on the aged (47.6) and that the Judaites were beaten and spat upon (50.6). No wonder that he expects a flood of immigrants as soon as Cyrus opens the gates of Palestine to these "captives." Little did he understand that more than half of the exiles had so firmly established themselves in the economy of the new land that return was practically impossible for them.

The contempt and derision which he pours over Bel and Nebo do not necessarily indicate Babylonian nativity. He saw these idols worshiped at the governor's court in Mizpah and in the soldiers' camps throughout the land. Perhaps he knew of some pusillanimous Judaites who had also accepted them, wishing to win the favor of the reigning Chaldeans.

Nor are the arguments from the similarity, or supposed similarity, between his text and that of the cuneiform inscriptions convincing (see, e. g., R. Kittel, in *ZAW*, 1898, p. 149 ff.; Stummer, in *JBL*, XLV (1926), p. 171 ff.; A. Jeremias, *Das Alte Testament im Lichte des Alten Orients*, p. 684 ff.; A. Jirku, *Altorientalischer Kommentar zum Alten Testament*, p. 202 ff.; L. Duerr, *Ursprung und Ausbau der israelitisch-juedischen Heilandserwartung*, p. 125 ff.). Many of the similarities are purely accidental; others do not depend on life in Babylonia itself, but could result from intimate acquaintance with imperial affairs even by a cultured and well-traveled provincial.

APPENDIX B

The Meaning of Ezekiel 1.1–2

The interpretation of these verses which I have accepted, namely that the "thirty years" of verse 1 date from the discovery of the Law and the reformation under Josiah, is the most ancient and natural one. It is accepted by Targum, ad loc.; *Seder 'Olam Rabba*, ch. 26, ed. Ratner, 58a; Jerome, in his commentary; and in modern times, Graetz, *Monatsschrift*, 1874, p. 518; Herrmann, *Ezekiel*, p. 10. Duhm, followed by Hoelscher, *Hesekiel*, p. 44, suggests that the era intended counted from the supposed beginning of the exile. The midrashic copyist who added the date, according to these scholars, remembered that Ezekiel had promised the restoration of Judah within forty years (4.6); and bearing in mind that the total length of the exile, according to Jer. 25.11, was to be seventy years, took it for granted that Ezekiel began to prophesy in the thirtieth year of the exile. More recently a number of commentators have suggested that the "thirtieth year" was of Ezekiel's own age (so K. Budde, in *JBL*, L (1931), p. 28; Kugler, *Von Moses bis Paulus*, p. 192; J. A. Bewer, in *AJSL*, L (1934), p. 98; and O. Eissfeldt in *Palaestinajahrbuch*, XXVII (1931), p. 66, note 1). Torrey, declaring the work to be pseudepigraphic, supposes that the writer intended to date it by the thirtieth year of King Manasseh. Others have attempted to emend the text, reading thirteen (from the reign of Nebuchadnezzar, Rothstein, Bertholet) or third (from the exile, Herntrich). During the past few years, the opinion has been gaining ground that "the thirtieth year" is really the last date in the book, following the "twenty-fifth year" by which chapter 40 is dated. This suggestion has been put forward in varying forms, by Merx, *Jahrbuecher fuer Protestantische Theologie*, IX, p. 73; Berry, *JBL*, LI (1932), p. 55; Albright, ibid., p. 96; S. Spiegel, *HTR*, XXIV (1931), p. 289. Another explanation, which apparently is gaining ground, is that put forward by Begrich (*Die Chronologie der Koenige von Isr. und Juda*, p. 206 f.) and accepted by Cooke in his Commentary on Ezekiel (p. 4), that the two dates are really identical, but represent the different traditions and calculations followed in Kings and Chronicles.

All these writers admit, however, the difficulties in the way of accepting their suggestions and justify us in endeavoring to study the question anew. The verses as they now stand read:

"Now it came to pass in the thirtieth year, in the fourth month, in the fifth day of the month, as I was among the captives by the River Chebar, that the heavens were opened, and I saw visions of God. *In the fifth day of the month*, that is the fifth year of King Jehoiachin's captivity, the word of the Lord came to Ezekiel, the son of Buzi the priest, in the land of the Chaldeans by the River Chebar" (Ez. 1.1–3).

In undertaking to explain the passage, it seems to me that we must not only reconcile the contradiction between the dates, but the curious repetition of the words, "in the fifth day of the month," which I have italicized. Their repetition is especially remarkable because the glossator (if it was a glossator who repeated the words) did not take the trouble to copy also the number of the month, as we should expect.

There can be little doubt that if the text before us were an ordinary Ms., we should be inclined, at first glance, to suppose that the words "that is the fifth year," etc., come from a marginal annotation, which began with a repetition of the words "in the fifth day of the month," to which they were attached; and that catchword and gloss were both taken over into the text by subsequent copyists.

The reasons for rejecting such an hypothesis with regard to the present text are clear:

1. No glossator, unless he was a contemporary of Ezekiel—and such an early glossator is unlikely — could possibly have known the exact date of Ezekiel's first prophecy, since the original date does not mention the time from which it is counted.

2. The number, "in the fifth year of King Jehoiachin's captivity," corresponds to the other dates given in the book (Ezek. 8.1; 20.1; 24.1; 26.1; 29.1; 31.1; 32.1; 40.1) all of which are reckoned from Jehoiachin's captivity.

3. It would be most natural for Ezekiel to date his prophecies by the years of Jehoiachin's captivity, the most important event in the prophet's own life.

4. No motive could be put forward for any glossator adding the words "the fifth year of King Jehoiachin" to the date; but various motives suggest themselves for the addition of the words the "thirtieth year" by a glossator.

These reasons, present in the minds of the commentators who dealt with the subject whether they were explicitly mentioned or not, are doubtless cogent; and compel us to accept the words, "in the fifth year of King Jehoiachin's captivity," as the original date of the prophecy.

But if the original dating of the book was that now found in verse 2, "in the fifth day of the month, that is the fifth year of the exile of King Jehoiachin," how does it happen that the month is omitted there and placed in the first verse?

The question has only to be put for the answer to suggest itself. The writer who put verses 1 and 2 in their present form wanted us to believe that verse 2 is an explanatory gloss to verse 1, and that is why he repeated the words "in the fifth day of the month," as a scribe might do when he is adding a marginal note into the text. The reason for his desire to make us think what was in his original text to be a marginal gloss has to be analyzed and studied to be understood.

Before we can do so, however, we must answer another question. Who wrote verses 1 and 2?

The answer can only be tentative. I believe, in view of what is said in the text, that the book of Ezekiel was revised by the prophet himself in his old age, when he had changed his views on some important questions which he had discussed and written about.

The answer to the main question, however, is less difficult. The reviser foresaw the interpretation which would be put on the combination of vv. 1 and 2 by people of his own and following generations. He realized that they would calculate backward from the fifth year of Jehoiachin's reign, and arrive at the eighteenth year of King Josiah, the year of the discovery of the Law, and take it that since he mentioned no other era, it was from the discovery of the Law that he was counting his thirty years. And, indeed, so far as the earlier Jewish tradition is concerned, he foresaw correctly, as has already been noted.

Since the original text was dated in the "fourth month, the fifth day of the month, in the fifth year of King Jehoiachin's captivity," he decided to add the altogether unnecessary note that this was the "thirtieth year" after the reformation. And then, to intensify the effect of this identification, he made the "thirtieth year" the principal date; and reduced the original reference to the fifth year of King Jehoiachin to an apparent gloss.

Why, it may be asked, however, did he not explicitly mention the event from which he was counting his era?

To have done so would have defeated his purpose. For it was his thought not merely to indicate that *he* counted his years by Josiah's Reformation, but that that was the normal period from which Judaites should count their era, after the destruction of their kingdom.

This type of teaching truths by innuendo and hinting at them may seem somewhat strange to moderns, but was characteristic of Ezekiel and a whole group of later writers, including the authors of the Book of Jubilees, Judith, the Testaments of the Twelve Patriarchs, and even such biblical works as Jonah, Ruth, etc., which have been discussed in the text.

APPENDIX C

Additional Controversies between the Sects

Besides the controversies mentioned in the text, there are some others which are well authenticated, and a number for which evidence has been adduced by various scholars. They are as follows:

I. The Authenticated Controversies.
II. Controversies mentioned in ancient records, but of doubtful authenticity.
III. Controversies attributed to the sects by modern scholars.
IV. A Controversy wrongly described as Sadducean.

I. The Authenticated Controversies

A. The Mishna, Yadayim 4.7, records that there was a controversy between the sects regarding the purity of the *nizzok.** The precise meaning of this word has, however, been the subject of considerable discussion. The commentators explain that it is a stream of water; and that the Sadducees maintained that when a liquid is poured from a clean into an unclean vessel, the stream of water joining the two vessels carries the uncleanliness from the lower one into the upper one. The Pharisees denied this. This interpretation, which is found in all the ancient commentaries, is based on a comparison of Mishna Yadayim with Mishna

* Cf. Supplement, pp. 716-718.

Makshirim, 5.9; and is accepted by Professor L. Ginzberg (*Eine unbekannte juedische Sekte*, p. 77). Nevertheless it presents grave difficulties, which have caused it to be rejected by a number of other scholars. The most important of these is the interpretation of the rejoinder made by the Pharisees in the argument which has been preserved on the question (Mishna Yadayim, loc. cit.). According to the record, "The Sadducees said to the Pharisees, We cry out against you, Pharisees, that you declare the *nizzok* pure. The Pharisees replied, We cry out against you, Sadducees, that you declare a stream of water which comes through a cemetery pure."

It is difficult to see how the answer of the Pharisees bears on the remark of the Sadducees. Professor Ginzberg maintains that the Pharisees argue that since all agree that water cannot become impure when it is "attached to the soil," it cannot take impurity from one vessel to another. But it is clear that such an argument is far from cogent. The difficulty led Geiger, in *Urschrift*, p. 147, to declare the whole controversy allegorical. According to him, the controversy really represents a political argument between the Herodians, whom he mistakenly identifies with the Sadducees, and the Pharisees. "You maintain," he makes the Herodians say, "that the impure descendants (the later Hasmoneans) are to be accepted as worthy because of their noble ancestry." The Pharisees reply, "You declare the stream which comes from the cemetery, pure," which is as much as to say, "Did not the dynasty of Herod attain the throne over the bodies of its opponents?" Leszynsky, *Die Sadduzäer*, p. 38 ff., interprets *nizzok* as honey. Zeitlin, *JQR*, N. S. VIII (1917–18), p. 67 ff. maintains that the discussion concerns the liability of vegetables to become impure while they are attached to the soil. I still believe as I did in 1929 (see *HTR*, XXII, p. 217) that *nizzok* means "aqueduct." The Pharisees held that water brought by an aqueduct was "pure" and fit for immersion; the Sadducees denied this. When the Pharisees were taunted for leniency by their opponents, they replied that the Sadducees permitted the use of water which is taken in an irrigation canal through a cemetery, showing that so long as the water remains attached to the soil it remains fit for the purposes of purification. They felt that they might justly infer from this that an aqueduct built into the ground would not prevent the water drawn in it from being used in a pool of purification (*mikveh*). I cannot, however, accept the interpretation of Ch. Tschernowitz (*Toledot Ha-Halakah*, II, 2, p. 289) that *nizzok* refers to water poured over the body. In order to maintain this curious view, he is compelled to resort to a violent emendation of the text of the Mishna, without any justification except that the new reading fits his theory.

B. There was a considerable difference between the sects regarding the law applying to a woman "with a flow"; but the details of this controversy are no longer clear (see Mishna, Horayot, 1.3, and compare Babli, ad loc., 4a; and also Mishna, Niddah, 4.2, which indicates that the sects disagreed also with regard to the law of menstrual impurity; for further discussion, see Ginzberg, *Eine unbekannte juedische Sekte*, pp. 30 and 226, where he shows that Ps. Solomon, 8.12, also attacks the Sadducees for their violation of the Pharisaic rules about these matters; the material is collected in Strack-Billerbeck, *Kommentar zum Neuen Testament aus Talmud und Midrasch*, V, p. 348).

C. A discussion between a Sadducee and Joshua Ha-Garsi (B. Shabbat, 108a) indicates a disagreement regarding the use of the skins of unclean animals for phylacteries. (With regard to this controversy see Leszynsky, *Die Sadduzäer*, p. 46, who denies that the Sadducees recognized the law requiring phylacteries, and therefore interprets the passage quite differently.)

D. There was a controversy between the sects regarding the right of the priests to eat the meal-offerings brought with animal sacrifices.* The Sadducees, siding as might be expected, with the priests, held that they could eat it; the Pharisees held that it ought to be consumed on the altar (*Megillat Ta'anit*, ch. 7, ed. Lichtenstein; op. cit., p. 338; cf. Mishna, Menahot, 6.2.)[1]

It is probable that the Sadducees had a *Book of Decisions*, *Sefer Gezerata*, in which the decisions rendered at least by the *Gerousia* were recorded. (So, apparently, also, Professor Ginzberg in *Eine unbekannte juedische Sekte*, p. 71.) The Pharisees, who believed in the preservation of the interpretations of the Law through oral tradition only, objected to the system of recording, as they objected also, doubtless, to many of the decisions which were included as precedents in the book. The day on which the Pharisees won the Sanhedrin to a rejection of the *Sefer Gezerata* was declared a half-holiday (*Megillat Ta'anit*, ch. 4; op. cit., p. 331).

E. Apparently there was also a disagreement between the scholars and certain sectarians, probably Sadducees, who considered it an ill omen if the High Priest, in drawing lots to decide which of the two he-goats was to be sacrificed to God and which was to be sent to Azazel on the Day of Atonement, drew the one for the sacrifice in his left hand (Yoma, 40b).

* Cf. Supplement, pp. 692-693.

II. Controversies Mentioned in Ancient Records, but of Doubtful Authenticity*

A. The Talmud maintains that only the Sadducees insisted on literal burning at the stake in executions, but this may be unhistorical, since one of the cases is cited as a precedent by R. Eleazar b. Zadok, a Pharisee (Mishna Sanhedrin, 7.2; B. Sanhedrin, 52b, and see N. Bruell in *Bet Talmud*, IV, p. 7).[2]

B. The gloss in the scholion to *Megillat Ta'anit*, ch. 4, ed. Lichtenstein in *Hebrew Union College Annual*, VIII–IX, p. 331, records three more controversies between the sects. While there can be little doubt that Wellhausen (*Die Pharisäer*, p. 61) is correct in rejecting the authenticity of the passage, it is altogether probable that the opinions it attributes to the Sadducees were actually held by them. The first of the three controversies there recorded concerns the *lex talionis*: the glossator maintains that the Sadducees accepted it literally, while the Pharisees rejected it. If this is true, it is probable that the interpretation put on it by the Sadducees was identical with that given by Josephus, *Antiquities*, iv. 8.35, according to which the maimed person was permitted to fix the amount of money he would accept instead of inflicting like punishment on his assailant. This is probably also the interpretation put upon the law by R. Eliezer ben Hyrcanus (Baba Kamma, 84a; Mekilta Mishpatim, ch. 8, p. 277).[3]

C. The second controversy recorded in the Scholion to *Megillat Ta'anit* concerned the proof of virginity in cases arising under Deut. 22.13. The Sadducees are said to have taken the verses literally, the Pharisees figuratively. This is altogether probable, for the more conservative Pharisees

* Cf. Supplement, pp. 721 ff.

also insisted on a literal interpretation of this verse, see Sifre, Deut. 237.

D. The third of this group of controversies, concerned the law of *halizah*. The Sadducees maintained that the sister-in-law who has been denied the levirate marriage must actually spit in the face of her brother-in-law, in accordance with a literal interpretation of Deut. 25.9; the Pharisees denied this.[4]

III. Controversies Attributed to the Sects by Modern Scholars

A. Geiger maintains that the Sadducees did not accept the rule which declares a woman "pure" for marital congress after the seven days of impurity for a son and the fourteen days of impurity for a daughter. His view, too, coincides altogether with what we know about the Sadducees and this controversy; but the evidence he offers to support the existence of a difference on the point is insufficient. See *Sadducäer u. Pharisäer*, p. 22; *Nachgelassene Schriften*, III, p. 316; *He-Haluz*, 5.29; 6.28 ff.; *Kebuzat Maamarim*, pp. 138 f., 163, and Ginzberg's notes to *Kebuzat Maamarim*, second edition, p. 385.

B. Geiger also maintains, quite erroneously in my opinion, that the Sadducees required the levirate marriage only from those who were "betrothed" (*arusot*), see *Kebuzat Maamarim*, p. 83, and the complete refutation in Ginzberg, *Eine unbekannte juedische Sekte*, p. 183.

C. Geiger further maintains that there was a controversy between the sects regarding the Levitical impurity of the bones and the hide of dead animals. According to him, the Sadducees, like the contemporary Samaritans and the later

Karaites, declared these impure; the Pharisees declared them pure (see *He-Haluz*, VI, p. 18; *ZDMG*, XVI, 717 f.; *Sadducäer und Pharisäer*, p. 15; *Nachgelassene Schriften*, III, 315). For a discussion of the subject, see B. Revel, *The Karaite Halaka*, p. 42, who demonstrates that the earliest Karaites did not accept the view of the impurity of the skin and bones of carcasses of animals. Cf., e. g., S. Schechter, *Documents of Jewish Sectaries*, II, p. 23.

D. Another controversy between the sects postulated by Geiger concerns the sacrifice of the paschal lamb on the Sabbath (*Sadducäer und Pharisäer*, p. 38 ff.). In order to arrive at this view, however, he is compelled (op. cit., p. 38, note 17) to identify the Bene Bathyra with Sadducean teachers, a view which is utterly without support in tradition. On the contrary, the fact that the Bene Bathyra finally submitted to Hillel when he declared that his Pharisaic masters, Shemaya and Abtalyon, had declared that the sacrifice might be offered, demonstrates that they were not Sadducees. Regarding the validity of Geiger's argument in this, see also A. Schwarz, *Die Controversen der Schammaiten und Hilleliten*, p. 17; B. Revel, op. cit., p. 41; and L. Ginzberg, *Eine unbekannte juedische Sekte*, pp. 98–99. The latter draws attention especially to the so-called Zadokite Document (ed. Schechter, in *Documents of Jewish Sectaries*, vol. I, p. 11, line 8) and the Book of Jubilees, 50.10–11, both of which apparently agree with the anti-Hillelite view. Yet neither work is Sadducean.

E. Leszynsky attempts to prove (*Die Sadduzäer*, p. 66, note 2) that there was a controversy between the sects regarding the observance of Purim. In support of his view he merely cites the fact that Purim is not mentioned in I Macc. 7.43, where the mention of the celebration of

Nicanor Day on Adar 13, the day preceding Purim, would make some reference natural. On the other hand, II Macc., which is clearly a Pharisaic work, does refer to Purim (II Macc. 15.36). Leszynsky also notes that Ben Sira in his list of the Jewish heroes makes no reference to Mordecai. Whether I Macc. can properly be called a Sadducean work is, however, open to doubt. It is altogether possible that the reason no mention is made of Purim in it and in Ben Sira is that both antedate the spread of its celebration, and perhaps the writing of the Book of Esther. It is obvious that the priests did not encourage the celebration of Purim, for they gave it no place in the Temple. On the other hand, it is altogether unlikely that the question of the observance of Purim arose early enough to become a sectarian issue.

F. Leszynsky maintains that one of the controversies between the sects dealt with the right of a scholar to "release" the vows of an individual; the extant rule permitting this was Pharisaic, according to him, and was rejected by the Sadducees (p. 48 ff.). While the evidence which he adduces as basis for this theory is inadequate, it is altogether probable from their general attitude toward such matters that the Sadducees denied the authority of scholars to release vows.

G. Aptowitzer (*Parteipolitik*, p. 31 ff.) also maintains that the legitimacy of the Davidic dynasty, which tradition derives from the marriage of Boaz with Ruth the Moabite, was a matter of dispute between the Pharisees and the Sadducees. The Sadducees, according to him, maintained that the marriage was null because of the prohibition of intermarriage with the Moabites in Deut. 21.4. The Pharisees, on the other hand, maintained that only Moabite men were prohibited to "enter the community" but not

Moabite women (Mishna Yebamot, 8.3). But the grounds which Aptowitzer advances in support of this hypothesis are entirely inadequate.

H. J. Mann, in *Jewish Quarterly Review*, N. S., VI (1915–16), p. 415, maintains that the Sadducees did not require a priest to defile himself in order to look after the burial of a *met mizvah*, i. e. an unidentified corpse. But while there may be some truth in this statement, his evidence is inconclusive (see Strack-Billerbeck, *Kommentar zum Neuen Testament*, II, p. 183; and Jeremias, *Jerusalem*, II B, p. 8).

IV. A Controversy Wrongly Described as Sadducean

The Mishna Yadayim, end, records a controversy between the Pharisees and a Galilean heretic regarding the propriety of dating ritual documents, like writs of divorcement, by the years of the Herodians and Roman rulers. While some later texts have replaced the original *min* with *Zadoki* in this passage, it is clear that the sectarian involved was not a Sadducee, but a Galilean nationalist, who opposed the recognition of the non-Davidic, and certainly of the Roman, rulers in Jewish ceremonial.

NOTES TO CHAPTER I

[1] Of works on the biblical period, mention may be made of Karl Budde, "The Nomadic Ideal in the Old Testament," in *New World*, December, 1895; published in German, in expanded form, in *Preussische Jahrbuecher*, 1896; F. Walter, *Die Propheten in ihrem sozialen Beruf und das Wirtschaftsleben ihrer Zeit*; F. Buhl, *Die sozialen Verhaeltnisse der Israeliten*; J. Herrmann, "Die soziale Predigt der Propheten" in *Biblische Zeit-und Streitfragen*, VI, 12; J. Koeberle, *Soziale Probleme im alten Israel und in der Gegenwart*; Johs Pedersen, *Israel, Its Life and Culture*; Max Weber, *Religionssoziologie*, vol. III; R. Kittel, *Geschichte*; and *Die Psalmen* (fifth and sixth editions); Wellhausen, *Israel.-jued. Geschichte*; Eduard Meyer, *Die Israeliten und ihre Nachbarstaemme*; his *Geschichte des Altertums*, II, 2, p. 178 ff.; and his *Ursprung u. Anfaenge des Christentums*, vol. II; Abram Menes, *Die vorexilischen Gesetze Israels*, and his "Die Sozialpolitische Analyse der Urgeschichte," in ZAW, XLIII (1925), pp. 33–62; Lurje, *Studien*; Causse, *Les "Pauvres" d'Israel*; Flight, "The Nomadic Idea and Ideal in the Old Testament," in *Journal of Biblical Literature*, XLII (1923), p. 158 ff.; Hans Schmidt, *Das Gebet der Angeklagten im Alten Testament*; Mowinckel, *Psalmenstudien*, parts 1–8; Albrecht Alt, "Die Rolle Samarias bei der Entstehung des Judentums," in *Festschrift Otto Procksch*, pp. 5–28; and his *Israel und Aegypten*; Louis Wallis, *God and the Social Process*, and I. Friedlaender, "The Political Ideals of the Prophets" in his *Past and Present*. For the post-biblical and rabbinical periods, see Abraham Geiger, *Urschrift*, *Nachgelassene Schriften*, and *Kebuzat Maamarim*; Meir Friedmann in his notes and introductions to his editions of the Mekilta and the Sifre, as well as scattered articles in *Bet Talmud*; David Hoffmann, *Einleitung in die halachischen Midraschim*; G. Dalman, *Arbeit u. Sitte in Palaestina*; J. Jeremias, *Jerusalem zur Zeit Jesu*, parts I, IIA, and IIB; A. Buechler, *Der Galilaeische 'Am-ha-'Ares des zweiten Jahrhunderts*; L. Ginzberg, *Eine unbekannte juedische Sekte*; and his epochal work *Mekomah shel ha-Halakah behokmat Yisrael*; Joseph Klausner, *Historia Yisraelit*; S. Dubnow, *Weltgeschichte des juedischen Volkes*, vols. I–II; S. Zeitlin, *the Second Jewish Commonwealth*; Salo W. Baron, *A Social and Religious History of the Jews*, vols. I–III.

[2] For a definition of these terms, see below, p. 619 f.

[3] The Herodians were the aristocratic adherents of the House of Herod. They are distinguished from the Sadducees and the Pharisees (see e. g. Mark 12.13); and doubtless were the assimilationist group of their time. The Sadduceans generally remained, in all probability, loyal to the memory of the Hasmoneans, while the Pharisees, of course, were opposed to both groups.

NOTES TO CHAPTER II

[1] Mishna Shebi'it, 9.2; Ketubot, 13.10; cf. Sanhedrin, 11b.

[2] Judges 11.1 ff. and I Kings 17.1.

[3] The Morning Bathers are mentioned in Tosefta Yadaim, end, p. 684; the Water Drinkers in Mekilta, Ed. Friedmann, 60b, Horowitz-Rabin, p. 200; and the Worshipers at Sunrise in Sifre, Deut., 48. In our texts the word "*harisim*"—literally "devotees of the sun"— has been altered or corrupted into *hasidim*, "saints." But the correct reading has been recovered by Hoffmann, *Midrash Tannaim*, Introduction, p. vii, and text, p. 42. (In spite of I. N. Epstein's remarks in *Tarbiz*, VIII (1936–37), p. 378, I am still convinced, with Hoffmann, that the correct reading in Sifre Deut. 48, as well as in Midrash Ha-Gadol, ad loc., is *harisim*; and that it is merely the infrequency of the word that led the copyists to substitute *hasidim* for it in most of the texts.)

[4] Yer. Sanhedrin, 10.6, 29c.

[5] This has already been noted by Professor L. Ginzberg, in *Eine unbekannte juedische Sekte*, p. 149; cf. also G. Kittel, *Die Probleme des palaestinischen Spaetjudentums und das Urchristentum*, p. 94. Perhaps nothing illustrates more vividly their scientific approach than the manner in which they preserved variant readings of the Scripture, retaining one for the written codices, and using the other for public reading. Cf. R. Gordis, *The Biblical Text in the Making*, p. 41 ff.

[6] 'Erubin, 13b.

[7] Yebamot, 14b.

[8] L. Finkelstein, *Akiba*, p. 42 f.

[9] Ibid., 294 ff., where a full discussion and demonstration of this is offered.

[10] See Tosefta Yoma, 1.8, p. 181; Babli, ibid., 19b; Tosefta Niddah, 5.3, p. 645; Babli, ibid., 33b; Josephus, *Antiquities*, XVIII, 1.4; XIII, 10.6; and XVII, 2.4.

[11] Micah 1.9; Cf. O. Procksch, in *Palaestinajahrbuch*, XXVI (1930), p. 19 f.; G. Dalman, ibid., XI (1915), 22, 39 ff.; A. Alt, in *ZDMG*, LXXIX (1925), 15.

[12] II Sam. 24.24. For the reasons governing David's choice, see Albrecht Alt, in *ZDMG*, LXXIX (1925), 14 ff.

[13] I Chron. 21.25.

[14] Cf. Josephus, *Against Apion*, I, 22, 197; and Jeremias, *Jerusalem*, I, p. 96. See also J. Beloch, *Die Bevoelkerung der griechisch-roemischen Welt*, p. 247; J. Juster. *Les Juifs dans l'Empire romain*, I, p. 210, note 2; Eduard Meyer, article "Bevoelkerungswesen (Bevoelkerung des Altertums)" in *Handwoerterbuch d. Staatswissenschaften*, II, 898–913; Ruppin, *Soziologie der Juden*, I, p. 69; and Salo W. Baron, in *Abhandlungen zur Erinnerung an H.P. Chajes* (Hebrew section), pp. 119, 120; and his most recent work, *A Social and Religious History of the Jews*, I, p. 131. The estimate given by Richard Zimmermann in "Bevoelkerungsdichte und Heereszahlen in Altpalaestina," in *Klio*, XXI (1927), 340, seems much too modest.

[15] Compare Jeremias, *Jerusalem*, IIB, p. 68.

[16] Mishna Sukkah, 3.8.

[17] Mishna Bikkurim, 3.8.

[18] Mishna Megillah, 4.8.

[19] Yer. Ketubot, ch. 5, end, 30c; Lamentations R. 1.16(50). It is interesting to note that the Babylonian Talmud (Ketubot, 65a), which usually indulges in the most extravagant hyperbole, prefers to minimize this particular incident, and maintains that the two *seahs* of wine were intended for a whole week. This doubtless is a reflection of the fact that wine is far less common, and therefore much more expensive, in Babylonia than in Palestine.

[20] Yoma, 18a.

[21] Lamentations R., loc. cit.

[22] Yer. Ketubot, loc. cit. The dinars are, of course, silver ones. In Lamentations R., loc. cit., the story is exaggerated, and the money is fixed in gold dinars.

[23] Gittin 56a; Lamentations R., 1.5 (32); cf. Josephus, *War*, V, 1.4; Tacitus, *Hist.*, V. 12.

[24] Josephus, *War*, IV, 3.1 ff.

[25] Jeremias, *Jerusalem*, IIA, p. 10 ff.; IIB, p. 94 ff.; Max Weber, *Religionssoziologie*, III, p. 37; M. Lurje, *Studien zur Gesch. d. wirtschaftlichen und sozialen Verhaeltnisse im israelitisch-juedischen Reiche*, p. 16; cf. also my remarks in *HTR*, XXII, p. 190 ff.; and in *Akiba*, p. 28 f.

[26] Shabbat 25a.

[27] The heave-offering (*terumah*) being about two and a half per cent of all produce, and the tithe which originally belonging to the Levites was usurped by the priests, were the most important of these. See Strack-Billerbeck, *Kommentar zum N.T.*, vol. IV, 2, p. 650; and *Akiba*, pp. 83 ff.

[28] Cf. the story of Eleazar ben Azariah (Baba Batra 91a), and Jeremias, *Jerusalem*, IIA, p. 14.

[29] L. Mitteis-U. Wilcken, *Grundzuege und Chrestomatie der Papyruskunde*, I, 1, p. 268; Jeremias, *Jerusalem*, IIA, p. 14; Brentano, *Das Wirtschaftsleben der antiken Welt*, p. 10 ff. For reference in other countries to the nobility who were engaged in international trade, cf. Rostovtzeff, *Economic Life*, p. 249; Robert von Pöhlmann, *Geschichte der sozialen Frage und des Sozialismus in der antiken Welt*, I, p. 133 ff.; and Beloch, *Griechische Geschichte*, I, 1, p. 307. Solon is said to have warned the rich to desist from attempts at increase of their wealth in these words, "Calm the eager tumult of your hearts; you have forced your way forward to a surfeit of good things. Confine your swelling thoughts within reasonable bounds" (I. M. Linforth, *Solon the Athenian*, p. 135). See further with regard to the general question, Brentano, op. cit., p. 64 ff.; and consider the conditions reflected in Aristotle's *Politics*, I, 3; and Plato's *Laws*, VIII, 831; IX, 870.

[30] Mishna Eduyyot 1.3. See, especially, G. Dalman, *Jerusalem und sein Gelände*, p. 197. For a similar situation in Rome, where the heights were in general occupied by richer classes and the valleys by the poorer classes, see Fowler, *Social Life at Rome*, p. 25.

[31] Mishna Baba Kamma 6.6.

[32] Mishna Baba Batra, 6.4; Sifre, Deuteronomy 229. Cf. Bauer, *Volksleben im Lande der Bibel*, pp. 43–44; and S. Krauss, *Talmudische Archaeologie*, I, p. 43.

[33] Mishna Baba Batra 1.6.

[34] Mishna Sukkah 2.7.

[35] Lev. 23.42.

[36] Yoma 38a.

[37] Jeremias, *Jerusalem*, IIA, p. 26; cf. Matthew 20.9; Tobit 5.15.

[38] On the basis suggested in the Mishna Pes., 8.7; 'Erubin 8.2.

[39] Yoma 35b.

[40] Hullin 84a.

[41] As Professor L. Ginzberg has shown in his *Mekomah shel ha-halakah behokmat Yisrael*, p. 27, this is clear from the fact that the Hillelites require the night sheet to have fringes if it is worn by day. The richer Shammaites, among whom the use of the sheet for clothing was unknown, forbid the use of fringes on it (Mishna 'Eduyyot 4.9).

[42] Cf. the expression *ben tobim* (the son of good people) for the child of a rich man (Mishna Shekalim 5.6; Sifre Deut. 116; Ketubot 67b); the expression *yekire yerushalaim* (the honored men of Jerusalem), Mishna Yoma 6.4; and *nashim yekarot* (the honored women) in Sanhedrin 43a, and Lamentations R. 4.16 (50); the "esthetically minded" men of Jerusalem (Mishna Gittin 9.9; Sanhedrin 23a, 30a, Masseket Soferim 14.14); "the seven good men of the city" (Megillah 26a); "the great men of Jerusalem" (Abot of R. Nathan, I, ch. 16, 63a; Yer. Hagigah 2.1, 77b).

[43] Sanhedrin 23a.

[44] Lamentations R. 4.2. Cf. Luke 14.17. The Egyptian parallels are given in L. Mitteis-U. Wilcken, *Grundzuege und Chrestomatie der Papyruskunde*, I, 1, p. 419.

[45] Mishna Kiddushin 4.5; Tosefta Sanhedrin 4.7, p. 421.

[46] See A. Buechler, in *Schwarz Festschrift*, p. 135, who recognizes the connection between this habit and the opposition to the marriage between uncles and nieces.

[47] Zadokite Document, in Schechter, *Documents of Jewish Sectaries*, vol. I, p. 5, line 7. With regard to the whole question see Schechter, ad loc., who, correctly in my opinion, cites the assertion of the Book of Jubilees that the early saints married their cousins as a parallel showing the antiquity of the issue (cf. Jubilees 4.15, 16, 20, 27, 28, 33; and cf. *HTR*, XVI (1923), 54; as well as Ginzberg, *Eine unbekannte juedische Sekte*, p. 31, who cites important parallels from other sects and works; Buechler in *JQR*, N. S., III (1912–13), 485 ff.; Schechter, ibid. IV (1913–14), 455; and S. Krauss in *Studies in Jewish Literature issued in honor of Professor Kaufmann Kohler*, p. 165.

[48] Tosefta Berakot 4.10, p. 9; B. Baba Batra 93b; Lament. R. 4.2.

[49] Pesahim 113a.

[50] Tosefta Berakot 4.8, p. 9; Baba Batra, loc. cit.

[51] Ketubot 106a; Sanhedrin 43a.

[52] Regarding polygamy among the patricians of Jerusalem see L. Ginzberg, *Eine unbekannte juedische Sekte*, pp. 24, 191; J. Jeremias, *Jerusalem*, IIA, p. 8 ff.; S. Krauss, *Talmudische Archaeologie*, II, p. 27 ff.; S. W. Baron in *Abhandlungen zur Erinnerung an Hirsch Perez Chajes*, Hebrew section, p. 90.

[53] The phenomenon of a socially lower class rejecting the cultural guidance of the upper class is unique, and doubtless accounts in part for the unique quality of the whole rabbinic tradition. Cf. F. Oppenheimer, "Machtverhaeltniss", in *Handwoerterbuch d. Soziologie*, 1931, p. 343 ff.

[54] Mishna Yoma 1.3, and 1.6. For other references to ignorant High Priests see Mishna Horayot, end, and Abot of R. Nathan, I, ch. 12, 28b.

[55] Sifre, Deut. 352.

[56] Deut. 18.1.

[57] Deut. 33.11; Sifre, ad loc.

[58] A. Buechler in *Schwarz Festschrift*, p. 135 ff.; J. Jeremias, *Jerusalem*, II B, 83 ff.; S. Klein in *Jued.-palästinisches Corpus Inscriptionum*, p. 12, note 9; and in *Monatsschrift*, LXXX (1936), p. 199; Aptowitzer in *HUCA*, V, p. 290; and Marmorstein in *PEF* Quarterly Statement, 1921, p. 188.

[59] This seems to be implied in Septuagint to Lev. 21.13; it is expressly maintained by Philo, in *De Monarchia*, II, 8 and 229; cf. Ritter, *Philo u. d. Halacha*, p. 73; A. Geiger, *Hehaluz*, 5.74; *Nachgelassene Schriften*, V, p. 133; see also Pineles, *Darkah shel Torah*, Vienna, 1861, p. 199; A. Buechler, in *Schwarz Festschrift*, loc. cit., and J. Jeremias, op. cit., II B, p. 11. It is possible that one of the purposes of Hillel's Mishna (preserved in Kiddushin 4.1), giving the order of classes in Israel, was the rejection of this rule.

[60] Mishna Ketubot 1.5.

[61] *Antiquities*, III, 12.2.

[62] Mishna Ketubot 2.9; cf., however, ibid., 1.10.

[63] Ibid., 2.9.

[64] Hence the sudden emergence of *Jehoiarib* as the first of all the priestly clans (I Chron. 24.7).

[65] Jeremias, op. cit., II B, pp. 16 and 54.

[66] Pesahim 57a; Josephus, *Antiquities*, XX. 9.2.

[67] See Jeremias, op. cit., II A, pp. 13 and 24; II B, p. 69.

[68] ʿArakin 11b. For further evidence regarding the social differences between the two groups of Levites, see Josephus, *Antiquities*, XX, 9.6; and cf. Targum Ps.-Jonathan to Ex. 29.30; and also Ezra 2.40; 7.7; 10.23; Neh. 10.29. For the controversy between the priests and the Levites regarding tithes, see Otto Eissfeldt, *Erstlinge und Zehnten im alten Testament*, Strack-Billerbeck, *Kommentar zum Neuen Testament aus Talmud und Midrasch*, IV, p. 656 ff.; and my *Akiba*, p. 84 ff.

[69] For modern parallels, see Bauer, *Volksleben im Lande der Bibel*, p. 9. For parallels outside of Palestine, and for the psychological significance of the opposition, see J. G. Thompson, *Urbanization, Its Effects on Government and Society*, pp. 3–38; and N. P. Gist and L. A. Halbert, *Urban Society*, p. 325 ff. See also, F. Oppenheimer, *System der Soziologie*, II, p. 345.

[70] See Skinner's note in his commentary to the passage (*Century Bible*); cf. also R. Kittel, *Geschichte*, II, 336. So also R. Gordis, in *JQR*, N. S., XXV (1934–5), 244. Cf., however, A. Menes, *Die vorexilischen Gesetze*, p. 69 ff.

[71] Isa. 5.3, et al. For another interpretation of this contrast see, however, O. Procksch, *Palaestinajahrbuch*, XXVI (1930), 38.

72 Compare for example the extravagant statement in Lamentations R. 4.2 that a Jerusalemite who married a provincial received as his dowry his weight in gold, while a provincial who married a Jerusalemite woman had to give her her weight in gold.

73 Perhaps it would be even better to render the expression "country-people" which conveys the same ambiguity in English as does *'am ha-arez* in Hebrew. The word *bur*, which in Mishnaic Hebrew is synonymous with *'am ha-arez* (but somewhat stronger), is likewise associated by G. R. Driver with the root meaning "outside," extended to "outside the city" and "wild, untamed, country." See *HTR*, XXIX (1936), 172; cf. also *baruta*, which is interpreted by R. Nathan ben Yehiel (*Aruk*, s. v. *bar*) as meaning "outside," and also implies "stupid." Felix Perles discovered what was probably the first reference to the *'am ha-arez* as a group opposed to the Scribes in the Psalms of Solomon, 8.23. The passage is usually translated: "(But) God hath shown Himself righteous in His judgments upon the *nations of the earth*" (Charles). Perles demonstrated, however, that the words ἔθνη τῆς γῆς are probably a mistranslation by the Greek of an original עמי הארץ. See *Orientalistische Litteraturzeitung*, V (1902), col. 335–336; and XIV (1911), col. 358. For evidence of differences between town and country in Hellenistic Egypt, similar in some respects to those in Judea, see L. Mitteis-U. Wilcken, *Grundzuege und Chrestomatie der Papyruskunde*, I, 1, p. 421. It is noteworthy that the term *agroikos*, literally "peasant," developed in Greek practically the same connotation of brutishness as the Hebrew *'am ha-arez* (see Heitland, *Agricola*, p. 117).

74 Mishna Abot, 2.5. Special interest may perhaps attach to the differences in manner between the scholar and the *'am ha-arez* cited by R. Benaiah, in reply to a question of R. Johanan (B.B. 57b). According to R. Benaiah, the scholar is more modest in his clothes, as well as more orderly in his household arrangements. "How can the bed of a scholar be recognized?" R. Johanan asks, finally. "It is a bed which has under it only sandals in the summer and shoes in the winter. The bed of the *'am ha-arez*, however, looks like a confused treasure house!"

75 Num. ch. 19.

76 Compare Katzenelson in *MGWJ*, XLIII (1899), pp. 1 ff., 97 ff., 193 ff.; XLIV (1900), 385 ff., 433 ff.

77 Lev. 15.1 ff.

78 Mishna Pesahim 5.5.

79 Cf. Num. 18.21 (First Tithe); Deut. 14.22 ff. (Second Tithe).

80 S. Krauss, *Talm. Archaeologie*, II, p. 164; G. Dalman, *Arbeit u. Sitte in Palaestina*, II, p. 32; Vogelstein, *Landwirtschaft zur Zeit d. Mishna*, p. 10 ff.; J. Wellhausen, *Skizzen und Vorarbeiten*, III; *Reste arabischen Heidentumes*, p. 170; Smith-Cook, *Religion of the Semites*, p. 534.

81 See Tosefta Shabbat, chs. 6(7), and 7(8), p. 117 ff. Compare also *Akiba*, p. 178 ff.

82 Deut. 6.8; 11.18.

83 Berakot 47b.

84 Mishna Hagiga, 3.4.

85 The Order Tohorot: "Pure Things."

[86] Hagigah 25a; Niddah 6b, according to the report of Ulla (ca. 300 C.E.), who says, "our colleagues purify themselves in Galilee." The interpretation of Rashi, according to which the Galileans prepared animals in purity in anticipation of the possible arrival of the Messiah, is unacceptable; but even if it be accepted, it implies the purity of the people, and hence the use of the ashes of the "red heifer."

[87] Berakot, loc. cit.

[88] Brentano, *Das Wirtschaftsleben der antiken Welt*, p. 72 f.; see especially note 1 on p. 73. Compare also below, p. 48.

[89] Pesahim 49b.

[90] Ibid.

[91] For a discussion of the subject see, e. g., F. Oppenheimer, *System der Soziologie*, II, p. 345 ff.; C. A. Beard, "The City's Place in Civilization," in *American City*, vol. XXXIX, No. 5, 1928, pp. 101–103.

[92] Both scholars retained their wealth after the year 70; this could hardly have happened to such nationalists without intervention. Cf. also Gittin 56b.

[93] Pesahim, loc. cit.

[94] Ibid.

[95] Ibid.

[96] Ibid. 49a.

[97] Baba Batra 8a.

[98] Leviticus R., 9.3.

[99] Pesahim, loc. cit.

[100] For the demonstration of this, see *Akiba*, pp. 17 and 320. For the general principle that the power of the nobility generally develops in the lowland, and especially on the coast, where the income from trade is joined to that from the rich soil, see M. Weber, article, "Agrargeschichte" (Altertum), in *Handwörterbuch der Staatswissenschaften*, I, 69a.

[101] M. Weber, *Religionssoziologie*, III, p. 64.

[102] G. A. Smith, *Historical Geography of the Holy Land*, 266 ff.; and see especially Josephus, *War*, IV, 8.2.

[103] The owners of the lands of Jericho were, to a large extent, priests of the upper classes; see Yer. Pesahim 4.1, 30d; B. Ta'anit 27a; and below, chapter IV.

[104] Pesahim 57a.

[105] For R. Eliezer, see e. g. Tosefta Ma'aser Sheni 5.16 (p. 96); R. Tarfon's residence in Ludd is implied in Mishna Baba Mezi'a 4.3 and Ta'anit 3.9; Hagigah 18a; Megillah 20a.

[106] W. F. Albright, *The Archaeology of Palestine and the Bible*, p. 131.

[107] Josh. 15.1 ff.; 18.11 ff. See particularly 18.22 and I Chron. 8.12.

[108] Esth. 2.5; cf. also II Chron. 11.12; 15.9; 17.17; et al.

[109] Philippians 3.5; Romans 11.1.

[110] See *Akiba*, pp. 169, 261.

[111] Sifre Deut. 352.

[112] Yer. Kilaim 9.3, 32b; Genesis R., 33.3, p. 306.

[113] Sifre Deut. 348. Cf. V. Aptowitzer, *Parteipolitik*, pp. 173 and 315. There is a similar controversy between R. Meir and R. Judah regarding the question of

who led Israel into the Red Sea. R. Meir maintains that the tribe of Benjamin sprang into the sea first, and that the princes of Judah actually threw stones at them in their anger at their having taken this precedence. R. Judah insists that the first to spring into the sea was Nahshon, the son of Aminadab, the prince of Judah (Mekilta, Beshallah, Vayyehi, ch. 5, p. 104 ff.).

[114] Mo'ed Katan 2a; cf. Tosefta, ibid., 1.1, p. 229. See also G. Dalman, *Arbeit und Sitte in Palaestina*, II, p. 42 f.

[115] I Macc. 5.15.

[116] Gittin 34b. The manager of Agrippa II's property, doubtless an eminent patrician in his own right, is said to have had two households in Galilee itself, one in Sepphoris, the other in Tiberias. In early biblical times, Gideon, living at Ophrah with most of his family, is recorded as having had a concubine, who lived in Shechem, and bore him a son, Abimelech (Judg. 8.31).

[117] S. Klein, *Beitraege zur Geschichte und Geographie Galilaeas*, p. 32 ff. The statement of R. Judah that the Galileans had "long ago written over their property to the prince" (Mishna Nedarim 5.5), may be a reminiscence of the fact that these lands originally belonged to the head of the nation and were distributed among the patricians on a feudal basis. The interpretation of the passage given in the *baraita*, B. Nedarim 48a, that the Galileans transferred their property to the Nasi, because they were prone to anger and wanted to save themselves from the effects of vows made in bursts of temper, need hardly be considered.

[118] Josephus, *Life*, 45.

[119] Mishna Baba Batra 4.7. The Mishna carefully distinguishes between the large walled city, and the ordinary unwalled city, which was in effect a hamlet. Cf. Mishna Ketubot 13.10. The Talmud fixes the normal population of a "city" at 120. (Mishna Sanhedrin, end of Chapter 1).

[120] Josephus, *Life*, 65.

NOTES TO CHAPTER III

[1] Comp. Shabbat 62b; Sanhedrin 19a; Yer. Horayot 3.5; See also S. Klein, in *Madda'e Ha-Yahadut*, I, 73 seq. and Jeremias, *Jerusalem*, II B, p. 91.

[2] Testament of Issachar, 3.5. For a similar situation in Greece, see Hesiod, *Works and Days*, Lines 695–697. Cf. *Akiba*, p. 304.

[3] Ketubot 82b; cf. Epstein, *The Jewish Marriage Contract*, p. 20 ff.; S. Zeitlin, *JQR*, N. S., XXIV (1933–4), p. 2; and see Tobit 7.14.

[4] Mishna Ketubot 1.5.

[5] Mishna Kiddushin 1.1. Mishna Ketubot 5.1 shows conclusively that the marriage contract was drawn up at the time of betrothal. R. Eleazar ben Azariah denies the right of the bride whose betrothal is annulled, to anything beyond the minimum dower, "for the husband executed the agreement only with the intention of having her as his wife."

[6] Mishna Ketubot 5.2. The expression "wedding" in English derives from a similar custom among the primitive Anglo-Saxons; wedding being the celebration

of the *wed* or pledge binding the bridegroom and the guardian of the bride to the carrying out of the marriage agreement.

[7] Mishna Ketubot 1.5. The custom may be as old as the Book of Chronicles, and the several "Matriarchal" marriages which he describes (cf. Ezra 3.61) may be intended to justify it. Cf. V. Aptowitzer, "Spuren des Matriarchats im juedischen Schrifttum," *H.U.C. Annual*, IV (1927), 10.

[8] Ketubot 12a; Tosefta, ibid. 1.4, p. 261; Yer. ibid.

[9] Mishna Baba Batra 6.4.

[10] Ketubot, loc. cit.; I do not deny, of course, that the custom may have been preserved in Judea and among the plebeians of Jerusalem from primitive times and that its origin may be due to special considerations of early times. The fact that the custom appears also in other countries would seem to indicate this (see E. A. Westermarck, *History of Human Marriage*, I, p. 205, note 3; II, p. 527; cf. also ibid., pp. 547, 550 f., 555 ff.). It seems altogether probable that in primitive times the union of the newly married couple took place as a matter of course in the tent which they shared with other members of the tribe; and that there was no sense of delicacy about the matter. Naturally, as some families grew in wealth and were able to obtain for themselves more considerable houses, they separated the newly married couple from the others, while the poorer families retained the ancient custom, rationalizing it as a means to ward off the dangerous attacks of spirits and devils. Indeed, it is a plausible surmise that the widespread superstitions about the dangers surrounding the bride and the bridegroom on their wedding night are really associated with the fact that they could not be granted the privacy which the developing sense of delicacy demanded, and some theory had to be developed for denying it to them. The continence practiced by the couple in different countries during the first nights of the wedding week may be the result of a compromise between the delicacy of the young people and the power of the rationalized custom, as well as the force of necessity, which prevented the bride and groom from separating themselves from their families and escorts. For the prohibition of conjugal relations during the first days of marriage, see e. g. Max Mueller, *Sacred Books of the East*, XXX, pp. 48, 51, 197, 267. While in Israel conjugal relations were not actually prohibited during the first days of marriage, the couple frequently refrained from them, as can be seen from Mishna Berakot 2.6. Cf. also Westermarck, *Marriage Ceremonies in Morocco*, p. 227, end. The curious Judean custom of searching the bride and groom before they entered the bridal chamber also has its parallels among other peoples; see Westermarck, op. cit., p. 228.

[11] See above, p. 41.

[12] Cf. W. R. Smith-S. Cook, *The Religion of the Semites*, p. 76; W. R. Smith, *Kinship and Marriage in Early Arabia*, p. 48 ff.; A. Bertholet, *Die Stellung der Israeliten und der Juden zu den Fremden*, p. 27 ff.; M. Sulzberger, in *JQR*, N. S., XIII (1922–23), p. 264 ff.; Johs. Pedersen, *Israel, Its Life and Culture*, pp. 40, 44. The passing of the centuries and the change of conditions has not, apparently, materially improved the situation of the family-less man or woman in rural districts, as is noted by R. M. MacIver, who remarks in his *Society*, p. 122, that "there is

little place for the man, and still less for the woman (in rural communities) whose orbit has not some family hearth as its focus."

[13] Mishna Ketubot 4.10. Cf. above, p. 43, where we have shown that the term, "Men of Jerusalem," was used exclusively for patricians. The sum of two hundred *zuz* mentioned in the text is the equivalent of about fifty dollars (1936) in actual gold value; but, of course, was considerably more in relation to purchasing power and the general standard of living.

[14] See above, ch. II, note 88. The traders of Jerusalem were especially condemned for hypocrisy, see Esther R. 1.3. For general discussions of the differences between city and country in social attitude, cf. Margaret Mary Wood, *The Stranger, A Study in Social Relationships*, pp. 204, 214, 223; P. Sorokin, *A Systematic Source Book in Rural-Urban Sociology*, I, pp. 242–8; P. Sorokin and C. C. Zimmerman, *Principles of Rural-Urban Sociology*, p. 320 ff.; P. Sorokin-C. C. Zimmerman-C. J. Galpin, *A Systematic Source Book of Rural Sociology*, I, p. 238; J. M. Williams, *The Expansion of Rural Life*, pp. 8 ff., 207 ff.; H. B. Woolston, "The Urban Habit of Mind," in *American Journal of Sociology*, XVII (1911–1912), pp. 602–14; R. E. Park, E. W. Burgess, and R. D. McKenzie, *The City*, pp. 217–225; Th. Petermann, "Die geistige Bedeutung der Grossstaedte," in *Die Grossstadt*, pp. 187–206; and most recently, R. M. MacIver, *Society*, p. 127. The use of *urbanus*, in the sense of urbane as well as urban, which testifies to a common recognition of the significance of town manners, dates back at least to the time of Cicero, who remarks in one of his letters to Appius Claudius Pulcher (*Epistolae ad familiares*, III, 8, 3), "In the first place, I never thought that you, a man not only of common sense, but also, to use the modern phrase (*ut hunc loquimur*), of culture (*urbanum*), derived any sort of pleasure from that sort of deputation."

[15] Semahot 3.6, p. 112.

[16] Ketubot 17a.

[17] Shabbat 153a.

[18] Semahot 10.15, p. 186.

[19] Ibid., 10.16. From the statement at the end, "R. Jose said, Why does one greet the bereaved in Judah on entering and on leaving? Because there is no mourning on the Sabbath day," it has been assumed that the whole *baraita* refers to greetings on the Sabbath day. But I doubt whether the text of R. Jose's statement is in order. On the other hand, there was, no doubt, a difference between the customs of Judea and Galilee regarding the offering of comfort to mourners on the Sabbath day. The Galileans, again because of their rural reserve and shyness, did not attempt to offer comfort on the Sabbath day; the Judeans did (Yer. Berakot 2.7, 5b; cf. B. Mo'ed Katan 22b). That *Darom* is Judah has been definitely shown by S. Klein in *Abhandlungen zur Erinnerung an H.P. Chajes*, Hebrew section, p. 285.

[20] J. Jeremias, *Jerusalem*, II B, p. 96.

[21] Mishna Pesahim 4.5.

[22] Felix Goldmann, *Der Oelbau in Palaestina zur Zeit der Mishnah*, p. 7; S. Krauss, *Talmudische Archaeologie*, II, 215; Loew, *Die Flora der Juden*, II, p. 289.

[23] Genesis R. ch. 20. For the difficulty of raising olives and vines in the same country, See Bauer, *Volksleben im Lande der Bibel*, p. 160.

[24] Gen. 49.20; cf. also Deut. 33.24; Sifre Deut. 355; Midrash Tannaim, ad loc., pp. 220–1; Mishna Menahot 8.3; Tosefta, ibid., 9.5, p. 526; B. ibid., 85b. The importance of the vine in Judea is testified to in Gen. 49.8 ff.; cf. also Nazir 31b.

[25] Shabbat 17a. For the probable occasion of this outburst, see *Akiba*, p. 44.

[26] Shabbat, loc. cit.

[27] See E. A. Westermarck, *History of Human Marriage*[5], p. 241 ff.; and cf. Judg. 21.19 ff. The "feast," par excellence, there referred to was doubtless the autumnal festival (I Kings 8.2 ff.). Cf. the discussion of the whole subject by J. Morgenstern, in *JQR*, N. S., VIII (1917–18), p. 31 ff. See also R. H. Kenett, *Ancient Hebrew Social Life and Custom*, p. 81.

[28] Mishna Ta'anit, end.

[29] This has already been noticed by A. Buechler, *Schwarz Festschrift*, p. 134.

[30] J. Morgenstern, in *H.U.C. Annual*, I, p. 23. The suggestion has been made that the custom of reading the laws of prohibited marriages on the afternoon of the Day of Atonement was intended to warn the participants in the celebration against the temptations aroused by the frivolities of the day (*Bet Talmud*, III, p. 344).

[31] Mishna Yoma 7.4.

[32] The patrician sage, R. Judah ben Bathyra, Pesahim 109a.

[33] Hullin 110a; Bezah 30a; Genesis R. 11.4, p. 91.

[34] Mishna Hullin 5.3.

[35] Shabbat 148b.

[36] Cf. Yoma 87a; *Shulhan 'Aruk, Orah Hayyim*, 605, and notes of Isserles ad loc.

[37] Yoma 87b. It is interesting to note that Maimonides, who could not conceive of anyone indulging in such an enormous banquet on the ninth of Tishri, changes the text slightly and makes it read, in his code, "lest he be strangled" at the meal, through some food entering his windpipe (*Yad*, *Hilkot Teshubah*, 2.7).

[38] Berakot 8b.

[39] The law is stated thrice: Ex. 23.19; 34.26; and Deut. 14.21.

[40] *Moreh*, III, ch. 48.

[41] *Folklore in the Old Testament*, III, p. 117.

[42] H. L. Ginsberg, *Kitebe Ugarit*, p. 79; S. A. Montgomery-Z. S. Harris, *The Ras Shamra Mythological Texts*, p. 75; for parallels see Ramsay, in *Encyclopedia of Religion and Ethics*, IX, 905a; and Max Radin, in *AJSL*, XL (1923–24), p. 209 ff., especially p. 217 f. W. R. Smith, in his *The Religion of the Semites* (third edition, with an introduction and additional notes by S. A. Cook, p. 221, note), accepts Maimonides's interpretation of the prohibition and refers to the fact that among the Arabs meat cooked with milk is a common dish. Regarding this, see also Musil, *Arabia Petraea*, II, 1, p. 39; III, p. 149; and cf. also Gen. 8.18. W. R. Smith indicates that in his opinion the custom of seething a kid in its mother's milk is somewhat associated with the conception of milk as transformed blood, and may be connected with the thought of eating meat and blood; see ibid. S. A. Cook in his additional notes to W. R. Smith, op. cit., p. 576, accepts the theory that the prohibition is based on "a singular compassionateness, and a sentiment against brutality or even unseemliness," and directs our attention to a similar rule laid down

in Lev. 22.28, prohibiting the slaughter of the parent and the young on the same day, as well as to Deut. 22.6, which prohibits taking the mother bird with its offspring. Meir Friedmann, in *Bet Talmud*, III, p. 351, draws attention to the fact that the birth of the young goats and the abundance of milk in the later spring months would naturally lead to the development of a custom of seething the kid in its mother's milk. It is probable that some association exists between this ancient custom and that still surviving in many Jewish communities of making Shabuot a festival celebrated by dairy foods. Indeed, a number of authorities permit a relaxation of the general rule prohibiting the eating of dairy foods within six hours after meat on this festival (*Kol Bo*, section 106, *Shulhan 'Aruk*, *Orah Hayyim*, 494, section 3, note of Isserles and commentaries.).

[43] Mishna Hullin 8.1 ff.

[44] Ibid. 8.4.

[45] Hullin 116a.

[46] Mishna, ibid., 8.1. One patrician scholar, Epikoulos, apparently agreed with Jose the Galilean (Tosefta Hullin 8.3, p. 509).

[47] Philo, *De Humanitate*, 19.142, ed. Cohn and Wendland, V, p. 309.

[48] *Shullhan 'Aruk*, *Yoreh De'ah*, 89.1. See note of Isserles and commentaries, ad loc., as well as references to the Talmud and the earlier codes.

[49] For the sake of completeness, mention must here be made of the distinction drawn by R. Judah ben Ilai (ca. 170 C.E.) between Galilee and Judah with regard to vows. "If a person says, 'Let this be heave-offering,' in Judah it is permitted, in Galilee it is prohibited; for the men of Galilee do not use the term heave-offering for the annual gifts to the Temple. If a person says, 'Let this be *herem*,' in Judah it is permitted, but in Galilee it is prohibited; for the men of Galilee do not recognize the *herem* of the priests" (Mishna Nedarim 2.4). The law derives its meaning from the fact that any statement must be interpreted on the basis of local usage; and furthermore, while gifts to the Temple are forbidden for secular use, those to the priests are permitted. If a person vows that something shall have the status of heave-offering for him, he may not use it if he lives in Judah, for there the term *terumah*, heave-offering, is frequently applied to the annual gift of half a shekel to the Temple, which is forbidden for secular use. In Galilee it is permitted, for he meant nothing more than that the subject of the vow should have the status of the priests' heave-offering, which may be used. The term *herem* is likewise ambiguous. It may be used for gifts either to the Temple or to the priests. In Judah, it may be assumed that a person declaring something *herem* meant to give it to the priests, for if he meant to give it to the Temple, he would use the more common expression *hakdesh*. In Galilee, however, the *herem* of the priests was unrecognized, and gifts were made to the Temple.

More closely related to the differences cited in the text is that recorded in Yer. Moed Katan 3.5, 82d, and Masseket Semahot 10.15, p. 186, according to which the Judeans would greet a mourner on the sabbath, while the Galileans would not.

There were other differences even more patently associated with the differences of geographical situation. In Judah, e. g., being a sheep-raising province, women were accustomed to weave wool, whereas those of Galilee worked with linen (Mishna

Baba Kamma 10.9). There were also differences in the weights and other measures between the two provinces (Mishna Terumot 10.8; Ketubot 5.9; Hullin 11.2). For differences of dialect between the provinces, see 'Erubin 53a, b; Kiddushin 6a; Genesis R. 26.7, p. 254; Matt. 26.73; Mk. 14.70. Cf. now, especially, A. Sperber, in *H. U. C. Annual*, XII–XIII (1937–38), pp. 149–153; for the special leniencies of the Judaites with regard to tithing certain types of food, Mishna Demai 1.1; for the Galileans' aversion to study, Yer. Shabbat 16, 15d, end; for their quarrelsome spirit, Nedarim 48a. Finally it must be noted that the "great men," i. e., the patricians, of Galilee are said to have been so fastidious that they used warm water for washing their hands before meals (Hullin 106a).

NOTES TO CHAPTER IV

[1] Pesahim 4.8.

[2] See below, p. 563 ff.

[3] I Sam. 15.22; the passage is probably much later than the time of Samuel the Prophet; yet it belongs, probably, to the earlier period of literary prophecy. See commentaries ad loc.

[4] Cf. Amos 5.28; Isa. 1.11; and the stories of the patriarchs, who are repeatedly described as building altars and calling on the name of the Lord, but not as sacrificing on the altars; cf. Gen. 12.7, 8; 13.18; 33.20; 35.7; and also the simple oil libations at Bethel described in Gen. 28.18; 35.14.

[5] See further regarding him, below, p. 575 ff.

[6] Abot 1.2.

[7] See further below, p. 576.

[8] The ascription of the reading of the *Shema'* to the Men of the Great Assembly is well authenticated. The Septuagint adds a special introduction to the verse Deut. 6.4, indicating that already at that time the passage was recognized as distinguished from the remainder of the Scriptures; in the famous Nash Papyrus (first published by S. A. Cook, in *Proc. Soc. Bibl. Arch.*, XXV (1903), pp. 34–56; see the recent discussion of it in H. Loewe, "Pharisaism," in *Judaism and Christianity*, vol. I, p. 141, note 3; and the magnificent reëxamination of all the relevant material in W. F. Albright, "A Biblical Fragment from the Maccabean Age: the Nash Papyrus," in *JBL*, LVI (1937), pp. 145–176), the *Shema'* immediately follows on the Decalogue; Josephus, *Antiquities*, IV, 8.13, knows of the *Shema'* as consisting of the three paragraphs. See I. Elbogen, *Der juedische Gottesdienst*, pp. 24 f., 582; and see also *REJ*, XCII (1932), p. 17 ff. For the antiquity of Mishna Tamid, which mentions the ceremony at the Temple, see L. Ginzberg, in *Journal of Jewish Lore and Philosophy*, I, 1919, p. 33 ff.

[9] Mishna Tamid 5.1.

[10] Cf. further, below, p. 579 ff.

[11] Mark 13.29; cf. Matthew 22.35.

[12] See I. Elbogen, op. cit., pp. 22, 26; L. Blau, *REJ*, XXXI (1895), 189 ff.; V. Aptowitzer, *MGWJ*, LXXIII (1929), p. 102 f.; A. Buechler, *Die Priester*, p. 176;

Epstein's review of it, in *MGWJ*, XL (1896), p. 144; and finally my remarks on the subject in *REJ*, XCII (1932), p. 7.

[13] At least this was the interpretation put on Lev. 23.14 by Jewish scholarship of the Second Commonwealth; see above, p. 115 ff.

[14] Regarding the sycamore trees, see Loew, *Flora d. Juden*, I, 1926, p. 274; S. Klein, in *Schwarz Festschrift*, p. 400. See also Tosefta Menahot 13.20, p. 533; ibid., Zebahim 11.17, p. 497.

[15] Matt. 12.1.

[16] Sifre Deut. 105, 95b.

[17] Yer. Ma'aserot 1.1, 48c.

[18] Luke 11.42.

[19] Pesahim 57a.

NOTES TO CHAPTER V

[1] The scribes were of course the leaders of the Pharisees; they did not constitute by any means the whole party. For the bibliography on the Pharisees and the Sadducees, see p. 711 ff.

[2] This has already been recognized by J. Jeremias, *Jerusalem*, II B, p. 139.

[3] Tosefta Megillah 4 (3).15, p. 226.

[4] Mishna Demai 2.3.

[5] Mishna Bekorot 5.5; Zabim 3.2; B. Mo'ed Katan 22b. See A. Buechler, *Der galilaeische 'Am Ha-'Ares*, p. 74.

[6] Mishna Hagigah 2.7.

[7] Tosefta Shabbat 1.15, p. 111; Yer. ibid.

[8] Josephus, *War*, II, 8.9 ff.

[9] Tosefta Demai 2.2, p. 47; Bekorot 30b. Cf. the severer regulations of Mishna Demai 2.2; are they to be associated with Rabbi Judah the Patriarch's personal antipathy to the *'am ha-arez*, which has been described above, p. 35?

[10] Tosefta, ibid., 2.14, p. 48.

[11] Bekorot, loc. cit.; Tosefta, Demai 2.13; Yer. ibid. 2.2, 22d.

[12] Ibid.

[13] Bekorot, loc. cit.; Tosefta, ibid., 2.12, where the text has apparently been emended to conform with that of Babli. The objection raised by the Talmud that according to the original text the Shammaites would be more lenient to the *'am ha-arez* than the Hillelites is hardly valid. There are several examples of sympathetic relationship between the Shammaites and *'am ha-arez*; cf. e.g. Mishna Oholot 5.2, 3; cf. Tosefta, ibid., 5.11, p. 603.

[14] This is implied in the incidents related below.

[15] Hence the process of expulsion was called *Niddui.*

[16] Mishna 'Eduyyot 5.6.

[17] Ibid.

[18] Baba Mezi'a 59b.

[19] Yer. Mo'ed Katan 3.1.

[20] The derivation of the name Sadducee from that of the High Priest Zadok was first proposed by Geiger, *Urschrift*, p. 100; and it has since been widely accepted (see Schuerer, *Geschichte*, II, 477, and the literature cited by him). On the other hand the record of a founder Zadok, mentioned in a legendary manner in Abot of R. Nathan, ch. 5, 13b, has been revived by Eduard Baneth, *Ursprung der Saddokäer und Boethosäer*, p. 35, who presumes that Zadok was a colleague of the early Pharisaic teachers, Jose ben Joezer and Jose ben Johanan. Most recently this view has found a champion in Eduard Meyer, *Ursprung*, II, p. 291. Nevertheless, it seems to me that Geiger's view must be accepted, especially as it alone explains the name Boethusians, which cannot be other than a popular synonym for Sadducees. The theory that the Boethusians were a special faction among the Sadducees, which I adhered to formerly, cannot, I think, be maintained in view of the fact that the Talmud uses the words interchangeably, and especially that Abot of R. Nathan, loc. cit. (which, however unacquainted it may have been with the origin of the sect, must have known much about its organization), is aware of no such division among the Sadducees. See also Geiger, *Urschrift*, p. 102; Aptowitzer, *Parteipolitik*, p. 191; but especially, L. Ginzberg, article "Boethusians," in *Jewish Encyclopedia*, and his discussions of the subject in *Eine unbekannte juedische Sekte*, p. 196. The derivation of the name from Boiotos, in *Ha-Zofeh*, IX, p. 288, is fanciful.

[21] Josephus, *Antiquities*, XIII, 10.6; XVIII, 1.3; Abot of R. Nathan, ch. 5, 13b.

NOTES TO CHAPTER VI

[1] Josephus, *War*, II, 8.14.

[2] *Antiquities*, XVIII, 1.3.

[3] *Antiquities*, XIII, 10.6; XX, 9.1.

[4] See above, ch. II, note 88 and ch. III, note 14. Good manners and even obsequiousness, and together with it, disingenuousness, are frequently found among non-urban races, but, as Westermarck points out, these traits can generally be traced to either oppression by the higher classes or to the influence of traders (*The Origin and Development of Moral Ideas*, II, p. 128 ff.; cf. also pp. 86, 96, and 146).

[5] Shabbat 30b.

[6] Abot 2.5.

[7] 'Arakin 16b; Sifra Kedoshim, 4.9, 89b.

[8] Cf. Sifre Deut. 1.

[9] Tosefta Hagigah 2.11, p. 236.

[10] Mishna Sukkah 2.7.

[11] Pesahim 69a.

[12] Tosefta Kelim, First Part, 1.6, p. 569.

[13] Sanhedrin 68a.

[14] Tosefta Yebamot 8.4, p. 250.

[15] Mishna Oholot 16.1; B. Shabbat 17a; 116a.

[16] Baba Mezi'a 85a.

[17] Berakot 28a. For the Shammaitic inclinations of R. Gamaliel see *Akiba*, pp. 304–306; and also A. Buechler, in *Bloch Festschrift* (*Sefer Ha-Yobel likebod R. Mosheh Aryeh Bloch*), pp. 21–30.

[18] Tosefta, Shekalim 2.1, p. 175. The text of Sifre, Deut. 79, is to be corrected in accordance with that found in the Tosefta; see *Tarbiz*, III (1931–32), p. 201.

[19] Tosefta Berakot 3.3, p. 5.

[20] 'Erubin 53b.

[21] Ibid.

[22] Yer. Yebamot, ch. 13, 13c.

[23] Sanhedrin 104b.

[24] Yer. Niddah 1.3, 49b; Semahot 2.11, p. 101.

[25] Ibid.; for Tabbita see Yer. Niddah 2.1, 49d; Lev. R. 19.4.

[26] Mekilta Bo, ch. 17, p. 68.

[27] Mishna Sukkah 2.1.

[28] Mishna Berakot 1.7.

[29] Shabbat 151b.

[30] Kiddushin 81b.

[31] Abot of R. Nathan, end; Kiddushin 31b.

[32] Yer. Nedarim 9.11, 41c. The war could not have been that of Bar Kokeba, for R. Ishmael died before its outbreak (*Akiba*, p. 268). His generosity may have been prompted partly by his revolutionary ardor, but is nevertheless remarkable (op. cit. p. 230).

[33] Mishna Nedarim 9.10.

[34] Berakot 28a.

[35] Shabbat 31a.

[36] 'Erubin 53b; cf. Lam. R., ch. 1, 28b.

[37] Ketubot 63a.

[38] Josephus, *Antiquities*, XVIII, 1.2. There were, of course, also some Sadducees who were learned in the Law. But since learning was not held in high regard by the sect, these were necessarily few and of little importance. So also V. Aptowitzer, *Parteipolitik*, p. 30; and L. Baeck, *Die Pharisäer*, p. 48.

[39] So the Resurrection, e. g., is discussed in the tenth chapter of Mishna Sanhedrin, in connection with the laws of capital punishment.

[40] Cf., e. g., Tosefta Shabbat 7(8), pp. 118–119.

[41] Josephus, loc. cit.

[42] See above, p. 28 ff.

[43] See p. 203 ff.

[44] Abot of R. Nathan, ch. 3, 7b.

[45] Abot 1.17. For the evidence of the Shammaitic tendencies of R. Simeon ben Gamaliel I, the author of this statement, see *Akiba*, p. 46 ff.

[46] Ibid. 1.15. For a further discussion of the question as it reappeared in rabbinic times, see *Akiba*, p. 49, 258 f.

[47] Sifre Deut. 41; Mekilta of R. Simeon 19.17, p. 100; Kiddushin 40b; Yer. Pesahim 3.7, 30b; ibid. Hagigah 1.7, 76c; Cant. R., ch. 2, on verse 14; see also *Akiba*, p. 260.

[48] Hence such expressions as are found in Mark 7.1 ff.; 12.38 f.; Matthew 6.5; 12.2 ff. etc.

[49] See *Akiba*, p. 304 ff.; cf. also A. Buechler, in *Bloch Festschrift*, p. 23.

[50] Berakot 28a.

[51] Assumption of Moses, 7.4 ff. The theory that the author is a Hillelite explains satisfactorily, I believe, the long mooted question of the meaning of this passage. It cannot be an indictment of the Romans, the Herodians, or the Sadducees, for the verse, "Do not touch me lest thou shouldst pollute me" (v. 10), could not apply to any of these. On the other hand, the writer being a Pharisee, as is admitted by all commentators, would hardly attack his own group, as is maintained by Jeremias (*Jerusalem*, II B, p. 120). It is clear, however, that being a member of the plebeian faction of the Pharisees, or the Hillelites, he might well accuse the patricians or Shammaites both of gluttony and claims to superior holiness.

[52] An anonymous *baraita* (B. Sotah 22b; Yer. Sotah 5.7, 20c) enumerates seven types of Pharisees, of various grades of piety. The expressions used are in several instances colloquial and no longer intelligible, yet obviously the author of the statement distinguishes "the Pharisee out of love," i. e. the one who observes the Law from love of God, from him who observes it out of fear of God, and from others who act from less worthy motives. R. Joshua ben Hananya, one of the leading plebeian scholars of his day (i. e. from about 80–118 C.E.), used to say, "A pious fool, a clever knave, an ascetic woman, and the sufferings of the Pharisees destroy the world" (Mishna Sotah 3.4). It is interesting to notice that in this statement the Hebrew word rendered by "sanctimonious" is *perushah*, meaning literally a "Pharisaic woman." Since R. Joshua himself was a leading Pharisee, however, it is clear that what he was objecting to was, in reality, the wife whose piety expressed itself in a reluctance to normal marital life as degrading or impure. The monogamous plebeians were less inclined to tolerate such abstinence in their wives than the provincials and patricians, among whom plural marriage was not unusual (cf. further the views of the Hillelites in Mishna Ketubot 5.6; Niddah 10.1; and see also ibid. 2.4). The word *perushim* occurs in passages where it cannot possibly have any other meaning than "ascetics"; see, e. g., Baba Batra 60b.

In this connection it should be noted, too, that the plebeians of later times were divided in their opinion of the place of woman in the cultural world. Apparently fearing the independent woman of their day, some of them, like R. Joshua (Mishna Sotah, loc. cit.), agreed with the provincials in their opposition to teaching the Torah to women. See also Mishna Ketubot 1.6–9, where R. Joshua refuses to accept the testimony of a seduced woman regarding the person who seduced her; Mishna Yebamot 15.2 f., where the Hillelites refuse to accept her testimony regarding the death of her husband so as to permit her to receive her husband's estates. See also *Akiba*, p. 300 f. This view was, however, resisted by a large faction of the Hillelites, whose leaders were R. Akiba and Ben Azzai. The views of Ben Azzai are illustrated by his statement, opposing both R. Eliezer ben Hyrcanus and R. Joshua ben Hananya, and holding that "one is commanded to teach one's daughter the Torah." Those of R. Akiba are reflected in a series of maxims which mark him as one of the foremost protagonists of the rights of women in history. He insisted that a woman who earned more than her maintenance cost was entitled to keep the remainder of her wages (Mishna Nedarim 11.4); that women have a right to use cosmetics in the period of "impurity" (B. Shabbat 64b; Yer. Gittin, end, 50d; Sifra Mezora', end); and he introduced other leniencies in this regard, which shocked his more conservative colleagues and disciples (Mishna Niddah 8.3). For a full discussion of his views, see *Akiba*, p. 187 ff.

NOTES TO CHAPTER VII

[1] For controversies between the sects, in addition to those described in this and the succeeding chapters, see Appendix C.

[2] Mishna Sukkah, chs. 4 and 5.

[3] Tosefta, ibid., 3.1, p. 195; see also below.

[4] Rosh ha-Shanah 16a; Yer. ibid. 1.3, 57a; Tosefta ibid. 1.12, p. 210; Tosefta Sukkah 3.18, p. 197. Indeed R. Akiba maintains that the water-pouring is biblically commanded (Yer. Sukkah 4.1, 54a; ibid. Rosh ha-Shanah 1.3, 57b). See further regarding the Sukkot ceremonies, Smith-Cook, *The Religion of the Semites*, p. 580 and literature there cited, as well as p. 644. Frazer, *Golden Bough*,[5] I, p. 247, cites similar ceremonies among other peoples. In vol. I, p. 303, he quotes parallels also to the "torches" used in these rain ceremonies. See also Dalman, *Arbeit und Sitte in Palaestina*, I, pp. 122, 148; and M. Friedmann, in *Graetz Jubelschrift*, p. 159 f. M. Friedmann regards the ceremonies of water-pouring and the carrying of the vegetables as extremely ancient, celebrated originally in connection with the agricultural festival of the *eighth* month, i. e. the first month of rain, and transferred by the Lawgiver to the seventh month in order to give the festival primarily an historical rather than an agricultural connotation. A similar suggestion has now been made by J. Z. Lauterbach in *H. U. C. Annual*, XI (1936), 24 ff.; and seems to be implied in S. Mowinckel, *Psalmenstudien*, V, p. 25 f.; as well as in J. Scheftelowitz, *Alt-Palaestinensischer Bauernglaube*, p. 93 ff.

[5] E. g. Ezekiel 46.23; Mishna Rosh ha-Shanah 1.2.

[6] Cf. Johs. Pedersen, *Israel, Its Life and Culture*, p. 35.

[7] G. A. Smith, *Jerusalem*, I, p. 15; and pp. 75–103; G. Dalman, *Arbeit und Sitte in Palaestina*, I, pp. 70–71; see also ibid. p. 176.

[8] E. Littman, in *Journal Asiatique*, N. S., XVIII (1901), p. 382, cited by Smith-Cook, in *The Religion of the Semites*, p. 575; Hoelscher, *Die Propheten*, p. 172, note 1; Derenbourg, in *Revue des Études Juives*, XLIV (1922), p. 124 ff. For abstinence in war, see Schwally, *Der heilige Krieg im alten Israel*, p. 55 ff., where the association of water-pouring with war generally is likewise discussed.

[9] The story shows clearly that Gideon knew that his visitor was an angel of the Lord, and that he was making a sacrifice to God out of the food which he had prepared. The historical authenticity of the incidents of Gideon and of Samuel do not of course bear on their value from the point of view of the development of the faith; see also Kittel, *Geschichte*, II, 248.

[10] Cf. Dalman, *Arbeit u. Sitte*, I, 1, p. 147.

[11] Diodorus Siculus, XIX, 94, ed. Fischer, p. 146.

[12] Mekilta, Jethro, p. 200.

[13] Yer. Pesahim 10.1, 37b.

[14] Nedarim 9b.

[15] Ibid; cf. Yer. Nedarim 1.3.

[16] The incident is recorded in Josephus, *Antiquities*, XIII, 13.5; in the Talmud Sukkah 48b, and Tosefta ibid. 3.16, p. 197.

[17] Cf. *JQR*, N. S., XVI (1924–5), 35, and 143.

[18] Mishna, Ta'anit 1.1.

[19] Mishna, Rosh ha-Shanah 1.2.

[20] Jubilees 6.23. For additional discussion of the question see *HTR*, XXII, p. 200.

[21] Jubilees 12.17.

[22] Lev. 23.15 ff.

[23] See Mishna, Menahot 10.3; Tosefta, ibid., 10.23, p. 528; B. ibid. 65a; Megillat Ta'anit, ed. Lichtenstein, in *HUC Annual*, VIII–IX, p. 324; cf. also Sifra, Emor, 12, 100d; Mishna Hagigah 2.4; Yer. Rosh ha-Shanah 2.1, 57d.

[24] Shabbat 86b; Mekilta, Beshallah, Vayyassa', ch. 1, p. 159; ibid. Jethro, Bahodesh, ch. 3, p. 212; Targum Ps.-Jonathan, Ex. 19.16. Though Philo and Josephus make no mention of the historical significance of Shabuot, they indicate that the offering of the Omer, the first sheaf of barley, must be made on the sixteenth of Nisan. See Philo, *De Specialibus Legibus*, II, 21, 176, ed. Cohn-Wendland, V, p. 129, l. 12; *De Decalogo*, 30, 160, IV, 304, l. 10; Josephus, *Antiquities*, III, 10.5.

[25] At the beginning of the book (1.1), Moses is commanded to come up to God on the mount to receive the tablets on the sixteenth day of the third month. This indicates the author's conviction that the Revelation had taken place the preceding day, the fifteenth of Sivan, which is his date for Shabuot (Jub. 6.17, but see next note). There may be some further allusion to the controversy in the Chronicler's representation that the covenant under Asa was made in the third month (II Chron. 15.10). This interpretation of the meaning placed on Shabuot by the book of Jubilees is generally accepted. It was already recognized by A. Epstein in *Eldad ha-Dani*, p. 156.

[26] The Pharisaic view is also explicitly supported by Targum Ps.-Jonathan on the passage in Leviticus. Peshitta, on the other hand, renders, "and after the last day of the Passover," showing that the translator agreed rather with the Book of Jubilees and the Falashas. See also Albeck, *Das Buch der Jubiläen u. die Halacha*, p. 16, and see *HTR*, XVI (1923), p. 41. For the doctrine of the Falashas, see *Tarbiz*, VII, pp. 129, 378, 387. A full discussion of the issue is to be found in D. Hoffmann, *Das Buch Leviticus*, p. 175; and *Die Zeit der Omer-Schwingung des Wochenfestes*. Whether the Karaites who held the same view as the Sadducees actually derived their teachings from records or remnants of the latter sect, a view upheld by Geiger and restated vigorously by S. Poznanski (on several occasions, see, e. g. *Gedenkbuch zur Erinnerung an David Kaufmann*, p. 173), has been questioned by Professor Louis Ginzberg (see, e. g., his *Kitbe Ha-Geonim*, *Ginze Schechter*, p. 478); as well

as by B. Revel, *The Karaite Halakah*, p. 14 ff. Prof. Ralph Marcus draws my attention to Josephus's record in *Antiquities* XIII, 8.4, telling that Hyrkan I, marching with his troops under Antiochus VII, caused the whole army to be delayed for two days because the Jews could not travel either on the Sabbath or on the festival of Pentecost which followed it. Whether that was merely a coincidence or the Hasmonean King, even in the early part of his reign, recognized the Sadducean interpretation of the festival, cannot be definitely ascertained.

[27] See Ezek. 45.18 ff.

[28] Sifra, Ahare, perek 3, 81a; Yoma 19b, 53a; Tosefta, ibid., 1.8, p. 181; Yer. ibid. 1.5, 39a.

[29] Mishna, Yoma 1.5.

[30] Dr. Julian Morgenstern calls my attention, however, to the fact that in the illicit offerings described in Lev. 10.1 and Num. 16.18, it appears that the incense was put on the fire before it was "presented before the Lord." It is altogether probable, he maintains, that the same order would be followed by those who made illicit, as by those who made prescribed, sacrifices. This argument is not, however, convincing. It is especially interesting to note that in Moses' command to Korah (Num. 16.17) there is no indication of the fact that the placing of the incense *on the fire* should precede the presentation before the Lord. In any event, those instances do not weaken the force of the argument from the text of Lev. 16.12, which plainly states that the incense is to be put on the fire *after* the priest has entered the Holy Chamber.

Leszynsky is unnecessarily literal when he maintains (*Die Sadduzäer*, p. 62) that since the High Priest is commanded to carry "his hands full" of incense, he must necessarily put the incense on the fire before entering the Holy Chamber; for, he argues, if the High Priest's hands were occupied with the incense, how could he carry the censer full of fire? The answer obviously is that the High Priest carried the two handfuls of incense not in his hands but, as the Mishna expressly states, in a container (Mishna Yoma 5.1). Even Leszynsky must assume an ellipsis in the verse, and agree that the incense was carried not in the priest's hands, but in the censer which contained the incense. What then is there more strange about the assumption that the incense was put into a second container than in the assumption that it was placed on the fire?

[31] *HUC Annual*, IV, 185 ff.; for an older explanation which probably interprets correctly the technical argument adduced by the Sadducees for their opinion, see *Bet Talmud*, IV, p. 268. Lauterbach's interpretation is, of course, partly anticipated by the remarks of Leszynsky, loc. cit. There is a striking parallel to this ancient difference between the country and city theology in some of the instances cited by Warren H. Wilson, in "Country versus City," published in *Papers and Proceedings, Eleventh Annual Meeting of the American Sociological Society*, XI (1917), p. 14.

[32] Mishna, ibid., 5.1.

[33] Mishna Parah 3.5; Tosefta, ibid., 3.8, p. 632. Cf. ibid., also 3.6.

[34] Hagigah 25a; Niddah 6b.

[35] Num. 19.11 ff.

[36] Mishna Zabim 5.12.

[37] Mishna Parah 3.7.

[38] Ibid.

[39] Ibid.

[40] The matter is most strongly emphasized by N. Bruell in *Bet Talmud*, I, pp. 240 and 270. His explanation, however, that the issue involved is the relative position of priests and laymen, seems far-fetched.

[41] Tosefta Parah 3.6, p. 632.

[42] Ibid., 3.8, p. 632.

[43] Josephus, *Antiquities*, XVIII, 1.4; Yoma 19b; Tosefta, ibid., 1.8, p. 181; Yer. ibid. 1.5, 39a.

[44] Tosefta Hagigah 3.35, p. 238; cf. also Yer. ibid. 3.8, 79d.

[45] Mishna Yadayim 4.7.

[46] Yer. Ketubot 8.11, 32c. There can be no doubt of the accuracy of this tradition in spite of the attempts of the Babylonian authorities to explain it away; cf. Shabbat 16b.

[47] Ibid.; cf. also B. Shabbat 15b.

[48] Cf. Lev. 11.32 ff.; Num. 19.14 ff.; 31.20–23.

[49] Benzinger, *Hebräische Archäologie*, pp. 70–71; and S. Krauss, *Talmudische Archäologie*, I, 58–75.

[50] II Macc. 5.25; cf. Josephus, *War*, I, 7.3; I Macc. 2.32.

[51] Yebamot 90b.

[52] Mishna Shabbat 7.1.

[53] A. Geiger, *Nachgelassene Schriften*, III, 287 ff.

[54] Compare G. Dalman, *Arbeit u. Sitte in Palästina*, I, p. 220 ff.; IV, p. 6 ff.

[55] Mark 14.67; Luke 22.55.

[56] Yoma 34b.

[57] Mishna Shabbat 1.3.

[58] Mishna Berakot 1.1.

[59] Mishna Pesahim 10.9; cf. Tosefta ibid, 10.12, p. 173; The patricians limited the time of the Passover celebration to the early evening. Compare also Jubilees 49.10, which requires the celebration to end by 10 P.M.

[60] Yer. Sotah 1.4, 16d.

[61] Mishna Berakot, loc. cit.

[62] Pesahim 4.4.

[63] Jeremias, *Jüdische Froemmigkeit*, p. 36.

[64] Mishna 'Erubin 6.2. For further discussions of the subject see Geiger, *Urschrift*, p. 147; *Jued. Zeitschrift*, II, p. 24; *Sadducäer u. Pharisäer*, p. 21; *Nachgelassene Schriften*, III, p. 290; *Kebuzat Maamarim*, p. 67; Ginzberg, *Eine unbekannte juedische Sekte*, p. 194; and also p. 159; Halevy, *Dorot Ha-Rishonim*, I C, p. 436; Leszynsky, *Die Sadduzäer*, p. 71.

[65] See G. Hoelscher, *Der Sadduzäismus*, p. 30 ff. It must be noted, however, that while Hoelscher's interpretation of the Civil Law is extremely helpful, his discussion of the controversies regarding ceremonial and his insistence that the Pharisees were literalists, are erroneous.

[66] Tosefta Yadayim 2.20, p. 684; Baba Batra1 15b; Yer. ibid. 8.1, 16a; Scholion

to Megillat Ta'anit, ch. 5, ed. Lichtenstein in *HUC Annual*, VIII–IX (1932), p. 334. Geiger (*Urschrift*, p. 143 f.) rather fancifully associated the view of the Sadducees with an alleged attempt to justify the Herodian seizure of the monarchy, holding that they derived the throne from the Hasmoneans, through Mariamne, the daughter of Alexandra, and the wife of Herod. Leszynsky (*Die Sadduzäer*, p. 88), on the other hand, finds the Sadducean view logical, but is unable to explain that of the Pharisees, except on the basis of the rather weak, technical argument, which they are said to have adduced in favor of their interpretation. Ch. Tschernowitz (*Toledoth Ha-Halakah*, I, 2, p. 327) is indeed compelled to admit that the view of the Sadducees is the more reasonable from a consideration of general social need; yet he considers that of the Pharisees superior from a purely juridical point of view. S. Poznanski in *JQR*, VIII (1896), p. 691 ff., and Aptowitzer, in *HUC Annual*, V (1928), p. 283 ff., maintain that the Sadducees actually permitted daughters to inherit on the same terms as sons. Professor Louis Ginzberg has, however, demonstrated that Poznanski's evidence rests on a copyist's error, in the text of Aaron ben Elijah's *Gan Eden*, 165d. See L. Ginzberg, *Ginze Schechter*, II, *Kitebe Ha-Geonim*, p. 470. Aptowitzer, who apparently realizes this, restates the theory without, however, adducing more cogent proof (op. cit.). See, however, also his work, "Die syrischen Rechtsbuecher und das mosaisch-talmudische Recht" (*Sitzungsberichte der Kais. Akademie d. Wissenschaften in Wien*, Band 163, *Abhandlung* 5, pp. 23, 81 ff.). In *HTR*, XXII (1929), p. 255 f., I advanced the theory that the Pharisaic view was based entirely on the sect's theological conception of immortality, and that the rule of the granddaughter's priority over the daughter was intended as a legal recognition of the fact that her father, though deceased, was really alive, in another world, and could inherit the property so as to hand it over to his child and to deprive his sister of her rights. I still believe that this thought may have played some part in the mental attitude of the Pharisaic judges toward the question. But certainly the issue of the division of the estates was far more important. That can be seen from the facts mentioned below.

[67] Mishna Baba Batra 9.9, 10, 11; see *Akiba*, p. 279 f.

[68] Mishna Ketubot 4.11. For Admon's patrician leanings, see *Akiba*, p. 300 ff.

[69] Tosefta Baba Batra 7.10, p. 408; Babli, ibid. 111a; Yer. ibid. 8.1, 16a. His view is also accepted by Simeon ben Yohai, a later patrician. The importance attached to the issue may be gauged from the rancor with which it was discussed in later times. Indeed, R. Nahman threatened to excommunicate anyone who decided in accordance with Zechariah's views on this subject (Babli, loc. cit.); and the Palestinian scholars said of the Babylonian judges who followed the ancient Sage that they were *hedyotot*, "unlearned" (Yer., loc. cit.). Such energetic expressions of opinion indicate deep social cleavages behind the quiet academic-juristic façade of ordinary talmudic discussion.

[70] *Code of Hammurabi*, section 3; see discussion by A. Jirku, *Das weltliche Recht im Alten Testament*, p. 102 f.

[71] Mishna Makkot 1.8; Sifre Deut. 190, 109b; Josephus, *Antiquities*, IV, 8.15; see Weyl, *Die juedischen Strafgesetze bei Flavius Josephus*, p. 83 ff.; D. Hoffmann, *Das Buch Deuteronomium*, p. 374.

[72] Cf. Deut. 17.7; Mishna Sanhedrin 6.4.

[73] See below, p. 162.

[74] For the change of view which developed when wrongful actions ceased to be considered purely civil and individual matters, and came to be regarded as wrongs against the state, see A. S. Diamond, *Primitive Law*, p. 304.

[75] The significance to be attached to intention, generally, was a matter of dispute between the plebeians and the patricians; and this doubtless played its part in the issue of false witnesses. For a discussion of the controversies regarding intention between the patricians and the plebeians among the Pharisees, see Ginzberg, *Mekomah shel ha-Halakah behokmat Yisrael*, p. 31 ff.; S. Zeitlin, *JQR*, N. S., XIX (1928–29), 268 ff.; Higger, *Intention in Talmudic Law.* The statement in the Talmud (Makkot 5b), supplementing that of the Mishna, that (according to Pharisaic law) the "false witnesses are not to be punished if the man against whom they testified has already been executed," is late and without any authority. It arose out of the opposition to capital punishment among the later Sages, but even among them it could only have been uttered when the Jews had lost all right over their criminal law. It would, of course, be absurd to suppose that the Pharisees, when they had judicial authority, punished false witnesses whose testimony had not led to execution, but refrained from punishing those whose testimony had resulted in the death of the accused (see A. Geiger, *Urschrift*, p. 140; Pineles, *Darkah shel Torah*, p. 172; I. H. Weiss, *Dor Dor ve-Doreshav*, I, p. 138). With regard to the main issue, it is interesting to note that in the story of Susanna, the false witnesses are executed, although Susanna had only been convicted, but not slain, on their testimony (Susanna, v. 61). But, as Charles maintains (*Apocrypha and Pseudepigrapha*, I, pp. 638, 651), it is altogether probable that the Book of Susanna was written to support the views of the Pharisees, and actually dates from the time of Simeon ben Shattah.

[76] The story is described in Mekilta, Mishpatim, ch. 20, p. 327; Tosefta Sanhedrin 6.6, p. 424; Yer. ibid. 6.5, 23b; and Babli Makkot 5b. Geiger, *Urschrift*, p. 141, has shown that the text in Mekilta is superior in naming Simeon ben Shattah as the judge who executed the false witness, and Judah ben Tabbai as the colleague who protested. According to our sources, which do not dare to attribute to Judah ben Tabbai (or in the variant texts, Simeon ben Shattah) Sadducean views, the protest was directed against the execution of the witness, because the law requires both witnesses to be found guilty of false testimony before either can be punished (Mishna Makkot 1.7). And it is said that Simeon executed the false witness, in spite of this, because he wanted to demonstrate the truth of the Pharisaic interpretation of the law, declaring witnesses punishable even though the person against whom they testified had not been executed.

The story as thus interpreted involves a number of difficulties. First, it seems incredible either that Simeon should not have known such a rule as the one providing that a single witness cannot be punished unless both are proved guilty, or that, if he knew it, he should intentionally have violated it. The supposition that he did it "in order to tear out of the heart of the Sadducees" their erroneous conception of the law, seems hardly sufficient to account for what is apparently nothing short of judicial murder. At the same time it seems difficult, on the ordinary interpretation of the story, to account for Judah b. Tabbai's words, "May I not see the consolation of Israel, if you have not shed innocent blood!" Certainly the blood was not innocently shed, since the witness had testified falsely. It was only for a technical reason that he could not be punished. Therefore under this interpretation, while on the one hand we cannot explain Simeon's highhandedness, no more can we understand Judah's words.

It seems to me probable that the case occurred before the establishment of the rabbinic rule that neither witness can be punished unless both are shown to have been guilty. Simeon was therefore within his rights in executing the witness who had given false testimony, even though there was no proof against his colleague. The difficulty lay rather in the fact that the person against whom he had testified had not yet been executed. He had been condemned to death by the decree of the court, but the new evidence impugning the testimony of the witnesses against him had been discovered in time to prevent his execution. Simeon nevertheless proceeded to execute the false witness, thus establishing the new rule that a witness can be punished for his false testimony, even if it led only to a wrong decision by the court and not to actual execution. Simeon was moved to give this new interpretation to the law because of the frequency of false testimony in his days. Compare his statement in Abot 1.9, "Ask the witnesses many questions and be careful with your words lest from them they should learn how to give false evidence." We know also that Simeon's own son was executed on the testimony of false witnesses (Yer. Sanhedrin 6.5, 23a). He considered it a matter of important social policy to extend the law against false testimony in this way. That Simeon was capable of drastic action when he felt there was need for it, we know from the story of his execution of eighty women in Ashkelon (Mishna Sanhedrin 6.4), and from what Josephus tells us of the actions of the Pharisees in the days of Queen Alexandra, when Simeon was their leader (*Antiquities*, XIII, 16, 2). The Pharisees accepted the decision of Simeon, although from Judah's words we can see that there was objection to it, while the Sadducees rejected it as an innovation.

[77] See G. Hoelscher, *Sadduzaeismus*, p. 31 ff.

NOTES TO CHAPTER VIII

[1] For a discussion of the Egyptian and Persian influence on the Jewish doctrine of the Resurrection, see Edwin Albert, *Die israelitisch-juedische Auferstehungshoffnung in ihren Beziehungen zum Parsismus*; A. Bertholet, *Die israelitischen Vorstellungen vom Zustande nach dem Tode*; idem, "Zur Frage des Verhaeltnisses von persischem und juedischem Auferstehungsglauben," in *Festschrift fuer F. K. Andreas*, p. 51 ff.; I. Scheftelowitz, "Der Seelen- und Unsterblichkeitsglaube im Alten Testament," *Archiv fuer Religionswissenschaft*, XIX (1916–9), 210 ff.; Gerhard Kittel, *Die Probleme des palaestinischen Spaetjudentums und das Urchristentum*, p. 78 ff.; Alex. Kohut, "Was hat die talmud. Eschatologie aus dem Parsismus aufgenommen," *ZDMG*, 1867, p. 552 ff.; R. Kittel, *Geschichte*, 3, 1, p. 252;

3.2, p. 744 ff.; Gressmann, *Der Ursprung der israelitisch-juedischen Eschatologie*; E. Boeklen, *Verwandtschaft der juedisch-christlichen mit der parsischen Eschatologie*; Eduard Meyer, *Ursprung u. Anfaenge d. Christentums*, II, pp. 57, 67 ff., 111 ff.; Bousset-Gressmann, *Die Religion d. Judentums*, 269, note; and 509 ff.; and August von Gall, *βασιλεία τοῦ θεοῦ*.

[2] Cf. L. Duerr, *Ursprung und Ausbau der israelitisch-juedischen Heilandserwartung*, especially pp. 69 ff., 102 f., 110 ff. H. Gressmann, *Der Ursprung der israelitisch-juedischen Eschatologie*, p. 193 ff.; J. Greenstone, *The Messiah Idea in Jewish History*; R. H. Charles, *A Critical History of the Doctrine of a Future Life in Israel, in Judaism, and in Christianity*, p. 83 ff.

[3] Isa. 53.9ff. See commentaries ad. loc.; Kittel, *Geschichte*, III, 1, p. 251, and Duerr, op. cit., p. 150 f.

[4] This we must assume in view of the absence of any real influence of Egypt on prophetic teachings in the First Commonwealth, in spite of the overwhelming cultural influence the southern empire must obviously have exerted on the whole of Palestine. Cf. below, p. 574 ff. for the Egyptian influence during later times.

[5] Gen. 50.2, 3, 26.

[6] See Dewey and Tufts, *Ethics*, pp. 78–80; Sorokin-Zimmerman, *Principles of Rural-Urban Sociology*, p. 345; P. A. Sorokin-C. C. Zimmerman-C. J. Galpin, *A Systematic Source Book in Rural Sociology*, I, p. 247; II, pp. 39, 48; Carpenter, *The Sociology of City Life*, p. 231; A. Vierkandt, "Sittlichkeit," in *Handwörterbuch der Soziologie*, p. 538; P. Kropotkin, *Mutual Aid*, p. 124 ff.; F. S. Bogardus, "The City, Spatial Nearness and Social Distance," in *Sociology and Social Research*, XIII (1928–1929), pp. 572–577; N. J. Spykman, "A Social Philosophy of the City," in E. W. Burgess, *The Urban Community*, p. 60; H. Maine, *Ancient Law*, p. 179 ff., and J. H. Kolb-E. de S. Brunner, *A Study of Rural Society*, p. 265. Cf., for a somewhat different approach to the problems involved, Gist and Halbert, *Urban Society*, p. 384.

[7] Cf. also Deut. 5.9; and see Berakot 7a.

[8] Jer. 12.1 et al. See further W. Eichrodt, in *Festschrift Otto Procksch*, p. 59 ff.

[9] See below, p. 415 ff.

[10] Cf. below, p. 226 ff.

[11] See below, p. 219 ff.

[12] Toy, *Judaism and Christianity*, p. 260.

[13] Mishna Abot 1.1; for the following remarks see Abot of R. Nathan, I, ch. 5, 13b.

[14] Dan. 12.2, 13. For a discussion of the significance of immortality and other-worldly punishments in various religions, see M. Landau, *Hoelle und Fegfeuer im Volksglaube, Dichtung and Kirchenlehre*; K. Kohler, *Heaven and Hell in Comparative Religion*.

[15] Josephus, *Antiquities*, XVIII, 1.3. For the controversy between the Pharisees and the Sadducees regarding the resurrection, see Schuerer, II, 459; Bousset-Gressmann, p. 273.

[16] Sanhedrin 10.1.

[17] See below, p. 579; *JQR*, N. S., XVI (1925–6), pp. 22, 143.

NOTES TO CHAPTER IX

[1] For a discussion of foreign influences on the Pharisaic doctrine of angels, see Eduard Meyer, *Ursprung u. Anfaenge*, II, pp. 63 ff., 95 ff.; R. Kittel, *Geschichte*, III, 2, p. 745 f.; Bousset-Gressmann, *Die Religion des Judentums*, p. 499 ff.; Stave, *Ueber den Einfluss des Parsismus auf das Judentum*; J. H. Moulton, *Early Zoroastrianism*, p. 286 ff.; G. W. Carter, *Zoroastrianism and Judaism*; Scheftelowitz, *Die altpersische Religion und das Judentum*; G. Kittel, *Die Probleme des palaestinischen Spaetjudentums und das Urchristentum*, p. 77 f.; and see also citations in note 1, to ch. VIII. With regard to the special questions discussed below, see in particular, L. Ginzberg, article "Anthropomorphism" in *Jewish Encyclopedia*, I. The *bene elohim* of Gen. 6.2 ff. do not form any real exception to the discussion of *malak* given in the text, as has been shown by J. W. Rothstein in *Budde Festschrift*, p. 150 ff.

[2] See further regarding this identification of persons with the head of the household, below, ch. XI, note 2; ch. XIV, note 6.

[3] I find that this interpretation of the theophany is apparently adopted also by B. Jacob, in his commentary on Genesis (*Das Erste Buch der Tora*), p. 438.

[4] Genesis R. 50.9, p. 525.

[5] The custom is mentioned in Rosh Ha-Shanah 16b; see also Genesis R. 44.12, p. 434; it is interesting to note that change of name is *not* cited in the *baraita* regarding the means of bringing change of fortune in Yer. Ta'anit 2, 65b. For parallels among other peoples see J. Scheftelowitz, *Altpalaestinensischer Bauernglaube*, p. 55 ff.; and R. Briffault, *The Mothers*, p. 8 ff. For a discussion of the significance of names among Semites generally, see M. Noth, in *ZDMG*, LXXXI (1927), 1 ff.

[6] Yoma 83b.

[7] *Sefer Hasidim*, ed. Wistinetski-Freimann, 363, p. 111; and 1552, p. 380.

[8] Baer, *'Abodat Israel*, p. 106.

[9] Cf. Bousset-Gressmann, *Die Religion des Judentums*, p. 320.

[10] See below, p. 461.

[11] Cf. Ezek. 9.2; 40.3; and also 3.12; 8.2; 11.24; 43.5; and see Bousset-Gressmann, loc. cit.

[12] For his Babylonian origin, see below, p. 504.

[13] Zech. 1.11, 13; 2.2, 7; 4.1; 6.4. Regarding the possibility of the influence of Zoroastrianism on prophecy at this early time, see Meyer, *Ursprung*, II, p. 95 ff.

[14] Ben Sira 51.12n (Hebrew text). The prayer of the Kingdom of God according to Rab, in the Additional Prayer for the New Year (*'Alenu*).

[15] See below, p. 468 ff. and 500 ff.; for a discussion of Isa. 63.9, see p. 489 ff.

[16] Eliphaz, 4.18; 5.1; 15.15; Bildad, 25.3; Elihu, 33.23.

[17] Mal. 3.1; I Chron. 21.1, 16, 18 ff.; Tobit 3.17; Dan. 3.25; 4.14; 6.23; 8.13; 10.5, 21; 12.1; 12.6; Jubilees 2.2, et al; Testament Levi 5.6, et al.

[18] Regarding these works see below, p. 195 ff.

[19] San. 109b.

[20] Cf. below, p. 601.

[21] Below, p. 557.
[22] Below, p. 216 ff.
[23] See also Ginzberg, *Eine unbekannte juedische Sekte*, p. 229.
[24] *War*, II, 8.7.
[25] Yoma 75b.
[26] Midrash Psalms, 104, 221b.
[27] Genesis R. 26.5, p. 247.
[28] Tosefta, Hagigah 2.2, p. 234.
[29] Mekilta of R. Simeon 6.3, p. 170.
[30] Abot of R. Nathan, I, ch. 1, 3a; cf. San. 59b.
[31] Gittin 90a. *Papus* is the spelling of the Babylonian Talmud for *Pappias*.
[32] Mekilta Beshallah, Vayyehi, ch. 6, p. 112.
[33] Mekilta of R. Simeon 14.25, p. 52.
[34] Mekilta Beshallah, Shirah, ch. 3, p. 126.
[35] Ibid., Jethro, Bahodesh, p. 239.
[36] Cf. Bousset-Gressmann, 322 ff.; Meyer, *Ursprung*, II, 106 ff.
[37] Jubilees 15.27.
[38] Cf., e.g., Mishna Hullin 2.4 with parallel *baraita* in B. Hullin 40a, and Tosefta, ibid., ch. 2. The significance of this difference was first pointed out by Professor Louis Ginzberg.

NOTES TO CHAPTER X

[1] Josephus, *Antiquities*, XVIII, 1.3.
[2] Abot of R. Nathan, I, ch. 5, 13b.
[3] See A. Menes, *Die vorexilischen Gesetze Israels*, pp. 13, 26.
[4] Diodorus Siculus, XIX, 94, ed. Fischer, p. 146. For the opposition to the building of houses in Israel, see Johs. Pedersen, *Israel*, p. 21, as well as the preference for a movable sanctuary recorded below, the attitude of the Rechabites as recorded in Jer. 35.7 ff., and the statement in II Samuel 11.11, that Israel and Judah were dwelling in tents. Does this mean that during a war period large numbers of civilians, too, returned to the nomadic habits of dwelling in tents, just as they grew long hair and withdrew from contact with women?
[5] For opposition to images of the Deity among other peoples than Israel, see Kittel, *Geschichte*, II, p. 82, especially note 2, and references there given; for a discussion of the use of stone images in Israel, see R. H. Pfeiffer, in *JBL*, XLV (1926), 211–222; and G. Dalman, "Ein neugefundenes Jahvebild," in *Palästinajahrbuch*, II (1906), 44 ff.
[6] Cf. Judg. 5.2; and commentaries ad loc.; also Kittel, *Geschichte*, II, p. 55, especially note 1; and p. 316. See also C. M. Doughty, *Travels in Arabia Deserta*, index, s. v. hair; J. Wellhausen, *Skizzen und Vorarbeiten*, III; *Reste arabischen Heidentumes*, p. 167; Smith-Cook, *Religion of the Semites*, p. 607; Frazer, *Folklore in the Old Testament*, III, p. 188 f.; Schwally, *Der heilige Krieg im alten Israel*,

p. 69 ff.; and especially H. Gressmann, "Die Haartracht der Israeliten" in *Budde Festschrift*, p. 61 ff.

Other regulations for a specially Israelitish mode of wearing hair are found in Lev. 19.27; with special reference to the priests, Lev. 21.5; Ezek. 44.20. In rabbinic times, equal emphasis was laid on avoiding arrangement of the hair which resembled that of the pagans, see Baba Kamma 83a; cf. also Me'i. 17a. For similar regulations in the Middle Ages, see my *Jewish Self-Government in the Middle Ages*, p. 233 ff.

[7] See also Ex. 33.6, where it is said that the Israelites were forbidden to wear their ornaments. It is interesting to note in this connection that metal seized in war generally had to be dedicated to God; it could not be used privately; see Josh. 6.19; II Sam. 8.11; I Kings 7.51; 15.15, 18; II Kings 12.19; and note G. Hoelscher, *Geschichte der israelitischen Religion*, p. 78.

[8] A. Jeremias, *Das alte Testament im Lichte des alten Orients*, p. 49.

[9] Smith-Cook, *The Religion of the Semites*, p. 158, 455, 481; and Schwally, *Der heilige Krieg im alten Israel*, p. 6 ff. For continence generally as a form of penance, see I Kings 21.27, and the interpretation given by Koehler, in *ZAW*, XXXIV (1914), p. 149; perhaps also implied in Jer. 29.6, in Baba Batra 60b, and in Cowley, *Aramaic Papyri of the Fifth Century B.C.*, p. 112, papyrus no. 30, line 20. See the interpretation of the passage given by Eduard Meyer, in *Der Papyrusfund von Elephantine*, p. 84, note 1.

[10] For Attica and Greece generally, see J. Hasebroek, *Griechische Wirtschafts- und Gesellschaftsgeschichte*, pp. 20 ff., 36; and especially 80 ff.

[11] For Ahab's cavalry, see Olmstead, *History of Palestine and Syria*, p. 384; the German translation of the original text in Gressmann, *Altorientalische Texte und Bilder*, I, p. 109, last line.

[12] Sellin, *Gilgal*, p. 17 ff., holds that the Gilgal mentioned in I Sam. 11.15 refers to a Gilgal near Shechem and not to the usual, well-known sanctuary near Jericho. But see, in opposition to him, Albrecht Alt, *Die Staatenbildung der Israeliten*, p. 27, note 22. Regarding the series of incidents here briefly referred to, see further, ch. XVI, and notes ibid. That the use of the stone images was really a symbol of assimilation to the Canaanites has already been noticed by Ed. Meyer, *Geschichte des Altertums*, II, 2, p. 227. See also Kittel, *Geschichte*, II, p. 390, and notes ibid.

[13] See above, p. 52 ff.

[14] *War*, II, 8.3.

[15] Ber. 43b.

[16] Cf. Matt. 26.8, where the complaint is ascribed to the disciples; in John 12.4, it is ascribed to Judas Iscariot. But it is clear that the narrative of Mark is the oldest.

[17] Tosefta Shabbat 7(8). 16, p. 118.

[18] Ibid.

[19] Zadokite Document, ed. Schechter, p. 1, line 19; see also Ginzberg, *Eine unbekannte juedische Sekte*, who draws attention to this passage, and shows that it is a parallel to the Assumption of Moses.

[20] Assumption of Moses 7.4 ff.

[21] Leviticus R. 13.4; 35.6; Pesikta of R. Kahana, 117a; Canticles R. on ch. 1, verse 4; cf. B. Hagigah 9b.

[22] Genesis R. 28.7, p. 266.

[23] Abot 2.8.

[24] Ibid. 6.4.

[25] Guedemann, *Geschichte des Erziehungswesens und der Cultur der Abendlaendischen Juden*, II, note XIV; Finkelstein, *Jewish Self-Government in the Middle Ages*, p. 293 f.; Abrahams-Roth, *Jewish Life in the Middle Ages*, pp. 161, 197, 299, 313, 316, 317; for parallels among other peoples, cf. Crawley, in *Encyclopedia of Religion and Ethics*, V, p. 58a; and J. M. Vincent, in *Encyclopedia of the Social Sciences*, XIV, p. 464.

NOTES TO CHAPTER XI

[1] Josephus, *Antiquities*, XVIII, 1.3. For an excellent discussion of the problem of Free Will in biblical and post-biblical writings, see Luetgert, *Das Problem der Willensfreiheit in der vorchristlichen Synagoge*; cf. also Eduard Meyer, *Ursprung u. Anfaenge*, II, p. 115 ff.; Walther Eichrodt, "Vorsehungsglaube und Theodizee im Alten Testament," in *Festschrift Otto Procksch*, pp. 45–70; and G. F. Moore, "Fate and Free Will in the Jewish Philosophies according to Josephus," in *HTR*, XXII (1929), pp. 371–389.

[2] Cf. Pollock and Maitland, *History of English Law*, II, p. 474 ff.; W. S. Holdsworth, *History of English Law*, II, p. 47; Holmes, *Common Law*, p. 11; Wigmore, *Harvard Law Review*, VII, p. 317; L. T. Hobhouse, *Morals in Evolution*, I, p. 92 ff.; E. A. Westermarck, *Origin and Development of Moral Ideas*, I, pp. 217 ff., 260 ff.; idem, *Ethical Relativity*, p. 162 ff.; Johs. Pedersen, *Israel, Its Life and Culture*, p. 132. It is interesting to note that even Plato, in his *Laws* (IX, 873), proposes that "If any beast of burden or other animal cause the death of anyone . . . the kinsmen of the deceased shall prosecute the slayer for murder . . . and let the beast when condemned be slain by them, and cast beyond the borders. And if any lifeless thing deprive a man of life, except in the case of a thunderbolt or other fatal dart sent from the gods — whether a man is killed by a lifeless object falling upon him, or his falling upon them, the nearest kin shall appoint the nearest neighbor to be a judge, and thereby acquit himself and the whole family of guilt. And he shall cast forth the guilty thing beyond the border, as has been said about the animals." Other examples of grave punishment of animals or even inanimate objects, even in comparatively modern times, are cited by Sir James Frazer in *Folklore in the Old Testament*, III, p. 415 ff. See also M. Higger, *Intention in Talmudic Law*, and S. Belkin, *The Alexandrian Halakah in Apologetic Literature of the First Century C.E.*, p. 57 ff.

[3] Cf., e. g., Josh. 7.24 ff. Cf. also the *Code of Hammurabi*, 229.

[4] "*Quod per eum non fuerit vitae remotior morti propinquior*," *Leges Henrici*, 90.11, cited by Pollock and Maitland, *History of English Law*, II, p. 470, note 2;

and W. S. Holdsworth, *History of English Law*, II, p. 53. The most amazing type of vicarious punishment, on the ground of the identification of the master with his household, is that of certain tribes who punish an injured husband if his wife commits adultery (see R. Briffault, *The Mothers*, II, p. 129).

[5] Pollock and Maitland, op. cit., p. 471.

[6] *Leges Henrici*, 90.7.

[7] Pollock and Maitland, op. cit., p. 473. According to Holdsworth (*History of English Law*, II, p. 53) it is said in the laws of Cnut "that, if stolen property is found in a man's home, it was at one time thought that his infant child was 'equally guilty as if it had discretion'—'but henceforth I most strenuously forbid it, and also many things that are hateful to God.' "

[8] It must be borne in mind, of course, that he came from the village of Anathoth.

[9] Cf. Isa. 6.10; 37.7; Jer. 20.7; 11.20; 12.3; 17.10; 20.12; Ezek. 14.9.

[10] See Joh. Fichtner, *Die altorientalische Weisheit in ihrer israelitisch-juedischen Auspraegung* (Beiheft z. *ZAW*, LXII), p. 47. Fichtner points out that while certain detailed ethico-religious maxims of the Proverbs are found, e. g., in the Wisdom of Amen-em-ope, they do not form a consistent and sustained approach such as is worked out in the biblical Wisdom Literature. For a detailed study of the passages involved see E. A. Wallis Budge, *The Teaching of Amen-Em-Apt*, especially pp. 11, and 100, for the older Egyptian moral teaching, and p. 103 ff. for the teaching of Amen-em-ope himself. There can be little doubt that the latter, of all the non-Israelitish writers, alone approached the purity of the plebeian ethics of Jerusalem. Yet, as Budge points out, even he "says nothing about a man's right behaviour to the women of his family, and seems to assume that the man who was wise enough to follow his teaching would need no advice on such private and domestic matters" (p. 131). He writes, Budge continues, "to enable a man to maintain a 'safe' position under all circumstances." And indeed these are practically Amen-em-ope's own words (pp. 140–141 of Budge's translation):

> To know how to return a suitable answer to him that has spoken to him,
> (and) to carry back a (satisfactory) report to the man who has despatched him on a mission,
> (and) will make him to follow a straight course on the roads of life,
> (and) will enable him to maintain his position of safety on earth,
> (and) will cause his heart to descend (or, enter) its case,
> (and) make him steer his course away from evil (or, the evil one)
> (and) make him to deliver himself from the mouth of the common folk (?)
> (and) to be applauded by the mouth of men of understanding."

[11] See Kittel, *Geschichte*, III, 2, p. 725.

[12] Ibid., p. 726.

[13] Cf. *Encyclopedia Britannica*, s. v. Proverbs, Book of; also *Encyclopedia Biblica*, s. v. Proverbs, Book of; see also Nowak in *Hastings' Encyclopedia*, s. v. Proverbs, Book of. Toy's view is adopted by Fichtner, op. cit., p. 7, who stresses the difference in ideology between Prov. 10–15 and 16.1–22.16; and also between 25–27, and 28–29.

[14] *Israels Spruchweisheit*, p. 33 ff.; cf. Fichtner, op. cit., p. 7.

[15] Cf. above, p. 177.

[16] See Erman, "Eine aegyptische Quelle der Sprueche Salomos," *Sitzgsber. d. Pr. Akad. d. Wissenschaften*, XV (1924), 86 ff.; H. Gressmann, "Die neugefundene Lehre des Amenemope u.d. vorexil. Spruchdichtung Israels," *ZAW* (1924), 272 ff.; W. O. E. Oesterley, "The Teaching of Amen-em-ope and the Old Testament," *ZAW* (1927), 9 ff.; Idem., *The Wisdom of Egypt and the Old Testament*; Kittel, *Geschichte*, III, 2, p. 722 ff.; Sellin, in *Deutsche Literaturzeitung*, 1924, col. 1873 ff.; Breasted, *The Dawn of Conscience*, p. 371 ff.; and Paul Humbert, *Recherches sur les sources Égyptiennes de la Littérature Sapientale d'Israël.*

[17] Shabbat 30b.

[18] Prov. 26.4–5.

[19] Meg. 7a.

[20] It may be argued with much plausibility that Purim originated as a provincial spring festival; and that it occurs exactly a month before Passover because in the Palestinian lowlands, spring arrived considerably before it did in Jerusalem, where the national festival was fixed. This suggestion is supported by the fact that one of the main aspects of Purim celebration was the meal (the *se'udah*) which was eaten at nightfall on the fourteenth day of Adar, just as the Passover meal was eaten at nightfall of the fourteenth day of Nisan. The lavishness of the Purim banquets (Meg. 7b) is strongly reminiscent of that associated with the provincial celebrations on the ninth of Tishri, concerning which see above, ch. III, F. And, indeed, just as on the ninth of Tishri, so on Purim, there was a tendency to prolong the meal into the evening; a tendency which the Sages, considering the meal associated with the holiday, resented (loc. cit.). Finally a number of customs, such as that of making bonfires, which are associated with Purim and survived even into medieval times, can only be explained on the basis of provincial origin (Cf. San. 64b; L. Ginzberg, *Geonica*, II, p. 3; B. M. Lewin, *Ozar ha-Geonim*, V, p. 74; N. S. Doniach, *Purim*, p. 72; I. Davidson, *Parody in Jewish Literature*, p. 21, note 33; I. Friedlaender, *JQR*, N. S., I (1910–11), p. 257; Frazer, *Golden Bough*, IX, 359 ff.; X, 106 ff.; S. Reinach, *Cults, Myths and Religions*, tr. from the French, p. 97 ff. H. Malter, "Purim" in *Jewish Encyclopedia*). It is noteworthy in this connection that the Temple authorities granted no recognition to Purim, refusing even to have the Hallel sung on it. It is one of the marks of the religious genius of the talmudic Sages that they transformed this festival into one of spiritual significance. The Mishna and the Tosefta omit all reference to the Purim dinner; they are concerned only with the reading of the Megillah, or Scroll of Esther, and the gifts to the poor. The Festival became for them one of good will and communal responsibility; one of its main aspects was the "Purim collection" which was intended to supply the poor with a festive meal (Tosefta Meg. 1.5, p. 222).

[21] Meg. 19a; Esth. R. 7.8.

[22] Contrast the rabbinic apology in Rashi, Esth. 2.10; also Ginzberg, *Legends of the Jews*, IV, 388.

[23] Ex. 28.3; 31.3. For parallels to Ben Sira's attitude toward labor, cf. F. Oppenheimer, *System der Soziologie*, II, p. 341 ff.

NOTES TO CHAPTER XII

[1] See further Gerhard von Rad, "Die levitische Predigt in den Büchern der Chronik," in *Festschrift Otto Procksch*, p. 113 ff.

[2] For a further discussion of the expression of class conflict in the Psalms, see Kittel, *Die Psalmen*, fifth and sixth eds., commentary on Ps. 64, p. 217 ff., and commentary on Ps. 86, p. 284 ff.; Hans Schmidt, *Das Gebet der Angeklagten im Alten Testament*; A. Causse, *Les "Pauvres" d'Israël*, especially p. 97 ff.; Mowinckel, *Psalmenstudien*, VI, p. 58 ff.

[3] Mishna Abot 3.15.

[4] Josephus, *Antiquities*, XVIII, 1.3.

[5] Josephus, *War*, II, 8.14.

[6] Ber. 33b.

[7] Josephus, *Antiquities*, XIII, 5.9.

[8] See discussion in *Akiba*, p. 203 ff.; cf. Bousset-Gressmann, p. 406 ff.; Schechter, *Some Aspects of Rabbinic Theology*, p. 170 ff.; and A. Marmorstein, *The Doctrine of Merits in Old Rabbinical Literature*.

[9] Mekilta Beshallah, Vayyehi, ch. III, p. 99.

[10] Apparently Abtalyon, like the later patrician scholar, R. Eliezer, believed that redemption from Rome could come through repentance, good deeds, and faith; while the plebeian Shemayah held that the "end" was fixed and irrevocable. For the patrician status of Abtalyon and the plebeian status of his opponent, see *Akiba*, p. 298; and Ginzberg, *Mekomah shel ha-Halakah*, p. 14 ff. In addition to the evidence there presented, the fact that Abtalyon had a Greek name would indicate patrician origin. The concern of his class with nationalist politics is indicated by the warning he gives them that lack of care in their words may lead to banishment, "and ye will go into exile into the place of bad waters, and the disciples who follow you will drink from them, and they will die, and so the Name of God will be profaned" (Abot 1.11). In other words, political quietism was essential for the preservation of the Law. Egypt or Babylonia, to which rebellious scholars might flee would not preserve the Law in pure form. Shemayah, addressing the plebeian pacifists, has no occasion to warn them against outward rebellion. He simply urges them to "love labor and hate office, and to avoid being taken cognizance of by the government." The last phrase does not mean warning them against holding office, but against taking any action which might lead to suspicion. That both Shemayah and Abtalyon were descended from proselytes is highly improbable. It is based, of course, on the insult offered them by the High Priest who, when they greeted him, replied contemptuously, "Let also the descendants of the heathen come in peace" (Yoma 71b). But the insult would have been just as effective if only one had foreign blood. In any event, Abtalyon's patrician standing would not be incompatible with the foreign marriage of one of his ancestors.

[11] Mishna 'Eduy. 5.7.

[12] San. 97b.

[13] Mishna Eduy. 2.9; Tosefta, ibid., 1.14, p. 456.

[14] See S. Schechter's note to his edition of the fragment of "Mekilta on Deuteronomy" in *JQR*, XVI (1904), p. 452 ff., and Hoffmann, in his edition of *Midrash Tannaim*, p. 62, note 9; compare, also, e. g., Mekilta of R. Simeon, 13.5, p. 32 (the parallel passage in Mekilta of R. Ishmael does not mention the merit of the fathers); ibid. 13.11, p. 35, where, however, the influence of the opposing school has become evident in the expression "by thy merit and the merit of thy ancestors." For other references see Ch. Albeck, *Untersuchungen ueber die halakischen Midraschim*, p. 16 f.

[15] Mekilta Beshallah, Vayyassa', ch. 1, p. 158.

[16] Cant. R. to ch. 3, verse 5.

[17] Abot 4.2.

[18] Suk. 52a.

[19] Abot 3.1.

[20] Ber. 60a.

[21] Bezah 16a.

[22] Mekilta, Jethro, Masseket Bahodesh, ch. 7, p. 229; compare Bezah, ibid.

[23] Mekilta Beshallah, Masseket Vayyassa', Ch. 2, p. 161.

[24] 'Ab. Zarah 18a.

[25] Gen. R. ch. 36, beg., p. 334.

NOTES TO CHAPTER XIII

[1] Josephus, *Antiquities*, XIII, 10.6.

[2] See Deut. 19.17; 21.2; 25.2; 25.7. For the Supreme Court in the Temple, see 17.8 ff., as well as 1.17.

[3] Cf. H. H. Schaeder in *Esra der Schreiber*, p. 39 ff.; Kittel, *Geschichte*, III, 2, p. 660 ff.; Gressmann, *Israels Spruchweisheit*, p. 47 ff. For the high position of the scribe in Babylonia, see Meissner, *Babylonien und Assyrien*, II, p. 328, (I owe this last reference to the kindness of Professor E. A. Speiser.)

[4] Schaeder, op. cit., p. 45 ff.

[5] Jubilees 4.17; 19.14; Testament Levi 13.2; John 7.15.

[6] See S. Kaatz, *Die muendliche Lehre und ihr Dogma*, parts 1–2. An interesting example of the superiority of authority over argument in reaching a decision is offered by the incident between Hillel and the Bene Bathyra (Pes. 66a). For the general tendency, cf. Mishna Peah 2.6; Yad. 4.3.

[7] *Monatsschrift*, LXXVI (1932), p. 532.

[8] Jubilees 30.2; cf. also Testament Levi 12.5, and "Aramaic and Greek Fragments" (ed. Charles, p. 254, line 15), where it is stated that Levi's age at the time of Dinah's rape was eighteen, which would make her age twelve, since she was six years younger (Jub. 28.14, 23). See *MGWJ*, loc. cit.

[9] Sifre Num. 112, p. 121.

[10] Mal. 3.10; Neh. 10.38; II Chron. 31.6 ff. See further discussions of this subject, by Ezekiel Kaufmann, in *Ziyyunim* (Memorial Volume for Simhoni),

pp. 101–115; and especially, the standard work of Otto Eissfeldt, *Erstlinge und Zehnten im alten Testament.*

[11] Tobit 1.7. For a discussion of the readings of the various Mss. of this book, see Eissfeldt, op. cit., p. 118 f.

[12] *JBL*, LII, 206, note 3; and see Jubilees 21.16; Testament Levi, 9.11; and the Old Testament of Levi in Charles' edition of the *Testaments of the XII Patriarchs*, p. 248, line 3.

[13] Mishna Ber. 1.1.

[14] Mishna Yoma 3.3.

[15] For the theory that sanctity as well as impurity can adhere to one's body and even to one's clothing, see Smith-Cook, *The Religion of the Semites*, pp. 452 ff., 655.

[16] Jubilees 21.12; Testament Levi 9.12; "Aramaic and Greek Fragments," published in Charles, *Test. of XII Patriarchs*, pp. 248–9; compare Mishna Tamid 1.3. See also *JBL*, XLIX (1930), p. 37.

[17] Tem. 16a.

[18] Shab. 14b. For a discussion of the origin of this rule see A. Buechler, *Der galiläische 'Am-ha-'Ares*, pp. 130–138; and G. Allon, in *Tarbiz*, IX (1938), pp. 186–188.

[19] Pes. 72b.

[20] Hul. 105a requires washing both before and after meals; the Talmud (ibid., 106a) is significantly more rigorous with regard to the ablutions for the heave-offering than with regard to other food. It is interesting to note that it is customary for priests who are about to recite the blessing of the people in accordance with Num. 6.22 to wash their hands only before the ceremony, and not after it (Sotah 39a). The earliest authority for this ablution is R. Joshua ben Levi, a teacher of the third century C.E. But there is good reason to believe that the custom is much older, as is evident from the norm, "immediately after the washing, follows the blessing" (Ber. 42a; but cited already in Mishna Men. 9.8). The reference to the "blessing" here was originally doubtless the "priestly blessing" and not the Grace after Meat, as Rashi maintains (Ber. ad. loc.), for if he were right, the text would have read, *Birkat Ha-Mazon.* The reason that the blessing of the priests is not followed by a second ablution is clearly that they do not touch any holy thing in the course of this ceremony.

[21] Yad. 4.6. For a discussion of this rule, see N. Bruell, in *Bet Talmud*, II, pp. 319 ff., 325, 368; and III, p. 49.

[22] Kelim 15.6.

NOTES TO CHAPTER XIV

[1] Mishna Shek. 1.1.

[2] Mishna Meg. 3.4.

[3] Mishna Shek. 4.2 ff.

[4] "Megillat Ta'anit," 1.1, Scholion, ed. Lichtenstein in *HUC Annual*, VIII–IX (1931–1932), p. 323; Men. 65a. The Pharisaic view is prescribed as norm in Sifre

Num. 142, p. 188; Sifre Zutta, ibid., 28.2, p. 322. Geiger (*Urschrift*, p. 136), followed by J. Derenbourg (*Essai*, p. 135), maintains, correctly, I believe, that the Sadducean view was supported by priests who led the Sect and who were anxious to protect the Temple's treasury, and spare it every possible expense. There was no conflict between these priests and the pious men of wealth who wanted to supply this sacrifice. J. Wellhausen's objection that the Temple treasury did not belong to the priests, but was a public fund (*Die Pharisäer und die Sadducäer*, p. 70), misses the point entirely. The priests were jealous of the rights of the Temple and anxious to enrich it, not because that benefited them individually, but because it was their institution. Everyday experience reveals similar interests by persons nowadays. The priests were especially moved to maintain this position because it happened that in this instance Scripture and precedent supported their view, Ezek. 45.17, and 46.13. According to the Septuagint, Syriac and Vulgate, which read "he shall offer" instead of "thou shalt offer," the "prince" is definitely obliged to provide the daily sacrifice. Indeed there can be little question that the masoretic reading *ta'aseh* (thou shalt offer) in the latter verse, as well as in 46.14, was substituted for the original *ya'aseh* (he, the prince, shall offer) just because of the susceptibilities on the question either by the Pharisees or their plebeian predecessors. Indeed II Macc. 3.3 expressly states that King Seleucus "actually defrayed, out of his own revenues, all the expenses connected with the ritual of the sacrifices." This can refer only to the daily sacrifice. Reference to a similar gift by the Persian government may be found perhaps in Ezra 6.9; 7.17 ff. It is true that rabbinic tradition distinguished these gifts from those subject to controversy by assuming that these gifts were made to the general fund of the Chamber, and for the provision of a specific daily offering (see R. H. 7a, bottom). But it is clear that the gifts of the Kings were not general gifts to the treasury of the Temple but were intended to provide for specific offerings, which is precisely what the Pharisees considered forbidden.

It is interesting to note, also, that the Chronicler, who ordinarily supports the views of the plebeians, in this instance gives his support to the patrician forerunners of the Sadducees. He specifically states that King Hezekiah provided the funds for the daily sacrifices (II Chron. 31.3). This is additional evidence in favor of Geiger's thesis that the Sadducees in defending the ancient custom were trying to protect the Temple's interests. For, obviously, the only reason which could move the Chronicler to desert his plebeians in this instance was his superior attachment to the Temple of which he was a Levite. His loyalty to the major institution overrode his class prejudice.

On the other hand, the view of the Pharisees is that found also in Josephus, *Antiquities*, III, 10.1. It is based, of course, on Neh. 10.33, which first established the payment of the third of a shekel as annual tax for the purpose of providing the Temple sacrifice. For further discussions of the question, see S. Krauss, in *Ha-Shiloah*, VIII (1901), p. 114; B. Revel, *The Karaite Halakah*, p. 37; R. Leszynsky, *Die Sadduzäer*, p. 68; S. Spiegel, in *HTR*, XXIV (1931), p. 268; Tschernowitz, *Toledoth Ha-Halakah*, I, 2, p. 260 f.

[5] Mishna Yad. 4.6.

[6] Ibid. In our texts of the Mishna a gloss has been added which confuses the argument. For a discussion of the correct text, see *HTR*, XXII (1929), 221, note 86. The question of extended personality in its relation to damages is discussed, of course, in practically all systems of law. Primitive law, generally, holds the slave-owner responsible for the acts of his slave, as indeed it must. This is usually explained on the theory of identification of personality, though there can be little doubt that the theory is merely a rationalization (a very acceptable one, from the slave-owner's point of view) of the necessary social rules. See with regard to this, Pollock and Maitland, *History of English Law*, II, p. 529; A. S. Diamond, *Primitive Law*, p. 510 ff.; Holmes, in *Harvard Law Review*, IV, p. 354 ff. (reprinted in Holmes, *Collected Papers*, p. 65 ff.); Wigmore, in *Harvard Law Review*, VII, p. 315; Hobhouse, *Morals in Evolution*, I, p. 91 f.; E. A. Westermarck, *The Origin and Development of Moral Ideas*, I, p. 267. It is altogether unnecessary to assume with G. Hoelscher, *Der Sadduzäismus*, p. 30 ff., that the Sadducean view was influenced by that of the Romans, though it may be true, to be sure, that the Sadducean judges were encouraged in their view by the fact that it resembled that of the Roman, and indeed most foreign, law.

Geiger, as usual, associates this controversy with a rather naive interpretation of the political events. According to him, the controversy arose with regard to the summons which the Sanhedrin issued to Herod to appear before it, when he had executed without due trial a certain Hezekiah, whom he accused of leading a band of brigands (Josephus, *War*, I, 10.6; *Antiquities*, XIV, 9.3). Herod appeared, but was set free (at least, so Geiger surmises). The Sadducees maintained, according to Geiger, that the reason for Herod's liberation was that he acted under the orders of King Hyrkan II, whose official he was, and insisted that the decision of the Sanhedrin to free Herod set a precedent for all such cases (*Urschrift*, p. 145). J. Wellhausen rightly rejects this ingenious but utterly untenable interpretation of the controversy (*Die Pharisäer*, p. 67). Yet he offers none which is more satisfactory. Leszynsky (p. 86) merely notes that the question of responsibility of masters for slaves is a "very complicated one" and that we need not be surprised at the inability of the Pharisees and the Sadducees to solve it. Tschernowitz (*Toledoth Ha-Halakah*, I, 2, p. 326 f.) simply says that we can "see that the Sadducees retained the older legal theory which puts slaves in the same category as domestic animals, while the Pharisees insisted on the development of jurisprudence and human progress." But he fails to indicate how the Pharisaic view represented progress.

While Geiger's interpretation of the conflicting views is clearly in error, he is certainly right in maintaining that the story of Herod, as told in the Talmud, indicates that in early times even the Pharisees accepted the Sadducean interpretation holding a master responsible for the injuries inflicted by his slave. For as the Talmud tells the story: "A slave of King Jannai slew a man. Thereupon Simeon ben Shattah said to the Sages, 'Let us put our minds to the matter and judge him.' They sent word to King Jannai, saying, 'Thy slave has slain a man.' When King Jannai had delivered the slave up for judgment, the Court sent him another message, saying, 'Come thou also hither . . . The owner of the ox must stand by his ox (when he is being tried).' When the King arrived, Simeon ben Shattah said to him, 'King Jannai, arise that the witnesses may testify against thee. For not before us dost thou stand, but before Him who spoke and brought the world into being'... Jannai, however, answered, 'Not as thou sayest, but as thy colleagues command.' Whereupon Simeon turned to the right, and saw the members of the Sanhedrin hiding their faces toward the ground; and he turned to the left and saw the other members of the Sanhedrin hiding their faces toward the ground. 'You are men of thought,' cried out Simeon, when he saw this, 'may the Master of Thoughts pay your penalty.' Immediately the angel Gabriel descended and smote them all to the ground. It was then that the rule was set down, 'The King may neither judge nor be judged' (San. 19a)." For a discussion of the significance of this ruling as a voluntary withdrawal by the Sanhedrin from a field where it found its views unenforceable, see M. Finkelstein, in *Harvard Law Review*, XXXVII (1924), 338 ff.

In spite of the legendary character of the talmudic story, there can be little doubt that it recalls an actual incident. Jannai has been substituted for Hyrkan II; Simeon ben Shattah for Sameas; and "the slave of King Jannai" for Herod. When these substitutions are recognized it becomes clear, as Geiger, I. H. Weiss (*Dor Dor ve-Doreshav*, I, p. 132), Wellhausen and Leszynsky recognize, that the talmudic story and that of Josephus refer to the same incident. Here again as in the other controversies regarding Civil Law (see above, p. 138 ff.) we find the Pharisaic view developing at a comparatively late period, when the judges of the sect were in charge of courts. This is in striking contrast to the controversies about the ceremonial law which, arising out of the lives of the people and the studies of the scholars, are more ancient than the Pharisaic Order itself.

[7] Kid. 43a. See I. H. Levinthal, "The Jewish Law of Agency," in *JQR*, N. S., XIII (1922–23), p. 159 ff.

[8] Mishna Shab. 1.7. For the division of the later plebeians and patricians on this subject, as well as for the deeper, social analysis of the differences, see *Akiba*, p. 287 ff.

[9] Mishna, Me'i. 6.1.

[10] Josephus, *Antiquities*, XIII, 10.6; XX, 9.1.

[11] Mishna San. 5.2.

[12] Mishna Mak. 1.10.

[13] Mishna San. 5.1.

[14] Mishna Mak. loc. cit.

[15] Mekilta Mishpatim, Kaspa, ch. 20, p. 328; Mekilta of R. Simeon 23.7, p. 156, and comp. Sifre Deut. 94, as emended and explained in *Tarbiz*, III (1931–32), p. 202; and also San. 37b.

[16] Ab. 2.6.

[17] B. M. 83b.

[18] Ber. 60b.

[19] Sifre, Deut. 32.

[20] Matt. 5.41.

[21] See above, p. 39.

NOTES TO CHAPTER XV

[1] San. 89a.

[2] Cf. Gist and Halbert, *Urban Society*, p. 359 ff.; Park, *The City*, p. 24 f.; N. Carpenter, *The Sociology of City Life*, p. 231 ff. While the last two books deal primarily with modern conditions, much of what they say applies, as can readily be seen, also to antiquity. See also Johs. Pedersen, *Israel, Its Life and Culture*, p. 24 ff., and M. Noth, "Die Ansiedlung des Stammes Juda auf dem Boden Palästinas," in *Palästinajahrbuch*, XXX (1934), p. 33. For the principle of equality and its influence on shepherd groups, see F. Oppenheimer, *System der Soziologie*, II, p. 265.

[3] W. F. Albright, *Archaeology of Palestine and the Bible*, p. 131.

[4] Cf. the remarks of so conservative a commentator as G. A. Smith in *The Book of the Twelve Prophets*, I, p. 220.

[5] See Kittel, *Geschichte*, II, p. 438. The story of Hosea's tragic marriage is generally accepted as authentic, although there have been attempts to reject it. See, e. g., L. W. Batten, in *JBL*, XLVIII (1929), 257 ff.; Hoelscher, *Die Propheten*, p. 426 f.; cf., however, most recently, C. Kuhl, in *ZAW*, LII (1934), p. 102 ff.; and U. Cassuto, *Poznanski Memorial Volume*, Hebrew section, pp. 115–35 and the literature cited by them; and also H. G. May, in *JBL*, LV (1936), 285 ff. The influence of the nomadic ideal, which, being part of the prophetic tradition, had its significance even for Hosea, was first recognized by Budde in his famous article in *Preuss. Jahrbuecher*, 1896, p. 57 ff., and is discussed further by P. Humbert in *Marti Festschrift* (*BZAW*, XLI [1925]), p. 158 ff.

[6] Practically all the commentators have noticed the difference between Amos's call to justice and Hosea's demand for truth. Yet they have identified the two concepts, as though both prophets were preaching the same social ideal. See, e. g., the excellent treatise of J. Herrmann, "Die Soziale Predigt der Propheten," in *Biblische Zeit- und Streitfragen*, VI, 12, p. 11 ff.; and W. Caspari, *Die israelitischen Propheten*, p. 60.

[7] See below, p. 468 ff. and cf. especially Isa. 44.11 ff.

[8] Cf. above, p. 220.

[9] That these passages are genuine is now generally admitted; see below, ch. XVII, note 16.

[10] G. A. Smith, *Jeremiah*, p. 5.

[11] Jeremiah does indeed beseech divine vengeance against his private enemies, but he is promised only just punishment for their sins (11.20; 20.12 ff.). The references to the vengeance of God in Jer. 50–51 belong, as is well known, to exilic prophets, concerning whom see below, p. 450. Zephaniah's reference to the fire of God's jealousy (1.18, 3.8) has nothing to do with the idea of jealousy as used by Nahum. The root *kana* came to mean anger, indignation and sense of outrage, rather than envy, among the later writers. Zephaniah uses it in that sense, just as Zechariah does (1.14). The difference between the provincial anthropomorphic

conception of God and the urban sophisticated view of Him persisted for many centuries, as has been demonstrated above, p. 119.

[12] Cf. Ezek. 4.13; see also below, p. 450 ff.; also Deutero-Zechariah, 9.14 ff.; see remarks of G. A. Smith regarding him in *The Twelve Prophets*, II, pp. 450, 460.

[13] B. Meg. 15a.

[14] The conceit significantly occurs but once more in Scripture, in the work of another urban plebeian, Eccl. 9.12, discussed above, p. 236.

[15] As Kittel remarks (*Geschichte des Volkes Israel*, III, p. 144), the study of Ezekiel has today reached an impasse between the rival analyses of Hoelscher (*Hesekiel, der Dichter und das Buch*) and Herrmann (*Ezechiel, uebersetzt und erklaert*). Since Kittel wrote, however, the discussion has been considerably advanced by the studies of Kittel himself, *Geschichte*, op. cit.; Kessler, *Die innere Einheitlichkeit des Buches Ezekiel*; Torrey, *Pseudo-Ezekiel and the Original Prophecy*; Buttenwieser, "The Date and Character of Ezekiel's Prophecies," in *HUC Annual*, VII, p. 1 ff.; Berry, *JBL*, XLIX (1930), 83 ff.; Shalom Spiegel, "Ezekiel or Pseudo-Ezekiel" in *HTR*, XXIV (1931), p. 245 ff., and "Toward Certainty in Ezekiel" in *JBL*, LIV (1935), 145 ff.; Budde, "Zum Eingang des Buches Ezekiel" in *JBL*, L (1931), 20 ff.; Otto Eissfeldt, "Ezekiel als Zeuge fuer Sanheribs Eingriff in Palaestina," in *Palaestinajahrbuch*, XXVII (1931), 58 ff., especially pp. 64–5; W. F. Albright, in *JBL*, LI (1932), 97 ff.; Torrey's replies to his critics, in *JBL*, LI (1932), 179 ff., ibid., LIII (1934), 291 ff.; Herntrich, *Ezechielprobleme*; and Alfred Bertholet, "Hesekiel," in *Handbuch zum Alten Testament*, Tuebingen, 1936. Yet it cannot be said that a satisfactory solution has been reached; for the reason, it seems to me, that textual criticism alone is insufficient to solve the problem. (The excellent commentary of G. A. Cooke in the *International Critical Commentary* appeared after this volume had been sent to press, so that I could use it only in the course of proof-reading. Cooke, too, draws attention to the "singular and complex personality" which "emerges from these writings;" and notes that "different strains of nature seem to have been woven into his character." He "united an intense imagination with a curious, even prosaic, love of detail." See commentary, p. xxvii.)

[16] Josephus, who approximately predicates this date (*Antiquities*, X, 6.3), may have had some traditional basis for his remarks. In any event, the fact that Ezekiel did not begin to preach until the year 592 B.C.E., may be taken as evidence that he was too young to do so before that time.

[17] Ezekiel's descent from the House of Zadok, the ruling priestly dynasty, has usually been assumed on the basis of 44.15 and similar passages. His father's wealth may be assumed from Ezekiel's acquaintance with various luxuries enumerated below and the likelihood of his having traveled to Tyre and Egypt, journeys which could only be undertaken by persons of means.

[18] In this and the following citation, I follow mainly Herrmann's and Hoelscher's reconstruction; cf. their commentaries.

[19] How objectionable this chapter seemed to one who had lived in Jerusalem, even for a time, can be seen from the prohibition against the public reading of it, issued by R. Eliezer ben Hyrcanus (Mishna Meg. end); and his violent anger

against the man who did choose it as a selection. "Go out and announce the disgrace of your mother," the enraged scholar shouted (Babli and Yer. ad loc.).

[20] Hoelscher considers this passage an editorial addition because of its uncouth implications (p. 63). But the very fact that, contrary to later usage, the food is described as *piggul* rather than *tamé*, shows that the text must be from Ezekiel. I consider it part of the original draft, because it is far more natural to suppose that Ezekiel in his later life (or a later editor) would try to soften an original harsh expression than that they would substitute a harsh expression for a cultured one.

[21] Yer. Yeb. 13.2, 14c; Ab. of R. Nathan, I, ch. 16, 32a.

[22] See Jer. chs. 30, 31.

[23] Ezek. 37.15 ff.; see also Gaster, *The Samaritans*, p. 11 ff. The same view was taken by R. Eliezer ben Hyrcanus, likewise a provincial (Mishna San. 10.4).

[24] See Paton, "The Case for the Post-Exilic Origin of Deuteronomy," in *JBL*, XLVII (1928), 322–358, and the literature cited by him.

[25] Such an episode seems to me implied in the visions Ezekiel has of the Temple. Even if we deny the prophet the authorship of Ezek. 40–48, there still remain among the undoubtedly genuine productions of his spirit prophecies which show intimate acquaintance with the Temple structure. The hypothesis that he visited the Temple and saw the secret idolatrous rites makes it unnecessary to attribute to him either clairvoyance or falsehood.

[26] Ezek. 8.3 ff.; cf. II Kings 21.3.

[27] The story of the death of Pelatiah ben Benaiah in Ezek. 11.13 is not clear. Did Pelatiah die while Ezekiel saw the vision? Or when he was describing it? The difficulty has confused the commentators, but it seems to me simple enough; Pelatiah was among the elders who sat before the prophet when he was describing the vision (8.1 ff.), and he was also originally among the worshipers whom Ezekiel had seen at the Temple. In his vision Ezekiel saw Pelatiah once more committing idol worship in the Temple. And as he was telling what he saw, Pelatiah fell dead. W. Staerk's interpretation of the scene as one connected with mystery religion does not seem well-founded. See his *Religion und Politik im alten Israel*, p. 16.

[28] R. Kittel, *Geschichte*, II, p. 462.

[29] It is evident from his prophecies about these peoples that he visited their countries; in no other way could he have obtained so intimate and detailed an acquaintance with their life as is exhibited in ch. 26 ff. The theory which denies Ezekiel's authorship of these chapters seems to me utterly unacceptable.

[30] Compare above, p. 32.

[31] Above, p. 21.

[32] Mekilta Beshallah, Vayyehi, ch. 6, p. 112.

[33] This reconstruction of the original draft of Chapter I may seem daring at first; but closer examination will show that it follows the suggestions of Herrmann (p. 13) who has demonstrated that verse 27 is immediately connected with the beginning of verse 4. The picture thus restored is clear, poetic and quite typical of the prophet in his early days. Herrmann, however, fails to see the contradiction between verse 1b, which places the theophany in heaven, and verse 4a, which places it on earth. Hoelscher recognizes the difficulty, but solves it erroneously,

I think, by assigning verse 1 to the editor (p. 44). For my own explanation of verse 4a, which corresponds more closely to Herrmann's, see below. In any event, the acceptance of verse 1 precludes the acceptance of 4a which definitely contradicts it, and indicates a better acquaintance with Babylonian cosmology, according to which the seat of God is in the North. The key to the original form of 4a is given by the difficult words *venogah lo sabib*: "with brightness round about *him*." As the words stand in our present text, the pronoun *lo* refers to *esh* "fire," but the word *esh* is *never* used in the masculine (see Albrecht, *ZAW*, XVI, 63, and Herrmann, *Ezechiel*, ad loc.). It seems to me clear that the use of the masculine *lo* indicates that *esh* is a "corrected" reading for *ish*, "man." The word *mitlakahat*, which follows *esh* in our text, and means, apparently, "blazing", must be omitted as an editorial gloss to prevent the reading of *esh* as *ish*. That the reading *lo* is correct and that the word *mitlakahat* is an editorial addition, is proven by v. 27b, where the phrase is repeated in the same form without *mitlakahat*. The word *umitokah*, in v. 4b, is futher to be omitted as an attempt to prevent the misreading of *esh* as masculine. As it stands now it makes the verse meaningless. Herrmann, who retains it, must in consequence omit the final words of the verse, "from the midst of the fire," and further take it to mean "and in it" rather than "and from it." It is interesting to note further that in 8.2, the LXX actually retains the reading *ish* rendering it by *andros*, where the Masoretic text has *esh*. In all this alteration of the Masoretic text, no change was made in the consonantal text, even when the masculine pronoun definitely betrayed the different reading of the original draft. Such loyalty to the original text indicates an affection for it which can hardly be reconciled with the hand of the glossator or editor; it would be natural only to the original author who, rejecting his original draft, yet wished to give it some immortality. See further regarding this below. The other emendations applying to vv. 27, 28, are simple and obvious. For quite a different approach to the subject, see O. Proksch, "Die Berufungsvision Hesekiels," in *Budde Festschrift*, pp. 141–149; also, L. Duerr, *Ezechiels Vision von der Erscheinung Gottes*, and now Bertholet, *Hezekiel.*

[34] I add the words, "as it were," here and above, to indicate the *kaf* in the word *kemareh*,—"I saw like the appearance of a man." In spite of his tendency toward anthropomorphism, the prophet does not, of course, ascribe human form to God; he merely insists as did the provincial sages of later times that God *sometimes* appeared in the form of a man. Even this, however, was objectionable to the advanced urban plebeians. For the substitution of *esh* for *ish* in this verse, see Hoelscher, pp. 69, and 72.

[35] *Sefer Hekalot* and *Shi'ur Komah* published in Jellinek, *Bet Ha-Midrasch* II, 41 ff., and III, 91 ff.; republished in Eisenstein's *Ozar Ha-Midrashim*, I, 107 ff.; II, 561 ff. Both were either interpreted allegorically or denounced as spurious by a whole series of philosophers; see Kaufmann, *Geschichte der Attributenlehre in der juedischen Religionsphilosophie*, pp. 11, 86 ff., 90, 217, 261, 359, 497; see also Ginzberg, "Cabbala" and "Anthropomorphism," in *J.E.*, I.

[36] *Yad*, *Hilkot Teshubah*, 3.7.

[37] See above, p. 32. Similarly, Deutero-Isaiah, below, p. 496. For the doctrine of intention, see also above, p. 196.

[38] In this, of course, I follow Hoelscher.

[39] Compare my remarks on Akiba and Paul the Apostle, in *Akiba*, p. 15 ff.

[40] In the light of the present reconstruction of the prophet's work, I see no reason to deny him the authorship of this passage, as is usually done.

[41] Compare the similar use of Sodom in rabbinic literature (Sifre, Deut. 43).

[42] Ezek. 3.17 ff.; 18.21 ff.; 33.10 ff. See also Hoelscher, p. 54.

[43] This, and the following remarks, are based on a reconstruction of the first four verses, which I derive essentially from Herrmann. His view seems to me demonstrated beyond doubt by the fact that LXX has retained at the end of verse 3 the original reading, "and the hand of the Lord was upon me," rather than "upon him," as the Masoretic Text has it. I have already indicated above how careful Ezekiel was to retain the consonantal text of his original draft, even permitting the betraying pronoun *lo* to remain in the masculine, though a feminine was required by his text.

[44] See Appendix B.

[45] It is characteristic of Ezekiel that he dates his prophecies by the reign of King Jeohaichin who was still generally recognized as the true King of Judah. This was the feeling of the other exiles, too, as can be seen from the general joy which greeted the release of King Jehoiachin (II Kings, end). In fact as late as IV Ezra, this feeling was still recognizable, and the author (ibid. 1.1) indicates that Saalthiel, the son of Jehoiachin, would use his father's, and not his uncle's life, as a basis for his reckoning.

[46] Jer. 51.1 ff.; for the authors of these passages, see below, p. 450.

[47] The device is known also among other peoples. In 1894, Professor Ludwig Quidde published a book entitled *Caligula, eine Studie uber römischen Caesarenwahnsinn*, which was generally taken to refer to the reigning Kaiser. (I owe this information to Mr. Rollo Ogden.) It may be argued against this theory that the prophecy which Ezekiel uttered actually applied to Tyre. To do this is to miss the point I am trying to make. Ezekiel was talking about Tyre, of course; but he read into her the evils which he knew were associated with Babylonia. In other words, we have here a case of psychological transference, of which many writers of history and biography are notoriously guilty.

[48] The theory that Babylonia is intended by Magog has already been advanced by Ewald, *Die Propheten des alten Bundes*, second edition, I, p. 531; English translation, IV, p. 182; and Meinhold, *Einfuehrung in das Alte Testament*, p. 236. Neither of these authors, however, has recognized the peculiar cipher which apparently produced the word Magog.

[49] The identification of Edom with Rome — the most common of all — occurs e. g. in 'Ab. Zarah 10a; Yoma 10a; Gen. R. 41(42). 2, p. 399; the identification of Assyria with other peoples is made in Gen. R. 16.4, p. 148; and there can be little doubt of the identification of Rome with the Egyptians in Mekilta, Beshallah, ch. 1, p. 94, et passim. For a similar and very amusing example of such a transference in the mind of a modern writer, see H. W. Nevinson, *Last Changes Last Chances*, p. 326.

[50] Indeed, the expression "Kingdom of Arrogance" is regularly used for Rome in the prayers.

[51] Shmarya Levin, *Youth in Revolt*, p. 29.

[52] P. Kropotkin, *Memoirs of a Revolutionist*, p. 359.

[53] Booker T. Washington, *Up from Slavery*, p. 7.

NOTES TO CHAPTER XVI

[1] After I had written this chapter, I noticed that V. Aptowitzer has already drawn attention to the opportunism of both the Hellenists and the Sadducees — the patricians of the period with which he is concerned — in his *Parteipolitik*, p. IX. For a curious parallel to the ultra-nationalism of the ancient Palestinian peasant in England, cf. Kent, *The Early History of the Tories*, pp. 31–35; and see also G. P. Gooch, *Nationalism*, pp. 40–49.

[2] Cf. Deut. 28.64; I Sam. 26.19; Ezek. 4.13; Amos 7.17.

[3] Sifre Deut. 37.

[4] Cf. II Kings 15.20, and commentaries, ad loc.; M. Weber, *Religionssoziologie*, III, p. 32 ff.; Meyer, *Geschichte des Altertums*, II, 2, p. 255; Lurje, *Studien*, p. 17; A. Menes, *Die vorexilischen Gesetze*, p. 70.

[5] "The Moral Equivalent of War," in *Memories and Studies*, p. 265 ff., reprinted from *McClure's Magazine*, August, 1910.

[6] For this as a general attitude of the city dweller, cf. John Bakeless, *The Economic Causes of Modern War*, pp. vii–viii, and 11–12.

[7] Compare the incident described in the letters of Zenon, in *Pubblicazioni della Società Italiana*; *Papyri greci e latini*, IV–VII, 406; cited and described by Tscherikower, in *Tarbiz*, IV (1932–33), p. 231 ff.

[8] Mishna, 'Uk., end.

[9] A reconstruction of the background of the Cain-Abel story, which has much in common with the above, is offered by Abram Menes in a brilliant article in *ZAW*, XLIII (1925), 46 ff. I cannot, however, follow him in his attempt to recover the original form of the story in our present text. The motif was, doubtless, borrowed from the Kenites, the text is original in Israel. For a further discussion of the story, see S. D. Goitein, in *Zion*, II (1937), 11. For the general characterization of the shepherd groups, see M. Weber, *Religionssoziologie*, III, 59 ff.; and cf. F. Oppenheimer, *System der Soziologie*, II, 270 and 276.

[10] Compare the similar belief of Ben Sira in the superiority of the scholar, cited above, p. 222; the clear partiality of the priests toward members of their class (see e. g., *Akiba*, p. 291, and Aptowitzer, *Parteipolitik*, esp. ch. V ff.); the idealization of the patriarchs as mechanics rather than shepherds, in the Book of Jubilees, which belongs to an artisan age (Jub. 11.23; cf. also Test. of Zebulun, 6.1 ff.); and the reconstruction of the patriarchs and prophets as rabbinic teachers in the rabbinic tradition (cf. Josephus's account of Abraham, *Antiquities*, I, 7.8; and that of David in Ber. 4a; 'Er. 53a; M. K. 16b). Similarly, Tenney Frank explains the high respect which the Roman peasant enjoyed in earlier American historiography

by the fact that America was still an agricultural people; with the rise of urban civilization, the judgment is being revised and historians tend to go to extremes in depreciating the ancient farmer (*Social Behavior in Ancient Rome*, p. 64).

[11] See above, p. 164.

[12] San. 39b.

[13] Weber, op. cit., p. 59 ff. Cf. also p. 245 ff. So also, O. Eissfeldt, *Krieg und Bibel*, p. 35 f.

[14] See Sorokin and Zimmerman, *Principles of Rural-Urban Sociology*, p. 339 ff.; A. S. Diamond, *Primitive Law*, p. 224.

[15] Cf. II Sam. 14.4; II Kings 6.26; 8.3 ff.

[16] Menes, *Die vorexilischen Gesetze*, p. 25. It is noteworthy that, as Beloch (*Griechische Geschichte*, I, 1, p. 347) points out, the similar assemblages in Greece gained power especially during the struggles between the King and the nobility.

[17] It was this dependence of the patricians on the peasantry for military assistance which in other countries, as in Israel, led to the reorganization of the State and the admission of the oppressed classes into political power. See regarding this Rostovtzeff, *A History of the Ancient World*, II, 33; Tenney Frank, *An Economic Survey of Ancient Rome*, I, 10; idem, *An Economic History of Rome*, 40; and M. Weber, "Agrargeschichte (Altertum)" in *Handwörterbuch der Staatswissenschaften*, I, 70a.

[18] See above, p. 186 ff.

[19] R. Kittel, *Geschichte*, II, pp. 54, 88 ff. Curiously enough the historians generally assume, in spite of I Sam. 4.1, 9, that the Philistines were the aggressors in these struggles. Yet, if they were, how can we explain the fact that they passed over the Judaites, their immediate neighbors, and concentrated their attack on the northern tribes. Eduard Meyer (*Geschichte des Altertums*, II, 2, p. 240) feels this difficulty, of course, but offers no solution to it. Albrecht Alt, who also considers the Philistines the aggressors, similarly struggles hard to explain why they should have sought control of the less fertile hill country, especially when they were apparently without sufficient numbers to occupy all the coastal plain (*Die Staatenbildung der Israeliten in Palaestina*, p. 6 ff.). He maintains that it is impossible to suppose that the untrained Israelite militia would dare attack the better equipped, well-disciplined Philistines. But in this assumption, he loses sight of the fierce faith of the Israelite tribes, and the confidence which their conquest of the hill country had given them. The assumption that the Philistines set out to establish for themselves an overlordship over the whole country, which indeed they ultimately obtained, seems to me less reasonable than the supposition, supported by the text of Scripture, that the Israelites coveted the coastal plain. This theory also is necessary to explain the terms of the covenants in Gen. 21.23 and 26.29, which are clearly intended to prevent Israelite aggression against the Philistines.

[20] R. Kittel, *Geschichte*, II, 82 f.

[21] I Sam. 2.13 f., 17. The accusation of impurity made in v. 17 is not found in all Mss. of the Septuagint, and may be secondary. Most probably, however, it reflects an old tradition regarding the sons of Eli, even if it was lacking in the orig-

inal source used by the editor of the Book of Samuel (see H. P. Smith, in *International Critical Commentary*, ad loc.).

[22] It is probable that both names, Hofni and Phinehas, are of Egyptian origin (see Eissfeldt, in *Religion in Geschichte und Gegenwart*, vol. II, s.v. Eli); see also Brown-Driver-Briggs, *Lexicon*, s.v. Phinehas; the authors consider the word Hofni of Sabaean origin.

[23] See p. 586 ff.

[24] Kittel, op. cit., 89 ff.

[25] See Kittel, op. cit., 91, note 3; and Wellhausen, *Israelit. und jued. Geschichte*, p. 51. Gunkel, too, seems inclined to accept the importance of Samuel, even on the basis of the meager material left intact by the critical analysts (see his article, "Samuel," in *Religion in Geschichte und Gegenwart*, V, 103). On the other hand, Eduard Meyer, *Geschichte des Altertums*, II, 2, p. 243; Alt, *Die Staatenbildung der Israeliten*, p. 18 f. and S. A. Cook, *Critical Notes on Old Testament History*, p. 34 f., are inclined to minimize his importance.

[26] I Sam. 7.16. See commentaries ad loc.; but compare Kittel, op. cit., p. 98.

[27] According to Josephus, *Antiquities*, VI, 3.2 (32), one was placed in Beth-el and the other in Beer-sheba.

[28] The supposed victory of Samuel over the Philistines in I Sam. 7.10 ff. would make the appointment of a King and his battles against the Philistines utterly inexplicable. But Kittel rightly points out that the rejection of the story of the battle does not invalidate the story of the gathering at Mizpah, which seems genuine (op. cit., 94 ff.). Regarding this pacifism, see below.

[29] For a recent recognition of the preëminent position of Samuel in the appointment of Saul, see O. Eissfeldt, *Die Komposition der Samuelisbuecher*, p. 7 ff. He recognizes I Sam. 10.21–27 as the oldest story of the appointment of the King.

[30] Saul's adherence to the YHWH worship in the beginning is sufficiently attested by the name of his oldest son, Jehonathan.

[31] Whether Saul ruled over a fully united Israel has in recent years been much disputed. The theory that he obtained the formal adherence of all the tribes, with the possible exception of Judah, is now generally accepted. Yet see, e. g., W. Erbt, *Die Hebraeer*, p. 55; Eduard Meyer, *Geschichte des Altertums*, II, 2, p. 42. With regard to the relation of the monarchical ideal to those of Canaan, cf. Pedersen, *Israel, Its Life and Culture*, p. 22.

[32] The usual rejection of I Sam. 13.8 ff. as a mere parallel to I Sam. 15.1 ff. seems to me not well founded. Smith, in the *International Critical Commentary to Samuel*, p. 21, has advanced cogent reasons for accepting I Sam. 13.8 ff. as belonging to the oldest stratum of the book. His opinion is also shared by Eduard Meyer (*Geschichte des Altertums*, II, 2, p. 244). O. Eissfeldt (*Die Komposition der Samuelisbuecher*, p. 11) assigns it to the middle stratum; see also his article "Samuelisbuecher" in *Religion in Geschichte und Gegenwart*, V, p. 104. The story of the rejection of Saul by Samuel in I Sam. 15.22 f. is of course a reduplication of 13.8 f. It is interesting to note, in this connection, that both stories deal with sacrifices, and both center in Gilgal. There can be little doubt therefore that they are derived from an old tradition which associated Samuel's quarrel with Saul with a sacrifice

in Gilgal. Probably, I Sam. 13.8 ff. has retained the more correct version of the first quarrel between the men. The compiler of the second tradition, built on the fact of Saul's battle with the Amalekites and his quarrel with Samuel concerning the *herem*, has seen fit to strengthen his story with the addition of some details which originally belonged to an entirely different incident. It was this confluence of the stories which made them resemble each other so completely. The story of the Amalekites, rejected by Smith, op. cit., as entirely fictitious, is accepted in its main elements by practically all the other writers, see Kittel, Gunkel, and Meyer, op. cit.; as well as Alt, *Die Staatenbildung der Israeliten in Palaestina*, p. 31. For further opposition to Gilgal, by later prophets, cf. Hos. 9.15, "All their wickedness is in Gilgal"; Amos 5.5, "For Gilgal shall surely go into captivity." Sellin (*Gilgal*) supposes that the original Temple of Gilgal was situated in a Gilgal near Shechem; and that subsequent writers transferred the traditions relating to that sanctuary to the one near the Jordan. What seems to me more probable is that later writers attempted to construct a theory for the importance which they knew attached to Gilgal, without justifying the Temple which had been established there. See, e. g., Josh. 5.9.

[33] The verse according to which Samuel commanded Saul to resort to Gilgal (I Sam. 10.8) contradicts the one which precedes it, and is almost universally rejected as a late gloss (Wellhausen, *Die Composition des Hexateuchs und der historischen Buecher des AT*, 245 ff.; Stade, *Geschichte des Volkes Israel*, I, p. 211).

[34] I Sam. 13.3; 14.1 ff.

[35] II Sam. 2.8. The name *Ish-bosheth* is of course substituted for Ish-baal by the scrupulous copyists; but the original form has been preserved in I Chron. 8.33; 9.39. Whether Ishui in I Sam. 14.49 is also a copyist's correction for Ishbaal or was another son of Saul is not yet determined (see Ewald, *Geschichte des Volkes Israel*, 3rd ed., III, p. 148). The fact that Saul's three (presumably, oldest) sons were killed in the battle of Gilboa, and Ishbaal, apparently still a very young man, survived, would seem to indicate that Ishui was simply an older child. Regarding David's son, Baal-yada, see below, note 49.

[36] That Meribaal was the original form of this name is now generally recognized (I Chron. 8.34; 9.40; see E. Nestle, *Israelitische Eigennamen*, p. 120 ff.).

[37] Hence it came about that Gibeon was the center of Benjaminite estates, see Josh. 18.25; 21.17; II Sam. 2.12 ff.; Solomon's sacrifice at Gibeon (I Kings 3.4) was doubtless intended to insure the loyalty to the Benjaminites; while the prominence given in Chronicles to the sanctuary in Gibeon reflects the importance of the tribe of Benjamin in the third century B.C.E. (Cf. I Chron. 16.39; 21.29; II Chron. 1.3, 13).

[38] See S. Klein in *Monatsschrift*, LXXX (1936), p. 204.

[39] The political significance of the attack on Amalek has already been recognized by Kittel, *Geschichte*, II, p. 106, note 3. That I Sam., ch. 15, has an historical kernel, even though the present form of the story may be late, can hardly be doubted. So, for instance, Eduard Meyer, *Geschichte des Altertums*, II, 2, p. 245; Eissfeldt, *Krieg und Bibel*, p. 14.

[40] The *herem*, or principle of destruction of booty, originated probably in the

thought of consecrating to God the first and most important part of material gained in battle, just as the first of the products of the earth were dedicated to Him. Nevertheless, there can be little doubt, in view of what has been said in the text, that the *herem* did become, in the hands of the earliest prophets, an instrument of propaganda against aggression. Whether it had the same significance outside of Israel, I am unable to say. See, however, S. Reinach, *Cults, Myths and Religions* (Eng. tr., Elizabeth Frost), p. 44 ff.; and cf. Schwally, *Der heilige Krieg im alten Israel*, p. 29 ff. For a reference to the *herem* principle outside of Israel, see the Mesha Inscription, lines 11–12.

[41] Wellhausen, *Israel.-juedisch. Geschichte*, p. 54.

[42] See, e. g., O. Eissfeldt, *Die Komposition der Samuelisbuecher*, p. 23.

[43] The creation of money economy and trade had actually led to the development of the royal power in Egypt (Brentano, *Das Wirtschaftsleben der Antiken Welt*, p. 8 ff.) and probably would have brought about similar centralization of authority in Israel, had the Davidic dynasty survived. For the failure of these results to follow in Northern Israel and in Greece, see below, p. 392 ff. For a recognition of the wider social and economic significance of David's military and political policies, see G. Hoelscher, *Geschichte der Israelitischen Religion*, p. 93; Margaret B. Crook, "Some Cultural Principles in Hebrew Civilization," in *JBL*, L (1931), p. 167; Franz Walter, *Die Propheten in ihrem sozialen Beruf und das Wirtschaftsleben ihrer Zeit*, p. 30 ff.; Johs. Pedersen, *Israel, Its Life and Culture*, p. 38 f.

[44] For the authenticity of the main tradition in II Sam. 7, see L. Rost, *Die Ueberlieferung von der Thronnachfolge Davids*, p. 47 ff.; O. Eissfeldt, *Die Komposition der Samuelisbuecher*, p. 33.

[45] For the children who bore "baal" names, see below.

[46] It is possible that the family of Barzillai which befriended David (II Sam. 17.27) was also admitted to the priesthood. This is a more likely explanation of the claims put forward by the sons of Barzillai in 538 B.C.E. (Ezra 2.61) than that which they actually made — according to the usual method of reconciling contradictory genealogies in ancient Palestine — that they were descended from the daughters of Barzillai. See also Kittel, *Geschichte*, II, p. 251.

[47] II Sam. 5.17; 8.1.

[48] Note that his first wife after he became king was the daughter of an Aramean King (II Sam. 3.3); and cf. also Gen. 38.2 ff.; 46.10; and see especially II Sam. 6.10.

[49] Indeed, in his old age, he actually named one of his sons Baal-yada, "Baal knows." Perhaps, he did this after the revolution of Absalom so as to win back the northern tribes and the lowlanders. At any rate, it is clear from II Sam. 5.13 ff. that Baal-yada was younger than Solomon. For the name Baal-yada, instead of El-yada, see I Chron. 3.5 ff.; 14.4 ff., and commentaries to Samuel, loc. cit.

[50] Compare Kittel, *Geschichte*, II, p. 226 f.

[51] See above, p. 189.

[52] The common assumption that the opposition to the whole system of royalty must be post-exilic seems to me to be without foundation. The cry, "Each man to your tents, O Israel," certainly original, shows how strong the desire for a return to the earlier feudalism was.

[53] I Kings 12.29.

[54] Cf. I Kings 12.25; his establishment of his capital in Shechem probably involved the reconstruction of its Temple. See also Olmstead, *History of Palestine and Syria*, p. 353.

[55] See Kittel, *Geschichte*, II, 280; Olmstead, *History of Palestine and Syria*, p. 354 ff.

NOTES TO CHAPTER XVII

[1] I Kings 20.34. This seems to me more probable than the assumption that he was compelled to surrender the privilege under duress (Kittel, *Geschichte*, II, p. 300; and less positively, Olmstead, *History of Palestine and Syria*, p. 369, as well as Wellhausen, *Israelit.-juedisch. Geschichte*, p. 70).

[2] For Omri's building exploits, see Olmstead, loc. cit.

[3] This interpretation of events is also accepted by G. Hoelscher, *Die Propheten*, p. 170. W. Erbt (*Die Hebraeer*, p. 116) finds the YHWH following in the general peasantry as opposed to the city patricianship. See, also, Franz Walter, *Die Propheten in ihrem sozialen Beruf und das Wirtschaftsleben ihrer Zeit*, p. 69 ff.; as well as the compact, but extremely interesting monograph of Justus Koeberle, *Soziale Probleme im alten Israel und in der Gegenwart*, p. 26 f. Cf. further, Sven Herner, "Athalia," in *Marti Festschrift* (*BZAW*, XLI [1925], 140). Similar conditions in Attica led to the reforms of Solon, see I. M. Linforth, *Solon the Athenian*, p. 49; Brentano, *Das Wirtschaftsleben der antiken Welt*, p. 38; and Hasebroek, *Griechische Wirtschafts- und Gesellschaftsgeschichte*, 164 ff. For the similar struggle in Rome, cf. Tenney Frank, *An Economic Survey of Ancient Rome*, I, p. 10, and *Cambridge Ancient History*, VII, pp. 452, 468, and 471. For a general discussion of the social phenomena, see Zimmerman, s. v. "Rural Society" in *Encyclopedia of Social Sciences*, XIII, 470, but especially Eduard Meyer, *Kleine Schriften*, I, p. 110 ff. The historical character of the incident at Mount Carmel is defended on other grounds by Albrecht Alt in *Festschrift Georg Beer*, p. 1 ff. (This reference and four or five other suggestions were given me by my friend, Dr. H. L. Ginsberg, who kindly read part of this book in page proof).

[4] Menander, cited by Josephus in *Antiquities*, VIII, 13.2 (324).

[5] The representatives of this faction were, of course, such prophets as those described in I Kings 20.35; 22.11 ff. See also, G. Hoelscher, *Die Propheten*, p .178 ff.

[6] This is apparently indicated in II Kings ch. 5. So also, Alfred Jeremias, op. cit., p. 618. For the high place of Aram in early prophetic thought, cf. the insistence of the patriarchs on the marriage of their children to Arameans (Gen. 24.10; 29.4 ff.); see also Deut. 26.5 where Jacob is called an Aramean; and the recognition of the prophetic powers of Balaam, the Aramaic soothsayer (Num. 23.7). It has even been suggested that there was a Syrian Judah at the northern end of Aram and it is claimed that several rulers in that region showed by their names that they were worshipers of YHWH. See Olmstead, *History of Palestine and Syria*, p. 251. Olmstead reminds us also that Gen. 31.24, 29 implies the worship of YHWH in Aram.

[7] II Kings 8.9. For a brilliant discussion of the issues raised in the text, cf. H. Gunkel, *Geschichten von Elisa.*

[8] Olmstead, op. cit., p. 399.

[9] Cf. *Cambridge Ancient History*, IV, p. 34 ff.

[10] Menes, *Die vorexilischen Gesetze Israels*, p. 16 ff.

[11] Cf. O. Eissfeldt (*Krieg und Bibel*, p. 47), who traces the development of the ethical concept that only righteous wars are "wars of the Lord" back to Amos. For a discussion of the issues which arose in this war and for varying interpretations of the policies of the prophet and the King, see K. Budde, "Jesaja und Ahaz" in *ZDMG*, LXXXIV (1930), p. 125 ff.; and cf. Begrich, "Der Syrisch-Ephraimitische Krieg," ibid., LXXXIII (1929), p. 213 ff.; Otto Procksch, *Der Staatsgedanke in der Prophetie*, p. 30; Willy Staerk, *Religion und Politik im alten Israel*, p. 4. Albrecht Alt, in his *Israel und Aegypten*, p. 67, indicates that the prophet was quite pro-Assyrian even at this time; yet I believe that to do complete justice to Isaiah, it is necessary to point out also the subtle difference between his policy and that of the King.

[12] The narrative in II Kings 18.4 has been rejected as post-exilic and spurious by many commentators, but has found a valiant defender in R. Kittel (*Geschichte*, II, p. 476).

[13] Compare Cowley, *Aramaic Papyri of the Fifth Century B.C.*, Introduction, p. xviii ff.; Eduard Meyer, *Der Papyrusfund von Elephantine*, p. 57 ff.

[14] Deut. 18.1 et al. See also Menes, *Die vorexilischen Gesetze*, pp. 8, 96 ff., 105 ff. and cf. also *Akiba*, p. 94 ff.

[15] Albrecht Alt, who accepts the general historicity of II Kings 20.12–20, places the incident about the year 720 B.C.E. (*Israel und Aegypten*, p. 67). The general interpretation of the opposition between King and Prophet on this issue remains unchanged.

[16] The genuine character of the Messianic prophecies in Isaiah has been disputed for some decades with much vigor. Even today, W. L. Wardle, in *The History and Religion of Israel* (Clarendon Bible, I), p. 188, maintains that they are of later age. While authorities are not altogether in agreement regarding the precise passages which come under this head, it is generally held that they include 2.2–4; 11.1–9; 32.1–5, 15–20. The tendency of most recent criticism has been, however, toward recognizing their authenticity; see commentary of Proksch, to Isa. 11.1 ff.; and A. Causse, *Les Prophètes d'Israël et les Religions de l'Orient*, p. 133 f. This tendency has been strengthened by the evidence adduced by various writers to show that the Messianic ideal arose not in post-exilic Israel under the influence of foreign systems of thought, but is inherent in the oldest strata of Hebrew literature. See Sellin, "Die israelitisch-juedische Heilandserwartung" in *Biblische Zeit- und Streitfragen*, V, 2–3; H. Gressmann, "Der Ursprung der israelitisch-juedischen Eschatologie," in *Forschungen zur Religion und Literatur des alten und neuen Testaments, Heft* 6; L. Duerr, *Ursprung und Ausbau der israelitisch-juedischen Heilandserwartung*. For the fundamentally religious character of the political views advocated by Isaiah and the other prophets, see especially F. Wilke, *Die politische Wirksamkeit der Propheten Israels*, p. 64 ff.

[17] See below, p. 581.

[18] See below p. 607.

[19] The correct interpretation of this passage, involving the interruption of the passage at this point, was first recognized by Eduard Meyer, see his article "Bevoelkerungswesen (Bevoelkerung des Altertums)" in *Handwoerterbuch d. Staatswissenschaften*, II, 898 ff. For a full discussion of the events see Albrecht Alt, article "Hiskia," in *Religion in Geschichte und Gegenwart*, vol. II; in *Israel und Aegypten*, p. 68 ff.; and "Nachwort ueber die territorialgeschichtliche Bedeutung von Sanherib's Eingriff in Palaestina," *Palaestinajahrbuch*, XXV (1929), pp. 80–88; W. Rudolph, "Sanherib in Palaestina," ibid., pp. 59–80; Otto Eissfeldt, "Ezechiel als Zeuge fuer Sanherib's Eingriff in Palaestina," ibid., XXVII (1931), pp. 58–66; Julius Lewy, *Orientalische Literaturzeitschrift*, XXXI (1928), col. 150 ff.; Otto Procksch, *Jesaia*, I, p. 460 and *Der Staatsgedanke in der Prophetie*, p. 35; I. Friedlaender, *Past and Present*, pp. 25, 59 ff.; S. Feigin, *Horeb*, II, pp. 17–36; *Ha-Doar*, XVI, 137, pp. 427–8; *Cambridge Ancient History*, III, pp. 388–91; Leo Honor, *Sennacherib's Invasion of Palestine*; U. Cassuto, article "Jesaja" in *Encyclopaedia Judaica*, IX. For a full discussion of the events see Albrecht Alt, *Israel und Aegypten*, p. 68 ff.; and "Nachwort ueber die territorialgeschichtliche Bedeutung von Sanherib's Eingriff in Palaestina."

[20] *Records of the Past*, vol. VI, p. 90 ff.; accessibly reprinted in the *Cambridge Bible, Isaiah* I–XXXIX, p. 18; for the whole period, see Jeremias, *Das Alte Testament im Lichte des alten Orients*, p. 590 ff.

[21] Yeb. 49b.

[22] See also A. Menes, *Die vorexilischen Gesetze*, p. 98.

[23] See also below, ch. XX. H. Winckler goes too far, however, in my opinion, when he assumes that there was intense prophetic activity during the reign of Manasseh (*Geschichte Israels*, I, p. 99). See, however, W. Staerk, *Das assyrische Weltreich im Urteil der Propheten*, p. 153.

[24] Whether the provinces which had been taken from Judah were restored to her in the days of Hezekiah is uncertain; there is good reason to believe that this occurred only in the time of Manasseh, see Albrecht Alt in *Palaestinajahrbuch*, XXV (1925), 87; and Otto Eissfeldt, ibid., XXVII (1931), 63. For the impoverishment of Judah during the last days of Hezekiah and the early days of Manasseh, see now also R. H. Pfeiffer in *JBL*, XLVII (1928), 184–6.

[25] II Kings 24.16; cf. ibid. 14; Jer. 24.1; 29.2.

[26] Jer. 51.59. The Septuagint indicates that the second delegation, too, was sent from Zedekiah, and that the King himself did not participate in it. Regarding the authenticity of the record in Jer. 50.59, see G. Hoelscher, *Die Propheten*, p. 289; as well as Peake's note in the *Century Bible*, Jeremiah II, p. 278; and his citations of older authorities.

[27] Cf. W. F. Albright in *JBL*, 1932, p. 103 ff., and references there given; see also his *Archaeology of Palestine and the Bible*, p. 172.

[28] It seems probable that Gemariah ben Shaphan who is recorded in Jer. 36.12 as the man in whose chamber Jeremiah read his scroll of prophecies to the people (Jer. 36.12) was a brother of this Ahikam, and therefore an uncle of Gedaliah.

Another member of the family, Elasa ben Shaphan, appears in Jer. 29.3 as the person who, as one of the commission sent by King Zedekiah to offer tribute to the Great King, bore with him an epistle from Jeremiah to the exiles.

NOTES TO CHAPTER XVIII

[1] See Kittel, *Geschichte*, II, p. 401 ff. and also Walther Eichrodt, in *Festschrift Otto Procksch*, p. 52 f.

[2] Cowley, *Aramaic Papyri of the Fifth Century B.C.*, p. 20.

[3] Shab. 145b.

[4] See note 6 below.

[5] Cf. Jer. 29.1, 4, 20; Lam. 1.1 ff.; 2.1 ff.; 4.2, 12, 22; contrast, however, the references to the exile of Judah in Jer. 1.3; 24.4; 28.4; 29.22; 40.1; 52.28 ff.; Lam. 1.3; I Chron. 5.41. Many of these passages are, of course, quite late.

[6] This is of course not to deny that the fortresses were destroyed and many provincial cities were burned to the ground. But the farmers, as a class, escaped unscathed. See Kittel, *Geschichte*, III, 1, p. 66 ff.; Albright, *Archaeology of Palestine and the Bible*, p. 172; Albrecht Alt, in *Festschrift Otto Procksch*, p. 15.

[7] For the importance of the trade routes which pass through Ludd, see Albrecht Alt, in *Palaestinajahrbuch*, XXI (1925), 48, and *ZDMG*, LXXIX (1925), 4; G. Dalman, *Sacred Sites and Ways*, p. 226; also *Palaestinajahrbuch*, IX (1913), 35 ff.

[8] At any rate the Idumeans, pressed by the Nabatean invasion of their country, spread throughout the southern section of Judah (see Kittel, *Geschichte*, III, 1, p. 70 ff.; especially, p. 72). Hence it came about that in rabbinic literature *Darom* (the later term for *Negeb*) is the equivalent of Edom or Idumea. (See Klein in *Abhandlungen zur Erinnerung an Z. P. Chajes*, Hebrew section, p. 284 ff.). Cf. Eduard Meyer, *Die Entstehung des Judentums*, p. 106.

[9] For Isaiah 13, 14, and 21 see R. Kittel, *Geschichte*, III, 1, p. 79 ff. Bewer, *The Literature of the Old Testament*, p. 196 ff., agrees regarding chapter 21, but apparently holds chs. 13, 14 to be products of Babylonia on the basis of their similarity to Babylonian poems (see Olmstead, *History of Palestine and Syria*, p. 541 ff.), but this argument does not seem to me conclusive and is entirely insufficient to outweigh the clear evidence of Palestinian environment. The evidence of the imagery used in Jer. 50–51.58, and the whole tone of those prophecies is equally convincing for their Palestinian origin.

[10] It is frequently stated that Lam. chs. 2 and 4 proceed from the same circles and perhaps even from the same author; cf. R. Kittel, *Geschichte*, III, 1, p. 98 ff.; Peake, "Jeremiah and Lamentations," in the *Century Bible*, II, 336–7; even Bewer, who recognizes the aristocratic origin of Lamentations ch. 4 (*The Literature of the Old Testament*, p. 189), suggests that ch. 2 also proceeded from the same pen (ibid., p. 190). The evidence of difference in point of view, however, as indicated in the text, seems to me convincing proof of difference of class origin.

[11] That the Psalm is the work of restored priests has been recognized by most commentators, see R. Kittel, *Die Psalmen*, p. 414; Mowinckel, *Psalmenstudien*,

V, p. 83 ff. (Cf. also the interesting interpretation of Hans Schmidt, in *Die Psalmen*, p. 138). Mowinckel, however, attributes it to the returning exiles of 538, which seems incredible in view of the anger displayed against the conquerors and the *silence* of the original text about Babylon (concerning which see note 12). Had the Psalm been composed after the destruction of Babylonia, she certainly would have been mentioned, as the guiltiest party.

[12] Mowinckel is, doubtless, right in taking it that the words *Bat babel ha-shedudah* of v. 8 were added later. They are not, however, a gloss (Mowinckel, op. cit., p. 84); they were added by a subsequent poet who, writing after Babylonia's fall, could not see the justice of invoking a curse on Edom, the minor foe, and forgetting the principal enemy.

[13] Jer. 29.22.

[14] See above, note 10.

[15] II Kings 24.14, 16; also Jer. 29.1.

[16] Jer. 29.5. It is interesting to see that the editor especially mentions the carpenters and the smiths in the heading of the chapter describing this letter, as if to indicate the people who were addressed in the epistle. He passes over in silence the seven thousand *gibbore ha-hayil* who are mentioned in II Kings 24.14.

[17] Jer. 29.24 ff.

[18] Sifre, Deut. 321, 138a; Seder 'Olam Rabba, 25, ed. Ratner, 57a; Yer. Sanhedrin 1.2, 19a; B. Sanhedrin 38a.

[19] See below, p. 609. Regarding the economic and social hardships which the exiles faced in Babylonia, see W. W. Kaplun-Kogan, *Die Wanderbewegungen der Juden*, p. 13 ff.; E. Klamroth, *Die juedischen Exulanten in Babylonien*, p. 31 ff., who shows that the situation in Babylonia was very difficult, and far from as happy as is usually supposed. See also, S. Daiches, *The Jews in Babylonia in the Time of Ezra and Nehemiah*; Hilprecht-Clay, *The Babylonian Expedition of the University of Pennsylvania*, Series A, vols. IX and X, E. Ebeling, *Aus dem Leben der juedischen Exulanten in Babylonien*. That the Pharisaic outlook on life, with its combination of universalism and particularism, described in the text, had its true origin in Babylonia, is demonstrated by L. Baeck, *Die Pharisäer*, p. 40; Schuerer, *Geschichte*, II, p. 465; V. Aptowitzer, *Parteipolitik*, p. 188.

[20] Kittel, *Geschichte*, III, 2, p. 363 f.

[21] For a discussion of the interaction of universalist and particularist elements in Judaism, see G. F. Moore, *Judaism*, I, p. 219 ff.; M. Guttmann, *Das Judentum und seine Umwelt*; Tschernowitz, *Toledoth ha-Halakah* I, 1, p. 256 ff.; Herford, *The Pharisees*; Bousset-Gressmann, *Die Religion des Judentums*, p. 3 ff.; Schechter, *Some Aspects of Rabbinic Theology*.

[22] Gen. 1.27; 5.2; the repetition of the thought indicates the emphasis placed upon it; cf. Gen. 2.22.

[23] Gen. 10.1 ff.; the names and territories of the nations can only be mentioned for one purpose, to show that they possess their lands from God, and that they must not be deprived of them.

[24] Lev. 25.1 ff., which prohibits the alienation of land from its original owner; Num. 26.52 ff., which prescribes the equal division of the land among the people;

the extension of the term *'am ha-arez* (in its original meaning of "gentry") to the whole population (Lev. 4.27; 20.2).

[25] Ex. 12.49; Lev. 16.29; 17.15; 18.26; 19.34; 24.22; Num. 15.15, 29; cf. also Josh. 8.33.

[26] Gen. 2.1; Ex. 35.2; Lev. 19.3; 23.3; Num. 28.9.

[27] Gen. 17.10.

[28] Lev. 11.1 ff.

[29] Lev. chs. 12–15.

[30] Ab. 1.1. For the convenience of the reader, I give the text as preserved in the Mishna, though I am convinced that the older version is that preserved in Abot of R. Nathan II, ed. Schechter, 1b, and implied in Abot of R. Nathan I, ibid. This text reads, "Moses received the Law from Sinai, and handed it over to Joshua, and Joshua to the elders, the elders to the judges, the judges to the prophets, and the prophets to Haggai, Zechariah and Malachi. Haggai, Zechariah and Malachi handed it over to the men of the Great Assembly." My reasons for preferring the text of Abot of R. Nathan are given in an article which will appear in *JBL* of this year (1938).

[31] B. B. 75a.

[32] Above, p. 264 ff.

[33] II Kings 25.27.

[34] I Chron. 3.18. It is interesting to note that the second son born after the release, when Jehoiachin had become accustomed to his new station in the Babylonian court, bore a purely Babylonian name, Shenazzar (regarding which see Meyer, *Entstehung des Judentums*, 75 ff.; R. Kittel, *Geschichte*, III, 2, p. 346). There may be some additional significance in the fact that his later sons bore again names with YHWH, see I Chron. ibid. Did the disappointment in the results of Amil-Marduk's favor drive the liberated King back into the arms of his people?

[35] For a more complete discussion of the issues raised in the text, see Appendix A.

[36] On no other hypothesis can we account for the breadth of mind displayed by this child of a peasant country. The wealth he saw in his home is reflected in a dozen prophecies. See for both conclusions, 42.10 f.; 43.3, 14; 54.11; 60.17.

[37] In most of these citations, I take Torrey's excellent rendering as a basis for the English text. I also accept his emendation of *zaddik* for *zedek*; but here, as so frequently, the word doubtless has the meaning "victorious."

[38] On this occasion, as on others, the prophet, feeling that he overemphasized his point in one address, tried to counterbalance it by stressing the very opposite truth in another. Chapter 41 describes Israel as engaged in battle with its enemies; chapter 42 shows that the battle is purely spiritual. Similarly chapter 50 scolds those who failed to return; chapter 51 welcomes those who did return. Chapter 52.13 ff. describes the struggle of Israel; chapter 54 hails its future glory. Chapter 59 is full of despairing condemnation; chapter 60 breaks forth into a song of rejoicing. This has partly been noticed by Torrey, *The Second Isaiah*, p. 443; and the recurrence of the phenomenon throughout the work is one of the evidences for its unity.

[39] The reference to Persian dualism does not indicate a late date for Deutero-Isaiah. (See R. Kittel, *Geschichte*, III, 1, p. 211).

[40] As H. H. Schaeder, *Iranische Beitraege*, I, pp. 220 f., has demonstrated, the original edict of Cyrus, promulgated in the Imperial Aramaic dialect, is still preserved in Ezra 6.3 f. For the limitations of the decree, see Albrecht Alt, in *Festschrift Otto Procksch*, p. 21 ff.

[41] For the identification of Sheshbazzar with the son of Jeconiah, see R. Kittel, *Geschichte*, III, 2, p. 346. For his position in the imperial government, see Albrecht Alt, loc. cit.

[42] Practically all the recent commentators have rejected 50.11 as a gloss (So L. Koehler, *Deuterojesaja*, p. 43; W. Caspari, *Lieder und Gottesspruecke der Rueckwanderer*, p. 105; and P. Volz, *Jesaia* II, p. 151). Only S. Mowinckel, in *ZAW*, XLIX (1931), 247, note 1, expresses some doubt regarding the rejection of the passage. The difficulty seems to be, however, that all the commentators take the verse to be a malediction, quite out of spirit with Deutero-Isaiah's prophecies generally — at least at this time of his life — and furthermore, that, as usually interpreted it has no connection with either what precedes or what follows. The commentators have, however, failed to grapple with the problem of interpreting the verse, even as a gloss. What does it mean? The words *lema'azebah tishkabun*, are usually interpreted, "In sorrow shall ye lie down." But the *lamed* in *lema'azebah* should certainly be a *bet* if that were the meaning. Furthermore, what sense can be made out of a verse, which reads:

"From My hand has this come to you,
In sorrow shall ye lie down?"

Why should any glossator have added such an absurd and meaningless statement?

The answer can be given through a slight emendation of the text, such as has been indicated in the translation. The words *lema'azebah tishkabun*, with the slight substitution of a *nun* for the *zadi* in *lema'azebah*, and the correction of *tishkabun* into the unusual Aramaic, and therefore easily corrupted word, *tisbakun*, give us a good text, which supplements the preceding phrases and leads on to the following.

"Out of My hand has this (the mission to the world) come to you;
For My sake shall ye adhere to it."

The root *sbk* occurs frequently in this sense in Aramaic and Syriac; its denominative forms *sobek* and *sebakah* occur in Scripture (II Sam. 18.9; II Kings 1.2; Job 18.8); its cognate root *shabaka* has the same meaning in Arabic. It is a plausible conjecture, therefore, that the word in our text originally read: *tisbakun*, but an early copyist (the corruption is found in the LXX) not recognizing the word, confused the letters *bet* and *kaf*, which are almost identical, took the *sin* for a *shin*, and read the familiar תשכבון for תשבכון. The corruption of the *lema'ani bah*, into *lema'azebah* followed almost as a matter of course.

[43] The expression "Holy One of Israel," which occurs ten times before this

(41.14, 16, 20; 43.3, 14; 45.11; 47.4; 48.17; 49.7; 54.5) occurs only thrice later, 55.5; 60.9, 14. The expression "God of Israel," which occurs in 41.17; 45.3; 45.15; 48.2; is repeated again only in 52.12. But the most amazing contrast occurs in connection with the use of Israel and Jacob in other connections, as can be seen from the following list:

A) References to Israel in chapters 40–51, inclusive:

1.	Why sayest thou, O Jacob, and speakest, O Israel	40.27
2.	But thou, Israel, art My servant, Jacob whom I have chosen	41.8
3.	Fear not, thou worm, Jacob, and ye men of Israel	41.14
4.	That created thee, O Jacob, and that formed thee, O Israel	43.1
5.	But thou hast not called on Me, O Jacob — O Israel	43.22
6.	And have given Jacob to the curse, and Israel to reproaches	43.28
7.	Yet now hear, O Jacob, My servant, and Israel whom I have chosen	44.1
8.	Fear not, O Jacob, My servant, and thou Jeshurun	44.2
9.	The name of Jacob . . . the name of Israel	44.5
10.	Remember these, O Jacob and Israel, for thou art My servant	44.21
11.	For the Lord hath redeemed Jacob . . . Israel	44.23
12.	For Jacob, My servant's sake, and Israel, Mine elect	45.4
13.	Israel shall be saved	45.17
14.	I said not unto the children of Jacob	45.19
15.	Shall all the seed of Israel be justified	45.25
16.	Hearken unto me, O House of Jacob and all the remnant of the House of Israel	46.3
17.	For Israel My glory	46.13
18.	Hear this, O House of Jacob . . . Israel	48.1, 12
19.	Hath redeemed His servant Jacob	48.20
20.	Thou art My servant, O, Israel	49.3
21.	To bring Jacob back to Him	49.5
22.	Thou shouldest be My servant, to raise up the tribes of Jacob, and restore the preserved of Israel	49.6

These twenty-three references occur in twelve chapters; in the remaining fifteen we have only seven references, in several of which neither Israel nor Jacob is recognized as a true unit.

They are as follows:

1.	Who gathereth the outcasts of Israel	56.8
2.	And show . . . the house of Jacob their sins	58.1
3.	And the Redeemer shall come unto . . . them that turn from transgression in Jacob	59.20
4.	The Mighty One of Jacob	60.16
5.	Great goodness toward the House of Israel	63.7
6.	And I will bring a seed out of Jacob	65.9
7.	As the children of Israel bring an offering	66.20

[44] Following Torrey's excellent reconstruction of the text.

[45] C. and D. Singer, "The Jewish Factor in Mediaeval Thought," in Bevan and Singer, *The Legacy of Israel*, p. 174 ff.

[46] For a discussion of the theory of Trito-Isaiah, and the problems connected with it, see Appendix A.

[47] I cannot accept Torrey's interpretation of these verses.

[48] Op. cit., p. 382.

[49] Torrey, op. cit., p. 111 ff.

[50] See above, p. 461.

[51] The reference to the eunuch and the stranger, and the unexpectedly broad universal outlook which appears in this passage, seem to imply some special situation. The discussion of whether the eunuch could be admitted "into the community of the Lord" revolved, apparently, about the interpretation to be put on Deut. 23.2. See Torrey, op. cit., p. 427.

[52] Amos 7.14.

[53] Cf. above, pp. 296 and 315.

[54] Above, p. 324.

NOTES TO CHAPTER XIX

[1] For the position he occupied as subservient to the Aramean officials of Samaria, see Albrecht Alt, in *Festschrift Otto Procksch*, p. 24.

[2] See above, p. 176.

[3] See above, p. 205.

[4] See above, p. 494.

[5] For a discussion of Haggai's attitude toward revolution, and whether his words were intended to have a practical application or were merely eschatological predictions, see J. Wellhausen, *Die Kleinen Propheten*, p. 170; Eduard Meyer, *Entstehung des Judentums*, p. 79 ff.; R. Kittel, *Geschichte*, III, 2, p. 455 ff.; and Olmstead, *History of Palestine and Syria*, p. 560 ff. For a recognition of the ethical limitations of Haggai's prophecy, and the marked differences between it and that of the earlier prophets, see so conservative a commentator as G. A. Smith, *The Book of the Twelve Prophets*, II, 252.

[6] That Haggai and Zechariah acted in opposition to one another is clearly indicated by the data furnished in the text; see Fleming James, in *JBL*, LIII (1934), 230 f.; and Otto Procksch, *Der Staatsgedanke in der Prophetie*, p. 56. The failure of historians to realize this, in spite of the almost universal recognition of the difference in attitude between Haggai and Zechariah, is due to the influence of Ezra 5.1, where the two prophets are coupled together. But as H. H. Schaeder says (*Iranische Beitraege*, I, p. 222), that verse is not part of the original document which the Chronicler used as his source for these chapters, but a paraphrase of a paragraph with which the Chronicler took some liberties. The government official who was the author of the original document would hardly be likely to refer, in any event, to the Jewish prophets and their influence on the people.

[7] For Zechariah's Babylonian origin, see G. A. Smith, *The Book of the Twelve Prophets*, II, p. 265. His family, that of Iddo, is expressly described, Neh. 12.4, as having returned from Babylonia under Cyrus. For his pacifist leanings, see G. A. Smith, op. cit., p. 281; R. Kittel, *Geschichte*, III, 2, p. 459 (who errs, however, in my opinion, in presuming that Haggai would have agreed with Zechariah). For Zechariah's relations to Ezekiel, see R. Kittel, op. cit., p. 457; G. A. Smith, op. cit., p. 312 ff.

[8] For the contrast between Zechariah's emphasis on the ethical life and Haggai's pure ritualism, see G. A. Smith, op. cit., p. 324; Olmstead, *History of Palestine and Syria*, p. 573.

[9] The lay leader of the Judaite community is mentioned in the famous appeal of the community of Yeb to the Persian Governor, Bagoas, printed in Cowley, *Aramaic Papyri of the Fifth Century B.C.*, p. 112. The leader at the time was "Ostanes, the brother of Anani"; see, ibid. p. 112, line 18 of the text. See also Sachau, *Drei aramaeische Papyrusurkunden*, p. 4 ff.; and Eduard Meyer, *Der Papyrusfund von Elephantine*, p. 70 ff. G. Hoelscher, *Geschichte der israelitischen Religion*, p. 143, note 2. Such a lay leader is also mentioned in II Chron. 19.11; and indeed a similar dual government is implied in Num. 27.19. There may be some relation between this early dual government and that instituted by the Pharisees, first in their own Order, and finally for the whole Synagogue, see *Akiba*, p. 298 ff.

[10] Cited by Eduard Meyer, *Ursprung u. Anfaenge d. Christentums*, II, 29.

[11] Neh. 7.6 ff.; Ezra 2.1 ff. Almost all of the clan names are missing from the corresponding records in Chronicles, showing that the clans had been dissolved by the time of the editor. The authenticity of the document, and Ezra's association with it, have finally been demonstrated by H. H. Schaeder, in *Esra der Schreiber*, p. 15 ff.

[12] Cf. I Chron. 9.7 and see R. Kittel, *Geschichte*, III, 2, p. 363.

[13] Compare the testimony of R. Eleazar ben Zadok, a patrician priest of the first century who belonged to this family. R. Eleazar recalls that he belongs to the clan of "Senaa, the son of Benjamin" and at the same time, knows himself as priest. He probably supposed that the one line of descent was maternal and the other paternal. This was a favorite manner of solving genealogical difficulties in antiquity. (See 'Er. 41a; the correct reading is given in Tosafot, ibid. Cf. also Aptowitzer, *Parteipolitik*, p. 95).

[14] Regarding him, see below, p. 587.

[15] See R. Kittel, *Geschichte*, III, 2, p. 337; cf. S. Klein, *MGWJ*, 1936, p. 199.

[16] Ezra 2.61; cf. I Chron. 24.10.

[17] Compare Mishna Ket. 2.7; and Babli, ibid., 24b.

[18] My father describes such a case, which came before him when he was rabbi in Baltimore, Md., about the year 1890. In accordance with the usual custom, he addressed a question regarding the matter to the famous Rabbi Isaac Elhanan Spektor, then Rabbi of Kovno. The case and the reply are recorded in my father's work, *'En Simeon*, beginning.

[19] Ezra 2.36 (=Neh. 7.39) does not know the family of Yoyarib; the principal priestly clan is Yedaiah. I Chron. 9.10 mentions Yedaiah first, Yoyarib second. This should probably be the reading also of Neh. 11.10, but our texts have, "Yedaiah, son of Yoyarib." Only in I Chron. 24.7 does Yoyarib at last attain primacy. See also V. Aptowitzer, *Parteipolitik*, p. XV ff.; Geiger, *Urschrift*, p. 204.

[20] For the earlier history of the Levites and their relations with the Aaronids, see primarily Eduard Meyer, *Die Israeliten und ihre Nachbarstaemme*; ibid., *Geschichte des Atertums*, II, 2, p. 306 ff.; R. Kittel, *Geschichte*, I, p. 522; II, pp. 91 ff., 521 ff.; A. Menes, *Die vorexilischen Gesetze Israels*, p. 1 ff.; for the later history, see R. Kittel, op. cit., III, 2, p. 392 ff.; Jeremias, *Jerusalem*, II B, p. 70 ff.; V. Aptowitzer, *Parteipolitik*, p. 145 ff.; and *Akiba*, 29 ff., 83, 278, 282.

[21] Mishna ʿAr. 2.4.

[22] Concerning him, see p. 38.

[23] R. Kittel, *Geschichte*, III, 1, p. 74 ff.; III, 2, p. 372.

[24] Shab. 31a; see also, M. Guttmann, *Das Judentum und seine Umwelt*, p. 75 ff.

[25] See Gen. R., 70.5, p. 802; Guttmann, loc. cit., note.

[26] Mishna Yeb. 6.5; Sifra, Emor, perek 1.7, 94b.

[27] I have followed, in general, Bewer's "Commentary on Joel," in *International Critical Commentary*, p. 50 ff. for the analysis of the work. That the work is composite was apparently the opinion also of G. A. Smith, *The Twelve Prophets*, II, p. 388, although he found himself unable to accept any of the theories current at the time of his writing. The fact that Joel reflects the ideas and mentality of the agricultural, rather than the urban, community has already been noticed by others. See, e. g., G. A. Smith, in his article, "Trade and Commerce," in *Encyclopedia Biblica*, IV, 5180–5181.

[28] The promise of rain is not simply the end of the drought; for the prophet specifically says, "Children of Zion, be ye glad, etc."

[29] G. A. Smith, who does not recognize the hand of the glossator in this passage, is forced, by the contradiction between this verse and the fourth chapter, to suppose that "all flesh" means only Israel; although menservants and handmaids are mentioned in the context. See G. A. Smith, op. cit., II, p. 428; see, however, Bewer, op. cit., p. 123.

[30] Cf., e. g., E. Sellin, *Das Zwölfprophetenbuch*, p. 274 ff.

[31] Cf. Jer. 49.7 ff.

[32] R. Kittel, *Geschichte*, III, 1, p. 72.

[33] See above, p. 360.

[34] Cf. Zech. 9.1; Sifre, Deut. 1.1, 65a.

[35] G. A. Smith, *The Book of the Twelve Prophets*, II, p. 449 ff. Kittel, *Geschichte*, III, 2, p. 691 ff.

[36] The usual rendering "against thy sons, O Javan" is to be corrected as indicated in the text. But even if we accept the traditional reading, the prophet is simply foreseeing Judah turning against Alexander and wresting his conquests from him.

[37] *Antiquities*, XI, 8.3 ff.

[38] See G. A. Smith, *The Book of the Twelve Prophets*, II, p. 465, note 8.

[39] Acts 15.29. See Eduard Meyer, *Ursprung und Anfaenge des Christentums*, III, p. 417; and cf. Lake, in *Jewish Studies in Memory of Israel Abrahams*, p. 256 ff.

[40] Ta'an. 16a.

[41] Deut. 23.4.

[42] Yeb. 76b. Or he may have limited the prohibition to unconverted Moabites.

[43] Prov. ch. 30.

[44] Following the interpretation of G. A. Smith.

[45] Hag. 2.7.

[46] The word *'al* in the text must, of course, be emended to *kol.*

NOTES TO CHAPTER XX

[1] Zech. 9.13; 10.6; 11.14; Obadiah, v. 18; cf. above, p. 530. See also R. Kittel, *Geschichte*, II, p. 470, where the problem of the remaining Israelites is discussed, and Assyrian monuments corroborating the story of the transplantations are cited. For the extent to which the land was denuded of its higher classes, see Olmstead, *History of Palestine and Syria*, p. 460, who compares the 27,290 captives reported as taken into exile from the land of Israel with the no more than 60,000 members of the gentry, who composed the higher classes in the far greater Israel of Menahem (II Kings 15.19 f.). So also, M. Gaster, *The Samaritans*, p. 16 ff. This is further implied in II Chron. 30.1 f.; and 34.6 f.; which doubtless reflects the true state of affairs in this matter. Cf. further, J. A. Montgomery, *The Samaritans*, pp. 50–55; S. Baron, *A Social and Religious History of the Jews*, I, pp. 214–18; III, p. 219; I. Ben Zevi, *Sefer Ha-Shomronim*, p. 16, and A. C. Welch, "The Share of Northern Israel in the Restoration of Temple Worship." in *ZAW*, XLVIII (1930), pp. 175–187.

[2] Mishna Yad., 4.4.

[3] Ezra 4.10; cf. also 4.2, where the claim is made that certain groups were transplanted by Essar Haddon. For the authenticity of the documents in Ezra 4.7 ff., see above, p. 479. The social cleavage between the deportees who were brought into Samaria and the Israelite peasantry who remained on the land has already been recognized by Albrecht Alt, *Festschrift Otto Procksch*, p. 10 ff.

[4] II Kings 17.25 ff.

[5] Kid. 75b.

[6] Jer. 31.19.

[7] Deut. 12.29; 27.12.

[8] This argument is not affected by Rothstein's ingenious interpretation showing that Haggai's "question" (2.11 ff.) bore on the Samaritan problem (J. W. Rothstein, *Juden u. Samaritaner*, 5 ff.). The force of the word *sham*: "there"— meaning Shechem — must not be overlooked. The authenticity of Ezra 4.1 f. is defended vigorously, and in my opinion successfully, by R. Kittel, *Geschichte*, III, 2, p. 433 ff. It is rejected, however, by H. H. Schaeder (*Esra der Schreiber*, p. 33).

[9] R. Kittel, op. cit., pp. 556, 599 ff.; cf. above, p. 530 ff..

[10] So also Albrecht Alt in *Festschrift Otto Procksch*, p. 27.

[11] For his position in the Persian government, and his authority, see Schaeder, *Esra der Schreiber*, especially pp. 39 ff., 49; and also Kittel, *Geschichte*, III, 2, 577, 581 ff.

[12] According to Kittel, we must assume that he was recalled (op. cit., p. 606 f.); Schaeder, however, seems less certain about the matter (op. cit., p. 38).

[13] In all this, I follow H. H. Schaeder, *Esra der Schreiber*, p. 5 ff., who accepts both the memoirs of Ezra and those of Nehemiah as authentic documents.

[14] Neh. 6.14. How completely secular and political the struggle must have seemed to the contemporary prophets becomes especially evident after a study of A. Alt's brilliant analysis of the issues in *Festschrift Otto Procksch*, pp. 27–28.

[15] Zech. 2.9.

[16] Testaments of the Twelve Patriarchs, Levi, 14.6.

[17] Cf. Ex. 20.24.

[18] See above, p. 432; and *Proceedings of the American Academy for Jewish Research*, 1931–2, p. 49 ff. The suggestion of the pre-exilic origin of the synagogue was warmly defended by Leopold Loew, see his *Gesammelte Schriften*, IV, p. 5 ff. For other theories of the origin of the Synagogue, cf. S. Krauss, *Synagogale Altertuemer*, pp. 52–66; J. Wellhausen, *Israelit. u. juedische Geschichte*, 184 ff.; R. Kittel, *Geschichte*, III pp. 112, 201; and A. Menes, in *ZAW*, L (1932), p. 268 ff.

[19] Ecclus. 51.23.

[20] For the probable importance of the Levites in this connection, see v. Rad, in *Festschrift Otto Procksch*, p. 113 ff.

[21] Meg. 29a; Targum Jonathan on Ezek. 11.16.

[22] Regarding the Sect of Damascus, see Schechter, *Documents of Jewish Sectaries*, I, p. 6, line 11; and the English translation in Charles, *Apocrypha and Pseudepigrapha*, II, p. 813; for the Essenes, see Schuerer, *Geschichte*, II, p. 663.

NOTES TO CHAPTER XXI

[1] Meyer, *Ursprung u. Anfaenge des Christentums*, II, 128 ff.; Tscherikower, *Ha-Yehudim ve-ha-Yevanim*, 194 ff.; S. Zeitlin, *The History of the Second Jewish Commonwealth*, p. 19 ff.

[2] Mishna Ab. 1.2; see above, p. 62.

[3] Cf. Abram Menes, *Die vorexilischen Gesetze Israels*, p. 90; and S. Zeitlin, *Proceedings of the American Academy for Jewish Research*, 1931–2, p. 156.

[4] Morgenstern maintains that the *'edah* as used in the Pentateuch, e. g., Num. 27.2; 35.25 et al., is a formal court consisting of representatives of the Community, see *HUC Annual*, VIII-IX (1931—2), pp. 86 and 118, notes.

[5] Zech. 13.4.

[6] See articles on the Canon and the Bible in the various encyclopedias; also G. Wildeboer, *The Origin of the Canon of the Old Testament* (tr. from the German); H. F. Ryle, *The Canon of the Old Testament*.

[7] B. B. 15a.

[8] For a discussion of this passage, see C. C. Torrey, *Pseudo-Ezekiel*, p. 19 f.; Shalom Spiegel in *HTR*, XXIV (1931), p. 278.

[9] See above, p. 63.

[10] Cf. *JQR*, N. S., XVI (1925–26), p. 41 ff.

[11] *JQR*, N. S., XXI (1928–29), p. 229, note 1.

[12] This is the oldest form of the statement, still preserved in Abot of R. Nathan, II, chs. 1–4, see ed. Schechter, 1b, 2a, and 7b. In Abot of R. Nathan, I, ch. 1, 1b, the form is given precisely as in Mishna Ab. 1.1: "Be deliberate in judgment, make many disciples, and set up a hedge about the Law." The reasons which led to this transformation of the original statement into the form it has in the Mishna and Abot of R. Nathan I, are discussed in a paper which is scheduled to appear in *JBL* for this year (1938).

[13] See, for example, Abot of R. Nathan, I, ch. 1, 2b.

[14] Josephus, *Antiquities*, XII, 3.3. The authenticity of this document is now generally recognized. See Eduard Meyer, *Ursprung u. Anfaenge des Christentums*, II, p. 127, note 2.

[15] It is important, of course, to distinguish this Simeon the Tobiad, from Simeon the Righteous, who was High Priest. For the theory that Benjamin in this passage means the priestly clan *Miyamin*, see later in this chapter.

[16] Josephus, *Antiquities*, XII, 5.1. That Menelaus was a Benjaminite and not a priest has been most vigorously asserted by Schuerer, *Geschichte*, I, p. 195; Meyer, *Ursprung*, II, p. 133; Jeremias, *Jerusalem*, IIB, p. 44; for further discussion see, however, A. Tscherikower, *Ha-Yehudim ve-ha-Yevanim*, p. 197, note 3; J. Klausner, *Historia Yisreelit*, I, p. 284; A. Buechler, *Die Tobiaden*, p. 10; S. Zeitlin, *The History of the Second Jewish Commonwealth*, p. 19, note 62; and pp. 62–66.

[17] Ecclus. chap. 44. For a further discussion of Ben Sira and his philosophy, see above, p. 219. For a recent discussion of his omission of Ezra's name, which remains a perplexing problem, see H. H. Schaeder, *Esra der Schreiber*, p. 37.

[18] Mishna Ab. 1.3. See above, p. 153.

[19] Gen. R. 65.22, p. 743.

[20] So also V. Aptowitzer, *Parteipolitik*, p. 196; Geiger, *Urschrift*, p. 215.

[21] *Akiba*, p. 298 ff.

[22] These are the famous Noachian laws, discussed fully in the Talmud, San. 56a; Tosefta 'Ab. Zarah 8.4, p. 473; Gen. R., ch. 16, p. 149; Pesikta of R. Kahana, 100b; and implied in the Book of Jubilees, 7.20 ff. Concerning that passage see *HTR*, XVI, p. 60; *JBL*, XLIX, p. 22; Ginzberg, *Legends of the Jews*, V, 193, note 67; M. Guttmann, *Das Judentum u. seine Umwelt*, p. 103; Albeck, *Das Buch der Jubiläen und die Halacha*, p. 34. Albeck alone denies any relation between the Noachian laws of the Talmud and those of the Book of Jubilees.

[23] For a discussion of the identity of the Hasmonean who first called himself King, see Graetz, *Geschichte*, III, 653; Schuerer, I, 274 ff.; and Aptowitzer, *Parteipolitik*, 13 ff.

[24] San. 11a.

[25] Mishna R. H. 1.7.

[26] Cf. *HTR*, XXII (1929), p. 258 ff.

[27] Josephus, *Antiquities*, XVII, 2.4.

[28] Yavitz, *Toledot Yisrael*, IV, 157 ff.; Halevy, *Dorot ha-Rishonim*, Ic, 360 ff.; Klausner, *Historia Yisreelit*, 99 ff.; Aptowitzer, *Parteipolitik*, p. IX.

[29] See above, p. 110.

[30] Sifra Behukkotai, beginning; Ta'an. 23a; Lev. R. 35.10.

[31] Josephus, *Antiquities*, XIV, 2.1.

[32] Josephus, *Antiquities*, XIV, 13.1.

[33] See *Akiba*, p. 46 ff.

[34] Mishna Yebamot 1.4; 'Erubin 13b.

[35] Berakot 19a.

[36] Ibid. 63a.

[37] Acts 15.22 f.

NOTES TO SUPPLEMENT CHAPTER I

[1] Cf. Joachim Wach, *Sociology of Religion*, pp. 264 ff.

[2] See below, pp. 754 ff.

[3] See text of this book, pp. 62 ff.

[4] See below, pp. 692, 721 ff.

[5] Jub. 1.14; 50.1–5. The author simply refers to the Jubilaic laws in Leviticus 25.8 ff.; and does not take the trouble to repeat them.

[6] See below, pp. 742 ff.

[7] Or rather "apostates." Naturally, the later Pharisees tried to give the word a more pleasant interpretation; and interpreted it to mean "ascetic"; cf. Sifra Kedoshim, beg.

[8] B. Temurah 15b. The "blemish" as will be seen, referred specifically to the controversies within Pharisaism; but the attitude toward Sadducism was itself a subject of controversy (see below p. 780 ff.)

[9] Regarding this document, see my discussion of the matter in *Ha-Perushim ve-Anshe Keneset ha-Gedolah*, pp. 60 ff.

[10] Neh. 9.1 ff.

[11] B. Sotah 48a.

[12] See text of this book, p. 272.

[13] Cf. *Harvard Theological Review* XXXI (1938), pp. 291 ff., XXXVI (1943), pp. 291 ff., and XXXVII (1944) pp. 1 ff.

[14] It would take me too far afield to discuss these issues here in detail; and I must reserve their analysis for another work.

[15] I owe this insight to my revered teacher Professor Louis Ginzberg who devoted to it his famous work, *Meqomah shel ha-halakah be-hokmat Yisrael*, now available in English, as the essay entitled, "The Significance of the Halachah for Jewish History," in Louis Ginzberg, *On Jewish Law and Lore*. Cf. *Akiba*, pp. 294 ff.

[16] Deut. 12.28.

[17] Mishna Yebamot 1.4.

[18] *Abot of Rabbi Nathan*, II, ch. 31, 34a.

NOTES TO SUPPLEMENT CHAPTER II

[1] Cf., e.g., Mishna Niddah 4.2.

[2] Cf. B. Niddah 33b; and see below, p. 778.

[3] See above note 2.

[4] See below, pp. 692, 738.

[5] Cf. the text of this book pp. 104, 116, 119, and also, see below, pp. 762 ff.

[6] See text of this book, pp. 102 ff.

[7] Zech. 14.16 ff.

[8] See above, p. 112.

[9] See Ezekiel Kaufmann, *Toledot ha-Emunah ha-Yisraelit*, III, 2, p. 323.

[10] Pp. 641-654, 718-720.

[11] See text of this book, pp. 115 ff. For a summary of the discussion of these passages until his time, see David Z. Hoffman, *Das Buch Leviticus*, pp. 175 ff., and cf. above, pp. 115 ff.

[12] Sifra Emor, *perek* 12, 100d.

[13] See below, pp. 702 ff., where I indicate that in all the talmudic passages dealing with this subject, the opponents of the Pharisees are called Boethusians. But, as will be seen, the Boethusian view antedated their sect, and presumably was inherited from the Sadducees.

[14] See this book p. 667, note 26.

[15] See p. 667, note 23.

[16] See above p. 116.

[17] See p. 667, note 26.

[18] Cf. *Mekilta Jethro*, *Bahodesh*, ch. 3, beg., and references there given. Cf., however, B. Yoma 4b, and references given by Professor Louis Ginzberg in *Legends of the Jews*, see Index, s.v. *Revelation*, *date of*. Perhaps the tendency of some later talmudic authorities, particularly of the School of R. Akiba, to understress the connection of Shabuot with the Revelation, is due to fear that the Torah might be equated with the Ten Commandments. See in relation to this apprehension, B. Berakot 12a.

[19] See this book p. 116.

[20] I Chron. 24.4; Mishna Ta'anit 4.2. The following argument is unaffected by the issue of the date of the origin of this arrangement. Doubtless from the beginning the priests were organized in clans, serving in rotation; and presumably the rules for division of the priestly emoluments were the same as in later times.

[21] Cf. Mishna Sukkah 5.7.

[22] Cf. Ezek. 45.18 ff.

[23] Perhaps the Sadducean view was that the word Shabbat in these passages was ambiguous; and that the court could choose which festival day or Sabbath (within the Passover week) it was to use. This might explain the fact that the Talmud does not impute the view that the *Omer* occurs after the weekly Sabbath to the Sadducees. It simply states that the "Boethusians hold that the *Omer*

cannot be cut (or should not be cut) on the evening after the festival day" (Mishna Menahot 10.3).

[24] This interpretation also seems to underlie the translation of the Peshitta.

[25] Tosefta Menahot 10.21, p. 528.

[26] Ibid.

[27] See Mishna Pesahim 4.8.

[28] Mishna Menahot 10.5.

[29] See text of this book, p. 116, and *Harvard Theological Review* XXXVI (1943), p. 19.

[30] Mishna Menahot 10.5.

[31] Ibid.

[32] Mishna Rosh ha-Shanah 2.1; but see especially Tosefta, ibid., ch. 1, end., p. 210.

[33] Below, p. 652.

[34] Sifra Emor, *perek* 10.2, 100a.

[34a] Apparently this is the view of Tosefta; cf. Professor Saul Lieberman, *Ha-Tosefta Ki-Fshutah, Kippurim*, III, p. 730, n. 37.

[35] Lev. 2.11; cf. my introduction to the *Facsimile Edition of the Sifra*, pp. 35 ff.

[36] See my discussion just mentioned.

[37] Sifra Ahare, *perek* 3.11, 81b.

[38] Mishna Yoma 5.1; see B., ibid., 49b; cf. Yer., ibid., 5.3, 42b, which describes the process somewhat differently, but still as a very difficult task.

[39] B. Yoma, ibid.

[40] Sifra Ahare, *perek* 3.11, 81b; B. Yoma 53a.

[41] See above, pp. 641 ff.

[42] Mishna Yoma 1.5.

[43] See below, pp. 697-699.

[44] Tosefta Yoma 1.8, p. 181, ed. Lieberman II, p. 222.

[45] See above, pp. 641 ff.

[46] Cf. text of this book, pp. 130 ff.

[47] Pp. 121 ff.

[48] Cf. Num. 19.9, and Sifre, ad loc., 124, p. 157.

[49] Lev. 22.6.

[50] Cf. Sifra Shemini, end.

[51] Pp. 661 ff.

[52] These norms were somewhat altered in later Talmudim, see below, pp. 676 ff.

[53] Cf. Sifra Shemini, *perek* 8.9, 53c.

[54] Cf. Mishna Kelim 1.1.

[55] Lev. 12.2, 5.

[56] Sifra Tazria, *perek* 1.7, 58d.

[57] Sifra Emor, *perek* 4.1, 97c.

[58] But cf. below, p. 665.

[59] See below, pp. 736-739.

[60] See text of this book, p. 123.

[61] Lev. 15.16. He is called *tamé* until evening, in the sense that he may not eat the sacrificial foods.

62 Lev. 15.24.

63 Mishna Yoma 1.1. Cf. Sifra, Zav, end.

64 Mishna Temurah 2.1; and cf. Maim. *Yad*, Biat Mikdash, 4.10.

65 B. Yoma 6b.

66 Ibid., 7a.

67 Sifre Deut. 78, p. 143, and references there given.

68 Mishna Zebahim 9.1 ff.

69 Mishna Pesahim 7.7. (It is interesting that this norm should occur in connection with the discussion of the paschal lamb, rather than in connection with the laws of sacrifices generally. Obviously, the norm is intended to reassure the pilgrims, coming to Jerusalem for the Passover, that even if the priest, offering the prescribed portions of their sacrifice on the altar, be impure, the validity of the sacrifice would be unaffected, unless the impurity were known.)

70 B. Pesahim 81b.

71 See text of this book, p. 274.

72 Tosefta, Yom ha-Kippurim, 1.16, p. 182, ed. Lieberman II, p. 226.

73 Cf. Tosefta Zebahim, 12.17, p. 498, which mentions the *tebul yom* offering sacrifice among those who commit a mortal sin (not punishable in human courts, however). Tosefta, however, does not mention the defiled priest; for he was subject to the more severe punishment of *hikkaret* from the moment he entered the Temple precincts. Apparently some Babylonian authorities had this text of the Tosefta, and that is why the question was raised as to whether a defiled person, who offered sacrifice, is subject to the punishment of death at the hands of Heaven or not, and the answer given was that he is not (B. Sanhedrin 82b). Later Babylonian authorities, who knew this *baraita* in another form, including reference to the defiled person, rejected the reply given by Rab Sheshet (ibid. 83a).

73a Mishna Nazir 7.4.

74 Sifra Hobah, *perek* 12.8, 23a.

75 A similar distinction between "lenient periods" and "severe periods" is made in Sifra Emor, *perek* 4.4, 97d. But the passage seems to be a quotation from that in Sifra Hobah. The evidence that the early Hasideans considered the *tebul yom* "pure" in every respect, save that he might not consume the sacrificial meat, in accordance with Lev. 22.7 seems clear. This remains true despite the efforts of the Babylonian Talmud and its commentaries to reconcile the statements deriving from the early Hasideans with the views of R. Akiba and his School. Much of the evidence for the early Hasidean views in this respect is presented in the text here, and in the book itself, pp. 121 ff. However, other evidence, too, is available.

Thus, according to Mishna Negaim 14.8, the healed leper, about to undergo the final ritual of his purification, had to bathe before entering the Temple court through the Gate of Nicanor. The immersion could be required only on suspicion that he might have had a seminal issue or become otherwise defiled during the night, for the healed leper had actually bathed the day before (Mishna, ibid. 14.3). The need for the bath immediately before the final rites of purification logically implied apprehension that somehow the healed leper had become defiled overnight, presumably through a nocturnal emission. R. Judah, who rejected the theory that anyone defiled could become "pure" the same day through bathing, insisted that the ritual bath before entering the Temple was unnecessary (Mishna Negaim 14.8). Had such a suspicion been entertained, the immersion would according to him have been useless. But R. Judah did not believe that a person about to be purified from the defilement associated with leprosy would conceal from the authorities any subsequent impurity which he had incurred. The practice followed at the Temple was instituted by the early Hasideans and Pharisees because they feared that even one about to undergo the rites of purification from leprosy (an impurity which involved many hardships) might indeed fail to tell of subsequent lighter impurity. On the other hand, they held that, even if the healed leper had suffered a seminal emission, the ritual bath made him a *tebul yom*, who was *tahor* and fit to enter the Temple.

The early Hasideans went further. They maintained, according to a *baraita* in B. Zebahim 32b, that a healed leper who had suffered a seminal emission on the day of his purification, could bathe, and then proceed with the usual rituals, despite the fact that he was a *tebul yom* — if this was necessary to enable him to participate in the Passover celebration the following evening.

The Talmud, following R. Akiba's view that a *tebul yom* was *tamê* and therefore punishable by *hikkaret* (complete perdition) if he entered the Temple court, is forced to explain that "because he was permitted to perform the ceremonies of purification despite his former leprous condition, the healed leper was also not barred by the emission." Indeed the *baraita* itself adds to the record of the ancient norm, "Although no other [known] *tebul yom* might enter the Temple court, this one might enter [by placing his head, fingers, and toes in the court], for a commandment, omission of which is punishable by *hikkaret*, supersedes one not involving that punishment." However, as already noted, it seems clear that the recorded Hasidean practice was actually based on the theory that a *tebul yom* might enter the Temple courts, and that the statement in the *baraita* was intended to reconcile that practice with the later view that he might not. While the Temple authorities might ordinarily reject the Hasidean and early Pharisaic lenient views in the actual practice of the Sanctuary, they did not dare deny the Pharisees or their predecessors this right on the eve of the Passover. Large crowds of Pharisaic sympathizers, who might cause a riot should one of the pilgrims held pure by the Hasidean or Pharisaic sages be declared impure by the priests, led the priests to allow conduct they considered forbidden.

The early Hasidean view is further reflected in a question asked of Ben Zoma. Referring to the ritual bath by the High Priest, before performing any act of worship on the Day of Atonement, the disciples of Ben Zoma asked why this bath was necessary since the High Priest had been kept within the Temple precincts all week, so that he might not become defiled, and was kept awake all the night of the Day of Atonement, lest he have a nocturnal emission. Ben Zoma replied, "If when entering from the outer courts to the Holy Shrine, in which the punishment of *hikkaret* is not involved, the High Priest is required to bathe on the Day of Atonement, how much more is he required to do so, when entering from the profane place into the Temple court," where the punishment of *hikkaret* might be involved (see Tosefta Yom ha-Kippurim 1.16, ed. Lieberman II, p. 226, and references and interpretation given in *Tosefta Ki-Fshutah*, ad loc., p. 744).

It seems clear that the questioners alluded to the High Priest only, who was known to be "pure" beyond any doubt. They did not refer to the average priest, required to bathe before entering the Temple courts, for his case was obvious. Such a priest, even if pure, had to bathe, so as to make no distinction among priests. Some priests might be impure; they would require ritual immersion. To prevent any resistance to this practice, all priests, even those claiming that they were undefiled and believed to be so, had to undergo immersion before entering the Temple for worship.

But surely the High Priest who had resided within the general Temple precincts for seven days before Yom Kippur, could be put in a class by himself and be excused from this preliminary immersion. Ben Zoma replied that since on this holy day the High Priest was required to bathe even on leaving the Temple courts to enter the Inner Shrine, it seemed logical that he should also bathe before entering the Temple courts from the less sacred places about them. (This reply would be irrelevant if the discussion concerned any other priest, for as *Tosafot Yeshanim* Yoma 30a points out, in that event Ben Zoma's argument could readily be refuted.) The requirement to bathe before entering the Sacred Shrine applied only on the Day of Atonement, and to the High Priest.

Other priests, entering the Temple structure on other days, to offer incense, or to kindle the lights, were not required to bathe. How then can we infer a norm relating to other priests from a norm established regarding the High Priest on the Day of Atonement? (The reply given by *Tosefta Yeshanim* is extremely forced.)

Moreover, Tosefta (Yom ha-Kippurim, 1.17, ed. Lieberman, p. 227) asserts that if either the High Priest or any other priest failed to bathe in the morning before the service, it was invalid. (According to Professor Saul Lieberman, *Tosefta Ki-Fshutah*, ad loc., this was also the reading of the Babli, loc. cit.). In order to maintain the position that the immersion required was not associated with suspicion of impurity, the commentators assume that the words "who has not bathed" were added simply because of their usual association with the remainder of the text. But this scarcely seems likely. It is far more probable that the service was invalidated because of the suspicion that a priest who had not bathed might be impure. The High Priest (although known to be ritually pure) was put in the same category as other priests by his colleagues who would not admit that the immersion required for them was due to suspicion of impurity.

But Ben Zoma's argument shows that according to him a High Priest failing to bathe before the morning service did *not* invalidate the sacrifice: for Ben Zoma equates such a failure on the part of the High Priest to undergo immersion with failure to bathe between one act of worship and another — a principle definitely rejected in the *baraita* just quoted. We must therefore conclude that the *baraita* transmits a record of actual Temple practice, according to which the authorities, submitting to the Hasidean demand that all priests bathe before entering the Temple to worship and that the High Priest bathe both before the beginning of the service and between each act of worship, denied that these ceremonies were in any way related to suspicion of ritual impurity. (Had they been, the bathing would, as already observed, have been useless; for a *tebul yom* was considered *tamê* by the Temple authorities.) However, according to Ben Zoma, the immersion of the priests before entering the Temple to worship was due only to the apprehension that they were impure. This view was resisted by the Shammaitic priests who, being Pharisees, required the immersion but did not associate it with impurity. That is why R. Judah could not accept Ben Zoma's argument. R. Judah held, first, with R. Akiba that a *tebul yom* was essentially *tamé*; and that the ritual bath would not change his status; and he also preserved the traditions of R. Eliezer (see B. Menahot 18a), deriving as so often from the Pharisaic Temple priests, according to which failure of the High Priest to bathe before the first act of worship invalidated the sacrifice, thus showing that the ritual bath was not associated with any suspected impurity.

There is further evidence that the early Hasideans did not forbid a priest who was a *tebul yom* to eat the heave-offering. The identification of the heave-offering with holy meat mentioned in Lev. 22.7, and which could not be eaten before evening if one became defiled, even if one had bathed (as shown in the text of this Supplement) and recorded in Sifra, *Emor*, *perek* 4.1 ff., 97c, is disputed by another passage in Sifra itself. It seems clear that according to Sifra, *Hobah*, *perek* 12.10, 23d, the holy meat discussed in Lev. 22.1 ff., is only sacrificial meat, and not the heave-offering at all. The Babylonian Talmud (Shebuot 6b), quoting that *baraita* in the Sifra, raises the question of its inconsistency with the general approach of talmudic law, according to which Lev. 22.1 ff. deals with the heave-offering as well as the sacrificial meat. No satisfactory answer is found to this inconsistency. Raba simply replaces the argument of the *baraita* with another, deriving from R. Judah the Patriarch. But it is obvious that R. Judah the Patriarch himself rejected the argument of Sifra, because he accepted the prevailing view of the School of R. Akiba, to which he adhered, namely, that Lev. 22.1 ff. deals with the heave-offering as well as the sacrificial meat. We are thus led to the conclusion that both R. Judah the Patriarch and, in a later century, Raba, recognized that the passage in Sifra *Hobah*, just referred to, follows an entirely different line of reasoning; and that according to it, Lev. 22.1 ff. deals only with sacrificial meat. (For further discussion of the difficulties involved in any other approach to the talmudic discussion in B. Shebuot 6b, see the commentary *Ezrat Kohanim* and *Tosefet ha-Azarah* on Sifra *Hobah*, loc. cit.)

It seems clear, too, that according to at least one authority, presumably the Hillelites, a woman was permitted to eat holy meat after nightfall on the fortieth day after childbirth, and a person suffering with a flow was allowed to do so after nightfall on the seventh day of his cure, provided they each had undergone the required ritual bath. The problem of the woman after childbirth is discussed in connection with the paschal lamb in Tosefta Pesahim 7,11, ed. Zuckermandel, p. 167 (ed. Lieberman is not yet available at the moment of this writing). The passage is cited in the Talmud, Keritot 10a, where the *amoraim* resort to a most complicated interpretation of the passage, in order to reconcile it with the prevailing attitude of the School of R. Akiba. Likewise, an unknown transmitter preserved in B. Pesahim 90b a tradition according to which a woman suffering "from a flow" but cured of the disease, may partake of the paschal lamb after nightfall, if the seventh day of her impurity occurred on the eve of the Passover and she bathed during the day. The transmitter was corrected by the talmudic authority to whom he cited his tradition; for the Mishna explicitly states (Pesahim 8.5) that such a woman may not partake of the paschal lamb until after nightfall on the *eighth* day following her cure, and provided of course she bathed the day before and offered the appropriate sacrifice of atonement on the eighth day itself. However, the passage in Tosefta dealing with the woman in childbirth, and the discussion in this note, suggest that the transmitter recorded the tradition accurately. The views he was reporting were those of the early Hasideans. Once more we note that these views are recorded in relation to the paschal lamb. We must assume that as a matter of practice the early Hasideans were in a position to enforce their point of view on the occasion of this sacrifice, although unable to do so otherwise. The Mishna which records the opposing view obviously follows the dominant position of the School of R. Akiba. But the earlier Hasidean authorities held that a woman during the period of purification after childbirth was *tahor*, except that she could not eat sacrificial meat or enter the Temple until nightfall at the end of the fortieth day (for a male child) or the eightieth day (for a female child). They further held that a person suffering from a flow, and healed, became *tahor* when bathing on the seventh day, although he might not eat sacrificial meat until after immersion and after nightfall that day, and a woman under such circumstances might not cohabit with her husband until nightfall that day.

More evidence pointing to this early attitude of the Hasideans may be marshalled. But that would lengthen this discussion inordinately. It seems patent that the issue of the red heifer arose out of that of the *tebul yom*; and that the early Hasideans considered the *tebul yom tahor* not merely in regard to the ceremonies of the red heifer, but in regard to the heave-offering, going into the Temple (except in the case of the woman after childbirth who is specifically forbidden to do so, Lev. 12.4), and even participating in Temple worship. (For further discussion of the talmudic passages bearing on the subjects touched upon in this note, and on closely related problems, see *Keren Orah*, on Zebahim 17a, as well as 32b, and other discussions cited there; *Siah Yitzhak* on Yoma 30b; *Gilyone ha-Shas* by R. Joseph Engel on Yer. Hallah 3.5 and citations there given; and Professor Saul Lieberman, *Tosefta Ki-Fshutah* I, Terumot, p. 382.

[76] Mishna Niddah 7.6.

[77] Maimonides, with his usual insight, seems to have recognized the difference of opinion on the subject among early talmudic authorities. He inferred from this difference of view that while the *tebul yom* is indeed barred from the Temple precincts, he is not subject to punishment if he entered them. Hence, as Meiri in his commentary to Sanhedrin (83a) observes, Maimonides enumerating in "Laws of the Sanhedrin," ch. 13.1, those guilty of *hikkaret* includes in one class all the "impure" persons who entered the Temple; whereas among those subject to mortal punishment from Heaven (ibid., section 2) he classifies separately the priest worshiping in impurity and the one worshiping as *tebul yom*. It is difficult to reconcile this statement of Maimonides with that cited in the "Laws of Entry into the Temple" (Biat Mikdash 3.14) according to which a *tebul yom* is subject to *hikkaret*

for entry into the Temple. Maimonides' remarks there have also presented other difficulties to the commentators, and it appears that some error has occurred in the transmission of the passage.

[78] Cf. the attempted explanations in Sifra Ahare, *perek* 6.4 ff., 82a.

[79] For further discussion of some of the issues raised in this analysis, cf. A. Geiger, *Kebuzat Ma'amarim*, second edition, pp. 89 ff., and cf. Professor Louis Ginzberg's note, ibid., p. 392.

[80] Cf. text of this book, p. 640.

[81] Lev. 6.16.

[82] Cf. above, p. 128.

[83] B. Shabbat 14b.

[84] Deut. 25.5.

[85] See text of this book, pp. 142 ff.

[86] See below, pp. 720 ff.

[87] Ibid.

[88] See text of this book, p. 144.

[89] See below, p. 774.

[90] See text of this book, p. 144, for references.

[91] Cf., e.g., Exod. 21.28.

[92] Sifra Behukotai, *perek* 12.7, 115a; the correct text is cited by me from the mss. in *Louis Ginzberg Jubilee Volumes*, Hebrew Section, pp. 306 ff.; and cf. note of Professor Saul Lieberman, there, p. 319. My explanation of the *baraita*, given there, should be corrected in accordance with what is stated here. Cf. also Mekilta, Mishpatim, ch. 10, ed. Horovitz, p. 285, 1.10.

[93] See, e.g., citations from ancient texts in James B. Pritchard, *Ancient Near Eastern Texts Relating to the Old Testament*, 1950, pp. 175, 189.

[94] Yer. Sukkah 4.1, 54b. According to R. Johanan the custom was instituted by the exiles who returned from Babylonia (ibid.). But other scholars maintain that the custom was a tradition going back to Moses, and was part of the Oral Law, revealed to him on Mt. Sinai. Cf. B. Ta'anit 3b, where R. Johanan, who ascribed the custom to returning exiles, as already noted, transmitted an earlier tradition to the effect that it was a tradition going back to Moses on Mt. Sinai. On the other hand, scholars like the very early Abba Saul (Yer., ibid.) and R. Nathan (B. Ta'anit, ibid.) derived the rule from the Written Law itself.

[95] See references in preceding note.

[96] See Sifre Num. 150, p. 196, and references there given; and cf. B. Sukkah 43b.

[97] See above, note 94.

[98] So R. Akiba in Sifre, loc. cit. Cf. also B. Ta'anit 25b. To the references given in note 6, to ch. VII, for parallels to the custom of water-libations outside Israel, add now those mentioned by Professor Saul Lieberman in *Hellenism in Jewish Palestine*, p. 132, note 44.

[99] See text of this book, p. 108.

[100] Tosefta Sukkah 3.1, p. 195; B. Sukkah 43b.

[101] See Maimonides, *Hilkot Kiddush ha-Hodesh* 7.1, 7; and cf. note of Rabad,

ibid. See also B. Sukkah 54b, and cf. also, ibid., 43b, and Tosafot, ad loc.; cf. also Yer. Aboda Zara 1.1, 39b, bottom; and B. Rosh ha-Shanah 19b.

[102] See references in preceding note.

[103] Maimonides, *Laws of the Sabbath* 25.6, and references there given in the commentaries.

[104] See below, pp. 754 ff.

[105] See text of this book, pp. 54 ff.

[106] P. 107.

[107] Cf. Mishna Sukkah 5.2.

[108] Ibid., 5.4.

[109] Ibid.

[110] Ibid., 5.1.

[111] Tosefta Sukkah 4.5, p. 198.

[112] Ibid., 4.4.

[113] Cf. *Akiba*, pp. 95 ff.

[114] Josephus, *Antiquities*, XIII, 10.6

[115] B. Sanhedrin 9b.

[116] Mishna, ibid., 4.1.

[117] Mishna Makkot 1.10.

[118] Ibid.

[119] Gen. 2.17.

[120] Ibid., 5.5.

[121] Shekalim 1.4.

[122] Cf. Notes to Supplement, Chapter I, n. 9, p. 882.

[123] Yer. Shekalim 1.4, 46b.

[124] Mishna Shekalim 1.1; cf. Mishna Megillah 3.5.

[125] This view, adopted later by many Pharisaic priests, is reflected in a statement of Rab Huna ben Joshua, preserved in the Talmud (B. Yoma 19a), while elsewhere in the Talmud the issue is raised without being resolved (B. Nedarim 35b).

[126] Mishna Yoma 1.5. The Talmud, loc. cit., reconciles this statement with the view of Rab Huna, cited in the preceding note, only with the utmost difficulty.

[127] Cf. Sifra Emor, *perek* 1.6, 94b.

[128] See above, pp. 655 ff.

[129] Cf. Mishna Zebahim 1.6. This Mishna seems to reflect the views of the Shammaitic priests, c.f. Sifra, Zav, *par.* 4.4, 33d, where part of it is cited in the name of R. Eliezer ben Hyrcanus, who frequently transmits Shammaitic traditions.

[130] So regularly in the *midrashim* from the School of R. Ishmael, doubtless drawing on Hillelite traditions (cf. Sifre Num. 143, p. 191, and references there given).

[131] Cf. Lev. 16.6, and the implications of the High Priest's confession over this bullock, of the transgressions of all the Aaronid priests (Mishna Yoma 4.2).

[132] Lev. 6.12 ff.

[133] Cf. Mishna Temurah 2.1.

[134] This seems to be implied in the statement of R. Judah cited in Sifra Ahare, *perek* 8.8, 83b; B. Yoma 61a; cf. Yer., ibid., 5.7, 43a.

135 Loc. cit.

136 Mishna Temurah 2.1.

137 Tosefta Temurah 1.17, p. 552.

138 Mishna Yoma 3.8; 4.2.

139 Lev. 16.11.

140 This seems implied in the rule that in the interim between the death of one High Priest and the appointment of another, the heirs of the first offer the sacrifice (Mishna Menahot 4.5).

141 Loc. cit.

142 Mishna Shekalim 1.4.

143 I hope to return elsewhere to a discussion of the nature of the sacrifice of the *Omer*.

144 Cf. S. Baer, *Abodat Israel*, p. 102; *Seder R. Amram*, ed. Frumkin, p. 288, variants.

145 Sifre Num. 43, p. 49, end. Another view is reflected in the interpretation of the verse given in Sifre Num. 39, p. 43, line 10, and cf. references there given.

146 See Sifre Num. 39, p. 43, line 10 and cf. references there given.

147 See above note 125.

148 See text of this book, p. 638.

149 Tosefta Sanhedrin 7.6, p. 426.

150 See text of this book, p. 135.

151 See text of this book, p. 272.

152 A controversy on the subject seems to be suggested by Mishna 'Eduyyot 5.5.

153 B. Shabbat 14b.

154 Sifra, Mezora, *perek* 4, end, 77a.

155 See text of this book, pp. 272 ff.

156 Cf. Sifre Num. 116, p. 133.

157 *Abot of Rabbi Nathan*, I, ch. 35, 52b.

158 See text of this book, p. 641.

159 *Kebuzat Ma'amarim*, second edition, pp. 88–89; and cf. notes of Professor Louis Ginzberg, there, pp. 390 f.

160 Above, p. 708.

161 Commentary to Exod., ad loc.

162 See above, pp. 708-709.

163 See Mekilta Mishpatim, ch. 10, p. 277.

164 Mekilta Mishpatim, ch. 8, p. 276, holds that the passage is to be explained literally. A murder intended for one victim, and resulting in the death of another, it insists, is punishable by death. This view is also upheld in Mekilta of R. Simeon, ad loc., p. 176, but it is disputed by R. Judah the Patriarch, who holds that in such instances only damages are due the husband for the death of his wife, for a person intending the death of one victim, and slaying another is free from capital punishment (see B. Sanhedrin 79a; Yer., ibid. 9.6, 27a). Doubtless, the majority view reflects that of the earlier priestly courts, who alone, at one time, could inflict capital punishment, and believed that they were precluded from accepting any "ransom" for a murder.

165 See above, p. 697.
166 Cf. Sifra, Emor, *perek* 20.7, 104d.
167 *Antiquities*, IV, 8.35.
168 Mishna Ketubot 1.5.
169 Mishna Rosh ha-Shanah 1.7.
170 Emor, *perek* 3.12, 97a.
170a While this volume was in press, the commentary of Rabbi Joseph Rosin (*Zafenat Paneah*) appeared under the editorship of Rabbi M. M. Kasher (Jerusalem, 5722). In the comment on Lev. 21.24 he interprets the passage in Sifra as is done herein, and suggests that the same interpretation applies to Sifre Num. 116.
171 Sifre Num. 116, p. 133.
172 Sanhedrin 2.6, 20c.
172a *Antiquities*, IV, 8.14.
173 Cf. my discussion of the subject in *Ha-Perushim ve-Anshe Keneset ha-Gedolah*, pp. 1 ff.
174 Mishna Ketubot 13.1.
175 Mishna Middot 1.2.
176 Mishna Sanhedrin 9, end.
177 Tosefta Kelim 1.6, p. 569.
178 Mishna Sanhedrin 7.2.
179 B. Sanhedrin 52b.
180 Yer., ibid., 7.2, 24b.
181 Sifra *Shemini Miluim* 26, 45a.
182 Ibid., 23.
183 Yer. Hagigah 2.2, 78a; B. Yebamot 90b.
184 Mishna Sanhedrin 1.3.
185 Sifre Num. 131, p. 172.
186 See above, pp. 722 ff.
187 See above, pp. 664 ff.
188 Sifra, Tazria, *perek* 1.7, final passage, 58d; and see Maimonides, *Issure Biah* 4.5
189 Maimonides, ibid., and references there given.
190 See text of this book, p. 642.
191 Ibid.
192 Cf. B. Shabbat 55b. This attitude is also implied in Sifre Num. 8, p. 13; and cf. references there given.
193 See *Kebuzat Ma'amarim*, second edition, p. 90; and notes of Professor Louis Ginzberg, ibid., p. 392.
194 See above, pp. 637 ff., 692.
195 See text of this book, p. 641.
196 Sifre Deut. 237, p. 270; cf. views of R. Eliezer ben Jacob cited above, and reflecting priestly tradition.
197 Sifre Deut. 235, pp. 268 ff.
198 This seems to be the view of R. Eliezer ben Jacob just cited.
199 Mishna Sanhedrin 1.1.
200 Both views are in opposition to those of the Sadducees, just mentioned.

[201] See text of this book, p. 642.

[202] Deut. 25.9.

[203] See text of this book, pp. 145 ff.

[204] P. 146.

[205] *Toledot ha-Emunah ha-Yisraelit* III, 1, pp. 185 ff.

[206] See *Mabo le-Mesektot Abot ve-Abot d'Rabbi Nathan*, pp. 213 ff.; cf. note of Chanoch Albeck to Mishna Sanhedrin 10.1.

[207] Cf. *Hilkot Teshuba* 8.2, and commentaries, ad loc.

[208] Loc. cit.

[209] *Torat ha-Adam*, Shaar ha-Gemul; see also the argument of Rabbi Samson ben Zeman Duran, in *Magen Abot*, Part I, 91a ff.

[210] Compare commentaries on Maimonides, loc. cit.; see also Meiri, Sanhedrin p. 334; cf. R. Margolis, *Margoliot ha-Yam*, Sanhedrin 90a, 4.23; 97b, 17; 107b, 20, and citations there given.

[211] Rabbi Joseph Albo, *Ikkarim*, IV, ch. 31.

[212] *Beer Sheba*, Sanhedrin, ch. XI.

[213] See above, pp. 161 ff.

[214] Cf. Pss. 30.10; 115.17; 118.17; and also Is. 38.18.

[215] Cf. A. M. Haberman, *Megillot Midbar Yehudah*, pp. 123 ff.; 127 ff.

[216] See above p. 742.

[217] I Kings 17.17 f.

[218] II Kings 4.34.

[219] See text of this book, p. 153.

[220] His view may have been shared by the rabbinic author of Sifre Deut. 64 (beg.), p. 130, a passage otherwise extremely difficult to explain, and which Rabbi Elijah of Wilna felt forced to emend radically.

[221] Cf. E. Neufeld in *Hebrew Union College Annual*, XXXI (1960), pp. 31 ff.

[222] See below, pp. 750-751.

[223] See text of this book, p. 153.

[224] *Abot of Rabbi Nathan*, I, ch. 5, 13b.

[225] Cf. Mishna Sanhedrin 10.2 which enumerates Balaam among those denied the Future Life, clearly implying that other Gentiles may share in it (B. Sanhedrin 105a).

[226] P. 148.

[227] See *Jewish Quarterly Review*, N. S., XVI (1925), pp. 22 f.

[228] Cf. text in *Jewish Quarterly Review*, N. S., XVI (1925), pp. 142 ff.

[229] Mishna Sanhedrin 10.1.

[230] See above, note 207.

[231] See above, pp. 170 ff.; 197 ff.

[232] *Harvard Theological Review*, XXXI (1938), pp. 306 ff.

[233] Cf. text of this book, pp. 181 ff.

[234] Mishna Abot 1.1.

NOTES TO SUPPLEMENT CHAPTER III

[1] See above, p. 628, note 1. Hillel's remark denying that the *'am ha-arez* can be a *hasid* (Mishna Abot 2.5) was clearly meant to be paradoxical. The *'am ha-arez* considered himself ultra-pious, because he took the observances which he cared for so seriously. The word *'am ha-arez* in Hillel's maxim should be taken literally, as Maimonides and other great commentators explain. The person who has not mastered the moral and intellectual virtues, which Hasideanism required, could not achieve saintliness, in Hillel's view. Moreover, Hillel held (loc. cit.) that the utterly illiterate, although fearful of transgression, could not be called *yeré het*, "one who is apprehensive of sin"; for he fears simply punishment and evil, and therefore is even more concerned over superstition than over the performance of the commandments.

[2] Cf. A. Geiger, *Kebuzat Ma'amarim*, second edition, pp. 94 f.

[3] Cf. Tosefta Sotah 13.10, p. 320; B., ibid., 48a. According to this record, a large number of the *'am ha-arez* would even separate the tithe. Raba, in Babylonia, held that most of them did (cf. B. Shabbat 13a).

[4] Cf. Tosefta, loc. cit.

[5] There is no evidence that the *'am ha-arez*, generally, violated the laws of the Sabbatical year by working in their fields. (Cf. Tosafot Ketubot 24a, catchword, *Raba*, and references given. Cf. also Mishna Shebi'it 9.1, and commentaries, ad loc.). The *'am ha-arez* was suspect of violating the law forbidding him to protect the grain which had grown in the field without being planted (ibid.) and of using the income derived from sale of his grain during the Sabbatical year for purposes forbidden by the Sages.

[6] Vayyikra R., beg.

[7] Cf. Yer. Gittin 4.3, 45d.

[8] Sifra, Behar, *perek* 2.3, 107a; B. Arakin 32b.

[9] See above, p. 703.

[10] See above, p. 646.

[11] Yer. Demai 4.1, 23d.

[12] Ibid.

[13] Tosefta Sanhedrin 3.4, p. 418.

[14] Tosefta Demai 2.2, p. 68.

[15] Mishna Hagigah 3.6.

[16] Yer. Demai 1.3, 22a.

[17] Tosefta Hagigah 3.19, p. 237.

[18] B. Hullin 35b.

[19] Cf. Sifra, Hobah, *perek* 12.8, 23a, b, and commentary of Rabad, ad loc.; cf. B. Shabbat 13b, and Tosafot, ad loc., catchword *Biyeme*; and *Abot of Rabbi Nathan*, I, ch. 2, p. 8.

[20] See above, note 11.

[21] Mishna Demai 2.5; cf. B. Hullin 6b.

[22] Cf. B. Baba Kamma 119a; and Hullin, loc. cit.

[23] Hullin, loc. cit.

[24] See pp. 754 ff.

[25] Cf. Tosefta Shabbat, ch. 7(8), p. 118, ed. Lieberman V, p. 26.

[26] Cf. Professor Saul Lieberman, *Sheki'in*, pp. 1 ff.

[27] P. 28.

[28] Cf. Mishna Bekorot 6.3.

[29] There is considerable evidence that even in comparatively late talmudic times, incense was offered by peasants, especially women, in their villages. Thus, R. José remarks that a wayfarer, passing a Jewish village, smelling the odor of incense, may not recite a blessing, "for Jewish women offer incense for magical purposes [i.e., to demons]." His colleagues denied this, and held that passing a Jewish village, a person detecting the smell of incense might recite a blessing (B. Berakot 53a). It is probably not an accident that R. José, knowing this custom, denied that one offering a sacrifice "on a rock or a stone" (as incense might be), although violating the law, is subject to no punishment (Mishna Zebahim 13.3). A generation earlier, R. José the Galilean had denied that one who sacrifices even a beast, slaughtered outside the Temple, is to be punished (ibid. 1). R. Eleazar b. Shammua, the colleague of the second R. José, having this approach in mind, declared that one incurs the penalty of *hikkaret* only if one sacrifices outside the Temple both the handful of the meal-offering, which should be offered on the altar, and *also* the incense (ibid. 6). To sacrifice the one without the other involved no penalty. He also held that one incurred punishable guilt only if one sacrificed the whole of the offering, which is set aside for the altar. One incurred no punishment for the sacrifice of simply a part of the offering appropriate for the altar (ibid. 4). R. José further maintained that two people offering a sacrifice together outside the Temple are not subject to punishment (see ibid. 3, quoted anonymously; but quoted in the name of R. José, Sifra Ahare, *perek* 10.2). One who offers the whole meal-offering, rather than the handful required, outside the Temple, incurs no punishment (Mishna Zebahim 13.5). All these leniencies regarding punishment were probably intended to free the person offering such sacrifice outside the Temple from fear of punishment; and to suggest, to those feeling a compulsion to offer such sacrifices, a way to do so, which did not quite resemble the Temple ritual. None of this would have been necessary, were not the customs of offering incense and meal-offerings widespread in the regions where R. José of Galilee, R. José b. Halafta, and R. Eleazar had special influence, and who therefore felt impelled to work out some compromise between the impulse to worship, and the letter of the Law. (Cf. above, note 26, and the reference to Professor Saul Lieberman's remark that Jews offered incense on the tenth of Tebet. Cf. also, Ch. Albeck, notes on Mishna Berakot 4.1.) It is apparently to the practice of offering incense outside the Temple that R. Ammi referred when he asked R. Samuel ben Nahman, "Why does Scripture say, 'And in every place incense is presented unto My Name, even pure meal-offerings' " (Mal. 1.10), whereas the Torah warns against sacrifices outside the Temple. The question would not have been raised had not R. Ammi known of the custom of

Jews to offer incense and meal-offerings outside the Temple; for no one denied that Gentiles might offer sacrifices to God anywhere (cf. B. Zebahim 116a). R. Ammi's question is the more curious since the prophet clearly was referring to sacrifices offered by Gentiles. Obviously, R. Ammi was concerned lest the verse seem to encourage the practice of Jews to offer meal-offerings and incense outside the Temple (see Tanhumah Ahare 9).

[30] Cf. B. Shabbat 9b, and Professor Louis Ginzberg's Commentary on the Yerushalmi, III, p. 51.

[31] Professor Ginzberg, ibid.

[32] B. Shabbat, loc. cit. et passim.

[33] Cf. above, p. 757.

[34] Cf. Mishna Sanhedrin 5.3.

[35] B. ibid., 41b.

[36] II Kings 23.30.

[37] Cf. A. Geiger, *Kebuzat Ma'amarim*, second edition, p. 94.

NOTES TO SUPPLEMENT CHAPTER IV

[1] Above, pp. 638 f.

[2] Cf. above, p. 629.

[3] Cf. below, pp. 771, 773 f.

[4] B. Kiddushin 66a.

[5] *Antiquities*, XIII. 10.5 f.

[6] B. Kiddushin, loc. cit.

[6a] Ibid.

[7] Abot 1.4.

[8] S. v. *Boethus*.

[9] Commentary on Baba Batra 115b.

[10] Hilkot Mamrim 3.3.

[10a] See, however, Professor Saul Lieberman, *Tosefta Ki-Fshutah*, IV, p. 870, and references there given.

[11] Mishna Abot 1.4, 5.

[12] *Abot of Rabbi Nathan*, II, ch. 11, beg. The omission of the statement in *Abot of Rabbi Nathan*, I, is certainly significant. Nevertheless, it is clear from the context, that the two Josés were followers of Antigonus.

[13] Bereshit R., 65.22, p. 742.

[14] Mishna Abot 1.5.

[15] Ibid., 1.6.

[16] Cf. Mishna Sanhedrin 10.1.

[17] See above, p. 750.

[18] Ps. Jonathan, Gen. 4.8.

[19] Cf. Mark 3.6; 12.13.

[20] B. 'Erubin 68b.

[21] See *Mabo* pp. 17 ff.

[22] Cf. Mishna Niddah 4.2; Tosefta Yoma 1.8, p. 181.

[23] Yer. Hagigah 2.2, 77d.

[24] Above, p. 705.

[25] Sifre Num. 112, p. 121. (R. Ishmael himself disagrees with the interpretation of Scripture there given, see ibid.).

[26] Cf. discussion of the subject in *Mabo*, p. 23. See Yer. Gittin, end, where the view reflected in *Abot of Rabbi Nathan*, I, is clearly ascribed to the Shammaites, and the alternative one to R. Akiba.

[27] B. Gittin 56b.

[28] Mishna Bezah 2.6.

[29] Cf. *Akiba*, p. 114.

[30] B. Berakot 29a.

[31] Mishna Abot 2.4.

[32] B. Sanhedrin 107b, in Dikduke Soferim; the passage is lacking in the current editions of the Talmud because of censorship.

[33] Yer. Shabbat 1.3, 3b.

[34] Cf. Maimonides, *Hilkot 'Erubin* 2.16, and commentaries.

NOTES TO SUPPLEMENT CHAPTER V

[1] See *Akiba*, pp. 42 ff.

[2] Above, pp. 633 f.

[3] See pp. 92 ff.; 279 ff.

[4] His invaluable work on the subject (now available in English translation, as the essay entitled, "The Significance of the Halachah for Jewish History," in Louis Ginzberg, *On Jewish Law and Lore*, pp. 77 ff.) remains the classic formulation of the doctrine.

[5] B. Temurah 15b.

[6] B. Baba Mezia 107b; cf. Yer. Shabbat 14.3, 14c; Vayyikra R., ch. 16, p. 363; Debarim R., ed. Lieberman, p. 80.

[7] Yer., loc. cit., cf. notes of Professor Saul Lieberman, in *Vayyikra R.*, ed. M. Margulies, p. 874.

[8] B. Berakot 44a.

[9] B. Shabbat 9b.

[10] Mishna Menahot 13.6.

[11] B. ibid. 107b.

[12] B. Yoma 55a.

[13] B. Nedarim 52b.

[14] B. Baba Mezia 40a.

[15] Ibid. 117a.

[16] Baba Batra 12a.

[17] B. Bekorot 30a.

[18] B. ad loc.

[19] This is the reading of the Yer. Terumot 11.4, 48a, according to R. Solomon Sirillo, see Professor Saul Lieberman, *Tosefta Ki-Fshutah, Demai*, p. 235.

[20] Professor Saul Lieberman, *Tosefta Ki-Fshutah*, loc. cit.
[21] Mishna Ma'aser Sheni 5.2.
[22] Yer., ad loc.
[23] Maimonides, Hilkot Ma'aser Sheni 2.2.
[24] B. Bezah 5b.
[25] Baba Mezia 105b.
[26] Yer. Mo'ed Katan 1.6, 80d.
[27] Yer. Nedarim 1.4, 40c.
[28] Yer. Ma'aser Sheni 5.5, 56b.
[29] Cf. Professor Saul Lieberman, *Hayerushalmi Kiphshuto*, p. 463.
[30] Cf. Professor Saul Lieberman, *Tosefta Ki-Fshutah*, *Hallah*, p. 798.
[31] Tosafot, Baba Kamma 36b, catchword *Veshel.*
[32] Baba Kamma 36b.
[33] Nimmuke Joseph on Baba Kamma 91a.
[34] Pp. 781 f.

ADDITIONAL NOTE

The Pharisaic View Regarding the Law of False Witnesses

The discussions both in the text of this book and the Supplement do not explain why the Pharisees punished false witnesses only if their villainy was discovered after the court's decision.

After all, they had *purposed* to harm their brother at the moment they testified. Why, then, were they unpunished unless the court based its decision on their testimony? Two different answers seem to have been given in the Pharisaic Schools, one by the Shammaites and Proto-Shammaites, the other by the Hillelites and Proto-Hillelites.

According to the Proto-Shammaites and Shammaites, one accused of a capital crime could escape the death penalty, *so long as judgment had not been rendered against him*, through payment of an appropriate fine, perhaps his value in the slave market or his weight in gold. (The sources are unclear on this point.) Only after the court's decision did the injunction (Num. 15.31) against accepting ransom in lieu of capital punishment apply. This tradition is clearly reflected in Sifra, Behukotai, *perek* 12.7, 115a. Thus so long as decision had not been rendered, witnesses accusing an innocent person of a capital crime could claim that they sought not the life of the victim, but to extort money from him or from his friends; for according to Sifra even another could pay the ransom, until the judgment had been given (see my emendation of the current text, on the bases of mss., in Louis Ginzberg, *Jubilee Volume*, Hebrew section, pp. 306 ff.).

As Professor Saul Lieberman points out (ibid., pp. 319 ff.), the case of Jonathan, who escaped the death penalty through popular ransom when he violated his father's oath on behalf of the people (I Sam. 14.45), was an instance of this rule. According to Midrash Shemuel 17, ed. Buber, p. 96, the people paid Jonathan's weight in gold to the Sanctuary and thus redeemed him.

Because a person subject to the *talio* (in other than capital cases) could redeem his limbs even after the court's decision, false witnesses in such cases could in this tradition escape punishment even after the decision, so long as the victim had not been maimed.

The alternative Pharisaic tradition, that of the Hillelites and their predecessors, denied that "eye for eye" should be taken literally under any circumstances. Hence false witnesses in cases of mayhem were guilty only of seeking to impose compensation on their victim and were subject only to monetary penalty.

On the other hand, false witnesses to capital crimes were even in this tradition subject to the *talio*, life for life, because their testimony could have led to the death of the accused. Yet even the Proto-Hillelites and the Hillelites did not consider the false witnesses punishable until the court had rendered a decision, based on their testimony. If exposed before the decision, the false witnesses apparently went unpunished. And this, despite the fact that (unlike the Proto-Shammaites and Shammaites) Proto-Hillelites and the Hillelites seem to have held that one accused of capital crimes could not ransom his life through monetary payment, even before the court's decision. This seems obvious from the tradition preserved in Mekilta Mishpatim, chap. 6, pp. 285 f.; Sifre Num. 161, p. 221, and was apparently the position preserved in the School of R. Ishmael.

However, according to the Proto-Hillelites and Hillelites, witnesses testifying against one could plead for the accused in mitigation of the crime until a decision had been rendered. This view is given anonymously in Sifre Num., loc. cit. It is further preserved by R. José b. R. Judah (of a much later generation) in Tosefta Sanhedrin 9.4, p. 429, and B. ibid., 33b. Indeed it seems possible that according to their view he could actually reverse his testimony until judgment was rendered (see Tosefta Sanhedrin 6.4, p. 424; see variant readings noted by Zuckermandel). Until the moment of decision, the witnesses could therefore claim that they did not *purpose* the execution of the person they accused. They had given false testimony, but had planned to speak in his favor and thus save him. This view seems to have originated in extremely ancient times, and to have been a basic issue of Proto-Hillelism, and therefore appears anonymously in Sifre, loc. cit.

The Sages, whose views are reflected in Mishna Sanhedrin 5.4, Tosefta, ibid., 9.4, p. 429 (anonymously), and in B. Sanhedrin, loc. cit., (anonymously) denied that witnesses could plead in mitigation of the charge, once they had given their testimony. These Sages seem to belong to the Proto-Shammaitic tradition. (The Proto-Hillelite tradition was followed by the Mishna underlying the Yerushalmi, as well as in Ms. Kauffmann, in Sanhedrin 4.1. However, in all other codices and editions, as well as in that underlying the Babylonian Talmud, the text there was emended to conform to the norm given in Mishna Sanhedrin, chap. 5, loc. cit.)

While, according to the Hillelite and Proto-Hillelite tradition, until decision has been rendered against him witnesses testifying to the guilt of the accused could claim that they would have saved him from execution through the plea of mitigating circumstances or through legal argument, they could make this claim only before judgment. Once judgment was given, while it could possibly still be reversed, as long as the accused was alive (Mishna Sanhedrin 4.1), it was obvious that the witnesses had *purposed* to take his life. They had not only testified falsely against him, but had failed to offer any plea on his behalf, so as to prevent judgment against him. Any belated plea in extenuation of the act with which they charged their victim could not save him from punishment. Therefore they were no longer in a position, if exposed as false witnesses, to claim that their intention was ultimately to save the accused from death.

Thus, the problem vexing to so many commentators, who wonder why one condemned to death was put in the same class as one executed, even though the court's judgment could be reversed until the last moment, seems resolved.

Later Rabbinic authorities who, following the Hillelite view, did not accept the principle that one accused of capital crime could purchase immunity before condemnation, emended the *baraita* in Sifra quoted above, in different ways. Their views are preserved in Sifra, loc. cit.; B. Ketubot 37b (two versions), Tosefta 'Arakin, 1.3, p. 543, but these need not be discussed here.

R. Akiba and most members of his School denied (like other Hillelites) that one accused of capital crime could redeem himself through monetary compensation even before the verdict. They also denied that a witness, having once given his testimony, could act as protagonist of the accused. (Hence their preservation intact of Mishna Sanhedrin, chap. 5, quoted above; and their emendation of Mishna Sanhedrin 4.1, in the manner reflected in most codices, edds., and the Babylonian Talmud, as well as in the anonymous view, opposing R. José b. R. Judah.) Yet they did not reject the ancient Pharisaic norm that perjured witnesses to a capital crime were subject to the death penalty as soon as their victim had been condemned by the court, even though this decision was still reversible, through the discovery of new evidence or a new argument for the defense.

They could reconcile these apparently contradictory positions only on the assumption that a person condemned to death, while still subject to rescue through new evidence, was at least in some respects legally dead, the chances of his rescue being remote. Hence they held that anyone offering the Temple either the value or the *erek* of such a person (one of the sums stipulated according to age and sex in Lev. 27.1 ff.) was free from payment (Mishna 'Arakin 1.3).

NOTES TO APPENDIX C

[1] See also Olitzki, *Josephus und die Halacha*, p. 42; H. Weyl, *Die juedischen Strafgesetze bei Josephus Flavius*, p. 101.

[2] It is interesting to note that while Josephus's *halakah* is, generally, that of the Pharisees, in this instance he agrees with the view of R. Eleazar b. Zadok, showing that the priestly-patrician Pharisees did not differ from the Sadducees regarding this question. See *Antiquities*, IV, 8.23, and cf. Weyl, op. cit., p. 104 ff.

[3] See Weyl, op. cit., pp. 98 ff.; and 156; and cf. also, for the view of Philo, Goodenough, *The Jurisprudence of the Jewish Courts in Egypt*, p. 139, and I. Heinemann, *Philons griechische und juedische Bildung*, p. 358 ff.; further discussion of the general subject by Amram, *JQR*, N. S. II (1911–12), p. 210; and in my article, "An Eye for an Eye," in *Menorah Journal*, 1936, p. 212.

[4] In this instance again Josephus agrees with the view attributed to the Sadducees (*Antiquities*, IV, 8.23); see Weyl, loc. cit.

BIBLIOGRAPHY

A. Ancient Sources

Hebrew Scriptures, unless otherwise noted, are cited according to the translation of the Jewish Publication Society, Philadelphia.

Septuagint. Ed. Swete, Cambridge, 1887–1894.
Peshitta. Mosul, 1887.
Vulgate. According to the edition of M. Hetzenauer, Ratisbon and Rome, 1922.
Apocrypha and Pseudepigrapha. Cited according to the translation included in R. H. Charles, Apocrypha and Pseudepigrapha of the Old Testament, Oxford, 1913 (except for special works cited below):
R. H. Charles, The Book of Enoch, Oxford, 1893.
R. H. Charles, The Book of Jubilees, London, 1902.
R. H. Charles, The Greek Versions of the Testaments of the Twelve Patriarchs, Oxford, 1908.
R. H. Charles, The Testaments of the Twelve Patriarchs, London, 1908.
New Testament. Cited according to the Revised Version, unless otherwise noted.

Mishna. Cited from the usual editions.
Tosefta. Ed. Zuckermandel, 1881; second edition with supplement of S. Lieberman, Jerusalem, 1938.
Ed. S. Lieberman, Zera'im, 1955.
Ed. S. Lieberman, Mo'ed, 1962.
Mekilta. Ed. Horowitz-Rabin, Frankfort, 1931. (The edition of J. Z. Lauterbach, vols. 1–3, Philadelphia, 1933–1935, appeared after the notes had been completed).
Babylonian Talmud. According to the usual editions. Where a treatise is cited without further indication, reference is made

to the Babylonian Talmud. References to Mishna, Tosefta, and Yerushalmi are specifically indicated.

Yerushalmi (abbreviated Yer.). Cited according to ed. Krotoschin, 1866.

Sifra. Ed. Weiss, Vienna, 1862.

Sifre Numbers. Ed. Horowitz, Breslau, 1917.

Sifre Deuteronomy. Ed. Friedmann, Vienna, 1864.
Ed. Finkelstein, 1939.

Mekilta of R. Simeon. Ed. D. Hoffmann, Frankfurt-am-Main, 1905.

Sifre Zutta. Ed. Horowitz, published as supplement to Sifre Numbers, cited above.

Midrash Tannaim. Ed. D. Hoffmann, Berlin, 1908.

Megillat Ta'anit. Ed. Hans Lichtenstein, *HUCA*, VIII–IX, (1931–1932), 318–351.

Seder 'Olam Rabbah. Ed. B. Ratner, Vilna, 1894; ed. Alexander Marx, including chapters 1–10, Berlin, 1903.

Abot of R. Nathan. Ed. S. Schechter, Vienna, 1886.

Masseket Semahot. Ed. M. Higger, New York, 1931.

Masseket Kallah. *In* Mesiktot Kallah, ed. M. Higger, New York, 1936.

Masseket Derek Erez. *In* Mesiktot Derek Erez, ed. M. Higger, New York, 1935.

Sheba' Mesiktot Ketanot. Ed. M. Higger, New York, 1930.

Masseket Soferim. Ed. J. Müller, Leipzig, 1878; ed. M. Higger, New York, 1937.

Midrash Rabbah. Cited from ed. Romm, Vilna (Exod. R., Leviticus R., etc.), except for the following:
Genesis Rabbah (Bereshit Rabbah), ed. Theodor-Albeck, Berlin, 1912–1932.
Lamentations Rabbah (Ekah Rabbah), ed. S. Buber, Vilna, 1899.

Pesikta of R. Kahana. Ed. S. Buber, Lyck, 1868.

Pesikta Rabbati. Ed. M. Friedmann, Vienna, 1880.

Midrash Samuel (Midrash Shemuel). Ed. S. Buber, Cracow, 1893.

Midrash Psalms (Midrash Tehilim or Shohar Tob). Ed. S. Buber, Vilna, 1891.

Midrash Proverbs (Midrash Mishle). Ed. S. Buber, Vilna, 1893.
Midrash Tanhuma. Ordinary editions, unless that of S. Buber, Vilna, 1913, is specifically designated.
Pirke de Rabbi Eliezer, Warsaw, 1852.
Sefer Hekalot (see below, A. Jellinek).

B. Literature on the Pharisees

The literature about the Pharisees and the Sadducees constitutes a veritable library. The most important material published until the year 1906, except for Hebrew works, is listed in Schuerer, Geschichte des juedischen Volkes im Zeitalter Jesu Christi, *fourth edition, Leipzig, 1907, 447 ff. Some few works of significance which were omitted from that list, the main discussions of the subject in Hebrew, and the principal publications since that time, are listed below. For the convenience of the student, it has seemed best to separate these works from the general bibliography which follows; and also, in the latter, to list separately rather than alphabetically, the editions and translations used of the standard reference works, the Hebrew Scriptures, the rabbinic texts, and the New Testament.*

I have made no attempt to include the vast number of books and articles written about the Qumram Sect, which deal incidentally with the Pharisees. They fall into a class by themselves, and are so many that it is quite impossible to list them here. The student will have to consult bibliographies in that field for this purpose.

I have also failed to include reference to the great commentaries on the Talmud, and on the classical codes based upon it, taking it for granted that the reader will understand the importance attaching to these books for understanding the Pharisees as well as their opponents. These include works emanating from Eastern Europe, and virtually ignored among all but a few Occidental scholars, such as the Or Sameah *on the code of Maimonides by Rabbi Meir Simhah of Dvinsk, and several which have been produced in the West. Of these the most important it seems to me are Professor Louis Ginzberg's* Commentary on the Talmud of Jerusalem, *Vols. I—IV, and Professor Saul Lieberman's* Tosefta Ki-Fshutah, *the first part of which has already appeared, and the second part of which is now in print. For the same reason, I omit reference to commentaries on classical talmudical works, appearing in Israel, even though they contain discussions of specifi issues raised by the phenomenon of Pharisaism. One of the mos important of these is Professor Chanoch Albeck's edition of th Mishna, with the commentary and supplementary notes. Reference to these works abound in the notes to the Supplement, and testify t their value for the studies here pursued.*

Abner, "Ha-Goremim ha-Kalkaliim ha-Hebrutiim shel Merida ha-Hashmonaim." *Ha-Shiloah*, XXIV (1911), 40 ff., 141 ff. 243 ff.

Abrahams, Israel, Studies in Pharisaism and the Gospels. Firs Series, Cambridge, 1917; Second Series, Cambridge, 1924.

Albright, W. F., From the Stone Age to Christianity; Monothe ism and the Historical Process. Baltimore, 1940. *See* Inde s.v. Pharisees.

———, Archaeology and the Religion of Israel. Baltimore, 1942 156.

*———, "Who Were the Pharisees?" *Menorah Journal*, XXVII No. 2 (April-June 1939), 232 ff.

Allon, G., "The Attitude of the Pharisees toward Roman Ru and the Herodian Dynasty." *Zion*, Third year, IV (July 1938), 300 ff.

———, "How Yabneh Became R. Johanan ben Zakkai's Resi dence." *Zion*, Third year, III (April, 1938), 183 ff.

*———, "Sociological Method in the Study of the Halacha." *In* Mehkarim be-Toledot Yisrael. II, Tel Aviv, 1958, 181 ff.

———, "Tehuman shel Hilkot Toharah." *Tarbiz*, IX, 2 (1938) 194.

Aptowitzer, V., Parteipolitik der Hasmonäerzeit im Rabbi nischen und Pseudoepigraphischen Schrifttum. Vienna, 1927.

Baeck, L., The Pharisees and Other Essays. New York, 1947.

Baer, F., "A Social and Religious History of the Jews" (comment on S. Baron's book) (Hebrew). *Zion*, Third year, IV (July 1938), 281–282.

Bamberger, S., Die Sadduzäer in ihrem Beziehungen zu Alexande Jannai und Salome. Frankfurt-am-Main, 1907.

* Asterisk identifies review of L. Finkelstein, The Pharisees.

BARON, SALO W., A Social and Religious History of the Jews. New York, 1937, I, 163–172; 218–223.

———, The Jewish Community, Its History and Structure to the American Revolution. Philadelphia, 1942. *See* Index s.v. Pharisaism and Pharisees.

*———, *JBL*, LIX (1940), 60–67.

*———, *Review of Religion*, IV, No. 2 (January, 1940), 196 ff.

BELLELI, LAZARE, Mélanges Hébraïques. Paris-Frankfort, 1895, 41–74.

*BENOIT, R. P. P., *Revue Biblique*, XLVIII, No. 2 (April, 1939), 280 ff.

BENTWICH, N., Hellenism. Philadelphia, 1919, 100–113.

BEVAN, E. R., "Jewish Parties and the Law." Cambridge Ancient History. New York-Cambridge, 1932, IX, 406–420.

BICKERMAN, E., "La Charte Séleucide de Jérusalem." *REJ*, C (1935), Nos. 197-198, 31.

BOKSER, B., Pharisaic Judaism in Transition. New York, 1935.

BOOTH, HENRY KENDALL, The Bridge Between the Testaments. New York-London, 1929, 20; 21; 37; 46 ff.; 150; 159.

BOX, G. H., Judaism in the Greek Period (Clarendon Bible, V). Oxford, 1932, 49–56.

———, "Pharisees." In *Encyclopedia of Religion and Ethics*, IX.

———, "Survey of Recent Literature on the Pharisees and the Sadducees." *Review of Theology and Philosophy*, IV, 1908, 129–151.

BRANSCOMB, B. H., Jesus and the Law of Moses. New York, 1930.

CASPARI, W., Die Pharisäer bis an die Schwelle des Neuen Testaments (Biblische Zeit- und Streitfragen, Series V, Heft 7). Berlin, 1909.

CASSUTO, UMBERTO, La Questione della Genesi. Florence, 1934, 31 ff.

CAUSSE, A., Du group ethnique à la communauté religieuse. Le problème sociologique de la religion d'Israël. Paris, 1937, 318 ff.

CHAJES, H. P., "Am ha-Arez e Min." *Rivista Israelitica*, III (1906), 83–96.

Charles, R. H., A Critical History of the Doctrine of a Future Life in Israel, in Judaism, and in Christianity. London, 1899.

———, Apocrypha and Pseudepigrapha of the Old Testament, Oxford, 1913.

Chwolson, D., Das letzte Passamahl. Leipzig, 1908, 115–120; 124–125.

———, Beiträge zur Entwicklungsgeschichte des Judentums. Leipzig, 1910, 15–21.

Cohen, A., "Jewish History in the First Century." *In* Judaism and the Beginnings of Christianity. London, 1920, 1–47.

Cohen, Morris Raphael, "Hoschander's The Priests and Finkelstein's The Pharisees." *In* Reflections of a Wondering Jew. Boston, 1950, 129–138.

*Danby, Herbert, *Journal of Theological Studies*, XL, No. 158 (April, 1939), 169 ff.

Daube, David, "Rabbinic Methods of Interpretation and Hellenistic Rhetoric." *HUCA*, XXII (1949), 239 ff.

Davaine, E., Le Sadducéisme, Étude historique et dogmatique. Montauban, 1888.

Deinard, S. N., "Perushim." In *Ozar Yisrael*, VIII (1912), 300–301.

Denney, J., "The Sadducees and Immortality." *Expositor*, Fourth Series, X (1894), 400–409.

Dubnow, S., Weltgeschichte des juedischen Volkes. Berlin, 1925–1928, 187–200.

Eerdmans, B. D., "Fariceen en Sadduceen." *Theologisch Tijdschrift*, XLVIII (1914), 1–26; 223–230; *See also* Oort, H., ibid., 214 ff.

Ehrenpreis, M., Talmud: Fariseism-Urkristendom. Stockholm, 1933.

Elbogen, I., "Einige neuere Theorien ueber den Ursprung der Pharisäer und Sadduzäer." *Jewish Studies in Memory of Israel Abrahams*, New York, 1927, 135–148.

———, "Judaism." In *Encyclopedia of Social Sciences*, VIII, 1932, 431 ff.

Enelow, H. G., "The Modern Reconstruction of the Pharisees." *In* Selected Works of Hyman G. Enelow, Privately Printed,

New York, 1935, IV, 116–134. Reprinted from *The Methodist Quarterly Review*, July, 1908.

FAIRBAIRN, A. M., "Jesus and the Jews." *Expositor*, Series I, VIII (1878), 431–449.

FAIRWEATHER, W., The Background of the Gospels. Edinburgh, 1908.

FARRAR, F. W., "The Results of the Exile and the Origin of Pharisaism." *Expositor*, Series I, V (second edition, 1879), 81–98.

FELTEN, I., Neutestamentliche Zeitgeschichte. 2d and 3d eds., Regensburg, 1925, I, 2, 403–414.

FINKELSTEIN, L., "The Pharisees: Their Origin and Their Philosophy." *HTR*, XXII (1929), 185–261.

———, Some Examples of the Maccabean Halaka. *JBL*, XLIX (1930), 2–42.

———, Akiba: Scholar, Saint, and Martyr. New York, 1936.

———, Ha-Perushim ve-Anshe Keneset ha-Gedolah. New York, 1950.

———, Mabo le-Mesektot Abot ve-Abot d'Rabbi Natan. New York, 1950, 129–138.

FOERSTER, W., Der Ursprung des Pharisaeismus. *ZNW*, XXXIV (1935), 35–51.

FRIEDLAENDER, M., Die religioesen Bewegungen innerhalb des Judentums im Zeitalter Jesu. Berlin, 1905.

GASTER, M., The Samaritans. London, 1925, 51–57.

GEIGER, A., *See* General Bibliography, Geiger, A.

GINZBERG, L., Eine unbekannte juedische Sekte. New York, 1922.

———, He'arot Shonot. Notes to the second edition of Geiger, Kebuzat Ma'amarim, Warsaw, 1910, 385–387; 392–393; 404–405.

———, Mekomah shel ha-Halakah be-Hokmat Yisrael. Jerusalem, 1931.

———, "The Religion of the Pharisee." *In* Students, Scholars and Saints. Philadelphia, 1928, 88–108.

———, Legends of the Jews. Philadelphia, 1909–1938. *See* Index s.v. Pharisees and Sadducees.

GOLDIN, JUDAH, "The Period of the Talmud." *In* L. Finkelstein,

The Jews: Their History, Culture, and Religion. New York, 1960, 115–216.

GRUENEBAUM, E., Die Sittenlehre des Judentums. 2d ed., Strassburg, 1878.

GUIGNEBERT, CHARLES, The Jewish World in the Time of Jesus, trans. S. H. Hooke. New York, 1951.

GUTTMAN, JEHOSCHUA, "Boethosäer." In *Encyclopaedia Judaica*, IV, 912.

GUTTMAN, MICHAEL, Das Judentum und seine Umwelt. Berlin, 1927.

HALEVY, I., Dorot Ha-Rishonim, I, 3. Frankfurt-am-Main, 1906, 358–546.

HEINEMANN, ISAAK, "The Attitude of the Ancients toward Judaism." *Zion*, Fourth year, IV (July, 1939), 269 ff.

HEINISCH, P., "Pharisäer." In *Lexikon fuer Theologie und Kirche*, VIII (1936), p. 214.

HERFORD, R. TRAVERS, Pharisaism, Its Aim and Method. London-New York, 1912.

———, What the World Owes to the Pharisees. London, 1919.

———, "The Significance of Pharisaism." *In* Judaism and the beginnings of Christianity, London, 1924, 125–166.

———, The Truth about the Pharisees. New York, 1925.

———, The Pharisees. London, 1924.

———, Judaism in the New Testament Period. London, 1928.

HOELSCHER, G., Geschichte der israelitischen und juedischen Religion. Giessen, 1922, 218–224.

HOLLMANN, G., The Jewish Religion in the Time of Jesus. English translation, London, 1909.

HOLTZMANN, H. J., Lehrbuch der Neutestamentlichen Theologie. Tuebingen, 2d ed., 1911, I, 27–60.

HOLTZMANN, O., Juedische Schriftgelehrsamkeit zur Zeit Jesu. Giessen, 1901.

———, Der Prophet Maleachi und der Ursprung des Pharisäerbundes. *Archiv fuer Religionswissenschaft*, XXIX (1931), 1–21.

HOOKE, S. H., "The Way of the Initiate." *In* Judaism and Christianity, I, edited by W. O. E. Oesterley, New York, 1937, 213–233.

HUSSEY, MARY D., "Origin of the Name Pharisee." *JBL*, XXXIX (1920), 66–69.

JACKSON, F., and LAKE, K., The Beginnings of Christianity. London, 1920, I, 1, 110–120.

JACKSON, F., Our Lord and the Pharisees. Leicester, 1910.

JEREMIAS, J., Jerusalem zur Zeit Jesu. II B, Leipzig, 1929, 115–140.

KARLIN, A., "Hillel." *Zion*, Fifth year, II (January, 1940), 170 ff.

KATZ, BEN ZION, " 'Al Ziddukim Rishonim ve-'Aharonim." *Ha-Doar*, XXIX (December 17, 1948), 173–174.

———, Perushim, Ziddukim, Kannaim, Nozrim. Tel Aviv, 1948.

KITTEL, G., Die Probleme des palaestinischen Spaetjudentums und das Urchristentum. Stuttgart, 1926.

KLAUSNER, J., Historia Yisreelit. II, Jerusalem-Tel Aviv, 1924, 99–115.

———, Jeshu ha-Nozri. 2d ed., Jerusalem-Warsaw, 1927, 216–227 (English translation by H. Danby, New York, 1925, 201–228).

KNOX, W. L., "Pharisaism and Hellenism." *In* Judaism and Christianity, II, edited by H. Loewe, London, 1937, 61–111.

KOHLER, K., "Pharisees" and "Sadducees." In *Jewish Encyclopedia*, IX, 661–666; X, 630–633.

KRANOLD, G., Pharisäer und Sadducäer. Beilage zum Jahresbericht des Realgymnasiums zu Magdeburg. Magdeburg, 1897.

LAGRANGE, M. J., Le Messianisme chez les Juifs. Paris, 1909.

LAUTERBACH, J. Z., "A Significant Controversy between the Sadducees and the Pharisees." *HUCA*, IV (1927), 173–207.

———, "The Sadducees and the Pharisees." *Studies in Jewish Literature, issued in honor of Professor Kaufmann Kohler*, Berlin, 1913, 176–198.

———, "The Pharisees and their Teachings." *HUCA*, VI (1929), 69–140.

———, "Midrash and Mishnah." *JQR*, N. S., VI (1915–1916), 55–95.

LESZYNSKY, R., Die Pharisäer und Sadduzäer. Frankfurt-am-Main, 1912.

———, Die Sadduzäer. Berlin, 1912.

———, "Pharisäer" and "Sadduzäer." In *Juedisches Lexikon.* Berlin, 1930, IV, 1, 894–895; IV, 2, 35–36.

LEVI, ISRAEL, "Bibliographie (Review of I. Elbogen, Die Religionsanschauungen der Pharisäer)." *REJ*, XLVIII (1904), 283 ff.

LIEBERMAN, SAUL, Hellenism in Jewish Palestine. New York, 1950.

LIGHTLEY, J. W., Jewish Sects and Parties in the Time of Christ. London, 1925.

LOEWE, HERBERT, "Pharisaism." *In* Judaism and Christianity, I, edited by W. O. E. Oesterley, New York, 1937, 105–192.

———, "The Ideas of Pharisaism." *In* Judaism and Christianity, II, edited by H. Loewe, London, 1937, 3–58.

MACGREGOR, G. H. C. and PURDY, A. C., Jew and Greek, Tutors unto Christ: The Jewish and Hellenistic Background of the New Testament. New York, 1936, 87–102.

MANN, J., "Jesus and the Sadducean Priests." *JQR*, N. S., VI (1915–1916), 415–422.

MANSON, THOMAS WALTER, Sadducee and Pharisee: The Origin and Significance of the Names. Manchester, 1938.

MARCUS, RALPH, "Pharisees, Essenes, and Gnostics." *JBL*, LXXIII (1954), 157 ff.

———, "The Pharisees in the Light of Modern Scholarship." *Journal of Religion*, XXXII, No. 3 (1952), 153 ff.

*MARGOLIOUTH, D. S., *Journal of the Royal Asiatic Society*, January, 1940, 115 ff.

MARGOLIS, M., and MARX, A., History of the Jewish People. Philadelphia, 1927, 153–160.

MARMORSTEIN, A., "Perushim." In *Ozar Yisrael*, VIII (1912), 302–303.

———, "Die Schriftgelehrten." *In* Religionsgeschichtliche Studien, II, Heft, Pressburg, 1912.

MARTI, K., Geschichte der Israelitischen Religion. Strassburg, 1903, 275 ff.

MESSEL, N., Die Einheitlichkeit der juedischen Eschatologie. Giessen, 1915.

MEYER, EDUARD, Ursprung und Anfaenge des Christentums. II, Stuttgart, 1921, 282–329.

MOFFATT, J., "The Righteousness of the Scribes and the Pharisees." *Expository Times*, XIII (1901–1902), 201–206.

MOORE, G. F., Judaism in the First Centuries of the Christian Era. Cambridge, 1927, especially pp. 56–71. (Partly published under the title, "The Rise of Normative Judaism," in *HTR*, XVII [1924], 307–373; XVIII [1925], 1–38).

NASH, H. S., "Pharisees." In *Hastings' one volume Dictionary of the Bible*, 1930, 719 f.

NEUMARK, DAVID, History of Dogmas in Judaism (Hebrew). Odessa, 1918, 165 ff.

OESTERLEY, W. O. E., "The Wisdom Literature: A Sage Among his People." *In* Judaism and Christianity, I, edited by W. O. E. Oesterley, New York, 1937, 59–83.

———, "The Apocalyptic Literature: A Seer Among his People." *In* Judaism and Christianity, I, edited by W. O. E. Oesterley, New York, 1937, 83–101.

———, The Jews and Judaism During the Greek Period. The Background of Christianity. London, 1941, 240–254.

OESTERLEY, W. O. E., and BOX, G. H., The Religion and Worship of the Synagogue. London, 1911, 120–139.

OESTERLEY, W. O. E., and ROBINSON, T. H., Hebrew Religion. New York, 1930, 330–332; 364.

OPPENHEIM, HAYYIM, "Mahaloket ha-Perushim u-Mitnaggedehem be-'Inyan 'Abodat Yom ha-Kippurim." *Bet Talmud*, IV (1884), 227–268.

PARKES, JAMES, "Rome, Pagan, and Christian." *In* Judaism and Christianity, II, edited by H. Loewe, London, 1937, 115–144.

PFEIFFER, ROBERT H., History of New Testament Times, with an Introduction to the Apocrypha. New York, 1949.

———, Introduction to the Old Testament. Revised edition, New York, 1948, 779.

PRAT, F., "Pharisiens." In *Dictionnaire de la Bible*, Paris, 1912, V, 205–218.

Rabin, S., Ziddukim. In *Ozar Yisrael*, IX (1913), 5–6.
Reines, Zev, Torah u-Musar. Jerusalem, 1954.
Riddle, D. W., Jesus and the Pharisees. Chicago, 1928.
Robinson, T. H., Jesus and the Pharisees. *Expository Times*, XXVIII (1916–1917), 550–554.
Robertson, A. T., The Pharisees and Jesus. New York, 1920.
Sachar, A. L., A History of the Jews. New York, 1930, 105–107.
Schechter, S., Some Aspects of Rabbinic Theology. New York 1910.
Schreiner, M., "Was Lehrten die Pharisäer." *Jahrbuch des Verbandes des Vereins fuer Juedische Geschichte und Literatur*, II 1898, 55–74.
Schwarz, A., La victoire des Pharisiens sur les Sadducéens en matière de droit successoral. *REJ*, LXIII (1912), 51–62.
Schweiger, Zvi, "Boethusians" (Hebrew). *Ha-Zofeh*, IX (1926) 288 f.
Segal, M. H., "The Names י"י and אלהים in the Books of the Bible." *Tarbiz*, IX, 2 (1938), 155.
Shaw, G., The Conflict of Jesus. Boston, 1916.
Sieffert, F., "Pharisees." In *New Schaff-Herzog Encyclopedia of Religious Knowledge*, IX, 8a–13b.
Simchoni, Y. N., Kitbe Yoseph ben Mattitiahu: Toledot Milhemet ha-Yehudim im ha-Romaim. Warsaw, 1923, 424 ff
Smith, G. A., Jerusalem, From the Earliest Times to A.D. 70 London, 1907.
Spiegel, S., Ezekiel or Pseudo-Ezekiel. *HTR*, XXIV (1931) 265–272.
Stade-Bertholet, Biblische Theologie des Alten Testaments II, Tuebingen, 1911, 295–322.
Staerk, Willy, Neutestamentliche Zeitgeschichte. Berlin-Leipzig, 1912.
Stein, M., "Yabneh and her Scholars." *Zion*, Third year, I (January, 1938), 118 ff.
Strack-Billerbeck, Kommentar zum Neuen Testament au Talmud und Midrasch. Munich, 1928, V, 334–352.
Thon, J., "Ha-Kittiyut be-Yisrael." *Sefer Zikkaron li-Kebo Shemuel Abraham Poznanski*. Warsaw, 1927, 193–203.

TOY, C. H., Judaism and Christianity, A Sketch of the Progress from the Old Testament to the New Testament. Boston, 1890.

TSCHERIKOWER, A., Ha-Yehudim ve-ha-Yevanim. Tel Aviv-Jerusalem, 1931, 259–269.

TSCHERNOWITZ, CH., Toledoth Ha-Halakah. II, New York, 1936, 217–351.

VOLZ, P., Juedische Eschatologie von Daniel bis Akiba. Tuebingen und Leipzig, 1903.

WAGNER, M., Die Parteiungen im juedischen Volke zur Zeit Jesu (Pharisäer und Sadducäer). Hamburg, 1893.

WEBER, MAX, Gesammelte Aufsaetze zur Religionssoziologie. III, Tuebingen, 1921, 401–442.

WEILL, JULIEN, "L'Essence du Pharisaïsme." *REJ*, LXV (1913), 1–15. (A Review of R. T. Herford, Pharisaism, Its Aim and its Method).

WEISS, I. H., Dor Dor ve-Doreshav. Berlin-New York, 1924, I, 114–123.

WELLHAUSEN, J., Israelitische und juedische Geschichte. Berlin-Leipzig, 1921, 275–294.

YAWITZ, ZEEB, Toledot Yisrael. IV, Berlin, 1911, 156–166.

YOEL, A., "Shitah Hadasha be-Heker Divrei Yemei Yisrael" (Review of Ben Zion Katz, Perushim, Ziddukim, Kannaim, Nozrim). *Ha-Doar*, XXVIII (July 9, 1948), 777 ff. *See also* in this Bibliography, Katz, Ben Zion.

ZEITLIN, S., The History of the Second Jewish Commonwealth. Philadelphia, 1933, 41–56.

———, "The Pharisees" (a review of Herford's The Pharisees), *JQR*, N. S., XVI (1925–1926), 383–394.

———, "The *Am Ha-Arez*." *JQR*, N. S., XXIII (1932), 45–61.

———, "Ha-Ziddukim ve-ha-Perushim." *Horeb*, III, 1937, 56–89.

———, "Nennt Megillat Taanit antisadduzaeische Gedenktage?" *MGWJ*, LXXXI (1937), 351–355.

———, "The Pharisees and the Gospels." *In* Essays and Studies in Memory of Linda R. Miller, ed. Israel Davidson. New York, 1938, 235–286.

C. General Bibliography

Aaron, Elijah ben, Gan Eden, Koslov, 1866.

Abhandlungen zur Erinnerung an Hirsch Perez Chajes, Vienna, 1933.

Abrahams, Israel, Jewish Life in the Middle Ages. (New edition by Cecil Roth). London, 1932.

———, *see* Jewish Studies in Memory of Israel Abrahams.

Adcock, F. E., "The Reform of the Athenian State." *Cambridge Ancient History*, IV, 26–58.

Aescoly, A. Z., "Ha-Halakah Ve-ha-Minhag ben Yehude Habash (Ha-Palashim)." *Tarbiz*, VII (1935–1936), 121–134.

———, "Teshubah le-Halakah." *Tarbiz*, VII (1935–1936), 380–387.

Albeck, Chanoch, "Das Buch der Jubilaeen und die Halacha." *In* Siebenundvierzigster Bericht der Hochschule fuer die Wissenschaft des Judentums in Berlin. Berlin, 1930.

———, Untersuchungen ueber die halakischen Midraschim. Berlin, 1927.

Albert, Edwin, Die israelitisch-juedische Auferstehungshoffnung in ihren Beziehungen zum Parsismus. Koenigsberg, 1910.

Albrecht, Karl, "Das Geschlecht der hebraeischen Hauptwoerter." *ZAW*, XVI (1896), 41–121.

Albright, William F., The Archaeology of Palestine and the Bible. New York, 1932.

———, "A Biblical Fragment from the Maccabaean Age: the Nash Papyrus." *JBL*, LVI (1937), 145–176.

———, "The Seal of Eliakim and the Latest Preexilic History of Judah, with Some Observations on Ezekiel." *JBL*, LI (1932), 77–106.

Alt, Albrecht, "Das Gottesurteil auf dem Karmel." *Festschrift Georg Beer*. Stuttgart, 1935, 1–18.

———, "Hiskia." *Die Religion in Geschichte und Gegenwart*, II, 1935–1937.

———, "Das Institut im Jahre 1924." *Palaestinajahrbuch*, XXI (1925), 5–58.

———, Israel und Aegypten. Die politischen Beziehungen der

Koenige von Israel und Juda zu den Pharaonen nach den Quellen untersucht. Leipzig, 1909.

———, "Jerusalems Aufstieg." *ZDMG*, LXXIX (1925), 1–19.

———, "Nachwort ueber die territorialgeschichtliche Bedeutung von Sanheribs Eingriff in Palaestina." *Palaestinajahrbuch*, XXV (1929), 80–88.

———, "Die Rolle Samarias bei der Enstehung des Judentums." *Festschrift Otto Procksch*. Leipzig, 1934, 5–28.

———, Die Staatenbildung der Israeliten in Palaestina. Leipzig, 1930.

AMRAM, DAVID W., "Retaliation and Compensation." *JQR*, N. S., II (1911–1912), 191–211.

ANDREAS, FRIEDRICH CARL, *see* Festschrift Friedrich Carl Andreas.

APTOWITZER, V., "בשכמל"ו, Geschichte einer liturgischen Formel." *MGWJ*, LXXIII (1929), 93–118.

———, "Scheeltoth und Jelamdenu." *MGWJ*, LXXVI (1932), 558–575.

———, "Spuren des Matriarchats im juedischen Schrifttum." *HUCA*, IV (1927), 207–240; V (1928), 261–297.

———, "Die syrischen Rechtsbuecher und das mosaisch-talmudische Recht." Sitzungsberichte der Kaiserlichen Akademie der Wissenschaften in Wien, CLXIII (1909).

ARISTOTLE, "Politics." (Translated by H. Rackham). London, 1933. *In* "The Loeb Classical Library."

BAER, S., Abodat Israel. Roedelheim, 1868.

BAKELESS, JOHN E., The Economic Causes of Modern War; A Study of the Period: 1878–1918. New York, 1921.

BANETH, EDUARD, Ursprung der Sadokaeer und Boethosaeer. Dessau, 1882.

BARON, SALO W., "Uklese Yisrael bi-Yeme Ha-Melakim." *Abhandlungen .... Chajes*. (Hebrew Section). 76–136.

BATTEN, L. W., "Hosea's Message and Marriage." *JBL*, XLVIII (1929), 257–273.

BAUER, LEONHARD, Volksleben im Lande der Bibel. Leipzig, 1903.

BEARD, CHARLES A., "The City's Place in Civilization." *American City*, XXXIX (1928), 101–103.

BEER, GEORG. *See* Festschrift Georg Beer.

BEGRICH, JOACHIM, Die Chronologie der Koenige von Israel und Juda und die Quellen des Rahmens der Koenigsbuecher. Tuebingen, 1929. *In* "Beitraege zur historischen Theologie."

———, "Der syrisch-ephraimitische Krieg und seine weltpolitischen Zusammenhaenge." *ZDMG*, LXXXIII (1929), 213–237.

Beitraege zur alttestamentlichen Wissenschaft; Karl Budde zum siebzigsten Geburtstag. Giessen, 1920.

BELKIN, S., The Alexandrian Halakah in Apologetic Literature of the First Century C.E. Philadelphia, 1936.

BELOCH, JULIUS, Die Bevoelkerung der griechisch-roemischen Welt. Leipzig, 1886.

———, Griechische Geschichte. 3 vols., Strassburg, 1904–1914.

BEN ZVI, I., Sefer Ha-Shomeronim. Tel-Aviv, 1935.

BENZINGER, IMMANUEL, Hebraeische Archaeologie. 3d ed., Leipzig, 1927.

BERRY, GEORGE, "The Title of Ezekiel (I 1–3)." *JBL*, LI (1932), 54–57.

———, "Was Ezekiel in the Exile?" *JBL*, XLIX (1930), 83–93.

BERTHOLET, ALFRED, "Zur Frage des Verhaeltnisses von persischem und juedischem Auferstehungsglauben." *Festschrift Friedrich Carl Andreas*. Leipzig, 1916.

———, Hesekiel. Tuebingen, 1936. *In* "Handbuch zum alten Testament."

———, Die israelitischen Vorstellungen vom Zustand nach dem Tode. Freiburg, 1899.

———, Die Stellung der Israeliten und der Juden zu den Fremden. Freiburg, 1896.

BEVAN, EDWYN R., Jerusalem under the High Priests. Five Lectures on the Period between Nehemiah and the New Testament. London, 1904.

———, and Charles Singer, The Legacy of Israel. Oxford, 1927.

BEWER, JULIUS A., *see* Smith, John M. P., Ward, William H., and Bewer, Julius A.

———, "Joel." A Critical and Exegetical Commentary on Micah, Zephaniah, Nahum, Habbakkuk, Obadiah and Joel. New York, 1911. *In* "The International Critical Commentary."

———, The Literature of the Old Testament in its Historical Development. New York, 1924.

———, "The Text of Ezek. 1:1–3." *AJSL*, L (1934), 96–101.

Billerbeck, P., *see* Strack, Hermann L. and Billerbeck, P.

Black, J. Sutherland, *see* Cheyne, T. K., and Black, J. Sutherland.

Blau, Ludwig, "Origine et histoire de la lecture du Schema et des formules de bénediction qui l'accompagnent." *REJ*, XXXI (1895), 179–201.

Bloch, Moshe A., *see* Emlekkonyv, Bloch Mozes. Budapest, 1905.

Boeklen, Ernst, Die Verwandtschaft der juedisch-christlichen mit der parsischen Eschatologie. Goettingen, 1902.

Bogardus, Emory S., "The City: Spatial Nearness and Social Distance." *Sociology and Social Research*, XIII (1928–1929), 572–577.

Bousset, Wilhelm, Die Religion des Judentums im Spaethellenistischen Zeitalter. (Edited by Hugo Gressmann). Tuebingen, 1926. *In* "Handbuch zum neuen Testament."

Breasted, James H., The Dawn of Conscience. New York, 1933.

Brentano, Lujo, Das Wirtschaftsleben der antiken Welt. Vorlesungen gehalten als Einleitung zur Wirtschaftsgeschichte des Mittelalters. Jena, 1929.

Briffault, Robert, The Mothers. The Matriarchal Theory of Social Origins. New York, 1931.

Briggs, Charles A., *see* Brown, Francis, Driver, S. R., and Briggs, Charles A.

Brown, Francis, Driver, S. R., and Briggs, Charles A., A Hebrew and English Lexicon of the Old Testament. Boston, 1906.

Bruell, N., "Ha-mahlekot ben ha-Perushim ve-ha-Ziddukim." *Bet Talmud*, I (1881), 240–245, 270–278.

———, "He'arot Shonot." *Bet Talmud*, IV (1884), 7–11.

Budde, Karl, "Habakuk." *ZDMG*, LXXXIV (1930), 139–147.

———, "Jesaja und Ahaz." *ZDMG*, LXXXIV (1930), 125–138.

———, "The Nomadic Ideal in the Old Testament." *New World*, IV (1895), 726–745. Translated from "Das nomadische Ideal im alten Testament." *Preussische Jahrbuecher*, LXXXV (1896), 57–79.

———, "Zum Eingang des Buches Ezechiel." *JBL*, L (1931), 20–41.

———, "Zwei Beobachtungen zum alten Eingang des Buches Jesaja." *ZAW*, XXXVIII (1919–1920), 58.

———, *see* Beitraege zur alttestamentlichen Wissenschaft; Karl Budde zum siebzigsten Geburtstag.

Budge, E. A. Wallis, The Teaching of Amen-Em-Apt, Son of Kanekht. London, 1924.

Buechler, Adolf, "Familienreinheit und Familienmakel in Jerusalem vor dem Jahre 70." *Festschrift Adolf Schwarz*. Berlin, 1917, 133–162.

———, Der galilaeische 'Am-ha 'Ares des Zweiten Jahrhunderts. Beitraege zur innern Geschichte des palaestinischen Judentums in den ersten zwei Jahrhunderten. Vienna, 1906.

———, "Halakot le-Ma'aseh ke-Bet Shammai bi-Zeman ha-Bayit ve-'ahar ha-Hurban." *Bloch Festschrift* (Hebrew Section). Budapest, 1905, 21–30.

———, "Review of Documents of Jewish Sectaries by S. Schechter." *JQR*, N. S., III (1912–1913), 429–485.

———, Die Priester und der Cultus im letzten Jahrzehnt des jerusalemischen Tempels. Vienna, 1895.

———, Die Tobiaden und die Oniaden im II. Makkabaeerbuche und in der verwandten juedisch-hellenistischen Litteratur. Vienna, 1899.

Buhl, Frants, Kanon und Text des alten Testaments. Leipzig, 1891.

———, Die socialen Verhaeltnisse der Israeliten. Berlin, 1899.

Burgess, Ernest W., ed., The Urban Community. Chicago, 1926.

———, *see* Park, Robert E., Burgess, Ernest W., and McKenzie, Roderick D.

Buttenwieser, Moses, "The Date and Character of Ezekiel's Prophecies." *HUCA*, VII (1930), 1–18.

———, "Where Did Deutero-Isaiah Live?" *JBL*, XXXVIII (1919), 94–112.

Cambridge Ancient History, The. 9 vols., New York, 1923–1936.

Cambridge Bible for Schools and Colleges, The. Cambridge, 1879–1930.

Carpenter, Niles, The Sociology of City Life. New York, 1931.

Carter, George W., Zoroastrianism and Judaism. Boston, 1918.

Caspari, Wilhelm, Die israelitischen Propheten. Leipzig, 1914.

———, Lieder und Gottesprueche der Rueckwanderer (Jesaja 40–55). Giessen, 1935. *In* "Beihefte Zeitschrift fuer alttestamentliche Wissenschaft."

Cassuto, U., "Jesaja." *Encyclopaedia Judaica*, IX, 4–13.

———, "Ha-Perek ha-sheni be-Sefer Hoshe'a." *Livre d'hommage à Dr. S. Poznanski.* (Hebrew Section). Warsaw, 1927, 115-135.

Causse, A., Les dispersés d'Israël. Les origines de la Diaspora et son rôle dans la formation du Judaisme. Paris, 1929.

———, Les "Pauvres" d'Israël (Prophetes, Psalmistes, Messianistes). Strasbourg, 1922.

———, Les Prophètes d'Israël et les religions de l'Orient. Essai sur les origines du monothéisme universaliste. Paris, 1913.

Century Bible, The. 11 vols., London, 1913.

Chajes, H. P., *see* "Abhandlungen zur Erinnerung an Hirsch Perez Chajes."

Clay, A. T., *see* Hilprecht, H. V., and Clay, A. T.

Cobb, William H., "Where Was Isaiah XL–LXVI Written?" *JBL*, XXVII (1908), 48–64.

Cook, Stanley A., Critical Notes on Old Testament History. The Traditions of Saul and David. London, 1907.

———, "The Fall and Rise of Judah." *Cambridge Ancient History*, III, 388–414.

———, "A Pre-Massoretic Biblical Papyrus." *Proceedings of the Society of Biblical Archaeology*, XXV (1903), 34–56.

———, *see* Smith, William R., Lectures on the Religion of the Semites.

Cooke, G. A., A Critical and Exegetical Commentary on the Book of Ezekiel. 2 vols., New York, 1937. *In* "The International Critical Commentary."

Cowley, Arthur E., Aramaic Papyri of The Fifth Century B.C. Oxford, 1923.

CRAWLEY, A. E., "Dress." *Encyclopaedia of Religion and Ethics*, V, 40–72.

CROOK, MARGARET B., "Some Cultural Principles in Hebrew Civilization." *JBL*, L (1931), 156–175.

DAHL, GEORGE, "Some Recent Interpretations of Second Isaiah." *JBL*, XLVIII (1929), 362–377.

DAICHES, SAMUEL, The Jews in Babylonia in the Time of Ezra and Nehemiah According to Babylonian Inscriptions. London, 1910.

DALMAN, GUSTAF, "Das alte und das neue Jerusalem und seine Bedeutung im Weltkriege." *Palaestinajahrbuch*, XI (1915), 17–38.

———, Arbeit und Sitte in Palaestina. 5 vols., Guetersloh, 1928–1937.

———, "Jahresbericht des Instituts fuer das Arbeitsjahr 1912–1913." *Palaestinajahrbuch*, IX (1913), 3–74.

———, Jerusalem und sein Gelaende. Guetersloh, 1930.

———, "Ein neugefundenes Jahvebild." *Palaestinajahrbuch*, II (1906), 44–50

———, Sacred Sites and Ways. Studies in the Topography of the Gospels. (Translated by Paul P. Levertoff). New York, 1935.

DAVIDSON, ISRAEL, Parody in Jewish Literature. New York, 1907.

DERENBOURG, HARTWIG, "Un Dieu nabatéen ivre sans avoir bu de vin." *REJ*, XLIV (1922), 124–126.

DERENBOURG, JOSEPH, Essai sur l'histoire et la géographie de la Palestine, d'après les Thalmuds et les autres sources rabbiniques. 1st part. Paris, 1867.

DEWEY, JOHN, and TUFTS, JAMES H., Ethics. New York, 1928.

DIAMOND, ARTHUR S., Primitive Law. London, 1935.

DIODORUS SICULUS, ed. Fischer. Leipzig, 1906.

DONIACH, N. S., Purim or the Feast of Esther. An Historical Study. Philadelphia, 1933.

DOUGHERTY, R. P., Nabonidus and Belshazzar, A Study of the Closing Events of the New Babylonian Empire. (Yale Oriental Series, XV). New Haven, 1929.

DOUGHTY, CHARLES M., Travels in Arabia Deserta. Boston, 1921.

Driver, G. R., "Textual and Linguistic Problems of the Book of Psalms." *HTR*, XXIX (1936), 171–195.

———, *see* Brown, Francis, Driver, S. R., and Briggs, Charles A.

Duerr, Lorenz, Ezechiels Vision von der Erscheinung Gottes (Ez. c. I, v. 10) im Lichte der vorderasiatischen Altertumskunde. Wuerzburg, 1917.

———, Ursprung und Ausbau der israelitisch-juedischen Heilandswartung. Berlin, 1925.

Duhm, Bernard, Das Buch Jesaia. Goettingen, 1902. *In* "Handkommentar zum alten Testament."

Ebeling, Erich, ed., Aus dem Leben der juedischen Exulanten in Babylonien. Babylonische Quellen. Berlin, 1914.

Eichrodt, Walther, "Vorsehungsglaube und Theodizee im Alten Testament." *Festschrift Otto Procksch.* Leipzig, 1934, 45–70.

Eisenstein, J. D., ed., Ozar ha-Midrashim. 2 vols., New York, 1915.

Eissfeldt, Otto, "Eli und die Eliden." *Die Religion in Geschichte und Gegenwart*, II, 104.

———, Erstlinge und Zehnten im alten Testament. Ein Beitrag zur Geschichte des israelitisch-juedischen Kultus. Leipzig, 1917.

———, Die Komposition der Samuelisbuecher. Leipzig, 1931.

———, Krieg und Bibel. Tuebingen, 1915.

———, "Samuelisbuecher." *Die Religion in Geschichte und Gegenwart*, V, 106–108.

———, "Uebersehene Angaben der Bibel zur Geschichte des Landes Juda unter den Assyren, Babyloniern und Persern. Ezechiel als Zeuge fuer Sanheribs Eingriff in Palaestina." *Palaestinajahrbuch*, XXVII (1931), 58–66.

Elbogen, Ismar, Der juedische Gottesdienst in seiner geschichtlichen Entwicklung. 2d ed., Frankfurt-am-Main, 1924.

Elbogen, J., Die Religionsanschauungen der Pharisaeer mit besonderer Beruecksichtigung der Begriffe Gott und Mensch. Berlin, 1904.

Emlekkonyv, Bloch Mozes, Budapest, 1905.

Encyclopedia Biblica. A Critical Dictionary of the Literary, Political and Religious History, the Archaeology, Geography and Natural History of the Bible. 4 vols., New York, 1899–1903.

Encyclopedia of Religion and Ethics. 12 vols., New York, 1908–1922.

Encyclopedia of the Social Sciences. 15 vols., New York, 1930–1935.

Epstein, A., "Buechler, Adolf, Prof. Dr., Die Priester und der Cultus im letzten Jahrzehnt des Jerusalemischen Tempels." *MGWJ*, XL (1896), 138–144.

———, ed., Eldad ha-Dani. Pressburg, 1891.

Epstein, Louis M., The Jewish Marriage Contract. A Study in the Status of the Woman in Jewish Law. New York, 1927.

Erbt, Wilhelm, Die Hebraeer. Kanaan im Zeitalter der hebraeischen Wanderung und hebraeischer Staatengruendungen. Leipzig, 1906.

Erman, Adolf, Aegypten und aegyptisches Leben im Altertum. (New edition by Hermann Ranke). Tuebingen, 1923.

———, "Eine aegyptische Quelle der 'Sprueche Salomos.'" *Sitzungsberichte der Preussischen Akademie der Wissenschaften*, XV (1924), 86–93.

Ewald, Heinrich G., Commentary on the Prophets of the Old Testament. (Translated by Frederick Smith). 5 vols., London, 1875–1881.

———, Geschichte des Volkes Israel. 3d ed., 8 vols., Goettingen, 1864–1868.

———, The History of Israel. 3d ed., 5 vols., London, 1876–1878.

———, Die Propheten des Alten Bundes. 2d ed., 3 vols., Goettingen, 1867–1868.

Feigin, S., "Mappalat Sanherib be-'Erez Yehudah." *Horeb*, II (1935), 7–36.

———, "Milhemet Sanherib bi-Yehudah." *Ha-Doar*, XVI (1937), 427–428.

Feitelowitz, J. N., "Ha-Halakot ha-Meshuarot shel ha-Palashim." *Tarbiz*, VIII (1935–1936), 373–379.

Festschrift, Adolf Schwarz, zum siebzigsten Geburtstage. Berlin, 1917.

Festschrift, Friedrich Carl Andreas. Leipzig, 1916.

FESTSCHRIFT, GEORG BEER, zum 70. Geburtstage. Stuttgart, 1935.

FESTSCHRIFT, OTTO PROCKSCH. Leipzig, 1934.

FICHTNER, JOHANNES, Die altorientalische Weisheit in ihrer israelitisch-juedischen Auspraegung. Giessen, 1933. *In* "Beihefte Zeitschrift fuer alttestamentliche Wissenschaft."

FINKELSTEIN, LOUIS, "The Birkat Ha-Mazon." *JQR*, N. S., XIX (1928–1929). 211–262.

———, "The Book of Jubilees and the Rabbinic Halaka." *HTR*, XVI (1923), 39–61.

———, "Ch. Albeck: Das Buch der Jubilaeen und die Halacha" (A Review). *MGWJ*, LXXVI (1932), 525–534.

———, "The Development of the Amidah." *JQR*, N. S., XVI (1925–1926), 1–43, 127–170.

———, "An Eye for an Eye." *Menorah Journal*, XXIV (1936), 207–218.

———, "The Institution of Baptism for Proselytes." *JBL*, LII (1933), 203–211.

———, "Introductory Study to Pirke Abot." *JBL*, LVII (1938), 13–50.

———, Jewish Self-Government in the Middle Ages. New York, 1924.

———, "La Kedouscha et les benedictions de Schema." *REJ*, XCIII (1932), 1–26.

———, "The Origin of the Synagogue." *Proceedings of the American Academy for Jewish Research* (1928–1930), 49–59.

FINKELSTEIN, MAURICE, "Judicial Self-Limitation." *Harvard Law Review*, XXXVII (1923–1924), 338–364.

FINKELSTEIN, S. I., En Simeon. St. Louis, 1924.

FLIGHT, J. W., "The Nomadic Idea and Ideal in the Old Testament." *JBL*, XLII (1923), 158–226.

FOWLER, WILLIAM W., Social Life at Rome in the Age of Cicero. New York, 1909.

FRAENKEL, Z., Ueber den Einfluss der palaestinischen Exegese auf die alexandrinische Hermeneutik. Leipzig, 1851.

FRANK, TENNEY, Aspects of Social Behavior in Ancient Rome. Cambridge, 1932.

———, An Economic History of Rome. Baltimore, 1927.

———, ed., An Economic Survey of Ancient Rome. 3 vols., Baltimore, 1933–1937.

FRAZER, JAMES G., Folk-Lore in The Old Testament. Studies in Comparative Religion, Legend and Law. 3 vols., London, 1918.

———, The Golden Bough. A Study in Magic and Religion. 2 vols., New York, 1929.

FRIEDLAENDER, ISRAEL, "Bonfires on Purim." *JQR*, N. S., I (1910–1911), 257–258.

———, Past and Present: A Collection of Jewish Essays. Cincinnati, 1919.

FRIEDMANN, M., "Jarobh-am oder die Theilung des Reiches." *Jubelschrift zum siebzigsten Geburtstage des Prof. Dr. H. Graetz.* Breslau, 1887, 131–161.

———, (abbreviated מא"ש) "Ta'ama d'Kera." *Bet Talmud*, III (1884), 351.

GALL, AUGUST F. VON, ΒΑΣΙΛΕΙΑ ΤΟΥ ΘΕΟΥ. Eine religionsgeschichtliche Studie zur vorkirchlichen Eschatologie. Heidelberg, 1926.

GALPIN, CHARLES J., *see* Sorokin, Pitrim A., Zimmerman, Carle C., and Galpin, Charles J., eds.

Gedenkbuch zur Erinnerung an David Kaufmann. Breslau, 1906.

GEIGER, ABRAHAM, "Betulah me-'Amav." *He-Haluz*, V (1860), 73–75.

———, Kebuzat Ma'amarim. 2d ed., Warsaw, 1910.

———, "Neuere Mittheilungen ueber die Samaritaner." *ZDMG*, XVI (1862), 714–728.

———, "Sadducaeer und Pharisaeer." *Juedische Zeitschrift fuer Wissenschaft und Leben*, II (1863), 11–54.

———, "Somekos ha-Ma'atik ha-Yevani." *He-Haluz*, V (1860), 27–31.

———, Uhrschrift und Uebersetzungen der Bibel in ihrer Abhaengigkeit von der innern Entwicklung des Judenthums. Breslau, 1857.

———, Nachgelassene Schriften. (Edited by Ludwig Geiger). 5 vols., Berlin, 1875–1877.

GEIGER, LUDWIG, ed., Abraham Geigers Nachgelassene Schriften. 5 vols. Berlin, 1875–1877.

GINSBERG, H. L., Kitbe Ugarit. Jerusalem, 1936.

GINZBERG, LOUIS, "Anthropomorphism." *Jewish Encyclopedia*, I, 621–625.

———, "Boethusians." *Jewish Encyclopedia*, III, 284–285.

———, "Cabala." *Jewish Encyclopedia*, III, 456-479.

———, Geonica. 2 vols., New York, 1909.

———, Ginze Schechter. Genizah Studies in Memory of Doctor Solomon Schechter. 2 vols., New York, 1928–1929.

———, The Legends of the Jews. 7 vols., Philadelphia, 1909–1938.

———, "Tamid. The Oldest Treatise of the Mishnah." *Journal of Jewish Lore and Philosophy*, I (1919), 33–44, 265–295.

GIST, NOEL P., and HALBERT, L. A., Urban Society. New York, 1933.

GLAHN, LUDVIG, and KOEHLER, LUDWIG H., Der Prophet der Heimkehr (Jesaja 40–66). Kopenhagen, 1934.

GOITEIN, S. D., "Ha-Makor 'ha-'Arabi' shel Yisrael ve-Dato." *Zion*, II (1937), 1–18.

GOLDMAN, FELIX, Der Oelbau in Palaestina zur Zeit der Mishnah. Pressburg, 1907.

GOLDMAN, SOLOMON, The Jew and the Universe. New York, 1936.

GOOCH, GEORGE P., Nationalism. London, 1920.

GOODENOUGH, ERWIN R., The Jurisprudence of the Jewish Courts in Egypt. Legal Administration by the Jews Under The Early Roman Empire as Described by Philo Judaeus. New Haven, 1929.

GORDIS, ROBERT, The Biblical Text in the Making: A Study of the Kethib-Qere. Philadelphia, 1937.

———, "Sectional Rivalry in the Kingdom of Judah." *JQR*, N. S., XXV (1934–1935), 237–255.

GRAETZ, H., "Die Echtheit des Buches des Propheten Ezechiel." *MGWJ*, XXIII (1874), 433–446, 515–525.

———, Geschichte der Juden von den aeltesten Zeiten bis auf die Gegenwart. 11 vols. in 13, Leipzig, 1897–1911.

———, *see* Jubelschrift zum siebzigsten Geburtstage des Prof. Dr. H. Graetz.

GREENSTONE, JULIUS H., The Messiah Idea in Jewish History. Philadelphia, 1906.

GRESSMANN, HUGO, Altorientalische Texte und Bilder zum Alten Testament. Berlin, 1926.

———, "Die Haartracht der Israeliten." *Budde Festschrift.* Giessen, 1920, 61–68.

———, Israels Spruchweisheit im Zusammenhang der Weltliteratur. Berlin, 1925.

———, "Die literarische Analyse Deuterojesajas." *ZAW*, XXXIV (1914), 254–297.

———, "Die neugefundene Lehre des Amen-em-ope und die vorexilische Spruchdichtung Israels." *ZAW*, XLII (1924), 272–296.

———, Die orientalischen Religionen im hellenistisch-roemischen Zeitalter. Berlin, 1930.

———, ed., Die Religion des Judentums im spaethellenistischen Zeitalter. Tuebingen, 1926.

———, Der Ursprung der israelitisch-jüdischen Eschatologie. Goettingen, 1905.

GRIHYA-SUTRAS, Rules of Vedic Domestic Ceremonies, The. Translated by Herman Oldenberg. The Sacred Books of the East. (Edited by Max Mueller). Vol. 30, Oxford, 1892.

GUEDEMANN, MORITZ, Geschichte des Erziehungswesens und der Cultur der Juden in Frankreich und Deutschland. Vienna, 1880.

GUNKEL, HERMANN, Geschichten von Elisa. Berlin.

———, "Samuel." *Die Religion in Geschichte und Gegenwart*, V, 104–106.

GUTTMANN, HEINRICH, Die Darstellung der Jüdischen Religion bei Flavius Josephus. Breslau, 1928.

HALBERT, L. A., *see* Gist, Noel P., and Halbert, L. A.

Handbuch zum neuen Testament. Tuebingen, 1909–1926.

Handwoerterbuch der Staatswissenschaften. 3d ed., 8 vols., Jena, 1909.

HARRIS, ZELLIG S., *see* Montgomery, James A., and Harris, Zellig S.

Harvard Theological Review, The. New York, Cambridge, 1908 et seq.

HASEBROEK, JOHANNES, Griechische Wirtschafts- und Gesellschaftsgeschichte bis zur Perserzeit. Tuebingen, 1931.

Hebrew Union College Annual. Cincinnati, 1904 et seq.

HEINEMANN, ISAAK, Philons griechische und juedische Bildung. Kulturvergleichende Untersuchungen zu Philons Darstellung der juedischen Gesetze. Breslau, 1932.

HEITLAND, WILLIAM E., Agricola. A Study of Agriculture and Rustic Life in the Greco-Roman World from the Point of View of Labor. Cambridge, 1921.

HERNER, SVEN, "Athalja." *Marti Festschrift.* Giessen, 1925, 137–141. *In* "Beitraege zur alttestamentlichen Wissenschaft."

HERNTRICH, VOLKMAR, Ezechielprobleme. Giessen, 1932. *In* "Beihefte Zeitschrift fuer alttestamentliche Wissenschaft."

HERRMANN, JOHANNES, Ezechiel. Uebersetzt und Erklaert. Leipzig, 1924.

———, Die soziale Predigt der Propheten. Berlin, 1911. *In* "Biblische Zeit- und Streitfragen."

HERZFELD, LEVY, Handelsgeschichte der Juden des Altertums. Braunschweig, 1879.

HESIOD, "Works and Days." Homeric Hymns and Homerica. (Translated by H. G. Evelyn-White). London, 1914. *In* "The Loeb Classical Library."

HIGGER, MICHAEL, Intention in Talmudic Law. New York, 1927.

HILPRECHT, H. V., and CLAY, A. T., The Babylonian Expedition of the University of Pennsylvania. Business Documents of Murashu Sons of Nippur. Series A, IX, X, Philadelphia, 1898–1904.

HOBHOUSE, L. T., Morals in Evolution. A Study in Comparative Ethics. New York, 1916.

HOELSCHER, GUSTAV, Hesekiel. Der Dichter und das Buch, eine literarkritische Untersuchung. Giessen, 1924.

———, Die Propheten. Untersuchungen zur Religionsgeschichte Israels. Leipzig, 1914.

———, Der Sadduzaeismus. Eine kritische Untersuchung zur spaeteren juedischen Religionsgeschichte. Leipzig, 1906.

HOFFMAN, DAVID, Das Buch Deuteronomium. Uebersetzt und Erklaert. 2 vols., Berlin, 1913–1922.

———, Das Buch Leviticus. Uebersetzt und Erklaert. 2 vols., Berlin, 1905–1906.

———, Zur Einleitung in die halachischen Midraschim. Berlin. *In* "Beilage zum Jahresbericht des Rabbiner-Seminars zu Berlin 5647 (1886–87)."

———, Zur Einleitung in den Midrasch Tannaim zum Deuteronomium. Frankfurt-am-Main, 1909. (Reprinted from *Jahrbuch der juedisch-literarischen Gesellschaft*, VI [1908], 304–323.)

———, Die Zeit der Omer-Schwingung und des Wochenfestes. *In* "Jahres-Bericht des Rabbiner-Seminars fuer orthodoxes Judentum pro 5634 (1873–1874)." Berlin.

Holdsworth, William S., A History of English Law. 4th ed., 9 vols., London, 1926.

Holmes, Oliver W., "Agency." Collected Legal Papers. New York, 1920. Reprinted from *The Harvard Law Review*, IV (1891–1892), 345–364; V (1892–1893), 1–23.

———, The Common Law. Boston, 1881.

Honor, Leo L., Sennacherib's Invasion of Palestine. A Critical Source Study. New York, 1926.

Horodezky, S. A., "Jerusalem." *Encyclopaedia Judaica*, VIII, 1115–1198.

Hoschander, Jacob, The Book of Esther in the Light of History. Philadelphia, 1923.

Humbert, Paul, "La Logique de la perspective nomade chez Osée et l'unité d'Osée." *Marti Festschrift*, Giessen, 1925, 158–166. *In* "Beiträge zur alttestamentlichen Wissenschaft."

———, Recherches sur les sources égyptiennes de la Littérature sapientale d'Israel. Neuchatel, 1929.

Huntington, Ellsworth, Palestine and its Transformation. Boston, 1911.

International Critical Commentary on the Holy Scriptures of the Old and New Testaments, The. New York, 1910 et seq.

Jacob, Benno, Das erste Buch der Tora, Genesis. Berlin, 1934.

James, Fleming, "Thoughts on Haggai and Zechariah." *JBL*, LIII (1934), 229–235.

James, William, "The Moral Equivalent of War." Memories and Studies. New York, 1911.

JELLINEK, A., ed., Sefer Hekalot. *Bet Ha-Midrasch*, II (1873), 170–176.

JEREMIAS, ALFRED, Das alte Testament im Lichte des alten Orients. Leipzig, 1930.

———, Juedische Froemmigkeit. 2d ed., Leipzig, 1929.

Jewish Encyclopedia, The. 12 vols., New York, 1901–1906.

Jewish Quarterly Review, The. New Series. Philadelphia, 1910 et seq.

Jewish Studies in Memory of Israel Abrahams. New York, 1927.

JIRKU, ANTON, Altorientalischer Kommentar zum alten Testament. Leipzig, 1923.

———, Das weltliche Recht im alten Testament. Stilgeschichtliche und rechtsvergleichende Studien zu den juristischen Gesetzen des Pentateuchs. Guetersloh, 1927.

JOSEPHUS, FLAVIUS, "Antiquities." (Translated by H. St. J. Thackeray and Ralph Marcus). 6 vols., London, 1926–1937. *In* "The Loeb Classical Library."

———, Complete Works. (Whiston's translation). 4 vols. in 3, New York, 1902.

Journal of Biblical Literature, The. 1882 et seq.

Jubelschrift zum siebzigsten Geburtstage des Prof. Dr. H. Graetz. Breslau, 1887.

JONES, H. STUART, and LAST, HUGH, "The Early Republic." *Cambridge Ancient History*, VII, 436–482.

JUDAH, B. SAMUEL (R. Yehudah he-Hasid), Sefer Hasidim. (Edited by Wistinetzki-Freimann). Frankfurt-am-Main, 1924.

JUSTER, JEAN, Les Juifs dans l'empire romain. Leur condition juridique, économique et sociale. Paris, 1914.

KAATZ, S., Die muendliche Lehre und ihr Dogma. Vol. I, Leipzig, 1922. Vol. II, Berlin, 1923.

KAPLUN-KOGAN, WLADIMIR W., Die Wanderbewegungen der Juden. Bonn, 1913.

KAUFMANN, DAVID, Geschichte der Attributenlehre in der Juedischen Religionsphilosophie des Mittelalters von Saadja bis Maimuni. Gotha, 1877.

———, *see* Gedenkbuch zur Erinnerung an David Kaufmann.

KAUFMANN, EZEKIEL, Matenot Ha-Kodesh, Ziyyunim. (Simhoni Memorial Volume). Berlin, 1929, 101–115.

———, Toledot Ha-'Emunah Ha-Yisre'elit. 2 vols., Jerusalem, 1937.

KENNETT, R. H., Ancient Hebrew Social Life and Custom as Indicated in Law, Narrative and Metaphor. London, 1933.

KENT, C. B. R., The Early History of the Tories, from the Accession of Charles the Second to the Death of William the Third (1660–1702). London, 1908.

KESSLER, WERNER, Die innere Einheitlichkeit des Buches Ezechiel. Dargestellt auf Grund einer methodischen Besinnung und in Auseinandersetzung mit Gustav Hoelschers "Hesekiel, der Dichter und das Buch." Herrnhut, 1926. *In* "Berichte des theologischen Seminars der Bruedergemeinde in Herrnhut."

KITTEL, R., "Cyrus und Deuterojesaja." *ZAW*, XVIII (1898), 149–162.

———, Geschichte des Volkes Israel. 4th and 5th eds., 2 vols., Gotha, 1921–1922.

———, Die hellenistische Mysterienreligion und das alte Testament. Stuttgart, 1924. *In* "Beitraege zur Wissenschaft vom alten Testament."

———, Die Psalmen. 5th and 6th eds., Leipzig, 1929.

KLAMROTH, ERICH, Die juedischen Exulanten in Babylonien. Leipzig, 1912.

KLEIN, HUGO, Das Klima Palaestinas auf Grund der alten hebraeischen Quellen. *ZDPV*, XXXVII (1914), 217–249, 297–327.

KLEIN, SAMUEL, "Arba' ve-'Esrim Bulaot she-bi-Yehudah." *Abhandlungen . . . Chajes* (Hebrew Section). 279–301.

———, Beitraege zur Geographie und Geschichte Galilaeas. Leipzig, 1909.

———, Juedisch-palaestinisches Corpus Inscriptionum (Ossuar-Grab- und Synagogeninschriften). Vienna, 1920.

———, "Kleine Beitraege zur Erklaerung der Chronik." *MGWJ*, LXXX (1936), 195–206.

———, "Weinstock, Feigenbaum und Sykomore in Palaestina." *Festschrift Adolf Schwarz*. Berlin, 1917, 389–402.

KOEBERLE, JUSTUS, Soziale Probleme im alten Israel und in der Gegenwart. Wismar, 1907.

KOEHLER, LUDWIG H., "Archaeologisches." *ZAW*, XXXIV (1914), 146–149.

———, Deuterojesaja (Jesaja 40–55). Giessen, 1923.

———, *see* Glahn, Ludvig, and Koehler, Ludwig H.

KOHLER, KAUFMANN, Heaven and Hell in Comparative Religion. With special Reference to Dante's Divine Comedy. New York, 1923.

———, "מקום und Makam." *ZAW*, XXXIV (1914), 73–74.

KOHUT, A., "Was hat die talmudische Eschatologie aus dem Parsismus aufgenommen?" *ZDMG*, XXI (1867), 552–591.

KOLBE, WALTHER, Beitraege zur syrischen und juedischen Geschichte. Kritische Untersuchungen zur Seleukidenliste und zu den beiden ersten Makkabaeer-buechern. Stuttgart, 1926.

Kommentar zum alten Testament. Leipzig, 1917–1924.

KRAUSS, SAMUEL, "Die Ehe zwischen Onkel und Nichte." *In* Studies in Jewish Literature issued in honor of Professor Kaufmann Kohler, Berlin 1913, 165–175.

———, "Huke Yehezke'el be-Yahasam 'el Torat Moshe." *Ha-Shiloah*, VII (1901), 109–118.

———, Synagogale Altertuemer. Berlin, 1922.

———, Talmudische Archaeologie. 3 vols., Leipzig, 1910–1912.

KROPOTKIN, PETER, Memoirs of a Revolutionist. Boston, 1899.

———, Mutual Aid. A Factor of Evolution. London, 1904.

KUGLER, FRANZ X., Von Moses bis Paulus. Forschungen zur Geschichte Israels. Muenster, 1922.

KUHL, CURT, "Neue Dokumente zum Verstaendnis von Hosea 2:4–15." *ZAW*, LII (1934), 102–109.

LAKE, KIRSOPP, "The Council of Jerusalem described in Acts XV." *Jewish Studies in Memory of Israel Abrahams*. New York, 1927, 244–265.

LANDAU, MARCUS, Hoelle und Fegfeuer in Volksglaube, Dichtung und Kirchenlehre. Heidelberg, 1909.

LAST, HUGH, *see* Jones, H. Stuart, and Last, Hugh.

LAUTERBACH, JACOB Z., "Tashlik. A Study in Jewish Ceremonies." *HUCA*, XI (1936), 207–340.

LEVIN, SHMARYA, Youth in Revolt. (Translated by Maurice Samuel). New York, 1930.

LEVINTHAL, ISRAEL H., The Jewish Law of Agency. *JQR*, N. S., XIII (1922–1923), 117–191.

LEWIN, B. M., Ozar ha-Geonim. 7 vols., Jerusalem, 1928–1935.

LEWY, J., "Sanherib und Hizkia." *Orientalische Literatur-Zeitung*, XXXI (1928), 150–163.

LICHTENSTEIN, HANS, "Die Fastenrolle, eine Untersuchung zur juedisch-hellenistischen Geschichte." *HUCA*, VIII–IX (1931–1932), 257–351.

LINFORTH, IVAN M., Solon the Athenian. Berkeley, 1919.

LITTMAN, ENNO, "Deux Inscriptions religieuses de Palmyre le Dieu." *Journal Asiatique*, N. S., XVIII (1901), 374–390.

Livre d'hommage à la mémoire du Dr. Samuel Poznanski, offert par les amis et les compagnons du travail scientifique. Warsaw, 1927.

LOEW, IMMANUEL, Die Flora der Juden. 3 vols. in 4, Vienna, 1924–1928.

LOEW, LEOPOLD, Gesammelte Schriften. 5 vols. Szegedin, 1889–1900.

LUETGERT, W., Das Problem der Willensfreiheit in der vorchristlichen Synagoge. Halle, 1906.

LURJE, M., "Materialistische Fragen zu der Evolutsie von der Yidisher Religie." (Yiddish). *Visenschaftleche Yorbicher* (Moscow), I (1929), 34–55.

———, Studien zur Geschichte der wirtschaftlichen und sozialen Verhaeltnisse im israelitisch-juedischen Reiche von der Einwanderung in Kanaan bis zum babylonischen Exil. Giessen, 1927.

MACIVER, ROBERT M., Society: Its Structure and Changes. New York, 1931.

MCCURDY, JAMES F., History, Prophecy and the Monuments, or Israel and the Nations. New York, 1914.

MCKENZIE, RODERICK D., *see* Park, Robert E., Burgess, Ernest W., and McKenzie, Roderick D.

MAINE, HENRY J. S., Ancient Law. Its Connection with the Early

History of Society, and its Relation to Modern Ideas. 3d American ed., New York, 1887.

MAITLAND, FREDERIC W., *see* Pollock, Frederick, and Maitland, Frederic W.

MALTER, HENRY, "Purim." *The Jewish Encyclopedia*, X, 274–279.

MARMORSTEIN, A., The Doctrine of Merits in Old Rabbinical Literature. London, 1920.

———, "A New Corpus Inscriptionum." *Palestine Exploration Fund Quarterly Statement*, 1921, 187–190.

MAY, HERBERT G., "An Interpretation of the Names of Hosea's Children." *JBL*, LV (1936), 285–291.

MAYNARD, JOHN A., "The Home of Deutero-Isaiah." *JBL*, XXXVI (1917), 213–224.

MEINHOLD, JOHANNES, Einfuehrung in das alte Testament, Geschichte, Literatur und Religion Israels. Giessen, 1919.

MEISSNER, BRUNO, Babylonien und Assyrien. 2 vols., Heidelberg, 1920–1925.

MENES, ABRAM, "Die sozialpolitische Analyse der Urgeschichte." *ZAW*, XLIII (1925), 33–62.

———, "Tempel und Synagoge." *ZAW*, L (1932), 268–276.

———, Die vorexilischen Gesetze Israels im Zusammenhang seiner kulturgeschichtlichen Entwicklung. Giessen, 1928. *In* "Beihefte Zeitschrift fuer alttestamentliche Wissenschaft."

MERX, A., "Der Werth der Septuaginta fuer die Textkritik des alten Testamentes." *Jahrbuecher fuer Protestantische Theologie*, IX (1883), 65–77.

METIN, ALBERT, Le Socialisme sans doctrines: la question agraire et la question ouvrière en Australie et Nouvelle-Zélande. Paris. 1901.

MEYER, EDUARD, "Die Bevoelkerung des Altertums." *Handwoerterbuch der Staatswissenschaften*. 3d ed., II, 898–913.

———, Die Entstehung des Judenthums. Eine historische Untersuchung. Halle a. S., 1896.

———, Geschichte des Altertums. 2d ed., 3 vols. in 5, Stuttgart, 1907–1937.

———, Die Israeliten und ihre Nachbarstaemme. Alttestamentische Untersuchungen. Halle a. S., 1906.

———, Julius Wellhausen und meine Schrift die Enstehung des Judentums. Halle a. S., 1897.

———, Kleine Schriften. 2nd ed., 2 vols., Halle a. S., 1924.

———, Der Papyrusfund von Elephantine. Dokumente einer juedischen Gemeinde aus der Perserzeit und das aelteste erhaltene Buch der Weltliteratur. 2d ed., Leipzig, 1912.

———, Ursprung und Anfaenge des Christentums. II, Stuttgart, 1921, 282–329.

Mitteis, L., and Wilcken, U., Grundzuege und Chrestomathie der Papyruskunde. Leipzig, 1912.

Monatsschrift fuer Geschichte und Wissenschaft des Judentums. 1852 et seq.

Montgomery, James A., and Harris, Zellig S., The Ras Shamra Mythological Texts. Philadelphia, 1935.

———, The Samaritans. The Earliest Jewish Sect, Their History, Theology, and Literature. Philadelphia, 1907.

Moore, George F., "Fate and Free Will in the Jewish Philosophies According to Josephus." *HTR*, XXII (1929), 371–389.

Morgenstern, Julian, "The Book of the Covenant. The Huqqim." *HUCA*, VIII–IX (1931–1932), 1–150.

———, "The Three Calendars of Ancient Israel." *HUCA*, I (1924), 13–78.

———, "Two Ancient Israelite Agricultural Festivals." *JQR*, N. S., VIII (1917–1918), 31–54.

Moses b. Maimon (Maimonides), Moreh Nebukim (Dalalat al-Hairin), ed. S. Munk. Paris, 1861–1866. (English translation by M. Friedlaender, second edition, London, 1928; Hebrew translation by Judah ibn Tibbon, Warsaw, 1872; Part I, in critical edition with commentary by J. Kaufman, Tel-Aviv, 1935).

Moulton, James H., Early Zoroastrianism. London, 1926.

Mowinckel, Sigmund, "Die Komposition des deuterojesajanischen Buches." *ZAW*, XLIX (1931), 87–112, 242–260.

———, Psalmstudien. Vol. I, Awaen und die individuellen Klagenpsalmen; vol. II, Das Thronbesteigungsfest Jahwes und der Ursprung der Eschatologie. Christiania, 1921–1922.

Mueller, Max, *see* The Grihya-Sutras Rules.

NESTLE, EBERHARD, Die israelitischen Eigennamen nach ihrer Religionsgeschichtlichen Bedeutung. Haarlem, 1876.

NEVINSON, HENRY W., Last Changes, Last Chances. London, 1928.

NIKOLSKI, N., "A Nay Buch vegn der Sotsial-Ekonomisher Geshichte fun Folk Yisroel." *Zeitschrift* (Minsk), II-III (1928), 165–184.

NOTH, M., "Die Ansiedlung des Stammes Juda auf dem Boden Palaestinas." *Palaestinajahrbuch*, XXX (1934), 31–47.

———, "Gemeinsemitische Erscheinungen in der israelitischen Namengebung." *ZDMG*, LXXXI (1927), 1–45.

OELGARTE, T., "Die Bethhoronstrasse." *Palaestinajahrbuch*, XIV (1918), 73–89.

OESTERLEY, W. O. E., ed., Judaism and Christianity. 2 vols., New York, 1937.

———, "The 'Teaching of Amen-em-ope' and the Old Testament." *ZAW*, XLV (1927), 9–24.

———, The Wisdom of Egypt and the Old Testament in the Light of the Newly Discovered 'Teaching of Amen-em-ope'. London, 1927.

OLDENBERG, HERMAN, *see* The Grihya-Sutras Rules.

OLITZKI, MARCUS, Flavius Josephus und die Halacha. Berlin, 1885.

OLMSTEAD, ALBERT T., History of Palestine and Syria to the Macedonian Conquest. New York, 1931.

OPPENHEIMER, F., "Machtverhaeltnis." *Handwoerterbuch der Soziologie*. Stuttgart, 1931, 338–348.

———, System der Soziologie. 4 vols., 8 parts, Jena, 1922–1935.

Palaestinajahrbuch des deutschen evangelischen Instituts fuer Altertumswissenschaft des heiligen Landes zu Jerusalem. Berlin, 1904 et seq.

PARK, ROBERT E., BURGESS, ERNEST W. and MCKENZIE, RODERICK D. The City. Chicago, 1925.

PATON, LEWIS B., "The Case for the Post-Exilic Origin of Deuteronomy." *JBL*, XLVII (1928), 322–358.

PAVRY, JAL D. C., The Zoroastrian Doctrine of a Future Life, from Death to the Individual Judgment. New York, 1926.

Peake, A. S., ed., Jeremiah and Lamentations. The Century Bible. London, 1913.

Pedersen, Johs., Israel. Its Life and Culture. 2 vols., Copenhagen, 1926.

Perles, Felix, "D. Chwolson: Beitraege zur Entwickelungsgeschichte des Judentums . . ." (A Review). *Orientalische Literatur-Zeitung*, XIV (1911), 357–359.

———, Zur Erklaerung der Psalmen Salomos. *Orientalische Literatur-Zeitung*, V (1902), 269–282, 335–342, 365–372.

Petermann, Theodor, "Die geistige Bedeutung der Grossstaedte." *Die Grossstadt. Vortraege und Aufsaetze zur Staedteaufstellung*. Dresden, 1903.

Pfeiffer, Robert H., "Images of Yahweh." *JBL*, XLV (1926), 211–222.

———, "Three Assyriological Footnotes to the Old Testament." *JBL*, XLVII (1928), 184–187.

Philonis Opera Quae Supersunt. Edited by Leopold Cohn and Paul Wendland. 7 vols. in 8, Berlin, 1886–1930.

Pineles, F., Darkah shel Torah. Vienna, 1861.

Plato, "Laws." The Dialogues of Plato. (Translated by B. Jowett). 3d ed., 5 vols., Oxford, 1924.

Poehlman, Robert von, Geschichte der sozialen Frage und des Sozialismus in den antiken Welt. 3d ed., 2 vols., Munich, 1925.

Pollock, Frederick, and Maitland, Frederic W., The History of English Law. 2d ed., 2 vols., Cambridge, 1911.

Poznanski, Samuel, "Jacob ben Ephraim, ein antikaraeischer Polemiker des X. Jahrhunderts." *Gedenkbuch zur Erinnerung an David Kaufmann*. Breslau, 1900, 169–187.

———, "Karaite Miscellanies." *JQR*, VIII (1896), 681–704.

———, "M. Klumel's 'Mischpatim'; F. Kaufman's אביב." *JQR*, XVI (1903–1904), 402–408.

———, *see* Livre d'hommage à la mémoire du Dr. Samuel Poznanski . . .

Procksch, Otto, "Die Berufungsvision Hesekiel." *Budde Festschrift*. Giessen, 1920, 141–149.

———, "Das Jerusalem Jesajas." *Palaestinajahrbuch*, XXVI (1930), 12–40.

———, Jesaia I, Uebersetzt und Erklaert. Leipzig, 1930.

———, Der Staatsgedanke in der Prophetie. Guetersloh, 1933.

———, *see* Festschrift Otto Procksch.

QUIDDE, LUDWIG, Caligula. Eine Studie ueber roemischen Caesarenwahnsinn. 2d ed., Leipzig, 1894.

RAD, GERHARD VON, "Die levitische Predigt in den Buechern der Chronik." *Festschrift Otto Procksch*, Leipzig, 1934, 113–124.

RADIN, MAX, "The Kid and Its Mother's Milk." *AJSL*, XL (1923–24), 209–218.

———, The Life of the People in Biblical Times. Philadelphia, 1929.

RAMSAY, W. M., "Phrygians." *Encyclopaedia of Religion and Ethics*, IX, 900–911.

REINACH, SOLOMON, Cults, Myths and Religions. (Translated by Elizabeth Frost). London, 1912.

REVEL, BERNARD, The Karaite Halakah and its Relation to Sadducean, Samaritan, and Philonian Halakah. Part I, Philadelphia, 1913.

Revue des Études Juives. Paris, 1880 et seq.

RIDDLE, DONALD W., "The Non-Septuagint Element in the Vocabulary of Paul." *JBL*, XLVII (1928), 74–90.

RITTER, BERNHARD, Philo und die Halacha. Eine vergleichende Studie unter steter Beruecksichtigung des Josephus. Leipzig, 1879.

ROSENTHAL, FRANZ, Vier apokryphische Buecher aus der Zeit und Schule R. Akibas. Leipzig, 1885.

ROST, LEONHARD, Die Ueberlieferung von der Thronnachfolge Davids. Stuttgart, 1926.

ROSTOVTZEFF, M., A History of the Ancient World. (Translated from the Russian by J. D. Duff.) 2 vols., Oxford, 1926–1927.

———, The Social and Economic History of the Roman Empire. Oxford, 1926.

ROTHSTEIN, JOHANN, "Die Bedeutung von Gen. 6: 1–4 in der gegenwaertigen Genesis." *Budde Festschrift*, Giessen, 1920, 150–157.

———, Juden und Samaritaner, die grundlegende Scheidung von Judentum und Heidentum. Leipzig, 1908.

Rudolph, W., "Sanherib in Palaestina." *Palaestinajahrbuch*, XXV (1929), 59–80.

Ruppin, Arthur, Soziologie der Juden. 2 vols., Berlin, 1930–1931.

Ryle, Herbert, The Canon of the Old Testament. An Essay on the Gradual Growth and Formation of the Hebrew Canon of Scripture. London, 1892.

Sachau, Eduard, Drei aramaeische Papyruskunden aus Elephantine. Berlin, 1908.

Sayce, Archibald H., ed., Records of the Past. Being English Translations of the Ancient Monuments of Egypt and Western Asia. 6 vols., London, 1889–1893.

Schaeder, Hans H., Esra der Schreiber. Tuebingen, 1930.

———, Iranische Beitraege. Vol. I, Halle, 1930.

Schechter, Solomon, Documents of Jewish Sectaries. Vol. I, Fragments of a Zadokite Work; vol. II, Fragments of the Book of Commandments by Anan. Cambridge, 1910.

———, "Genizah Fragments." *JQR*, XVI (1903–1904), 425–452, 776–777.

———, "Reply to Dr. Buechler's Review of Schechter's 'Jewish Sectaries.'" *JQR*, N. S., IV (1913–1914), 449–474.

———, Some Aspects of Rabbinic Theology. New York, 1910.

———, Studies in Judaism. 3 vols., Philadelphia, 1896–1924.

Scheftelowitz, J., Alt-Palaestinensischer Bauernglaube in religionsvergleichender Beleuchtung. Hanover, 1925.

———, Der altpersische Religion und das Judentum. Unterschiede, Uebereinstimmungen und gegenseitige Beeinflussungen. Giessen, 1920.

———, "Der Seelen- und Unsterblichkeits-glaube im alten Testament." *Archiv fuer Religionswissenschaft*, XIX (1916–1919), 210–232.

Schmidt, Hans, Das Gebet der Angeklagten im alten Testament. Giessen, 1928.

———, Die Psalmen. Tuebingen, 1934.

Schuerer, Emil, Geschichte des juedischen Volkes im Zeitalter Jesu Christi. 3d and 4th eds., 3 vols., Leipzig, 1901–1911.

———, A History of the Jewish People in the Time of Jesus Christ. 5 vols., Edinburgh, 1886–1890.

SCHWALLY, FRIEDRICH, Der Heilige Krieg im alten Israel. Leipzig, 1901. *In* "Semitische Kriegsaltertuemer."

SCHWARZ, ADOLF, Die Controversen der Schammaiten und Hilleliten. Ein Beitrag zur Entwicklungsgeschichte der Halachah. Part I, Vienna, 1893.

———, *see* Festschrift Adolf Schwarz.

SELLIN, ERNST, Geschichte des israelitisch-juedischen Volkes. 2 vols., Leipzig, 1924–1932.

———, Gilgal. Ein Beitrag zur Geschichte der Einwanderung Israels in Palaestina. Leipzig, 1917.

———, "Die israelitisch-juedische Heilandserwartung." *BZS*, Series V (1909), Nos. 2–3.

———, ed., Kommentar zum alten Testament. 9 vols., Leipzig, 1917–1932.

———, "Die neugefundene 'Lehre des Amen-em-ope' in ihrer Bedeutung fuer die juedische Literatur- und Religionsgeschichte." *Deutsche Literaturzeitung*, XLV (1924), 1873–1883.

———, Das Zwoelfprophetenbuch. Leipzig, 1922.

SIMPSON, D. C., "Book of Proverbs." *Encyclopaedia Britannica* (14th ed.), XVIII, 644–646.

SINGER, CHARLES, *see* Bevan, Edwyn R., and Singer, Charles.

———, and Dorothea Singer, The Jewish Factor in Mediaeval Thought. *The Legacy of Israel.* Oxford, 1927, 173–282.

SINGER, DOROTHEA, *see* Singer, Charles, and Singer, Dorothea.

SKINNER, J., The Book of the Prophet Isaiah, Chapters XL–LXVI (Introduction). Cambridge, 1902. *In* "The Cambridge Bible for Schools and Colleges."

———, ed., Kings. The Century Bible. London, 1913.

SMITH, GEORGE A., The Book of the Twelve Prophets, Commonly called the Minor. 2 vols. London, 1928.

———, The Historical Geography of the Holy Land, Especially in Relation to the History of Israel and of the Early Church. 7th ed., New York, 1900.

———, Jeremiah. 4th ed., New York, 1929.

———, "Trade and Commerce With Trade Routes." *Encyclopaedia Biblica*, IV, 5145–5199.

SMITH, HENRY P., A Critical and Exegetical Commentary on the Books of Samuel. New York, 1899. *In* "The International Critical Commentary."

SMITH, JOHN M. P., WARD, WILLIAM H., and BEWER, JULIUS A., A Critical and Exegetical Commentary on Micah, Zephaniah, Nahum, Habakkuk, Obadiah, and Joel. New York, 1911. *In* "The International Critical Commentary."

SMITH, WILLIAM R., Lectures on the Religion of the Semites. The Fundamental Institutions. (With an introduction by Stanley A. Cook). 3d ed., New York, 1927.

———, Kinship and Marriage in Early Arabia. (Edited by Stanley S. Cook). London, 1903.

Society of Biblical Archaeology, The. *Proceedings*, XXV, London, 1903.

SOROKIN, PITRIM A., and ZIMMERMAN, CARLE C., Principles of Rural-Urban Sociology. New York, 1929.

———, ZIMMERMAN, CARLE C., and GALPIN, CHARLES J., eds., A Systematic Source Book in Rural Sociology. 3 vols., Minneapolis, 1930–1932.

SPERBER, ALEXANDER, "Hebrew Based upon Greek and Latin Translations." *HUCA*, XII–XIII (1937–1938), 103–274.

SPIEGEL, SHALOM, "Toward Certainty in Ezekiel." *JBL*, LIV (1935), 145–171.

SPYKMAN, NICHOLAS J., "A Social Philosophy of the City." *The Urban Community*. Chicago, 1926, 55–64.

STADE, BERNHARD, Geschichte des Volkes Israel. 2 vols., Berlin, 1887–1888.

STAERK, WILLY, Das assyrische Weltreich im Urteil der Propheten. Goettingen, 1908.

———, Religion und Politik im alten Israel. Tuebingen, 1905.

STAVE, ERIK, Ueber den Einfluss des Parsismus auf das Judentum. Haarlem, 1898.

STUMMER, FRIEDRICH, "Einige Keilschriftliche Parallelen zu Jes. 40–66." *JBL*, XLV (1926), 171–189.

SULZBERGER, MAYER, The Am Ha-aretz. The Ancient Hebrew Parliament. A Chapter in the Constitutional History of Ancient Israel. Philadelphia, 1909.

———, "The Status of Labor in Ancient Israel." *JQR*, N. S., XIII (1922–1923), 245–301, 397–459.

Tacitus Claudius, The Histories. (Translated by C. H. Moore). 4 vols., London, 1925–1937. *In* "The Loeb Classical Library."

Thompson, John, Urbanization. Its Effects on Government and Society. New York, 1927.

Torrey, Charles C., "Certainly Pseudo-Ezekiel." *JBL*, LIII (1934), 291–320.

———, "Ezekiel and the Exile. A Reply." *JBL*, LI (1932), 179–181.

———, Pseudo-Ezekiel and the Original Prophecy. New Haven, 1930.

———, The Second Isaiah. A New Interpretation. New York, 1928.

Toy, C. H., "Proverbs." *Encyclopaedia Biblica*, III, 3906–3919.

Tufts, James H., *see* Dewey, John, and Tufts, James H.

Vierkandt, Alfred, "Sittlichkeit." *Handwoerterbuch der Soziologie.* Stuttgart, 1931, 533–545.

Vincent, J. M., "Sumptuary Legislation." *Encyclopaedia of the Social Sciences*, XIV, 464–466.

Vogelstein, Hermann, Die Landwirtschaft in Palaestina zur Zeit der Mishnah. Part I, Berlin, 1894.

Volz, Paul, Jesaia II uebersetzt und erklaert. Leipzig, 1932. *In* "Kommentar zum alten Testament."

Vom alten Testament: Karl Marti zum siebzigsten Geburtstage. Giessen, 1925. *In* "Beitraege zur alttestamentlichen Wissenschaft."

Wallis, Louis, God and the Social Process. A Study in Hebrew History. Chicago, 1935.

Walter, Franz, Die Propheten in ihrem sozialen Beruf und das Wirtschaftsleben ihrer Zeit. Freiburg, 1900.

Ward, William H., *see* Smith, John M. P., Ward, William H., and Bewer, Julius A.

Wardle, W. L., The History and Religion of Israel. *In* "The Clarendon Bible," I. Oxford, 1936.

Washington, Booker T., Up From Slavery. An Autobiography. New York, 1901.

WEBER, MAX, General Economic History. (Translated by Frank H. Knight). New York, 1927.

———, "Agrargeschichte (Altertum)." *Handwoerterbuch der Staatswissenschaften*, I, 52–188.

WELCH, ADAM C., "The Share of N. Israel in the Restoration of the Temple Worship." *ZAW*, XLVIII (1930), 175–187.

WELLHAUSEN, J., Die Composition des Hexateuchs und der historischen Buecher des alten Testaments. Berlin, 1889.

———, Die kleinen Propheten. (Skizzen und Vorarbeiten, V). Berlin, 1892.

———, Die Pharisaeer und die Sadducaeer. Eine Untersuchung zur inneren Juedischen Geschichte. 2d ed., Hanover, 1924.

———, Reste arabischen Heidentums. (Skizzen und Vorarbeiten, III). Berlin, 1887.

WESTERMARCK, EDWARD, Ethical Relativity. New York, 1932.

———, The History of Human Marriage. 5th ed., 3 vols., New York, 1922.

———, Marriage Ceremonies in Morocco. London, 1914.

———, The Origin and Development of Moral Ideas. 5th ed., 2 vols., London, 1912–1926.

WEYL, HEINRICH, Die juedischen Strafgesetze bei Flavius Josephus in ihrem Verhaeltnis zu Schrift und Halacha. (Mit einer Einleitung: Flavius Josephus ueber die juedischen Gerichtshoefe und Richter). Berlin, 1900.

WICKS, H. J., The Doctrine of God in the Jewish Apocryphal and Apocalyptic Literature. London, 1915.

WIGMORE, JOHN H., "Responsibility for Tortious Acts: Its History." *Harvard Law Review*, VII (1893–1894), 315–337, 383–405, 441–463.

WILCKEN, U., *see* Mitteis, L., and Wilcken, U.

WILDEBOER, G., The Origin of the Canon of the Old Testament. An Historical Inquiry. (Translated by B. W. Bacon). London, 1895.

WILKE, FRITZ, Die politische Wirksamkeit der Propheten Israels. Leipzig, 1913.

WILLIAMS, JAMES, The Expansion of Rural Life. The Social Psychology of Rural Development. New York, 1926.

WINCKLER, HUGO, Geschichte Israels in Einzeldarstellungen. Vol. I, Leipzig, 1895; vol. II, Leipzig, 1900.

WOOD, MARGARET, The Stranger. A Study in Social Relationships. New York, 1934.

WOOLSTON, HOWARD, "The Urban Habit of Mind." *American Journal of Sociology*, XVII (1911–1912), 602–614.

ZEITLIN, SOLOMON, An Historical Study of the Canonization of the Hebrew Scriptures. *Proceedings of the American Academy for Jewish Research* (1931–1932), 121–158.

———, Megillat Ta'anit as a Source for Jewish Chronology and History in the Hellenistic and Roman Periods. Philadelphia, 1922.

———, "Note on the Relation of the Slavonic Josephus to Josippon." *JQR*, N. S., XIX (1928–1929), 77–78.

———, "The Origin of the Ketubah." *JQR*, N. S., XXIV (1933–1934), 1–7.

———, "Takkanot Ezra." *JQR*, N. S., VIII (1917–1918), 61–74.

Zeitschrift fuer die alttestamentliche Wissenschaft. Giessen, 1881 et seq.

Zeitschrift der deutschen morgenlaendischen Gesellschaft. Leipzig, 1847 et seq.

ZIMMERMAN, CARLE C., "Rural Society." *Encyclopaedia of the Social Sciences*, XIII, 469–471.

———, *see* Sorokin, Pitrim A., and Zimmerman, Carle C.

———, *see* Sorokin, Pitrim, A., Zimmerman, Carle C., and Galpin, Charles J., eds.

ZIMMERMAN, RICHARD, "Bevoelkerungsdichte und Heereszahlen in Alt-Palaestina." *Klio*, XXI (1927), 340–343.

INDICES

INDEX TO PASSAGES CITED

This index includes references to the Hebrew Scriptures, the New Testament, Apocrypha, Pseudepigrapha, Babylonian and Palestinian Talmuds, Mishna, Tosefta, and other rabbinic works, as well as Philo and Josephus.
The numbers on the right refer to pages. The numbers in parentheses refer to footnotes. An asterisk following a number in parentheses indicates that the reference occurs in the note and not in the text proper.

HEBREW SCRIPTURES

Genesis

1.27 . . . 461 (22)
2.1 . . . 462 (26)
2.17 . . . 708 (119)
2.22 . . . 461 (22)
3.8 . . . 161
3.22 . . . 161, 183
4.15 . . . 708
4.16 . . . xxiii
4.17 . . . 187
5.2 . . . 461 (22)
5.5 . . . 708 (120)
ch. 6 . . . 751
6.2 ff. . . . 160 (1)*
6.6 . . . 161
7.16 . . . 161
8.18 . . . 58 (42)*
9.20 . . . 109
10.1 ff. . . . 461 (23)
10.2 . . . 338
10.6 . . . 424
11.4 . . . xxiii, 187
11.5 . . . 161
12.7,8 . . . 62 (4)*
13.11 . . . 379
13.18 . . . 62 (4)*
15.6 . . . 201
15.16 . . . 355
15.18 . . . 355
16.2 . . . 163
16.13 . . . 169
17.5 . . . 169
17.10 . . . 462 (27)
17.15 . . . 169
18.2 . . . 164
18.22 ff. . . . 167
19.1 ff. . . . 379
19.15 ff. . . . 168
21.21 . . . 423
21.22 f. . . . 354
21.23 . . . 362 (19)*
22.15 ff. . . . 168
24.10 . . . 407 (6)*
25.22 . . . 566
25.27 . . . 187
26.29 . . . 362 (19)*
28.18 . . . 62 (4)*, 191
29.4 ff. . . . 407 (6)*
29.30 . . . 169
30.3 . . . 163
31.24,29 . . . 407 (6)*
32.25 . . . 164
32.28 . . . 169
33.4 ff. . . . 379
33.20 . . . 62 (4)*
35.4 . . . 188
35.7 . . . 62 (4)*
35.14 . . . 62 (4)*
38.2 ff. . . . 377 (48)*
38.8 . . . 170
38.9 . . . 163
46.10 . . . 377 (48)*
49.8 ff. . . . 52 (24)*
49.14 . . . 44
49.20 . . . 52 (24)
50.2–3 . . . 146 (5)
50.26 . . . 146 (5)

Exodus

3.2 ff. . . . 168
7.3 . . . 197
7.5 ff. . . . 190
12.49 . . . 462 (25)
18.20 . . . lxix
18.22 . . . lxvii
20.20 . . . 184
20.21 f. . . . 190
20.24 . . . 562 (17)
21.1 ff. . . . lxxix
21.7 . . . lxxix
21.10 . . . lxxix
21.13 . . . 721
21.22 ff. . . . 721
21.24 ff. . . . 722
21.28 . . 197, 698 (91), 708
21.29 ff. . . . 162
21.35 . . . 162

22.15..............xciv
22.16............lxxviii
23.16..............104
23.19.......xciv, 58 (39)
23.21..............169
24.10–11...........656
26.1 ff..............189
28.3...........221 (23)
28.29..............712
28.38..............712
29.1...............712
30.1 ff..............281
30.11 ff.............711
30.15..............282
30.18 ff.............273
30.20..............cviii
31.3...........221 (23)
32.3...............188
33.6...........188 (7)*
33.18..............656
33.20..............656
34.22..............104
34.26.......xciv, 58 (39)
35.2...........462 (26)
35.3...........131, 660

Leviticus

2.11...........655 (35)
3.3................xcv
3.17...........xcv, xcvi
4.18 ff.............xcvii
4.27...........461 (24)
6.9 ff..........xcvi, 692
6.12 ff.........713 (132)
6.16...........692 (81)
6.17...............xcvi
7.16...............cxv
7.22 ff..............xcvi
7.26...............xcv
7.27...............xcv
9.2................xcii
9.4................xciii
9.5................xciii
10.1..........119 (30)*
10.8 ff..............693
10.10..............661
11.1 ff..........462 (28)
11.24..............668
11.27..............668
11.28..............668
11.32 ff.........129 (48)
11.38...............53
11.39..............668
11.40..............668
chs. 12–15......462 (29)
12.1...........663 (55)
12.4......670, 678 (75)*
12.5.......663 (55), 736
ch. 13..............735
14.8...............669
ch. 15..............652
15.1 ff...........27 (77)
15.5...............668
15.6...............668
15.7...........122, 668
15.11..............719
15.13..............669
15.16......122, 672 (61)
15.18..............668
15.20..............668
15.24..........672 (62)
15.25.............xcviii
15.27..............668
15.32..............668
16.6..........713 (131)
16.11.........714 (139)
16.12.....119, 119 (30)*
16.21..............712
16.28..............670
16.29..........462 (25)
17.10 ff.............xcv
17.15..........462 (25)
18.3...............424
18.26..........462 (25)
19.3...........462 (26)
19.6...............xcvi
19.8...............cxv
19.18..........xcii, 304
19.20 ff.............790
19.27..........187 (6)*
19.34..............462
20.2...........461 (24)
21.5...........187 (6)*
21.8...............712
21.20,23.............xci
21.24..............725
22.1 ff.........678 (75)*
22.4 ff..............689
22.6...........661 (49)
22.7..........687 (75)*
22.7 ff..............670
22.28..........58 (42)*
ch. 23..........ciii, 649
23.3...........462 (26)
23.10 f..............641
23.11..........641, 646
23.14.......67 (13), 651
23.15..........116, 646
23.15 ff.........115 (22)
23.16..............641
23.22...............69
23.24..............646
23.32.......57, 646, 647
23.39..............646
23.42.......15 (35), 105
24.6 ff..............709
24.12..............709
24.19 ff.............722
24.22..........462 (25)
25.1 ff....cxviii, 461 (24)
25.8 ff....lxxxii, 629 (5)*
25.29.............lxxix
25.29 ff.......lvi, lxxxii
25.35 ff..........lxxxiii
27.1 ff.............901*
27.29..............699

Numbers

5.1 ff...........lxxxviii
5.2 ff..............669
5.11 ff...........lxxvii
6.2 ff..............188
6.22..........278 (20)*
6.27...............715
11.8...............656

15.4 ff.............693
15.7,10.............693
15.15..........462 (25)
15.17 ff.............792
15.20.............682
15.29..........462 (25)
15.31.............899*
15.32.............709
15.34.............709
15.37–41.............64
16.17.........119 (30)*
16.18.........119 (30)*
16.22.............150
18.1.............726
18.1 ff.............712
18.5.............727
18.7.......682, 726–727
18.21.......28 (79), 270
18.21 ff.............28
18.24.............69
18.26.............270
18.26 ff.............cxiv
18.28.............681
ch. 19..27 (75), 652, 674
19.7.............670
19.8.............670
19.9...666 (48), 665, 686
19.10.............670
19.11 ff.........122 (35)
19.12.............666
19.13.............686
19.14 ff.........129 (48)
19.18..........665, 686
19.19.............665
21.22.............355
23.7..........407 (6)*
25.7.............735
26.12.............150
26.52 ff.........461 (24)
27.2..........577 (4)*
27.8..........139, 694
27.19.........508 (9)*
28.9..........462 (26)
29.13 ff.............cxi
30.3 ff.............xci
31.20–23.......129 (48)
31.22..........129, 693
35.25..........577 (4)*
35.31.............723
35.32 f.............699
35.34.............734
35.38.............712

Deuteronomy

1.15.............729
1.17..........261 (2)
1.18 ff.............lxvii
4.6.............95
5.9..........150 (7)
6.4–9.............63
6.8..........29 (82)
6.9.............29
7.10.............150
8.17.............201
8.18.............202
11.13–21.............64
11.18..........29 (82)
11.20.............29
11.26.............202
12.23.............xcv
12.28..........633 (16)
12.29..........551 (7)
13.6,17,26.............xci
14.21......xciv, 58 (39)
14.22 ff.............28
14.22–23.............270
14.25.............272
14.29.............270
15.2.............lvi
15.22 ff..........28 (79)
16.13.............104
16.18.............lxxiii
17.6.............lxxxvii
17.7..........143 (72)
17.8 ff....lxvii, lxix, lxxii, lxxiv, lxxv, 261 (2)
17.9.............lxix
17.15.............cxxvii
17.16.............189
18.1...20 (56), 420 (14), 509
18.6.............420
19.15.............lxxxvii
19.17..........261 (2)
19.18 ff.............723
19.19......142, 144, 696
19.21.............696
21.2..........261 (2)
21.4.............818
21.5.............lxxvii
21.8.............734
21.16.............268
21.18.............268
21.19.............lxxviii
22.6..........58 (42)*
22.13........lxxviii, 815
22.13 ff........lxxv, 738
22.15 ff.............740
22.23.............xciv
22.26.............199
22.29.............lxxviii
23.2..........491 (51)*
23.4..........541 (41)
23.8.............424
23.10.............663
23.15.............188
24.15.............lxxx
24.16.............150
24.22.............xci
25.2..........261 (2)
25.6.............169
25.7..........261 (2)
25.9......741 (202), 816
26.5......407 (6)*, 423
26.14.............663
27.12..........551 (7)
27.21.............35
28.64..........346 (2)
30.15.............202
30.19.............202
32.10.............729
33.4.............36
33.11..........21 (57)
33.24..........52 (24)

Joshua

1.8.................95
5.9...........367 (32)*
5.11...............116
6.19...........188 (7)*
7.24 ff...........197 (3)
8.33...........462 (25)
15.1 ff....lxxxii, 39 (107)
18.11 ff.........39 (107)
18.22..........39 (107)
18.25.........367 (37)*
21.17.........367 (37)*

Judges

2.1................169
3.19...............190
5.2.........187 (6), 188
5.24...............352
5.30...............347
6.19...............108
8.31..........41 (116)*
11.1 ff.............7 (2)
11.30...............xci
13.7...............189
13.18..............169
14.3...............362
14.18..............362
16.1 ff..............362
21.19..............363
21.19 ff.........55 (27)

I Samuel

1.11...............189
1.28...............189
2.2................737
2.13 f.,17.......363 (21)
2.22...............363
4.1,9..........362 (19)*
5.4................362
7.6................108
7.10 ff.........365 (28)*
7.16...........365 (26)
10.8..........367 (33)*
10.21–27......366 (29)*
11.14..............191
11.15.........190 (12)*
13.3............367 (34)
13.4 ff..............191
13.7...............190
13.8 ff.........367 (32)*
14.1...........367 (34)
14.45..............899*
14.49.........367 (35)*
ch. 15.........368 (38)*
15.1 ff.........367 (32)*
15.22.............62 (3)
15.22 f........367 (32)*
21.6...............188
22.7...............347
26.19.......346 (2), 444
28.9...............368

II Samuel

2.8............367 (35)
2.12 ff.........367 (37)*
3.3...........377 (48)*
3.37...............374
4.4................367
5.13 ff.........377 (49)*
5.17...........377 (47)
6.10..........377 (48)*
6.21...............376
ch. 7..........376 (44)*
7.2................189
8.1............377 (47)
8.4................189
8.6................379
8.11...........188 (7)*
9.6................367
10.1 ff..............379
11.11......187 (4)*, 188
11.15..............403
14.4...........360 (15)
17.27.........377 (46)*
18.9..........482 (42)*
20.1...............381
21.1 ff..............377
21.8...............367
23.16..............108
24.1...........196, 230
24.24.......11 (12), 377

I Kings

3.4...........367 (37)*
4.9 ff...............383
6.7................190
7.51...........188 (7)*
8.2 ff..........55 (27)*
8.23–53............565
8.30...............433
8.41–43............433
11.5...............383
11.26..............383
12.16..............385
12.25..........387 (54)
12.29......191, 387 (53)
14.2 ff..............387
15.15,18........188 (7)*
15.27..............388
16.9 ff..............389
16.24..............390
17.1..........7 (2), 399
17.17 f........745 (217)
18.18..............400
18.34..............108
18.37..............197
19.15 f..............401
19.16..............402
19.20..............402
20.35..........405 (5)*
21.1 ff.............lxxxiii
21.3...............403
21.4...............397
21.19..............403
21.27..188 (9)*, 397, 404
22.11..............406
22.11 ff.........405 (5)*
22.21..............196
29.36..............759

II Kings

1.2...........482 (42)*
3.2................407
3.20...............759
4.1...............lxxix
4.23...............563

4.34..........745 (218)
ch. 5............407 (6)
5.17...............444
6.26...........360 (15)
8.3 ff...........360 (15)
8.9.............407 (7)
8.11...............407
8.12...............410
9.30 ff..............396
10.15...............408
10.18...............410
11.17...............412
11.18...............412
11.20...........24, 411
12.3...............414
12.12...............414
12.13...............414
12.14...............414
12.16...............414
12.19..........188 (7)*
14.6...............150
14.21...............415
15.5...............415
15.19 f.........547 (1)*
15.20...........346 (4)
16.10 ff.............417
16.15...............759
17.25 ff..........549 (4)
18.4......418, 418 (12)*
19.18...............301
20.12–20......421 (15)*
20.16 ff.............421
20.34...........390 (1)
21.3...........319 (26)
22.12...............442
22.15 ff.............438
22.17...............301
23.9...............437
23.30..........761 (36)
24.14.440 (25), 455 (15), 456 (16)*
24.16..440 (25), 455 (15)
25.12...............442
25.27..........465 (33)
25.30.........334 (45)*

Isaiah

1.11..............62 (4)
2.2–4.........423 (16)*
2.7...............191
2.7 ff...............415
3.14 ff...............301
3.18 ff...............191
5.3.............24 (71)
5.8............267, 302
6.6...............171
6.10........197, 202 (9)
7.4...............416
7.12...............201
7.21...............191
7.25...............192
8.16...............95
8.23...............40
10.1 ff..............302
11.1 ff.........302, 423, 423 (16)*
11.1–9........423 (16)*
ch. 13.....450, 450 (9)*
ch. 14.....450, 450 (9)*
ch. 21.....450, 450 (9)*
22.9 ff..............202
chs. 24–27.....145, 178, 536, 742
24.1 f...............536
24.13 ff.............537
24.21..........173, 536
24.23...............537
25.7...............537
26.15...............537
26.19......145, 173, 536
30.1–3.............422
30.26...............543
31.9...............428
32.1–5........423 (16)*
32.15–20......423 (16)*
33.7 f...............428
ch. 34..............450
chs. 34–35..........801
ch. 35..............450
37.7...........202 (9)
37.19...............301

38.18..........743 (214)
chs. 40–55......801, 802
chs. 40–66..........803
40.1...............446
40.7...............469
40.9...............804
40.19–20...........301
40.27.........483 (43)*
ch. 41.........473 (38)*
41.2 ff..............471
41.7...............301
41.8..........483 (43)*
41.14.........483 (43)*
41.16.........483 (43)*
41.17.........483 (43)*
41.18...............804
41.20.........483 (43)*
41.25...............471
ch. 42.........473 (38)*
42.1 ff..............474
42.10 f........468 (36)*
42.19...............176
43.1..........483 (43)*
43.3.468 (36)*, 483 (43)*
43.14.........468 (36)*, 483 (43)*
43.22.........483 (43)*
43.28.........483 (43)*
44.1..........483 (43)*
44.2..........483 (43)*
44.5..........483 (43)*
44.11 ff..........300 (7)
44.12...............301
44.21.........483 (43)*
44.23.........483 (43)*
44.23 ff.............477
44.26...............176
45.1 ff..............478
45.3..........483 (43)*
45.4..........483 (43)*
45.10...............479
45.11.........483 (43)*
45.15.....479, 483 (43)*
45.17.........483 (43)*
45.19.........483 (43)*

45.25 . . . . . 483 (43)*
46.3 . . . . . 483 (43)*
46.13 . . . . . 483 (43)*
47.4 . . . . . 483 (43)*
47.6 804
48.1 . . . . . 483 (43)*
48.2 . . . . . 483 (43)*
48.12 . . . . . 483 (43)*
48.17 . . . . . 483 (43)*
48.20 . . . . . 483 (43)*, 804
49.3 . . . . . 483 (43)*
49.5 . . . . . 483 (43)*
49.6 . . . . . 483 (43)*
49.7 . . . . . 479, 483 (43)*
49.9 804
ch. 50 . . . . . 473 (38)*
50.2 481
50.4 ff. 482
50.6 804
50.10 ff. 482
50.11 . . . . . 482 (42)*
ch. 51 . . . . . 473 (38)*
51.2 482
51.6 484
51.8 482
51.12 482
51.18 483
52.11 803
52.11 f. 484
52.12 . . . . . 483 (43)*
52.13 ff. . . . . . 473 (38)*
52.13–53.6 486
53.9 ff. 145 (3)
53.10–11 486
ch. 54 . . . . . 473 (38)*
54.5 . . . . . 483 (43)*
54.11 . . . . . 468 (36)*
54.11 f. 489
54.14 490
55.1 ff. 492
55.5 . . . . . 483 (43)*
chs. 56–66 802
56.6 ff. 494
56.8 . . . . . 483 (43)*
56.12 493
57.2 ff. 493
58.1 . . . . . 483 (43)*
58.6 ff. 495
ch. 59 . . . . . 473 (38)*
59.1 ff. 496
59.20 . . . . . 483 (43)*
ch. 60 . . . . . 473 (38)*
60.9 . . . . . 483 (43)*
60.14 . . . . . 483 (43)*
60.16 . . . . . 483 (43)*
60.17 . . . . . 468 (36)*
63.7 . . . . . 483 (43)*
63.9 . . . . . 176 (15)*
63.17 496
65.3 ff. 497
65.9 . . . . . 483 (43)*
65.14 497
ch. 66 605
66.1 ff. 498
66.20 . . . . . 483 (43)*
66.23 498
66.24 606

Jeremiah

chs. 1–3 305
1.3 . . . . . 446 (5)*
2.11 ff. 432
5.4 ff. 19
5.26 ff. 303
7.34 24
8.10 ff. 303
9.22 ff. 304
10.3 301
11.20 . 202 (9), 307 (11)*, 324
12.1 . . . . . 151 (8)
12.3 . . . . . 202 (9)
13.3 200
14.11 565
15.19 565
17.5 201
17.10 . . 200, 202 (9), 324
17.21 136
18.3 14
20.7 . . . . . 202 (9)
20.12 . . . . . 200, 202 (9)
20.12 ff. . . . . . 307 (11)*
22.13 304
24.1 . . . . . 440 (25)
24.4 . . . . . 446 (5)*
25.2 415
25.11 806
26.24 442
28.4 . . . . . 446 (5)*
29.1 . . 441 (26), 446 (5), 455 (15)
29.2 . . . . . 440 (25)
29.3 . . . . . 442 (28)*
29.4 . . . . . 446 (5)
29.5 . . . . . 456 (16)
29.6 . . . . . 188 (9)*
29.7 445
29.20 . . . . . 446 (5)
29.22 . . 446 (5)*, 453 (13)
29.24 ff. 456 (17)
chs. 30–31 . . . . . 317 (22)
31.19 . . . . . 551 (6)
34.16 305
35.6 109
35.7 ff. . . . . . 187 (4)*
36.12 . . . . . 442 (28)*
36.22 132
37.12 347
39.11 ff. 442
40.1 . . . . . 446 (5)*
41.2 447
43.2 447
49.7 ff. 526 (31)
chs. 50–51 . 307 (11)*, 450
50–51.58 . . . . . 450 (9)*
50.59 . . . . . 441 (26)
51.1 ff. 335 (46)
52.28 ff. . . . . . 446 (5)*

Ezekiel

ch. 1 328
1.1 . . . . . 323 (33)*
1.1–3 807
1.2 808
1.4 . . . . . 323 (33)*

1.5 ff. . . . 171
1.5–2.10 . . . 323
1.27 . . . 323 (33)*
1.28 . . . 323 (33)*
3.12 . . . 172 (11)
3.17 ff. . . . 329, 331 (42)
3.26 . . . 330
4.1 . . . 328
4.1 ff. . . . 318
4.6 . . . 806
4.10 . . . 316, 328
4.13 . . . 308 (12), 346 (2)
5.1 . . . 328
ch. 8 . . . 323
8.1 . . . 319 (27)*, 808
8.2 . . . 172 (11)
8.3 ff. . . . 319 (26)
8.12 . . . 321, 452
8.16 ff. . . . 319
9.2 . . . 172 (11)
9.6 ff. . . . 318
10.2 . . . 171
11.13 . . . 319 (27)*
11.24 . . . 172 (11)
14.9 . . . 202 (9), 324
14.14 . . . 330
15.4 . . . 315
16.3 . . . 317
16.4 ff. . . . 315
16.15–25 . . . 316
16.49 . . . 331
16.59 ff. . . . 551
17.3 ff. . . . 314
18.4 . . . 330
18.5 ff. . . . 331
18.21 ff. . . . 331 (42)
18.22 . . . 333
18.24 . . . 333
18.25 . . . 333
19.2 ff. . . . 315
19.10 ff. . . . 315
20.1 . . . 808
20.40 . . . 551
22.6 ff. . . . 331
ch. 23 . . . 316
24.1 . . . 808
24.16 . . . 317
ch. 26 ff. . . . 321 (29)*
26.1 . . . 808
28.1 ff. . . . 337
29.1 . . . 808
31.1 . . . 808
31.3 ff. . . . 314
31.10 ff. . . . 338
32.1 . . . 808
32.2 ff. . . . 322
33.1 ff. . . . 329
33.10 ff. . . . 331 (42)
33.11 . . . 329
33.30 ff. . . . 326
33.31 ff. . . . 314
34.2 ff. . . . 332
34.17 ff. . . . 332
35.10 . . . 551
37.15 ff. . . . 317 (23), 551
38.10 ff. . . . 339
38.23 . . . 340
ch. 40 . . . 807
ch. 40 ff. . . . 328
chs. 40–48 . . . 318 (25)*
40.1 . . . 808
40.3 . . . 171, 172 (11)
43.5 . . . 172 (11)
44.15 . . . lxxiv, 314 (17)*
44.20 . . . 187 (6)*
45.8 . . . 333
45.17 . . . 283 (4)*
45.18 ff. . . . 117 (27), 644 (22)
46.13 . . . 283 (4)*
46.14 . . . 283 (4)*
46.23 . . . 103 (5)
47.13 . . . 333
48.1 ff. . . . 551
48.35 . . . 552

Hosea

2.6–9 . . . 297
2.12–14 . . . 297
2.16 f. . . . 192
3.3 . . . 298
4.1–2 . . . 299
5.1 . . . 299
7.3 ff. . . . 300
7.11 . . . 300
8.6 . . . 300
9.10 . . . 357
9.15 . . . 367 (32)*
10.4 . . . 299
10.13 . . . 299
11.1 . . . 356
11.8 . . . 356
12.2 . . . 300
12.8 . . . 300
12.9 . . . 299
13.2 . . . 300
13.14 . . . 357

Joel

1.8 f. . . . 520
1.12 . . . 519
1.13 ff. . . . 519
2.12 ff. . . . 521
2.15 ff. . . . 520
2.22 ff. . . . 524
2.27 . . . 524
3.1 ff. . . . 525
3.3 f. . . . 526
4.1 f. . . . 524
4.4 ff. . . . 522
4.9 . . . 521
4.13 . . . 522
4.18 . . . 523
4.19 . . . 522

Amos

1.3 . . . 410
2.6–7 . . . 294
2.8 . . . 294
2.12 . . . 109
3.10 . . . 294
4.1 . . . 295
5.5 . . . 367 (32)*
5.12 . . . 295
5.28 . . . 62 (4)

7.12 294
7.14 . . . . . 294, 492 (52)
7.17 . . . . . 346 (2)
9.7 356

Obadiah

v. 15 f. 527
v. 18 . . . . . 530, 547 (1)
v. 20 527

Jonah

3.5–10 538
4.8–11 539

Micah

1.9 . . . . . 11 (11)

Nahum

1.2 ff. 306
1.4 306
1.8 306
1.11 308
2.1 309
2.7 307
3.1 308
3.4 308
3.5 ff. 307
3.10 307
3.12 306
3.16 . . . . . 306, 309
3.17 306

Habakkuk

1.2–3 311
1.13 311
1.14 310
1.15 310
2.1 309
2.11 309
2.12 309
2.15 309
2.17 309
2.20 310

Zephaniah

1.8 . . . . . 311, 432
1.12 312
1.13 312
1.18 . . . . . 307 (11)*
2.3 312
3.1 ff. 312
3.8 . . . . . 307 (11)*

Haggai

1.2 501
1.6 502
1.10 502
1.12 506
1.13 176
2.6 ff. 503
2.7 . . . . . 545 (45)
2.11 ff. . . . . . 555 (8)*
2.16 ff. 502
2.19 502
2.23 503

Zechariah

1.11 . . . . . 173 (13), 507
1.13 . . . . . 173 (13), 507
1.14 . . . . . 307 (11)*
1.16 507
2.2 . . . . . 173 (13)
2.6 504
2.7 . . . . . 173 (13)
2.9 . . . . . 506, 560 (15)
2.15 506
3.2 173
4.1 . . . . . 173 (13)
4.2 504
4.6 506
4.7 506
5.2 504
5.7 504
6.1 504
6.4 . . . . . 173 (13)
6.11 504
7.4 519
7.4 f. 505
7.9–10 505
8.16,17 505
chs. 9–11 518
9.1 . . . . . 527 (34)
9.7 533
9.8 ff. 533
9.9 189
9.13 . . . . . 529, 530, 547 (1)
9.14 530
9.14 ff. 308 (12)
9.15 532
10.3 534
10.3 ff. 530
10.6 . . . . . 547 (1)
10.6 f. 531
11.4–5 531
11.7 531
11.8 f. 532
11.11 532
11.14 . . . . . 547 (1)
chs. 12–14 534
12.2–3 542
12.7 542
12.8 542
12.12 599
13.4 . . . . . 577 (5)
14.2 542
14.3 542
14.3 ff. 543
14.5 542
14.7 543
14.8 544
14.16 ff. 542, 639 (7)
14.16–17 700
14.16–19 112
14.20 ff. 545
14.21 545

Malachi

1.6 557
1.7 557
1.8 557
1.8 ff. 557
1.10 . . . . . 759 (29)*
2.7 557
2.10 558

2.11 . . . 558
2.12 . . . 558
2.13 ff. . . . 558
3.1 . . . 177 (17)
3.8 ff. . . . 271
3.10 . . . 271 (10)
3.22 . . . 399

Psalms

19.8 . . . 269
19.9 ff. . . . 95
20.8 . . . 189
30.10 . . . 743 (214)
33.16–18 . . . 244
34 . . . 177
37.1–5 . . . 243
37.16–17 . . . 243
37.23 . . . 243
51.8–12 . . . 244
51.17–19 . . . 245
51.20–21 . . . 245
64 . . . 240 (2)*
68.28 . . . 39
73.2–14 . . . 242
73.18–19 . . . 242
73.22–26 . . . 242
74.8 . . . 563
78 . . . 177
78.25 . . . 181
82 . . . 751
86 . . . 240 (2)*
86.1–14 . . . 245
86.11 . . . 246
91 . . . 177
93 . . . 246
93.1–2 . . . 247
94–99 . . . 246
94.7 . . . 244
94.8–9 . . . 244
94.20–21 . . . 244
95.1–7 . . . 247
96.1–13 . . . 247
97.1–9 . . . 248
97.10 ff. . . . 248
99.6 . . . 249
103 . . . 177
103.20 . . . 756
104 . . . 177
104.12 . . . 182
114.16 . . . xci
115.4 . . . 301
115.10–11 . . . 744
115.17 . . . 743 (214)
118.17 . . . 743 (214)
118.25 . . . 705
119.50 . . . 94
119.71 . . . 94
119.92 . . . 94
119.97 . . . 94
122.3 . . . 11
135.1–12 . . . 249
135.15 . . . 301
136 . . . 249
136.10–20 . . . 250
137 . . . 453 (11)*
137.8 . . . 453 (12)*
141.2 . . . 760

Proverbs

chs. 1–9 . . . 204
1.5–8 . . . 207
1.7 . . . xxxvii
1.15 . . . 205
2.1–9 . . . 205
2.20 . . . lvii
3.1–4 . . . 207
3.5–12 . . . 208
3.16 . . . 205
3.28 . . . 204
6.1 . . . 204, 205
6.6 . . . 205
6.29 . . . 205
7.10–20 . . . 204
8.19 . . . 204
9.10 . . . 572
chs. 10–15 . . . 211 (13)*
10.1–22.16 . . . 211
10.2 . . . 210
10.3 . . . 210
10.4 . . . 208
10.15 . . . 208
10.22 . . . 210
11.28 . . . 210
12.24 . . . 209
13.4 . . . 209
13.8 . . . 209
14.20 . . . 209
14.24 . . . 209
15.3 . . . 210
15.11 . . . 210
16.1 . . . 210
16.1–22.16 . . . 211 (13)*
16.4 . . . 227
16.8 . . . 210
17.18 . . . 209
18.10 . . . 210
18.11 . . . 209
19.4 . . . 209
19.10 . . . 209
19.21 . . . 210
20.24 . . . 211
20.27 . . . 215
21.1 . . . 210
21.2 . . . 211
22.7 . . . 209
22.17–18 . . . 215
22.17–24.22 . . . 213
22.29 . . . 214
23.1–2 . . . 214
23.10–11 . . . 214
24.17 ff. . . . 214
chs. 25–27 . . . 211 (13)*
chs. 25–29 . . . 211
25.21 ff. . . . 214
26.4–5 . . . 215 (18)
chs. 28–29 . . . 211 (13)*
28.19 . . . 209
ch. 30 . . . 541 (43)
30.2–3 . . . 212
30.5–9 . . . 212
30.10 . . . 212
30.13–14 . . . 213
30.21 ff. . . . 213
30.24 ff. . . . 213

Job

1.21 . . . 288
1.22 . . . 288
3.19 . . . 231
4.18 . . . 177 (16)
5.1 . . . 177 (16)
5.15 ff. . . . 232
8.20 . . . 233
9.23 . . . 233
9.29 ff. . . . 233
11.13 ff. . . . 233
12.6 . . . 233
15.15 . . . 177 (16)
18.8 . . . 482 (42)*
20.18 ff. . . . 232
25.3 . . . 177 (16)
31.13 ff. . . . 232
33.23 . . . 177 (16)

Ruth

1.16 . . . 540
2.23 . . . 787

Lamentations

1.1 ff. . . . 446 (5)
1.3 . . . 446 (5)*
ch. 2 . 451 (10)*, 453, 454
2.1 ff. . . . 446 (5)
2.14 . . . 454
2.19 . . . 454
3.6 ff. . . . 226
3.21–24 . . . 227
3.31–38 . . . 227
ch. 4 . . . 451 (10)*, 454
4.2 . . . 446 (5)
4.2–7 . . . 452
4.12 . . . 446 (5)
4.20 . . . 452
4.22 . . . 446 (5)

Ecclesiastes

1.16 . . . 236
1.18 . . . 236
2.11 ff. . . . 238
2.18 . . . 237
3.9 . . . 237
3.15 . . . 239
3.16 . . . 236
3.19 ff. . . . 237
4.1 . . . 236
4.5 . . . 238
5.4 . . . xci
7.11 . . . 238
7.15 . . . 236
8.8 . . . 239
9.2 ff. . . . 237
9.11 . . . 237
9.12 . . . 236, 310 (14)*
10.9 ff. . . . 239
10.10 . . . 239
10.16 . . . 238
10.18 . . . 238
11.9 . . . 240
12.7 . . . 240

Esther

2.5 . . . 39 (108)
9.19 . . . 216

Daniel

3.25 . . . 177 (17)
4.14 . . . 177 (17)
4.24 . . . 155
4.27 . . . 155
6.23 . . . 177 (17)
8.13 . . . 177 (17)
9.16 . . . 155
9.19 . . . 155
9.21 . . . 760
10.5 . . . 177 (17)
10.21 . . . 177 (17)
12.1 . . . 177 (17)
12.2 . . . 154 (14)
12.6 . . . 177 (17)
12.13 . . . 154 (14)

Ezra

2.1 ff. . . . 511 (11)
2.36 . . . 513 (19)
2.40 . . . 23 (68)*
2.59 . . . 461
2.61 . . 377 (46)*, 512 (16)
3.61 . . . 46 (7)*
3.64 . . . 480
4.1 ff. . . . 554, 555 (8)*
4.2 . . . 549 (3)*
4.7 ff. . . . 549 (3)*
4.10 . . . 549 (3)
4.13 . . . 559
4.16 . . . 559
5.1 . . . 504 (6)*
6.9 . . . 283 (4)*
7.7 . . . 23 (68)*
7.17 ff. . . . 283 (4)*
9.4 . . . 760
10.23 . . . 23 (68)*

Nehemiah

5.5 . . . lxxix
6.12 ff. . . . 561
6.14 . . . 560 (14)
7.6 ff. . . . 511 (11)
7.39 . . . 513 (19)
9.1 ff. . . . 631 (10)
10.29 . . . 23 (68)*
10.33 . . 282, 283 (4)*, 710
10.38 . . . 271 (10)
10.38 ff. . . . 282
11.10 . . . 513 (19)*
12.4 . . . 504 (7)*

I Chronicles

3.5 ff. . . . 377 (49)*
3.18 . . . 466 (34)
4.18 . . . 556
5.41 . . . 446 (5)*
8.12 . . . 39 (107)
8.33 . . . 367 (35)*
8.34 . . . 367 (36)*
9.7 . . . 511
9.10 . . . 513 (19)*
9.39 . . . 367 (35)*
9.40 . . . 367 (36)*
11.18 . . . 113
14.4 ff. . . . 377 (49)*

16.39.........367 (37)*
21.1.......177 (17), 230
21.16,18 ff......177 (17)
21.25...........11 (13)
21.29.........367 (37)*
24.4...........653 (20)
24.7..22 (64)*, 513 (19)*
24.7 ff..............512
24.10..........512 (16)
28.3...............595
29.11–19...........229

II Chronicles

1.3,13.........367 (37)*
2.13...............556
11.12..........39 (108)
14.10..............228
15.9...........39 (108)
15.10.........116 (25)*
16.7–9.............229
17.17..........39 (108)
19.8 ff............lxvii
19.11..........508 (9)*
20.12..............229
20.37..............229
29.34..............275
30.1 f..........547 (1)*
31.3...........283 (4)*
31.6 ff..........271 (10)
32.4...............544
33.11..............434
34.6 f..........547 (1)*

VERSIONS

Septuagint

Lev. 21.13.......21 (59)
Lev. 23.15..........116
Deut. 6.4........63 (8)*
Ezek. 1.3......334 (43)*
Ezek. 8.2......323 (33)*

Targum Jonathan

Ezek. 1.1...........806
Ezek. 11.16.....568 (21)

Targum Ps.-Jonathan

Gen. 4.8........769 (18)
Exod. 19.16.....116 (24)
Exod. 29.30.....23 (68)*
Lev. 23.15.....117 (26)*

Peshitta

Lev. 23.15.....117 (26)*

APOCRYPHA

Tobit

1.7............272 (11)
3.17...........177 (17)
5.15............15 (37)
7.13...............xciv
7.14............44 (3)*

Judith

8.15...............218
8.27...............218
9.11...............218
12.8...............127
13.16..............218

Ben Sira

4.29...............221
7.17...............223
8.12...............222
10.11..............153
10.30–11.1.........223
11.11..............223
13.21..............222
15.11 ff............224
15.14..............177
17.27..............153
21.27..............177
25.24..............224
26.29–27.20.........220
31.3–4.............221
33.16..............221
38.25–33...........221
41.3...............153
ch. 44.........590 (17)
50.26..............589
51.12 n.........174 (14)
51.23..........566 (19)

I Maccabees

1.39–41............156
2.32...........130 (50)
5.15...........40 (115)
7.12...............594
7.43...............817

II Maccabees

3.3............283 (4)*
3.4................583
4.9................585
4.10...............585
4.12 ff.............586
4.24...............586
4.47...............590
5.25...........130 (50)
15.36..............818

Susanna

v. 61.........144 (75)*

PSEUDEPIGRAPHA

Testaments of the XII Patriarchs

Reuben
2.2................251
3.3 ff..............251

Simeon
2.7................251
3.1................251

Levi
5.6............177 (17)
9.11...274 (12), 678–679
9.12...........277 (16)
12.5............268 (8)
13.2............264 (5)
14.6...........562 (16)

Judah
16.1...............251

Issachar
3.5 .... 44 (2)

Zebulun
6.1 ff. .... 353 (10)*

Dan
1.6 251

Gad
1.9 251
3.1 251

Asher
1.5 252
7.1 178

Aramaic and Greek Fragments
ed. R. H. Charles
(Old Testament of Levi)
p. 248, 1.3 .... 274 (12)
p. 248, 1.9 .... 277 (16)
p. 254, 1.15 .... 268 (8)

Jubilees
1.1 .... 116 (25)
1.14 .... 629 (5)
2.2 .... 177 (17)
2.30 civ
3.9 ff. 737
4.15 .... 16 (47)*
4.16 .... 16 (47)*
4.17 .... 264 (5)
4.20 .... 16 (47)*
4.27 .... 16 (47)*
4.28 .... 16 (47)*
4.32 cxv
4.33 .... 16 (47)*
5.13 252
6.9 ff. xcvii
6.17 .... 116 (25)*
6.22 civ
6.23 .... 113 (20)
7.20 ff. 597 (22)
7.28 ff. xcvii
11.23 .... 353 (10)*
12.17 .... 114 (21)
13.9 cxiv
13.26 cxiv
15.27 .... 184 (37)
16.22 .... cxi, cxii
16.25,29 cxi
16.31 .... cv, cvi
19.14 .... 264 (5)
21.6 xcvii
21.9,10 xcvii
21.12 .... 277 (16)
21.16 .... 274 (12), 679
21.18 xcvii
22.30 cxix
23.31 cxv
28.14,23 .... 268 (8)*
30.2 .... 268 (8)
32.4 cxi
32.10 cxiv
32.11 cxv
32.14 746
34.18 cxii
34.19 cxii
49.10 .... 133 (59)*
49.17 746
49.18 cxiv
49.20 746
49.22 .... civ, cxi
50.1–5 .... 629 (5)
50.8 civ
50.8 ff. 130
50.10–11 817

Psalms of Solomon
5.4 ff. 252
8.12 813
8.13 (12) .... xciv, xcix
8.23 .... 25 (73)*
9.7 252

I Enoch
25.5–7 147
45.1 178
69.9–11 230

IV Ezra
1.1 .... 334 (45)*

Assumption of Moses
7.4 ff. .. 98 (51), 193 (20)

Zadokite Document
(ed. Schechter)
p. 1, 1.19 .... 817, 848*

GOSPELS

Matthew
5.41 .... 289 (20)
6.5 .... 97 (48)*
12.2 ff. .... 97 (48)*
20.9 .... 15 (37)
22.35 .... 64 (11)
26.8 .... 192 (16)*
26.73 .... 60 (49)*

Mark
3.6 .... 770 (19)
7.1 ff. .... 97 (48)*
11.23 .... 69 (15)
12.13 .... 4 (3)*, 770 (19)
12.29 xvi
12.34 xvi
12.38 f. .... 97 (48)*
13.29 .... 64 (11)
14.4 192
14.67 .... 132 (55)
14.70 .... 60 (49)*

Luke
11.42 .... 70 (18)
14.17 .... 16 (44)
22.55 .... 132 (55)

John
7.15 .... 264 (5)
12.4 .... 192 (16)*

Acts

5.34 . . . xvi
15.22 f. . . . 622 (37)
15.29 . . . 535 (39)
23.6 . . . xvi
23.8 . . . 179

Romans

11.1 . . . 39 (109)

Philippians

3.5 . . . 39 (109)

JOSEPHUS

Against Apion

I, 22, 197 . . . 11 (14)

Antiquities

I, 7.8 . . . 353 (10)*
III, 10.1 . . . 283 (4)*
III, 10.5 . . . 116 (24)*
III, 12.2 . . . 21 (61)
IV, 8.13 . . . 63 (8)*
IV, 8.14 . . . 183 (172a)*
IV, 8.15 . . . 142 (71)
IV, 8.23 . . . 815 (2)*, 816 (4)*
IV, 8.35 . cxxi, 724 (167), 815
VI, 3.2 (32) . . . 365 (27)
VIII, 13.2 (324) . . 399 (6)
X, 6.3 . . . 314 (16)*
XI, 8.3 ff. . . . 531 (37)
XII, 3.3 . . . 581 (14)
XII, 5.1 . . . 587 (16)
XIII, 5.9 . . cxxiv, 255 (7)
XIII, 8.4 . . . 117 (26)*
XIII, 10.5 . . . cxxiv
XIII, 10.5 f. . . . 763 (5)
XIII, 10.6 . . lviii, lxxxvii, xc, cxxiv, 10 (10), 80 (21), 83 (3), 261 (1), 286 (10), 707 (114)
XIII, 13.5 . . . 110 (16)
XIII, 16.2 . . . 144 (76)*
XIV, 2.1 . . . 615 (31)
XIV, 9.3 . . . 284 (6)*
XIV, 13.1 . . . 618 (32)
XVII, 2.4 . . . cxxv, xv, 10 (10), 609 (27)
XVIII, 1.2 . . . cxxvii, 91 (38), 93 (41)
XVIII, 1.3 . . . 80 (21), 82 (2), 158 (15), 186 (1), 195 (1), 253 (4)
XVIII, 1.4 . . . 10 (10), 126 (43)
XX, 9.1 . 83 (3), 286 (10)
XX, 9.2 . . . 23 (66)
XX, 9.6 . . . 23 (68)*

Life

45 . . . 41 (118)
65 . . . 41 (120)

War

I, 5.2 . . . lviii, cxx
I, 7.3 . . . 130 (50)
I, 10.6 . . . 284 (6)*
II, 8.3 . . . 192 (14)
II, 8.7 . . . 180 (24)
II, 8.9 ff. . . . 77 (8)
II, 8.14 . . . lviii, cxx, 82 (1), 253 (5)
IV, 3.1 ff. . . . 14 (24)
IV, 8.2 . . . 38 (102)
V, 1.4 . . . 13 (23)

PHILO

De Decalogo

30, 160 . . . 116 (24)*

De Humanitate

19, 142 . . . 60 (47)

De Monarchia

II, 8 . . . 21 (59)
II, 229 . . . 21 (59)

De Specialibus Legibus

II, 21, 176 . . . 116 (24)*

MISHNA

Berakot

1.1 . . . 133 (58, 61), 274 (13)
1.7 . . . 88 (28)
2.6 . . . 47 (10)

Peah

2.6 . . . 266 (6)*

Demai

1.1 . . . 60 (49)*
2.2 . . . 77 (9)*
2.3 . . . 76 (4)
2.5 . . . 758 (21)

Shebi'it

9.1 . . . 756 (5)*
9.2 . . . 7 (1)
10.3 . . . lvi

Terumot

10.8 . . . 60 (49)*

Ma'aser Sheni

5.2 . . . 790 (21)

Hallah

2.6 . . . 792
4.10 . . . 683

Bikkurim

3.8 . . . 13 (17)

Shabbat

1.3 . . . 133 (57)
1.7 . . . 286 (8)
7 . . . xc
7.1 . . . 131 (52)
7.2 . . . lxiv

'Erubin

6.2 . . . . . 137 (64)
8.2 . . . . . 15 (38)
10 c

Pesahim

1.6 676
4.4 . . . . . 135 (62)
4.5 . . . . . 51 (21)
4.8 . . . . . 61 (1), 647 (27)
5.5 . . . . . 27 (78)
6.1 . . . . . c, cvi
7.7 . . . . . 673 (69)
8.5 . . . . . 678 (75)*
8.7 . . . . . 15 (38)
10.9 . . . . . 133 (59)

Shekalim

1.1 . . . . . 281 (1), 711 (124)
1.4 . . 710 (121), 714 (142)
4.2 ff. 282 (3)
5.6 . . . . . 16 (42)*
8.6 676

Yoma

1.1 . . . . . 672 (63)
1.3 . . . . . 20 (54)
1.5 . . . . . cxxiv, cxxx, 119 (29), 658 (42), 711 (126)
1.6 . . . . . 20 (54)
3.3 . . . . . 275 (14)
3.8 . . . . . 714 (138)
4.2 . . 713 (131), 714 (138)
5.1 . . 119 (30)*, 120 (32), 657 (38)
6.4 . . . . . 16 (42)*
7.4 . . . . . 56 (31)

Sukkah

2.1 . . . . . 87 (27)
2.7 . . . . . 15 (34), 84 (10)
3.8 . . . . . 13 (16)
chs. 4,5 . . . . . 102 (2)
4.1 cv
4.2 cv
4.4,5 cv
4.5 cvii
4.8 701
5.1 . . . . . 706 (110)
5.2 . . . . . 705 (107)
5.4 . . . . . 706 (108, 109)
5.7 . . . . . 643 (21)
5.7–8 645

Bezah

2.6 . . . . . 777 (28)

Rosh ha-Shanah

1.2 . . cxi, 103 (5), 113 (19)
1.7 . . . 603 (25), 725 (169)
2.1 . . . . . 652 (32)

Ta'anit

1.1 . . . . . 111 (18)
3.9 . . . . . 38 (105)
4.2 . . . . . 643 (20)
4.8 . . . . . 55 (28)

Megillah

3.4 . . . . . 281 (2)
3.5 . . . . . 711 (124)
4.8 . . . . . 13 (18)
4.10 . . . . . 316 (19)*

Mo'ed Katan

1.1 lxiv

Hagigah

1.6 xciii
1.8 . . . . . lviii, xc
2.3 cxii
2.4 . . . . . 116 (23), 653
2.6–7 691
2.7 . . . . . 76 (6)
3.4 . . . . . 30 (84)
3.6 . . . . . 757 (15)

Yebamot

1.4 . . . 620 (34), 634 (17)
6.5 . . . . . 516 (26)
8.3 819
15.2 ff. . . . . . 99 (52)*

Ketubot

1.4 xciv
1.5 . . . . . 21 (60), 45 (4), 46 (7), 725 (168)
1.6–9 . . . . . 99 (52)*
1.10 . . . . . 21 (62)*
2.7 . . . . . 512 (17)
2.9 . . . . . 21 (62), 22 (63)
4.10 . . . . . 48 (13)
4.11 . . . . . 141 (68)
5.1 . . . . . 45 (5)
5.2 . . . . . 45 (6)
5.6 . . . . . 99 (52)*
5.8 786
5.9 . . . . . 60 (49)*
13.1 . . . . . 730 (174)
13.10 . . . . 7 (1), 41 (119)*

Nedarim

1.1,3,4 xcii
2.1 xcii
2.4 . . . . . 60 (49)*
3.1 xcii
5.5 . . . . . 41 (117)*
6.1 784
6.5 784
8.4 787
9.1 . . . . . xcii, xciii
9.10 . . . . . 89 (33)
11.4 . . . . . 99 (52)*

Nazir

7.4 . . . . . 677 (73a)

Sotah

1.4 lxxxviii
1.8 lxxxix
3.4 . . . . . 99 (52)*

Gittin

9.9 . . . . . 16 (42)*

Kiddushin

1.1 . . . . . xciv, 45 (5)
4.1 . . . . . 21 (59)*
4.5 . . . . . 16 (45)

Baba Kamma

1.2 . . . lxxii
3.1 ff. . . . lxv
3,4 . . . lxv
4.3 . . . lxxii
6.4 . . . lxxxi
6.5 . . . lxiv
6.6 . . . 15 (31)
8.6 . . . 793
9.1 ff. . . . lxv, lxxx
10.9 . . . 60 (49)*

Baba Mezi'a

ch. 3 . . . lxiv
3.4 ff. . . . lxv
3.8 . . . 784
4 . . . lxv
4.3 . . . 38 (105)
4.6 . . . lxvi
5 . . . lxvi
6 . . . lxvi
6.4 ff. . . . lxiv
7 . . . lxvi
8.1 ff. . . . lxiv
10 . . . lxvi
10.2 . . . 785

Baba Batra

1.1 . . . lxvi
1.2 ff. . . . lxvi
1.6 . . . 15 (33), 785
2 . . . lxvi
4 . . . lxvi
4.7 . . . 41 (119)
4.8 . . . lxvi
5 . . . lxvi
5.1 . . . lxvi
6.4 . . . 15 (32), 46 (9)
7.1 ff. . . . lxvi
9.9,10,11 . . . 140 (67)

Sanhedrin

1.1 . . . 740 (199)
1.3 . . . 734, 734 (184)
1.6 . . . 41 (119)
3 . . . lxxiii
3.1 . . . lxxiii
4 . . . lxxvii
4.1 . 708 (118), 900*, 901*
5.1 . . . 287 (13)
5.2 . . . 286 (11)
5.3 . . . 761 (34)
5.4 . . . 900*
6.4 . . . 143 (72), 144 (76)*
7.2 . . . 732 (178), 815
9, end . . . 732 (176)
10.1 . 158 (16), 750 (229), 769 (16)
10.2 . . . cxv, 749 (225)
10.4 . . . 317 (23)*

Makkot

1.7 . . . 144 (76)*
1.8 . . . 142 (71)
1.10 . . . 287 (12, 14), 708 (117, 118)

Shebuot

6.1 . . . lxxix

'Eduyyot

1.2 . . . 793
1.3 . . . 14 (30)
2.9 . . . 256 (13)
2.10 . . . cxxii
3.3 . . . 789
4.9 . . . 16 (41)*
5.5 . . . 718 (152)
5.6 . . . 78 (16, 17)
5.7 . . . 256 (11)
8.3 . . . 728

Abot

1.1 . . . 153 (13), 463 (30), 580 (12)*, 753 (234)
1.2 . . . lxxi, 63 (6), 576 (2)
1.3 . . . 590 (18)
1.4 . . . 765 (7), 766 (11)
1.5 . . . 766 (11, 14)
1.6 . . . 767 (15)
1.9 . . . 144 (76)*
1.11 . . . 256 (10)*
1.12 . . . lxxxix
1.15 . . . 96 (46)
1.17 . . . 96 (45)
2.4 . . . xc, 778 (31)
2.5 . . . 26 (74), 83 (6), 754 (1)*
2.6 . . . 288 (16)
2.8 . . . 193 (23)
2.9 . . . cxxi
3.1 . . . 258 (19)
3.15 . . . cxxix, 253 (3)
4.2 . . . 257 (17)
6.4 . . . 193 (24)

Horayot

1.3 . . . lxxv, xcvii, 813
3.8 . . . 20 (54)

Zebahim

1.6 . . . 711 (129)
2.1 . . . cix, 675, 689
6.2 . . . xcvi
9.1 ff. . . . 673 (68)
13.1 . . . 759 (29)*
13.3 . . . 759 (29)*
13.4 . . . 759 (29)*
13.5 . . . 759 (29)*
13.6 . . . 759 (29)*

Menahot

4.5 . . . 714 (140*, 141)
6.2 . . . 814
8.3 . . . 52 (24)
9.8 . . . 278 (20)*
10.3 . 116 (23), 646 (23)*, 653
10.5 . . 648 (28), 651 (30), 652 (31)
13.6 . . . 783 (10)

Hullin

2.4 . . . 185 (38)

5.3 . . . . . 56 (34)
8.1 . . . . . 60 (46)
8.1 ff. 59 (43)
8.4 . . . . . 59 (44)
11.2 . . . . . 60 (49)*

Bekorot

5.5 . . . . . 76 (5)
6.3 . . . . . 759 (28)

'Arakin

1.3 . . . . . 901*
2.4 . . . . . 514 (21)
9.4 . . . . lvi, lxxxiii, lxxxiv

Me'ilah

6.1 . . . . . 286 (9)

Temurah

2.1 . . . . . 672 (64), 713 (133, 136)
7.6 c

Tamid

1.1 681
1.3 . . . . . 277 (16)*
5.1 . . . . . 63 (9)

Middot

1.2 . . . . . 731 (175)
1.9 681
5, end 727–728

Kelim

1.1 . . . . . 662 (54)
1.9 cviii
15.6 . . . . . 279 (22)

Oholot

5.2,3 . . . . . 77 (13)*
16.1 . . . . . 86 (15)

Nega'im

14.3 . . . . . 678 (75)*
14.8 . . . . . 678 (75)*

Parah

3.1 . . . . . 666, 672
3.2 666–667
3.3 667
3.5 . . . . . 121 (33)
3.6 667
3.7 . . . . . 123 (37, 38, 39)
11.4 . . . . . 676–677, 689

Niddah

2.4 . . . . . 99 (52)*
4.2 . . . . 637 (1), 773 (22), 813
5.8 lxxviii
7.6 . . . . . 678 (76)
8.3 . . . . . 99 (52)*
10.1 . . . . . 99 (52)*
10, end xcix

Makshirim

5.9 . . . . . 716, 812

Zabim

3.2 . . . . . 76 (5)
5.12 685
15.12 . . . . . 123 (36)

Yadayim

4.3 . . . . . 266 (6)*
4.4 . . . . . 548 (2)
4.6 . . . 279 (21), 283 (5)*, 284 (6)
4.7 . . . . . lxiv, 128 (45), 716, 811, 812
4.8 819

'Ukazin

3.12 . . . . . 349 (8)

TOSEFTA

Berakot

1.1 (ed. L., p. 1) 685
3.3, p. 5 . . . . . 86 (19)
4.8, p. 9 . . . . . 17 (50)
4.10, p. 9 . . . . . 17 (48)

Demai

2.2, p. 47 . . . . . 77 (9)
2.2, p. 68 . . . . . 757 (14)
2.13 . . . . . 77 (11, 12)
2.14, p. 48 . . . . . 77 (10)

Ma'aser Sheni

5.16, p. 96 . . . . . 38 (105)

Hallah

1.17 (ed. L., p. 276) . . 787

Shabbat

1.1, p. 1 lxiv
1.15, p. 111 . . . . . 77 (7)
6 (7) and 7 (8), p. 117 ff. 29 (81)
7 (8).16, p. 118 . 192 (17), 193 (18)
7 (8), p. 118 (ed. L., V, p. 26) 759 (25)
7 (8), pp. 118–119 . 92 (40)

Pesahim

7.11, p. 167 . . . . 678 (75)*
10.12, p. 173 . . . . 133 (59)

Shekalim

2.1, p. 175 . . . . . 86 (18)

Yoma (Yom ha-Kippurim)

1.4 (ed. L., II, p. 221) . . 681
1.8, p. 181 . . . . . 10 (10), 118 (28), 126 (43)
1.8, p. 181 (ed. L., II, p. 222) . 659 (44), 773 (22)
1.16, p. 182 (ed. L., II, p. 226) . . . . . 674 (72), 678 (75)*
1.17 (ed. L., II, p. 227) . 678 (75)*

Sukkah

3.1, p. 195......103 (3), 702 (100)
3.1, p. 195 (ed. L., p. 266).........cvi, cvii
3.16, p. 197.110 (16), 701
3.18, p. 197......103 (4)
4.1, p. 198 (ed. L., II, p. 272)...........cxii
4.4, p. 198.....706 (112)
4.5, p. 198.....706 (112)
4.23................cix
4.23, p. 200 (ed. L., p. 277).............cvii

Rosh ha-Shanah

1.12, p. 210......103 (4)
1, end, p. 210...652 (32)

Megillah

1.5, p. 222.....216 (20)*
4 (3).15, p. 226...75 (3)

Mo'ed Katan

1.1, p. 229......40 (114)

Hagigah

2.2, p. 234......183 (28)
2.11, p. 236.......84 (9)
3.19, p. 237.....757 (17)
3.35, p. 238.....128 (44)

Yebamot

8.4, p. 250.......86 (14)

Ketubot

1.4, p. 261........46 (8)

Sotah

1.6, p. 293.......lxxxviii
3.1, p. 295........lxxxix
13.10, p. 320...755 (3,4)

Baba Batra

7.10, p. 408.....142 (69)

Sanhedrin

3.4, p. 418......757 (13)
4.7, p. 421......16 (45), 757 (130)
6.6, p. 424......144 (76)
7.6, p. 426.....717 (149)
9.4, p. 429.........900*
13.7 ff., p. 435......cxxii

'Eduyyot

1.14, p. 456.....256 (13)

Horayot

1.17, p. 474........xcvi

'Abodah Zarah

8.4, p. 473......597 (22)

Zebahim

11.17, p. 497.....68 (14)
12.17, p. 498........cix, 675 (73)

Hullin

ch. 2..........185 (38)*
8.3, p. 509......60 (46)*

Menahot

9.5, p. 526.......52 (24)
10.21, p. 528.647 (25, 26)
10.23, p. 528....116 (23)
13.20, p. 533.....68 (14)

'Arakin

1.3...............901*
1.3, p. 543.........901*

Bekorot

2.12............77 (13)

Temurah

1.17, p. 552....713 (137)

Kelim

I, 1.6, p. 569..cvii, cviii, cix, 85 (12), 732 (177)

Oholot

5.11, p. 603.....77 (13)*

Parah

3.6, p. 632.....121 (33), 124 (41), 667
3(2).8, p. 631.......cxxx
3.8, p. 632.....121 (33), 125 (42)

Niddah

5.3, p. 645.......10 (10)

Yadayim

2.20, p. 684.......9 (3), 139 (66)

BABLI

Berakot

2b.................685
4a...........353 (10)*
7a..............150 (7)
8b..............58 (38)
12a...........642 (18)*
19a............621 (35)
28a.....86 (17), 89 (34), 98 (50)
29a............778 (30)
33b.............253 (6)
42a...........278 (20)*
43b............192 (15)
44a.............782 (8)
47b.....29 (83), 32 (87)
53a...........759 (29)*
60a............258 (20)
60b............288 (18)
63a............621 (36)

Shabbat

9b....759 (30), 760 (32), 783 (9)
13a............755 (3)*
13b............758 (19)
14b.......278 (18), 689, 693 (83), 718 (153)

15b............128 (47)
16b.......128 (46*, 47)
17a.....53 (25), 54 (26), 86 (15)
25a.............14 (26)
30b.....83 (5), 215 (17)
31a....90 (35), 516 (24)
55b..........737 (192)
62b..............43 (1)
64b............99 (52)
86b...........116 (24)
104a...............cxxi
108a...............814
116a............86 (15)
145b...........445 (3)
148b............56 (35)
151b............88 (29)
153a............49 (17)

'Erubin

13b......9 (6), 620 (34)
41a..........511 (13)*
53a..........353 (10)*
53a–b..........60 (49)*
53b.....86 (20), 87 (21), 91 (36)
68b........770 (20), 775
102a.................c

Pesahim

49a.....35 (96), 36 (99)
49b.........33 (89, 90), 34 (93, 94, 95)
57a....38 (104), 23 (66), 71 (19)
66a............266 (6)*
69a.............84 (11)
72b...........278 (19)
81b............673 (70)
90b..........678 (75)*
109a............56 (32)
113a............17 (49)

Yoma

4b...........642 (18)*
6b............672 (65)
7a............673 (66)
10a..........340 (49)*
18a.............13 (20)
19a.........711 (125)*
19b....10 (10), 118 (28), 126 (43)
34b............132 (56)
35b.............15 (39)
38a.............15 (36)
40b...............814
49b........657 (38, 39)
53a...118 (28), 658 (40)
55a...........784 (12)
61a..........713 (134)
71b..........256 (10)*
75b...........181 (25)
83b.............170 (6)
87a.............57 (36)
87b.............57 (37)

Sukkah

43b...cvi, cvii, 700 (96), 702 (100, 101)
48b.......110 (16), 701
52a............258 (18)
54b..........702 (101)
55b................cxi

Bezah

5b............791 (24)
16a.........259 (21, 22)
30a.............56 (33)

Rosh ha-Shanah

7a.............283 (4)*
16a.............103 (4)
16b.............170 (5)
19b..........702 (101)

Ta'anit

3b...........700 (94)*
16a............539 (40)
23a...........612 (30)
25a................cxxi
25b............700 (98)
27a..........38 (103)*

Megillah

7a.............216 (19)
7b............216 (20)*
15a............309 (13)
19a............217 (21)
20a............38 (105)
25b...........316 (19)*
26a............16 (42)*
29a............568 (21)

Mo'ed Katan

2a.............40 (114)
16b...........353 (10)*
22b.....50 (19)*, 76 (5)

Hagigah

9b.............193 (21)
13b................xxiii
18a............38 (105)
25a....31 (86), 121 (34)

Yebamot

14b...............9 (7)
47a f.............cxxvii
49b............421 (21)
60b..................c
76b...........541 (42)
90b..130 (51), 734 (183)
101b.................c

Ketubot

3a.................lxxi
12a......46 (8), 47 (10)
17a.............49 (16)
24b............512 (17)
37b...............901*
63a.............91 (37)
65a............13 (19)*
67b............16 (42)*
82b.........xciv, 44 (3)
106a............17 (51)
110b..............xxiii

Nedarim

9b.........109 (14, 15)

35b....711 (125*, 126*)
48a..41 (117)*, 60 (49)*
52b............784 (13)

Nazir

31b............52 (24)*

Sotah

22b.......xxiii, 99 (52)*
39a...........278 (20)*
48a....632 (11), 755 (3)

Gittin

34b............41 (116)
36b.............lvi, lvii
56a.............13 (23)
56b...34 (92)*, 777 (27)
90a............183 (31)

Kiddushin

6a.............60 (49)*
31b.............88 (31)
40b.............97 (47)
43a.............285 (7)
66a.......cii, 763 (4, 6)
75b.............550 (5)
78a..................c
81b.............88 (30)

Baba Kamma

6b...............lxxii
27b..............lxxvi
36b...........793 (32)
55b..............lxxxi
82a...............lxxi
83a...........187 (6)*
84a.................815
84b..............lxxvi
107a.............lxxix
119a..........758 (22)

Baba Mezi'a

3a.................lxxx
40a...........785 (14)
59b............79 (18)
83a................lvii
83b............288 (17)
85a.............86 (16)
105b...........791 (25)
107b............782 (6)
117a...........785 (15)

Baba Batra

36...............cxxvii
8a..............35 (97)
12a............786 (16)
15a.............578 (7)
57b............26 (74)*
60b...99 (52)*, 188 (9)*
75a............464 (31)
91a.............14 (28)
93b..........17 (48, 50)
111a...........142 (69)
115b...........139 (66)

Sanhedrin

3b.................lxxx
9b............708 (115)
11a............602 (24)
11b...............7 (1)
19a.....43 (1), 284 (6)*
23a...lxxiii, 16 (42*, 43)
30a............16 (42)*
33b.................900*
37b............287 (15)
38a............456 (18)
39b............354 (12)
41b............761 (35)
43a....16 (42)*, 17 (51)
52b......733 (179), 815
56a............597 (22)
59b............183 (30)
64b...........216 (20)*
68a.............85 (13)
79a..........723 (164)*
82b...........675 (73)*
83a.......cix, 675 (73)*
83b.................675
87a................lxxv
89a.............292 (1)
97b............256 (12)
104a.................cxv
104b.............87 (23)
105a..........749 (225)*
107b............778 (32)
109b............178 (19)

Makkot

5b.........144 (75*, 76)
8b...................686

Shebuot

6b.............678 (75)*

'Abodah Zarah

10a...........340 (49)*
17a..................xvi
18a........xix, 259 (24)

Horayot

4a...................813

Zebahim

32b...........678 (75)*
116a..........759 (29)*

Menahot

18a...........678 (75)*
65a....116 (23), 283 (4)
85b..............52 (24)
107b............783 (11)

Hullin

6b......758 (21, 22, 23)
35b.............758 (18)
40a............185 (38)*
84a..............16 (40)
105a...........278 (20)*
106a.60 (49)*, 278 (20)*
110a.............56 (33)
116a.............59 (45)

Bekorot

30a.............786 (17)
30b....77 (9, 11, 12, 13)

'Arakin

11b..............23 (68)

16b..............83 (7)
32b.............756 (8)

Temurah

15b.....631 (8), 782 (5)
16a............277 (17)

Keritot

10a...........678 (75)*

Me'ilah

17a............187 (6)*

Niddah

6b.....31 (86), 121 (34)
33b.....10 (10), 637 (2)
65a..............lxxviii

YERUSHALMI

Berakot

2.7, 5b.........50 (19)*

Demai

1.3, 22a........757 (16)
2.2, 22d......77 (11, 12)
4.1, 23d.....756 (11, 12)

Kilaim

9.3, 32b........39 (112)

Shebi'it

6, end..............684

Terumot

11.4, 48a.......789 (19)

Ma'aserot

1.1, 48c.........70 (17)

Ma'aser Sheni

1.1.................791
5.2............790 (21)
5.5, 56b........792 (28)

Shabbat

1.1.................lxiv
1.3, 3b.........778 (33)
1.5, 3c...........77 (7)
14.3, 14c......782 (6, 7)
16, 15d........60 (49)*

Pesahim

3.7, 30b.........97 (47)
4.1, 30d.......38 (103)*
5.5, 32c............792
10.1, 37b.......109 (13)

Yoma

1.5, 39a.......118 (28), 126 (43)
5.3, 42b.......657 (38)*
5.7, 43a...713 (134, 135)

Shekalim

1.2.................lvii
1.4, 46b.......711 (123)

Sukkah

4.1, 54a........103 (4)*
4.1, 54b........700 (94)

Rosh ha-Shanah

1.3, 57a.........103 (4)
1.3, 57b........103 (4)*
2.1, 57d........116 (23)

Ta'anit

2.65b..........170 (5)*

Megillah

4.1, 75a............lxxi
4.12, 75c.......316 (19)

Hagigah

1.7, 76c.........97 (47)
2.1, 77b........16 (42)*
2.2, 77d........774 (23)
2.2, 78a.......734 (183)
3.8, 79d........128 (44)

Mo'ed Katan

1.1.................791
1.6, 80d........791 (26)
3.1..............79 (19)

Yebamot

ch. 13, 13c......87 (22)
13.2, 14c.......317 (21)

Sotah

1.4, 16d........133 (60)
5.7, 20c........99 (52)*

Ketubot

1.5, 25c..........46 (8)
5.12, 30c.............13
8.11, 32c.......128 (46)

Nedarim

1.3.............109 (15)
1.4, 40c........792 (27)
9.11, 41c........88 (32)

Nazir

8.1, 57a............674

Gittin

4.3, 45d.........756 (7)
9.11, 50d.......99 (52)*
end...........776 (26)*

Baba Batra

8.1, 16a.......139 (66), 142 (69)

Sanhedrin

1.2, 19a........456 (18)
2.6, 20c.......729 (172)
3.2,21a............lxxiii
6.5, 23b........144 (76)
7.2, 24b.......733 (180)
9.6, 27a.......723 (164)
10.6, 29c..........9 (4)
11.4, 30a.....lxxv, lxxvi

Aboda Zara

1.1, 39b.......702 (101)

Horayot

1.3...............xcvii
3.5..............43 (1)

Niddah

1.3, 49b......87 (24, 25)
2.1, 49d........87 (25)*

MINOR TREATISES

Abot of R. Nathan

I, 1, 1b.......463 (30)*, 580 (12)*
I, 1, 2b........580 (13)
I, 1, 3a........183 (30)
I, 2, 8.........758 (19)
I, 3, beg..........lxxxix
I, 3, 7b.........96 (44)
I, 5, 13b....cxxiii, cxxix, 80 (20*, 21), 153 (13)*, 186 (2), 748 (224), 764 ff., 778
I, 6, 14a.....cxxiii, cxxix
I, 12, 28b.......20 (54)
I, 16, 32a......317 (21)
I, 16, 63a......16 (42)*
I, 23, 38b............lv
I, 35, 52b....lxxxiv, 720 (157)
I, 35, 53a...........681
I, 36, 53b ff........cxxii
I, 41, 67a..cxxi, 88 (31)
II, 1–4.........580 (12)
II, 1b.........463 (30)*
II, 31, 34a......635 (18)

Semahot

2.11.........87 (24, 25)
3.6.............49 (15)
10.15...........50 (18)
10.16...........50 (19)

Soferim

14.14..........16 (42)*

MEGILLAT TA'ANIT

ch. 1...........116 (23)
1.1, scholion.....283 (4)
ch. 4...............814
ch. 4, scholion.......815
ch. 5, scholion..139 (66)
ch. 7...............814

SEDER 'OLAM RABBAH

ch. 25..........456 (18)
ch. 26..............806

TANNAITIC MIDRASHIM

Mekilta

Bo
ch. 17, p. 68.....87 (26)

Beshallah, Vayyehi
ch. 1, p. 94....340 (49)*
ch. 3, p. 99......256 (9)
ch. 5, pp. 104 ff. 40 (113)*
ch. 6, p. 112....184 (32), 322 (32)

Beshallah, Shirah
ch. 3, p. 126....184 (34)

Beshallah, Vayyassa'
ch. 1, p. 158....257 (15)
ch. 1, p. 159....116 (24)
ch. 2, p. 161....259 (23)

Jethro, 'Amalek
ch. 2..............9 (3)
p. 200.........109 (12)

Jethro, Bahodesh
ch. 3, beg.......642 (18)
ch. 3, p. 212....116 (24)
ch. 7, p. 229....259 (22)
p. 239..........184 (35)

Mishpatim
ch. 1, p. 246.......lxxix
ch. 2, p. 253.......lxxix
ch. 3, p. 257.......lxxix
ch. 3, p. 258.......lxxix
ch. 6, pp. 285 ff.....900*
ch. 8, p. 276..723 (164)*
ch. 8, p. 277........815
ch. 10, p. 285, 1.10 699 (92)
ch. 10, p. 277..722 (163)
ch. 20, p. 327...144 (76)
ch. 20, p. 328...287 (15)

Mekilta of R. Simeon

6.3............183 (29)
8, p. 176.....723 (164)*
13.5...........257 (14)
13.11..........257 (14)
14.25..........184 (33)
19.17...........97 (47)
23.7...........287 (15)

Sifra

Hobah
perek 12.1, 22d...lv, 684
perek 12.8, 23a..678 (74)
perek 12.8, 23a,b.758 (19)
perek 12.10, 23d 678 (75)*

Zav
par. 4.4, 33d...711 (129)
perek 8.6, 33b.......676
perek 12.1, 35c......xcvi
end............672 (63)
end, 37, 43a........666

Miluim
beg...............cxii

Shemini Miluim
23............733 (182)
26, 45a........733 (181)

Shemini
beg. lv
perek 2.4, 47b xcv
perek 8.9, 53c . . . 662 (53)
end 661 (50)

Tazria
perek 1.7, 58d . . 663 (56), 736 (188)

Mezora'
perek 4, end, 77a 719 (154)
perek 9.12, 79c . . 99 (52)*
end lv

Zabim
perek 8.4, 79a . xcviii, xcix

Ahare
perek 3, 81a 118 (28)
perek 3.11, 81b . . 656 (37), 658 (40)
perek 6.4 ff., 82a . 678 (78)
perek 8.8, 83b . . 713 (134)
perek 10.2 . . . . . 759 (29)*

Kedoshim
beg. 631 (7)
perek 4.9, 89b 83 (7)

Emor
perek 1.6, 94b . . 711 (127)
perek 1.7, 94b . . . 516 (26)
perek 3.12, 97a . 725 (170)
perek 4, 97c 689
perek 4.1, 97c . . . 663 (57)
perek 4.1 ff., 97c 678 (75)*
perek 4.4, 97d . . 678 (75)*
perek 10.2, 100a . 654 (34)
perek 12, 100d . . 641 (12)
perek 12, 110d . . 116 (23)
perek 12.1, 100d ci
perek 20.7, 104d 723 (166)

Behar
beg. lxxxii
perek 2.3, 107a . . . 756 (8)

Behukkotai
perek 1.1, 110d . . 612 (30)
perek 12.7, 115a . 699 (92), 899*

Sifre Numbers

8, p. 13 . . . . . . 893 (192)*
12, p. 18 lxxxix
39, p. 43 . 715 (145*, 146)
43, p. 49 . . . . . . 715 (145)
112, p. 120 cxxii
112, p. 121 . . . . . . 270 (9), 775 (25)
116 . . . . 893 (170a)*
116, p. 133 . . . . 683, 719 (156), 726, 727 (171)
124, p. 157 . 661 (48), 687
125, p. 161 . . . . . 678, 686
129, p. 166 687
131, p. 172 . . . . 735 (185)
142, p. 188 . . . . . 283 (4)*
161, p. 221 . . . . 900*

Sifre Zutta

Num.
5.2, p. 228 cviii
18.7, pp. 292–293 . . . 682, 683, 687
28.2, p. 322 . . . . . 283 (4)*

Sifre Deuteronomy

1 . . . . 84 (8)*
1.1 . . . . 527 (34)
15, p. 25 730
32 . . . . 288 (19)
37 . . . . 346 (3)
41 . . . . 97 (47)
43 . . . . 331 (41)*
48 . . . . 9 (3)
64, p. 130 . . . . 746 (220)*
78, p. 143 . . . . . . 673 (67)
79 . . . . 86 (18)
94 . . . . 287 (15)
105 . . . . 70 (16)
116 . . . . 16 (42)*
152, p. 205 lxxv
160, p. 211 729
190 . . . . 142 (71)
205, p. 241 734
208, p. 243 734
229 . . . . 15 (32)
235, pp. 268 ff. . 739 (197)
237 816
237, p. 270 . . . . 739 (196)
321 . . . . 456 (18)
348 . . . . 40 (113)
351, p. 408 . . . . . 729, 734
352 . . . . . 20 (55), 21 (57), 39 (111)
355 . . . . 52 (24)

Midrash Tannaim

Deut.
13.9, p. 65 lxxxviii
31.24 . . . . 52 (24)

LATER MIDRASHIM

Genesis Rabbah

11.4, p. 91 . . . . 56 (33)
ch. 16, p. 149 . . . 597 (22)
16.4, p. 148 . . . . 340 (49)*
ch. 20 . . . . 52 (23)
26.5, p. 247 . . . . . 182 (27)
26.7, p. 254 . . . . . 60 (49)*
28.7, p. 266 . . . . . 193 (22)
33.3, p. 306 . . . . . 39 (112)
36.1, p. 334 . . . . . 260 (25)
41 (42).2, p. 399 340 (49)*
44.12, p. 434 . . . . . 170 (5)
50.9, p. 525 . . . . . . 168 (4)
65.22, p. 742 . . . 594 (19), 766 (13)
70.5, p. 802 . . . . . 516 (25)

Leviticus Rabbah

beg. 756 (6)
9.3 . . . . 36 (98)

13.4 . . . . 193 (21)
16, p. 363 . . . . 782 (6)
19.4 . . . . 87 (25)*
35.6 . . . . 193 (21)
35.10 . . . . 612 (30)

Deuteronomy Rabbah

(ed. Lieberman)

p. 80 . . . . 782 (6)

Canticles Rabbah

1.4 . . . . 193 (21)
2.14 . . . . 97 (47)
3.5 . . . . 257 (16)

Lamentations Rabbah

1, 28b 91 (36)
1.5 (32) 13 (23)
1.16 (50) . 13 (19, 21, 22*)
4.2 . . . . . 16 (44), 17 (48), 24 (72)*
4.16 (50) . . . . 16 (42)*

Esther Rabbah

1.3 . . . . 48 (14)*
7.8 . . . . 217 (21)

Tanhumah

Ahare 9 . . . . 759 (29)*

Pesikta of R. Kahana

100b 597 (22)
117a 193 (21)

Midrash ha-Gadol

Deut.
11.22 . . . . 9 (3)*

Midrash Shemuel

17, p. 96 . . . . 899*

Midrash Psalms

104, 221b 182 (26)

RASHI

Esther
2.10 . . . . 217 (22)*

SEFER HASIDIM

W-F, 363, p. 111; and 1552, p. 380 . . . 170 (7)

INDEX TO SUBJECTS

Aaron, lxxxix, cxvi, 713, 714, 725–726.
Aaronids, and proselytes, 516; and Hellenists, 583–584; relations with Levites, works on, 878. *See* Priests.
Abba Saul, 890.
Abbahu, 789.
Abel, 709, 769.
Abel-meholah, Elisha meets Elijah at, 402.
Abimelech, priest of Nob, 370–371.
Abishai, 381.
Abner, 372, 373–374, 375.
Abot of R. Nathan, on origin of Sadducees and Boethusians, 764–772, 775–778, 897.
Abraham, cvi; determined rainfall on Rosh ha-Shanah, 114; and moral responsibility of the individual, 149–150; visited by angels, 164–165, 174, 354; hospitality of, 165–167; a shepherd, 353; pacifist, 354; promised Canaan by God, 358; symbol for Cyrus, 471; source of inspiration to Second Isaiah, 482.
Abraham ben David of Posquières, quot., 323–324, 676.
Absalom, 380–381.
Abtalyon, and free will, 256, 852; and paschal lamb, 730, 817.
Acts of the Apostles, 179, 180.
Adam, 708, 738.
Adeni, Solomon, 794.
Admon, patrician judge, 141–142; and Hanan, 731.
Adultery, punishment of, 733, 734.
Aggression, policy of, *See* Militarism.
Agricultural products, taxes on, 28, 69–72; purity of, 30.
Agrippa II, 13.
Agur ben Yakeh, Wisdom of (Prov. 30), 211–213, 541.
Ahab, King, cavalry of, 189, 395, 848; and Divine Providence, 196; reign of, 390–406, 411.
Ahaz, King, 320, 416-417, 430, 513, 759.
Ahaziah, King, 406, 408, 411.
Ahijah of Shiloh, 385, 387.
Ahikam, 442, 870.
Akaba, Gulf of, 378.
Akabiah ben Mahalalel, 78, 79, 620; quot., 256.
Akiba, xlii, li, lv, lxxvii, cxxii, cxxix, cxxxi, 796–797; disciples of, 1, 96; School of, 39, 627; marriage of, 45; and Eliezer ben Hyrcanus, 78–79, 84–85; at Academy, 83–84; humility of, 90, 91; and study of Law, 103; and Sukkot festival, 103, 701, 838; on inheritance, 140; and angels, 181, 182; and anthropomorphism, 322; literary power of, 464; loyal Pharisee, 620; (and views of School) on *tebul yom*, 676–678, 684, 686–689, 885, 888–889; on judicial leniency, 708; (and views of School) on Sadducees, 774–777; on menstrual laws, 776; and *Abot of R. Nathan*, 776–777, 897; on Johanan ben Zakkai, 776–777; (and views of School) on descendants of Hillel, 777; and Babylonian academies, 777–778; and women's rights, 837–838; and Shabuot, 883.
Quoted: on early dislike of scholars, 33; on righteousness, 86; on angels, 183–184; on poverty 194; on free will, 253, 256–257; on capital punish-

ment, 286–287; on love of God, 288; on Sabbatical year, 786.
Albo, Joseph, 743.
Alcimus, 593–595, 766.
Alexander the Great, 529, 878; conquers Persia, 570. *See also* Obadiah, Deutero-Zechariah.
Alexander Jannaeus, xxiii, 76, 110, 611–612, 638, 698, 701–703, 705, 763, 774.
Alexandra, Queen, *See* Salome.
Alfasi, Isaac, 794.
'am ha-arez, as applied to early provincials, xli, 25–32, 826, 894–895; later meaning of, 32–36, 629, 754, 760–761, 872; rules *re*, quot., 34; antonym of Pharisee, 76–77, 834; lack of culture of, 83–89; Elijah and, 401–402; gain power, 411–413; appoint a king, 439; piety of, cxx, 629; and observance of Sabbath and festivals, 660, 703–704, 756–759, 895; and Levitical purity, 664, 673–674, 690, 757–758; and offerings, 631–632, 647–648, 755, 757–758, 895; and pagan rituals, 759–760; and resurrection, 744–745, 754; and *halizah*, 741. *See also* Elisha, Jehu, Hanael.
'am Judah, variant of *'am ha-arez*, 415.
Amalekites, 368–369, 866.
Amasa, 381.
Amaziah, King, 415.
'amidah prayer, 750.
Amil Marduk, 335, 465–466, 873.
Ammi, 791, 896.
Ammonites, 366–367, 379; Joshua ben Hananya on, 547–548.
Amos, 19, 175, 341; his concept of equality analyzed, 294–295; comp. with Hosea, 300, 301, 357, 358, 858; as universalist, 356, 564.
Ancestor worship, 742, 744–746, 747.
Angelology, cxviii f.; of pre-exilic religion, 160–171, 744; exilic, 172; Pharisaic *vs.* Sadducean doctrines of, 173–185, 751–753; in Proverbs, 212; in Second Isaiah, 490; of Zechariah, 505; of Isaiah chs. 24–27, 536; of Trito-Zechariah, 542; of Hasidim, 574, 600; works *re* foreign influence on Pharisaic, 846.
Animals, controversy *re* purity of, 816–817.
Anthropomorphism, in early biblical records, 161–162; absent in later prophets, 307; of Ezekiel, 316–317, 322–323, 861; in later mystical works, 323–324; and sacrificial system, 655–656, 712. *See also* Angelology.
Antigonus, 618–619.
Antigonus of Socho, 95, 153, 154, 588, 590, 764–767, 769, 772, 775, 778, 897.
Antiochus Epiphanes, 8, 147, 154–157, 512, 563, 584, 590–593.
Antiochus III, 581–582.
Antipater, 614–615, 616, 618.
Antony, 618.
Anxiety, futility of, 258.
Aphek, first battle of, 363–364, 365; second battle of, 371.
Apocalypses, Isaiah, 24–27; analyzed, 536–537, 540, 541.
Apocalyptic literature, xlix f., 638.
Aptowitzer, V., cit., 818–819.
Arabah, 378, 382.
Aram-zoba, conquered by David, 378, 379, 380; consolidated, and Israel, 390; Ahab fears, 394; and Elijah, 401, 405–406, 868; after Ahab, 407–410; and Judah, 416, 423.
Aramaic, version of Bible, and anthropomorphism, 161–162; language of North, 553.
Aretas, 614–616.
Aristobulus, King, 610–611.
Aristobulus II, King, 612–617.
Aristocracy. *See* Patricians, Sadducees, Hasmoneans.
Aristophanes, quoted, xxiv.
Ark of the Covenant, 189, 319, 363, 364, 376.

Arrogance, sin of, 155, 228, 331, 340.
Artaxerxes, 559.
Asa, King, 839; reason for defeat of, 228–229; Ben-hadad helps defeat Baasa, 388, 411.
Assimilationism, 61, 66, 152, 154, 172, 351, 361, 363, 377, 384, 513, 555–559, 821. *See also* Hellenism; Manasseh; Ezra; Marriage, mixed.
Assumption of Moses, 193.
Assur-bani-pal, 434, 435, 436, 548.
Assyria, immigrants to Palestine from, 7; revolts against, 25; vices of, denounced by Nahum, 308–309; uses Jewish kingdom as buffer state, 416–436 *passim*, 869; purposes of, in dispersion of Israelites, 547–548; reason for Hezekiah's rebellion against, 550.
Astarte, worship of, introduced into Temple, 431. *See also* Idol-worship.
Athaliah, Queen, 24, 395–396, 407, 411, 413, 430, 513.
Atonement, Day of, lix, ci, cxii ff., anecdote *re*, 13; festival of, 54–58, 705–706, 713–714, 831; Pharisees and Sadducees on, 107, 114–115, 118–121, 127, 629, 639, 649, 654–660, 840; lights on, 134–135; performance of ceremonies, 265, 276–277, 670–672, 702, 783–784, 886–887; portion from Second Isaiah read on, 495; Supreme Sabbath, 646–647.
Autumn Festival, 15, 54–55, 831.

Baal, worship of, 1, 3, 28, 228, 345, 361, 365, 367, 369, 405, 407, 411, 417, 419, 426, 450, 705, 759; Hosea denounces, 295–298, 300; Jezebel introduces, 394–395; Jehu and, 410. *See also* Idol-worship.
Baasa, 388.
Babylonia, revolts against, 25, 550; Day of Atonement in, 56; exile in, 171–172, 262, 263, 328, 335, 853, *see also* Exile, Babylonian; suzerainty of Judah, 318–321; Ezekiel's hostility to, 335–340; uses Jewish kingdom as buffer state, 420–442 *passim;* fall of, 476–479; conditions reflected in Talmud, 782–783.
Babylonian academies, 715, 777, 797.
Bacchides, 594.
Baeck, Leo, lvii.
Balaam, cxv, 894.
Bar Kokeba, rebellion of, cxxxii f., 31, 836.
Barley, cut before the Omer in Jericho, 67, 839; first sheaf of, cut from fields, and Shabuot, 115; and calendar, 602.
Barzillai family, 867.
Bath-sheba, sin of, comp. with that of Naboth, 403.
Beer-sheba, shrine of, 365, 865.
Ben Azzai, 45; quot., 32, 85, 86.
Ben Bokri, 710–711.
Ben-hadad, 388, 407.
Ben Sira, 96, 152, 154, 178, 301, 566, 818, 881; quot., 153, 177; analyzed, as a patrician philosopher, 220–225, 588–590, 745, 748, 772, 863.
Benaiah ben Jehoiada, 382, 826.
Bene Bathyra, and sacrifice of paschal lamb, 730–731, 817; and authority *vs.* argument, 853.
Benjamin, tribe of, 24, 39, 290, 511, 512, 583, 828.
Benjaminites, 366–370, 372–373; accept David as King, 374; revolt against David, 381. *See also* Saul.
Beruriah, quot., 86, 87.
Bet Din Ha-Gadol. See Gerousia.
Beth-el, shrine at, 191, 295, 362, 365, 387, 549, 564, 865.
Beth-horon, 383.
Betrothal, length of, 450. *See also* Marriage, Wedding.
Biblical Law. *See* Scripture, Inheritance, False witnesses, etc.
Biblical period, works of, 821.
Bi-partisan control of Government, 9,

877. *See also* Oral Law, Great Assembly, Pharisees.
Boethus, 642, 764–768, 775.
Boethusians, origin of, 654, 762–779; comp. with Sadducees, cvi f., cxxiii, 770, 773, 777–779, 835; apostasy and corruption, 652–654, 775–778; opposed to Pharisees, 641–642, 649, 652–654, 658–660, 701–704, 705, 708, 883.
Boion, on tithing, 71.
Book of Jubilees. *See* Jubilees.
Book of Palaces (*Sefer Hekalot*), 323.
Book of the Pious, quot., 170.
Booty from "holy" war, and Samuel *vs.* Saul, 368–369, 866–867.
Bousset, W., xlviii f.
Bracton, quot., 198.
Bunyan, John, comp. with Pharisees, xviii.
Buzi, 318, 320.

Caesar, 618.
Cain, 709, 769.
Cain-Abel story, as pacifism, 351–354, 863.
Calebites, 515, 556.
Calendar, controversy *re*, 601–603; determination of new moon and festivals, c, 642, 652–654, 702, 725, 761.
Cambyses, 500.
Canaan, Israel in, 62, 116, 186, 358, 359, 362; David and, 377, 378.
Capital punishment, lxxv ff., in Jerusalem, 17, 287, 607, 843–844; Sadducees *vs.* Pharisees *re*, 696–697, 699–700, 708–709, 732–734, 735–736, 740–741, 815, 892; and Resurrection, 836. *See lex talionis.*
Carchemish, battle of, 318, 439, 440.
Cassuto, U., 721.
Cave Sect, 744.
Celibacy, 44, 45.
Ceremonies, ancestral, farmers' devotion to, 345–346; plebeians' devotion to, 349–350. *See also* Sacrifices, Temple, Marriage, etc.
Chaldeans, Habakkuk foresees conquest of Judea by, 310–311; Ezekiel admires, 335; and Judah, 420–421. *See also* Babylonia.
Charles, R. H., trans. quot., 147.
Childbirth, woman after, 642, 662–663, 670, 678, 736–739, 888–889. *See* Impurity.
Children, 162, 197, 268.
Christianity, and Pharisaism, 1, ix; spread of, in provinces, xi, xiv–xv, 32; and Decalogue, 65; and non-resistance to evil, 288–289.
Chronicles, 177, 178, 271, 272, 511, 556, 577; as plebeian philosophy, 228–230.
Circumcision, of exilic period, 172; of angels, 184; and Priestly Code, 462; Hellenists and, 571, 585; and priests, 674–675. *See also* Samson.
City, and country, xxiii–xxvi, lxi ff., 24–26, 32–34, 36, 37, 82, 308, 828; ancient texts on, 43; women in, 47; artisans of, cf. with peasants, 60; social attitude of, 149, 200, 202, 293, 342, 357.
City of refuge, 700, 713, 723.
Civil Law, lxxviii ff., and inheritance, 138–139, 841; protects landowners, 267; on responsibility of masters for slaves, 857. *See also sub* Individuality.
Civil War, 611–612.
Clan-consciousness, of aristocrats, 149, 293, 359; of priests, 792.
Class-consciousness, in Jerusalem, 16, 132; plebeian, 230–234, 236–240. *See also* Benjamin, Judah.
Clothing, sheet as, 16, 824.
Coffin, Henry Sloane, 628.
Commerce, of Jerusalem and Judah, 14, 416, 418, 433–434; David's policy *re* 382–384; of northern kingdom, 390–394, 867; of foreign countries, 823.
Conscription, law on, 597.

Copper mines, of Transjordan, 378, 382, 386, 387, 390, 392.
Corpse, unidentified. *See Met Mizvah.*
Corvée, Solomon's, 383, 385, 392.
Country gentry, 25, 33, 34, 41, 346, 350, 358, 430, 446, 515.
Court of Priests, 684, 689, 724–736.
Courts of justice, lxvi ff., 724, 727, 730–732; penalties in, Pharisees *vs.* Sadducees, 83, 286–287, 708–710, 721. *See also* Sanhedrin, False witnesses.
Craftsmen, 24, 41, 83, 264, 328, 446.
Criminals. *See* Courts of justice.
Croesus, 469, 470.
Cultural guidance, plebeians reject, of patricians, 19, 824.
Culture. *See* Social grace, Patricians, Plebeians, Provincials, etc.
Cutheans, 548. *See also* Samaritans.
Cynicism, plebeian, 230–234, 236–240; ended by Maccabean victories, 250.
Cyrus the Great, 173, 467, 468, 469–470, 471, 474, 476–480, 500, 509, 873.

Damascus, Sect of, xviii, xcix, 291, 568, 880; province of Israel, 379; Israel loses, 382; aids Judah, 388; Aristobulus invades, 613.
Daniel, Book of, 154–155, 177, 178, 536, 578, 592.
Darius, 500, 503, 507, 508.
David, cxvi, establishes Jerusalem, 11, 12, 378; provincials' loyalty to dynasty of, 25; and use of horses, 189; proposes build sanctuary, 189, 376; and Divine Providence, 196, 229; a shepherd, 353; prestige of, 355; wars of, 370–374, 378–379; king of united Israel, 374–380; resistance to, 380–381.
Davidic dynasty, modern scholar's view *re* legitimacy of, 818–819.
Decalogue, in Temple service, 63, 65; equated with Torah, 883.
Demetrius, 593.
Democracy, of resurrection, 147–148; of plebeian philosophy, 212–213; of plebeian law, 268–269; David's, 374, 376; of Babylonian exiles, 460–462. *See also* Equality.
Determinism, of provincials, 254–255. *See also* Fatalism.
Deutero-Isaiah. *See* Second Isaiah.
Deuteronomy, 271–272, 437, 439, 464, 551.
Deutero-Zechariah, 518, 519; as a rural prophet, analyzed, 528–532; interpolations in, 532–534.
Dietary laws, on fowl with milk, 58–60, 831–832; and Priestly Code, 462; conversion of provincials to, 534–535. *See also* Olives, Wine.
Dispersion. *See* Exile, Babylonian.
Divine Providence, 195–197; and plebeian philosophy, 226–230, 252–254; Job's disbelief in, 231–234; in appendices to Job, 234–235; and Psalms, 242–246, 248, 249; accepted by all Pharisees, 255, 606; in Zephaniah, 312; Hasidim and, 574, 600. *See also* Plebeians, philosophy of; God; Nationalism; Second Isaiah.
Divorce, 21, 44.
Doctrine, formulation of, 573. *See also* Hasidim, history of.
Dosa ben Arkenas, 731, 789.
Drunkenness, a rural sin, Hosea denounces, 295.
Dubnow, S., lix f.
Duhm, B., cit., 490; and Second Isaiah, 801, 803.
Duplicity, Hosea denounces, 295.

Ebiathar, 371, 377.
Ecclesiastes. *See* Koheleth.
Edom, province of Israel, 379; Israel loses, 382; ally of Babylonia, 449, 452–453, 871; Obadiah and, 526, 527, 528, 530; John Hyrkan conquers, 587–598. *See also* Idumeans.

Ego, consciousness of, 150, 158; development of, 196–202. *See also* Moral responsibility, Resurrection.
Egypt, influence of, on Proverbs, 213–214; loses suzerainty of Judah, 318, 388; effect on Ezekiel of visit to, 321–322, 335; Ezekiel uses, to denounce Babylonia, 336, 337; uses Jewish kingdom as buffer state, 420–440 *passim;* conquered by Persia, 500, 508; reason for Hezekiah's confederacy with, 550. *See also* Tobiads.
Ehud, at Ha-Pesilim, 190.
Elah, 388.
Elasa ben Shaphan, 870.
Elbogen, Ismar, lx.
Eleazar ben Arak, 719.
Eleazar ben Azariah, cxxxi, 85, 259, 783, 828.
Eleazar ben Shammus, 896.
Eleazar ben Zadok, 733–734, 815, 877, 882.
Eleazar ha-Kappar, 109; quot., 728.
Eleazar of Modin, 516.
Elephantine papyri, 419.
Eli, 737.
Eliakim, 439. *See also* Jehoiakim.
Eliezer ben Enoch, 78.
Eliezer ben Hyrcanus, xcii, cvii ff., cxxiii, 1, 34, 38, 78–79, 87, 133, 184, 317, 516, 620, 673, 721, 722–723, 724, 736, 796, 827, 837, 852, 888, 891; quot., 32, 32–33, 84, 85, 256, 732, 859.
Eliezer ben Jacob, 731, 739, 893; quot., 734.
Elihu, appendix of, to Job, 235.
Elijah, 7, 19, 196–197, 729, 745; and Samaria, 395, 397–398, 399–407; later estimates of, 398–399.
Elijah, Gaon of Wilna, xvii, xxxvii, xlii.
Elisha, 402, 407–408, 410, 745.
Elisha ben Abuyah, 79.
Emancipation of women, in plebeian law, 268–269. *See also* Women's rights.
Embalming, and resurrection, 146.
Employees, treatment of, in Jerusalem, 16–17.
En-gedi, produce of, 38.
England, law of retaliation in, in twelfth century, 197–198.
Enoch literature, 146–147, 152, 177, 178, 179, 230.
Ephraimites, 317, 362–366, 372; accept David as King, 374; after David, 385; and Deutero-Zechariah, 532, 534; as the Samaritans, 547. *See also* Samuel.
Epicurean, 751, 775.
Equality, human, Pharisees *vs.* Sadducees on, 284, 342–343, 516; prophetic ideal of, 292–294, 342–343, 858; ideal lacking in Hosea, 300–301; Isaiah, 301–302; Jeremiah, 302–305; Micah, 305–306; lacking in Nahum, 306–309; Habakkuk, 309–311; Zephaniah, 311–312; Ezekiel, 324–334, 341; Second Isaiah, *see sub* Universalism; urban, 535–541. *See also* Clan-consciousness, Democracy.
'erub, civ, 135–138, 639, 649, 719–720.
Esarhaddon, 431.
Essenes, xxxviii, cxvi, cxix f., 9, 77, 180, 192, 254–255, 291, 568, 880; and Hasideans, 573.
Esther, Book of, cit., 39, 177, 179, 818; analyzed as patrician philosophy, 216–217; comp. with story of Judith, 216–219; writing of, attributed to Sages, 578.
Ethical tradition of Jews, 203–204; Amen-em-ope's maxims comp. with, 850.
Eulogy, forms of, 48–50.
Eve, 738; sin of, and free will, 224–225.
Excommunication, origin of, 79–80.
Executions. *See* Capital punishment.
Ezekiel, ignores Shabuot, 117, 644; principle of individual moral responsibility, 150, 324, 325, 330; individual reward and punishment, 151, 333;

views regarding angels, 171, 172, 744, 752; and free will, 202; Book of, 312 ff.; relationship to the Temple, 318 ff.; visits to Tyre and Egypt, 321 ff.; change in style and interest, 326–327; and social injustice, 330 ff.; and equality of man, 332; and centralization of worship, 334; denounces Babylonia, 335 ff.; and Gog and Magog, 338–339; comp. to Second Isaiah, 467–468; promises union of Judah and Ephraim, 551–552; plan for Ideal Model Commonwealth, 551–552; and Synagogue, 566; and resurrection, 745.

Exile, Babylonian, historical significance of, 443–445; classes deported to, 446, 451, 455, 456; culture of Palestine during, 447; Jeremiah's followers in, 456–465, 872; early hope for a restoration, 465–466; Ezekiel and, 466–467; under Cyrus, 479–481; Second Isaiah with, 489; Haggai with, 504–505.

Exodus, quot., 104, 131, 168, 184, 273, 282; cit., 162, 169, 188, 189, 190, 197, 281.

Ezra, lxxi, xxxvi, 263, 461, 480, 510–511, 512, 558–559, 561, 562–568 *passim*, 590, 636, 761.

Falashas, 603, 641, 647.

False witnesses, lxxiii, Sadducees *vs.* Pharisees on law of, 142–144, 696–698, 843–844.

Farmers, and artisans, 37, 38, 60; of lowland, cf. with those of highland, 39, 40, 290; and Joel, 179; and social conflict, 294, 342; and Nahum, 308; and Kenites, 352; worship of, 345, 419, 431; *see also* Provincials, Patricians, *'am ha-arez.*

Fatalism, and Divine Providence, 195–197. *See also* Free will.

Fate, three views of, 195; plebeians' free will *vs.*, 202, 224, 251–254. *See also* Fatalism, Determinism.

First Commonwealth. *See* Social strata, Israel, Judah, Militarism, Pacifism, etc.

Flogging, 83–84.

Food. *See* Dietary laws.

Frazer, Sir James, 58.

Free will, 184; Fate *vs.*, 202, 224, 251–254; psalmists' denial of, 244, 245–246; works on, 849. *See also* Moral responsibility; Patricians, philosophy of.

Freedom, growth of concept of. *See* Equality, prophetic ideal of.

Funeral rites, 49–50, 830.

Galilee, lxi, 7; sociological strata of (chart), *see sub* Palestine; purity of produce of, 30, 827; survival of purification ceremony in, 31; social structure of, 40–42; customs of, comp. with Judah, 43, 60, 832–833; marriage customs of, 46, 47; widow's rights in, 48; funeral rites in, 49–50; olive-growing in, 52–54; and eating of fowl with milk, 59; and tithing, 72; its views of Pharisees' urbanity, 97; lights on Sabbath and Day of Atonement in, 134; use of oil in, 192; Phoenicians buy strip of, 382; offers help to Judea, 619; resurrection in, 751; harvest in, 787. *See also* Paschal lamb; Passover; Atonement, festival of.

Gamaliel I, 620.

Gamaliel II, cxxi, 34, 87, 133, 770, 775–777, 836; Academy of, 83; quot., 86, 89, 98, 278.

Gaumata, 500.

Gedaliah, 442, 447, 448, 870.

Geiger, A., lviii, l ff., cit., xlii, 131, 630, 637, 692, 720, 781, 816–817.

Gemariah ben Shaphan, 870.

Genesis, 331, 709.

Gentiles, and Sabbath law, 285–286,

770, 776; intermarriage with, 562; in new Commonwealth, status of, 597; equality of, 605; and immortality, cxv, 749, 894; and sacrifices, 896.
Geonim, period of, xli, xciv; schools of, 794.
Gerousia, 576–577, 582–583, 607–608, 762. *See also* Sanhedrin.
Gershom, Rabbenu, 263.
Gezer, 383.
Gibeah, seat of Philistine governor, 365, 372.
Gibeon, 367–368, 372, 377, 381, 866.
Gilgal, shrine at, 190–191, 363, 365, 367, 848, 865–866.
Ginzberg, Louis, lii, cit., xxii, xl–xli, 635, 716, 781.
Gischcala, olive trees of, 52.
Glassware, purification of, 128–130.
Gluttony, 193.
God, wrath of, 150, *see also* Vengeance; impersonal angels of, 160–172; and Job, 234; as origin of human thought—Ezekiel, 324; Ezekiel's mature conception of, 333–334; changing conception of, 443–445. *See also* Divine Providence, Anthropomorphism.
Grace after meal, 854; quot., 58, 579.
Graetz, H., lii.
Great Assembly, 576–580, 711, 753, 833. *See also* National Assembly.
Gressmann, H., liv, cit., 211.

Habakkuk, 306, 316, 341; comp. with Nahum, 307; social concept of, analyzed, 309–311.
Haberim, 757–758.
Hadrian, persecutions of, 31, 85, 96, 259, 563.
Haggai, 176, 177, 501–504, 505–508, 876, 877.
Hair, significance of uncut, 187, 188–189, 847; arrangement of, 848.
Hakoz, family, 512.
Halevy, I., lii.
Halizah, Sadducees *vs.* Pharisees *re*, 741, 816. *See also* Marriage, levirate.
Hanan ben Abishalom, 731.
Hananiah ben Hezekiah ben Gorion, 259.
Hand washings, for Temple, 273–277, 718–719; before and after meals, 278, 719–720, 854; after contact with a holy scroll, 278–279, 718.
Hanina (Segan ha-Kohanim), 676.
Hanina ben Hama, quot., 782–783.
Hanina ben Teradyon, 86, 259.
Ha-Pesilim, temple at Gilgal, 190–191.
Hasidim (Hasideans), 1, 3, 29; scholars' interpretation of Law against Sabbath reaping, 69; quot., 94; resurrection, 152–157, 742, 748–751, 754, 769; interpolations of, in Proverbs, 205–206, 208, 210–211, 227; appendices of, to Job, 234–235; glosses of, to Koheleth, 237–240; glosses of, to Psalms, 248, 249; and Divine Providence, 251; humanitarianism of, 541; history of, 573–574; reason for prestige of, 574–580; and Antiochus Epiphanes, 592–593; and laws of purity, 668–669, 677, 679–681, 684, 686–688, 690–692, 757–758, 885–889; and priesthood, 679, 680, 695, 711–716; and Great Assembly, 711; and sacrifices, 712–715; comp. to *'am ha-arez*, 754–755, 757–759, 761; opposition to Sadducees, 717–718, 762, 772; Sages of Israel, 762–763, 767–768, 773–774, 779. *See also* Pharisees, Essenes.
Hasmoneans, 14, 20, 22, 67, 80, 110, 639, 680, 734, 762, 821; and Hasideans and Pharisees, 157, 705, 762–763, 771, 773–774, 777–778; and free will, 251; militarism of, 593–596, 598; new aristocracy, 596–605, 610–619; and priesthood, 638, 683, 691–692; and Sadducees, 763, 770. *See also* Hyrkan, John; Maccabeans, Sadducees.
Hazael, 407, 409, 410.

Health, Levitical laws as rules of, 27–28.
Heavenly Chariot, controversy over, 182–183; Ezekiel's conception of, 328, 334.
Heave-offering, 632, 664, 669–671, 676, 677, 679–685, 687–689, 719, 736, 755, 789, 823, 888–889.
Hebron, 381.
Hecataeus of Abdera, 509.
Helene, Queen, 15.
Heliodorus, 584.
Hellenism, 1, 3, 22, 66, 152, 154, 312, 412; aristocracy and, 570–571, 574–575, 610; plebeians and, 571–573; Sadducean party heir of, 608. *See also* Tobiads.
Herem. *See* Booty.
Herford, R. Travers, lii ff.
Herod, cxiv, cxxvi f., cxxxi, 22, 67, 80, 285, 512, 618–619, 765, 768, 770, 773–774, 856, 857.
Herodians, 3, 13, 33; and *Shema'*, 66; and *nizzok*, 812; defined, 821.
Hezekiah, King, 417–430, 431, 433, 435, 437, 438, 550, 747, 855, 870.
High Priest, lix, history of office of, 22–23, 80; under Persia, 508; and Hasidism, 574–576; and Pharisees, xxxix-xl, 630–632; exegesis of Scripture, 629, 637, 654, 658; and Sadducism, 654, 778; in Hasmonean period, 638–639, 680, 683; and sacrifices, 655–660, 667, 671–674, 678–680, 681, 706, 712–715, 784, 886–888, 891–892; as judge, 730–732. *See also* Priests, Tobiads, Sukkot, Heave-offering, Calendar.
Hikkaret, 885, 886, 889, 896.
Hillel, xli, li, 15, 84, 773, 777, 795–796; and purity of olives, 53; meekness of, 83, 89–90; pupils of, 96, 124, 259; and Heavenly Chariot, 182; and proselytes, 516; School of, 619–620; *see also* Hillelites; and sacrifice of paschal lamb, 730, 817; and authority *vs.* argument, 853; disagreement with Shammai, 792–793. Quoted: on *'am ha-arez*, xli, 26, 894–895; on teachers, 83; on poverty, 193; on anxiety, 258; on Divine Providence, 287–288.
Hillelites, 1, 3, 10, 627, 633, 731, 777, 796, 824, 891; and work during Passover festival, 51; and purity of wine, 54; and size of *mahol*, 55; and eating fowl with milk, 60; humility of, 90–91; and ritual purity, 668, 676, 683–685, 687–689, 888; and inheritance, 696; and slaves, 697–698; and *lex talionis*, 722–724; and *'am ha-arez*, 834. Quoted: on praise of bride, 49; on Shammaites, 98, 837.
Hisda, lxxvii, 782.
Hofni, 363–364, 865.
Holiness, Pharasaic view of, 634, 649; Sadducean view of, 634; pagan view of, 655–656; in army, 664.
Holy of Holies, 118–120, 277, 654–658, 728, 784, 886–887.
Honi, quot., 615.
Horses, uses of, 189, 383, 384, 395, 534.
Hosea, 171, 294, 308, 315; quot., 192; social teachings of, analyzed, 295–301, 858; politics of, 356–358.
Hoshaya, 684.
Huldah, prophetess, 438, 442.
Humanitarianism, in Jerusalem, 17. *See also* Equality, Universalism.
Huna, Rab, lxxvii.
Huna ben Joshua, 891.
Huxley, Thomas, quoted, xvii.
Hyrkan, ben Joseph ben Tobiah, 580–581, 583, 584–585.
Hyrkan, King John, cxxvi, 157, 274, 425, 597–598, 606–608, 610, 638, 762–763, 771, 773–774, 777–778.
Hyrkan II, King, 612–618, 856, 857.

Idol-worship, xcvii, identified with luxury, 191, 655; Jeremiah denounces, 305; effect of, on Ezekiel, 319–321,

324–325; Solomon and, 383, 384; Jeroboam and, 387; Jezebel introduces, 394–395; at Mizpah, under Babylonia, 449. *See also* Baal worship, Elijah, Temples, Second Isaiah, etc.

Idumeans, cxxvi, rule Judea, 614–619. *See also* Edom.

Images, opposition to, 187, 847.

Immortality, cxv, cxxi f., 631; and nationalism, 749; and inheritance, 842. *See* Resurrection.

Impurity, sources of, xcviii ff., 26–27, 662–663, 665–671, 672–676, 678, 681, 686, 690–691, 718–719, 736–738, 758, 812–813, 885–886, 888–889.

Individual, recognition of. *See* Moral responsibility, Free will.

Individuality, absence of conception of, in pre-exilic times, 162–163, 846; name and, 169–170, 846; *re* masters and slaves, 283–285, 856–857; *re* accessory before the fact, 285; growth of concept of, *see* Equality, prophetic ideal of. *See also* Free will.

Inheritance, Pharisees *vs.* Sadducees on rights of daughters to, 138–142, 650, 694–696, 842. *See also* Widow's rights.

Intention, deed *vs.*, 197, 200, 496, 849. *See also* Vengeance, False witnesses.

International Right, Isaiah's doctrine of, 416. *See also* Universalism.

Irrigation, in Palestine, 28; *see also nizzok*.

Isaac, sacrifice of, 167, 168; a shepherd, 353; pacifist, 354.

Isaiah, 24, 146, 176–178, 191, 202, 310, 311, 312, 316, 341, 406, 450, 564, 605, 742, 744, 745, 747, 751; his concept of equality, analyzed, 301–302; rise of, 415; pacifist doctrines *re* foreign allegiance, 416–431 *passim*, 438. *See also* Second Isaiah, Apocalypses.

Ishbaal, 367, 372, 373, 374, 375, 866.

Ishmael, li, lv, xciii, 1, 86–88, 96, 181–185, 256–257, 620, 686–687, 787, 796, 836, 897; quot., 181, 727; School of, 683, 685–686, 774–775, 891.

Ishmael ben Phiabi, 124.

Israel, efforts to unite, *see* Samuel, Saul, David, Solomon; southern kingdom, *see* Judah; northern kingdom, 390–410; as a buffer state, 417, 423; list of references to, in Second Isaiah, 875. *See also* Samaria, Obadiah, Deutero-Zechariah.

Israel Baal Shem, Rabbi, xxi.

Isserlein, Israel, 263.

Jabesh-gilead, 366, 374–375.

Jacob, cxii, embalmed, 146; a shepherd, 353; pacifist, 354; list of references to house of, in Second Isaiah, 875.

Jacob, (R.), 714.

Jacob Tam, 792–795.

James, William, cit., 346.

Jannai, King, 76. *See also* Alexander Jannaeus.

Jason, High Priest, 586, 591.

Jebusites, David's treatment of, 377.

Jedaiah, clan of, 596, 878.

Jehoahaz, King, 439, 441.

Jehoash, King, 411–415.

Jehoiachin, King, 440, 465–466, 873.

Jehoiakim, King, 132, 320, 334, 439–440, 585, 862.

Jehoiarib, clan of, 513, 825, 878.

Jehonadab, 408.

Jehoram, 407–408, 411.

Jehoshaphat, King, lxvii ff.; and Divine Providence, 229; joins Ahab against Aram, 406, 411.

Jehu, 408–410, 411.

Jephthah, 7.

Jerahmeelites, 515, 556.

Jeremiah, 12, 14, 18, 24, 150, 151, 172, 176, 202, 298, 306, 307, 310, 315, 317, 320, 324, 341, 357, 450, 550, 564, 744, 870; denounces social oppression, 302–304; his concept of equality, analyzed, 304–305; foreign policy of,

436–442 *passim;* during Exile, 445, 455, 472; forced into Egypt, 447.
Jeremias, A., cit., 135, 138.
Jericho, lxi, produce of, 38, 647–648, 827; transfer of estate titles of, to Temple, 38, 68; customs of, 61–72; climate of, 131–132.
Jeroboam, and shrine at Beth-el, 191; and Ephraimite corvée, 383, 385; king of northern tribes, 385–388.
Jerusalem, lxi ff., 7; sociological strata of (chart), *see sub* Palestine; social structure of, 11–23, 627, 643–644, 647–648, 751–753, 761, 789 f.; tax for poor of, 28, 69–72, 270–272; influence on Judea and Galilee, 43, 60; widow's rights in, 48; funeral rites in, 49–50; climate of, 132, 378; concept of freedom in, 293; Ezekiel rejects primacy of, 317–318; income of, 382; destroyed, 442, 449, 591, 777; hopes for rebuilding of, *see* Second Isaiah; rebuilding of, 501; rebuilding of wall, 559–561; Pharisees in, 628, 630, 632–633, 774; in Persian and Hellenistic periods, 639, 746–748; traditions of, 647, 651–652, 704, 707–708, 788; judges in, 699, 724, 731; doctrine of immortality in, 747–748. *See also* Paschal lamb, Passover, Pilgrims, Tithes.
Jezebel, 394–398, 400, 403, 406, 408, 409–410.
Jezreel, plain of, 40, 107, 371, 388; Ahab's capital, 400, 408.
Joab, 373–374, 381.
Job, Book of, 151, 152, 176–177, 178, 179, 541, 750; analyzed as plebeian philosophy, 231–235; quot., 288.
Joel, 178–179; as a rural prophet, analyzed, 518–523, 524, 525–526, 878; interpolations in, 523–524, 525, 532.
Johanan ben Nappaha, lxxiii f., 782, 789, 791, 890.
Johanan ben Nuri, 84; quot., 83.
Johanan ben Zakkai, cxxx, 33–34, 90, 96, 124–125, 182, 286, 620, 651–652, 710, 731, 776–777, 791, 826; quot., 124, 279, 635, 710, 728–729.
Johanan the Hauranite, 84.
Jojarib family, 596.
Jonah, Book of, 521, 537–540, 810.
Jonah Gerondi, xli.
Jonathan, 367, 370, 375, 865.
Jonathan ben Mattathias, 157, 594–595, 638.
Jonathan, (R.), 686–687.
Joram, King, *see* Jehoram.
Jordan. *See* Transjordan.
Jose ben Halafta, 1, 757, 760, 784–785, 830, 896; quot., 785, 787.
Jose ben Hanina, 785.
Jose ben Joezer, cxxix, 130, 594, 691, 766, 782, 835, 897.
Jose ben Johanan, 766, 771, 835, 897.
Jose the Galilean, 59, 86, 96, 793–795, 896.
Joseph, cxii, embalmed, 146.
Joseph, (R.), 733.
Joseph ben Kismah, quot., 259.
Joseph ben Tobiah, 574–575, 580–581, 587.
Joseph ibn Habib, 794.
Josephus, xlvii ff., 10, 21, 41, 77, 80, 91, 96, 102, 110, 124, 126, 180, 185, 192, 195–196, 251, 254, 531, 581, 587, 609, 615, 616, 700–701, 708, 724, 730, 736, 763, 815. Quoted: on attitude to Pharisees, xv; on Pharisees *vs.* Sadducees, 82, 261; on Law among Pharisees, 91, 93; on Fate *vs.* free will, 253; on Aristobulus II and Hyrkan II, 614; on Pompey's siege, 617.
Joshua, lxxxii f., 464, 641, 654.
Joshua, Book of, quot., 95, 116.
Joshua ben Hananya, i, lxxi, cvi, cxxxi, 86, 90–91, 103, 182, 256, 516, 547–548, 620, 673, 685, 706–707, 796; quot., 32, 547–548, 706, 837.
Joshua ben Korha, quot., 288.

Joshua ben Levi, 792, 854.
Joshua ben Perahya, 597, 766, 771, 778.
Joshua Ha-Garsi, 814.
Joshua, High Priest, 501, 504, 507.
Josiah, King, 11, 314, 319, 320, 334, 435–439, 441, 442, 550, 565, 747.
Josiah, (R.), 686, 727, 784.
Jotham, as regent, 415.
Jubilaic system, cxv ff., 756.
Jubilees, Book of, xlvii ff., lxxviii, 113–114, 116, 177–179, 184, 252, 268, 274, 276, 277, 536, 601, 603–605, 629, 641, 647, 651, 810, 817.
Judah, land of highlanders, 24, 39, 828; as kingdom, 386–388; social conflict in, 410–417; trade of, 416; as a buffer state, 416–440; subjected by Babylonia, 440–442; during Exile, 445–451, 551, 871; *see also* Second Isaiah; Sheshbazzar appointed governor under Cyrus, 480; exiles return to, 480–481, 509; Zerubbabel governor, 500–508; Persian governors appointed, 508. *See also* Provincials, Judea, Judaites, Ezekiel, Carchemish, Haggai, Zechariah, Persia.
Judah ben Bathyra, 183.
Judah ben Ilai, 1, 109, 651–652, 714–715, 735, 776, 783–789, 793, 827–828, 885–886, 888, 891; quot., 49, 710, 786, 832.
Judah ben Mattathias, 593–594, 691.
Judah ben Tabbai, 612, 767, 771, 774, 778, 843, 844; quot., 144, 697.
Judah the Patriarch (the Prince), lxxvii, 39–40, 185, 834, 888, 892; quot., 35, 86.
Judaites, and Samuel *vs.* Saul, 368–369; and David, 370–374, 378, 381; after David, 383, 385–388; Athaliah and, 395; effect of return of, on Samaritans, 553; results on, of Samaria's rejection, 555–559, 757; signs of maturity of, 561; friendly with Samaritans, 561. *See also* David, Judah.
Judea, 7, 8–9; sociological strata of (chart), *see sub* Palestine, also social strata; purity of produce of, 30; social structure of, 37–40, 627, 748, 753; customs of, comp. with Galilee, 43, 60, 832–833; marriage customs of, 45, 46; widow's rights in, 48; funeral rites in, 49–50; wine-making in, 54; and eating of fowl with milk, 59; climate of, 131–132, 660; lights on Sabbath and Day of Atonement in, 134; belief in resurrection in, 158; simple life in, 187, 192; and tithing, 272, 786; concept of freedom in, 293; under Idumean ruler, 618–619; spread of Pharisaism in, 751; harvest in, 787. *See also* Paschal lamb; Passover; Atonement, festival of.
Judgment, four periods of, Sadducees *vs.* Pharisees on, 113–114.
Judith, 127–128, 810; comp. with Esther, 217–219.
Justice, social, *see* Equality, human; Vengeance, Reward and punishment; political, *see* Courts of justice.

Kaddish prayer, 750.
Karaites, 134, 737, 779, 817, 839.
Kaufmann, E., 742.
Kedusha, 752.
Kenites, 515, 556, 863. *See also* Cain-Abel story.
Kidron, Valley of, 647.
Kings, Books of, 281, 334, 434, 549, 761.
Koheleth, 750; analyzed as plebeian philosophy, 235–240.
Krochmal, N., 781.

Lamentations, 3rd chap. analyzed as plebeian philosophy, 226–227; 4th chap., nationalist, 451–453; 2nd chap., pietist, 453–455.
Land laws, attempts to enforce, 290–291.
Land-ownership, development of, 38–

39; social effects of, and Amos, 293–295; effect of use of money on, 393–394.

Lauterbach, Jacob Z., lvii, explanation of Day of Atonement controversy, 119–120, 655.

Lay associate of High Priest, 508, 877.

Learning, patricians' early contempt for, 18; priests' lack of, 20; provincials' lack of, 29; Pharisees' respect for, 91–95; patricians' later views of, 95–96, 836; and Great Assembly, 579–580. *See also* Scribes, Oral Law, etc.

Legal institutions, development of. *See* Oral Law.

Legalism, development of, during Babylonian Exile, 462–465.

Leszynsky, E., cit., 817–818.

Levirate marriage. *See sub* Marriage.

Levites, rivalry of, with priests, 2, 513–514, 582, 825; classes of, 23, 514, 825; tax for support of, 28, 69–72, 270–272, 631–632, 681 f., 755; mentors of plebeian farmers, 37–38, 514; property owners, 514–515; and Temple, 705–707, 711; in judicial procedure, 729–732; works on relation of, with Aaronids, 878.

Levitical laws of purity. *See* Purity.

Leviticus, 115, 644, 649, 693–694.

Lex talionis, lxxvi f., cxv, cxxi, Sadducees *vs.* Pharisees *re*, 639, 696–697, 720–724, 736, 815, 882.

Liberalism, of Pharisees, 9–10; of Levites and Scribes, 23.

Lieberman, Saul, cxxxiii f., cit., 685, 789, 792, 897, 898, 899.

Living, standard of, in Jerusalem, 13, 16, 830; patrician *vs.* plebeian, history, 186–192; later struggle for simple, 192–194, 847; Pharisees' *vs.* Sadducees', 186, 193.

Lots, scholars *vs.* Sadducees *re* drawing, for sacrifice of he-goats, 814.

Loyalists, 588–596 *passim.* *See also* Simeon II, Nationalism.

Luther, M., li.

Ludd, produce of, 38; and commerce of Jerusalem, 447.

Maccabean Age, philosophy of, and after, 250–260.

Maccabeans, lx, 7, 13, 40, 67, 74, 116, 117, 120, 121, 130, 312, 425, 594, 638, 671, 766. *See also* Hasmoneans.

Maccabees, Books of, 512, 587, 589, 644.

Maimonides, xli, xciv, 58, 323, 464, 676, 743, 751, 765, 798, 831.

Malachi, 177, 179; quot., 271, 399, 557–558.

Manasseh, King, 319, 320, 430–435, 437, 438, 513, 550, 565, 870.

Manichaeism, xii.

Mann, J., cit., 818.

Marital congress, laws *re*, 662–666, 668–670, 672, 734–739, 758, 816, 889.

Marriage, xciii; among Pharisees, 9; of near relatives, 16, 824; among priests, 21–22, 23, 825; Deuteronomy quot., on, 34–35; plural, 18, 41, 43, 665, 824, 828, 837; customs of, 43–47, 829; contract, 45, 48, 828; levirate, 163, 169–170, 695, 740–741; 816, 824; mixed, 555–559, 561–562, 589; and festivals, 791. *See also* Monogamy.

Martyrdom, Jeremiah on, 320; religious, in Jerusalem, 431; Hasids and, 592–593.

Materialism, of lower classes in time of Jeremiah, 18; of priests, 21, 638, 643–645. *See also* Patricians, philosophy of.

Mattathias of Modin, 156, 593.

Meal-offerings, 713–715, 759–760, 896; Sadducees *vs.* Pharisees *re*, 692–693, 814.

Measurement of the Height (*Shi'ur Komah*), 323.

Media, Ten Tribes exiled in, 326, 444, 479.
Megiddo, 439.
Meir, lxxiii, xcii, cviii, 1, 39, 40, 79, 86, 133, 170, 677, 714, 740–741, 776, 783–784, 791–792, 827–828; quot., 34, 184, 260.
Meir of Rothenburg, 263.
Mendelssohn, Moses, xxii.
Menelaus, High Priest, 512, 586–587, 590–591, 881.
Menorah, purification of, 128–129.
Menstrual impurity, xcvii ff., 637, 666, 668–670, 672, 776; Sadducees *vs.* Pharisees *re*, 813. *See also* Purity, laws of.
Merodach-baladan, 420.
Messianic hopes, 8, 73, 145, 189, 335, 503, 507, 600, 629, 635, 747, 827, 869.
Met mizvah, 819.
Metals, impurity of, Sadducees *vs.* Pharisees on, 128–130, 649, 693–694.
Meyer, Eduard, xlviii f., cit., xxvi, xxxvii.
Micah, 12, 176, 298; his concept of equality, 305–306.
Micaiah, 405–406, 426.
Michal, 370, 376.
Militarism, farmer's, 346–347; patrician's 350–351, 361, 864; Shiloh priest's, 362–364; Saul's 366–371; David's, 370–374, 377, 378; Solomon's, 384; Ahab's, 405–406; Elisha and, 407; revolts against Babylonia, 440–442; of Haggai, 503–504; Hasmoneans', 593–596, 598. *See also* Deutero-Zechariah.
Milton, John, quoted, xviii.
Minhah prayer, 707, 759–760, 783.
Mishna, interpretation of, 1–2; growth of, 93; recitation of, 650.
Mithraism, xi.
Mixed marriages. *See sub* Marriage.
Mizpah, shrine at, 108, 365, 865; and Babylonian governors, 449, 471, 804.
Moab, province of Israel, 379; Law and, 541, 879.
Modesty, of Galileans *vs.* Judeans, 47.
Modin, village of, and laws of purity, 30.
Molin, Jacob, 263.
Money, 867; introduction of economy of, during Ahab's time, 393–394.
Monogamy, and marital life, 837.
Monotheism, early, 166.
Moore, G. F., lii ff.
Moral responsibility, individual, 149–151, 167, 197, 225, 284; deed *vs.* intention, 202, 849–850; Ezekiel and, 324, 325, 329–334; and Babylonian exiles, 489; and Second Isaiah, 490. *See also* Free will.
Mordechai, a Benjaminite, 39, 818.
Morning Bathers, 9, 822.
Mortgages, farm, and money, 394.
Moses, lxvii, ciii, cxviii, cxxv, God's appearance to, 168, 656; and Oral Law, 266, 701; a shepherd, 353; Elijah comp. with, 399; power of expression of, 464; derivation of Law from, 463, 873.
Mount Carmel, Elijah's assembly on, 400.
Mount Horeb. *See* Elijah.
Mount of Olives, red heifer ceremony on, 123, 127, 667; and paschal meal, 757.
Musaf prayer, 707.

Nabopolassar, 435.
Naboth's vineyard, lxxxiii, 397, 402–403, 404, 405.
Nadab, 388.
Nadab, and Abihu, 733.
Nahman, lxxvi, 842.
Nahmanides, xli, 743.
Nahum the Elkoshite, 310, 450; philosophy of, analyzed, 306–309.
Nasi, 774
Nathan, (R.), 890.

Nathan ben Yehiel, 765.
Nathan the Prophet, and built sanctuary, 189–190, 376; quot., 184.
National Assembly, 400.
Nationalism, movement toward, 66–67, 73–74, 852; farmers', 344, 345–347; of prophets, 355–356; and foreign sympathy, 425; of Babylonian exiles, 451–453; of Haggai, 503–504, 506; and marriage, 555–556. *See also* Social strata, Loyalists, Simeon II, Second Isaiah.
Nazirites, 188, 365.
Nebuchadnezzar, lxiii, arrogance of, 155; conquers Judah, 439–442, 449; and seditious prophets, 453; Cyrus upholds plans of, for Negeb, 479. *See also* Babylonia.
Nebuzaradan, 442.
Necho, Pharaoh, 439.
Necromancers, and Saul, 368.
Nehemiah, 136, 271, 282, 508, 512, 559–561, 631, 711, 761.
Nehunyah ben Hakkanah, 683.
Nergal-Shar-Usur, 335, 466–467.
New Covenanters, 9.
New Year, celebration, 54; Additional Prayer for the, 846.
Nicanor, 594.
Nisan, fourteenth day of, not observed in Jericho, 61. *See also* Paschal lamb.
Nittai the Arbelite, 597, 766, 770.
Nizzok, Sadducees *vs.* Pharisees *re*, 716–718, 811–813.
Noachic laws, ciii, 597, 881.
Nomadic culture, 295–296, 352–353, 858, 863.
Non-aggression, doctrine of. *See* Pacifism.
Non-resistance to evil, 287–289.
Numbers, Book of, 271.

Obadiah, 391, 400, 518; as a rural prophet, analyzed, 526–528, 529, 530.
Oil, use of, 192–193.
'olam ha-ba, 741–743, 749–750, 769.
Olives, purity of, 52–54.
Omer, ci, 641–642, 646–653, 715, 773, 883.
Omri, 388–389, 390, 391, 392, 868.
Onias, II, 575.
Onias III, 584–585, 587.
Opportunism, a patrician policy, 344, 375, 384, 386, 391; effect of Ahab's, on prophecy, 391–392. *See also* Social strata, Hezekiah.
Oral Law, 180, 600; rejected by Sadducees, 261, 266, 777; early development of, 261–267; as adjustment of Written Law, 267–270; on tithes, 270–272; on hand washings, 272–280; accepts system of land-ownership, 289, 701, 890.
Original sin, 224–225.

Pacifism, of early Pharisees, 287, 345, 347–350; of patricians, 351; and Cain-Abel story, 351–354; of patriarchs, 354–355; of plebeians, 361, 852; of Samuel, 364–366, 368–369; of Zechariah, 504, 506; Darius trusts Judah's, 508; in Second Zechariah interpolation, 534; Nehemiah *vs.* urban prophets', 560; reconciled with militarism, *see* Hasmoneans, militarism of. *See also* Isaiah, Hasidim.
Paganism, priests and, 637–638, 643, 647, 660; and incense, 655, 657–658, 896; and water-libations, 704, 707; and *'am ha-arez*, 759–760; and immortality, 747. *See also* Idol-worship.
Palestine, 2; sociological strata of, last decade of Second Commonwealth (charts), 4–5; provinces of, 7; twentieth-century, 516–518; a single unit, 550; sociological conditions of, reflected in law, 782–783; schools of, 797. *See also* Jerusalem, Judea, Galilee, Jericho.
Pappias, 322; quot., 183.

Pardo, David, 727.
Parents, authority of, Biblical *vs.* plebeian law on, 268–269
Paschal lamb, sacrifice of, 50–51, 678, 730, 746, 817, 885, 889
Passover, ci, 27, 50–51, 103, 115–117, 126, 133, 601–602, 632, 641–643, 646–649, 652–654, 757, 841, 883, 885–886, 889
Passover *Haggada*, 751–752
Patriarchs, pacifism of, 354–355
Patricians, as a class, 4; income of, 14; and learning, 18, 95–96, 754; and provincials, 24, 761, 826; philosophy of, xl, 204–209, 214, 216–219, 220–225, 246–251, 632–633, 748–751, 773, 789, *see also* Opportunism, Militarism; and Oral Law, 261, 266, 269–270; and tithing, 270–271; in David's kingdom, 377, 380–381; after Solomon, 383–385; under Ahab, 393–394; foreign sympathies of early, 424–425, 440; under Josiah, 437–438; old, under Persia, 510–511; and Hellenism, 570–571, 574–575, 610, *see also* Tobiads; in Pharisee-Sadducee controversies, 627–628, 630, 634, 648, 651, 655, 660, 767; and background of Sadducism, 753. *See also* Sadducees, Hasmoneans, Shammaites, Senaa, etc.
Paul, a Benjaminite, 39.
Peasant revolt, 409. *See also* Hazael, Jehu.
Pentateuch, norms of, l; Sabbath reading of, 134; and "angel of the Lord," 165, 179; and sanctuaries, 189; and hand washing, 274; and human equality, 342–343; *re* "Ammonite," 547; *re* Ten Tribes, 552; Samaritans accept authority of, 561. *See also* Priestly Code.
Pentecost, celebration of, 13, 103, 265, 600. *See also* Shabuot.
Peraea, 7. *See also* Transjordan.
Persia, officials of, and patricians, 201, 509; provincials under, 25, 510; appoints Jewish governors, 480, 500; places own governor over Judah, 508; rural prophets under, 518–534; and rebuilding Jerusalem's wall, 559; Alexander conquers, 570. *See also* Cyrus, Darius.
Personality, name signifies, 169–170; extended, 285–286, 856–857.
Pesah. *See* Passover.
Pestilence, Jews' comparative immunity to, 273.
Peter, 132.
Pharisaism, spread of, ix; and Christianity, x; and Moslem influence, x; a political slogan, 76; survey of, 99–100; history of, 606–609; 611–619; fissure in party, 619–620; legacy of, 636, 780, 797–798.
Pharisees, accusations against, xv, 97–100; and prophetic teaching, xvi, 627–630, 753; and Puritans, xvii; and Rabbinic Judaism, xxi, xl; and urban life, xxiii, 627–630, 632–633; theology and ethics of, xxxvii–xl, 627–636, 748 f., 752–753; organization of, 1, 3, 76, 631, 763, 821; divisions within ranks of, xl, 255–260, 285, 633–634, 637, 696, 738, 740, 780–798; comp. to Essenes, xxxviii; on immortality, xliii, 626, 741–751, 754, 764, 767, 769, 772–773, 777; and Temple and priesthood, 23, 628–634, 652, 771, 774; open-mindedness of, 9–10, 634, 780, 822; and *Shema'*, 66; and Sabbath reaping, 69; on tithing, *see* Tithes; comp. with Sadducees, 80–81, 82–83; and learning, 91–97; controversies with Sadducees, 101–144, 279, 281–285, 630, 632–636, 637–753, 811–819, *see also* Oral Law; and hand washing, 275–277, 278–280; and foreign allegiance, 425; and Synagogue, 569, 631; and Hasideans, 573, 606; demands of, from Queen Salome, 612–613; comp.

with *'am ha-arez*, 628–629, 631–632, 754, 757–761; and Hasmoneans, 762–763, 771, 773; break with Sadducees, 631, 762–779; leaders of, 766–767, 771, 774; seven types of, 837. *See also* Pharisaism; Shammaites, Hillelites, Purity, Society for enforcement of.
Philanthropy, in Jerusalem, 17.
Philippi, battle of, 618.
Philistines, Abraham's treaty with, 354; marriage with, forbidden, 355, 362; subjection of Israel to, 363–367, 865; Benjaminite raid on, 367–368; and David, 371–372, 377–378; and Jeroboam, 387–388; and Assyria, 426, 429, 430.
Philo, 60.
Phineas, 735.
Phinehas, 363–364, 865.
Phoenicians, in Galilee, 382; Omri's treaty with, 390; Ahab vassal of, 394, 401.
Phylacteries, Sadducees *vs.* Pharisees *re*, 814.
Pietists, faith of, 66, 74; maxims of, 205–206, 208, 210–211; appendices of, to Job, 234–235; glosses of, to Koheleth, 237–240; and Psalms, 243–246, 248, 249; under Manasseh, 432–433; among Babylonian exiles, 453–455. *See also* Hasidim.
Pilgrims, to Jerusalem, 27, 643–644, 648–649, 663, 683, 704–705, 707, 720, 745, 746–747, 757, 791, 885.
Pineles, H., lii.
Plebeians, as a class, 4, 627–628, 630, 648, 694–695; homes of, 14–15; wages of, 15; and learning, 18, *see also* Scribes, Prophets; as spiritual mentors, 19–20; and provincials, 24–25; and Fate *vs.* free will, 202, 224, 251–254; philosophy of, 211–213, 215, 217–219, 226–246, 248, 249, *see also* Nationalism; law of, *see* Oral Law; in David's kingdom, 379–380; after David, 383–389; and Ahab, 393–394, *see also* Elijah; foreign sympathies of early, 424, 440; effect of Sennacherib's raid, 430, 431, 433–435; and Hellenism, 571–573, 581, *see also* Hasidim; and Hasmoneans, 599–605. *See also* Pharisees; Exile, Jeremiah's followers in; Loyalists; etc.
Poetry, replaced by prose, 463–464.
Polygamy, in Jerusalem works on, 824. *See also* Marriage, plural.
Pompey, conquest by, 65–66, 615–618.
Population, of Jerusalem, 11–12, 609.
Prayer-meetings, pietists establish private, 432, 563–565, 880. *See also* Synagogues.
Predestination, and free will, 252–253.
"Priestly Code," 461, 872.
"Priestly blessing," 278, 854.
Priests, lxii ff., rivalry with Levites, 2, 513–514, 582, 792; lack of learning among, 20; as landowners, 20–21, 290–291, 508–509; as mentors of landowners, 37; suspicious of Pharisees, 76; criticized by psalmist, 244; as psalmists, 246–250; and Law, 264–266, 633, 638, 643–645, 647; Levites required to tithe for, 270; David and, 377; Jehoash and, 413–414; under Persia, 508–514, 652, 704, 748; Malachi shows corruption of, 557; and synagogues, 567–568; status of, 628–630, 709–716; and pagan rites, 637–638, 643, 647; materialistic interests of, 638, 643–645; and laws of purity, 661–692 *passim*, 718–719, 884–888; uncircumcised, 674–675. *See also* Hand washings.
Prophets, 1 f., true and false, 1–3, 292, 426, 441, 454, 493–494; and resurrection and immortality, 152, 743, 745–746, 747, 749; and angels, 171, 744, 751–753; birthplaces of, Sages' method of determining, 309; David and,

376, 377; Jeroboam and, 387; Ahab and, 391-392, 394–406 *passim;* from Ahab to Jehoash, 408–411; Jehoash and, 413–414; and village temples, 418–420; and Isaiah, 426; under Manasseh, 431–433; under Josiah, 436–437; of exilic Palestine, 450–451; types of, in Babylonia, 451–455; become legalists, 462–463; rural, during Persian period, 518–534, *see also* by name; urban, 534–541, *see also* Apocalypses, Trito-Zechariah; ethical lesson *re*, 539–540; synagogues and, 563–565; last of true, 577–578; and pagan beliefs, 646, 742–744, 759. *See also sub* Equality, Prophets by name, etc.

Prosbul, lvi.

Prose, replaces poetry, 463–464.

Proselytes, c, among Babylonian exiles, 461, 491, 872; of the Pharisees, 498–499; Zechariah welcomes, 506; in Second Commonwealth, 515–516; and dietary laws, 535; Samaritans as, 550; as wives, 556, 561; Law *re*, 597; Idumeans as, 598, 614; Aristobulus and, 610.

Proverbs, Book of, 177, 572, 748; history of, 203–204, 211, chs. 1–9, analyzed, 204–208; examples of patrician philosophy in, 208–209, 214; pietistic maxims, 210–211; examples of plebeian philosophy in, 211–213, 215; Sages and, 215–216, 257.

Provincials, Palestinian, lxi ff., 24–37; philosophy of, 254–255, 257, 342; prophets of, 518–534. *See also* Judah, Ephraimites, etc.

Psalmists, and resurrection, 152, 744–746; and angels, 177, 181–182, 751.

Psalms, 453, 871; history of, 240–241; philosophy of, analyzed, 241–250; glosses to, 245, 248, 249.

Pseudepigraphic literature, lxxx.

Purification ceremony. *See* Red heifer.

Purim, observance of, in Book of Esther, 216, 851; modern scholar raises controversy *re*, 817–818.

Puritanism, its relation to Pharisaism, liii f., xvi; accusations against, similar to those against Pharisees, xx.

Purity, xcviii ff., laws of, 17, 26–28, 30–32, 180, 629; boundary lines of, 30; of olives, 52–54; of wine, 54; and Priestly Code, 462; Trito-Zechariah on, 544–545; Sadducees *vs.* Pharisees on, 661–691 *passim*, 811–813, 816–817, 885–889; and *'am ha-arez*, 757–758; Society for enforcement of; issue of organization of, 74–75, 606, 834; unique characteristics of, 75–76; "Separatists," 76; political aspect of, 76, *see also* Pharisaism; rules of admission and expulsion, 77–78, 834; cases of expulsion, 78–79; number of members, 609. *See also* Pharisees, Red heifer, Hand washings, Geiger, Impurity, *Tebul yom.*

Qumram sect and scrolls, xxxviii, l, lxxiv, cxvi, cxix, cxxxiii.

Rab (Abba Arika), lvii, lxxvii, 782–783.

Raba (Abba ben Joseph), lvi, 888, 895.

Rabbah ben Hanan, lvii.

Rachel, grave of, 39.

Rain ceremony. *See* Sukkot week

Ramah, shrine at, 365.

Rapaport, S. J. L., cit., xlii.

Ras Shamra inscriptions, 58.

Rashi, cit., xli, 676, 726.

Rebellion, Jeremiah opposes, 320. *See also* Pacifism.

Red heifer, ceremony of, lxxvii ff., 17, 27, 31, 649, 702, 734; Pharisees *vs.* Sadducees on, 121–128, 661–692, 889.

Reformation. *See* Josiah.

Rehoboam, 385.

Resurrection, cxv, cxix, confession of faith in, 110–112; Pharisees *vs.* Sadducees on, 145–159, 742–751, 765, 767–768, 772–773, 775, 845; poor man's hope for, 145–152, 773; democracy of, 147–148, 750, 894; and moral responsibility, 149–151; opponents of, 152–153; and persecutions of Antiochus Epiphanes, 154–157; and belief in angels, 178, 536, 574; and nationalism, 749; *'am ha-arez* and 754; and capital punishment, 836; works *re* foreign influence on Jewish belief in, 844–845.

Revelation on Sinai, and Shabuot, 116, 642, 650–651, 883; and Pharisaic tradition, 650; denial of, 751.

Reward and punishment, Ezekiel's teaching on, 333; Second Isaiah's teaching on, 497.

Ritual documents, controversy *re* dating, 819.

Roman Law, 139, 142, 694, 695. *See also* Civil Law.

Rome, Great Rebellion against, lxxxiv ff., cxxxi; conquest of Palestine, 8, 13, 31, 33, 66, 282, 447, 615–619, 685, 777; courts under, 724. *See also* Titus, Vespasian, Pompey, etc.

Rosh ha-Shanah, 113, 114. *See also* New Year.

Russia, described in synagogues of Czarist regime under cipher, 340–341.

Ruth, Book of, lxxxiii, 540–541, 556, 810.

Saadia Gaon, xli, 464.

Sabbath, prohibition against reaping on, 69; fighting on, 130, 156–157; Pharisees *vs.* Sadducees on kindling lights for, 130–135, 649, 660–661; Pharisees *vs.* Sadducees on merging households on, 135–138, 718–720; of exilic period, 172; observance of, xcvii f., civ, 258–259, 703, 708, 709, 714, 756, 758–759, 770, 776, 779; of *shekalim*, 281; and extended personality, 286–287; and "Priestly Code," 462; among Babylonian exiles, 454, 489; Nehemiah on, 560; visits to prophet customary on, 563; Hasmoneans and, 599; meaning of, 643, 645–647, 660; comp. with *shabbatu*, 646, 660, 756, 759; Supreme, *see* Day of Atonement; sacrifice of paschal lamb on, 817; traveling on, 840.

Sabbatical year, 756, 786, 791, 895; cycle, 663, 755.

Sacrifices, xci f., 62, 655, 705, 707, 711–712, 719, 727, 783, 833; of exilic period, 172; criticized by psalmist, 245; daily, Pharisees *vs.* Sadducees on, 282–283, 710–716; out of Temple, 757, 759–760, 896. *See also* Lots, Paschal lamb, *Tebul yom*, Red heifer, Meal-offering, Day of Atonement, *Omer*.

Sadducees, li ff., 1, 3, 608, 821; comp. with Pharisees, 10, 80–81, 82–83, 97; priests as, 23; and *Shema'*, 66; comp. with Shammaites, 83; controversies with Pharisees, 101–144, 279, 281–285, 630, 632–636, 637–753; number of, in Palestine, 158; gluttony of, 187, 193; reject Oral Law, 261, 266, 269–270, 277, 279; origin and social background of, 633–634, 637, 643, 724, 748–751, 753, 762–779, 835; in Pharisaic tradition, 637, 771–773, 774–776, 777–779; comp. with Boethusians, 652–654, 770, 773, 777–779; and plural marriage, 665; and Hasmoneans, 762–763, 770; and resurrection and immortality, 741–751, 764–765, 767–769, 772–773, 775, 777; and Sanhedrin, 772, 774. *See also* Patricians, Hasmoneans, Priests, High Priest.

Sages, and word "Baal," 29; and tithing, 70; and angels, 180–185; and use of oil, 192; and Proverbs, 215–216; and Book of Esther, 217; *re* social teaching of prophets, 292; *re* birthplaces of prophets, 309; and use of symbols for persecutors, 340; on

Jonah story, 538–539; collect and edit prophets, 578. Quoted: on tithing, 71; on literary power, 464; on Queen Salome, 612. *See also* Atonement, festival of; Scholars; Sages by name; etc.
Sages of Israel, *see sub* Hasidim.
Salanter, Israel, xxii, xl.
Salome, Queen, cxx, cxxvi, 130, 275, 610, 611, 612–613, 697, 774, 778.
Samaria, 7, 11, 40; Hosea denounces sins of, 298–300; as Omri's kingdom, 390; Ahab's comp. with Jerusalem, 392; Assyria conquers, 417–418, 547; under Cyrus, 480. *See also* Israel, Ahab, Jezebel, Elijah.
Samaritans, 816; descendants of Ten Tribes, 547; character of, 548–549; folkways, 549–553; break with Judaites, 553–555, 757; complain of Judaites to Persia, 559; struggle with Nehemiah, 560; friendly with Judah, 561; and Antiochus Epiphanes, 591; John Hyrkan conquers, 597; text of Scripture of, 737.
Samson, 355, 362.
Samson of Sens, 792.
Samuel, 190–191, 364–369, 371, 379, 385, 405, 833, 865; Book of, 62
Samuel ben Meir, 765.
Samuel ben Nahman, 896.
Sanhedrin, and change in marriage customs, 44; place of meeting of, 63; and Society for enforcement of purity, 77; Shammaites at meetings of, 84; and purification of metals, 129; *vs.* Menelaus, 590; Hasmoneans and, 597–603, 773–774; disbanded, 607–608; reformed, 612–618; and Pharisees, 629, 772–774, 779; and judicial leniency, 709; jurisdiction of, 726–731, 735; tribal, 736; and responsibility of masters for slaves, 856–857. *See also* Courts of Justice, *Gerousia*.
Sargon, 420.
Satan, evil attributed to 230–231; as author of Job's troubles, 235.
Saul, 190–191, 366–371, 372, 373, 374, 375, 377, 865.
Scholar *vs.* provincials, after Second Commonwealth, 33–36; Shammaitic, quot., 83–89 *passim;* in *Gerousia*, 576–577, *see also* Sanhedrin. *See also* Scribes.
School, punishment in, 83–84.
Schuerer, E., xlviii f.
Scribes, liberalism of, 23; organize Society for enforcement of purity, 74, 76, 93, 834; and pedagogics, 92–93; history of, 262–267; later meaning of word, 279–280; position of, in Babylonia, 262, 853. *See also* Scholars, Pharisees.
Scripture, reading of in Temple, 63–65; and Pharisees *vs.* Sadducees, 101–102; and plebeian law, 268–269; and foreign powers, 423–424; prose and poetry in, 463–464; Pharisees preserve variant readings of, 822.
Second Commonwealth, 0, 2, 7; sociological strata of Jewish Palestine during last decade of (charts), 4–5; opposition between city and country during, 24; agricultural taxes of, 28; landownership during, 38–39; angelology of, 177–185; and psalmists, 246; social conflicts *re* foreign allegiance in, 425; social strata of, 515, 630; sects in, 639, 648.
Second Isaiah, 145, 175, 176, 521, 747; teachings, analyzed, 467–499; unity of Isaiah, 40–66, 801–803; date of, 803; home of, 803–805; list of references to Israel and Jacob in, 875.
Second Zechariah. *See* Deutero-Zechariah.
Sects and societies, rise of, in Judea, 9.
Seleucids, officials of, and patricians, 20, 512, 581, *see also* Tobiads; provincials under, 20. *See also* Syria.

Seleucus IV, 584, 855.
Self-support, of women. *See* Inheritance, Widow's rights.
Senaa, clan of the, 457, 511–512, 877.
Sennacherib, 420, 426–429, 430.
"Separatists." *See* Purity, Society for enforcement of.
Sepphoris, 41, 782.
Septuagint, 116.
Seraiah, clan of. *See* Jedaiah.
Shabuot, ci, ciii ff., 105, 113, 115–119, 126, 599, 629, 639, 641–654, 773, 832, 839–840, 883. *See also* Pentecost.
Shalmaneser III, 409.
Shalmaneser IV, 417–418.
Shammai, cxxiii, 773, 795; comp. with Hillel, 83; preparation for Sabbath—his anxiety, 258–259; and proselytes, 516; School of, 619, *see also* Shammaites; on size of loaf, 792–793. Quoted: on purity of olives, 53; on learning, 96; on principal's guilt in crime of agent, 285.
Shammaites, li, cxxiii, 1, 3, 633, 770, 777, 796–797, 824, 891; quot. on praise of bride, 49; and work on fourteenth of Nisan, 51; and purity of olives, 52–54; and size of *mahol*, 55; and eating fowl with milk, 59–60; ill manners of, 83–89; gluttony of, 193; and extended personality, 285–286; on Shabuot, 653; judicial principles of, 659, 697, 722–724; on laws of purity, 676, 683–685, 687–690, 776, 888, 897; and *'am ha-arez*, 834.
Sharon, plain of, 107.
Sheba, 381.
Shechem, 11, 385, 387, 549, 551, 591, 868.
Shekalim, 281–283, 710–711, 715, 854–855.
Shekinah, 160.
Shema', omission of response in Jericho, 61–67, 578, 579; response to, quot., 64, 66; and pietists, 66, 578, 833; and angels, 752; quot., 63.
Shemayah, and Divine Providence, 255, 852; and sacrifice of paschal lamb, 730, 817.
Shemoneh 'Esreh, 110–112.
Sheshbazzar, 480, 500, 874.
Sheshet, 885.
Shiloh, priests at, 362–364.
Siloah, 667.
Simai, 675.
Simeon, tribe of, 377, 385.
Simeon ben Azzai, 837; quot., 257.
Simeon ben Boethus, 80.
Simeon ben Gamaliel I, 102–103, 620, 707, 776–777, 836.
Simeon ben Gamaliel II, 79, 96; quot., 55, 287.
Simeon ben Lakish, lxxiv, 785.
Simeon ben Mattathias, 595–596, 638.
Simeon ben Shattah, 44, 128–129, 144, 612, 694, 697–698, 767, 771, 778, 843–844; quot., 856–857.
Simeon ben Yohai, 1, 39, 182–185, 714–715, 735, 842.
Simeon ben Zoma, lv, 886–888; quot., 258.
Simeon the Pious, cvii ff., 85.
Simeon II (the Righteous), 62–63, 95, 109, 152, 154, 464, 575–576, 581, 583–584, 588, 629, 680, 762, 764, 767; quot., 63. *See also* Great Assembly.
Simeon the Tobiad, 583.
Simhoni, J. N., lvii.
Sins of the fathers, punishment for, 150, 197, 225.
Slaves, lxxix f.; liability of owner for damages of, 283–285, 698–699; Jeremiah denounces seizing of freedmen for, 305.
Social grace, of Pharisees *vs.* Sadducees, 82–83, 835; Shammaites' lack of, 83–89; Galileans' view of Pharisees', 97.
Social strata, of Commonwealth, and equality, 342, *see also* Equality; and

international policy, 344, 351, *see also* Universalism; history behind different political views of, 358–374, 385–389, *see also* Kings by name; of early Restoration, 515. *See also sub* Palestine; Exile, Babylonian.

Social struggle. *See* Equality, Landownership.

Sodom, and individual responsibility, 150; inhospitality of, to angel visitors, 166, 167–168, 178; arrogance of, 331.

Solomon, King, cxiv, 376, 719–720, 866; cavalry of, 189, 383; Koheleth attributed to, 235; resistance to, 382, 385; mercantile policies of, 382–384; prayer of, at dedication of Temple, 432–433, 565.

Solomon ibn Aderet, xli.

Sosenk, 387–388.

Spektor, Rabbi Isaac Elhanan, xxii.

Spengler, Oswald, xxv.

Sukkot week, ci, civ f., 13, 84, 87, 629, 643, 720; Pharisees *vs* Sadducees on, 102–115, 611, 700–708; biblical origins of, 103–107, 638–639; plebeians and, 265–266; works on, 838.

Superstitions, provincial, 28–29, 896; Law forbade use of, 92; *re* resurrection, 146, 742–743, 744–745. *See also* Ancestor worship.

Supreme Court, of Temple, 261, 853. *See also* Oral Law, Priests, etc.

Synagogues, *Shema'* in, 64, 579; omit Decalogue, 65; and doctrine of future life, 158, 747, 750; origin of, 563–565; development of, 566–568, 631, 880; importance of, 568–569; Great Assembly and, 578–579. *See also* Prayer-meetings.

Syria, lxxiii ff.; conquest of Palestine, 8; decree of on Jewish worship, 762. *See also* Antiochus Epiphanes, Tobiads, Seleucids.

Talio. *See Lex talionis.*

Talmud, xxiii, 1, 2, 795–797; sociological basis for differences in, 780–798.

Tarfon, 38, 96, 708, 827; quot., 14, 86, 88, 278, 286–287, 687.

Taxes, on agricultural products, 28, 69–72; for Temple, 281–283, *see also Shekalim;* Solomon's 383; in Judah, under Babylonia, 449; classes exempt from, under Antiochus III, 582. *See also* Tithes.

Tebel, 755.

Tebul yom, ci, 126–127, 661–692, 736–738, 885–889; works on, 889.

Tekoa, a barren land, 294.

Temple, in Jubilees, cii; David's choice of site for, 11, 822; priests of, 12, *see also* Priests; servants of, 12, *see also* Levites; ceremonies, 13, *see also* Pentecost, Atonement, etc.; artisans, income of, 15; destruction of, 31, 282, 337, 442; ownership of Jericho property, 38, 68; boundary dispute, 39–40; *Shema'* in, 62–64, 578; and Sadducean influence, 81; candelabrum, purification of, 128–129; building of, 190, 383, 384; and psalmists, 245, 246; fuel for altar of, 277, 582; source of revenue, 281–283, 710–711, 715; plebeian loyalty to, 289–290; Ezekiel's attitude to, 318–321; Ezekiel's idea of restored, 328, 332, 334; Jehoash's legislation *re*, 413–414; *vs.* village altars, 418–420; Solomon's prayer at dedication of, 432–433, 565; under Cyrus, 480; rebuilding of, 501, 508, *see also* Haggai; builder of, a half-Jew, 556; officials of, and Synagogue, 567, 568–569; and Antiochus III, 582; Antiochus Epiphanes and, 590–593; Judah and, 593–594; Demetrius and, 594; Pharisees and, 631, 652, 771, 774; defiled by Ahaz, 759. *See also* High Priest, Priests, Levites, Tobiads, Pilgrims, etc.

Temples, controversy *re* luxurious, 187, 189–191; Ezekiel's early attitude toward provincial, 318; prophets disapprove village, 418–420, 428, 429–430; under Manasseh, 431; and Jeremiah, 436–437; Second Isaiah denounces, 494, 497–498; Joel and, 520; Ezra and, 562–563, 567–568. *See also* Synagogues.
Ten Tribes, 7, 317; exile of, in Media, 327, 444; descendants of, *see* Samaritans.
Testament of Levi, 274.
Testaments of the Twelve Patriarchs, lxxviii ff., 44, 177, 178, 179, 251–252, 268, 274, 276, 277, 561–562, 603–604, 810.
Theism, early, 166.
Third Commonwealth, 516–518.
Tiberias, 41.
Tibni, 389.
Tiglath-pileser, 416.
Tigranes, 613.
Tithes, cxiv f., 28, 69–72, 270–272, 631–632, 663, 671, 677, 681 f., 746, 755, 786, 790–792, 823. *See also* Taxes.
Titus, conquest of, 22, 41.
Tobiads, history of Hellenizing movement of, 580–587.
Tobiah, 560.
Tobit, 177, 179, 272.
Torah, Pharisees and, 9–10, 629, 632–633, 749; and Shabuot, 116; poverty and study of, 193; and Divine Providence, 197; and human equality, 342–343; and pacifism, 351–355; ambiguities of, 633–634, 698–699, 780; principles of justice, 708–710, 721–723, 734–735; change in interpretation of, 782.
Torrey, C. C., cit., 325; on Second Isaiah, 801–802; on Ezekiel 1.1–2, 806.
Tosafists, xli, 676, 786, 792–794.
Toy, C. H., quot., 153; cit., 211.
Trajan, 88.
Transjordan, 7, 187, 366, 371, 372, 374, 378–379, 386, 387, 392.
Treaties, Hosea denounces contradictory, 299–300.
Trito-Isaiah, is there a, 489, 801–802.
Trito-Zechariah, predicts world conflict and its results, 542–545, 574; ends period of prophecy, 577.
Tyre, effect on Ezekiel of visit to, 321–322, 335; Ezekiel uses to inveigh against Babylonia, 336–337, 862; David and, 377; Solomon visits, 383; Omri and, 390, 392; Exile deflects Jerusalem's commerce to, 447, 449.
Tyropoean valley, 14, 15.

Universalism, plebeians', 344–345, 347–350; of Amos, 356; of Second Isaiah, 490–496; of urban prophets, 535–541. *See also* Social strata, Equality.
Urban-rural conflict, xxiii, lxi ff., 627–628, 630, 632–633.
Urbanity. *See* Social grace.

Vengeance, and punishment, 197–199; Law-giver decides against, 199; divine, in Nahum, 307–309, 858; in Joel, 522, 524–526.
Vespasian, conquest of, 13, 31, 776–777.
Village shrines. *See* Temples.
Virginity, Sadducees *vs.* Pharisees *re* proof of, 739–741, 815–816.
Vows, xci ff., 188–189; modern scholars' view of "release" from, 818; R. Judah ben Ilai quot. on, of Galilee and Judah, 832.

War. *See* Militarism.
Water Drinkers, 9, 109, 822.
Water-libations, ci, civ f.; Pharisees *vs.* Sadducees on, 102 ff., 180, 192, 629, 638–639, 650, 700–708, 774, 890. *See also* Sukkot.
Water supply, of Jerusalem, 106.

Weber, Max, lix.
"Wedding" and betrothal, 828–829.
Weiss, I. H., lii.
Wellhausen, J., xlviii f., cit., 630.
Widow's rights, 47–48.
Wine, purity of, 54; *vs.* water-libations, 107–110; cost of, in Babylonia and Palestine, 823. *See also* Joel, Deutero-Zechariah.
Wisdom literature, *see* Proverbs, Job, Koheleth.
Women's rights, 837–838. *See also* Inheritance, Widow's rights, Emancipation.
World conflict, Trito-Zechariah predicts, and its results, 542–545, 574.
Worship, form of, patrician, plebeian, provincial comp., 345.
Worshipers at Sunrise, 9, 822.
Writing, ceremonies involving, in Jerusalem *vs.* provinces, 29; word, synonymous with liberal education, 264.

Yabneh, 447, 710, 776.
Yannai, anecdote of peasant and, 35–36.
Yeb, island of, 444. *See also* Elephantine papyri.
Yedaiah. *See* Jedaiah.
Yehoyarib. *See* Jehoiarib.
Yom ha-Kippurim. *See* Atonement, Day of.
Yoyarib. *See* Jehoiarib.

Zadok, lxxiv, 22, 80, 377, 763–768, 775, 834.
Zadokite Document, 193, 817.
Zadokites, 22, 80, 586. *See also* Sadducees.
Zechariah, 112, 171, 173, 175–176, 178–179, 504–507, 639, 876–877. *See also* Deutero-Zechariah, Trito-Zechariah.
Zechariah ben ha-Kazzab, 22, 142.
Zedekiah, King, 406, 441, 862, 870.
Zeira, quot., 792.
Zekut abot, 255–257.
Zephaniah, 307, 310, 316, 431; his concept of equality, 311–312.
Zerubbabel, 500–508 *passim.*
Zidon, commerce with, 390; Jezebel introduces gods of, 394–395.
Zimri, 388–389.
Zoroastrianism, xii, 173, 470, 478, 846.